Pamphlets:Labor, vol.1.

1. Berry, J:M. $3,000,000 state loan, to provide a home of its own for every family in the state.
2. Butterworth, Benjamin. The eight-hour law...1890.
3. Dean, John. Address to convention of Mountain City div.172, Order of railway conductors...1891.
4. Drage, Geoffrey. Old-age pensions.
5. George, Henry. Thou shalt not steal; an address before the anti-poverty society.
6. The Boycotter.
7. Illinois arbitration board. Sustains labor unions; finding of Arbitration board in Sattley strike case.
8. Hotchkiss S:M. Practical suggestions on labor organization...1881.
9. Hours of labor: manufacture of coarse & fine cotton goods.
10. Labor strikes...since passage of McKinley tariff act.
11. The law relating to labour unions...as laid down by recent judgments.
12 & 13. Liberty & property defence league. Annual report 1894-95 & 1897
14. The farmers want to know: challange of the State Grange of Penn. to the Home market club of Boston, & its reply...
15. Moore, H:L. Von Thuenun's theory of natural wages.
16. Nash, Joseph. The relations between capital & labor in the U.S...1878.
17. Commissioners of the State bureaus of labor statistics Report on the industrial, social & economic conditions of Pullman, Ill.
18. Peabody, A.P. The rights & dangers of property...1872
19. Phillips, T:W. Nonpartisan industrial commission...18
20. Quincy, Josiah. Moderate houses for moderate means: an argument for cheap trains...
21. Richardson, G:M. The gospel of work.
22. Wright, C.D. Letter of the com. of labor...showing the direct cost of labor in the manufacture of 1 ton of steel rails in the U.S., Gt. Brit. & Europe.
23. Waterhouse, Sylvester. The advantages of educated labor in Missouri...1872.
24. Weeden, W:B. Arbitration & its relation to strikes.
25. Weeks, J.D. Report on the practical operation of arbitration & concilation...in England.
26. Brown, William. The claims of capital considered.
27. Workingmen's loan assoc. Origin & system.
28. Wright, A.O. Distribution of profits: a new arrangement of that subject.

PRICE TEN CENTS.

$3,000,000 State Loan,

TO PROVIDE

A Home of its Own for Every Family

In the State.

It is a plan to assist those who deserve help, and will not beg. To accomplish this great good a State Loan of $3,000,000 is required. It will be amply secured by the homes.

From 1860 to 1875 our State legislatures gave away over two million dollars, without the remotest prospect of a direct return; partly as follows:—

Museum of Zoology,	over	$300,000	For the Colleges,	over	300,000
Agricultural College,	"	300,000	" Deaf & Dumb,	"	300,000
Institute of Technology,	"	350,000	" Idiotic & Blind,	"	550,000

Now it is benevolent to furnish good homes to the Idiotic who cannot appreciate them; would it not be equally well, and as truly benevolent to build homes for deserving citizens not idiotic, who can appreciate them.

Think of the palaces we have erected at Danvers, Worcester, and elsewhere, for the insane, two of which, for housing only 1500 lunatics, costs more than this bill asks for to comfortably house a sane million.

Think of the happiness of the noble-hearted, shrewd and good contractors, who by the prospect of a good contract and money to be made in the future, could spend their time, and employ suitable men to explain to the legislature how much these unfortunate wards of the state needed a palace to live in.

Think of the happiness of the doctors and attendants, housed also in the palace at *good* salaries, and shop keepers happy in furnishing supplies at *good* prices.

Think of the *happy* farmers made more so by the *state* agricultural college *assisting* them to educate their sons in a special class education that will give them advantage over the laborers and their sons, who cannot avail themselves of it, *their* last dollar is taken to pay rent.

Think of the *happy* landlords (housed in their own home), made more so by the state *assisting* them to educate their sons in the *best paying* trades at a school of Technology that will give them an advantage over any mechanic in the state who uses *his* last dollar to pay rent.

Think of the *happy* Bank Presidents and Millionaires made more so by the state *assisting* them to give their sons a collegiate education, that will still further increase the inequality of chances between their family and that of wage and salary earners, who use *their* last dollar to pay rent.

These things are good in their *place;* but is it not *commencing* at the wrong end? Is it not better for the government to use its strength to help the *mass* of people, instead of a class?

> " He's but a wretch, with all his lands,
> That wears a narrow soul."

The last cent being taken from these poorer men to pay excessive rent to landlords, they *can't* educate *their children* at college, however smart and promising they may be.

Equality of *opportunities* (and such equality our government is established to create), can only be given in colleges by the state furnishing board free to scholars who properly improve their opportunities.

.. this work, no clique can *make money*, it is wholly for the *benefit of the people;* yet these very reasons will operate against it. Friends! look this case up carefully, for the enemies to the measure will *spell out* every single word in this bill, in their endeavors to get information by which, in an oily way, to do all the damage they can to the work.

Think of the many other buildings as costly as palaces, built by the state, where the most hardened and infamous criminals are healthfully fed, comfortably housed, warmly clothed, carefully nursed if sick, and kept in the finest physical condition possible, to be used by avaricious contractors to compete with honest, hard-working and deserving mechanics, who find it almost impossible to furnish the wants of their families from the mere pittance which they now earn.

Perhaps it is all right to give the prodigal son a hearty welcome, perhaps it is all right to use up sentimental charity on infamous and hardened criminals, and criminally careless paupers; but I do claim and insist that a chance shall be given sensible men and women, to help by their kindly aid the deserving mechanics, who will die before they will beg, like the chance that is given the Board of State Charities to help the pauper poor and hardened criminals.

If the government had done its duty before this and given these same criminals a little well timed friendly aid, many of them would never have become such.

The DUTY of our state government being to equalize, it is not the way to do it by lifting those that are up still higher; but to give a lift to those who are down and thus try to bring them up to an equality with their more *favored brothers.*

And now one other subject of the state's beneficence demands our attention: the Museum of Zoology, where are preserved the *precious* REMAINS of snakes and polliwogs long since defunct, never having been quite as sensitive or deserving our care as human beings, and now less so than when in life; but *they* are carefully housed and tended, even expensively so.

Are the men elected to *wisely* distribute the funds raised from the taxation of labor? Are these men insane or idiotic that they thus care for senseless and inanimate things, and leave living human flesh and blood to suffer?

We will, at great expense to ourselves, instruct these legislators that it is their first duty to house men, women and children in comfortable homes, before so much as one cent is taken from our treasury, to house snakes, stones, etc., etc., etc.

We will go one step further. Churches are made into palaces, and God's poor go shelterless. Christ said, "feed the hungry," and "inasmuch as ye have done it unto one of the least of these, my brethren, ye have done it unto me." These words mean something.

If Christ came to us today would we let him starve, would we let him go naked, would we let him go with no roof over him, and think to honor and satisfy his requirements by our costly church buildings? We know better. He plainly tells us that we feed, clothe and shelter him, when we feed, clothe and shelter his poor. Yet palaces are built for churches, and God's poor starve (or go shelterless). *Is this right?*

Friends, don't let this become any party measure, make one party on it, the PARTY OF RIGHT; let us take up this work unselfishly, both parties joining hands. And friends of the measure, don't, *don't*, DON'T, under any circumstance, pair on this measure with any one; lose your vote first, and we know what we are advising, we are sure on this question, don't pair with any one; lose your vote first.

It is hard for the advocate of this measure, after sacrificing health, business and money on account of opposition, to find it necessary for the good of the work, to be compelled to state that he is not interested even in the remotest degree, in the lumber trade, land, or any other business, by which he can derive the slightest benefit from his work; it involves anxiety and loss alone to him. He does not receive any money aid to assist him, and no salary or honors, so-called, could ever tempt him to do this work for the state. Wealth and position have no value except to accomplish some good purpose. The kindly advice and hard labor of two trusted friends who are helping him, he values more than anything else. The three rely wholly and completely on the happiness to be created by this measure, as the most valuable recompense for the labor invested; it is their ambition

"To scatter plenty o'er a smiling land
And read their history in a nation's eyes."

A native of Salem, he asks the most searching scrutiny; as those who rarely see unselfish work done, are hard to be convinced. *****

> "Ye friends to truth, ye statesmen who survey
> The rich man's joys increase, the poor's decay,
> 'Tis yours to judge, how wide the limits stand
> Between a wealthy and a happy land."

A bill will be presented to the next legislature for the purpose of assisting any family in the state into a home of their own, by the state loaning every town and city $5,000, and an additional $1,000 for every thousand in excess of five thousand inhabitants; the work to be carried on by associations guaranteed by said cities and towns; the state loan to be repaid by a perpetual ground rent, to be used first to pay off the bonds, and after that to accumulate to assist the occupants of the land or their children into a home, should they ever need it. This ground rent will repay the state in less than forty years' time.

The bill will necessitate a loan of

$3,000,000.

Some never dare do anything unless they have a precedent for it; so we will give a few from our state records.

Acts to aid railroads were passed as follows:—

Boston and Portland,	$50,000.	Troy and Greenfield, over	$900,000.
Andover and Haverhill,	100,000.	Boston and Albany,	3,000,000.
Norwich and Worcester,	400,000.	New York and New England,	5,000,000.
Eastern,	500,000.	Hoosac Tunnel, over	23,000,000.

Brothers, what are we doing? Lending the credit of our *commonwealth to a class of men*, TO HELP THE RICH STOCK-HOLDERS of the New York and New England and other railroads to make money with, just what our constitution expressly forbids, and neglecting to loan it to the people, the mass of citizens, to be used to furnish them with homes, to make them happy and to increase their happiness, just what our constitution expressly requires us to do.

This was loaned to help rich men as a class, the poor did not apply for the loans; the roads were just starting and poor men could not invest in them, and all know rich men never build railroads and issue stocks and bonds or get state loans to help the poor, or, in fact, any one else but themselves; they did it to make money, using the state's credit to do it with, and the state lost millions by the operation. The loan asked for to provide the people with homes of their own will create a million times more happiness among our citizens, and the security given is a thousand times better than a railroad ever has given, or ever can give.

No *class* legislation is asked in *this* bill, but it is to give to every one, rich and poor alike, a chance to get a home. Our state constitution says: "Government is * * * * for the happiness of the people, * * * * NOT *for the* PROFIT OF ANY CLASS OF MEN," and further on it says, "It shall be the duty of the Legislatures * * * * to encourage * * * * rewards and immunities, to countenance and *inculcate* the principles of humanity and general * * * * benevolence, public and private charity, * * * * and *generous* sentiments among the people.

This loan can be raised in England, where most of our loans have been raised, so it will not diminish the working capital of our state.

By taxation of the property thus newly created here, the state will reap a benefit in money, of many times the amount of the loan.

The state has spent over *twenty-three million* dollars on the Hoosac Tunnel, and there is no prospect of a return for this enormous investment. It was started to help a railroad corporation, yet only about one-tenth that amount is here asked to help every man, woman and child in the state; no one class of rich people, but all classes, and at the end of twenty-five years we will have a perfect garden state, blooming all over with comfortable, happy homes, instead of a hole in a mountain which the state would make money to give away, *under proper restrictions* as to its use, as she is losing on it at the following rate per year, and we will only go back ten years.—in

1874.	Tunnel cost over 12 millions.		1879.	Tunnel cost over 19 millions.	
1875.	" " " 15	"	1880.	" " " 20	"
1876.	" " " 17	"	1881.	" " " 21	"
1877.	" " " 18	"	1882.	" " " 22	"
1878.	" " " 18 1-2	"	1883.	" " " 23	"

That is enough to make any one feel sad, who wishes for the happiness of the people. The state *will lose* more on the loan made on account of the rich corporators of the New York and New England railroad than is here asked for, to build homes for *all* our people. *Just think of that.*

Now those were only loans, LOANS of the *credit* of the state, but sometimes the legislature *gives* away money, as we have already proven.

Some lawyers at first thought that building associations, formed under a law like the one proposed, would be too tightly tied up to allow them to do the greatest amount of good they were capable of; but *experience* in this state, at Lynn, has taught that this is not so; and if any additional tie can be put on such associations to PREVENT *them* or *their members* FROM *making money, even in the most* INDIRECT *way out of them, it will be best to make it today.*

This plan is shorn of every possibility of financial gain to those engaged, as it involves labor, and loss alone, pecuniarily.

"All may save self, but minds that
Heavenward tower,
Aim at a wider power,
Gifts on the world to shower."

BE TRUE.

"Thou must be true thyself
If thou the truth would'st teach;
Thy soul must overflow, if thou
Another's soul would'st reach;
It needs the overflow of heart
To give the lips full speech.

Think truly, and thy thoughts
Shall the world's famine feed;
Speak truly, and each word of thine
Shall be a fruitful seed;
Live truly, and thy life shall be
A great and noble creed."

Some timid hearts—destitute of courage—quiver in every nerve if bold, sharp, interested persons, to gain selfish ends, cry out—"this or that is inexpedient"—"this or that can't be done." Such timid ones submit and claim the patience as a virtue—forgetting that

"Patience in cowards, is tame hopeless fear;
But in brave minds a scorn of what they bear."

Manly and courageous men dare attempt a noble object; and, daring, win. Cowards fear attempt, and by their fear and cowardice lose all—when the fact bold and plain, is—

"It is not just as we take it—
This mystical world of ours;
Life's field will yield, *what we make* it."

The most despicable are those, who, wishing to do the right—lack the courage; how can one hesitate to enlist in a noble cause? *One*, only one earnest champion on the floor of the House or Senate, will draw others—then concentration and persistence will surely end in victory. A brave man, seeing the right, never gives up till the cause is won.

Extracts from the Constitution of Massachusetts.

All * * * * are born FREE and EQUAL and have *certain* NATURAL * * * * *rights* * * * * in fine that of * * * * OBTAINING HAPPINESS.

Government is * * * * for the * * * * HAPPINESS *of the* PEOPLE * * * * NOT for the profit * * * * of any * * * * class of men.

The legislature *ought* FREQUENTLY TO ASSEMBLE * * * * *for making* NEW LAWS, as the COMMON GOOD *may require.*

The end * * * * of government is * * * * to FURNISH * * * * individuals * * * * THEIR NATURAL rights, and the BLESSINGS of *life.*

Whenever * * * * NOT *obtained*, the PEOPLE *have* A RIGHT to *alter* the *government* * * * * for THEIR *happiness.*

The PEOPLE * * * * HAVE A RIGHT to *institute government*, and to *reform*, alter, or totally change *the same*, when THEIR * * * * HAPPINESS REQUIRES IT.

The PEOPLE *have* A RIGHT * * * * to *give instructions to their representatives.*

FREQUENT *recurrence to the fundamental* principles of the constitution * * * * *are* ABSOLUTELY NECESSARY * * * * *to maintain a free government.*

The whole foundation of our government is "EQUALITY of opportunities," the further we depart from that, the weaker grows the fabric of our state, until finally it will fall, if WE neglect to strengthen the foundations.

Those extracts show that lack of courage, alone, prevents us enjoying this happiness. The brave men who devised our constitution did all they could for us; they had the wisdom to plan, but it was beyond their power to furnish us the courage to carry it out. It needs action on our part, and true, hard, and earnest work—for

"Happy were men if they but understood
There is no happiness but in doing good."

Many today worship the gold, not the man—and

"The base wretch who hoards up all he can
Is praised and called a thrifty man."

Success is pleasant, but principle is best,

"Where honor or where conscience does not bind,
No other tie shall shackle me."

The advantages of the ownership of homes by families, as a means of happiness, is better understood by women than men, and manly men value a true woman's advice.

A bill will be presented to the next legislature for a state loan of $3,000,000 to our cities and towns to help the citizens into homes of their own.

Don't ask the opinion of those who rent houses, or are interested in mortgages directly or indirectly, or of those who do not need a home at present.

The moment you hear an opinion given against any endeavor made to house our citizens in homes of their own, look for a selfish motive, and ninety-nine times out of a hundred you will find it comes from one who rents property, or from some one selfishly interested either directly or indirectly.

COMMONWEALTH OF MASSACHUSETTS.

IN THE YEAR ONE THOUSAND EIGHT HUNDRED AND EIGHTY-FIVE.

AN ACT

TO PROMOTE THE ESTABLISHMENT OF BENEVOLENT BUILDING ASSOCIATIONS THROUGHOUT THE COMMONWEALTH.

Be it enacted by the Senate and House of Representatives in General Court assembled, and by the authority of the same, as follows:

Method of Incorporation and General Powers.

SECTION 1. Twenty-five or more persons, over twenty-one years of age, who associate themselves together by an agreement in writing, with the intention of forming a corporation for the purpose of purchasing and holding real estate within this Commonwealth, of improving the same for homes to be owned by their occupants, and of selling houses and lots payable at cost on instalments to persons who shall occupy the same under its rules, shall, upon complying with the provisions of the five following sections, be and remain a corporation for said purposes, with all the liabilities, duties and restrictions set forth in this act, and in all general laws which now are or may hereafter be in force relating to such corporations.

NOTE. These corporations cannot depreciate, but *must* IMPROVE real estate. No person can speculate in real estate through them by purchasing a house and lot, for he must *occupy* it for a home while it is being paid for. The corporations cannot permanently hold real estate, but *must sell* within a very limited time. (See sections 11, 29 and 31.) In this matter of homes, where she is directly interested, woman is placed on the same footing as elsewhere in the General Statutes.

It is necessary that a large number *shall sign the agreement*, in order to find among them enough unselfish ones to attend the meetings and run the work without pay.

SECT. 2. The agreement shall set forth the fact that the subscribers thereto associated themselves with the intention of forming a corporation for the purposes stated in the preceding section, and the town or city—which shall be within this Commonwealth—in which it is located.

NOTE. To prevent misunderstandings from the commencement, it is important that some definite agreement should be made and signed.

SECT. 3. Each subscriber, before subscribing to said agreement, shall contribute and pay to a person agreed upon by all the subscribers as a temporary treasurer, the sum of five dollars, which shall be for an admission fee; and the further sum of one dollar and twenty cents, which shall be for the first annual assessment, and said temporary treasurer shall pay over all sums of money so paid to him, to the treasurer of said corporation as soon as one is elected.

NOTE. Twenty-five persons are allowed, by existing laws, to form a money making building association; seven can form a benevolent association. It was thought if a town could not furnish twenty-five liberal enough to give $6.20 each to start one of these benevolent associations, there would not be interest enough felt to run it properly. If not obliged to pay the money *before* signing, many would sign with no intention to pay.

SECT. 4. The first meeting shall be called by a notice signed by one or more of the subscribers to such agreement, who shall have made the payments required by the preceding section, stating the time, place and purpose of the meeting, a copy of which notice shall, seven days at least before the day appointed for the meeting, be given to each subscriber who shall have made such payments, or left at his usual place of business or place of residence, or deposited in the post-office post-paid and addressed to him at his usual place of business or of residence; such notice shall contain the names of all signers of the agreement. And whoever gives such notices shall make affidavit of his doings, which shall be recorded in the records of the corporation.

NOTE. It is actually necessary for the good of the work that very careful notice shall be given of the first meeting; to get a full attendance of the members to start the work properly. And a list of all signers are sent to each member, that they may have sufficient time before the meeting to make enquiries as to the ability of those he wishes to vote for as officers.

SECT. 5. At such first meeting, including any necessary or reasonable adjournment, an organization shall be effected by the choice by ballot of a temporary clerk, who shall be sworn; and by the adoption of by-laws; and by the election by ballot of a president (who shall also be first director), vice president, treasurer, assistant treasurer, clerk, assistant clerk, and of second, third, fourth, fifth, sixth and seventh director; but at no meeting shall any person, who has not subscribed the agreement of association and made the payments provided by section three, vote or be eligible to any office. The temporary clerk shall make and attest a record of the proceedings until the clerk has been chosen and sworn, including a record of such choice and qualification.

NOTE. The right of adjournment prevents an organization being hastily formed with consequent liability to errors. The by-laws should be very carefully examined before adoption. The commissioner of corporations could probably furnish a better model to form on than any other person in the state. Election of officers by ballot instead of by voice vote, prevents a distribution of the loud-mouthed ones in different parts of a hall, each instructed to shout for the election of a man agreed on beforehand by some clique, instead of giving competent men and women equal opportunity to hold office. No person being eligible to office at the first meeting except signers of the agreement, every one has had opportunity to make enquiries as to the character and ability of all officers before voting, and after that, as but one office becomes regularly vacant each month, it will be hard for an incompetent man to get the place.

SECT. 6. The president, treasurer, clerk and a majority of the directors shall forthwith make, sign and swear to a certificate, setting forth a true copy of the agreement of association, with the names of the subscribers thereto, the date of the first meeting and the successive adjournments thereof, if any, and shall submit such certificate, and also the records of the corporation, to the mayor of the city or chairman of the board of selectmen of the town in which the corporation is located. Said mayor or chairman shall thereupon cause the same to be submitted to the city council or to a town meeting, as the case may be, and said council or town meeting shall immediately vote upon the question of endorsing the corporasion. If such endorsement shall be voted in the manner provided by section seven of the twenty-ninth chapter of the Public Statutes for votes for incurring debts, the aforesaid mayor or chairman shall transmit said certificate and records, together with an attested copy of said vote, to the commissioner of corporations, who shall examine the same, and who may require such other evidence as to the facts of the case as he may judge necessary. The commissioner, if it appears that the requirements of this and the preceding sections, preliminary to the establishment of the corporation have been complied with, shall certify that fact and his approval of the certificate by endorsement thereon, and immediately notify the aforesaid officers of the corporation thereof. Such certificate shall thereupon be filed by said officers in the office of the secretary of the commonwealth; who, upon the payment of the fee of five dollars, which shall be in full for filing and recording the certificates required by this section, including the issuing of the certificate of organization by the secretary, shall cause the same, with the endorsement thereon, to be recorded, and shall thereupon issue a certificate in the following form:—

NOTE. The responsibility attaching to a sworn statement will tend to a more perfect organization. The signatures and oaths of the three most responsible officers, and a majority of the directors, to a certificate containing the names of all subscribers with particulars, together with the records, gives those who are to endorse or reject, ample means of judging whether it will be to the advantage of the city or town.

As such endorsement guarantees the state from loss on account of these chosen men and women, the same rule is used in regard to the vote on it as on that for money appropriations. The city or town thus becomes responsible to the state, and must make good the loss to the state if any occurs.

Should such endorsement be given, an examination of the association must be made by the State Commissioner of Corporations exactly the same as for any other kind of corporation formed under the general laws, and for money-making building associations like the Saving Loan and Fund.

COMMONWEALTH OF MASSACHUSETTS.

BE IT KNOWN, that wheaeas [here the names of the subscribers to the agreement of association shall be inserted] have associated themselves with the intention of forming a corporation under the name of [here the name of the corporation shall be inserted, the figures of the name being spelled out in full] for the purpose of purchasing and holding real estate within this Commonwealth, of improving the same for homes to be owned by their occupants, and of selling houses and lots payable at cost on instalments to persons who shall occupy the same under its rules, with a capital not to exceed five hundred thousand dollars, and have complied with the provisions of the statutes of this Commonwealth in such cases made and provided, as appears from the certificate of the president, treasurer clerk and directors of said corporation, duly approved by the commissioner of corporations, and recorded in this office; now, therefore, I [here the name of the secretary shall be inserted], secretary of the Commonwealth of Massachusetts, do hereby certify that [here the names of the subscribers to the agreement of the association shall be inserted] their associates and successors are legally organized and established as, and are hereby made an existing corporation under the name of [here the name of the corporation shall be inserted] with the powers, rights and privileges, and subject to the limitations, duties and restrictions which by law appertain thereto. Witness my official signature hereunto subscribed and the seal of the Commonwealth of Massachusetts hereunto affixed this day of in the year [in these blanks the day, month and year of execution of the certificate shall be inserted].

The secretary shall sign the same, and cause the seal of the commonwealth to be thereto affixed, and such certificate shall have the force and effect of a special charter, and shall be conclusive evidence of the existence of such corporation.

NOTE. The above certificate and form of organizing a corporation by the first six sections of this bill are almost identical with the form of organizing a corporation under the general laws, except the guarantee of the aldermen and council and the town.

SECT. 7. Not more than one such corporation shall be formed for each twenty thousand inhabitants, and one additional for the remainder, if any.

NOTE. $20,000 is thought to be enough for the state to invest in any one of these corporations. It is better to have two of $20,000 each, than one of $40,000. (See section 36.)

SECT. 8. The names of such corporations shall be assigned to them by the secretary of the Commonwealth in the certificate provided by section six, and shall be as follows: The Massachusetts Benevolent Building Association, Number [here a number shall be inserted, which shall be One for the first such corporation, and shall be increased by one for each successive corporation so formed thereafter.]

NOTE. The name being assigned by the secretary of the state will prevent confusion arising from a similarity of names.

SECT. 9. Such corporations shall have a seal, which shall be attached to all sealed documents executed in its name and behalf, and which shall have the words Massachusetts Benevolent Building Association upon it in a circle, with the number of the corporation in figures in the centre thereof.

NOTE. The designation of the corporations by numbers will make all these corporations branches of one state system and more easily operated as such.

SECT. 10. Every such corporation may hold real and personal estate for the purposes aforesaid, not exceeding five hundred thousand dollars in value, and it may receive and hold, in trust or otherwise, as a part of said sum, funds received by gift or bequest, to be by it devoted to the purposes for which it is incorporated.

NOTE. $500,000 is the amount that can be held by any benevolent association formed under the general laws, and an association of this sort being formed and worked to advantage in any city or town, no matter how small, furnishes a nucleus to which benevolent persons will add to as they see the good it will accomplish, thereby doing needed good in their own country. instead of converting the heathen of foreign lands.

SECT 11. No such corporation shall occupy any real estate belonging to it for offices in which to transact its business; nor use its funds or property or any part thereof except for the purposes for which it is incorporated.

NOTE. It will be the best policy for the state to prohibit these associations from occupying their real estate for offices, as such occupation would finally lead to the erection of costly buildings, and the next step would be to costly salaries, all of which extravagancies would be at the expense of the benefits intended to be given the citizens at large.

SECT. 12. Such corporations may make by-laws not repugnant to the laws of the Commonwealth, and annex penalties for the breach thereof, not exceeding five dollars for each offence.

NOTE. Similar penalties are allowed to be annexed to violations of the by-laws of corporations formed under the general laws.

Officers and Members and their Rights, Duties and Meetings.

SECT 13. Any person residing in a town or city in which any such corporation shall be located, and being married or over twenty-one years of age, may become a member of said corporation upon making application to the officers of the same, and paying an admission fee of five dollars; but no person shall be at the same time a member of more than one such corporation.

NOTE. It is thought best to fix the amount of the admission fee—which is required as a guarantee of good faith and genuine interest—at five dollars; this limitation and the limitation on the assessments (section 15) will always keep the work in the hands of the people, and thus prevent a close corporation ever being formed from them. $10 was tried at Lynn, but is found to be too high. If experience shows that a less sum will effect the desired result, it may be reduced by future legislation.

SECT. 14. No shares shall be issued in any such corporation, but each member shall have an equal vote at its meetings. No person, by any vote or action of the corporation or otherwise, shall ever have a better opportunity than another to obtain the benefits which said corporation is designed to confer, except that no person not a member, shall be given the right to occupy and purchase a home, when a member, present at the meeting at which the right is drawn desires the right.

No member of such corporation shall directly or indirectly derive any pecuniary profit from the same, except the right to draw a house and lot as provided by this act; and in case he draws such right his membership shall be suspended, and he shall not act as such until he has paid for the house and lot in full, or has given up his privilege, and a full settlement has been made between him and the corporation. No salary shall be paid to any officer, nor any bond or security required from him.

No such corporation shall make any gift or loan, and no transfer or loan of any property belonging to it shall be allowed except a regular sale by authority of the corporation.

NOTE. Sections 25 and 26 render the giving of a bond or security unnecessary. The design of these corporations is to give every homeless citizen an equal chance to get a home. That no person may, through wealth, influence or cunning get an extra advantage beside, no member is allowed to have any profit, salary or possible gain, except this chance. Shares are issued in corporations to be traded upon, and piled up in the hands of a few who control all the votes; here each has an equal chance and vote, and no certificates are issued for the poor man to sell for a mess of pottage. By this plan no man can work for his own selfish interest, and his only interest in the corporation will be to promote the general interest of the members.

A good lawyer, or a sensible man, when he reads the words "no member of such corporation. shall directly *or indirectly* derive any pecuniary profit from the same, will know that this is not a money making scheme; but fools will hunt for a selfish motive, as some are now hunting for perpetual motion, with as good a prospect of finding it."

No loan or gift is allowed because in Lynn it was found to create hard feeling if such were refused by an officer. By placing it beyond their power this is avoided.

SECT. 15 No assessment shall be laid upon a member of any such corporation to exceed one dollar and twenty cents per annum.

NOTE. The business must be done economically, and members are not to be taxed for unnecessary expenses, such as finely carpeted offices, lithographed letter heads, and other vain luxuries, the cost of which ought to go towards housing the homeless.

SECT. 16. Regular meetings of such corporations shall be held on the first Monday evening of each month, at eight o'clock. Special meetings may be held upon other days, at the same hour and place as regular meetings, under such rules as the by-laws of the corporation may prescribe.

Twelve members, one of whom must be an officer, shall be necessary to constitute a quorum at any meeting. But a less number may hold a regular meeting for the purpose only of receiving payments, and if both the treasurer and assistant treasurer be absent, they may elect a treasurer *pro tempore*, to whom the payments may be made. Four members of the board of directors shall constitute a quorum of that board.

NOTE. If there is a regular meeting night for these corporations throughout the state everybody will understand and remember it; and a man cannot so well illegally join more than one corporation. The advantage is similar to that of a uniform day for elections. Payments must be received at a regular meeting night, and it will sometimes occur that no quorum is present.

SECT. 17. No person shall be elected to any office in such a corporation of which he is not a member; and any officer can be removed from office by a four-fifths vote of the members present, provided not more than two officers are removed at any one meeting.

NOTE. By the last clause sudden evolutions in office are prevented.

SECT. 18. The term of office in such corporations shall expire at regular meetings as follows:

In January, the office of	Seventh Director.
In February, that of	Assistant Clerk.
In March, that of	Sixth Director.
In April, that of	Clerk.
In May, that of	Fifth Director.

In June, that of Assistant Treasurer.
In July, that of Fourth Director.
In August, that of Treasurer.
In September, that of Third Director.
In October, that of Vice President.
In November, that of Second Director.
In December, that of President and First Director.

NOTE. This plan prevents a regular succession, by which incompetent men being regularly promoted through a sort of good natured courtesy, can arrive at the higher offices. As but one office becomes vacant at a time, each officer's character and ability are examined more closely than if all were to be elected at one time; and it also prevents any sudden change in the official body. Notice particularly the regular order in which they become vacant.

Endeavors will be made to throw out this section to prevent the *gradual* change of officers, and have all offices become vacant at the same time, thus compelling an almost entire reelection of the former officers to prevent sudden change in so many departments at one time; also enabling tricksters to combine, and by trading votes with each other vote themselves into office over and over again, until finally, honest members finding they could not control, would leave, when the tricksters would claim members could not be found to even supervise the work without pay, and would in the end get fat salaries out of it, which workmen would have to pay.

SECT. 19. In case there should fail to be an election to any office in any such corporation upon its becoming vacant, the member who has not held said office during any part of the preceding term, and who is not then holding office, and who has within a year held the highest office in the corporation which has been held by such a person, shall assume said vacant office and hold the same until an election is had, which shall be as soon as may be. Officers shall rank in the order in which they are named in section five.

No officer shall be elected to the same office two successive terms, and no member shall hold two offices at the same time except that the president shall also be first director.

NOTE. This prevents a vacancy occurring in case there is no election. By the constant change here provided, no person is allowed to foist himself into an office perpetually, and feel that he runs it, and can do as he pleases with it, perhaps embezzle, and nobody meddle with him.

No man ever was or ever will be *essential* to the success of the work of any office, position or cause.

SECT. 20. The board of directors subject to this act and the by-laws of any such corporation shall receive, invest, manage and apply to the purposes of the corporation, all funds and estate of such corporation, and may sell and transfer any of said estate. It shall make all agreements for and purchases of labor, stock and land; *provided*, that no contract or conveyance shall be made for more than the amount of three hundred dollars without a previous vote by the corporation authorizing the same.

NOTE. The directors should never be allowed to make a contract for a larger amount than $300 for if it is done, the supervision is taken further from the people; and for the good of the work it is actually necessary that the main management should be as near the citizens as possible.

SECT. 21, If at any time the officers of any such corporation are unable to give the time necessary for a proper performance of their duties, the board of directors may be authorized by such corporation to employ persons not members of the same to assist said officers. No person shall be so employed till approved by said corporation, nor during any part of two successive years, nor for any longer time than the pleasure of the corporation. Such persons shall receive such compensation as said corporation shall determine, at the rate of not exceeding four hundred dollars each per year. An equitable proportion of the amount paid for such compensation, shall be added to the cost of each house sold. Not more than two such persons shall be employed at one time; nor more than one when the amount of capital of said corporation is less than twenty thousand dollars.

NOTE. By employing persons not members of the association, changing them every year, and putting the wages low, the position is prevented from being a prize for the control of which members might contend. These places will be a valuable assistance to promising young people not established in life, who can thus earn a trifle, which will be quite an item to *them* under the supervision of older heads, and at the same time gain valuable experience, and, to some extent, prove their fitness for more lucrative and responsible situations.

Strong endeavors will be made to weed this clause out so as to run it into paying offices. Enemies will contend that those who have occupied one year will be better qualified to act two; this would be so if any one person ever did know *everything* and was also the most honest, but that never has happened, and a man NEVER *died* but a better man could be found to fill his place. Besides, leave a man in office over a year and he begins to think that office is for his benefit instead of for that of the people. This feeling increases so rapidly the longer the position is held, that even the people begin to think it is so, and don't dare to question the master. Use reason every time and you will make fewer mistakes in life; trust in yourself above all others.

SECT. 22. The commissioner of corporations shall prepare and cause to be manufactured, a sufficient number of blank record and account books, and such other blank forms as he may deem expedient, in uniform style, to be determined by him; and said books and forms shall be furnished at cost to any such corporation which shall apply therefor. All such corporations shall conform to the forms so prescribed.

NOTE. Uniformity in method will simplify the work, and the commissioner will have the benefit of suggestions arising from the experience or all in devising the one best method for all. See note on section 9.

SECT. 23. It shall be the duty of the officers of such corporations to cause to be kept a full list of the members of said corporations and their residences; and also two full sets of accounts by double entry, showing all matters or transaction affecting the property of said corporations; one to be kept by or under the direction of the treasurer, and the other by or under the direction of the clerk; each set of said accounts shall be kept in separate buildings.

NOTE. This section is designed to prevent the possibility of loss of the accounts and most important records of a corporation, by fire or otherwise.

Methods of Doing Business.

SECT. 24. At every regular meeting of any such corporation the records and all books belonging to said corporation shall be open to the inspection of any editor of a newspaper or periodical published in the Commonwealth, and to the chairman of the selectmen of the town, or the mayor of the city in which said corporation is located, or such person as he may designate; and any such editor or other person may copy such extracts as he may see fit from the records.

NOTE. This work being of public interest, the newspapers will, by means of this section, be enabled to prevent any questionable transactions being secretly carried on, by exposing them, if commenced. Belonging to a city or town as much, if not more, than anything else they own, it should be under the direct supervision of their duly elected officers, and this section places it there.

SECT. 25. Such corporations shall designate some bank or banks at which it shall deposit its moneys.

No person or persons shall have authority to endorse or cash checks made payable to the order of any such corporation; except that the treasurer, or in his absence, the assistant treasurer may endorse such checks for deposit only in the aforesaid bank or banks, to the credit of said corporation's account.

Payments to any such corporation shall be valid only when made by check payable to the order of said corporation and duly honored, unless the amount of said payment is actually deposited in said bank at some time to the credit of said corporation: *provided*, that an officer's return of satisfaction upon any execution issued in favor of any such corporation shall have the usual effect; but said officer shall be bound to pay the amount collected to the corporation by a check duly honored in the same manner as to any other person.

All money or checks received by any such corporation shall at once be deposited in the bank or banks which said corporation has designated as provided for by this section.

NOTE. The trouble and risk of handling considerable sums of money, with the consequent risk of robbery and loss, is avoided by the provisions of this section.

By means of this section no money belonging to such corporations is allowed to pass through the hands of any person on its way into the bank, unless the careless ones who are too lazy, and the mean ones who are too close to buy a *bank check*, choose to take the risk of any loss which may happen to the corporation by their negligence in paying cash, and give bonds for the treasurer which they virtually have to under this section for such neglect on their part.

SECT. 26. No money shall be paid by any corporation except upon bills audited and approved by the clerk, or in his absence by the assistant clerk, to whose satisfaction they shall be proved correct.

The clerk shall at once report in writing to the president, or in his absence to the vice president, the amounts of all bills approved by him, with the name of the party to whom each is due.

All payments shall be by check on the bank in which the corporation deposits, signed by the treasurer, or in his absence by the assistant treasurer, and sealed with the seal of the corporation. All checks shall be made payable to the payee or order, three days from date, and shall never be antedated.

All instruments under seal shall be executed by the treasurer in the name and behalf of the corporation. The treasurer shall give and receive receipts for everything received or parted with by the corporation however small may be its value.

The seal of the corporation shall always be in the custody of the president, or, in his absence, of the vice president, and shall be affixed to any paper only by said custodian after careful inquiry as to the propriety thereof.

NOTE. In Section 25, very careful provision is made to prevent any loss to the fund of the association on its way into the bank; and this section prevents any improper abstraction of money from the bank after it is there, and is far preferable to a careless handling of money, secured by the giving of a bond as security for it, as in most other corporations, which bond is seldom paid in case of loss. This system renders a bond unnecessary, and officers in these corporations will not be elected because of their wealth and ability to furnish a bond, but because of their good character; the security of three well known men of character is better than all the bonds in the world. Endeavors will also be made to throw out these two sections by enemies. The consent of three men holding the three most responsible positions in the corporation is actually necessary before one cent can be drawn, and even then not until three days afterwards. The seal being in possession of the president, no bond or deed can be executed by the treasurer without his knowledge and supervision. The giving and receiving of receipts prevents dispute in every case.

SECT. 27. All contracts for labor shall be made by the job, and shall contain a time stipulated for completion; times for paying instalments as the work progresses, the amounts being so fixed that a balance sufficient to protect the corporation from loss shall always be due until seven days after the work is finished; and a provision for a penalty in case of violation of the terms of the contract sufficient to protect the funds or the corporation from loss. The terms of the contract shall be fixed by the board of directors, and all agreements for stock, labor or land shall be in writing, signed by a majority of the board of directors, and by the other parties to the contract.

Such agreements shall contain a statement that to the best of the knowledge and belief of the contracting parties, no member or members of the corporation have any pecuniary interest in said agreement except as members of the corporation.

NOTE. Those who are experienced in building will see clearly, upon reflection, that for the success of the work of this corporation it is absolutely necessary that labor should be performed by the job, and not by the day. No business man would be likely to sign the statement provided for by the last paragraph with the consequent liability for damages in the future, unless it were strictly true.

As it will be for the best interests of the people that the stock should be purchased, and the labor contracted for separately, the limit of seven days will be sufficient to protect most any such corporation from loss on account of labor. Every endeavor should be made to so arrange matters that the workingman can take the work, which he often could not compete for if credit had to be obtained and given by him on the stock, this will enable him to get more pay for his labor and will prevent bloated contractors standing by with hands in their pockets and oaths in their mouths, gathering in from the working people $10 per day for the profanity they invest in the job.

Contractors of course will fight the bill for it is so arranged that they cannot make fortunes out of it.

SECT. 28. No purchase shall be made by any such corporation upon credit, and all the business of said corporation shall be done for cash so far as practicable. No title shall be given by any such corporation to any real estate sold by it until full payment has been received for the same.

NOTE. Compelling associations to buy for cash, enables them to buy stock at low prices, makes their trade desirable, and the enormous quantities they will buy throughout the state, will make such competion for their trade, that they will be able to obtain in the end the *lowest* prices, keeps them constantly on a solid basis, and prevents speculation and failure from hard times. Not all the corporations will have the requisite financial talent for doing a credit business.

SECT. 29. Not over one-tenth of the cash in the treasury of any such corporation shall at one time be paid or agreed to be paid for real estate bought by said corporation, nor shall any real estate be purchased by any of said corporations so long as it owns any real estate not allotted to parties to be bought by them on instalments, but this shall not apply to payments by a corporation on account of houses and lots previously assigned and forfeited for failure to meet payments.

NOTE. Experience has taught that one-tenth the amount of money on hand is about the proportion that should be used in purchasing land for this purpose. If more is found to be needed, any future legislature can easily alter the amount. It is important that too much should not be tied up in dead land; those who have dealt in real estate will easily understand the importance of this. It is not intended to buy large tracts, and establish colonies of those who are just struggling into homes, to be called some slurring local name by envious people who have more wealth, and are afraid the owners will eventually outstrip them in means and social standing.

If allowed to purchase at any price, land monopolists finding the people were in the market for the land, would put it at such extortionate prices that most of the loan would be in land instead of in dwellings. On the page of figures you can see how easily half the money *could* be invested in land, if land monopolists force the people to do so.

SECT. 30. No land shall be bought by the corporation until the title has first been examined and passed by a competent attorney, and a warranty deed shall be insisted upon by the corporation. The corporation shall sell land by quit-claim deed only. All buildings when completed shall be kept fully insured until they pass out of the hands of the corporation.

NOTE. A quit-claim deed gives all the corporation ever has, subject only to the limitations and restrictions distinctly expressed in the deeds; the buyer should not require the corporation to insure his title, besides taking the great care to see that it is good, which is required in this section.

Methods of Disposing of Property.

SECT. 31. Whenever such a corporation is ready to erect a house, the right to occupy and buy said house, with the lot upon which it is to be situated, shall be drawn by lot at the next regular monthly meeting, all members present having an equal chance to draw the right. The successful person shall receive the bond provided by section thirty-four, as soon as the house is ready for occupancy, and have all the rights guaranteed thereby.

The right to occupy and buy houses shall be drawn at regular intervals so far as convenient, and rights may be drawn through the winter, though the corporation may not be ready on account of the season of the year to begin building, provided there are funds in the treasury at the time of drawing sufficient to build all houses drawn. In such case the houses shall be built as speedily as possible when the season opens.

If no member wishes the right due notice shall be given, and at the next meeting any person eligible to membership shall be allowed to draw the right on the same terms as a member, and with the same rights if successful.

The person drawing a right shall in all cases act as an overseer without pay, of the construction of the house, and report to the clerk in writing as soon as possible any waste of stock, defect in workmanship, or failure to fulfil the terms of the contract, that may come under his observation, and all such reports shall be considered by the board of directors.

Any person drawing a right, may, if he has a lot considered by the directors suitable to build a house upon, deed the same to the corporation for a nominal consideration, and have his house built upon it, and the amount he is to pay shall not include any charge for the lot.

NOTE. If a person does not feel interested enough in getting a home, to appear at the meeting, he would be very likely to fail to pay for one. By drawing for homes throughout the winter hope is kept alive in all, and they should not be drawn ahead, as it consequently decreases hope.

No person would naturally be so much interested in the erection of the building as the prospective owner, and beside the regular supervision of the association, an extra hand is secured in him.

By the last section provision is made for those who can afford a large lot, to obtain a house on the same without detriment to other members of the corporation, as no larger amount will be taken from *the fund* to provide the land than would be required for a less costly piece of ground. The 1-10 ground tax will make it desirable for families to content themselves with a small piece of land.

SECT. 32. So long as any person is ready to buy of any such corporation a house and lot costing not over three hundred dollars, said corporation shall furnish no house and lot costing more than that sum, nor so long as a person is ready to buy and pay for a house of the following dimensions and containing four rooms, shall any such corporation build any wooden house of different dimensions or style than as follows: twenty-eight feet long by thirteen feet wide, with a straight flight of stairs three feet wide running up in the centre, having eleven steps of eight inch rise leading to a landing which shall be eight inches below the upper floor; the side sills shall be made from lumber twenty-eight feet long by six inches square, having a piece cut from one corner twenty-eight feet long four inches wide and two inches thick, leaving a ledge on the lower inside edge of said sill two inches square on which the lower floor joists are to rest; the end sills shall be thirteen feet long by four inches square, the ends of which are to fill places on the ends of the side sills from which four-inch cubes have been cut; the lower floor joists seventeen in number, of two by six inch lumber twelve feet four inches long; two of the lower floor joists shall be placed one on each side of the centre of the side sills one foot seven inches distant therefrom, two of the upper floor joists and two sets of rafters shall be directly above them in their respective places; the upper floor joists twenty in number of two by six inch lumber thirteen feet long, leaving seven feet, six inches in the clear between them and the lower floor joist; the corner posts fourteen feet long by five inches square, having a piece cut from one corner two inches square and fourteen feet long; there shall be forty side studs of two by three inch lumber fourteen feet long set fourteen inches from each other, commencing at the corner posts and setting towards the centre; the sixteen end studs of the proportionate length and set in place in like manner; the plates of two by three inch lumber; there shall be seventeen sets of rafters of two by three inch lumber cut for a half pitch roof; the collar beams of two by three inch lumber, nailed in their places so as to leave seven feet six inches in the clear between them and the upper floor joist; the furring of one by three inch lumber; the floors of single matched boards; the base boards six inches wide; the corner and saddle boards four and five inches wide; the side fascia boards eight inches and the end ones six inches wide; no coving shall be added until the house is fully paid for; the shingles and clapboards shall be of spruce.

The doors shall be six feet six inches long, two feet four inches wide and an inch and a quarter thick; the front doorway shall enter from opposite the lower landing of the stairs; the front doors shall have the two largest panels made of plain ground glass; plain rim-locks or catches shall be used on the doors; the windows shall be an inch and a quarter thick and contain four lights each of twelve by twenty four inch glass; the chimney shall rest on a stone or on the ground and be built five bricks to the course, and run up in as near the centre of the house as the stairs will allow in the room designed to be used for a kitchen; the house shall rest on fourteen posts, one at each corner, one at each end, and four on each side, no cellar being furnished,—nor a brick house of different style and dimensions from said wooden house, except that the roof joists may be longer and three inches wider, and the foundation shall be of stone or brick, which may include a cellar.

When there is no demand for houses of the style above described, only houses of the same general style, but thirteen feet wide by forty feet long and containing six rooms, shall be furnished so long as a person shall desire such a house. The chimney for the additional rooms shall run up through the ridge and through the same rooms as the other chimney.

When there is no demand for houses of the foregoing styles, only houses of the same general style, but thirteen feet wide by forty-six feet long containing eight rooms, shall be furnished, so long as a person shall desire such a house. If wished the six and eight roomed houses may be obtained in the brick buildings erected by adding one or two stories extra.

Any person buying a house and lot worth more than three hundred dollars of said corporation, shall pay ten per centum of its cost at the time of receiving the privilege of buying it, and the balance in instalments the same as in the case of other houses and lots.

NOTE. An inexpensive style of house is to be built so long as there is a demand for it, that those who are most in need may first be benefitted, and also that a larger number may participate in the benefits, as more houses can thus be built from a given fund in the same length of time. A uniform style is required for these houses, as experience has shown it to be more generally satisfactory, and the houses being built by wholesale will be built much cheaper. The payment of ten per cent. in advance on the more expensive houses, falls on the class best able to bear it, protects the corporation against too great single risks of non-payment of instalments, and those who feel it too burdensome ought to be more economical in their selection of a house, and thus at the same time be surer of success in getting their homes, and leave the state the extra funds to use in furnishing other citizens with homes.

After the occupant of any wooden house has paid for the same, he can easily build a cellar under it, and by not having the expense of one to pay for when first starting, he is the more sure of paying for his home. In brick houses the cellar cannot be conveniently dug after the frame is built, and whenever it is possible it should be included in the original work of the contractor. These houses are small, but they give four rooms, each twelve feet square, and it is much better to build a home that can be paid for by the occupants, than an extravagant one which they cannot buy.

The small four roomed homes can easily be paid for by single women and by thus making them independent we confer one of the greatest blessings on them and on the human race at large. Many a helpless woman has been forced into a repulsive marriage for lack of a home; the curses of which only a few weeks experience in a divorce court makes plain to the most skeptical. Man ought to have reached that plane of civilization in which some thought can be spared from self to advance the interest of those whose main fault is loving them. The ten per cent. payment in advance on all houses costing over $300, will force people to be economical and happy instead of extravagant and unhappy in endeavoring to outdo others. If to surpass each other in character was made half as earnest an aim as to outstrip in style, this world would be a happy place to live in.

The rich laugh at and ridicule those who try to equal them, as all of us would a monkey endeavoring to equal us in dress and style. Strenuous endeavors will be made to make the limit $500,- for the benefit of contractors. Experience has taught that $300 is the proper limit at present. Future legislatures can alter if needed. If $500 limit is made, then for the success of the plan, a proportionate increase of the time for payment is actually necessary, for many people will not be able to pay $100 per year for five years.

SECT. 33. All land when bought by any such corporation, must be divided at once into suitable sized lots by the board of directors, who shall apportion the cost value among said lots, taking into account desirability and relative situation. Such lots may afterwards be sold singly, or two or more may be joined in one.

NOTE. A more correct and impartial appraisal can be made in the first place than after private interests in the land, or parts of it, have been attached. There is especial danger that the best locations will be valued too low comparatively, and go off rapidly, while the rest remain as dead stock. Experience has taught that the easiest way to get at the proportionate value of the land, is to reckon the value of the smaller lots, in combination with the value of the houses proposed to be erected thereon.

SECT. 34. Whenever a person shall obtain the right to occupy and buy a house and lot to be provided by such a corporation, a bond for a deed, signed and sealed by the treasurer on behalf of the corporation, shall be given to him, and if the cost of said house and lot amounts to three hundred dollars or more, there shall be appended to such bond a copy from the records of the corporation, attested by the clerk, showing that the obligee has duly obtained the right to receive such bond. Said bond shall contain the provisions of this and the following section in regard to payment for the estate, the effect of failure to pay, and the giving of the deed therefor; and shall also contain a statement that said bond is given under the authority of this act, and subject to the provisions thereof. The amount to be paid for the estate shall be its actual cost, computed by the directors as exactly as possible, including the fair proportionate cost of the land, cost of building house, of insurance, searching title, making out papers, drainage, grading and other improvements; it shall also include such necessary expenses as may be incurred by the corporation on account of said estate, between the time of giving the bond and the time of giving the deed; except the last named item, the amount shall be specified in the bond, and the penalty of the bond shall be the same amount. The first instalment shall be paid at the next regular meeting after the house is ready for occupancy, the advance payment, if any is necessary, having been made as provided in section thirty-two, the amount of his admission fee being credited to the obligee, if he was a member of the corporation when he obtained the right to buy said estate, when he has paid for the remainder of its cost, deducting the amount of said admission fee. The remainder of the amount specified in the bond shall be paid in forty-eight equal instalments, except as hereinafter provided. one to be made at each successive regular monthly meeting, the remainder of the cost, if any, to be paid in the same manner in successive monthly instalments of the same amount as those previously made, until all is paid.

Every person obtaining the right to occupy and buy such a house and lot, shall after making four full payments on the same, have the privilege of omitting to pay not to exceed one instalment the first six months, or two instalments the first year, or three instalments the first sixteen months, or four instalments the first twenty months, or five instalments the first two years, or six instalments the first twenty-eight months, or seven instalments the first thirty-two months, or eight instalments the first three years, or nine instalments the first thirty-nine months, or ten instalments the first forty-two months. or eleven instalments the first forty-five months, or twelve instalments the first four years; provided all such omitted instalments are paid by him before the end of the fifth year. But all estates must be fully paid for within five years. and the terms of payment shall be the same for all buyers, unless otherwise provided by this act.

Every person upon paying the first instalment due upon the house and lot, shall have the right to occupy the same without payment of rent or interest so long as he shall continue to pay the instalments as above provided. Any buyer may pay for his estate as much faster than is required by his bond as he may see fit; no expenditure shall be made upon the houses and lots, except as ordered by the corporation, until the buyer has received his deed.

The treasurer, without special authority, shall give a quit-claim deed as soon as any estate is seasonably paid for in full, and not before. Said deed shall be signed and sealed by the treasurer on behalf of the corporation, and shall recite as its consideration the giving of the bond and the payments made, stating the then exact aggregate amount, with all restrictions and conditions under which it has been sold.

NOTE. By this section buyers are carefully protected from the disasters that hard times often bring on the careless and improvident, as it allows twenty five per cent of the payments to be deferred; consequently buyers are encouraged by these deferred payments to form a sort of reserve fund, as a security against a possible inability to pay future instalments. By preventing the occupants from making any improvements before the property is paid for, we protect them from themselves by preventing their laying out their money on the property of some one else. Experience has taught that most persons are so anxious to get full possession of the estates, in order to commence their improvements, that payments will be made a long time before they become due. In case the buyer belonged to the association, the five dollars he paid as an admission fee is kept for him as a nest egg, by which to help meet his last payment; after struggling thus for so many years to pay for the place, this will be welcome help at the last moment, when his endurance is becoming exhausted.

As the bond has to be sealed by the president as per section 26, the association is guarded from loss.

The occupant not being allowed to improve the property until it belongs to him is an extra security furnished to protect and is entirely different from what *land* LORDS wish done: they will allow the most extravagant improvements on their property if a tenant will pay for it.

SECT. 35. Whenever any person, holding or being entitled to a bond or deed, shall fail to keep the provisions of such bond, he shall immediately vacate the house and lot for which he holds said bond, and surrender the same to the corporation from which he obtained it; and should he fail to do so the board of directors may recover possession of said house and lot, in the manner provided by chapter one hundred and seventy-five of the Public Statutes, and it shall be their duty to at once recover possession of the same in that or some other suitable manner; upon recovering such house and lot, the corporation shall pay to the treasurer of the commonwealth for the benefit of the person who held a bond therefor an equitable compensation for what said person has invested upon said house and lot, deducting therefrom any expense incurred in recovering possession. In case of any dispute as to the amount of such compensation, said house and lot shall be sold at auction, and after deducting the unpaid instalments due, expenses of sale, and any other expenses which said corporation has necessarily incurred on account of said house and lot, the balance, if any, shall be paid to the treasurer of the commonwealth. The treasurer upon the payment of any sum to him under the provisions of this section shall at once issue a certificate therefor in the same manner and with the same effect as those authorized in section thirty-nine of this act.

No person shall be allowed to transfer or assign any right under a bond, nor the right to receive a bond or to occupy a house belonging to such a corporation, to any other person, but shall surrender the right to said corporation if he does not choose to keep it himself.

NOTE. Everything is against the interests of the associations, and in favor of the interest of the individuals; objection is made to this by many, but as the whole purpose for which the corporations are established is for the interest of individuals, it seems only right to make the law so as to effect that end. If any person is allowed to transfer a right there would be combination of those who did not want a house for themselves, to draw it for some friend.

Any family not owning a home would have to pay as much per month for rent, so if *all* they paid in was *lost* to them they would be no worse off than they are to-day, paying rent. But the aim of the government being to furnish homes for every family in the state, provision is here made by which if through carelessness or any unforseen circumstances a family miss their payments, most of what is paid in each time will accumulate in the state treasury to help them in paying for the next house taken, until finally enough is saved to furnish the family the home aimed for. It also prevents the thriftless improvident class from using this as a means to accumulate from rent thus saved enough to go on a summer excursion at the expense of present benefits to their family, and future cost to the community. At an auction sale the association can make *one* bid which must be sufficient to repay the amount due the state fund; whatever the estate brings above that amount is deposited in the state treasury for the future benefit of the family giving up the house.

Relations to State; Conditions of Sale.

SECT. 36. There shall be paid from the treasury of the Commonwealth to every such corporation one thousand dollars on the first Tuesday of every month succeeding that in which the certificate of incorporation provided by section six is issued to said corporation: *provided*, that the whole amount paid to corporations formed in any city or town shall not exceed five thousand dollars in a town containing not more than five thousand inhabitants: and in cities and towns containing more than five thousand inhabitants one thousand dollars for each thousand inhabitants, and an additional thousand dollars for the remainder, if any; nor exceed twenty thousand dollars to any one corporation; and that no payment of money shall be made to any corporation while it has more than five hundred dollars cash in its treasury.

For the purpose of meeting any expenses that may be incurred under the provisions of this act, the treasurer is hereby authorized upon the order of the governor and council, to issue scrip or certificates of debt to an amount not exceeding three million dollars, which shall be expressed in such currency and shall bear such rate of interest, not exceeding four per centum per annum, as the governor and council may direct, and shall be redeemable in not less than twenty nor more than fifty years from the date thereof; and said treasurer shall sell or otherwise dispose of the same as he may deem proper, subject to the approval of the governor and council. To provide for the payment of the scrip or certificates of debt to be issued under the authority of this act, a sinking fund is hereby created to be composed of whatever premium may be received from the sale thereof, (and its accumulations of interest), beyond the cost of preparing and negotiating the same, and so much of the receipts from ground rent as provided for by section thirty-eight of this act, as together with its accumulations of interest and the said premium and its accumulations will be sufficient to pay said scrip at maturity. The said fund, together with its accumulations of interest, shall be invested as is now or may be provided by law for the investment of such funds, and shall be pledged and held as the sinking fund hereby established, and shall be used for the redemption and payment of said scrip or certificates of debt, and for no other purpose whatever.

NOTE. It is best not to have too much ready money for these corporations to handle, until the corporators are somewhat used to the business; consequently it is to be given to them monthly in small instalments. By borrowing the money in a foreign country, we avoid taking it, or keeping it, from any industry in our own state; and as we bring in the capital from abroad, no property already in this state will be on account of this act exempted from taxation, and so no additional burden of taxation is laid on any citizen, but the reverse will be proved a fact; for, besides improving business, on account of the extensive building operations it will necessitate, it will increase the value of unimproved real estate, and so, enormously enlarge the taxable property, thus relieving those now burdened with taxation.

The state has loaned millions on millions of dollars to the rich corporators of many railroads which they used to make money with for themselves, and it was known and fully understood that they would do so when the loans were made. The state spends *permanently* and will continue to do so, millions of dollars to educate our citizens, care for our poor, for our insane, and for our idiots.

Yet here is only a *temporary* loan asked for with the best of security offered, to establish an educational system for married people, that will prove a proper and well timed help to many thousand deserving citizens who are struggling for a home.

The premium received from the sale of the bonds at 4 per cent., together with its accumulations, if invested as the law now requires, sinking funds to be invested will be sufficient to repay the whole $3,000,000 at the end of 20 years; so all that will have to be provided for will be the yearly interest; and the ground rent at the lowest rate possible will *surely* pay that inside of 40 years, and shrewd scholars will quickly see how it will be done in 20 years time on account of increased valuation of the real estate.

This section loans even the smallest towns $5000, and over a dollar apiece for every man, woman and child in every city or town in the state. $20,000 is enough for the state to invest in any single risk, and if many such sums were lost to the state, it would not amount to much when compared with the happiness created by the successful associations.

SECT. 37. Towns and cities may, by vote, grant to such corporations the free use, for its meeting and offices, of any room or rooms belonging to said towns or cities. They shall be liable to pay to the Commonwealth, any amounts due to the same from any such corporations located within their respective limits; and may recover in an action of contract from any such corporation any amount so paid on its account.

NOTE. The corporations are completely under the direction and control of the citizens, even more so than the municipal governments, and it will be good policy for the municipality to loan rooms for the use of these corporations. The money paid by the state, is in effect, a loan of the state's credit to the cities or towns, and is made in this manner to encourage thrift and frugality. By this means, we get the great benefit of making an extensive state system. It is in reality an educational plan, like the school system, designed to train married people in protecting their families from want, and giving them "happiness and the blessings of life."

The millions invested every year in education of the children of the poor in book knowledge is now considered all right, and so will millions invested to educate the people in home life be considered all right in the future.

If a city or town is indifferent they need not take the loan; but as it costs them nothing it would be mean in any city or town to oppose any other in obtaining that which is for the happiness of their citizens.

SECT. 38. All lands sold by any such corporation shall forever after be subject to a yearly payment of ten per centum of the assessed valuation of said land (excluding buildings) for the year, which sum shall be a lien on said land, to be enforced by the party to whom such payment is to be made, in the same manner as liens for taxes on real estate may now be enforced by the city or town to which said taxes are payable.

Said payment shall be made to such corporation as originally sold said land, or to such corporation or officer as may hereafter be designated by law, on or before the first Monday in October of each year; and said corporation shall before the first Monday in December, and after the first Monday of November of each year pay over to the treasurer of the Commonwealth all moneys in its possession received from this source; said payment shall be used by said treasurer, first, to pay the interest on the loan provided for by section thirty-six of this act, and the excess, if any, shall be added to the sinking fund provided for by said section, except as is hereinafter provided for.

NOTE. Ten per cent. is about the amount allowed to be invested in land: that is, a $900 house could be put on a $100 lot, then the payment per year to the state, on account of land rent, would be but $10. The payments can be made in the latter part of the year easier than at any other time, and the money is placed in the state treasury as early as can be conveniently done. The amount can be easily paid, and it is a fair demand that the state may be gradually reimbursed by those whom its bounty has aided, and afterwards helped in giving aid to others who need it. The ground rent will surely repay the state for all expenses incurred in 40 years; one-tenth seems a small amount but it will repay the state in that time.

SECT. 39. At any time after the first Monday in October, and before the first Monday in November, any person over twenty-one years of age, and not under guardianship, may make affidavit and prove to the satisfaction of the president, treasurer and clerk, or a majority of them, of any such corporation that he has for at least nine months of the year next preceding said first Monday in October, actually resided upon land originally sold by said corporation; a like affidavit and proof may be made by any such person in behalf of any person under twenty-one years of age, or under guardianship. As soon as the total amount paid to the treasurer of the commonwealth by any such corporation as provided in section thirty-eight shall be sufficient to pay interest on all amounts which said corporation shall have received from the commonwealth (except any received upon the certificates provided for by section thirty-five) and its proportion of the amount of the scrip authorized by section thirty-six which would remain unpaid if the said sinking fund were at that time applied to the payment of said scrip, (such proportion to be the same as that which the amount received by said corporation from the commonwealth bears to the total amount of said scrip, issued, said corporation shall with each payment so made thereafter to the treasurer of the Commonwealth, transmit a certificate signed by the president, clerk and treasurer, and sealed with the seal of the corporation, showing the names and residences of all persons whose residence during the current year has been proved to said corporation as provided for in this section. The treasurer of the Commonwealth shall thereupon issue, through said corporation, to each person contained in said list, a certificate stating that such person is entitled to an amount which is to be determined by dividing the whole amount received in that year from such corporations who have fully reimbursed the Commonwealth, by the total number of names contained in all lists transmitted by them as provided by this section, fractions of cents being disregarded. Said certificates shall be sealed with the seal of the corporation, through whom they are distributed, and shall not be transferable or negotiable, except as hereinafter provided, and shall be void in the hands of any other person than the hands of the ones to whom they were originally issued. Said certificates shall be received by any corporation formed under the provisions of this act, in lieu of cash, from any person who has received from said corporation the privilege of occupying and buying a house and lot therefrom, or the husband or wife of such person, as a final payment on said house and lot when sufficient to pay all due upon it. Said corporation shall thereupon be paid from the treasury of the Commonwealth the amount of all such certificates as it shall present to the treasurer of the Commonwealth, upon proving that it has given to the person to whom they were issued, or the husband or wife of such person, a deed of a house and lot under the provisions of this act. In case of persons holding said certificates moving from the state, the treasurer of the Commonwealth may cash the same on receiving proof that the holder has given to the person to whom they were issued, or the husband or wife of such person, a deed of a house and lot out of the state. Said certificates shall be received or cashed in no other way than as herein provided.

NOTE. These provisons are designed to compel those who have been helped to homes by the corporations to contribute their mite, when enjoying the consequent increase in their prosperity, to extend the same blessing to other citizens, and by means of this section the money for the ground rent returns to the family who pays it; and in the case of children, their certificates are allowed to accumulate until married or of age, when they are assured of a home of their own with a little exertion. If one of our citizens finds it for the advantage of him and his family to leave the state, our humanity ought to be large enough to be willing he should be happy anywhere and also willing to do all that can rightlv and justly be done on our part to effect that end.

SECT. 40. Every bond and deed executed by such corporations shall contain the the following clause: "Subject, however, to the condition that no intoxicating liquor shall ever be sold on said premises, but said condition not to be enforced by any entry at a time when the record title shows the fee to belong to a person who has actually resided upon the premises since acquiring the title under which he holds said fee, and that his title was acquired subsequently to the time when the last sale of intoxicating liquor occurred upon the premises." Whenever any corporation enters for breach of this condition upon any land of which it shall have given a deed, it shall at once become the duty of the treasurer thereof to execute a full quitclaim deed of the same in the name of said corporation, to the city or town in which said corporation is located, for the use of the public schools of said city or town.

NOTE. These houses are for small homes, and it is not desirable that the occupants of them should be allowed to retail liquor out of jugs in a petty way, as would inevitably be done, if at all, from such small dwelling houses. Every reflecting man, however much he may be opposed to sumptuary laws, which restrict the liberty of the citizen and commercial freedom, must be opposed to such a traffic; while this does not in any way interfere with the dealer in liquors, who complies with the provisions of our license laws, and invests capital in establishing convenient shops for satisfying the demands of the people in a law-abiding way. On the contrary, it protects them from the competition of a legion of petty tenement or dwelling house dealers who are responsible to no law; are the smugglers of the trade; and have done much to bring odium upon a business which should be conducted only under proper restrictions.

It is customary for a certain class of so-called reformers to speak of those who believe in licensing the sale of intoxicating beverages and their use in moderation by those whose health requires them, and of men in business who are engaged in this branch of trade, by various disgusting names such as pirates, scoundrels, thieves, robbers, villains, and destroyers of homes. Perhaps when a wise, well-considered, and conservative measure like the one here proposed, equally removed on the one hand, from that which would ruin a whole branch of business and all connected with it, however indirectly, and on the other from anarchy and unregulated liberty comes up, the people will learn by a yea and nay vote who are their true friends; and that it is not the most radical and loud-mouthed who *do* most for their welfare.

SECT. 41. Every householder having a family, shall be entitled to an estate of homestead, as provided in chapter one hundred and twenty-three of the Public Statutes, in any house and lot purchased by him of any such corporation, and all the provisions of said chapter shall apply to said estate, but said estate shall be exempt from attachment, levy on execution, and sale for the payment of debts contracted by him at any time, whether before or after acquiring said estate.

NOTE. Many men and women of family, working for less than one dollar a day, by lack of work, sickness, or many other causes, are so overwhelmed by debt that the chance of ever meeting their liabilities is hopeless. Yet they go struggling manfully on, feeling under the circumstances every man is an enemy and every law against them. They have small chance of passing through insolvency, as those can who have enjoyed wealth or controlled extensive business; is it not well, is it not good policy for the state to encourage these men by trying to establish them in a home which no unmerciful Shylock can take from them after the state by its liberality through these corporations has given it to them? The policy is already sanctioned in our homestead laws, but a man cannot by them gain immunity for his home from debts already contracted. Yet it is conceded by all parties that some relief should be given the poor man burdened with hopeless debt. See Gov. Robinson's inaugural, in which he advocates measures designed to bring the insolvency laws more easily and cheaply within their reach. This will only exempt $800. Besides it would be poor encouragement for the benevolent men and women who are to do the work, to do so feeling it is only to put more money into some wealthy person's coffers.

SECT. 42. All property, both real and personal, held by any such corporation, so long as it shall remain the property of said corporation and shall be used for the purposes and under the provisions of this act, shall be exempt from taxation.

NOTE. As many corporations as choose, composed of seven or more persons can form under the general laws and hold property to the amount of five hundred thousand dollars exempt from taxation. As the money which the corporations contemplated by this act are to use will be brought in from outside the state, the exemption will not increase the burden of taxation for other citizens, but will tend in the end to measurably relieve all from it.

SECT. 43. The treasurer of every such corporation shall, on the second Monday of each month, send to the commissioner of corporations a correct balance sheet showing the financial condition of said corporation; together with a statement of the amount paid for land, the number of houses built and the number paid for since the last statement, and also the number built and the number paid for together with the original and last assessed value of land purchased since said corporation was established, and the assessed value of the said land including buildings thereon: and said commissioner shall report annually to the legislature a summary of the condition of all such corporations, to be made up from such reports.

NOTE. It is best for the interests of the citizens for the state to keep a close eye on all these corporations. Besides it is important to watch their working and observe by statistics the effect of their operations, that their value may be better appreciated and we may learn by experience to improve them.

SECT. 44. Any treasurer violating the provisions of the preceding section shall forfeit the sum of five dollars, for the use of the public schools of the city or town in which the corporation of which he is treasurer is located.

NOTE. The penalty in this section is added to prevent any ignoramus or absent-minded blunderer from taking the office and doing the damage that would necessarily result, and the use of such money in the manner provided for will tend to prevent future repitition.

SECT. 45. In case any such corporation shall be formed in the city of Lynn, the Lynn Workingmen's Aid Association is hereby authorized upon a majority vote to transfer all its property to said corporation, and when such conveyance shall be made, chapter one hundred and ninety-five of the acts of eighteen hundred and eighty, incorporating said association, is hereby repealed.

NOTE. The Lynn Association was the pioneer, and has proved the practicability and wonderful efficiency of this plan in helping those who are down; but as this work is now laid out on a system throughout the state it can be better prosecuted in Lynn under the general system than by an indedendent corporation with necessarily limited means.

SECT. 46. The provisions of this chapter may be amended or repealed so as to affect existing corporations at the pleasure of the general court; the general court may by special act dissolve any corporation subject to said provisions; and no such corporations shall be dissolved in any other manner. In case any corporation shall be so dissolved, the treasurer of the Commonwealth shall take charge of all its property and preserve the same in a distinct fund. Upon the formation of another such corporation in place of the one dissolved, in the city or town in which said corporation was located, said fund, together with the balance if any which should have been paid to the dissolved corporation under the provision of section thirty-six if it had not been dissolved, shall be paid thereto in the same manner in which it is provided by section thirty-eight that money shall be paid by the Commonwealth to such corporations; said corporation shall receive no further grant from the state and shall be liable to make the same payments to the Commonwealth as the dissolved corporation would have been liable to make, had it continued.

NOTE. By this, a perfect control of these corporations is retained by the legislature, in whose hands, it is clear, full power over its organizations should ever remain. Strong opposition to this measure is sure to come from those who are revelling in luxury from the proceeds of rents wrung from the necessities of citizens by renting houses to them; but they will not offer their real reason for opposition, which will be the desire to make money by excessive charges for their tenements, but concoct some other reason entirely foreign to the real one, and by their smooth, oily way of putting it will bamboozle fools, and get them to side with such opposition; the opposition of the renters of property to this plan, will be avoided in the legislature, because the rules expressly forbid any member serving on a committee or voting on any question where his private right is immediately concerned, distinct from the public interest. When the yea and nay vote is called on this measure, it will plainly show how our legislators stand on the great question of administering the government so as to help the people and secure to them and their descendants the blessings our commonwealth was founded to secure.

Method of Incorporation and General Powers.

1. Incorporators No., age, purpose.
2. Agreement, nature of.
3. Payments in advance.
4. First meeting, how called.
5. First meeting, proceeding.
6. Incorporation; certificate; approval, endorsements.
7. Corporations, distribution of.
8. Name.
9. Seal.
10. Property, power of holding.
11. Property, not for offices.
12. By-laws.

Officers and Members and their Rights, Duties and Meetings.

13. Membership, conditions of.
14. Members equal. No salary.
15. Assessment on members limited.
16. Meetings, time of holding, Quorum.
17. Officers to be members. Removal of officers.
18. Office terms and tenure.
19. Election, failure of.
20. Directors, duties of.
21. Assistance, employment of.
22. Stationery furnished by state at cost.
23. Records, what and how kept.

Methods of Doing Business.

24. Records open to editors and city and town officials.
25. Payments to associations, Bank designated.
26. Payments by associations, Receipts, Sealed instruments.
27. Contracts and Agreements.
28. Credit prohibited.
29. Purchase of real estate, restriction on.
30. Title, insurance.

Methods of Disposing of Property.

31. Rights to buy, how allotted.
32. Styles of houses to be built first, smallest allowed.
33. Land to be divided and appraised.
34. Payments, time for, omitted instalments, Deeds.
35. Rights untransferable and forfeiture, what done with payments made.

Relations to State. Conditions of Sale.

36. Aid from the State, amount of Sinking fund.
37. Guarantee by towns; rooms loaned.
38. Ground rent, perpetual, State to receive the same.
39. Ground rent distributed to residents to pay for homes. Proof of residence.
40. Liquor selling condition.
41. Homestead law, and sold subject to.
42. Taxation, exemption.
43. Reports to State.
44. Reports, penalty for not making.
45. Lynn Association may surrender charter.
46. Dissolution by legislature.

HELP BEFORE OR AFTER.

DEAR SIR:—

In 1877, Gov. Rice in his address said, "the aggregate outlay for public and private charity is very large, amounting to $4,500,000, paid during the year 1876;" one-third by the state, one-third by cities and towns, one-third private institutions; and this does not take into account the millions spent by the plain people in charity.

Would it not be better to LOAN $3.000,000 today to house the citizens in homes of their own, and thus make them all independent, than spend $3,000,000 per year a short distance in the future, to take care of only a very few of them? The state government is formed for the purpose of conferring "happiness and the blessings of life on the people," and let us see it do its duty.

In 1880 our state contained 19 cities and 327 towns.

On account of the close packing of tenants by heartless *land* LORDS in the wards containing workingmen and women, there were four thousand two hundred and fifty-eight more deaths among these people than would have happened had the same number been housed on the less closely packed land of towns in our state.

That is the number of honest, hard-working people *murdered each year* by the greedy grasping *land* LORDS in cities, and is equal to blotting out of existence the inhabitants of over 15 of our small towns *every year.*

Each of those murders of working people, allowed by our government to be perpetrated by avaricious *land* LORDS, plundering and murdering for gold, causes pain and sorrow as intense as any we can feel, to equally loving hearts in the breast of these working men.

J. M. B.

If increase of wealth is the highest aim of Statesmen, this should be carefully read.

DEAR SIR:—**$51,522,576** can be made in sixty years by the state loaning **$3,000,000** to build homes for its citizens, as a bill to be brought before the Legislature provides. **$2,714,000** will be the amount necessary to supply every city and town with their allowance; the balance of the $3,000,000 loan can be used to pay interest for a few years.

Columbus knew of a new world without seeing it, and offered its wealth to his native state, and they scornfully refused it.

Another may offer wealth untold to his native state, and have it refused. It was *not the fault* of Columbus that he knew it; he did not have too much brain, but those who refused it had too little.

In 1876 the governor proved that $4,500,000 was spent in *charity.*

The happiness of our citizens ought to be the only aim of statesmen; if it were they would delight to read this.

The following figures show in detail only PART of the enormous benefits the state at large will derive at the end of 60 years, from an investment of $3,000,000 in the manner proposed in the Bill before the Legislature for the purpose of furnishing the citizens of our state with homes of their own.

The state treasurer can get a premium on 4 per cent. bonds of $3,000,000 sufficient for a sinking fund which can be invested so as to pay the whole of the bonds at maturity, so interest on it ends in twenty years.

In twenty years the receipts from taxes and ground rent will more than suffice to pay the interest on a $3,000,000 loan.

The average of taxes throughout the state is $15 per thousand of valuation; the return from that source will be enormously in advance of these figures from the increased valuation of this and the adjoining property on account of the improvements.

Only one-tenth of the cash in the treasury of a corporation on the first of each month is allowed to be invested in land during that month; and only one-tenth of the value of the land is paid back as ground rent; my figures do not take into account any increased value of the land that will come on account of its being built on and improved.

The direct return from ground rent will be much greater than these figures show, for suppose $10,000 to be on hand, only $\frac{1}{10}$ can be invested in land, during that month, or $1,000. Now suppose two houses, each worth $500 are built on the land, and both houses and land disposed of, there is still $8,000 in the treasury, and on the first of the next month one-tenth or $800 more of the original $10,000 can be invested in land, and so on.

The Lynn experiment showed an increase in the value of the last two lots of *land* bought of 400 per cent. in one year's time.

TOTALS OF FIGURES.

Real estate created,	$34,739,200
Amount from taxes,	14,329,920
Ground rent,	9,553,280
	$58,622,400
Less 1 per cent. for land gross	586,224
	58,036,176
Less interest,	6,513,600
Net total,	$51,522,576

This is only just the simple return in money value, and if this value at compound interest were taken into account, the amounts would be almost fabulous.

Now try to imagine the increased value to all property. Then dream of the future results.

The total of happiness (experience with legislation has taught me) is not to be considered in the State House, except by a very few.

J. M. B.

No. of years.	Value of the real estate created each year.	Amount receiv'd from taxes each year.	Amount rec'd from ground rent each yr.
1	$2,714,000		
2	542,800		
3	542,800		
4	542,800		
5	542,800		
6	542,800	$40,710	$27,140
7	542,800	48,852	32,568
8	542,800	56,994	37,996
9	542,800	65,136	43,424
10	542,800	73,278	48,852
11	542,800	81,420	54,280
12	542,800	89,562	59,708
13	542,890	97,704	65,136
14	542,800	105,846	70,564
15	542,800	113,988	75,992
16	542,800	122,130	81,420
17	542,800	130,272	86,848
18	542,800	138,414	92,276
19	542,800	146,556	97,704
20	542,800	154,698	103,132
21	542,800	162,840	108,560
22	542,800	170,982	113,988
23	542,800	179,124	119,416
24	542,800	187,266	124,844
25	542,800	195,408	130,272
26	542,800	203,550	135,700
27	542,800	211,692	141,128
28	542,800	219,834	146,556
29	542,800	227,976	151,984
30	542,800	236,118	157,412
31	542,800	244,260	162,840
32	542,800	252,402	168,268
33	542,800	260,544	173,696
34	542,800	268,686	179,124
35	542,800	276,828	184,552
36	542,800	284,970	189,980
37	542,800	293,112	195,408
38	542,800	301,254	200,836
39	542,800	309,396	206,264
40	542,800	317,538	211,692
41	542,800	325,680	217,120
42	542,800	333,822	222,548
43	542,800	341,964	227,976
44	542,800	350,106	233,404
45	542,800	358,248	238,832
46	542,800	366,390	244,260
47	542,800	374,532	249,688
48	542,800	382,674	255,116
49	542,800	390,816	260,544
50	542,800	398,958	265,972
51	542,800	407,100	271,400
52	542,800	415,242	276,828
53	542,800	423,384	282,256
54	542,800	431,526	287,684
55	542,800	439,068	293,112
56	542,800	447,810	298,540
57	542,800	455,952	303,968
58	542,800	464,094	309,396
59	542,800	472,236	314,824
60	542,800	480,378	320,252
	$34,739,200	$14,329,920	$9,553,280

Are all our Citizens entitled "to happiness and the blessings of life" under the State Constitution?

DEAR SIR:—

Some claim that it is not the place of our state government to loan money to its cities and towns to enable them through benevolent associations to build up their section of the state by furnishing homes and conferring "happiness and the blessings of life" on the citizens.

If we pay the least attention to our constitution it is not only the place, but the explicitly stated duty of our government to do everything that tends to that happiness.

Now in regard to the state carrying on the building business—the state is not to do it—the benevolent associations do it; and the towns and cities guarantee the state from losses on their account; and the state only overlooks them through its commissioner of corporations, something like our school system only far less costly, as it does every other corporation, only more closely; and the state government reserves full and complete control over them in every respect, and can stop all or any one of them without a moment's warning.

Now in regard to our state not having an inherent incontestible right to go into *any business* for the purpose of conferring "happiness and the blessings of life" on its citizens.

The United States is in the expressing business to an enormous extent, expressing letters, papers, books and packages to all parts of the world, and a bill was reported in the last Congress to the Senate for her to go into telegraphing. The nation builds ships, and manufactures guns, cannon, etc., etc.; it also cares for our rivers and harbors.

Our state owns and runs the Troy and Greenfield railroad, builds roads in Mashpee and elsewhere, builds a railroad and a Hoosac tunnel; makes and trades in building lots on the Back Bay, etc., etc.

The counties build highways, bridges, etc.; the cities and towns, streets, sidewalks, schools, etc., etc., for the benefit of the citizens.

But better yet, better than all else, the United States government, realizing what a great benefit it is to the nation for every family to own its home, confers "happiness and the blessings of life" on its citizens by *giving* them valuable farms; and still better, will give a farm even to the unfortunate foreigners who leave their homes and state so regretfully on account of the mismanagement of the governing powers, UNDER OUR HOMESTEAD LAWS.

Now what is the result so far as our state is concerned? The Western States by the homestead laws of *giving* a farm to every family, are attracting many of our most ambitious, most intelligent and best citizens to them, and the western states are being rapidly built up at the expense of Massachusetts.

All know what a wonderful growth the West can show, and it is almost entirely on account of families being able there to get homes of their own; cut off the homestead laws and see how quickly that western growth would stop.

Now the design of this bill for homes is, to extend the benefits of the homestead laws to our citizens, and thus confer "happiness and the blessings of life" on them right here at home, instead of compelling families to move thousands of miles out west to get it; and thus build up our own Commonwealth instead of another, without the ultimate cost of one cent to the State, but by ONLY *a temporary loan* of three million dollars.

The Massachusetts Bureau of Labor Statistics shows that only one family in a hundred of our wage or salary class owns its homes, and even forty-four per cent. of these are mortgaged, and the average mortgage on said homes owned by the males is $977.00 and homes of the females $688.00. Can any statesman read these frightful figures and not dread the future of our commonwealth? Any reader of history knows what disaster is eventually in store for us, if we cannot get wisdom enough in the state house to change these figures for the better.

Bold, heartless men in all times, to gain some selfish ends often cry out this or that can't be done, this or that is unconstitutional, bringing the word unconstitutional up from the pit of their stomach, so that it sounds like a doleful sound from the tomb, and enables them to chill the very marrow in the bones of timid men or cowards,—and in the confusion of shudders thus brought on they gain their point; and afterwards have a good hearty laugh over the trembling of the scared fools whom they deceived.

If anything that is to benefit our citizens is unconstitutional, we can very easily make it constitutional, for our constitution says so in the most positive terms.

By the Statutes of 1874, chapter 364, the legislature undertook to authorize the city of Boston to raise money and loan it upon mortgage at current interest to the owners of land in Boston, the buildings upon which had been destroyed in the great fire, to rebuild upon the said land.

Upon complaint of certain tax-payers of Boston this was declared unconstitutional, not being a tax for a public use. (111 Mass. Report, 454.)

It might be, it was said, that the results would be more beneficial than some grants for public uses; but it is the character of the object, whether it is a *public use* or not, that determines.

A public use was declared to be one whose direct object is to benefit inhabitants of the state "as a community and not as individuals." If this is the nature of the object, "however limited and unimportant the interests to be promoted," or though "it practically affects only a small portion of the inhabitants or lands of the commonwealth," the court cannot interfere with the action of the legislature, and this is still true, although the act " may not be productive, practically, of public advantage." Otherwise the act is not within the power of the legislature, however beneficial it may be.

This act, it was said, was to raise a fund to be distributed "by separate loans to numerous individuals, each one independent of any relation to the others, or to any general purpose, except that of aiding individual enterprise in matters of private business. The property created would remain exclusively private property, with no restriction as to the character of the buildings to be erected or the uses to which they should be devoted, and with no obligation to render any service or duty to the Commonwealth or the city,—except to repay the loan—or to the community at large or any part of it."

It is to be noticed that the persons who could receive the aid of this loan were merely a particular number who had lost by a certain fire, and it was not open to the public nor to any particular community, nor indefinite class, but only to certain particular individuals. In the decision of the case it is stated that enterprises rendering facilities, "of which the whole community may rightfully avail itself," may be constitutionally aided by loans from the state, and as illustrations are mentioned, railways, who as common carriers "hold their franchises charged with this duty and trust for the performance of the public service;" aqueducts, from which any citizen on the line has a right to purchase water; saw and grist mills, which must serve all who apply on reasonable terms; drains and sewers.

Now the act we propose furnishes funds for the benefit indifferently of *all* members of the community; the beneficiaries are not "independent of each other or of any general purpose, except that of aiding individual enterprise," the purpose being an educational one, viz.:—to render citizens independent, and establish them in homes, make them industrious and thrifty, and to prevent them from becoming public charges—a purpose already recognized by the exemption from taxation of small estates. The property created does *not* remain absolutely the property of the purchasers, but is charged with various restrictions, under which it is highly important for the interests of the community that real property should be held, but with which land cannot well be charged unless taken for public uses, and so charged by the state for the benefit of the community. The holders of the land are to be ever after subject to an annual payment for public purposes; and there are careful restrictions as to the "character of the buildings erected and the uses to which they are to be devoted."

Hence it will be seen that this proposed act differs in almost every essential particular from the one declared unconstitutional, and directly subserves public uses in many ways.

It is constitutional for the government to help the poor—it is unconstitutional to help the rich—as our government's end is to equalize, and that end can only be ached by helping the working class; for if we help the rich we increase the equality.

J. M. B.

A LEGAL TRIAL FOR RIGHT.

)EAR SIR:—

In the Constitution of Massachusetts, Article 1, acquiring property and *enjoying* life is declared one of the *rights* of ALL men. Article 7 says, the *government* is

FOR the *happiness* of the people; it also explicitly says that *government is instituted for that purpose*—and when happiness is not obtained, government may be altered or totally changed to secure it.

Under our system of government, many men and women work hard nearly every day and cannot by any possibility acquire property. The Massachusetts labor statistics show this; and that happiness and contentment are not secured to the people no argument is needed to prove.

It is customary for the governing class who neglect their duty to these citizens to try to clear themselves of responsibility by blaming them for wasting money in liquor and in other ways. How much money will a man have to waste on unnecessary things who earns but $1.50 per day, and pays the bills of his family, as 90 per cent. of them do pay? This brings the charge of the enormous sums wasted on liquors to the door of the wealthier class, where it belongs.

One of the strongest desires of humanity is the desire to own a home; it is the fountain from which flows in profusion the greatest happiness and the choicest blessings of life. The taxes paid by these people should secure to them so reasonable a desire, instead of being spent in drilling military to shoot them down for being discontented, and in building prison cells with the necessary and costly appliances for their homes. It is proposed to consolidate in one regiment all the troops in Boston to make them more effective in shooting down the citizens in case of a riot—is it not better to prevent than to stamp out a riot? Is it not a wiser statesmanship to willingly loan $3,000,000 to content and make our citizens happy, than be compelled to expend $5,000,000, as Pennsylvania is now doing in vain efforts to repair the the damage done by the unhappy and discontented of only one city—Pittsburg?

Remember the object of our government is to make the people happy—it is formed for that purpose. Are our legislators actuated by that consideration? Is that the aim and object of all that is said and done in legislative halls? Is that the aim and object of all money appropriations?

Selfish ones will do their best to gain a false reputation as watch dogs of the treasury, by attempting to kill the bill to provide homes for the people when before the legislature, in which there is no money or profit to them, that they may use that false reputation to gain some selfish end.

Sharpers in an argument often give faint praise to a good work to gain the confidence of others, so as to more effectively destroy it by an appearance of fair dealing; rather give me an open and avowed enemy; then one knows how to meet them. Not only will they oppose it but they will induce the ignorant ones to do so.

To the ignorant brain this plan that can be so easily worked, seems as impossible as the construction of a locomotive would be to the legislators of a kingdom of Central Africa. Imagine a creative brain like one of our first inventors, trying to show them by drawings how to build and equip a railroad that would bring happiness and the blessings of life to their nation.

To fully appreciate the ignorance of the ignoramuses of today, all that is necessary is to imagine them with their pompous airs and the law-making power in their hands, dressed in the every day clothes of the laborer.

Clothes are the making of most men, and if you will but imagine the opposers of this bill in such clothing, you can the better take the measure of their arguments; look beyond the clothes, look for the manliness, the intelligence, the generosity, particularly notice the independence of the defenders of this bill which would make them manly in any dress or position, either as mechanics or as statesmen. Opposition to good measures is nothing new; everything good had to make a beginning; no good ever started without determined opposition from the selfish and ignorant; inventors and discoverers have always suffered and been abused for their good works before this, and will have to suffer and be abused to the end of time, it is their encouragement and too often their reward.

Some claim because this work is new it ought not to be tried; if every one had so thought humanity's advance would have been slow; to whom does the world owe its progress? Certainly not to the conservative man who never originated a new idea, and who condemns and opposes that of another; if conservatives had complete control in past ages, we would today have occupied the caves of the primitive man.

Others object that the bill *may* not be perfect; every law has to be tried and proved, every constitution amended.

It is customary to point to the accumulated generosity of ages to prove that this age is generous, but all we should credit ourselves with, is what is now being done. We see accumulations of immense fortunes in the hands of few; we see all crimes increasing in our state, until now the per cent. is higher than ever before. The mass are dissatisfied, unhappy. Why is this? Are you trying earnestly as a part of the government to make *happiness* for the people? Is that your aim? Then I am glad, for that by the words of the constitution, is what you were elected for, and I love to see a man do his duty.

The committee report reference to the next general court. Why this delay of a whole year on a bill so important to the happiness of the people? Such a report by the committee is an acknowledgement of merit in the bill asked for. Reference to the next general court, in so vital a matter, is an acknowledgement of a lack of intelligence and ability in this; is not the legislature of this year as able and as competent to judge of the merits of this plan as the next is likely to be? Sit the whole year out rather than leave this question undecided, and your constituents will make no complaint of work so decidedly to their advantage.

J. M. B.

WHO PAY THE TAXES?

DEAR SIR:

It has been stated that this matter of homes for the people ought to be referred to the tax payers for decision.

We are willing to agree to this proposal; and then the question arises who are the tax payers?

Tax payers are those who really pay the taxes; and they are the salary and wage classes.

Proof. We will suppose a man to be letting out a tenement house for $100 per year. Now if some great war measure makes it necessary for the government to put a tax on all estates, and he has to pay $100 on account of it, any sensible man knows that not only he, but every other man who is letting property, will more than double their rents on account of that war tax, and the wage or salary class pay it by an increased rent, the poor cannot live out of doors, so must pay it all. Thus it is with every kind of merchandise, the dealers having a large number of articles to sell, can raise the price on any one, and so make themselves whole on any taxation.

But salary or wage workers having only one article to sell—their labor, are detected at once when they raise on the price; and as the capitalist can often get along without them for a long while when they strike, they are often unjustly starved into submission; and sometimes, when goaded by their wrongs into overt acts, it is called a riot, and the militia are called out to shoot them down. But it will be said that these landlords and merchants also pay the advanced rates. True, but they tuck it on to what they have to sell and the labor sellers eventually pay all, for the laborer *can't* tuck on.

Now who are the state? Certainly the people. The government is only formed for a purpose; what is that purpose? It is to furnish "happiness and the blessings of life" to the citizens. The citizens are the state, and if they choose to impose a tax to provide themselves with homes, instead of building Hoosac Tunnels, or loaning their money to wealthy corporators of railroads, &c., &c., we know they have the right to do so under the constitution.

Some sharp, bold lawyers, in the opposition, will try to scare the ignorant and timid by looking as solemn as owls, and saying this measure of homes for the people is unconstitutional; and endeavor to kill it by delay in asking a Supreme Court decision which is slower than death. The able lawyers that will support the bill are not to be scared so easily; but even the most ignorant man ought to know any good measure can be quickly made constitutional.

But some say enough able men cannot be found in the cities and towns of this Commonwealth to run these associations. In the city of Lynn they are able to run such an association successfully, and I don't think any representative will claim his constituents are any less able.

Any town of our Commonwealth with one of these associations and a capital of only $5000 can by this system house one family every week, if they are only as able as the citizens of Lynn. And, on account of the many buildings of exactly the same size and style being built all over the state, the price of them will get down to the very lowest figure, and thousands will get a home who could not buy one at present rates.

Generous men appreciate the labors of the men in the legislature, who are doing their best to pilot a $3.000,000 loan through to promote these Benevolent Building Associations for providing homes for the people; which experience in Lynn by a like association, has proven will accomplish this object.

By no possibility can these kind men of the legislature get any riches or fame in return for their labors that always come from assisting the wealthy; but on the contrary it is decidedly against their interest as lawyers to do so; and they are intelligent enough to know it; yet manfully, they help a good cause.

It is beyond my comprehension how it is possible for even mean men to oppose them, but they do, and get pleasure from it besides. But to more easily win they try to cloak their delight by a sorrowful look, as if they were opposing the good work regretfully. Shame upon such hypocricy! Why can't they come out like men and tell the real reason?

If this enmity would only come out plain and plump and show itself, we could easily overcome it, but it will be the snake in the grass kind, that will not say, "it will hurt our pocket books, so we must oppose you," but conjure up some false reason. Some have property which they rent, some are interested in mortgages, some have other selfish motives and still others aim to be judges; and judges must be made of conservative stock, and conservative means to oppose anything new, no matter how good.

This is a measure which will do more to make women happy than anything else. A home of her own to a true woman is one of her high aims. Who can be good associating with the vile in a low tenement house?

The independent home makes the independent family and independent citizen.

The Board of State Charities say in their report that although it costs more for the time being to give outside help to the poor, in the long run it is cheaper; but it is *better* to start before charity begins; and have the government help workingmen, the same as it has helped the wealthy class.

J. M. B.

DO RIOTS PAY?

Dear Sir:—

The Boston Advertiser of April 5th says:—"Apropos of the Cincinnati Riots, it may be stated that some months ago the city of Boston was divided into sections, and the different districts assigned to officers of the Cadets to be examined with a view to the best way of treating them in case of disturbances. What were the points of vantage, how they were best approached and held, what buildings could be most effectively occupied by troops, and how great a force would be needed in each instance, were among the practical questions considered."

During the Great Fire the dens and cellars of Boston vomited forth—for pillage—such a thieving, lawless crowd that every *wise* citizen was startled, and thought with dread of the evil that was sometime sure to result from this volcanic element. Content the poorest first.

The New York city, Pittsburg and Cincinnati Riots, prove to *wise* men that if something is not speedily done to direct this dissatisfied element into right channels and contentment, disastrous consequences are eventually in store for Boston and other cities of our loved Commonwealth.

Fools are in the habit of laughing at dangers *before they come*, and running away in the hour of peril; brave men shrink from impending evils and try to avert them by concessions and wise measures, but will risk life to quell the disturbances brought on by the short sighted economy of these same fools.

The dissatisfied element owning no property have nothing to lose, and think they have everything to gain by getting work through rebuilding the structures they destroy; this is a disagreeable fact which we will have to meet, if we do not take measures today to prevent it. The percentage of crime in Massachusetts was greater during the past year than ever before.

Our state house is in dangerous proximity to some of the slums of Boston. In a few minutes and before the military could get out, a mob could fire it and do incalculable damage. Prevent it by wise measures now.

The Pittsburg riot has proven that shooting them down costs more than housing them.

The Massachusetts Bureau of Labor Statistics shows that only one in a hundred of the wage and salary class owns his homes, and even forty-four per cent. of these are mortgaged, and the average amount of the mortgage on the homes owned by the males is $977, and of females $688; this showing is enough to make any one with a kind heart feel sad.

A careful reading of history has taught, that men entrusted with power are generally so blinded by it that they become arrogant, and instead of trying to improve the character of the laboring class by a little encouragement in time, the element they could once have easily directed becomes unmanageable and destructive.

These *so-called wise* rulers are in reality the dangerous class for they foolishly think it to be a sign of fear on their part to assist these people today to avoid disasters to the state in the future.

The relation between governors and governed should not be that of threats on the one side and punishment on the other; but wise policy does all possible to promote prosperity and content among its laboring class, and then preserves order at all hazards.

Let us see what these riots cost, for shrewd men always examine a business before they enter it. The annual cyclopedia of 1877 reports over 100,000 men out of employment on account of the Pittsburg riots. In 1878 it reports $710,000 appropriated by the STATE of Pennsylvania to pay simply the cost of the military to suppress the riot. Think of the lives lost besides.

In 1879 the committee on Ways and Means of the State of Pennsylvania, reported a bill appropriating four million dollars to pay the losses incurred by the Pittsburg riot; bear in mind that enormous damage was done in a few days time, in a city whose wealth was insignificant compared with that of Boston. But that was in Pittsburg, the fools will say,—and when a riot comes in Boston, the fools in Pittsburg, then grown wise, will say,—O, that riot is in Boston.

How much better it would have been to spend a less amount of money to make the few citizens of Pittsburg property owners and contented, than for the state to waste such an enormous sum in a vain effort to repair the mischief resulting from their discontent.

It was held that Alleghany County, Penn., was not liable for the damage done by the Pittsburg riot because it was general, not local, and that the state was constitutionally liable for the restitution of property lost through general riot and mob violence.

A decision was cited proving that any property damaged or destroyed while being used as a barracks, or while in possession of state or national authorities, and destroyed by the enemies, should be paid for by the state or nation. It was further urged that it was no riot, but an insurrection brought about by suffering from depression, occasioned by the panic.

As soon as the proclamation by the Governor was issued, calling out the troops to suppress the insurrection, the state assumed control and responsibility, and this was done before a shot was fired or a torch was lighted; the state was therefore liable in equity and was morally bound to pay for the damage occasioned by the mob at that time.

Now no matter who has to pay for it, any sensible man can see that it is a much greater loss to that state than the loss of four million, seven hundred and ten thousand dollars spent in attempts to repair the damage.

Is there not wisdom sufficient in the country to so appropriate half as much as here wasted in riots, as to transform these rioters into prudent, industrious citizens, striving to pay for their homes, and with this object to labor for, no leisure left for lawlessness and violence?

It shocks one to read the article quoted from the Advertiser,—where in the coldest of blood, you see the preparations being made with the utmost deliberation to send these starving, misdirected, unfortunate ones to their coffins, to make misery for their families, and probably paupers and convicts of many. Yet that is respectable, that is wise, that is good, while we who are trying to avert such disasters are called fanatics, for determinedly and persistently *begging* the Legislature to give these poor citizens their rights under the constitution, which is expressly stated to be happiness and the blessings of life.

You loaned millions to the rich corporators of railroads for them to make money with; yes, some say, but the state has given that up *now*.

Are the reasonable demands of the mass of our citizens for a loan of money to supply them with homes to be denied?

But do you refuse to aid railroads? Then why is that law in the Public Statutes that cities and towns can give them aid; the LAW is there yet to help them.

All know families are more content and happier in homes of their own.

The Pittsburg riot cost over five millions of dollars, and many lives; the Cincinnati riot, valuable and costly property, and also much life. Think of that value spent in furnishing homes for these misguided citizens, to be paid by easy payments.

Had this riotous element owned real estate, they would think at once their property might get damaged, but would certainly be taxed to pay all damage done; so each one would then have become a self constituted policeman.

How much better to listen to the conservative measures of wise men, and avert such disasters and waste of property, by the intelligent investment of a much less sum, making the people all owners of real estate, and thereby changing them from lawless violators, to the most conservative promoters of peace and good order.

Is it not better to loan three millions of dollars today, to content dissatisfied citizens in our own state, whom you know to be rightly dissatisfied, because the government is not giving them the happiness and blessings of life our constitution says the government is founded for, than to spend five millions of dollars in attempts to repair the damege that the Pittsburg riot shows that they are capable of doing in any city.

New York, during the Cincinnati riot was flooded with circulars in the localities where mobs would be most likely to form, and the whole police force there had to be on the alert, showing that there is some unknown secret organizations in our midst, ready to encourage this element into lawlesseness, unless we, by wise measures, content it.

J. M. B.

Do Homes for the People Pay?

DEAR SIR:—

The Massachusetts Bureau of Labor Statistics shows that only one in a hundred of our wage class owns his home, and even forty-four per cent. of these homes are mortgaged, and the average mortgage on said homes owned by the males is $977, and on the homes owned by the females, $688; think of the struggles and trials they must make to meet that payment of interest, beside taxes, insurance, repairs, water rates, sewerage, etc.

A man or woman who owns a home of his own is seldom concerned in a riot. History for thousands of years proves this fact. Discontent creates trouble, riot, war. Content—happiness, concord, peace. Nothing so much conduces to content families as owning their homes. The majority in our state do not own their homes. Consequently the majority are discontented. For political motives liars will deny the above. The state is created for the happiness of the people, not for the benefit of any class.

A class are deriving a profit by our system of leglslation that they would not get under a primitive government, and are not entitled to under our constitution.

If, as our constitution says, "government is for the happiness, and to confer the blessings of life on the people," and the majority of our people are unhappy and have not the blessings, if the government can do anything further to promote their happiness and does not do so, it fails in its duty.

All these people ask, is their right under our constitution, which is the enjoyment of happiness and the blessings of life.

If, as our constitution says, "Whenever **** not obtained, the people have a right to alter the government **** for their happiness," it seems as if they are not asking too much for the government to assist them in getting homes.

Millions of dollars have been loaned to railroads for a rich class to make money; let us now give a benefit open to all, rich and poor alike.

Millions of dollars are given to colleges to help rich men educate their sons, from which poor men, on account of their poverty, not only cannot get a benefit, but these colleges instruct those who are already able and forehanded so highly, that the poor stand no chance in after competition with them; these poor ones are so poverty-stricken, that they cannot avail themselves of the offer of an education by simply paying their board.

The argument is used against this bill for furnishing homes for the citizens, that it will not be a benefit to the rich, as they would not use them; that is their fault; no matter how poor or how rich one is, he can avail himself of the opportunities at any time if he wish; but from a college, poverty operates to bar poor men as a class from its benefits, yet the state gives aid to them.

Some state officials act as if they thought our government was created for their exclusive benefit, and as if the State House and its contents of men and books constituted the *state* of Massachusetts, and that their duty is wholly done if they perform the routine work and draw their pay, but they are only the government servants. This idea ought to be forced out of their brains, and the new thought introduced that they should as a return for the salary they get be on the continual study to increase the happiness of the citizens of the state.

This bill asks for a LOAN to help these poor people, and rich alike, if they wish, into pleasant, happy homes.

That they painfully need and must have help in their strnggles and endeavors to comfortably house their loved wives and little ones, the following figures from the Lynn Experiment plainly show.

For after the advocate of this measure has given the same help to the unfortunate ones there, that the state is now asked to give all its cities and towns, and the association through whom it is being done has economized in every direction to build cheaply, so as to make the load so light that it could be easily carried, it is still so heavy with all the other calls of a family to supply that the *per cent.* of failures to pay for the homes is as follows, and I have plainly seen them work hard for the money and struggle in every way to meet the payments.

45 per cent. of the families could not pay for their homes.
44 per cent. of the families paid for their homes.
11 per cent. of the families have not yet paid them.
—
100 per cent.

If these figures do not convince our legislators that something must be done for these unhappy ones, and the pressing need of doing it at once to preserve the fabric of our state, an angel from heaven could not convince them.

Yet from the manner some legislators, who are paid for their work by the state, receive my arguments, one would think me almost a criminal for trying to convince them; think for a minute, ye intelligent ones, can it be a pleasure for me to sacrifice business, money and health? Can it be pleasure for a high-spirited man to haunt the corridors of the State House to get a chance to obtain justice for these poor unfortunate ones; beg for these poor citizens' rights who are not able to argue for themselves, who can't spend a cent to help me, but must struggle with might and main every moment to keep their families from starvation?

Nothing is asked for myself; no benefit can the state confer on me; for I leave when this bill is through for fields of labor in other states.

Ye wise ones, don't smile to think I lack intelligence to realize the magnitude of the work undertaken; without a friend in the Legislature to help me, though I would be glad of one, *I am determined to win;* and bear in mind, others as well as John Brown, may reach a hand out of the grave and accomplish their work for the oppressed.

But how much more generous on your part to grant these men what you know to be a right and reasonable request, and save further expenditure of my time and strength.

Nothing is to be gained by evasions and delays on the part of this body to whom I appeal today. If fifty years are required to carry this bill successfully through, fifty years shall be given. This day do the work of today and think of that $4,710,000 spent to repair the damage done by the misguided citizens of Pittsburg, in riots.

Millions of dollars and thousands of lives were freely GIVEN by our Commonwealth to secure "happiness and the blessings of life" to the colored race in other states. Are the white race who lack these two essentials in our own state any less precious, any less dear? Many of us who risked life for the blacks in another state, would give it today for the blacks and whites in our own.

Would the New York, Pittsburg and Cincinnati riots have happened had the people been happy and contented?

I ask this year a recorded vote of both branches, and this virtually leaves the question with the people, and they will send those they wish either to advocate or oppose the bill.

Certainly no honest man can be afraid to trust his constituents with the knowledge of his position on this very important matter, and a recorded vote will do it, except for those who dodge the vote.

Please help me obtain that recorded vote. J. M. B.

How Workingmen are Housed outside and inside of Massachusetts.

Dear Sir:—

In Europe, at Antwerp, Belgium, the size of cottages is fixed by law at forty superficial yards for each family; our proposed law for the *smallest* cottages contemplates over forty superficial yards for each family.

It is considered a great privilege in Belgium to be allowed to occupy these houses, as according to the rules of the Bureau of Benevolence they are only rented to respectable well conducted citizens, the tenant being also subjected to certain restrictions: 1. They can only be occupied by persons named in the lease. 2. The tenant is not allowed to underlet or take any persons in as lodger without the express consent in writing, of the administrators, neither is he permitted, without written authority, to pursue any trade or business other than that specified in the lease; nor, for health reasons, to keep on the premises pigeons, rabbits, pigs, or other animals. 3. Each tenant is expected to deposit, by the way of security, on taking possession, either the sum of $18.60, on which he receives interest at the rate of five per cent. a year, or a sum of $4.65 in cash, the remainder to be paid by instalments of 10 cents per week. The example set by the erection of these model dwellings is, no doubt, a step in the right direction.

In Maine and New Hampshire the working classes generally live in detached cottages one and a half and two stories high, with from three to six rooms.

In Buffalo, N. Y., the industrial classes almost invariably occupy detached cottages built of wood.

In Philadelphia about one-half the industrial classes occupy separate houses; of those living in separate houses about one-half are owners, the others paying rent.

The French workmen sent here to examine the condition of our laboring class, go back content with their lot, as it is much better than ours.

Algeria; here, as in all great cities of France, artisans cannot obtain cottages or separate houses, but occupy apartments in large buildings. These are badly ventilated and drained; and the difference between children who have always inhabited these crowded rooms, and those who have been brought up in the country, is very striking.

In Switzerland the majority of artisans own their cottages.

The above are extracts from the labor reports of Mass.

Brothers:—If in the Reports on Labor for 1870, at the State Library, you read on from page 165 you will see that our wage class *need your help* to get a home; and after reading of the miserable tenements some of them occupy, they will be sure to get your assistance and sympathy.

To read from page 519 of 1871 Report would shock the nerves of the devil himself; read pages 213 and 437, Report of 1872; read report of 1873; read page 386, Report of 1875; read page 32, Report of 1876. J. M. B.

A good Child makes a good Citizen, a bad one, a Criminal.

Dear Sir:—

The moral good of our commonwealth requires that boys and girls should keep at school, not at work. The Massachsetts Bureau of Statistics says:

"But 35 + per cent. of heads of families are able by their individual earnings to supply their family needs."

"64 + per cent. rely upon the assistance of wives and children."

"26 per cent. of their children work."

"In the larger places the percentage of assisted is the greatest."

"Only 9 per cent. of the unskilled workmen get along without assistance."

"Only 55 per cent. of the families save money."

"Their average yearly saving is but $24.74."

"35 per cent. of the families make both ends meet."

"10 per cent. of the families have to run in debt."

"The *skilled* mechanic receives $2.50 per day on the average."

"The ordinary laborer receives on an average $1.50 per day."

"Women's wages are 82 cents per day."

"The women's average of wages is lower partly because some of them work in families and get their board."

"The average of the whole wage class is $1.23 per day."

"The average number of days they were employed is 290 +."

"Only one out of a hundred own their homes."

"In an examination into the condition of the working population of a state, there is no more important fact to be discovered than the proportion of people who possess, in fee simple, the houses which shelter them. No statement as to the occupations, earnings, expenses, etc., is of much value that is not accompanied with the facts relating to this point."

"Summary of results, an insignificant proportion of workingmen, whose condition we investigated, are *able* to own their own homes."

"Among them the families containing the greatest number of child workers occupy the most crowded rooms and the inferior class of tenements.

"Nearly one-half the unskilled laborers live in *inferior* tenements.

If we can assist, and by some system direct the exertions of the heads of the families of these working people, and show them how to spend wages to the best advantage, and enable them to get a home of their own, surely we are not only conferring a great benefit on them but a benefit on the poor, struggling, unfortunate hard-worked women, who are their wives, and through them a benefit on their children, and through them all an enormous benefit on the state at large.

But some cavillers say it is not the business of the state to do this; then what is the business of the state?

Who are the state? The citizens, certainly. And are they not to be allowed to benefit themselves, or is the state composed wholly of office-holders, whose whole duty after looking out for self, is to pass laws for the benefit of landlords?

And now in order to enable the landlords and holders of mortgages on the vile dens called tenement houses, described in the labor reports as in our Commonwealth, to live in luxury on the hard earnings wrung from the labor of these poor unfortunate ones, are we for a moment to be so foolish as to listen to their well guarded arguments and the shrewd ones of their friends, favoring them in continuing this bare-faced robbery? I think the time is now reached when intelligent legislators cannot be led by them to oppose the will of the majority of the people.

They say it is not the place or the duty of the state to help get homes for its citizens; then whose duty is it? Whose duty is it to confer happiness and the blessings of life on its citizens?

The true reason for the opposition of the holders of mortgages and the owners of tenements lies in this. No rich man nor any one else can make money out of this bill; but it will tend to materially reduce the profits of some by curtailing their mortgages and rents, which accounts for the fierce opposition to this measure.

Let them tell the truth of their opposition, for cloak it as they may we know it is wholly selfish.

It is because they or their friends can't make money out of it.

Only the kind, the good, the true, the courageous will dare oppose this class, and advocate the cause of the workingman, and in a lawful manner obtain him his rights under the constitution, which are happiness and the blessings of life.

J. M. B.

"The vainly proud, the selfishly ambitious,
Shall they o'er ride the fortunes of mankind,
Or shall their teachings false and schemes pernicious,
By honest wrath be scattered to the wind?"

IS THIS TO COME?

DEAR SIR:—

The reading of "Uncle Tom's Cabin" sent many of us to the war, to leave it only at Lee's surrender; we gave our health and strength and we were willing to give our lives to protect the poor unfortunate blacks, and give them their natural rights, which were happiness and the blessings of life.

The task master of the South took the labor of the blacks but gave them in return enough food for their families, for it did not pay him to starve his own property. He clothed and housed them comfortably, and if they were sick saw them doctored and nursed, and when old age came on, public sentiment required the owners to protect, feed, clothe, and house them, and at death give a Christian burial.

The task master of the North, by a wage system that is devilish, takes the labor of the whites, and gives in return a pittance which does not furnish enough food for many of their families, or why the need of free soup and pauper asylums? Some northerners are cruel enough to starve human beings they do not own; clothing or housing their help is of *no* interest to many of them, and to get a doctor or nurse is done only by a few; to care for old age or burial of a faithful employee is rarely thought of.

Think you if we gave health and strength, and were willing to give our lives for the black brothers as they were then situated, that we lack the courage to do the same today for our white brothers almost starving at the north?

Although those southern task-masters did wrong and stole the labor of their help, they did not begin to make the money from the blacks that under another system the northern task-masters make from their help. The wealth of the principal task-masters in the two sections North and South plainly proves this fact.

The southern task masters, as a rule, did not begin to revel in the luxury wrung from the labor of the black, that the northern task-masters do from the hard work of the white.

As a rule the black did not have to work half as hard, or with near as much earnestness as a white at the north does to get a bare living.

Now any sensible man knows our wage class at the north has to live in better condition than the blacks at the south on account of the cold weather; he has many heavier expenses on account of that cold; most of them are pressed every month for money to buy food and clothing for their families, which monthly and six weeks' payments make still harder.

The average daily pay of the laboring man is $1.50. How do the thousands on thousands get on who have less than the average? God and themselves only know; they keep it to themselves and struggle on. The grave opens for them, the poor-house for their families.

Brothers we feel sorry, but are we doing *our* duty by them? let us not *talk* but *work* for their relief, work to get them their "natural rights" which our constitution says is "happiness and the blessings of life."

We know they are not getting their rights; do you wonder if in their rough lawless way, the only way in which they know how to try for their rights, they follow as near as they can the instruction of our constitution, and by mob violence try to totally change the government, as the constitution says may be done by the people when they don't get "happiness and the blessings of life"?

The state furnishes the benevolent persons who compose the State Board of Charities, with permanent buildings, and gives them enormous sums to assist the unfortunate poor who *will* beg. Our Bill contemplates the state only *lending its credit* to furnish homes and happiness to men and women who will *not* beg.

The Saving Loan and Fund Associations, money making institutions, which, in almost every circular they issue try to convince readers that their main aim in life is to get working men into homes of their own, were out in force to oppose this measure before the committee; they want to help the working man into a home, but they ought to add at the end of their circulars, "provided said workingmen pay them a good fat interest," even more than the savings banks exact. Their mortgages average about a thousand dollars each, which virtually bar a poor man out, as it would be rather hard for a man of family to pay that amount with interest, from his wages of $1.50 per day, after feeding and clothing a family from it with the incidental expenses.

One of the men who spoke for them is mistaken in thinking that as able men as are associated with him could not be found in other parts of our commonwealth to run these corporations; I know they would *not*, as he said, "run them into inextricable confusion;" there is brain outside of the Boston and other Saving Loan and Fund Associations.

The banks used the same argument in opposing the gentleman when getting charters for his pet organizations, and pretended to hold the same views in regard to them.

This will hurt their prospects for money making, and so from selfish motives they oppose it.

One employee at the State house opposes this bill but he has four houses to rent, so he puts in solid work by confidential slurs to members.

Some men know so little about benevolence, they think this work in which no one can get a salary or make a cent either directly or indirectly, will start at once with a rush, and the money will go flowing out of the state treasury like water. Every lover of the welfare of the state might well pray for this, but the benevolent men will come forth so slowly to work it without pay, that it will be a slow and steady growth, slower than it would otherwise be on account of the opposition it will get from landlords, and holders of mortgages.

J. M. B.

UNCONSTITUTIONAL.

A civil question addressed to even a BOOR, carries with it a natural right to a civil answer. To dispel the *least* doubt our state constitution explicitly says, *every* citizen has a *right* to address a petition to the legislature; that RIGHT carries with it a plainly understood and incontestible RIGHT to an answer of some kind from the Legislature, which is composed of two branches, the Senate and House; an answer from ONLY ONE of which is NOT an answer from the Legislature. Yet in a clearly unconstitutional manner, the Senate and House have each sets of rules and rulings, by which either branch can neglect to answer a petition, and also prevent the other branch from answering it. Such a ruling was made by the Speaker at the last session, and a petition was so buried, not only robbing one citizen of his rights, but it clearly usurped the power of the other branch of the Legislature; but as *only one* person was injured by it, and as he could not help himself, he was sat down on and the petition was not answered by *either* branch; but if any legislature expects respect for laws it makes, it can best obtain it by respecting laws which are made to govern itself.

In Rules, Senate 55, and House 100, when there is no rule bearing on the subject, Cushing shall decide. Now the only thing to sustain a ruling that the Senate should not have a chance to discuss said petition and try to substitute a bill that might have been acceptable to the House, is Cushing, page 887, as follows: "It is not the usage for one of two houses of a legislative body to inform the other by what numbers a BILL has passed; nor where a BILL from the other house has been rejected, does the house, in which the proceedings take place, give the other any notice of the rejection, or return the BILL to that house; but the matter passes *sub silentio* to prevent unbecoming altercations." Now that is wholly in relation to a BILL and is entirely foreign to this case. This case was on a petition, *a report of a* JOINT *commiteee*, and a PROPOSED *substitute bill.*

And Cushing's decision directly bearing on the subject is as follows: "In Massachusetts, joint committees, consisting of unequal members of the two branches, are appointed by a concurrent act; are employed about the ordinary business of legislation; constitute one homogeneous committee; and make their report indifferently in either branch. These committees, as to their form and authority, and modes of proceeding, *do not differ* from the common select committee of a single branch, EXCEPT *that every vote, in relation to them and their proceedings,* MUST *be concurrent.*" So *constitutional* Justice demands an answer of some kind to that petition. J. M. B.

Who are the people to *rightly* decide in regard to the *benefit conferred on the citizens*; THOSE who receive the benefits, *or* THE SELFISH ONES who oppose the work, or THOSE, who, without examining into the matter, *are determined* NOT *to be convinced?*

Selfish men have *always* opposed the advance of any good work, and will do so for a long time to come, so it has been in this case. This is a small thing today, without strength and without Influence; but *every* GREAT and GOOD WORK started weak and small, and only grew up to large dimensions after many years.

I have tried my native state; if not allowed to work it here, like others who have had the same experience in their own country, I can go elsewhere, for I can and will make it a great success somewhere.

If *kindly* feelings force us to spend the enormous sums that we do, to care for our paupers and helpless ones, many of whom are made so by their own fanlt, would it not be GOOD POLICY, as well as a proof of a kindlier feeling, to give *just* a LITTLE *help* to the *really deserving poor and almost helpless ones*, who are struggling with might and main to avoid becoming paupers and a permanent burden on the state?

Law made to Protect Bones of the Wealthy Dead, before it is made to Protect Live Flesh on the Bones of Workingmen and Women.

In 1880, the Lsgislature *at first* refused to charter an association in Lynn to house workingmen and women; but at the same time they were making a law for the *better* protection of the bones of the wealthy in the *ancient* grave-yards; and I could hardly contain my anger to hear the grand speeches made in the Legislature at that time, of the importance of protecting the SACRED (?) BONES of governors and other notorious men of former days, when the same Legislature had rejectcd a bill, only a few days before, that was to provide for the comfortable housing of workingmen and women in our state. JOHN M. BERRY.

From Mrs. C. H. Richmond
May 1892

THE EIGHT-HOUR LAW.

SPEECH

OF

HON. BENJAMIN BUTTERWORTH,

OF OHIO,

IN THE

HOUSE OF REPRESENTATIVES,

THURSDAY, AUGUST 28, 1890.

WASHINGTON.
1890.

SPEECH

OF

HON. BENJAMIN BUTTERWORTH.

The House having under consideration the bill (H. R. 9791) constituting eight hours a day's work for all laborers, workmen, and mechanics employed by or on behalf of the Government of the United States or by contractors doing work or furnishing material for the Government, and providing penalties for violation of the provisions thereof—

Mr. BUTTERWORTH said:

Mr. SPEAKER: I want to ask the gentleman in charge of the bill whether it prohibits a man from making a contract with another to work more than eight hours per day, if both desire to do so and neither of them is in the employ of the Government.

Mr. CUTCHEON. That is just what it does.

Mr. CONNELL. It does except in special cases where there is some necessity for it.

Mr. BUTTERWORTH. And who is to decide when the special necessity arises?

Mr. CONNELL. The parties can decide that for themselves, and if they make a mistake they are amenable to the court, as they ought to be.

Mr. BUTTERWORTH. Who is to determine when there has been a violation of the law, or when there has been a mistake?

Mr. CUTCHEON. As stated by the gentleman from Pennsylvania, that is a question of fact to be determined by the jury.

Mr. BUTTERWORTH. I understand my friend from Nebraska insists if I take employment to work nine hours a day by my own consent, in order to secure the additional compensation, I am robbing somebody else of employment, and that that is the point in this bill.

Mr. CONNELL. The point is to give everybody a chance to get work.

Mr. FARQUHAR. That is just what the bill does.

ERECTING A GOVERNMENT ARISTOCRACY.

Mr. CUTCHEON. No; the bill does not. We are simply erecting a Government aristocracy.

Mr. BUTTERWORTH. Let me ask the gentleman if this law is expected to apply in any case except in regard to Government employés?

Mr. FARQUHAR. Not at all.

Mr. BUTTERWORTH. It certainly is not pretended that it can reach beyond the employés of the Government.

Mr. TURNER, of New York. That is all that it does and what it is intended to do.

Mr. BUTTERWORTH. My friend is in error. I think the bill in terms goes far beyond that. It in express terms seeks to control private contracts between citizens, if the employer happens to have a contract with the Government to supply material or render service, though neither party is in fact working for the Government or in its employ.

I submit, touching this intermeddling in the private affairs of the citizen, that it might be very well for my friend to work but eight hours a day if he had only a wife, or himself, to support, while it might be necessary for me to have the increased compensation for working ten hours a day if I had to support a wife and twelve children. Now, we ought not to try to regulate by statute, I think, the precise number of hours that a man not in the employ of the Government shall work, unless, at the same time, we can adopt some regulation to limit the number of children that he should have, and generally regulate or fix the limit of his necessities and the range and measure of his responsibilities.

Mr. CONNELL. But half a loaf is better than no loaf at all.

Mr. BUTTERWORTH. That is true; but we have not come to the half loaf yet, and in this country there are loaves enough for all, if we have fair play, coupled with industry, economy, and sobriety.

Mr. CONNELL. And that is the theory upon which this bill is framed.

WE DO NOT WANT THE GOVERNMENT TO MEDDLE.

Mr. BUTTERWORTH. It is a question, I will say to my friend, whether under this bill our Government is not getting too paternal and meddling in matters that are none of its business. I think from the evidence brought before me that possibly men working eight hours a day will in many lines of industry accomplish as much as they would working ten under the old régime. That is the testimony that has been adduced before the Commissioner of Labor and otherwise, but that does not determine the question as to the individual right of an American freeman to sell without the meddlesome interference and restriction of the Government the only thing that God gives him to sell, that is his labor, in order to provide for his family and better his condition.

Mr. TUCKER. Or cotton-seed oil.

Mr. BUTTERWORTH. No matter what it is, whether it be cotton-seed oil, as my friend suggests, or his wheat, corn, or labor, or whatsoever else he has got.

Mr. MUTCHLER. As a lawyer, do you believe any statute can be enacted that will prevent a man from doing that?

Mr. BUTTERWORTH. I do not, and if that is true, then my honored friend will see that this act would be nugatory. But I am discussing the wisdom, or want of wisdom, of attempting, to the proposed extent and in the manner proposed, to restrict the freedom and inherent right of the free citizen. I do not think we can do so constitutionally. And if we could, we should not do so.

Mr. MUTCHLER. That is what I think.

Mr. BUTTERWORTH. We are all concerned, and properly concerned, in protecting the rights of the American citizen. There is no man in America who is fit to associate with who does not eat his bread in the sweat of his face, no matter in what honorable vocation he labors.

Mr. MUTCHLER. But there is no legislation that can say I dare not work ten hours if I choose to do it.

Mr. CUTCHEON. This bill says it.

BUT

THE BILL ABRIDGES A CITIZEN'S RIGHTS.

Mr. BUTTERWORTH. Clearly if this bill abridges the constitutional right of the citizen it ought not to pass.

Mr. MUTCHLER. No law can say I shall not work over eight hours.

Mr. BUTTERWORTH. Gentlemen will correct me if I am wrong in my construction of the bill. It is better to be right than to attempt merely to please a considerable number of people, for any political advantage that may come to us as a result of pleasing them. Now, I understand that if this bill should become a law and if I have a contract to deliver to the United States at Fort Leavenworth 1,000 tons of hay, and employ my neighbor to help me bale the hay for delivery to the Government, or to help me to haul it to the place of delivery, and I agree with him to work ten or nine hours a day, or permit him to do so with or without increased pay, I become a criminal, and would be liable under this bill to fine and imprisonment.

Mr. WADE. That provision has been stricken out.

Mr. BUTTERWORTH. I understand that is the proposition pending.

Mr. WADE. That has been stricken out.

Mr. BUTTERWORTH. No, sir, that provision has not yet been stricken out, and the bill as it now stands would cover the case I have supposed.

Mr. CUTCHEON. Any Government work.

Mr. McCOMAS. If the gentleman will allow me, as that section now stands it reads, by an amendment offered and adopted:

That all contracts hereafter made by or in behalf of the Government.

And down in line 8:

Such corporation, person, or persons under such contract, to permit or require.

It is limited strictly and sharply to Government employment, and does not affect the citizen in the matter of personal employment.

A CASE IN POINT.

Mr. BUTTERWORTH. That is just what I want to get at. You say it limits it to Government employment. In terms it does not do so. In the case I put, my neighbor whom I might employ would in no sense be in Government employment.

I desire to ask the gentleman from Maryland [Mr. McCOMAS], in order to get at the true import of the language of this bill so far as it has been modified: let us suppose that I am employed to build a tunnel for the Government, no matter where, or to do any work, to transport goods, if you please, from one place to another. Suppose it was the preference and a prime necessity of those who were employed by me, and my own preference, that we should work ten hours a day, and we should agree to it; suppose I should pay the men for the increased hours of work, and they should do it. I understand that under this bill I would be liable to fine and imprisonment. Is that so?

Mr. CUTCHEON. Yes; if you even permitted them to do it.

Mr. BUTTERWORTH. If I even permitted them to do it?

Mr. CUTCHEON. Yes, you would have to go to prison.

Mr. McCOMAS. When you make a contract as a Government officer you are prohibited from making, as one of the terms of that contract, any agreement which requires or permits more than eight hours a day as part of that Government contract. That is the whole of it.

Mr. STEWART, of Vermont. That is to say, that men who make contracts shall not modify them.

Mr. McCOMAS. An officer of the Government shall not do it; that is all. It says that in all contracts made on behalf of the Government, by a Government officer, he shall not, in any such contract, as the bill now stands, put in the body of that contract any requirement or permission to do more than eight hours' labor.

THE PURPOSE OF THE BILL EXPLAINED.

Mr. BUTTERWORTH. As I understand my friend, it provides that, if I have a contract with the Government to do certain work, for instance to construct a railroad to transport supplies from one point to another, to construct a tunnel, to cut and deliver 10,000 cords of wood, or any other work, if in the prosecution of that work the men who are engaged in it as employés, for me, work more than eight hours a day, although we may mutually desire to work nine hours and to increase the pay on the basis of the longer hours, or if I permit that, I will be liable to fine and imprisonment. Is that so?

Mr. McCOMAS. That is the purpose of this bill; in the case of the Government-contracting, so far it makes him an official of the Government.

Mr. BUTTERWORTH Now, Mr. Speaker. I do not believe that the cause of labor, which is the cause of mankind, the cause of ourselves and our children, can possibly be promoted by an act of that kind. If I thought so I would vote for it. Let us pause and reflect a moment upon what we are doing. Have we indeed reached a point in this free country that the freemen of the land are not allowed, although every man interested—the employer and the employed—desires to work nine hours a day with increased compensation—that we can not do it without the employer becoming a criminal under the law and liable to fine and imprisonment? If so, then it seems to me the Government has become thoroughly and utterly paternal and our privileges as freemen are being shamefully abridged.

What may we not look for, what may we not fear if such legislation as this is even possible? The excuse is that there is not work enough for all. If it be true that there is not work enough for us to do—if that be true, and if we are forced to recognize that fact, which I do not in any wise believe, then let us resort to some other remedy.

ADOPT ANOTHER REMEDY IF NECESSARY.

It seems to me that the highest right of an American freeman is to utilize the time and the faculties that God has given him to feed himself and his children; and instead of depriving the citizen of this inestimable boon, which is the birthright of every freeman in my country, a right that has been purchased at the cost of forty centuries of conflict waged in the interest of larger liberty for men, I would close the gates of Castle Garden for a little season at least against that kind of immigration which is depriving the boy and girl of America of the rights and opportunities they ought to enjoy.

Mr. TRACEY. But it is the American boy and girl who ask for the passage of this law.

Mr. WADE. Will the gentleman allow me to ask him a question?

Mr. BUTTERWORTH. One single moment.

Now, no one on this floor need to say that he is more the friend of labor than another. It is not true. There is hardly a man who has a seat in this House who did not begin life surrounded by conditions that compelled him to work and struggle with adversity, and no one here but won his spurs by wisely utilizing the very privilege which this bill would strike down. The honorable gentlemen about me achieved the success that has marked their careers by extra hours devoted to work. Gentlemen, this is not a mere question of votes as a result of a demonstration on behalf of labor. There is involved in this bill the question whether the time and ability of every American freeman is his own and to be enjoyed, or whether both belong to the Government to be employed only and to the extent permitted by the Government. I insist that one of the highest and most sacred rights of an American citizen is perfect freedom to employ his time and his faculties as he sees fit, and that the right to say I shall only work eight hours, whether I want to or not and whatever my necessities, involves the right to say what, when, and how much I may eat and sleep.

To regulate the hours of labor, as it is done in most of the States, is a very proper but a very different thing from saying I shall not work over eight hours if I want to, or that the man who hires me, at my request, to work ten hours and pays me for it is a criminal.

CIVIL LIBERTY IS INVOLVED.

I believe myself that eight hours is better. I believe in providing that limitation upon the requirement by the Government, but when you go beyond and say that a man who has contracted to deliver to the Government this, or that, or the other, that when I contract, or you contract, to deliver to the Government 10,000 tons of hay, or a million bushels of oats, or to construct a railroad from point to point—when you say that I or you shall not agree with those whom we employ to work nine hours a day, you deprive each of them of one of the highest rights and most important privileges of an American freeman.

When you make a criminal of me for giving these men a larger opportunity you deprive an American citizen of one of the most important elements of civil liberty, and if the law does not extend to the subcontractor and the subcontractor under him, you put it into the power of the contractor to stand aside and simply sublet his contract and thus escape the provisions of the law. If we intend to experiment with Bellamy's theory as described in Looking Backward, the provision of this bill which we are discussing is a very natural and proper step.

Mr. CUTCHEON. This provision does extend to the subcontractors.

Mr. BUTTERWORTH. Undoubtedly; and, if it is right, it is right in the abstract, and, if I may not have the right to agree with my friend here to work nine hours a day, it must be because it is a wrong that anybody should have or enjoy that right, since it rests upon the principle that no man has the right to work over eight hours a day, lest if he do he rob somebody else of a job. And yet the effort is made, and successfully, to show that men will accomplish as much in eight hours as they have been accustomed to accomplish in ten; and, if that be true, where does the increased opportunity for employment come in? If it is right for the Government to say to me: "You, as a contractor, shall not employ your neighbor to work nine hours a day," it must follow, as I have suggested, that it is wrong in the abstract, for clearly that contract which would be wrong in the matter of cutting wood nine hours a day for A, who is a contractor, would be equally wrong for B, who is not a contractor, under the Government.

Mr. LAWLER. Why, then, should it be applied to your Departments? They work seven hours in them.

THE REAL QUESTION AT ISSUE.

Mr. BUTTERWORTH. I do not object to their working seven hours or six hours. I would prefer six hours myself. My friend might prefer five. [Laughter.] That is not the point. My friend misapprehends the real point in this controversy.

Mr. LAWLER. Right here it appears that there is no issue raised in the case of these men who are receiving payment of three thousand and four thousand or five thousand dollars, but there is in those who work by the day's work.

Mr. BUTTERWORTH. My friend from Illinois is raising another and a totally different question. Whenever they work extra time they should be paid for it. This has nothing to do with it. I am talking about this clause in the bill which would make you a criminal if you should enter into an agreement with your neighbor to work or permit him in his own interest to work nine hours a day.

Mr. MORGAN. Do you not, as a matter of fact, work from twelve to thirteen hours a day?

Mr. BUTTERWORTH. I do so, and there is not a member on this floor who does not find it necessary to work as much. And my observation is that any man that makes a success in life and gets ahead does it by working longest and best, of course of his own accord. One word more, for I want to get at the root of this matter. I am an American citizen and I have no patience with anybody that is a recent transplant who tells me how to love my country and how to stand by it, or to instruct me as to its opportunities and its glories and at the same time intimates that he is more a friend to the homes of my country than I am. [Applause.]

Mr. LAWLER. These men love their country just as much as you do.

Mr. BUTTERWORTH. Certainly those you refer to do; those I refer to do not. I refer to this because I have been criticised by some persons, not members of this House, but recent importations, men who never struck a blow for the freedom of the country they left and who brought nothing to our own that could add to its moral or mental elevation, who represent servile instincts and lawlessness, and yet these same creatures would assume to teach us what freedom is and how to throw around American institutions and American freemen the only true safeguards of both.

A PREMIUM PUT UPON DULLNESS.

Mr. FARQUHAR. There are foreigners on this floor just as good citizens for the country as you are.

Mr. BUTTERWORTH. I have not a doubt of it and I have never said otherwise.

But now, Mr. Speaker, to return to the question, if the Government says to me that I shall not hire A or B or that A or B shall not hire me, even if we both agree, recognizing the necessity to both to work nine hours a day, it must be because it is inherently wrong.

Mr. WADE. Yes, and it is.

Mr. BUTTERWORTH. Very well. If it is inherently wrong, as my friend from Missouri [Mr. WADE] says, then by all the rules of morals and logic the law ought to apply to every man in private life as well as to contractors and subcontractors of the Government.

BUT

Mr. WADE. And that is how we want to make it. [Laughter.]

Mr. BUTTERWORTH. Undoubtedly. Your purpose is to handicap industry and perseverance and offer a premium on dullness and sloth. Now, I will put this question to my distinguished brother from Missouri [Mr. WADE]: If I can not dispose of my time and service, the only capital which God gives me with which to earn my bread and win larger opportunity for my children as I please, in what sense am I a freeman? And if we go on in the same direction how long will it be until I am a serf?

Mr. LAWLER. We answer that by saying that we are legislating here for American mechanics working for the United States Government, and we do not propose to interfere with private individuals.

Mr. BUTTERWORTH. Certainly. You are legislating their liberties from them. The difference between my friend from Illinois [Mr. LAWLER] and me is that I would leave to every mechanic, the father of every family in this country, the widest possible liberty, while my friend would abridge the man's liberty. In other words, while pretending or attempting to reduce his hours of labor he would deprive him of his freedom as a citizen. Thank heaven, no such proposition was ever sprouted in American soil. It has about it no trace of the spirit that belongs to American institutions. It belongs to a soil and a country where the government is everything and where the citizen is nothing.

Mr. LAWLER. Organization of trades has been found necessary for the protection of those men and their families in this country.

THIS IS NOT AN AMERICAN IDEA.

Mr. BUTTERWORTH. I understand that, but I am not talking about that, but am objecting to robbing workmen of their liberty under the pretense of enlarging their opportunity.

Mr. LAWLER. But you are leading towards it.

Mr. BUTTERWORTH. We are talking about different things. I am talking about the authority of this Congress to say to individuals that they shall under no circumstances, so far as contracts to render service to a Government contractor are concerned, be permitted to work more than eight hours per day, no matter what may be the conditions, no matter what may be the surroundings. That is something new in my country. I may be wrong. This is a period of evolution and I may be wrong about this, but for me and my house, until there is a stress, until I find that there is no remedy except to abridge the liberties of American freemen to do as they please with the time and faculties which God has given them by which to earn their bread, I do not propose to adopt this method, at least until I lose all my confidence in and respect for the manhood of my countrymen.

Mr. HENDERSON, of Iowa. Will the gentleman yield for a question?

Mr. BUTTERWORTH. Yes, sir.

Mr. KERR, of Iowa. Mr. Speaker, I rise to a question of order. I desire to know who is controlling the time on this side. I understood the Chair to state some time ago that the gentleman from Pennsylvania [Mr. MUTCHLER] was to control the time in opposition to the bill.

The SPEAKER *pro tempore*. The Chair will state to the gentleman that the gentleman from Nebraska [Mr. CONNELL], in charge of the bill, is entitled to control practically an hour's time if he desires to do so in favor of the bill. The gentleman from Pennsylvania

[Mr. MUTCHLER] was recognized to control the time in opposition to the bill, but the gentleman from Pennsylvania occupied so much time as he wished and did not manifest a desire to use any more, and unanimous consent was given to the gentleman from Michigan [Mr. CUTCHEON] to offer an amendment, to which he addressed himself. Then, nobody rising to oppose the bill except the gentleman from Ohio, the gentleman from Ohio was recognized.

A CERTAIN LIMITATION IS PROPER, BUT——

Mr. MUTCHLER. Mr. Speaker, after the gentleman from Ohio [Mr. BUTTERWORTH] has concluded I shall ask to control the balance of the time in opposition to the bill.

The SPEAKER *pro tempore.* So much time in opposition to the bill as shall remain after the gentleman from Ohio [Mr. BUTTERWORTH] concludes will be controlled by the gentleman from Pennsylvania [Mr. MUTCHLER.]

Mr. BUTTERWORTH. Now, Mr. Speaker, so far as the rule of conduct in the navy-yards and in the other departments is concerned, I quite agree to the policy of fixing a day's work at eight hours, but I have not yet got quite so far along in making serfs of my countrymen that I am willing to say that a man is a criminal because he permits his employé to work nine hours under a contract to furnish supplies to the United States.

Mr. CUMMINGS. Does not the gentleman know that under the laws of the different States men, women, and children are forbidden to work in cotton-mills and other factories twelve, fourteen, and sixteen hours a day?

Mr. BUTTERWORTH. I understand that employés shall not be required to work excessive hours, but I do not know of any State in which men are placed in the position of being punished as criminals if they agree by contract with those who work under them that they shall work nine or ten hours a day.

Mr. CUMMINGS. There is a penalty provided for the violation of the law in Massachusetts and in New York; and does the gentleman mean to tell me that the General Government has no right to prescribe that men shall work eight hours per day on work that is done for the Government?

Mr. BUTTERWORTH. Undoubtedly the Government has a right to fix the time during which its employés shall render service; and not only that, but I believe that such a limitation as to the number of hours required is proper. But that is another question——

Mr. CUMMINGS. If the State provides a penalty for the violation of its State law, why has not the General Government the right to provide a penalty for the violation of its law?

Mr. BUTTERWORTH. My friend must observe that the law to which he calls attention is wide apart from the provisions of this bill to which objection is urged. They are totally unlike. The question is as to the range of the bill, how far you may rightly go without subverting the liberties of the people.

SHOULD WE BY LAW COMMIT A WRONG?

I agree with my friend, and always have done so, with regard to the proper limit of the hours of work; and the law in all the States, I believe, provides that in the absence of any contract to the contrary a day's work shall be ten hours, eight hours, or whatever number may be specified. But this goes further—much further. It applies to subcontractors, no matter where and how employed—not specially in any factory, department, or bureau, but wherever through-

BUT

out the United States workmen may be engaged, not by the Government, but by a contractor or subcontractor, who may be engaged to build a ship, or improve a waterway, or the like; he may not permit a workman to be employed over eight hours a day under penalty of going to prison; no matter how scarce labor may be, no matter though there be work for a thousand men and only a hundred to do it, without regard to any circumstances of this kind, I become a criminal, liable to fine and imprisonment, if I hire my friend or (which is more likely) if he hires me to work nine hours a day.

Mr. CUMMINGS. If the contractor takes a contract under that specification, how can it be wrong?

Mr. BUTTERWORTH. But the question is whether we should compel a contract which does wrong to the rights of the individual citizen.

Mr. CUMMINGS. The law, if passed, makes the specification.

Mr. BUTTERWORTH. That is true, but the question is as to the wisdom of the law, even if it was constitutional.

Mr. CUMMINGS. If a law of this kind violates the right of the individual citizen, why does not a similar law with regard to work in the factories of Massachusetts violate the rights of the individual citizen?

Mr. BUTTERWORTH. My honored friend is comparing two laws which are unlike both in provision and object. No such law as this would be valid in any State in this Union. The circumstances may be entirely different. The law of Massachusetts relates specifically to factories; it refers to certain conditions which are pointed out, and limits the number of hours that may be required as a day's work. The trouble with this bill, as my friend will observe, is that it is general in its application. It is not to enlarge the opportunity of the workman, but to abridge his liberty.

Mr. CUMMINGS. It relates simply to contracts under the Government.

THIS BILL WOULD MAKE CITIZENS SERFS.

Mr. BUTTERWORTH. Undoubtedly, but to all kinds of contracts; and operates to restrict the highest rights of the citizen to work according to the necessities of his condition, and, although there may be but one hundred men to do a thousand men's work, yet it makes me a criminal if I employ a hundred men or one man to work for a greater length of time daily than eight hours.

Mr. CUMMINGS. You understand that when you take the contract.

Mr. BUTTERWORTH. Certainly; but we should not provide for making such a contract.

Mr. McCOMAS. If the gentleman will allow me a moment I wish to ask him this one question: Has he noticed that the section as now amended is limited strictly to contracts made by the Government for the performance of work? It does not apply to the furnishing or the manufacturing of materials, but simply provides that when there is a contract to work for the Government the party shall not be required or permitted under such contract to work more than eight hours a day. That is the whole of it.

Mr. BUTTERWORTH. My friend must certainly see that there is a very broad distinction between being an employé of the Government and being an employé of a citizen having a contract with the Government for supplies, whether in one line or another.

Mr. SMITH, of Illinois. I desire to ask the gentleman from Ohio a question.

Mr. EVANS. May I ask the gentleman a question?

The SPEAKER *pro tempore* (Mr. PAYSON). The gentleman from Ohio [Mr. BUTTERWORTH] is still entitled to the floor.

Mr. BUTTERWORTH. I beg pardon of my friend for having trespassed so much upon his time.

The objection to this bill as it is reported to the House is that it leaves the citizen little better than a serf. It turns civilization backward, instead of forward. It has some excellent provisions, such as that wherein it seeks to compel the observance of the law by bureaus and Departments of the Government in the matter of the number of hours of labor that are required of those in the employ of the Government. Beyond that there is, I fear, more politics than wisdom in the bill.

CONTEMPT IS DUE THE POLITICAL DEMAGOGUE.

The statement made upon the floor of the House to-day that a law which makes it a penitentiary offense for a man to contract with his neighbor to work nine or ten hours a day, getting larger compensation therefor, is an enlargement instead of an abridgment of opportunity, is brilliant in the extreme; and the pretense that anybody upon this floor has, during this discussion, suggested that it was unwise to limit the day's labor so far as Government employés are concerned to eight hours is wholly gratuitous and sounds very like an attempt to go on dress parade for political campaign purposes. The issue here is as to the proper limitation upon the exercise of governmental power in interfering to control and abridge the liberty of the citizen in disposing of his time and opportunity according to his necessities and desires.

Those who carefully study the relation between capital and labor, between employer and employé, and who address themselves intelligently, as well as earnestly, to making those relations what they should be, in the interest of all concerned, are entitled to all honor, and I am glad to recognize the thoroughly unselfish devotion of many members upon the floor of this House in their efforts to restrain the exactions of capital in that wherein it appears to be heartless. Verily, they are entitled to their reward. But I have nothing but contempt for the mere actor in the arena of politics, who sighs over that about which he has no honest concern and becomes demonstrative about economic questions of which he has little knowledge and no wisdom.

Every gentleman upon this floor who, in the line of his own experience, knows what it is to earn his bread, must realize the truth and force of the fact that the present and future prosperity of his children, and those who come after them, will be found in preserving to each citizen the largest liberty consistent with the public safety, and such member can not be other than a friend of the workmen of our country, and he can not fail to realize, also, that we are a nation of laborers, all workmen, some in one field of endeavor and some in another, but none the less all workmen, striving to provide for those who depend upon us and to aid those among whom our lot has been cast to achieve the success upon which their comfort and happiness in large measure depend.

INTELLIGENT CONVICTION AND HONEST EFFORT NEEDED.

The economic and social problems that confront us will be found difficult enough to solve when men bring to the work intelligent conviction and honest effort. We will not be helped any by the mere gratuitous lip service of the pretended friends of labor, nor by the unintelligent efforts of those who have not given the subject studious investigation and careful thought.

I desire to submit, in conclusion, that the intelligence and saving common sense of the people of this country are too often underrated, and there is too little disposition to accord to principle and to clean personal character the power and influence that attach to both.

Outrages upon liberty have been most frequently committed in the name of liberty. It is so with labor. The wrongs that have been inflicted upon the workmen of my country are most frequently the result of the efforts of those who assume to be their special friends and champions. A friend who lacks discretion is more dangerous than an avowed enemy, and zeal without intelligent guidance is like a ship without ballast or rudder. I repeat, we are a nation of laborers. We are the Government, and we can enlarge the opportunity of all without restricting the proper liberty of any. The bill will be greatly improved by the amendments offered by the gentleman from Maryland [Mr. McCOMAS], the gentleman from Michigan [Mr. CUTCHEON], and others.

It is to be regretted that it still has embodied in its provisions a plain and direct assault upon the inherent right and most sacred privilege of every workman in the United States, and it may be doubted whether the good accomplished can sufficiently atone for the evil which may result from the adoption of the measure unless it shall be further amended. It is to be hoped that the provision to which I have called attention may be modified before the bill goes from this Capitol.

SUCCESS IS WON BY LONG EFFORT.

There is a thought or two I wish to add to what has been said touching the wisdom and justice of abridging by law the right of a citizen to use his time and ability as he pleases in order to provide for his necessities and those of his family. It not only strikes a blow at the liberty of the citizen, but it offers a premium on idleness and vice, while it rebukes and condemns industry and perseverance.

The proposition that in this goodly land, which would support a population of 500,000,000, there is not employment and room for 65,000,000 and that we must by law restrict the opportunity of each citizen to earn bread, and by the same logic limit the quantity and quality of what he eats, will not for a moment stand the test of critical examination. Yet that is just what this bill proposes.

Why, gentlemen, there is not a man about me whose whole life has not been a protest against the principle and policy of this bill. There is not a member who hears me whose life would not be a flat failure if he had been controlled by the principle of this measure. There stands in front of me my good friend from New York, AMOS CUMMINGS. If his success is due to any one thing more than another it is to the fact that he has worked more hours and worked harder than his competitors, and by so doing has left them behind in the race, and as a result he has won honorable distinction in the councils of the nation. He works now not less than fourteen hours a day. Here on my right is my equally worthy friend, General HENDERSON, of Iowa. I know that he never saw the day he worked less than twelve hours. His honorable position here attests the wisdom of his course. The same is true of my friends FARQUHAR, CUTCHEON, BUCHANAN, of New Jersey, and the other honorable members here. Nor is that all. I do not know of any one on or off this floor who does not owe his success in life, whether in business or politics, to extra effort and longer hours, and the idea that somebody else has been robbed thereby is utterly at variance with the fact.

NOT BY IDLENESS AND WASTEFULNESS.

Yet this bill proceeds on the theory that we can make equal yoke-fellows of idleness and industry, economy and wastefulness, and secure to all equal thrift by limiting the opportunity of each, and sending to the penitentiary as a felon the employer who gives to either an extra hour's work for an extra hour's pay. That is the idea of the chairman of the Committee on Labor. It is the idea which finds expression in this bill as reported to the House. And so captivating to the mere politician are the supposed political advantages that will accrue to its supporters, that one gentleman hops about and frantically shrieks for the "yeas and nays" in order to go on record himself for or put some member on record against this folly.

The worst features of the bill have been eliminated by the vote of the House, but there remains still the fatal defect which marks it, a meddlesome abridgment of the personal liberty of the citizen, and to that feature I am and will continue to be unalterably opposed. Nor will it be necessary to resort to the "yeas and nays" in order to apprise my constituents what my convictions are upon this subject or any other. If they trust me, I much prefer that it be because of their knowledge instead of their ignorance of my official conduct.

From Prof. H. C. Adams
July, 1887

ADDRESS

—OF—

HON. JOHN DEAN

—TO—

CONVENTION OF

MOUNTAIN CITY DIVISION No. 172, ORDER OF RAILWAY CONDUCTORS, UNITED LODGE No. 174, BROTHERHOOD OF RAILWAY TRAINMEN, AND ALTOONA LODGE No. 287, BROTHERHOOD LOCOMOTIVE FIREMEN.

—HELD—

AT ALTOONA, PENN'A.

—ON—

SATURDAY, SEPTEMBER 5TH, 1891.

HOLLIDAYSBURG, PA.
D. & F. J. OVER, BOOK AND JOB PRINTERS.
1891.

ADDRESS

—OF—

HON. JOHN DEAN,

To Convention of Mountain City Division No. 172, Order of Railway Conductors, United Lodge No. 174, Brotherhood of Railway Trainmen and Altoona Lodge No. 287, Brotherhood Locomotive Firemen, held at Altoona, Pennsylvania, September 5, 1891.

MR. CHAIRMAN, MEMBERS OF CONVENTION, LADIES AND GENTLEMEN:

A great Englishman, Lord Macaulay, great both as an author and statesman, sixty years ago, argued impliedly, that, a government, such as that of Great Britain, made up of monarchy, aristocracy and democracy, king, lords and commons, was the best yet devised by the wit of man. His attention was called to ours, a democracy, without king or lords, as an illustration of good government. He did not deny that there was less crime, less poverty here, as great security for life and property, a more equal distribution of wealth than in England, consequently greater happiness, but, he replied: "The case of the United States is not in point; in a country where the necessaries of life are cheap and the wages of labor high; where a man who has no capital but his legs and arms may expect to become rich by industry and frugality, it is not very decidedly for the advantage of the poor to plunder the rich, and the punishment for doing so would very speedily follow the offence; but in countries where the great majority live from hand to mouth, and in which vast masses of wealth have been accumulated by a comparatively small number, the case is widely different; immediate want is at times craving, imperious and irresistible. It has steeled men to the fear of the gallows and urged them on the point of the bayonet. If these men had at their command, that gallows and those bayonets, what is to be expected? The increase of population is accelerated by good government; the better the government the greater the inequality of conditions; the greater the inequality of conditions the stronger are the motives which impel the populace to spoliation. As for America, I appeal to the twentieth century."

Well, we are very near the time fixed for hearing and determining that appeal; we are on the verge of it; nine years more and we are in the twentieth century. Has our government failed in the essential elements of government, the protection of life, person and property? this, the great Englishman thought, could only be accomplished with the aid of a king and an aristocracy; a democracy guided and held in check by kingly power and aristocratic conservatism.

Are there any indications of failure to meet its responsibilities on the part of our government? The time being so near, there should be some black clouds to announce the coming storm; are there any? I see none; do you?

It was conceded by him that a democratic form of government, a government wholly "of the people, by the people and for the people," had resulted in as great happiness to the people of this country as the people of Great Britain were enjoying under theirs. But, says he, the case is not in point; wait seventy years, until population increases, until wealth increases, and you will see! I have heard a few despondent Americans talk in the same strain; public servants are venal, the Republic is a failure, says one; labor is becoming importunate, aggressive and lawless; it antagonizes capital, and threatens the security of property; our government cannot stand, says another; wait and see! What do we see? every sign pointing to the utter failure of all the doleful predictions. We are not calling for kingly power to repress the turbulent, nor for an aristocracy to check the mad progress of a democracy. A government based on the intelligence and patriotism of the whole people has proved strong, is to-day powerful. Public opinion, the opinion of the "populace," is expressed in the law of the land; this opinion, thus expressed is administered and enforced by courts and executives; the populace submit to and obey their own laws; their sheriffs hang and imprison those who violate them; their troops put down anarchists and rioters who attempt to overthrow this public opinion. Every law on our statute book is but the opinion of the populace. You, speaking through your representatives, enacted these laws, your governors approved them, your courts and sheriffs enforce them, and this, not in theory, but in fact; for, though occasionally bad laws are passed, as soon as time demonstrates they are bad, their repeal follows. This is, and must be the case; for if, in a government of the people, bad laws be of long continuance, or if laws necessary to the happiness of the people be not enacted, then the majority of the people are either corrupt or indifferent to their interests, which is not true now and never was true. Where the representative must answer often to the people, bad laws must have short lives; for, as President Lincoln said, "You can cheat some of the people part of the time, you can cheat all the people some time, but you can't cheat all the people all the time." If, then, you and I make a law to control our actions, why should we not be bound by it? Why should we not yield implicit obedience to it and aid in its enforcement? We need no king to compel obedience; it has back of it the sovereignty of those who made it.

Our government is inherently strong, at the same time gives scope to the largest individual freedom; it is the best government, and as Macaulay predicted, has resulted in a vast increase in population and wealth. But this great increase in population and wealth has brought no increased strain on the government. From ten millions to seventy millions is a great stride in population; from wealth estimated at $300 per capita to wealth estimated at $1,000 is a great stride in riches. But the result is not as predicted; relatively this wealth has not been concentrated in fewer hands; the great mass of the people do not live from hand to mouth; labor has not become cheaper and food dearer; there is not greater inequality of condition, wealth is more equally distributed than ever. I admit that a few collossal fortunes have been made; the Astors, foreseeing the advantages of New York City as a seaport, and its future commercial supremacy, by investing and re-investing for three generations in New York City real estate are estimated now at over one hundred millions of dollars; the limited fortune of the grandfather, the old German fur-trader has become a great one. Jay Gould is estimated at over one hundred millions, probably much of it acquired by questionable methods in manipulating railroad securities; the same methods would hardly succeed now; what was only sharp practice twenty years ago, is in most cases now by law a crime. The Rockafellers, through the "Standard Oil Trust," are said to have accumulated fortunes of over one hundred millions; but now by law all trusts which interfere with trade are illegal; those in existence cannot live, new ones will not be born. I might name some others, but compared with the population, or compared with the millions of moderate fortunes they are rare; it is not desirable that they should be many; I have no apprehension that they will be. The manipulation of railroad and other securities, whereby the few gain largely and the many lose, was easy twenty years ago, it is now hard, and I mistake the plain tendency of our laws, if twenty years hence it is not almost if not altogether impossible.

But no law will, no law ought to restrain honest individual effort to better one's condition, either for his own gratification or for the advantage of his family, and so long as individual effort in this direction is not curbed, there will be large fortunes made by the few compared with the more moderate ones of the many. Take any young man, say of twenty-one years to-day, let him have good health, work hard, live on the barest necessaries of life, carefully invest and re-invest his savings, let him have shrewdness, foresight, a minimum of conscience in a bargain, the probability is that forty years hence, he would be, as compared with his neighbors, a very rich man; but few of his neighbors would envy him his fortune acquired by such effort. And a large fortune, when compared with those of prudent men, may sometimes be quickly acquired by a bold speculation. Within the last sixty days any man, with one hundred thousand dollars, rash enough to bet it on the produce exchange, that wheat would go up, could have made probably two hundred thousand more; but some other rash man or men, would have bet the same amount that it would not go up, or would go down, and they would have lost what the other won; and a prudent man, with more foresight than most of us have shown, with a moderate fortune twenty years ago, by investing and re-investing it in Altoona real estate, would to-day have been very rich as compared with the majority of his fellows. Rare miserliness, rare recklessness, rare foresight, will result in rare large fortunes. But notwithstanding these rare cases, the tendency on the whole, during the last sixty years, has been toward a more equal distribution of the large aggregate increase of the wealth of the country, by making the poor richer; the process has been a leveling up one not a leveling down. No one will deny that this large increase in wealth the unexampled prosperity of the country to-day, is in large measure, due to the construction of railroads; this wealth to a certain extent, in one sense may be said to have been created by railroad corporations; and in using the word corporation, I do not have in mind the legal definition, but I include every one connected with it, from stock-holder to brakeman.

The building of railroads may really be said, to have commenced only forty years ago; there was a limited mileage before that time, but then, commenced that vast system of construction which has put the locomotive to-day in every populated corner of the country; from that day to this, millions upon millions of capital have been invested in railroad building; there have been paid out alone, in one form or another, in the construction of the main line of the Pennsylvania Railroad between Philadelphia and Pittsburg with its connecting branches, two hundred millions of dollars. This immense sum was distributed among all those helping to build it; to the diggers and ditchers, to the lumbermen who furnished the ties and timber, to the iron manufacturer who delivered the rails; to the mechanics, the stonemason, bricklayer, carpenter, machinist, carbuilder and everyone who helped; those who furnished the two hundred millions have in place of their money the ownership of the road; they hold as evidence of this title, seventy-seven millions in bonds and one hundred and twenty-three millions in stock. This is the first distribution of railroad money, the expense of construction. Of course, the people who paid out this money expect a return in interest and dividends year by year; an income must be earned:

here come in all the complicated problems of railroad management, requiring in their solution, sound judgment, fair dealing, alertness of intellect, never-ending reflection and deliberation; traffic, passenger and freight, must be had; it will not come unless there be reasonable rates; what is a reasonable rate? The answes to this question depends on circumstances so varied, that any one who will take the trouble to read the mass of testimony given by railroad experts and shippers before the Congressional committees and "Inter-state Commerce Commission" will find that no answer has yet been given which would satisfy all interested. The object of the railroad officer is, to fix a rate so high, that money enough will be raised in the shape of gross receipts, to maintain the road and equipment in good condition, pay fair wages to all the employes, interest on the bonds and a reasonable dividend to the stockholder. If the rate be too high, traffic is discouraged, receipts fall off, men are discharged and the road goes down. If the rate be too low, a large business is done with no profit and bankruptcy comes sooner or later. In the division of the gross receipts, wages generally absorb more than one-half and this comes out first; then material and equipment are paid for; then interest on bonds is paid, then if anything be left the stockholders get it; if nothing be left the stockholders get that, too—more than once in the history of the Pennsylvania Railroad, a road carefully and conservatively managed has it happened, that the stockholders got nothing.

All the millions of dollars expended in construction, all the millions annually earned from operating the railroad are distributed, bringing comfort and abundance to innumerable homes and quickening every form of business life. All property real and personal along the line, or in parts of the country tributary to it, appreciate in value. The owner of a tract of coal land worth $5 per acre not reached by a railroad, as soon as the railroad touches it gets $50 or $100. His coal was valueless because it could reach no market; the railroad takes it to market and enriches him; and so with almost every species of property. By quickness of movement the scarcity of food in one part of the country is immediately supplied from another; neither famine nor famine prices seem to be again possible since the era of railroads.

So necessary has the railroad now become to our lives, that it has been truthfully said, our prayer "give us this day our daily bread," without them, could not be answered, unless by miracle.

As I have said, the wealth thus produced is not unequally distributed ; all have shared in it, all will continue to share in it; fair wages have been paid, fair wages will be paid, otherwise the railroad from its very nature cannot be a success ; the most perfect machinery, rolling stock brought by science and experience to the highest possible condition cannot move a single passenger or ton of freight without the engineer, fireman, conductor, brakeman ; the movements of machinery must be started and controlled by intelligence; the machinery cannot think; it must obey the directions of those who do ; and all these millions of capital thus invested, to be productive, must have the services of the engineer, fireman, conductor and brakeman to direct and control the movements of the train. A successful railroad here demands the highest grade of efficiency ; the highest grade is always in demand ; that quick intelligence, that fidelity to trust, which bears without murmuring hardships and faces danger and death without a tremor, contributes towards the wealth created by the railroad ; they share also in the distribution of it As the methods of operation and the character of the equipment have advanced in the last forty years so there has been a corresponding advance in the skill, and value of the services of all the employes. Forty years ago, the first railroad I knew, was the Portage, at Hollidaysburg; Col. Jesse R. Crawford, who was Assistant Superintendent of the road and still resides in Gaysport, informed me yesterday, that his salary was $700 per year ; that Eli Yoder, one of the best locomotive engineers on the road, he died only a few years ago and may have been known to many of you, got $1.50 per day ; the fireman got 75 cents, sometimes a little more. To be conductor on a passenger train was considered a very high position and one always sought after ; that paid $2.00 per day. Maj. Crawford did not tell me so, but when he named over the conductors, the late Gov. Geary, Col. Wm. B. Piper and Major Adams, it occurred to me, that this position might have been awarded to the most active Democrats ; and when he named the late Maj. John Brotherline as conductor, when the Whigs for a short time had control, I thought possibly the same rule might have been followed by the opposite party. Laborers received 75 cents per day and this was considered good wages.

Now notice the advance; the locomotive engineer averaged last year on the Pennsylvania Railroad $1,230, the firemen $690, the conductor $1,050, the brakemen $630. This indicates, not only the great advance in the skill and intelligence of the men receiving the wages, but also the tendency to equality of distribution in the wealth earned by the railroad. Nor is it true that this, more than 200 per cent. advance in wages, has been followed by a corresponding increase in the cost of living. Mr. Jonathan Stouffer, a tailor, residing in Hollidaysburg, and who did business there forty years ago, says he made clothes for men working on the railroad; a good Sunday or dress suit was made of pilot or beaver cloth and cost complete from $36 to $40; he said, I am making one now of beaver cloth, such as I speak of, for a clergyman; it will cost $38, but the material is much finer and better than that used by me forty years ago; a suit of that same quality of material would now cost about $25.

Mr. A. L. Holliday, who kept a general store, put in my possession one of his old day books, showing sales to customers; I have made a thorough examination of it and find that flour was then sold at $8.75 per barrel—it is now sold for $5. Calico 12½ cents, now not over 5 cents per yard; sugar 12½ cents, now 5 cents; coffee 15 cents, now 28 to 30; muslin 12 cents, now 5 cents; potatoes the same as now, 50 cents per bushel; cured meats about 5 cents more than now per pound. Nearly all food and clothing classed as necessaries of life are cheaper than forty years ago. Rent, an important item in cost of living is higher; railroads have largely appreciated the value of real estate; this has been followed by an increase in rent of 50 to 100 per cent.

If wages have risen 200 per cent., and this has been followed by no corresponding increase in cost of living, then, unless capital in railroads has received a disproportionately large return, the man with no capital but his arms and legs, as Macaulay expresses it, must be getting relatively richer instead of poorer;

it is not necessary for me to state to this audience, that returns on railroad investments have been getting less; the bonds on this road which once were six and seven per cent., are now 4½; the stock which once returned 10 per cent. now gets 5; a similar reduction on the returns of capital has been experienced in nearly every railroad in the land.

This large increase in wages, with no corresponding increase in cost of living, must to a considerable exrent, have taken the form of savings and have become invested capital in some shape or other, thus tending to an equalization of wealth; of course a large part of this margin has been consumed in comforts and luxuries to which the best paid railroad man 40 years ago was a stranger; homes have been made more attractive by articles of ornament and comfort; the table has been supplied with a greater variety and better food; the family has been better clothed; the children better educated; but even with all this expenditure for new comforts, and new pleasures in life, there is still left a larger margin, a greater ability for accumulation, than could be had from any possible savings forty years ago.

Take Altoona itself; it is almost exclusively a railroad city; its business to great extent, is dependent on the monthly payments of three or four hundred thousand dollars made by the lailroad company for wages and material; does this three or four millions annually paid out here concentrate itself in a few hands, so that the rich grow richer and the poor poorer? For the purpose of information I this week examined the assessments in the office of the County Commissioners. The assessed value of the real estate of the city for county and State purposes is nearly twelve millions of dollars; this is owned by something over three thousand five hundred persons; I suppose, to-day the city has about seven thousand voters; one-half of them then own real estate; the greater number of the assessments are specified as half lot, one lot and two lots; the valuations run generally, from one thousand to four thousand dollars, being strong evidence to my mind that one-half the voters here own their homes. When we consider that the business of the city is almost wholly industrial, and in consequence, such a large proportion of the population is made up of young men between the ages of 21 and 30 years, who as yet, have had no time to accumulate, the conclusion is irresistible, that this large wealth, poured out here monthly by the railroad company does not tend to make the rich richer and the poor poorer; does not tend to inequality of condition as Macaulay predicted. But not to rest on inference, I went further, and noted the occupations of the 356 lot owners as returned from the 1st ward; these 356 were put down as owning $1,794,225 worth of real estate; of these 22 are laborers, 20 carpenters, 13 painters, 12 machinists, 11 car builders, 8 blacksmiths, 6 engineers, 6 butchers, 6 conductors, 3 tailors, 3 plasterers, 3 firemen, 3 tinners, 3 printers, 2 brakemen, 2 gas-fitters, 1 moulder, 1 saddler, 1 shoemaker; the remainder is made up of clerks, foremen, mail-carriers, ticket agents, lawyers, physicians and gentlemen; of a few the occupation is not given; a few are widows; some are wives whose husbands doubtless out of affection or as a precaution against financial disaster, put in them the title to the home; in seven instances alone, did the record show any considerable individual wealth in real estate. These seven owned each $20,000 or over; eight persons owned property valued between ten and twenty thousand dollars; twenty-six owned property valued between five and ten thousand dollars, leaving the balance of the property in the ward to be divided between 315 persons owning $5000 or less; if the property were divided exactly equal between the 356 owners it would give then about $5000 each, but as 41 persons own more than $5000, it leaves about $4000 each to 315 persons, about as near equality of distribution as can be had. This was the only ward in which I noted the occupations of the owners and extent of ownership; but I have no reason to believe the other wards of the city will show any greater inequality; on the contrary, am informed by reputable persons who know; that the other wards show nearer an equality than the 1st. So far then, as railroads have stimulated the production of wealth, or have distributed it, it has not been concentrated in a few hands; the mass of the people have grown richer.

Nor is there any foundation for the assertion often made of antagonism between the capital invested and the labor which operates the railroad. The railroad in its essential features is a huge co-operative enterprise, in which the stock holder furnishes the capital and the men employed the labor; the gross receipts are divided among all who co-operate to make the road a business success. Neither is it true, that the rich alone own the road; I do not know the facts as to other roads, but the reports of the Pennsylvania Railroad show over 25,000 owners of stock, the large majority residents of the State; go where you will it has the reputation of being progressively yet wisely managed; the character of all its employees stands high; disputes between them and the company have been rare; as a result, its stock has become a favorite investment with all classes; many of those who hold it, have in it their all. Any one standing near the paying teller's window after a dividend has been declared and noticing those who receive their dividends will be surprised how few of them, in their appearance, give evidence of wealth; many of them, aged men and women, often in faded and thread-bare clothes, drawing their dividend on five, ten, twenty or thirty shares.

Doubtless some very rich men own stock in large amounts, but the aggregate value of the stock is probably distributed about in proportion to the real estate of Altoona

Why then, should shere be any antagonism between those connected with railroads? The stockholder wants a fair return for his money; the men want fair wages; the passenger and shipper want a fair rate; the success and prosperity of all are contingent on the success and prosperity of the road; therefore acting from a purely selfish motive, self-interest, harmony must be maintained or injury to all follows. But outside of the selfish motive, all who co-operate in the enterprise are subject to the same moral laws that are binding on others. We often hear it said a corporation has no soul; this is not true; it has just the soul of those who compose it, the stockholders, officers and employees; the same soul as any other form of business enterprise; it has just such morality as they have, no more and no less. The stockholder in contributing his money, the officer in undertaking the management, the men engaging to run it, are just as much bound by good morals as men in any other kind of business. The Christian rule "do unto others as you would have them do to you," is binding upon every true man, whether he operates a railroad or carries a hod; it is imperative, cannot be shirked or violated with impunity by any one; we do not always live up to it, but we all, Christian, Jew and Infidel profess to try to.

The 25,000 stockholders say, we want a fair return on our money invested; the 24,000 employees say, in view of the nature of our employment, the risks incident to it, the hardships we endure, we want fair wages; if a demand on the part of either for more than this be gratified, the common enterprise suffers either directly or indirectly; the payment of unreasonably high dividends or unreasonably high wages demands the exaction of unreasonably high rates; if these be unreasonably high traffic is repressed, shipments and travel fall off, down go gross receipts.

What is fair or reasonable to each and all, is the difficult question the railroad officer has to answer; to him is confided a high trust, affecting in its administration the lives and fortunes of stockholders, employees, shippers and all others interested in the road; there can be no real antagonism between the capital under his care and the men employed under his management any more than there can be antagonism between the fuel that makes the steam and the driving wheels of the locomotive which move the train. He tries to work for the vast interests intrusted to him by the rule "do unto others as you would have them do to you" and so do you; under this rule you all co-operate for a common purpose. There is no other right rule, at this day, there is no other practical rule, than the short and simple one announced by the Carpenter of Galilee.

No. 2. (New Series).

From

LIBERTY AND PROPERTY DEFENCE LEAGUE.

(To uphold the principle of liberty, and guard the rights of labour and property of all kinds against undue interference by the State; and to encourage Self-help versus State-help.)

OLD-AGE PENSIONS

BY

GEOFFREY DRAGE,

SECRETARY TO THE

LIBERTY AND PROPERTY DEFENCE LEAGUE.

PUBLISHED BY THE

LIBERTY AND PROPERTY DEFENCE LEAGUE,

7, Victoria Street, London, S.W.

1895.

PRICE ONE PENNY.

LIBERTY AND PROPERTY DEFENCE LEAGUE.

(To uphold the principle of liberty, and guard the rights of labour and property of all kinds against undue interference by the State; and to encourage Self-help versus State-help).

COUNCIL, 1894-5.

OLD-AGE PENSIONS.*

THE present agitation with regard to old-age pensions seems to call for a somewhat fuller statement of the case.

The almost daily experience of the Labour Commission was that there already existed laws and officials to remedy the grievances laid before it, but the laws were not known and the officials not efficient. What seemed at every step to be necessary was not so much far-reaching plans of reform as a careful attention to the details of administration. In this pamphlet I desire to point out that as far as we can at present judge this is the case with the grievances of the aged poor.

Before dealing with the extent and causes of old-age pauperism in England, as well as the remedies which suggest themselves, it may be well to consider briefly the old-age pension schemes at present in force in Europe.

The German invalid and old-age insurance scheme is part of a comprehensive scheme of social insurance for the working classes. It was originally promoted by Prince Bismarck partly in deference to the prevalent feeling in Germany that something must be done, partly to take the wind out of the sails of the Socialists. The sick and accident insurance law was passed in 1883, the law on old-age and invalid insurance, with which we are concerned, was passed in 1889, and only came into force in 1891. The details of the law are probably well known to my readers, but, should they wish to refresh their memories, I may be, perhaps, allowed to refer them to my report to the Labour Commission on Germany, in which full particulars are given. I desire here merely to indicate the financial, social, economic, administrative, judicial, and political objections to the law, which can already be fairly urged as arguments against any similar plan for England.

Financially the scheme is eventually intended to be self-supporting, but there is no sign at present that it will ever be able to dispense with the State subsidy, which begins at £320,000 and is estimated to rise gradually to £3,450,000 in the 80th year. The premiums are levied half from the employer, half from the workman, and the calculations are based, as far as the portions of the law which refer to invalids are concerned, chiefly on the statistics of one industry—the railway industry. Further, in adjusting the amounts of the contributions, it was impossible to calculate with any precision the extent to which such contingencies as sickness, military service, and want of employment

* The substance of this pamphlet appeared in the form of two letters to the "Times," on January 7th and 15th, 1895.

might affect the regularity of the payments, and I may add that statistics as to the probable invalidity and mortality of women are wanting. Again, it was calculated that the administrative expenses would not materially increase, but they have already done so.

From a social standpoint it is to be remembered that some of the friendly societies already existing are recognized by the Government, subject to their conferring benefits equal to those of the law, and subject to certain other provisions. It is not yet clear what effect the law will have on societies not so privileged, but it is clear that the relations between employer and employed have not improved as was expected, nor have strikes diminished. Further, there is not yet sufficient evidence to warrant the statement that can be made with regard to Denmark, that the family tie and the sense of responsibility for blood relations have been weakened. But the law does a distinct injustice in partially excluding from its operation widows and married women, who notoriously in every country form a large percentage of the aged poor. It is true that a woman who ceases to earn wages on her marriage may receive back the amount of her previous contributions, but by so doing she forfeits all claim to a future pension in old age or invalidity; or if instead of receiving this sum she prefers to keep up her claim to a pension, it can only be at a higher rate of contribution. A widow again may, on the death of the husband, receive back the amount of his contribution, but a comparatively small lump sum of this nature cannot provide for her old age. Lastly, we have still to learn its effect in increasing or diminishing charity.

From an economic point of view, the burden on the employers is alreadys everely felt. They not only complain of the sums they have to pay in premiums, which already apparently form a considerable tax on industry; but they declare that their clerical staff will not be able to do the work imposed on them in this connection, and they demand official help. In some cases the employers have even found themselves obliged to pay the men's premiums as well as those which they themselves are bound to pay in order to avoid stirring up dissatisfaction. Hitherto, it is stated, the employers have continued their contributions to existing friendly societies, but should they cease to do so, it appears that the men will absolutely be worse off under the existing law than they were before. In any case, the employer will probably not feel as much bound to help old servants as he did before, and there is evidence to show that wages have already been lowered in the case of those benefited by the Act, and the whole income has thus been actually reduced. The workmen and their friends complain that the age, 70, at which the old-age pension becomes due is too high, and the pensions, which vary from £5 6s. to £9 11s., are too low. Moreover, since no person is entitled to an old-age pension who has not insured for 30 years, or to an invalid pension unless insured for five years, there are numerous persons who are forced to pay the contributions but never derive any benefit under the law. The Socialists add that, whereas under the Poor Law the expenses fell chiefly on the middle classes, the workmen now not only have to pay their contributions, but have also to bear the burden of the Imperial subsidy. Graver still are the following objections from an economic point of view to the law in question. The law rests, of course, in the first instance, on a passport system which is necessary for the identification of the beneficiaries, but which we should find intolerable in England. Further, in spite of the employment of a large number of honorary officials, the number of paid officials, both central and local, has been largely increased, and the cry is, as we have seen, still for more. The cards to which the stamps used in payment of the premiums are affixed have already required the erection of special buildings for their storage, and grave inconvenience has been caused by what seemed a simple method of utilizing the services of the Post Office in this connexion. It is worthy of note that no general decrease has been recorded in the cost of administering the Poor Law; at Cologne the expenses have actually increased; on the other hand, at Berlin a slight decrease has been notified.

From an administrative and judicial point of view, I will only briefly advert, first to the fact that the body of what is called administrative law, that is, the law which gives special privileges to officials, has increased, and then to the grave result that an immense number of applications under the law (60,000 up to July, 1893) have been refused. Under the old-age part of the schemes 245,013 persons applied, and 193,114 were recognized as admissable, 42,984 were refused absolutely. Naturally, this points to an increase of malingering and fraud, quite apart from the delay and vexation of appeals to higher Courts.

Politically, the measure was intended to be a message of peace, but from all parties in Germany come the same complaints as to the vexatious obligations of the law. My friend, Mr. Graham Brooks, records that, whereas the other social insurance laws were received with a strange lack of interest and no hint of gratitude and enthusiasm by the working classes, the apathy of the insured in the case of the old-age insurance scheme often becomes open and uncompromising dislike, especially in South Germany. The measure has been something in the nature of a political bribe, and a bribe which has failed. So far from contenting the Socialists, it has given them a fresh grievance.

If the German scheme of partial old-age pensions has been unsuccessful, the Danish scheme of complete old-age pensions in the form of out-door relief for destitution seems to have had even worse results.

No country had till recently done so much as Denmark to encourage thrift and self-help, but the Act which was passed in 1891 and came into force in 1892, providing for pensions to the deserving poor, is positively a premium on destitution. The details are probably well known to my readers. I have given them at length in my report to the Labour Commission on

Denmark. The scheme is practically a system of unlimited outdoor relief at the discretion of the guardians, half the expense being borne by the State. The results of the law are not so well known as they deserve to be. Early in 1894 complaints became rife that the benefit funds supported by the employers were being broken up, that the friendly societies were in difficulties, and, worse still, that the money in the savings banks was being drawn out and squandered. The ties between parents and children, as well as those between master and servant, had already been seriously weakened. To crown all, as a result of the system, wages were being reduced.

It may be too soon to judge of the eventual effect of either the German or the Danish scheme, but at present they appear to have done little, if any, good.

I will now deal with old-age pauperism in England and Wales, giving first some particulars as to the extent and causes of the present evils, and then dealing with the measures which are intended either to prevent or palliate those evils.

I may perhaps lay claim to some small personal experience in the matter, for, in addition to what slight information was laid before the Labour Commission on the subject, I am a member of some standing of the Manchester Unity of Oddfellows. I have known something of the administration of the Poor Law both in town and country, and I have analysed with great care the works of Mr. Booth and other English and foreign writers on the subject. Mr. Booth assures us that the number of aged persons in England and Wales in receipt of Poor-Law relief is not less than 30 per cent. of those above the age of 65, and, as the well-to-do classes must be subtracted, Mr. Chamberlain estimates that one person in $2\frac{1}{4}$ of the aged poor must be numbered among the pauper class. In the first place, I should like to point out that these statistics include persons in receipt of medical relief; and such relief is often given to persons far removed from pauperism and received by them as conveying no stigma. The Act of 1885 removed the disqualification which such relief up till then attached to voting for certain local government offices; but the number applying for such relief would in some unions equal the whole of the indoor and outdoor paupers.

A reduction of 50 per cent. has taken place in the number of paupers during the last 40 years, and that Mr. Chamberlain attributes to the stringent administration of the Poor Law and the great prosperity of the nation. He adds that the reduction has only taken place in the outdoor paupers. I venture to think that the immense growth of thrift, temperance, and education are important contributory causes, and further that there has been a substantial, though comparatively slight, diminution of the indoor and also of the aged pauper.

The causes of the evil may be divided into two classes—(*a*) Moral causes, in consequence of which the pauper has very largely to thank himself for his position; and (*b*) economic or social causes over which the pauper has no control.

It is with regard to the first that I venture with all respect to differ from Mr. Chamberlain. I should be inclined to say that intemperance, want of thrift, and, most of all, want of backbone, are in a majority of cases the cause of destitution in old age.

The chief economic cause of old-age poverty is generally low wages, such as the casual labourer in towns or the agricultural labourer in the country receives. But Mr. Little's report to the Labour Commission showed that skilled agricultural labourers such as carters, receive on an average as much as 17s. 2d. in earnings, while ordinary labourers receive on an average 15s. 11d., and Mr. Little adds that, in purchasing, 16 shillings now is equivalent to a sovereign 20 years ago, as far as the necessaries of life are concerned. I feel that sufficient stress has not been generally laid on the short period over which the power of earning lasts for some workers, especially in the case of women; but for agricultural labourers this period is generally much more prolonged than in most other employments. Even when an agricultural labourer gets past earning full wages, he can often get employment at odd jobs in the country, and where he is known as a decent fellow an effort is very frequently made to provide him with such work as he can do. In other kinds of work the increased stress and rapidity of industrial occupations is much felt by the aged workers, and this adds to their difficulty in finding employment; while last, but not least, amongst the causes of old-age poverty there is the density of the population in towns.

In addition to the above there are certain local causes. Comfortable infirmaries, as in London, attract those who would not otherwise accept relief, and the action of the local clergy and landowners, as well as the local administration of the Poor Law, may contribute to swell or lessen the numbers of the aged poor. Last of all, unsound friendly societies naturally bring about widespread distress, and local doles have been known to pauperize a neighbourhood.

There being the causes, it is obvious that there is no panacea, and, what is more, there are two questions that present themselves—first, how to prevent the existence of the evil; and, second, how to alleviate the trouble which already exists. Under each of these heads we have to consider whether the action of State or of the individual is preferable, and whether in some cases the one should or should not supplement the other.

State remedies to prevent old-age poverty rest on the argument that many paupers could not help their poverty and should not be degraded by pauper relief. It is impossible for the State to investigate the question of merit; hence the question of desert cannot be raised. The State cannot apply the test of destitution, for if it waits till the poor are destitute they will already be under the stigma of pauperism. The State must, then, undertake to maintain all persons above a certain age. Mr. Charles Booth therefore proposes that all persons above 65 should receive 5s. a week from the State. Apart from the objection at once made that the age is too high and the sum paid too low to afford a solution, there are a number of more general obstacles to the scheme. In the first place the duty of the State to support all its members has not yet been recognized, and involves a general scheme of State Socialism. The expense involved is so great that it would probably be difficult to find a statesman at present whether Socialist or not, to propose to set aside from 17 to 20 millions a year for the object. There is the moral difficulty of the discouragement of thrift, as well as the economic difficulty of the withdrawal of so much capital from use and its effect on wages. There is the disastrous effect which would probably be exercised, as we have seen in Denmark, on friendly societies and trade-union funds, quite apart from such practical questions as to whether the pensioners are to be allowed to go on earning wages. What, one may ask, is to prevent them spending the five shillings on a spree and returning to the poorhouse? Then there are the fundamental difficulties of administration and identification without a passport system, which we are not yet prepared to tolerate. All these have to be faced, quite apart from the fact that the whole plan is an experiment from which the State will not be able to recede.

To the State and Socialist methods are opposed the individual or self-help methods hitherto adopted of providing for old age out of former earnings, with the help of friendly societies, trade-unions, and savings banks. The system involves three things. First, the economic possibility of thrift—*i.e.*, the necessary margin between wages and necessary expenditure—which, except in the case of the casual and part of the agricultural labourers, is generally possible. Secondly, there must be the moral possibility of thrift—*i.e.*, self-control, forethought, self-denial, and what I have called "backbone." It is here that education, temperance, and the sympathy of the upper classes can help. Lastly, there must be the external inducement to thrift of secure and advantageous investments.

There are already greater inducements than formerly, and thrift is an ever-increasing quantity; witness the growth of the friendly societies, building societies, co-operative societies, and trade-unions, which have now funds amounting in all to 100 millions sterling. Anything that strengthens or assists these societies is therefore a help. The friendly societies have funds amounting to 25 millions sterling. They began their work when the principles of insurance were not understood, and as the science has become better known they have manfully set to work to place their funds on a sound actuarial basis. I can see no reason why they should not succeed as well with the superannuation fund which they have just taken up. The problems they have already solved were far harder. They are in every way more fitted to deal with such questions than a State department could be. For instance, a fixed age for the commencement of the superannuation benefit is unpopular and undesirable; local considerations come in, and must be given due weight. A society might find itself able to make provision to grant to a man not likely to live long an earlier payment, acting on medical and actuarial advice, or the money might be made returnable to him. All these details about which, when they are the precedents of a vast department, there is so much difficulty, can be much better solved in this way. Much can be learnt, too, from foreign attempts at old-age pensions, and it will probably be found desirable, *inter alia*, that sick pay should cease when the superannuation pay begins.

Special difficulties are (as Mr. Brabrook's and Mr. Ludlow's evidence before the Labour Commission showed) connected with trade union funds, which cannot well be kept separate for different purposes, the paramount object of these societies being to maintain the rate of wages if necessary at the cost of a strike. These difficulties are not, however, insuperable. Special provision might be made to meet them, and suggestions were made before the Labour Commission for further regulating friendly societies, and building societies especially, with a view to insuring their solvency.

The advantages of the individual system are immense. It is simple and economical; it is elastic. It is an education in the art of government to the working man. It makes considerable additions to the productive wealth of the country, and it has already proved itself an immense success.

The most important suggestion with regard to the assistance of the voluntary efforts by the State is one suggested by Mr. Chamberlain, which amounts to a system of State contributory pensions. Mr. Chamberlain has himself enumerated the objections which have been made to it. They seem to be much the same as those which we have seen to apply to the German system of insurance, which is compulsory, whereas Mr. Chamberlain's would be voluntary to the insured. There are, however, some objections which should be mentioned here. The scheme would not reach the poorest; it would be an unfair benefit to one class for which the whole country would be taxed. It is hard on societies not benefited by it. The benefits contemplated are not very great, while the fact of the age being fixed makes the scheme resemble a deferred annuity, which is unpopular with working men. In addition to these there are the administrative difficulties, which would be even greater in England than in Germany, as we have not got a trained bureaucracy, and our experience is that as soon as the bull's-eye of public opinion is turned off a department it is apt to become sluggish.

Near akin to the State contributory pension are the State subsidies for friendly societies, which have also been connected with Mr. Chamberlain's name. To these, perhaps, the chief objection is that they necessitate a State control, and this State control would probably be looked upon as a State guarantee. State subsidies are open to many of the objections mentioned above.

I have before alluded to Government annuities, which are not popular with the working man. They are said not to provide as good terms as the friendly societies; but that is reasonable, for the Government security entitles it to better terms than a private society could get.

Lastly, there are the Government savings banks, which, one would think, might play a greater part than they have done hitherto if better known.

None of the old-age pension schemes referred to above are expected by their supporters to remove old-age poverty in the next thirty or even fifty years, so we shall for some time to come have the aged poor with us, if indeed we shall not always have them. It remains to consider what we can do in detail now at once. There are two methods open to us—the adoption of the scheme now in force in Denmark, to which I need not now revert, and our own Poor Law, which I will proceed to explain.

The principle of the English Poor Law is that a man must not starve, that a pauper must receive only the necessaries of life, so as not to make him better off than the independent poor, and the life of the pauper must be accompanied by such drawbacks as to make it undesirable.

The harshness of such a law is, as Dr. Aschrott has well shown, not in the law itself, but in the administration. As a matter of fact, the guardians have an almost absolute discretion in the administration, and are able to remove almost all the abuses of which complaint has hitherto been made.

The objections to outdoor relief are well known; they led to the passing of the present Act in 1834. The guardians can, however, grant it if they think fit. The chief other objections which one hears made with regard to the Poor Law, especially in the country, are the harshness and dictatorial tone of the relieving officer, the routine life of the workhouse, the monotony of the diet, the confinement in the house or grounds, the want of privacy, and the association with unpleasant companions—all of which can be remedied by the action of the guardians. The whole question, in fact, of what is known as classification is in their hands; they can place the deserving paupers in separate cottages, and have, I believe, done so in some cases; and they can remedy one great and well-known grievance by the appointment of trained nurses.

Amongst the other grievances one hears mentioned are those connected with the maintenance of paupers by their relations, and the law of settlement. It seems only just that blood relations, such as parents, grandparents, and children, who alone are liable, should have such a responsibility, but the one undoubted grievance which requires an Act of Parliament is that relating to the law of settlement; it seems that the abolition of the power of removal of the destitute might be considered.

With regard to the officials, the overseers merely raise rates, but it is on the guardians, who are unpaid, and the paid officials, the relieving officers, masters, and matrons, that so much depends. When there is a strong chairman to the board it does not seem to matter much what the policy of the board is if it is systematically carried out and if sufficient attention is given to the numerous cases considered.

An attempt should undoubtedly be made to get better officials by higher salaries, and, above all, to enlist the services of women both as guardians and as relieving officers.

To sum up, I believe that a steady, sympathetic administration of the existing law, combined with minor legislative amendments and a more careful management of existing charities, endowed and unendowed, will do much to remedy the grievances complained of. Much can be done by the joint action of boards of guardians with such institutions as the Charity Organisation Society and the clergy. In fact, what is wanted here, as elsewhere, is not heroic legislation, but individual attention to the petty grievances of everyday life in the administration of the Poor Law, combined with a cordial recognition of what the working men have done to help themselves. It is by the resolute application of common-sense remedies to individual difficulties as they occur, and by the development of the spirit of local self-government as opposed to the action of any central department, that we shall successfully solve the social problem in so far as, humanly speaking, it ever can be solved.

GEOFFREY DRAGE,

Secretary.

Liberty & Property Defence League,

7, Victoria Street,

Westminster, S.W.

February, 1895.

Copies of this pamphlet can be had on application to the Secretary, at 7, Victoria Street, at the price of 2s. *per* 100 (*net*).

"THOU SHALT NOT STEAL

from

ESS, BY HENRY GEORGE, BEFORE THE ANTI-POVERTY SOCIETY.

ond public meeting of the Anti- ociety was held in the Academy of w York, on Sunday evening, May auditorium was densely crowded, people being turned away to have e Academy a second time. Henry addressed the meeting as follows:

cGlynn (great applause)—Dr. McGlynn applause)—Dr. McGlynn (great ap-)—in Chickering hall last Sunday night t was a historic occasion. He was right. a priest of Christ, standing on Sunday on a public platform and addressing a t audience—an audience embracing men women of all creeds and beliefs—should claim a crusade for the abolition of pov- y, and call on men to join together and rk together, to bring the kingdom of God earth, did mark a most important event. reat social transformations, said Mazzini, ver have been and never will be other than e application of great religious movements. pplause.) The day on which democracy all elevate itself to the position of a relig- us party, that day will its victory begin. Great applause.) And the deep significance of the meeting last Sunday night, the mean- ing of this Anti-Poverty society that we have joined together to inaugurate, is the bringing into the struggle of democracy the religious sentiment, the sentiment alone of all senti- ments powerful enough to regenerate the world. (Applause.)

The comments made on that meeting and on the institution of this society are sug- gestive. We are told, in the first place by the newspapers, that you cannot abolish poverty because there is not wealth enough to go around. We are told that if all the wealth of the United States were divided up there would only be some eight hundred dollars apiece. Well, if that is the case, all the more monstrous then is the injustice which to-day gives single men millions and tens of millions, and even hundreds of millions. If there really is so little, then the more injus- tice in these great fortunes. But we do not propose to abolish poverty by dividing up what wealth there is, so much as by creating more wealth. We propose to abolish poverty by setting at work that vast army of men, estimated last year to amount in this country alone to one million, that vast army of men only anxious to create wealth, but who are now, by a system which permits dogs in the manger to monopolize God's bounty, de- prived of the opportunity to toil. (Applause.)

Then again, they tell us, you cannot abolish poverty because poverty always has existed. Well, if poverty always has existed, all the more need for our or its abolition It has existed We ought to be tired of it; let us get rid of it. (Applause.) But I deny that poverty, such poverty as we see on earth to-day, always has existed. Never before in the history of the world was there such an abundance of wealth, such power of producing wealth. So marked is this that the very people who tell us that we cannot abolish poverty, attribute it in almost the next breath to over-production. They virtu- ally tell us it is because mankind produces so much wealth that so many are poor; that it is because there is so much of the things that satisfy human desires already produced, that men cannot find work, and that women must stint and strain. Poverty attributed to over- production; poverty in the midst of wealth; poverty in the midst of enlightenment; pov- erty when steam and electricity and a thou- sand labor saving inventions have been called to the aid of man, never existed in the world before. There is manifestly no good reason for its existence, and it is time that we should do something to abolish it. (Applause.)

There are not charitable institutions enough to supply the demands for charity; that seems incapable of being supplied. But there are enough, at least, to show every thinking woman and every thinking man that it is utterly impossible to eradicate poverty by charity, to show everyone who will trace to its root the cause of the disease that what is needed is not charity, but justice—the con- forming of human institutions to the eternal laws of right. (Applause.) But when we propose this, when we say that poverty exists because of the violation of God's laws, we are taunted with pretending to know more than men ought to know about the designs of Omnipotence. They have set up for them- selves a God who rather likes poverty, since it affords the rich a chance to show *their* goodness and benevolence; and they point to the existence of poverty as a proof that God wills it. Our reply is that poverty exists not because of God's will, but because of man's disobedience. (Applause.) We say that we do know that it is God's will that there should be no poverty on earth, and that we know it as we may know any other natural fact. The laws of this universe are the laws of God, the social laws as well as the physical laws, and He, the Creator of all, has given us room for all, work for all, plenty for all. If to-day people are in places so crowded that it seems as though there were too many people in the world; if to-day thousands of men who would gladly be at work do not find the opportunity to go to work; if to-day the competition for employment crowds wages down to starvation rates; if to-day, amid abounding wealth, there are in the center of worse off than savages in any it is not because the Creator has been niggardly; it is simply because of our own injustice—simply because we have not carried the idea of doing to others as we would have them do unto us into the making of our statutes. (Great applause.)

This Anti-poverty society has no patent remedy for poverty. We propose no new thing. What we propose is simply to do justice. The principle that we propose to carry into our laws is neither more nor less than the principle of the golden rule. We propose to abolish poverty by the sovereign remedy of doing to others as we would have others do to us; by giving to all their just rights. And we propose to begin by assuring to every child of God who, in our country, comes into this world, his full and equal share of the common heritage. Crowded! Is it any wonder that men are crowded together as they are in this city, when we see men taking up far more land than they can by any possibility use, and holding it for enormous prices? Why, what would have happened if, when these doors were opened, the first people who came in had claimed all the seats around them, and demanded a price of others who afterward came in by the same equal right? Yet that is precisely the way we are treating this continent. That is the reason why people are huddled together in tenement houses; that is the reason why work is difficult to get; the reason that there seems, even in good times, a surplus of labor, and that in those times that we call bad, the times of industrial depression, there are all over the country thousands and hundreds of thousands of men tramping from place to place, unable to find employment. (Applause.)

Not work enough! Why, what is work? Productive work is simply the application of human labor to land; it is simply the transforming into shapes adapted to gratify human desires, the raw material that the Creator has placed here. Is there not opportunity enough for work in this country? (Applause.) Supposing that, when thousands of men are unemployed and there are hard times everywhere, we could send a committee up to the high court of Heaven to represent the misery and the poverty of the people here, consequent on their not being able to find employment. What answer would we get? "Are your lands all in use? Are your mines all worked out? Are there no natural opportunities for the employment of labor?" (Applause.) What could we ask the Creator to furnish us with that is not already here in abundance? He has given us the globe, amply stocked with raw material for our needs. He has given us the power of working up this raw material. If there seems scarcity, if there is want, if there are men who cannot find employment, if there are people starving in the midst of plenty, is it not simply because what the Creator intended for all has been made the property of the few? (Great applause.)

In moving against this giant wrong, which denies to labor access to the natural opportunities for the employment of labor, we move against the cause of poverty. We pro- [illegible] to abolish it, to tear it up by the roots, [illegible] employment for every man. We propose to disturb no just right of property. As Dr. McGlynn said last Sunday night, we are defenders and upholders of the sacred right of property—that right of property which justly attaches to everything that is produced by labor; that right which gives to every one a just right of property in what he has produced—that makes it his to give, to sell, to bequeath, to do whatever he pleases with, so long as in using it he does not injure any one else. That right of property we insist upon, that we would uphold against all the world. To a house, a coat, a book—anything produced by labor—there is a clear individual title, which goes back to the man who made it. That is the foundation of the just, the sacred right of property. It rests on the right of the individual to the use of his own powers, on his right to profit by the exertion of his own labor; but who can carry the right of property in land that far? Who can claim a title of absolute ownership in land coming from the man who made it? (Applause.) And until the man who claims the exclusive ownership of a piece of this planet can show a title originating with the Maker of this planet; until he can produce a decree from the Creator declaring that this city lot or that great tract of agricultural land, or that coal mine, or that gas well, was made for him—until then we have a right to hold that land was intended for all of us. (Great applause.)

Natural religion and revealed religion alike tell us that God is no respecter of persons; that He did not make this planet for a few individuals; that He did not give it to one generation in preference to other generations, but that He made it for the use during their lives of all the people that His providence brings into the world. (Applause.) If this be true, the child that is born to-night in the humblest tenement in the most squalid quarter of New York, comes into life seized with as good a title to the land of this city as any Astor or Rhinelander. (Tumultuous applause.)

How do we know that the Almighty is against poverty? That it is not in accordance with His decree that poverty exists? We know it because we know this, that the Almighty has declared, "Thou shalt not steal." (Applause.) And we know for a truth that the poverty that exists to-day in the midst of abounding wealth is the result of a system that legalizes theft. (Great applause.)

The women who by the thousands are bending over their needles or sewing machines thirteen, fourteen, sixteen hours a day; these widows straining and striving to bring up the little ones deprived of their natural bread-winner; the children that are growing up in squalor and wretchedness, underclothed, underfed, under-educated even, in this city without any place to play—growing up under conditions in which only a miracle can keep them pure—under conditions which condemn them in advance to the penitentiary or the brothel—they suffer, they die, because we permit them to be robbed, robbed of their birthright, robbed by a system which disinherits the vast majority of the children that come into the world. (Great applause.) There is enough and to spare for them. Had they the equal rights i[illegible] estate which their Creator has given [illegible] would be no young girls forced to unwomanly toil to eke out a mere existence, no widows finding it such a bitter, bitter struggle to put bread in the mouths of their little children; no such misery and squalor as we may see here in the greatest of American cities (applause), misery and squalor that are deepest in the largest and richest centers of our civilization to-day. (Great applause.)

These things are the results of legalized theft, the fruits of a denial of that commandment that says, "Thou shalt not steal." (Applause.) How is this great commandment interpreted to-day, even by the men who pretend to preach the gospel? "Thou shalt not steal." Well, according to them, it means: "Thou shalt not get into the penitentiary." (Laughter.) Not much more than that with any of them. You may steal, provided you steal enough, and you do not get caught, and you may have a front seat in the churches. (Laughter and applause, and cries, "That is so!") Do not steal a few dollars—that may be dangerous, but if you steal millions and get away with it, you become one of our first citizens. (Applause.) "Thou shalt not steal;" that is the law of God. What does it mean? Well, it does not merely mean that you shall not pick pockets! It does not merely mean that you shall not commit burglary or highway robbery! There are other forms of stealing which it prohibits as well. It certainly means (if it has any meaning) that we shall not take that to which we are not entitled, to the detriment of others. (Great applause.)

Now, here is a desert. Here is a caravan going along over the desert. Here are a gang of robbers. They say, "Look! There is a rich caravan; let us go and rob it, kill the men if necessary, take their goods from them, their camels and horses and walk off." But one of the robbers says, "Oh, no; that is dangerous; besides, that would be stealing! Let us, instead of doing that, go ahead to where there is a spring, the only spring at which this caravan can get water in this desert. Let us put a wall around it and call it ours, and when they come up we won't let them have any water until they have given us all the goods they have. (Applause.) That would be more gentlemanly, more polite and more respectable; but would it not be theft all the same? (Great applause.) And is it not theft of the same kind when men go ahead in advance of population and get land they have no use whatever for, and then, as people come into the world and population increases, will not let this increasing population use the land until they pay an exorbitant price? That is the sort of theft on which our first families are founded. (Applause.) Do that under the false code of morality which exists here to-day and people will praise your forethought and your enterprise, and will say you have made money because you are a very superior man, and that anybody can make money if he will only work and be industrious! (Laughter and applause.) But is it not as clearly a violation of the command, "Thou shalt not steal," as taking the money out of a man's pocket? (Applause).

"Thou shalt not steal." That means, of course, that we ourselves must not steal. But that we must not suffer anybody else to steal if we can help it? (Applause.) "Thou shalt not steal." Does it not also mean, "Thou shalt not suffer thyself or anybody else to be stolen from?" (Applause.) If it does, then we, all of us, rich and poor alike, are responsible for this social crime that produces poverty. (Applause.) Not merely the men who monopolize land—they are not to blame above anyone else, but we who permit them to monopolize land are also parties to the theft. The Christianity that ignores this social responsibility has really forgotten the teachings of Christ. Where He in the gospels speaks of the judgment, the question which is put to men is never, "Did you praise me?" "Did you pray to me?" "Did you believe this or did you believe that?" It is only this: "What did you do to relieve distress; to abolish poverty?" To those who are condemned, the judge is represented as saying: "I was ahungered and ye gave me not meat, I was athirst and ye gave me not drink, I was sick and in prison and ye visited me not." Then they say, "Lord, Lord, when did we fail to do these things to you?" The answer is, "Inasmuch as ye failed to do it to the least of these, so also did you fail to do it unto me; depart into the place prepared for the devil and his angels." On the other hand, what is said to the blessed is, "I was ahungered and ye gave me meat, I was thirsty and ye gave me drink, I was naked and ye clothed me, I was sick and in prison and ye visited me." And when they say, "Lord, Lord, when did we do these things to thee?" the answer is, "Inasmuch as ye have done it unto the least of these ye have done it unto me." (Applause.)

Here is the essential spirit of Christianity. The essence of its teaching is not, "Provide for your own body and save your own soul!" but, "Do what you can to make this a better world for all!" It was a protest against the doctrine of "each for himself and devil take the hindermost!" It was the proclamation of a common fatherhood of God and a common brotherhood of men. (Applause.) This was why the rich and the powerful, the high priests and the rulers, persecuted Christianity with fire and sword. It was not what in so many of our churches to-day is called religion that pagan Rome sought to tear out—it was what in too many of the churches of to-day is called "socialism and communism," the doctrine of the equality of human rights! (Great applause.)

Now imagine when we men and women of to-day go before that awful bar that there we should behold the spirits of those who in our time under this accursed social system were driven into crime, of those who were starved in body and mind, of those little children that in this city of New York are being sent out of the world by thousands when they have scarcely entered it—because they did not get food enough, nor air enough, nor light enough, because they are crowded together in these tenement districts under conditions in which all diseases rage and destroy. Supposing we are confronted with those souls, what will it avail us to say that we individually were not responsible for their earthly conditions? What, in the spirit of the parable of Matthew, would be the reply from the judgment seat? Would it not be, "I provided for them all. The earth that I made was broad enough to give them room. The materials that are placed in it were abundant enough for all their needs. Did you or did you not lift up your voice against the wrong that robbed them of their fair share in what I provided for all?" (Great applause.)

"Thou shalt not steal!" It is theft, it is robbery that is producing poverty and disease and vice and crime among us. It is by virtue of laws that we uphold; and he who does not raise his voice against that crime, he is an accessory. The standard has now been raised, the cross of the new crusade at last is lifted. Some of us, aye, many of us, have sworn in our hearts that we will never rest so long as we have life and strength until we expose and abolish that wrong. We have declared war upon it. Those who are not with us, let us count them against us. For us there will be no faltering, no compromise, no turning back until the end. (Great applause and cheering.)

There is no need for poverty in this world, and in our civilization. There is a provision made by the laws of the Creator which would secure to the helpless all that they require, which would give enough and more than enough for all social purposes. These little children that are dying in our crowded district for want of room and fresh air, they are the disinherited heirs of a great estate.

Did you ever consider the full meaning of the significant fact that as progress goes on, as population increases and civilization develops, the one thing that ever increases in value is land? Speculators all over the country appreciate that. Wherever there is a chance for population coming; wherever railroads meet or a great city seems destined to grow; wherever some new evidence of the bounty of the Creator is discovered, in a rich coal or iron mine, or an oil well, or a gas deposit, there the speculator jumps in, land rises in value and a great boom takes place, and men find themselves enormously rich without ever having done a single thing to produce wealth.

Now, it is by virtue of a natural law that land steadily increases in value, that population adds to it, that invention adds to it; that the discovery of every fresh evidence of the Creator's goodness in the stores that He has implanted in the earth for our use adds to the value of land, not to the value of anything else. This natural fact is by virtue of a natural law—a law that is as much a law of the Creator as the law of gravitation. What is the intent of this law? Is there not in it a provision for social needs? That land values grow greater and greater as the community grows and common needs increase, is there not a manifest provision for social needs—a fund belonging to society as a whole, with which we may take care of the widow and the orphan and those who fall by the wayside—with which we may provide for public education, meet public expenses, and do all the things that an advancing civilization makes more and more necessary for society to do on behalf of its members? (Great applause.)

To-day the value of the land in New York city is over a hundred millions annually. Who has created that value? Is it because a few land owners are here that that land is worth a hundred millions a year? Is it not because the whole population of New York are here? Is it not because this great city is the center of exchanges for a large portion of the continent? Does not every child that is born, every one that comes to settle in New York, does he not add to the value of this land? Ought he not, therefore, to get some portion of the benefit? And is he not wronged when, instead of being used for that purpose, certain favored individuals are allowed to appropriate it? (Applause.)

We might take this vast fund for common needs, we might with it make a city here such as the world has never seen before—a city spacious, clean, wholesome, beautiful—a city that should be full of parks; a city without tenement houses; a city that should own its own means of communication, railways that should carry people thirty or forty miles from the City hall in a half hour, and that could be run free, just as are the elevators in our large buildings; a city with great museums, and public libraries, and gymnasiums, and public halls, paid for out of this common fund, and not from the donations of rich citizens. (Applause.) We could out of this vast fund provide as a matter of right for the widow and the orphan, and assure to every citizen of this great city that if he happened to die his wife and his children should not come to want, should not be degraded with charity, but as a matter of right, as citizens of a rich community, as co-heirs to a vast estate, should have enough to live on. (Applause.) And we could do all this, not merely without imposing any tax upon production; not merely without interfering with the just rights of property, but while at the same time securing far better than they are now the rights of property and abolishing the taxes that now weigh on production. We have but to throw off our taxes upon things of human production; to cease to fine a man that puts up a house or make anything that adds to the wealth of the community; to cease collecting taxes from people who bring goods from abroad or make goods at home, and put all our taxes upon the value of land—to collect that enormous revenue due to the growth of the community for the benefit of the community that produced it. (Applause.)

Dr. Nulty, bishop of Meath (great applause), has said in a letter addressed to the clergy and laity of his diocese that it is this provision of the Creator, the provision by which the value of land increases as the community grows, that seems to him the most beautiful of all the social adjustments; and it is to me that which most clearly shows the beneficence as well as the intelligence of the creative mind; for here is a provision by virtue of which the advance of civilization would, under the law of equal justice, be an advance toward equality, instead, as it now is, an advance toward a more and more monstrous inequality. (Applause.) The same good Catholic bishop in that same letter says: "Now, therefore, the land of every country is the common property of the people of that country, because its real owner, the Creator, who made it, hath given it as a voluntary gift unto them. 'The earth has He given to the children of men.' And as every human being is a creature and a child of God, and as all His creatures are equal in His sight, any settlement of the land of this or any other country that would exclude the humblest from his equal share in the common heritage is not only an injury and a wrong done to that man, but an impious violation of the benevolent intention of his Creator." (Great applause.) And then Bishop Nulty goes on to show that the way to secure equal rights to land is not by cutting land up into equal pieces, but by taking for public use the values attaching to land. (Applause.) That is the method this society proposes. I wish we could get that through the heads of the editors of this city. We do not propose to divide up land. (Laughter.) What we propose to do is to divide up the rent that comes from land; and that is a very easy thing. (Applause).

We need not disturb anybody in possession, we need not interfere with anybody's building or anybody's improvement. We only need to remit taxes on all improvements, on all forms of wealth, and put the tax on the value of the land, exclusive of the improvements, so that the dog in the manger who is holding a piece of vacant land will have to pay the same for it as though there were a building upon it. In that way we would treat the whole land of such a community as this as the common estate of the whole people of the community. And as the Sailors' Snug Harbor, for instance, out of the revenues of comparatively a little piece of land in New York can maintain that fine establishment on Staten Island, keeping in comfort a number of old seamen, so we might make a greater Snug Harbor of the whole of New York. (Great applause.)

The people of New York could manage their estate just as well as any corporation, or any private family, for that matter. But for the people of New York to resume their estate and to treat it as their own, it is not necessary for them to go to any bother of management. It is not necessary for them to say to any land holder, this particular piece of land is ours, and no longer yours. We can leave land titles just as they are. We can leave the owners of the land to call themselves its owners; all we want is the annual value of the land. Not, mark you, that value which the owner has created, that value which has been given to it by improvements, but simply that value which is given to the bare land by the fact that we are all here—that has attached to the land because of the growth of this great community. (Applause.) And, when we take that, then all inducement to monopolize the land will be gone, (applause); then these very worthy gentlemen who are holding one-half of the area of this city idle and vacant will find the taxes upon them so high that they either will have to go to work and build houses or sell the land, or, if they cannot sell it, give it away to somebody who will build houses. (Great applause.)

And so all over the country. Go into Pennsylvania, and there you will see great stretches of land, containing enormous deposits of the finest coal, held by corporations and individuals who are working but little part of it. On these great estates the common American citizens who mine the coal, are not allowed even to rent a piece of land, let alone buy it. They can only live in company houses; and they are permitted to stay in them only on condition (and they have to sign a paper to that effect) that they can be evicted at any time on five days' notice. The companies combine, and make coal artificially dear here and make employment artificially scarce in Pennsylvania. Now, why should not those miners, who work on it half the time, why shouldn't they dig down in the earth and get up coal for themselves? (Applause.) Who made that coal? There is only one answer—God made that coal. Whom did he make it for? Any child or any fool would say that God made it for the people that would be one day called into being on this earth. (Applause.) But the laws of Pennsylvania, like the laws of New York, say God made it for this corporation and that individual; and thus a few men are permitted to deprive miners of work and make coal artificially dear. (Applause.)

A few weeks ago, when I was traveling in Illinois, a young fellow got in the car at one of the mining towns, and I entered into conversation with him. He said he was going to another place to try and get work. He told me of the condition of the miners, that they could scarcely make a living, getting very small wages and only working about half the time. I said to him, "There is plenty of coal in the ground; why don't you employ yourselves in digging coal." He replied, "We did get up a co-operative company, and we went to see the owner of the land to ask what he would let us sink a shaft and get out some coal for. He wanted $7,500 a year. We could not raise that much." Tax land up to its full value and how long can such dogs-in-the-manger afford to hold that coal land away from these men? And when any man who wants work can go and employ himself, then there will be no million or no thousand unemployed men in all the United States. (Applause.)

The relation of employer and employed is a relation of convenience. It is not one imposed by the natural order. Men are brought into the world with the power to employ themselves, and they can employ themselves wherever the natural opportunities for employment are not shut up from them. No man has a natural right to demand employment of another, but each man has a natural right, an inalienable right, a right given by his Creator, to demand opportunity to employ himself. (Great applause.) And whenever that right is acknowledged, whenever the men who want to go to work can find natural opportunities to work upon, then there will be as much competition among employers who are anxious to get men to work for them as there will be among men who are anxious to get work. Wages will rise in every vocation to the true rate of wages, the full, honest earnings of labor. That done, with this ever increasing social fund to draw upon, poverty will be abolished, and in a little while will come to be looked upon as we are now beginning to look upon slavery—as the relic of a darker and more ignorant age. (Great applause.)

I remember—this man here remembers (turning to Mr. Redpath) even better than I, for he was one of the men who brought the atrocities of human slavery home to the heart and conscience of the north—I well remember, as he well knows, and all the older men and women in this audience will remember, how property in human flesh and blood was defended just as private property in land is now defended; how the same charges were hurled upon the men who protested against human slavery as are now made against the men who are intending to abolish industrial slavery. (Applause.) We remember how the dignitaries of the churches, and the opinion of the rich members of the churches branded as a disturber, almost as a reviler of religion, any priest or any minister who dared to get up and assert God's truth—that there never was and there never could be rightful property in human flesh and blood. (Applause.)

So it is now said that men who protest against this system, which is simply another form of slavery, are men who propose robbery. Thus the commandment, "Thou shalt not steal," they have made, "Thou shalt not object to stealing." When we propose to resume our own again, when we propose to secure its natural right to every child that comes into being, such people talk of us advocating confiscation—charge us with being deniers of the rights of property. The real truth is that we wish to assert the just rights of property, that we wish to prevent theft. (Applause.) Chattel slavery was incarnate theft of the worst kind. That system, which made property of human beings, which allowed one man to sell another, which allowed one man to take away the proceeds of another's toil, which permitted the tearing of the child from the mother, and which permitted the so-called owner to hunt with bloodhounds the man who escaped from his tyranny—that form of slavery is abolished. (Applause.)

So far as that goes the command, "Thou shalt not steal," has been vindicated, but there is another form of slavery.

We are selling land now in large quantities to certain English lords and capitalists who are coming over here and buying greater estates than the greatest in Great Britain or Ireland; we are selling them land, they are buying land. Did it ever occur to you that they do not want that land? They have no use whatever for American land; they do not propose to come over here and live on it. They cannot carry it over there to where they do live. It is not the land that they want. What they want is the income from it. They are buying it not that they themselves want to use it, but because by and by, as population increases, numbers of American citizens will want to use it, and then they can say to these American citizens, "You can use this land provided you pay us one-half of all you make upon it." What we are selling those foreign lords and capitalists is not really land; we are selling them the labor of American citizens; we are selling them the privilege of taking, without giving any return for it, the proceeds of the toil of our children. (Applause.)

So here in New York you will read in the papers every day that the price of land is going up. John Jones or Robert Brown has made a hundred thousand dollars within a year in the increase in the value of land in New York. What does that mean? It means he has the power of getting so many more coats, so many more cigars, so much more wine, drygoods, horses and carriages, houses or food. He has gained the power of taking for his own so much more of these products of human labor. But what has he done? He has not done anything. He may have been off in Europe or out west, or he may have been sitting at home taking it easy. If he has done nothing to get this increased income, where does it come from? The things I speak of are all products of human labor—some one has to work for them. When the man who does no work can get them, necessarily the men who do work to produce them must have less than they ought to have. (Applause.)

This is the system that the Anti-poverty society has banded together to war against, and it invites you to come and swell its ranks. It is the noblest cause in which any human being can possibly engage. What, after all, is there in life as compared with a struggle like this? One thing and only one thing is absolutely certain for every man and woman in this hall, as it is to all else of human kind—that is death. What will it profit us in a few years how much we have left? Is not the noblest and the best use we can make of life to do something to make better and happier the condition of those who come after us—by warring against injustice by the enlightenment of public opinion, by the doing all that we possibly can do to break up the accursed system that degrades and embitters the lot of so many? (Applause.)

We have a long fight and a hard fight before us. Possibly, probably, for many of us, we may never see it come to success. But what of that? It is a privilege to be engaged in such a struggle. This we may know, that it is but a part of that great, world wide, long continued struggle in which the just and the good of every age have been engaged; and that we, in taking part in it, are doing something in our humble way to bring on earth the kingdom of God, to make the conditions of life for those who come afterward, those which we trust will prevail in heaven. (Long continued applause.)

The Landlord.

Mathilde Blind.

"To him belonged the glens with all their grain;
To him the pastures spreading in the plain;
To him the hills whence falling waters gleam;
To him the salmon swimming in the stream;
To him the forests desolately drear,
With all their antlered herds of fleet-foot deer;
To him the league-long rolling moorland bare,
With all the feathered fowl that wing the autumn air.

For him the hind's interminable toil;
For him he plowed and sowed and broke the soil;
For him the golden harvests would he reap;
For him would tend the flocks of woolly sheep;
For him would thin the iron-hearted woods;
For him track deer in snow-blocked solitudes;
For him the back was bent, and hard the hand,
For was he not his lord, and lord of all that land."

Thy Kingdom Come.

O God, and still Thy children suffer want!
And haggard fathers seek from day to day
For work in vain, and babies cry for bread,
And heartsick mothers with dry eyes look on,
Too sad to weep, too hopeless far to pray,
As happy Christians do, "Thy kingdom come."

Thy kingdom come. How often has the prayer
Gone up to Thee since Christ, the poor man's friend,
First told His humble followers how to pray.
From million homes the prayer goes up to-day
To thee, and still no answer dost Thou send,
Or so it seems, for want and crime are here.

And yet, O Father, wherefore the delay?
Whose fault that want and crime walk hand in hand?
Whose fault but ours, for wealth enough is here.
But selfish Greed, and Ignorance, and Fear,
A band of triple tyrants, rule the land
And thwart the prayer they offer day by day.

O God! I see a home—a million homes
So poor and comfortless, bare even to tears:
Nor paint, nor carpet on the hard, rough floor;
Some chairs, a table, bed and stove, no more;
And they have lived in such a home for years,
And still the prayer goes up, "Thy kingdom come."

And hard the father toils through long, long hours;
The mother drudges, and the children, too,
Must work to eke out the poor meager fare.
No chance for knowledge to gain entrance there;
No chance the gentler virtues there to woo,
But chance enough for all the evil powers.

And when the father drinks—the children swear,
Or steal, or worse—and bitterness and hate
Fills every heart where should be only love—
With cold philosophy free thinkers prove
'Tis law that millions dooms to such a fate;
'Tis God, the Christians say, then wherefore care?
Or wherefore vex and sadden all our years
In feeling all the woes of wretched men
Whom God has doomed to toil, and want, and sin,
That the elect, the wealthy few, may win
Leisure for wisdom, virtue, joy, and then,
At last, a place where comes not death or tears?

We do not like to hear of poverty,
That hot bed of disease, and sin, and crime.
We preach that thrift and virtue is its dower.
With eyes, we see not. Have we lost the power?
Has self and greed, then, made us deaf and blind?
And made our worship worse than blasphemy?

We quote, "Ye always with you have the poor,"
And make a prophecy of what was meant
But as a statement of the facts that then
Existed. But a time in vain seek, when
The Christ or prophet in God's Bible lent
His voice to justify so curst a state.

Let us not dare to pray—giving the while
A paltry sum, degrading charity,
To those our ignorance or greed has robbed
Of justice, their divine inheritance,
And doomed them slaves when God has made them free.
Let us not dare to pray "Thy kingdom come!"

Let us not dare, till we have done our part
With voice or pen or freeman's vote to win
Them justice and to blot this deadly stain
From off our souls. Nor ignorant remain
Of all their wrongs, for ignorance is sin.
Let us not dare to harden still the heart.

For God is just. He will avenge the wrong
Done to his children by their brothers here.
The silent, voiceless agony ascends
From prisoned souls to Him in heaven, and lends
New strength to outraged laws divine.
Then fear eternal justice, sure, and swift and strong.

—MRS. ELIZABETH JOHNSON.

Pictou, Ont., April 13, 1887.

TO APPLICANTS FOR MEMBERSHIP

The object and principles of the ANTI-POVERTY SOCIETY are set forth on the other side of this sheet.

Aside from the initiation fee all contributions will be voluntary. Envelopes addressed to the Treasurer will be distributed through the hall at each meeting. Contributions may be placed in these and handed to the collectors, or the envelope can be taken home and mailed as addressed.

To those willing to make regular contributious, envelopes for use each week will be furnished.

Though money for hall rent, printing and other expenses is absolutely necessary, members who will work can be just as useful as those who contribute money; and all who are willing actively to engage in distributing tracts, or in otherwise promulgating the principles of the Society, are requested to notify the Secretary.

To each applicant will be sent a certificate of membership, signed by the President and Secretary,

EDWARD McGLYNN, President.

MICHAEL CLARKE, Secretary,
1996 Fulton avenue, Brooklyn.

BENJAMIN URNER, Treasurer,
6 Harrison street, New York.

The objects of the Anti-Poverty Society are sufficiently explained in the blank form of application for membership given below. Persons wishing to join the society can cut out and fill in the blank and send it, with one dollar initiation fee, to the treasurer, Benjamin Urner, 6 Harrison street, New York.

ANTI-POVERTY SOCIETY.

Believing that the time has come for an active warfare against the conditions that, in spite of the advance in the powers of production, condemn so many to degrading poverty and foster vice, crime and greed, the undersigned desires to become a member of the Anti-Poverty Society. The object of the Society is to spread, by such peaceable and lawful means as may be found most desirable and efficient, a knowledge of the truth that God has made ample provision for the needs of all men during their residence upon earth, and that poverty is the result of the human laws that allow individuals to claim as private property that which the Creator has provided for the use of all.

Name..

Address..

Inclosed please find One Dollar Initiation Fee.

HOUSES NOT BOYCOTTED.

WE ASK OUR FRIENDS TO PATRONIZE THEM.

There will be from 20,000 to 50,000 copies of the BOYCOTTER printed and distributed weekly in Atlanta and adjoining towns on the various Railroads leading into the city.

[OVER.]

THE BOYCOTTER

OL. I. PUBLISHED BY ATLANTA TYPOGRAPHICAL UNION, NO. 48. NO. I.

Organized Labor has been forced into this measure of Boycotting after every other attempt to settle the differences had failed. The *Constitution* has systematically blacklisted the printers of Atlanta for over three years, for the sole reason that they joined Typo. Union No. 48—a society instituted by printers for the elevation of their craft, (a society just as necessary to the printer as the Odd Fellows, Knights of Honor or any other secret or benevolent institution, one of its objects being to take care of its sick and indige .t members and to bury the dead), and to secure a higher degree of workmanship. You are asked to boycott the names on this list (which means not to trade with them) for the reason that they patronize our enemy, the *Constitution*. This request is intended to apply to our friends everywhere—those coming from the country as well as those in Atlanta. This fight is one purely of DEFENCE, and is waged by Organized Labor and the different Trades Unions which have seen fit to espouse the cause. The *Constitution* commenced the war without other reason than opposition to and contempt for not only Organized, but for all Labor. Remember the motto of the great K. of L., "AN INJURY TO ONE IS THE CONCERN OF ALL." (For boycott on *Constitution* see *Working World* each week.)

The farmers are equally interested in the fight against this monopolistic sheet, and they ought to spend their money where they know it will not go into its coffers.

You are earnestly requested not to trade with a ıy house on this list, or buy any article named in it.

DRY GOODS.

J. M. HICH,

M. RICH, & BRO., JOHN KEELY,
McCONNELL & JAMES, JOHN RYAN,
CHAMBERLIN JOHNSON & CO.

CLOTHING.

GEORGE MUSE, HIRSCH BROS.,
JAS. A. ANDERSON.

JEWELERS.

FREEMAN & CRANKSHAW,
J. P. STL /ENS, D. N. FREEMAN,
ER. LAWSHE.

GROCERS.

PETER LYNCH. J. J. DUFFY.

ART GOODS.

E. A. HORNE & CO.

FURNITURE.

P. H. SNOOK. A. J. MILLER.

TOYS.

C. S. SCHUESSLER.

MISCELLANEOUS.

Thompson, Langdon & Co., Corsets; Atlanta Lumber Company; **Royal Baking Powder**; F. M. Ferris & Co., Hams; Stone Mountain Granite Co.; Hathaway, Soule & Harrington, Shoes; Freeman & Gillies, Artistic Furniture; Chattahoochee River Brick; Southern Seed Co.; Louisiana State Lottery; Atlanta Rubber Co.; Dr. Price's Flavoring Extracts, McDonald's Fire and Water Proof Cement, Ladd's Lime, James Means' Shoes.

BOOKS AND STATIONERY.

"OLD BOOK STORE,"

JOS. VAN HOLT NASH, E. H. THORNTON.

WHOLESALE COMMISSION.

W. F. STOKES & CO., ELAM JOHNSON & CO.,
CHANDLER BROWN & CO., WYLY & GREENE.

CROCKERY.

McBRIDE.

COAL.

J. C. WILSON, J. C. BRIDGER.

WHOLESALE TOBACCO.

W. A. RUSSELL & CO.

REAL ESTATE.

FRIERSON & SCOTT, SAM'L W. GOODE,
G. W. ADAIR, R. H. KNAPP,
GHOLSTIN & KROUSE, E. M. ROBERTS & CO.
A. S. TALLY, SMITH & DALLAS,
RICE & WILSON. KEY & JONES,
G. H. EDDLEMAN & CO.

PROPRIETARY MEDICINES.

Hunnicutt's Rheumatic Cure, Tutt's Pills, B. B. B., Clingman's Tobacco Remedies, Ayer's Cherry Pectoral, Cuticura Remedies, Wilbor's Cod Liver Oil, French Hospital Remedies, Quinn's Pioneer Blood Renewer, Dugro's Ailiamentary Elixir, Cheney's Expectorant, Bull's Cough Syrup, Mrs. Winslow's Soothing Syrup, Angostura Bitters, Hall's Lung Balsam. Johann Hoff's Malt Extract, Tropic Fruit Laxative, Pennyroyal Pills, Rosadalis, Holmes' Sure Cure, Taylor's Cherokee Remedy, Henry's Carbolic Salve, Schenck's Mandrake Pills, Dr. Sweet's Infallible Liniment, Johnson's Anodyne Liniment. Carter Medicine Co.

This list will be corrected weekly, and all new advertisers added to it. Those wishing to cease patronizing the *Constitution* until this trouble is over can address the "Committee," 49½ S. Broad St., and their names will be dropped from this list.

[OVER.]

SUSTAINS LABOR UNIONS.

Finding of Arbitration Board in Sattley Strike Case---It Recommends That the Company Recognize the Union.

Finding Discusses the Question in an Advanced Light----Decision of Great Importance.

[From The Illinois State Journal, Springfield, Dec. 29, 1901.]

The decision of the state board of arbitration in the Sattley case, which was announced yesterday, sustains the right of workingmen to belong to a labor organization. This is said to be the first instance in which a state arbitration board has assumed to pass upon this question. Controversies referred to arbitration usually relate to wages. In the Sattley case the board found that practically the sole cause of the strike now on at the plow works was the demand of the men for a recognition of their union and the refusal of the company to grant the demand. This made the issue one of unionism.

Although the Sattley company was represented at the hearing before the board, it was not a party to the application and therefore is not bound by the board's findings. The decision, therefore, is only of an advisory nature, rendered in the hope that the recommendations contained in it will be acted upon and result in a settlement of the present difficulty.

The decision reviews the facts of the case quite exhaustively. On the vital point, the "recognition of the union," the board recommends that this be a part of the terms of settlement, the precise scope of such recognition to be defined by written agreement. While making clear that, so far as strictly legal rights are concerned, there can be no question of the right of an employer to employ whomsoever he chooses or the right of the employe to work for whomsoever he chooses, the board points out that there are certain obligations due between employer and employe, and from both to the public, quite distinct from those defined by constitution and statute.

The tendency of the age, it is contended, in the direction of co-operation and organization, in the commercial and industrial relations of men, is irresistible, and the questions to be met are properly those of regulation.

The arbitration board is composed of Frederick W. Job of Chicago, chairman; Chauncey B. Geiger of Ashley, representative of the employers, and Walter A. Mathis of Clinton, representative of organized labor. J. McCan Davis of this city is secretary.

TEXT OF THE DECISION.

Discussion of the Entire Case and Finding of the Board.

STATE OF ILLINOIS, }
State Board of Arbitration. }

Springfield, Dec. 28, 1901.

In the matter of the application of the striking plow workers lately employed by the Sattley Manufacturing Company, of Springfield, Ill.

Application filed December 14, 1901.

Hearing at Springfield, December 18 and 19, 1901.

The petition in this case comes from the striking plow workers and bears 114 signatures. The grievances complained of are stated as follows:

"The said employes have made substantially the following demands of said company:

"1. The recognition of Plow Workers' Union No. 9,460.

"2. The restoration of the scale of wages in force prior to Sept. 1, 1901.

"3. The reinstatement of all employes, in their respective places, who were laid off, locked out, or discharged without cause since Oct. 16, 1901.

"4. That the minimum wage scale for common labor be fixed at $1.50 per day.

"The said company has refused to grant these demands."

Prior to the hearing the Sattley Manufacturing company was given an opportunity to join in the petition, but declined to do so. The company, however, was represented at the hearing by its secretary and treasurer, Mr. S. E. Prather, and by its attorney, S. P.

Wheeler, Esq. A motion to dismiss the petition was entered by the company on the ground that this board had no jurisdiction to conduct an inquiry upon the petition, the chief reasons assigned being in substance that the signers of the petition were not employes of the Sattley Manufacturing company at the time of the filing of the petition, and that the board has no authority to entertain a petition where a strike has been inaugurated and is in existence at the time of the filing of the petition. The motion to dismiss was overruled, and the board proceeded to hear such evidence as was offered. The striking plow workers were represented by Mr. George F. Paul, secretary of Plow Workers' Union No. 9,460, and by E. L. Chapin, Esq. The privilege of cross-examining witnesses was accorded to the attorney for the Sattley Manufacturing company. No objection was made to this by the legal representative of the men; but as one witness declined to answer a question propounded by the attorney for the company, on the ground that the company had not joined in the petition, it is proper to state that under the law it is the express duty of the board, in conducting an inquiry as to the causes of any difference between an employer and his employes, whether upon the petition of one or both sides, "to hear all persons interested therein who may come before them." The manifest purpose of the law is that the board shall ascertain all the facts of the case under investigation, and in order to facilitate the inquiry it was deemed proper to permit all interested parties to participate in the examination of witnesses.

History of the Case.

The Sattley Manufacturing company is engaged in the business of manufacturing plows and other agricultural implements at Springfield, Ill. The history of its difficulty with its employes, briefly stated, is as follows:

On Oct. 1, 1901, there was a cut in the piece-price schedule in the paint shop, ranging from 5 to 20 per cent, according to the class of work. The company claimed that, owing to the installation of a "trolley" in 1900, the individual employe in the paint shop could turn out much more work and that the company was entitled to share in the saving. There was at the same time a radical cut in the piece schedule in the wood shop, amounting, in the case of balance cultivator frames, to a reduction of 50 per cent. It appears from the evidence that the cut in the wood shop was made by the foreman without the knowledge or consent of the officers of the company, and without previous consultation with them; but this fact was not known to the men at the time. These wage reductions appear to have occasioned some alarm among the plow workers. A rumor was circulated that there was to be a general cut of wages throughout the shops.

On Oct. 14, Plow Workers' Union No. 9,460 was formed with a membership which embraced a large majority of the employes—two-thirds, it is conceded by the company. Previous to this date men had been employed without reference to the question of membership in the union. "Never," it is stated on behalf of the company, "during the twelve years prior to October, 1901, had there been any substantial difference or controversy between the Sattley Manufacturing company and its employes." The officers of the company, it appears, looked with extreme disfavor upon the threatened unionizing of their shops. For the purpose, it is alleged, of establishing a wage scale which should prevail throughout the year, unless changed by mutual consent, and in the hope that the removal of the apprehension of a reduction of wages would take from the minds of its employes the desire to join the union, the company closed its plant on Wednesday, Oct. 16, announcing that on Saturday, Oct. 19, a new wage scale would be posted, and that employes desiring to return to work should notify the proper officials of their desire to do so.

New Employes Engaged.

Only a few of the men gave notice of their intention to return to work, and accordingly, on Sunday, Oct. 20, the company began a search for new employes. During the ensuing three days there were conferences between the company and a committee representing the men who had not returned to work. On Wednesday, the 23d, an understanding was reached between the company and the committee. Among other things it was arranged that the men who returned to work should sign the following agreement:

Springfield, Ill., Oct., 1901.

"I agree, in taking a place with the Sattley Manufacturing company, to accept ...... cents per hour, net, for time employed, as full compensation for services rendered; same rate to prevail for extra time put in on nights; and to faithfully and diligently serve them to the best of my ability unless prevented by sickness, or desiring to take a position elsewhere, in which case I agree to give them three days' notice of my intention to quit; and I promise, during the manufacturing season of 1902, to make no demand upon them for an increase of wages, nor to unite with other employes in any concerted action with a view to securing greater compensation. I further agree to a strict compliance with the printed rules of the company."

(Signed)..........

A written memorandum of the terms of the agreement was drawn up and signed by the company and by a committee of the men, and was subsequently approved by Plow Workers' Union No. 9,460.

What Agreement Provided.

Among other things this agreement provided that if the old employes came back on Thursday morning (the 24th) the company would put to work from 40 to 50 per cent of them at that time, and that the others would be taken back as the company could find places for them, not later than the date of the completion of the new building then in course of construction; that the company have the right to retain in its employ all of the new men then working and to put to work all new men who had been promised employment, provided they should apply for their positions "within a few days;" and that as soon as possible, "and within three months," the company would make up a piece schedule and submit it to its employes, which should not be less than the old day schedule. Under this arrangement a large number of the men returned to work.

On Nov. 25 a committee of the employes waited on the company and submitted a written statement calling attention to "the hostile attitude of some of your representatives who have of late called before them certain employes and urged them to surrender their membership in Plow Workers' Union No. 9,460 of the American Federation of Labor, and who have resorted to very questionable tactics to bring about the dissolution of our union. Indications point to a continuance of this very unfair and unwarranted abuse of authority, and it does not seem likely to cease unless the company will give us recognition." The statement also embodied the four demands above referred to as contained in the application to this board.

Waited on the Company.

On the following morning (Tuesday, Nov. 26) the committee again waited on the company and stated that unless the company acceded to their demands by noon of that day the employes would be called out on a strike. The company desired until Friday, the 29th, to consider the matter, but the only extension of time obtainable was until 5 o'clock of the afternoon of the 26th.

The company posted a notice calling attention to the agreements previously entered into and claiming that it had not violated any part of the same. "We think we have fully complied with all of the obligations undertaken by these agreements," the notice stated. "We are, however, willing to confer with any committee of our employes in regard to any acts of ours which you claim constitute a breach of any obligations we have undertaken by the agreements we have entered into."

The conference between the officers of the company and the committee of the employes on Tuesday, the 26th, related almost entirely to the question of the recognition of the union. No understanding being arrived at, the union employes at 5 o'clock that afternoon went out on a strike. The strike then inaugurated is still on. The company has employed non-union men to take the places of the strikers. The total number of men at work Dec. 18 (the date of the hearing before this board), according to the statement of the secretary and treasurer of the company, was 254. The number at work on the date of the strike (Nov. 26) was 285.

Question of Recognition.

While the statement of grievances set forth in the petition contains four distinct propositions, it is clear, from the evidence presented at the hearing, that there is no substantial difference between the company and the men on any except one of these propositions. This is the demand of the men for the recognition of the Plow Workers' union. The other demands are all of a subordinate nature. With the question of unionism settled, we are of the opinion that all questions of wages will be easily and satisfactorily adjustable. The demand for a minimum wage scale of $1.50 per day, for instance, affects only a small number of men. Heretofore the lowest wages paid for common labor at the Sattley shops has been $1.25 per day; but it is in evidence that of the 285 men in the employ of the company on the date of the strike, only thirteen were receiving as low as $1.25 per day. The company claims that this rate is intended to apply only to new men who perform common labor. Owing to the small number of men affected, we have no doubt that the company would be willing to concede the demand on this point. As to the scale for piece work, there appears to be no difference between the company and the men worthy of serious controversy.

In our view of this case it appears that the present situation is due to four circumstances, to-wit: (1) An exaggerated alarm on the part of the company as to the probable difficulties that would follow recognition of the union; (2) a well founded belief on the part of the men that the company was making an effort to break up the union; (3) an insistence on the part of the men for a recognition of their union more strict than the company was willing to concede; and (4) a misunderstanding as to what constituted a violation of the agreement entered into between the company and the men under date of Oct. 23, 1901.

Legal Rights Not Determined.

We are not called upon in this case to determine legal rights or obligations. These are left to the courts, where they have been determinable from time immemorial. The law creating this board expressly provides that it shall have jurisdiction only where there is a difference "not involving questions which may be the subject of an action at law or bill in equity." While the rights prescribed by law are superior to all others, and must forever remain so in a free government, yet there are certain obligations due between employer and employe, and from both to the general public, quite distinct from those defined by constitution and statute, and so generally recognized that the law itself has taken cognizance of them. It is for the adjudication of controversies arising from these obligations that such tribunals as the state board of arbitration have been erected. So far as strictly legal rights are concerned, it will not be questioned that an employer, unless bound otherwise by contract, is at liberty to employ whomsoever he chooses, and that the workingman has the like liberty of working for whomsoever he chooses; and that the law does not, and cannot consistently with the fundamental principles of civil liberty, undertake to say whether a man shall or shall not belong to a labor union.

Yet it is impossible to ignore, and futile to try to check, the tendency of the age, in the commercial and industrial relations of men. It is distinctively an age of co-operation—of the achievement of results by concerted and harmonious action for the common good of all. We witness today combinations of capital of a magnitude scarcely dreamed of so recently as a quarter of a century ago. There have been, in connection with some of these combinations, results that have created widespread alarm. Yet, in the sober second thought of the nation, it is conceived that these combinations are a necessary part of commercial progress; that the evils that have arisen from them are of a purely incidental nature, and that ultimately these will be minimized or completely eradicated by proper regulation.

Unions Not Necessarily Bad.

So, likewise, the tendency toward co-operation—to organize for the common good and to attain a common end—has extended to the industrial masses to such an extent that the labor union is now found in almost all trades and occupations. That men in these organizations, suddenly clothed with large power, have sometimes exercised it unwisely, and that the men composing the rank and file of the organization have sometimes acted upon bad counsel, is undeniable. Yet this is far from proof that such organizations are intrinsically bad. On the other hand growing experience has shown them, when judiciously conducted, to be a powerful agency for good. Whatever evils are justly chargeable to labor unions may be traced to incompetent or unwise management or leadership.

We fail to perceive any reason for denying to workingmen the same right to combine for their mutual benefit and protection as is exercised with great freedom by their employers. The labor union is based upon the recognition of the potency of organization. Men have learned that in the great industrial struggle the individual is but an atom. If he have a grievance, standing alone, he is powerless to redress it. In all respects he is at a decided disadvantage in his relations with his employer. But when he has the united co-operation of his fellow-employes, he is supported by a power that at least must command attention.

We have but to glance back a century to perceive the phenomenal changes that have come in the relations between employer and employe, and between individual citizens generally. Customs deemed wise and necessary then would be absurd and intolerable now. So there have come changes in the laws. In former times the concerted action of workingmen in quitting the service of an employer was adjudged a criminal conspiracy; but today the right of workingmen to strike is recognized by legislatures and courts, and it is only when striking men resort to violence or intimidation that they incur the penalties of the law.

Company's Position Criticized.

In the case under consideration, while the Sattley Manufacturing company, as is admitted, had a perfect legal right to employ whomsoever it chose, we are of the opinion that the company has assumed an unwise attitude toward the Plow Workers' union. This company itself has recognized the benefits to be derived from cooperation, not only by taking a corporate form for the conduct of its business, but by its membership in the Northwestern Plow Manufacturers' association. This association, while its avowed object is purely social, has endeavored in a measure to fix the prices of the articles manufactured by its members by "recommending" price lists to be followed from year to year. That the association has gone no farther than to "recommend" certain prices appears to be due to the existence of an anti-trust law; and the fact that its "recommendations" have not been followed uniformly in nowise changes the object sought to be accomplished.

We make no criticism of the Sattley Manufacturing company for its membership in the Plow Manufacturers' association. The object of the association, however it may be stated, is to secure for its members some common advantage. We can perceive no impropriety in conceding a similar privilege to the men employed by the Sattley Manufacturing company—the privilege of uniting themselves into an organization for their common benefit and protection.

The whole controversy in this case appears to hinge upon what is implied by the term "recognition of the union." It is in evidence that the ordinary meaning of this term is that only union men shall be employed; that if the company employs a man who does not belong to the union, and if he refuses to join the same, he shall be discharged; that if any man is discharged by the company the union shall have the right to investigate the cause of the discharge, and, if found to be unjust, to insist upon the reinstatement of the man. The officers of the Sattley Manufacturing company were of the opinion that "recognition of the union" in this sense involved such a surrender of the management of their business that they could not conduct the same with satisfactory results. They made the argument that there is at present no "union" plow factory in the United States, in the sense here set forth, and that to "unionize" their own shops would place them at a decided disadvantage with their competitors.

Agreement Was Not Broken.

We shall not enter into a discussion of the contract made between the company and the men under date of Oct. 23. The company claims that it was guilty of no violation of this contract, and this claim appears to be sustained by the evidence; if any agreement was broken by the company it was a verbal one, and was not the written contract above referred to; but it is clear that the men were of the opinion, and honestly so, that the company had been guilty of bad faith, and that for this reason they were justified in ignoring their agreement not to unite in a concerted demand for higher wages, or to quit the service of the company without three days' notice. As is almost invaribaly the case in controversies of this kind, possibly neither side was wholly free from fault.

We regard the present difficulty as exceedingly unfortunate and a satisfactory adjustment of it an object much to be desired. Many of the men now on strike had been in the employ of the company from the time the plant was founded twelve years ago. Their relations with the company, prior to the present difficulty, had been harmonious. Some of them had built their own homes, and in general they had become identified with the city in which they resided.

The employer owes it not only to himself but to the community in general to promote permanency of employment among his employes. He who builds a home, or entertains the hope of doing so, is likely to be a superior workman and a superior citizen. The man who feels that his employment is permanent enjoys a sense of security for the future. There is then an incentive for him to possess a home, to accumulate his savings, and to take an active and beneficial interest in the affairs of his community, his state and his country. There should be an avoidance of all conditions which will tend to foster a vast army of migratory men, without certain employment, without home ties, and without a substantial interest in citizenship. It is to the interest of all to provide, in every way possible, for the permanent employment of men. It is for this reason that in the case under consideration we deem the present relations between the Sattley Manufacturing companw and its old employes to be a misfortune to be deplored by the entire community.

Recommendations of the Board.

As this is a case in which the board of arbitration has no power to render a decision that may be enforced by legal process, we make the following recommendations, in the hope that they will be acted upon by the parties to this controversy and result in a settlement thereof:

1. That the Sattley Manufacturing company meet a committee of its old employes with a view of making an arrangement by which employment may be provided for all or a part of them, as may be found practicable.

2. That the terms of re-employment include "recognition of the union" by the Sattley Manufacturing company, the precise meaning of this term to be defined by written agreement; but that, in any event, the company shall not deny to the men the right to be members of the Plow Workers' union and shall not discriminate against the

members of such union or endeavor to persuade them to withdraw from the same.

3. That the terms of settlement be embodied in a contract covering a specified period, and shall include an agreement on the part of the company not to discharge men, and on the part of the emloyes not to leave the service of the company without a specified notice.

4. That said coutract provide that, in case of future differences arising between the company and the men, the same shall be referred to arbitration without a strike or lockout—the arbitrators to be either the state board of arbitration or persons mutually agreed upon.

We regard this case, in its present status, as one requiring mutual concessions, and we urgently request the reopening of negotiations between the company and the men with a view to effecting a settlement; and in this connection we hereby tender such further service of this board, or of its individual members, as may be required to accomplish the end in view.

(Signed)

Frederick W. Job, Chairman,
Chauncey B. Geiger,
Walter A. Mathis,
State Board of Arbitration.

J. McCan Davis, Secretary.

Practical Suggestions on Labor Organization.

A Paper read at the Twenty-sixth Annual Meeting of the American Social Science Association at Saratoga, N. Y., Sept. 2, 1891.

BY

SAMUEL M. HOTCHKISS,

Commissioner of the Bureau of Labor Statistics, Hartford, Connecticut.

PRACTICAL SUGGESTIONS ON LABOR ORGANIZATION.

BY SAMUEL M. HOTCHKISS, OF HARTFORD, CONN.

The interests of capital and labor are not identical, but they need not and should not conflict. Each is essential to the other, and justly entitled to its fair share of the benefits which they jointly produce. No plain law has yet been discovered for the settlement of this account, by which the scales of justice have been made to balance. Nearly two thousand years ago a carpenter's son proposed a plan which did not meet with much favor at the time, but has since commanded some attention as applicable to the settlement of such questions. Unfortunately, its principles have not been conspicuous in the treatment of this question by either party.

The laborer has found that he cannot stand alone in the modern industrial struggle. Mechanical invention and immigration have encroached upon his opportunities for remunerative employment, till he has met the emergency in the only way open to him. Labor organization is the natural and necessary outgrowth of conditions for the existence of which he is not responsible.

It aims to unite the mass of workers to maintain and advance their common interests. If this aim could be fully realized, the irresponsible use of the vast power of such organization might prove a serious danger to society. This danger, however, is not likely to be realized. The masses may be stirred to united action to attain a specified end, like the movement for shorter hours of labor, but experience has proved that they cannot be held permanently together. Only a small proportion is efficiently organized. The permanent value of their organization will depend upon a just use of its power and the degree in which it is made mutually beneficial to employer and employed.

The laboring men knew what they wanted, but did not know the best way to attain it. Their want of discrimination in the use of unaccustomed power was one leading cause which brought labor organization into public disrepute. Capital, which did not understand the reason for the movement, regarded it as a dangerous impertinence, and was quick to take advantage of its mistakes to array the forces of society against it. Employers made the great mistake of fighting organization instead of assisting their workmen to distinguish and utilize the good, and avoid the evil involved in it. But recently there has been a most salutary change in the treatment of this question by both sides.

The attitude of employers toward labor organization down to a recent period, and the radical change which is taking place, is aptly illustrated by the relations between the hat manufacturers and the trades-unions in Danbury, Conn., which are among the oldest in the State and country. The unions were organized in 1850, when the manufacturers began a struggle to maintain their independence of the unions, which lasted for thirty-five years. During this whole period strikes and shop calls were of daily occurrence, and often paralyzed business. The labor cost of an order could not be safely predicted, nor the time when it could be completed. Frequent periods of idleness subjected the working people and tradesmen to serious inconvenience and loss. Finally, the hat manufacturers, tired of the wasteful struggle, proposed to the unions that both parties cease hostilities and seek peaceful means for the settlement of difficulties without the interruption of business.

Upon a suggestion from the trades-unions, the manufacturers organized the Manufacturers' Association, which entered into permanent agreements with each union, by which provision was made for the adjustment of all questions, including wages, through committees, and, in case of disagreement, by arbitration. Non-union workmen were admitted to the unions, and all the factories submitted to union rules.

This common-sense action in Danbury, in 1885, practically closed the vexatious warfare which had prevailed for a whole generation. For six years business has met with no interruption, except the lockout in November, 1890, caused by the attempt of the Trimmers' Union to withdraw from the compact, which did not succeed, and the principle was established that neither party can withdraw from the compact without the consent of the other.

The vitality of the trade idea is illustrated by an incident which occurred during this contest. The Trimmers' Union is composed of women and girls to the number of seventeen or eighteen hundred. The Manufacturers' Association, fearing that the course of the trimmers would endanger the trade agreements, decided to destroy their union. But, with all the combined power and influence which the seventeen wealthy corporations in the association could bring to bear, their effort failed, and the ranks of the union remained unbroken. Fortunately, the association and all of the unions sustain the integrity of the trade agreement, and there is no prospect of further disturbance.

It is interesting to note that the dissatisfaction of the trimmers grew out of the introduction and use of machines and the principle of subdivision of labor in trimming hats; and, further, that, while members of the union were displaced, the innovations made it possible for a union shop to make cheap grades of hats at a profit, using high-priced union labor, in competition with non-union shops, using low-priced non-union labor. It not infrequently happens that loss in one direction, by reason of such changes, is partially or wholly compensated by gain in another.

The experience of the last six years in Danbury clearly demonstrates that it is possible for capital and labor, by perfecting instead of fighting organization, to maintain the just rights of both parties and harmonize clashing interests without resort to force.

Fortunately, the prevailing assumption that organized labor has no right to any voice in the adjustment of wages and other conditions, vitally affecting the laborer, that employers are bound to respect, is giving place to more just and reasonable views. The superior advantages which wealth, education, and commanding business and social relations confer on employers, should be used to supplement the honest efforts of the less favored working class, in seeking equitable adjustment of difficulties for the existence of which neither is responsible, but which both must face.

The dissatisfaction of the laboring man with his present limitatations is one of the hopeful signs of progress. The first President Dwight, President of Yale College one hundred years ago, in referring to the indisposition of the Englishman of that day to attempt to grow out of the condition in which he was born, said, "If an Englishman is born to the wheel-barrow, he never will aspire to the hand-cart." In A.D. 1100 a charcoal-burner named Purkess found the dead body of William II., son of the Conqueror, who had been shot with an arrow in the New Forest, and carried it jolting in his rough cart to Winchester cathedral. "Lineal descendants of this man are reported living in the same spot, who have constantly been proprietors of a horse and cart, but never attained to the possession of a team" (more than one beast). They occupy the same rank to-day as their ancestor who furnished rough transportation for the carcass of the second Norman king eight hundred years ago.

The fact that the working people of America are stirred with ambition for solid advancement in life is cause for profound satisfaction. Labor organizations have contributed largely to the public good in this country and Europe, in awakening and fostering the manly ambition of the working people.

A large proportion of the members of the unions is from the less intelligent classes of the working people. In many of the trades intelligent mechanics who receive liberal wages do not feel personal need of organization and prefer to act independently. Labor organization suffers for want of the help of these men, whose higher intelligence and wider experience would insure wiser and more conservative leadership. Most unions restrict membership to actual workmen This is probably wise; but unions suffer serious loss by the promotion of their best men to positions of trust, which disqualifies them for membership. It is a curious fact that in these changed relations overseers and managers often become unfriendly to the system, and labor difficulties are sometimes aggravated by the jealousy of workmen of overseers and bosses promoted from the ranks.

The loyalty and unselfish fidelity of the members to the unions, and their willingness to share their earnings with fellow-unionists, can in almost all cases be implicitly relied upon, however great the inconvenience may be to themselves and their families.

The Knights of Labor are entitled to the credit of organizing and developing the principle of settling disputes by means of friendly conference and arbitration. It is a reasonable and common-sense method, and should receive universal encouragement. Owing to the complex character of the organization, the masses of the working people prefer the simpler form adopted by the trades-unions, which they can easily understand.

While the unions were not, like the Knights of Labor, special advocates for the peaceful settlement of difficulties by arbitration and conciliation, the principle has now been practically adopted by all organizations.

The enrolled membership of the unions is small compared with the mass of the working people, but it has the advantage of organization. A dozen men thoroughly organized have greater efficiency than hundreds or even thousands without it. While their mistakes have been numerous, trade organizations, as a whole, have exerted a powerful, progressive influence. All the State bureaus of labor statistics and that of the United States were established through their direct efforts. Imperfect as the organization is, it affords the best and almost the only practical means for direct communication with the laboring people. The work of the bureaus of labor statistics is greatly aided by this means of intercourse. Ballot reform, and especially the adoption of the official ballot, was strenuously advocated by all labor organizations long before its importance received public recognition; and it is through their direct efforts that the system has been so extensively adopted. Their agitation for this cause and for weekly payments, factory inspection, shorter hours of labor, and other reforms, has met with marked success.

But their greatest efforts have been expended upon questions affecting wages. In this field, which appeals directly to their most pressing needs as well as to their selfish instincts, their intelligent leaders have found the greatest difficulty in convincing the rank and file that wages cannot be permanently increased on a falling market, and that the organization which is designed to help the laboring man to obtain justice can only be legitimately used, under proper conditions, to secure a just advance or to prevent or retard an improper decrease, and that permanent success can only come to the union or to him personally from a course that will promote the mutual good of employer and employed.

Extended observation justifies the belief that these views are now generally held by union men. Many employers frankly say that under such conditions the unions can be as beneficial to them as to the workmen. Numerous instances have recently been reported in Connecticut in which employers have advised their employees to organize, believing that it would result to their mutual advantage.

An extensive builder and contractor recently said, referring to the unions of carpenters, masons, bricklayers, hod-carriers, and others connected with the building trades, that he had no objection to these organizations. He said that he saw no reason why the laboring people had not as good a right to organize and to say who should be admitted to their several trades, and to do what they could to obtain liberal remuneration, as ministers, lawyers, and doctors had to organize their societies and unions, and to say who should be permitted to practise or officiate in their several professions; under what conditions their members should be permitted to earn their daily bread, and to fix their fees for professional services; or as business men had to combine to promote their interests. He said that the unions had never complained of his discharge of men for cause. He further said the average workmen furnished by the unions were superior to the average under the old system. Answers to inquiries of prominent builders in other cities and towns in Connecticut were in substantial accord with those referred to. Jevons says,* "All classes of society are trade unionists at heart, but differ chiefly in the boldness, ability, and secrecy with which they push their respective interests."

In connection with the foregoing opinions of builders and contractors, it is proper to note that there are others, especially among the smaller contractors, who are restive under the new order of things and who do not accept the situation willingly. But, so far as these inquiries have extended, the opinion seemed to prevail that, on the whole, in the building trades the unions are helpful to both employer and employed.

Contractors say that they find little embarrassment on account of any advance in the labor cost falling on the property owner by reason of fewer hours of daily labor in the building trades. The opposition to the unions, based on the theory that capitalists will not build if remunerative wages are paid, seems to be hardly justified by the facts. Capitalists who have been interviewed say substantially that they are not only willing, but prefer, that labor should be liberally paid. Inquiry and observation in other manual trades and employments show similar results, but varying according to the conditions affecting each particular trade.

The question whether the union will be advantageous or otherwise to the contractor, and especially to the employees, depends upon the intelligence, good judgment, and business qualifications of the contractors and union officials. Either party wanting these favorable conditions may make the relations of capitalists, contractors, and employees intolerable. Experience seems to justify the conclusion that the union admits of reciprocal relations which may make it advantageous to both parties and to society.

The effectiveness of trade organization in mechanical industries comes far short of that attained in the manual trades. In all man-

*Preface to "State in Relation to Labor."

ufactories labor is struggling to find its proper adjustment in the sweeping changes from manual to mechanical production. The average intelligence required in the masses of working people employed in all factories becomes lower and lower as inventive genius multiplies the means for mechanical production. Major Bent, president of the Pennsylvania Steel Company, said in a recent address, referring to their large works at Steelton, near Harrisburg, Penn.: "When that plant was started, the average wages of our men was above four dollars per day. Now the average is about one dollar and seventy-five cents per day." Numerous cases showing equally radical changes might be cited.

It is here that intelligent labor encounters its hardest conditions. All the operatives in a given occupation may suddenly find their occupation abolished. Continued production of a given article often depends upon keeping the labor cost from advancing or forcing a reduction. The employer is as much perplexed as the employee. The demand of the union for increased wages is met with the assurance that the increase demanded would result in closing production, or in substituting mechanical means for accomplishing the work now performed by human hands. Many of the large manufacturers keep in their employ experts and inventors for the purpose of reducing the labor cost of production by improving their labor-saving machines. A single illustration is in point.

The manager of one of the largest manufactories of hardware in Connecticut recently said that two years ago they were manufacturing an article at a cost of six dollars and fifty cents per dozen, which involved the labor of fifty-seven men. They were able to sell the article at a profit of fifty cents per dozen. A competing establishment was manufacturing the same article, but at a cost which gave the first the advantage in the market. A committee of the union called upon the manager and urged an increase of wages. He showed them the facts as stated, and that the proposed advance would give the trade to the competing firm. He further informed them that, if the labor cost was increased, it would compel them to do most of the work by machinery. The demand was pressed, and the advance granted. The result was that in a few months machinery was built by the aid of which seven men produced more goods than had been produced by the fifty-seven formerly employed, at a cost of only three dollars and fifty cents per dozen. Of course, the result displaced fifty of the men employed in the manufacture of that one article. Numerous similar incidents might be cited in other lines of manufacture. The radical changes in methods of production in all mechanical industries render any permanent solution of the intricate problem in these lines extremely difficult, if not impossible.

It is true, however, that there are mechanical industries, limited in their extent, in which labor organization meets reasonable success in influencing the conditions of labor.

In one of these, having but seven manufactories in the whole country, only skilled operatives trained to that work can be profitably employed. The limited number of operatives are closely organized in unions which have succeeded in securing remunerative wages. The occupations are similar to those in another line of industry requiring a similar grade of skill, which employs thousands of operatives who are not efficiently organized. The lowest wages paid in the organized industry are two dollars per day. Nearly all, however, earn from three to three and a half dollars per day, and in some cases four and four and a half dollars; while operatives of the same grade in the other line receive wages varying from ninety cents to one dollar and a quarter, and in rare instances one dollar and a half per day. The proportion who receive as much as one dollar and a quarter per day is small.

But for the close organization of the skilled operatives in the limited industry, by means of which apprenticeship and admission to their unions are limited and controlled, equally skilled operatives in the similar line would immediately become competitors for their places, and wages would fall to the lower scale. In maintaining liberal compensation, this union does no wrong to the manufacturers, since all are subject to the same conditions, and the difference in the increased labor cost of goods to the consumer is infinitesimal.

It would be a public benefit if the thousands engaged in the similar occupations referred to could secure to themselves like remunerative wages instead of the present beggarly income of ninety cents to one dollar and a quarter per day, which necessitates the employment of wife and children in the mills in order to secure a daily income equal to that of the father alone in the other similar employment; while the public who consume the goods, notwithstanding the modern craze for the bargain counter, would willingly pay the increased labor cost in the purchasing price of the goods.

In some trades the efficiency of local unions is supplemented by the action of those in other places whose members use the products of the former's labor. This is illustrated by the case of the local unions of quarrymen, and the unions of stone masons, stone cutters, and carmen who use or handle the quarry products. The local unions of quarrymen were materially assisted in their strikes for shorter hours with increased pay by the refusal of unions to use or handle their products for building or other purposes in New York and other large markets till their demands were complied with, which seriously embarrassed, and in some instances stopped, the business of the quarry companies.

Many of the most intelligent workmen believe that the agitation of the movement for shorter hours of labor will prove to be the most effective agent for the equitable adjustment of the general labor problem. It is the leading question in all of the labor organizations to-day.

The absurd theory that a man can perform as much work in eight hours as he can in ten is not held by the working people. They believe that, if the hours of labor are reduced 20 per cent., it will require a corresponding increase of laborers to perform a given amount of labor in a given time. They further believe that, if the percentage of decrease in the hours of labor is greater than the percentage of the unemployed, there will necessarily be appreciation in wages.

The agitation for shorter hours has awakened general public sympathy for the movement. Intelligent employers say that the objections are not to the change itself, but to the practical difficulties which must be encountered in bringing it about in important lines of mechanical industries where it will meet its gravest difficulties. But the movement has met with practical success in the building and some other manual trades, and indications favor its general success.

Wages under an eight or nine hour day will be adjusted on precisely the same principles which control under a ten-hour day, and should be treated as an independent question. If combined with the movement for shorter hours, it will be sure to give the impression that the object of the latter is merely to increase wages.

The use of the strike, boycott, lockout, and black list, has fallen into disrepute, but is by no means obsolete. Of these objectionable expedients, the black list is the least excusable and the most unpopular. It is a system of terrorism borrowed from the dark ages, and is utterly unworthy of the otherwise honorable men who still permit its use. No employer is willing to admit that it has ever been employed in his establishment, and yet in disguised and hidden forms it prevails wherever there is an attempt to enforce the requirements of organized labor. It prevails to the greatest extent in places where organization is most effective.

It is a serious fact that officers of unions and members of committees who are conspicuous in maintaining contested union interests are very likely to find themselves practically blacklisted. Discharge is never attributed to this cause, and frequently does not immediately follow the offence; but sooner or later some plausible excuse, like "dull times," is utilized to drop the objectionable hand, who will be refused work in other factories. Many cases might be cited in proof of these statements. Some skilled hands are received back after a limited period of enforced idleness.

Tradesmen and professional men often decline to serve as arbitrators, because they are afraid that connection with sharply contested arbitration might injure their business by incurring the displeasure of one side or the other.

In Danbury one leading hat firm declined to join the Manufacturers' Association, but complied with the union rules. Their factory forms an asylum for men and women who have been practically blacklisted in the other shops. They are among the best workmen and women in the trades. It is invaluable to the unions, because it enables them to draw the ablest unionists for officers and members of committees from this shop's crew, as it is termed, all of whom are beyond the reach of the dreaded blacklist.

The danger to employees in forming unions and taking positions as officers and members of committees is still real, and is encountered in almost all lines of industry.

In mercantile lines agreements are made between employers that they will not employ a man or woman discharged by another employer in their line, or who leaves such employer without his recommendation for honesty and efficiency. It would be difficult to find recorded evidence of such agreement; but numerous cases could be cited which prove the existence of this form of practical blacklisting. The fact remains that in mercantile as well as mechanical pursuits the practice prevails to an extent bordering on conspiracy.

The laboring people, as a rule, have small confidence in the efficacy of profit-sharing and similar plans for securing to them their share of the products of their labor. Nearly all prefer the plan of fixed wages, which are not subject to contingencies and conditions with which they are wholly unfamiliar. The system works smoothly when there are profits to be distributed; but, when the frequent intervals of depression occur, and there are no profits, the question of fair dealing in the manipulation of the accounts is almost sure to be raised. Even if the workmen were admitted to an inspection of the books, it would be of little practical service, because they are not familiar with methods of book-keeping and the principles of business management. In Connecticut at least they believe that the practical effect of all such schemes is to reduce wages sufficiently to discount all receipts from so-called profit-sharing. They have a shrewd suspicion that in some way the dividend to the employee is provided for to the profit of his generous employer.

An interesting experiment under the name of Gain-sharing attempts to obviate this objection to the profit-sharing plan. Here, too, the advantage to labor is challenged by the laborers, because the accounts are all kept by the employers, for which service they appropriate one-half of the gains, if any there be. They control the wages of their men, and many of the employees believe that in practical operation the depreciation in wages will in some way more than balance their half of the gains. It is evident that the success of any of these plans for profit-sharing presupposes a degree of intelligence in the average workingmen and of their confidence in employers which has not yet been attained.

The revolution in public thought and sympathy on the subject of labor organization during the last five years is remarkable. When the observations upon which these remarks are based began five years ago, reasonable and intelligent men among the organized laboring people, in referring to their efforts for labor reform, used the following truthful language: —

"We are not understood by the public, our actions are misrepresented, and our motives are misjudged; we have never had opportunity to lay before the public a fair expression of our ideas on the labor question; our papers published in the interest of labor reform are only read by a few of the laboring people; the public press will not exchange with our papers or copy articles which fairly represent our views. In reporting our meetings, they only ridicule us for our failures and mistakes. The public is ignorant of the merits of our cause, and we are condemned without a hearing."

To-day the secular and religious newspapers freely open their columns to the broadest discussion of the interests of labor and labor organization, and fully and fairly report all of their meetings in their news columns. In magazines and innumerable other publications, in the pulpit and on the platform, the subject is treated and discussed by the ablest minds in professional and business life.

Study of its practical features has a large place in the departments of political and social science in all of our schools and colleges, under professors and teachers who are almost to a man radical in their ideas of industrial progress and reform. Social science and economic associations provide for open discussion of the subject, in which representatives of the workingmen and their societies are invited to give free expression to their views and participate in the discussions.

While the greatest efforts of labor organizations have been expended upon questions affecting wages, it is doubtful whether the advantages reaped by the laboring people from their contests with capital at all compare with the results of their efficient educational and benevolent work, and their efforts for the establishment of bureaus of labor statistics, ballot reform, weekly payments, factory inspection, shorter hours of labor, and other reforms of lasting value to society.

The contest between capital and labor is by no means ended, but the time must come when each will have learned that its interests can in no way be served by hostile relations. Improved conditions will not come through sudden revolution, but through the slower process of evolution. That passion and prejudice have blinded and warped the better judgment of both sides in such a sharply contested field is not strange. Selfish cupidity will continue to retard, but cannot stop, progress. The best interests of society are inextricably involved in the contest. Legal enactment may be helpful in attaining special ends, but public opinion is the court of final appeal. No organization of capital or labor can long maintain itself in opposition to an enlightened public sentiment. Once make the facts in the case clearly evident, and the final public verdict will demand justice.

It is the privilege and the duty of labor organizations to give to the public full and authentic statistics relating to this subject. In such educational work lies their highest and most effective usefulness.

HOURS OF LABOR.

Manufacture of Coarse and Fine Cotton Goods.

Half-truths are as great source of error as untruths, and sometimes give rise to errors which are of the most persistent class. One of these half-truths which is now pressed into the service of the labor agitators is that the North, and particularly Massachusetts, enjoys climatic advantages over the South for spinning cotton. The point is made that the South cannot contend with us in spinning fine yarns, because that industry cannot be carried on in the South without creating artificial moisture in the mills. It is impossible for those who are advocating a forcible reduction of the hours of labor to deny, and in fact they do not deny, that the situation of Southern spinners with reference to the supply of raw material gives them an advantage over northern manufacturers ; nor can it be disputed that the advantage is increased by the low price of labor in that part of the country, and by the absence of laws limiting the hours of labor.

But it is urged, these Southern spinners are restricted by the inexorable laws of nature to the production of coarse goods. They are prohibited by their climate from making the finer qualities, unless they will go to the expense of creating artificial humidity in their mills. Here, then, is the opportunity of Massachusetts to improve the quality of her goods and to take a market in which she can have no Amercan rival.

This sounds plausible, and it is surely calculated to tickle the vanity of a Massachusetts man. To one who knows but little about the cotton manufacturing industry, it may seem like a proposition to abandon crude things and devote our attention to the production of articles more in keeping with Massachusetts "culture."

The aspect changes when it is explained that on the one hand the assertions upon which the suggestion is based are only half true; and that on the other hand they would be of little or no consequence if they were wholly true.

The facts regarding the advantages and disadvantages depending upon difference in climate, are simply these: There is no part of the United States where fine yarns, technically known as such, can be spun without the use of artificial moisture; there is no part of the country where coarse yarns and the coarser medium yarns cannot be spun in the natural atmosphere of a mill. The climate of Southern Massachusetts—but of Rhode Island and Connecticut as well—is such that rather finer yarns can be spun successfully in the natural atmosphere than in the South. That is all there is in this suggestion.

Now what are "coarse" and what are "fine" goods? and what is the relative market for each? A cloth made of No. 32 warp and No. 36 filling is technically known as coarse goods. It is cloth made of yarn that can be spun as well in the South as in the North without any artificial moisture. It is of such, or of coarser cloth, that the shirt upon your back and the sheet upon your bed are made. It is of coarse spun yarn that the standard print cloths are woven, which afterwards become calicos and prints. It is from such yarn that most of the ginghams are made, and by far the largest part of ladies' underwear.

In short, fully nine-tenths of all the cotton cloth consumed in the country, and not only that, but nine-tenths of all that would be consumed, if purchasers had their choice between fine and coarse goods at the same price, is cloth known to the trade as coarse, and, as has been said, cloth that may be made in the South on absolutely equal terms so far as atmospheric humidity is concerned.

Another point may be mentioned which seems to have been overlooked. Manufacturers are now turning their attention more and more to the weaving of goods for exportation. An arrangement has lately been concluded, as every one knows, which is expected to give access for our domestic cotton goods into Brazil. It is expected that the policy that brought about this arrangement will be successful in opening other markets to these goods. And what grade of cotton cloth, is it supposed, will be exported to the Latin-American peoples, if a trade with them should be created? Coarse goods, surely. The export trade to China is already far more extensive than people generally suppose; for the largest part of our exportation of domestics is shipped overland through Canada and Vancouver, and does not appear at all in the general statistics of trade. Every yard of the goods so exported is coarse spinning. Do those who advocate a change in the labor laws think it is of no consequence that the legislation they propose may — should their suggestion to spin finer goods be adopted — force Massachusetts mills to abandon all hope of a share in the export trade? How far would a monopoly of the market for cloth for baby clothes go, as compensation for the loss of the market for nine-tenths of the domestic consumption and the whole foreign market?

But even if the market proposed as an alternative for that in which we now have a footing, were larger than it is, it could not be occupied except at a large expenditure for new plant. A factory cannot shut down on Saturday night after running on yarn of a certain fineness and start up on Monday morning on yarn of a different number. Increased fineness in goods produced means more machinery as well as different machinery. To adjust mules and spinning frames to the spinning of cotton of a particular number is a work requiring time and care. Of course it is not worth while to dwell on this point, after it has been shown that the suggestion under consideration is worthless. For when it is true that a quarter of the present spindle capacity of Massachusetts alone is equal to the production of all the fine goods for which there is a demand, it is idle to think of changing the machinery in use until it is suggested what shall be done with the three-quarters of the spindles which must be stopped in any event, if Massachusetts is to abandon the production of coarse goods.

The truth is there is a total absence of reasonableness in the suggestion that manufacturers can do better than to follow the policy that has heretofore guided them,— a policy of endeavoring to find out what the public demands and to supply that want. It comes in the guise of a proposition for the benefit of manufacturers. It is really a suggestion that they go out of business altogether.

INCREASE IN WAGES—DECREASE IN HOURS OF LABOR.

The last report of the Bureau of Labor Statistics of the State of New York, just issued, shows that the hours of labor have been decreased in more than 2,000 factories in that State in one year, and that the wages of labor have been advanced in more than 1,900 cases against 441 in which they have been reduced.—*Speech of Hon. J. P. Dolliver, of Iowa, in H. R., March 29,* 1892.

LABOR STRIKES.

Disturbance of Labor—Hostile and Inimical Relations between Employer and Employee since Passage of McKinley Tariff Act.

Among the many remarkable statements made by the Senator from Missouri in his speech of June 28, I find the following:

> I am prepared to show by irrefutable testimony that never in the history of this country has there been such disturbance of labor, never such hostile and inimical relations between employer and employee, never such prostration of agricultural interests, never such a limiting and narrowing of foreign markets, never such disaster brought about in so short a time, as by this infamous legislation.

It will be noticed that this sentence contains three distinct charges in regard to the operations of the act of 1890, and these I propose to take up seriatim. The first of these is that there had never been such disturbance in labor, never such hostile relations between employer and employee, as were brought about by the act referred to. In support of this allegation the Senator submitted and had printed in the "Record" a long list of alleged "wage reductions, shut-downs, lock-outs, and strikes in protected manufactures which had taken place since the passage of the McKinley bill from data collected by Hon. John De Witt Warner for the New York World." This list covers the time between December 4, 1890, and June 18, 1892, a period of eighteen months.

The statement shows that during this period seventy-seven strikes occurred in the United States. If we assume that these figures are accurate, and it will be seen from an examination of the other papers furnished by the same gentleman that he has **a decided tendency to overstate in his statistics,** it may be profitable to make a comparison between the number of strikes occurring as alleged since the passage of the act of 1890, and in the years which preceded it.

Many of the items in the list of strikes and reductions are inserted several times, apparently in order to swell the number.—*Speech of Hon. N. W. Aldrich, of R. I., in U. S. Senate, July* 26, 1892.

Statistics of Strikes in United States Prior to 1890—Ten Times as Many Strikes in 1890 as Reported in Senator Vest's Statistics for Eighteen Months—Number of Employees Involved.

Having this comparison in mind, I requested the Commissioner of Labor to furnish me with statistics of strikes in this country for the years prior to 1890, and, if possible, to give me comparative statistics of strikes which have taken place in Great Britain within the period covered by his American statistics.

In answer to this request I have received the following table, showing the number of strikes and the number of employees involved in each year, from 1880 to 1890, inclusive, in the United States:

YEARS.	Number of Strikes.	Employees Striking and Involved.
1880	610	......
1881	471	129,521
1882	454	154,671
1883	478	149,763
1884	443	147,054
1885	645	242,705
1886	1,411	499,489
1887	872	345,073
1888	679	211,016
1889	643	177,298
1890	798	201,682

It will be noticed that the number of strikes in this country varied from 433 in 1884 to 1,411 in 1886; the average number of each year for the whole period being 625. The number reported in 1890 is 798, being more than ten times as many in this single year as reported by Mr. Warner for the eighteen months covered by his statistics.—*Ibid.*

Strikes in Great Britain, the Paradise of Tariff Reformers—Great Durham Strike in England—Remarkable Freedom from Strikes and Labor Troubles in this Country since Passage of McKinley Act—No Reduction of Wages—Wage Earnings Exceptionally High—Wages of Bar Rollers in Pittsburg Mills $15.25 Per Day, etc.

Available statistics show that in Great Britain, the paradise of tariff reformers, 3,164 strikes occurred in 1889. The British Board of Trade officially report 1,028 strikes in 1890, with 392,981 persons involved in 738 of these.

It will be seen by a comparison of the relative number and importance of strikes in the United States and in Great Britain for the year 1890 that the number was much greater in the latter country, and that the number of persons involved was more than three times as great in proportion to the number of persons engaged in useful occupations in the respective countries.

In the recent strike in Durham (English) district 100,000 coal miners went out, and remained idle from March 12 to June 1, when they accepted a reduction of 10 per cent. in wages. This strike involved the closing down of one hundred blast furnaces in addition to the suspension of mining operations.

The statistics submitted by the Senator from Missouri confirm in a striking manner the judgment of every intelligent observer, that there has been a remarkable freedom from strikes and labor troubles in this country since the passage of the Tariff Act of 1890. It can be said that at no time in the history of the country has labor been so constantly and profitably employed, and at such satisfactory wages, as in the period referred to. **No person in the United States, with the capacity and willingness to work, is out of employment.**

It is true that a reduction of wages has taken place in a limited number of establishments producing iron and steel; but the fact should not be overlooked that, even with this reduction, the average wages are still much higher than in any of the other great industries. The earnings in some departments are exceptionally high; for instance, the average net earnings of bar rollers in all the Pittsburg mills is $15.25 per day, and the net earnings in wire rod rolling are even higher than this.

Mr. Warner's table contains several items in regard to reductions in wages said to have been made in the Rhode Island and Fall River cotton mills, in November, 1890, and in 1891. I can say, on the authority of the representatives of the mills in question, that these statements are entirely **untrue, and that no such reductions took place.**

From such examination as I have been able to make, I can say that the various statements in regard to the reductions of wages in cotton mills **are equally untrue.**—*Ibid.*

Strikes no Connection with Tariff—Immemorial Contest between Capital and Labor—Streets of Free-Trade London Resound with Tramp of Thousands of Strikers against Reduction of Wages—Strikers' Curses Loud and Deep—400,000 Mine Workers, in Free-Trade England, out on a Strike.

A few days ago the *pro tempore* leader of the House on that side, with a disingenuousness unworthy of him, inveighed against the protective system because certain coal-miners in Alabama, certain iron-workers in Pennsylvania, had struck for higher wages. He knows that the tariff had no connection with these strikes. He knows that in all climes, at all times, since man first looked into the eye of his fellow, capital and labor have been engaged in contests which a Christian civilization has lessened in number and reduced in bitterness, but has not yet learned to prevent. He knows that not long since the streets of free-trade London resounded to the tramp of marching thousands, strikers, not for an advance, but against a reduction of wages. Men, and women too, who in Trafalgar Square, in presence of the bronze figure of England's great captain on the seas, in curses loud and deep denounced the policy that on land made beggars of her own. He knows that to-day four hundred thousand mine-workers in free-trade England, out on a strike, have laid their paralyzing hand on England's trade.

And if the gentleman from Tennessee, appealing in an assembly such as this, not to reason, but to passion and prejudice, is enamoured of this subject of strikes, let me commend him to the recent history of his own State, where freemen—mine-workers—were turned out to the winter's blast, hungry and workless, by convicts put in their places to sate the greed of Democratic mine-owners. That strike, like all the others, bore no relation to the tariff, nor did the tariff bear any relation to it. Man's avarice on one side or on the other accounts for them all, tariff or no tariff.—*Speech of Hon. John Dalzell, of Pa., in H. R., April 2, 1892.*

Labor's Condition in America Better than Anywhere Else in the World.

In the issue of the American Economist of January 29, 1892, I find an article upon "American Wages." It is brief and to the point, and I quote from it with the statement that the figures given are shown by every official and unprejudiced unofficial statement on the subject to be correct:

Our import duties are laid with a view to covering the difference in cost of production here and abroad.

Labor cost, or wages, constitute fully 90 per cent of this cost of production.

Consequently our workmen receive nearly all the benefit derived from protection.

It is conceded by all that American wages are from 60 to 150 per cent higher than in England, and from 100 to 1,000 per cent greater than in other countries.

The American farm laborer gets on an average $20 a month and found, while the English farm laborer gets but $8.

The American iron-workers get $5.50 per ton for puddling, while the Englishman gets but $2.

The American potter gets three times as much for the same work as the English workman.

Our textile workers earn from two to three times as much as the textile workers in England.

And so we might go through every trade and occupation, skilled and unskilled, and we would find that a day's labor in the United States is worth double, and more, the same work in England. This is equally true whether paid by time or piece.

Not only do our workmen receive much better wages than the laborers abroad, but they receive more than our own laborers did half a century ago, when we had a free-trade tariff.

In fact, as Labor Commissioner Carroll D. Wright has just said: "The condition of the wage workers of the United States, viewed in all respects, is better now than at any previous period in our history."

Not only are wages higher, but the cost of living has not increased. There has, moreover, been a general decrease in the hours of labor, all of which tends to better the condition of the American wage earner in every way.—*Speech of Hon. J. A. Dolph, of Ore., in U. S. Senate, March* 11, 1892.

From the Publishers
Oct. 10, 01

THE

LAW RELATING

TO

LABOUR UNIONS

As regards their Legal Liabilities in connection with Picketing, Coercion, and Intimidation; the Right to Sue and be Sued, and the Consequent Liability of their Funds;

AS LAID DOWN BY RECENT JUDGMENTS.

Price Sixpence.

ISSUED BY THE
EMPLOYERS' PARLIAMENTARY COUNCIL,
7, VICTORIA STREET, WESTMINSTER.

1901

CONTENTS.

THE LAW RELATING TO LABOUR UNIONS.

THE

LAW RELATING TO LABOUR UNIONS.

ALLEN *v.* FLOOD.

THE following summary, taken from the *Morning Post*, December 15th, 1897, gives the facts in this first of the important series of labour-union test cases. The case was originally known as Flood and Taylor *v.* Allen :—

"Messrs. Flood and Taylor were working shipwrights duly qualified in their trade. They were engaged in April, 1894, by the foreman of the Glengall Iron Company (Limited) to work at repairs on the ship *Sam Weller*. At some previous period of their careers these two men had worked at iron work on an iron ship. The Boilermakers' Union holds that shipwrights ought not to work at iron work on an iron ship, and that such work ought to be reserved exclusively for boilermakers, members of their union. Accordingly Mr. Allen, a delegate of the Boilermakers' Union, went to see the managing-director of the Glengall Iron Company, and gave him to understand that, unless Flood and Taylor were discharged, all the members of the union then in the Company's service would cease work. The Company employed far more boilermakers than shipwrights, and the two shipwrights to whom exception was taken were discharged. There was no contract between them and the Company; theirs was merely a day-to-day engagement, but, in the ordinary practice, they would not have been discharged, except for misconduct, until the repairs on which they were employed had been finished. There appears to have been no secrecy about Allen's communication to the Company, and no doubt that the discharge of the two shipwrights was occasioned by it. The two shipwrights thought that Allen by that communication had injured them, and that the law of England would give them redress, so they brought an action against him. The action was tried before Mr. Justice Kennedy, and the jury thought they had been injured and ought to have redress to the extent of £20 apiece. Allen appealed. The

Court of Appeal [consisting of the Master of the Rolls (Lord Esher), Lords Justices Lopes (afterwards Lord Ludlow) and Rigby] held that he had done wrong, and that he ought to pay the £40. Allen then appealed to the House of Lords, which called to its aid no less than eight judges, six of whom [viz., Justices Hawkins (now Lord Brampton), Cave, Wills, Grantham, Lawrance, and North] agreed with Mr. Justice Kennedy, the jury, and the Court of Appeal, while two [Justices Mathew and Wright] thought that he had acted within his legal rights. Yesterday the Judicial Peers gave their judgments; three of them [viz., Lords Ashbourne and Morris and the Lord Chancellor (Lord Halsbury)] agreed with the Lower Courts, but six of them [Lords Herschell, Watson, Macnaghten, Davey, Shand, and James] held that Allen had acted within his rights. Accordingly the decision of the House of Lords is that Allen was within his rights, and that Flood and Taylor have no legal ground for complaint, and must pay the costs of the three trials."

* * * * * *

It would appear from the recent decision in Quinn *v.* Leathem that the importance of Allen *v.* Flood has been much exaggerated, and that it does not go to anything like the extent generally supposed. According to the judgment of Lord Lindley in Quinn *v.* Leathem, Allen *v.* Flood establishes two propositions. "The first and important proposition is that an act otherwise lawful, although harmful, does not become actionable by being done maliciously, in the sense of proceeding from a bad motive and with intent to harm or annoy another. ......The second proposition is that what Allen did infringed no right of the plaintiffs, even although he acted maliciously and with a view to injure them......Truly, to inform a person that others, *not under the control of the informant*, will annoy or injure him unless he acts in a particular way cannot of itself be actionable, whatever the motive or intention of the informant might have been." It will thus be seen that the element of threat is entirely eliminated from Allen's proceedings, and the proposition for which the case has usually been quoted falls to the ground. The question is further dealt with later.

QUINN *v.* LEATHEM.

The original action (under the name of Leathem *v.* Craig) out of which this appeal to the House of Lords arose was tried before Lord

Justice FitzGibbon at the Belfast Assizes in July, 1896. Leathem, the plaintiff, was a butcher at Lisburn, near Belfast, and he had in his employment one, Robert Dickie, who had been with him for ten years. Leathem had been in the habit of sending meat to the value of about £30 a week to a butcher in Belfast named Andrew Munce. Craig and the other defendants formed themselves into a duly-registered trade union under the title of "The Belfast Journeymen Butchers Assistants' Association," and shortly afterwards demanded that the plaintiff should dismiss Dickie from his service, which he refused to do. As he was threatened with various unpleasant consequences by the union, the plaintiff had an interview with Craig and other leading members, and offered that, if they would accept his men as members, he would pay whatever fines and demands the union might have against them. The union refused this offer, and insisted that the men should be put out to walk the streets for twelve months as punishment. The plaintiff refused to yield, and, in consequence, pressure was brought to bear upon his servants to leave him, and upon Munce to discontinue taking meat from him. The trade union also issued "black lists" upon which were the names of Leathem and other butchers who had offended against the society's rules. The plaintiff alleged that this course of conduct constituted a legal wrong for which he was entitled to recover damages, and in the result the jury awarded him £250, for which amount and costs judgment was entered. The defendants subsequently moved that judgment should be entered for them or a new trial ordered. The arguments were heard in the Queen's Bench Division in Ireland before Lord Chief Justice O'Brien, Chief Baron Palles, and Justices O'Brien and Andrews, and on November 22nd, 1898, after waiting for the decision in Allen *v.* Flood, the Court (Chief Baron Palles dissenting) refused the motion. The defendants appealed to the Court of Appeal in Ireland, and on May 2nd, 1899, the appeal was dismissed, the Court consisting of the Lord Chancellor of Ireland (Lord Ashbourne), the Master of the Rolls (Right Hon. A. M. Porter), and Lords Justices Walker and Holmes. The defendants finally took the case to the House of Lords, and the original verdict has been unanimously upheld by the judgments delivered on August 5th, 1901, by the Lord Chancellor (Lord Halsbury) and Lords Macnaghten, Shand, Brampton, Robertson, and Lindley, who thereby affirmed the decision of the Court of Appeal in Ireland, and dismissed the appeal, with costs.

* * * * * *

The argument of the appellant assumed that Allen *v.* Flood had decided that the threats alleged to have been used by Allen were lawful, and it was argued that the threats in this case were of the same nature, and that the only possible distinction between the two cases was that the jury negatived conspiracy in Allen's case, and affirmed it in the case of Quinn and those who acted with him. It seems clear, however, from the judgment that the Lords do not admit the legality of threats to bring about a strike or lock-out, and that they consider that the threats *alleged* to have been uttered by Allen, but not proved, would have been just as actionable as the threats in this case, and equally so whether there was a conspiracy or not. A few extracts will make this clear. The Lord Chancellor said: "Now the hypothesis of fact upon which Allen *v.* Flood was decided by a majority in this House was that the defendant there neither uttered nor carried into effect any threat at all. He simply warned the plaintiffs' employer of what the men themselves, *without his persuasion or influence*, had determined to do." The following passage from the able judgment of Lord Lindley deals with the two questions of conspiracy and threats: "It was contended at the Bar that, if what was done in this case had been done by one person only, his conduct would not have been actionable, and that the fact that what was done was effected by many acting in concert makes no difference. My Lords, one man without others behind him who would obey his orders could not have done what these defendants did. One man, exercising the same control upon others as these defendants had, could have acted as they did; and, if he had done so, I conceive that he would have committed a wrong towards the plaintiff, for which the plaintiff could have maintained an action. I am aware that in Allen *v.* Flood Lord Herschell expressed his opinion to be that it was immaterial whether Allen said he would call the men out or not......If Lord Herschell meant to say that as a matter of law there is no difference between giving information that men will strike and making them strike, or threatening to make them strike, by calling them out when they do not want to strike, I am unable to concur with him."

LYONS *v.* WILKINS.

The case of Lyons *v.* Wilkins was decided on February 3rd, 1898, by Mr. Justice Byrne in the Chancery Division of the High Court of Justice. The plaintiffs, who are wholesale leather bag manufacturers, sought an injunction to restrain the secretary of the Amalgamated Society of Fancy Leather Workers, and others, from watching their premises, and persuading persons not to work for them. They also sued to restrain the publication of a libel in two letters written by the secretary to the fathers of youths in their employ, pointing out the "gross unfairness of their sons working for a starvation wage of twelve shillings a week," when they might be earning twenty-eight. Mr. Justice Byrne decided both issues in favour of the plaintiffs. He held that watching and besetting of their premises had been clearly proved at the trial, and made perpetual the interlocutory injunction which had been granted by Mr. Justice North in February, 1896. As regards the letters, an injunction was not pressed for, as the strike was over. But the Judge distinctly held that they constituted an actionable wrong, and awarded the plaintiffs damages, which he limited, however, to five pounds, in view of the fact that the libels were not repeated, and did not remain long in the hands of the recipients. The case, being one of clear picketing, was not affected by the Allen *v.* Flood judgment.

On November 29th and December 1st, 1898, the Appeal was heard before the Master of the Rolls (Sir Nathaniel, now Lord, Lindley) and Lords Justices Chitty and Vaughan Williams. On December 20th judgment was given, upholding the original decision. In the course of his judgment the Master of the Rolls said :—

> "The truth was that to watch or beset a man's house with a view to compel him to do or not to do what it was lawful for him not to do or to do was wrongful and without lawful authority, unless some reasonable justification for it was consistent with the evidence. Such conduct interfered with the ordinary comfort of human existence and the ordinary enjoyment of the house beset, and would support an action for nuisance at Common Law; and proof that the nuisance was for the purpose of peacefully persuading other people would afford no defence to such action. Persons might be peacefully persuaded, provided that the method employed to persuade was not a nuisance to other people.......It was all very well to talk about peaceable persuasion, and to draw fine lines between persuasion and giving information. The line might be fine; but in this case there was no difficulty whatever in coming to the conclusion that what was done was watching and besetting, as distinguished from attending in order merely to obtain or communicate information."

The final Appeal to the House of Lords was entered by the defendants, but was abandoned on February 7th, 1901, the officials of the labour unions which had guaranteed the cost deciding not to contest the judgment of the Court of Appeal.

* * * * * *

Prior to the action of Lyons *v.* Wilkins it had been very generally assumed that the proviso in Section 7 of the Act of 1875 (see Appendix) legalises what is called "peaceful picketing"—in other words, it was supposed that, although violence and intimidation were illegal, the statute allowed workmen who had a difference with their employer to attend at or near the employer's premises with the object of inducing other men, by argument and persuasion, either to leave or to refuse to accept employment with the master whose premises were picketed. It has now been decided that the words of the Act, "to obtain or communicate information," are to be understood literally, and do not cover the totally different procedure of argument and persuasion.

The legal position being thus settled, every employer should, not only in his own interest and that of employers generally, but in the interest of men who are willing to work and desire to be protected from molestation, insist that pickets confine themselves to their legitimate and legal business, and do not attempt to enter into argument with persons approaching or leaving the works. If they refuse to do so, proceedings should at once be taken against them. These proceedings may be either by way of injunction, as in Lyons *v.* Wilkins, or may be taken summarily before magistrates. In some specially aggravated cases an injunction may be the best remedy, as the power of the Court to order imprisonment for breach of it is unlimited; but, as a general rule, the simpler and cheaper remedy of summary proceedings will probably be found sufficient.

TAFF VALE RAILWAY COMPANY *v.* AMALGAMATED SOCIETY OF RAILWAY SERVANTS.

This case arose out of the strike on the Taff Vale Railway in the summer of 1900. Picketing took place at the Cardiff Station of the Great Western Railway and elsewhere, which was clearly illegal according to Lyons *v.* Wilkins, and the Taff Vale Railway Company applied for injunctions against two officials of the Amalgamated Society of Railway Servants, and also against the Society itself. Both injunctions were granted by Mr. Justice Farwell, the latter on September 5th, 1900; that against the two officials was not challenged, but that against the Society was taken to appeal, with the result that the Court of Appeal [consisting of the Master of the Rolls (Sir A. L. Smith) and Lords Justices Collins and Stirling], on November 21st, 1900, dissolved the injunction. The main argument influencing this decision was that a trade union is neither a corporation, a partnership, nor an individual; and is therefore not an entity known to the law, and could only be sued in virtue of an express statutory provision, which does not exist in the Trade Union Acts. The Railway Company appealed to the House of Lords, and on July 22nd, 1901, that body reversed the decision of the Court of Appeal and restored that of Mr. Justice Farwell. The Lords [the Lord Chancellor (Lord Halsbury), and Lords Macnaghten, Shand, Brampton, and Lindley] unanimously held that where the Legislature creates a body capable of owning property and acting by agents there must be an implied liability to be sued for wrongs committed by its agents for its benefit, and, of course, a corresponding right to sue for wrongs committed against it.

* * * * * *

Reference must be made to two cases previous to the Taff Vale case—viz., Charnock *v.* Court (judgment given April 12th, 1899) and Walters *v.* Green (judgment given August 8th, 1899), both of which were decided by Mr. Justice Stirling, and in both of which an interlocutory injunction was asked for and granted.

In the first case the plaintiffs originally sued on behalf of themselves and all other members of the union of master joiners at Halifax, and the action was brought against the president, the secretary, and a member of the executive committee of the Halifax branch of the Amalgamated Society of Carpenters and Joiners, the writ being afterwards amended by adding the whole of the members of the union, twenty-six in number, as plaintiffs. The injunction granted restrained the defendants from picketing the landing stage at Fleetwood or the railway station at Halifax and other places for purposes of persuasion and so forth.

In the second case the plaintiffs were master builders, carrying on business in Hull and neighbourhood, and members of the Hull Master Builders' Association. The defendants were officials of various labour unions at Hull and also of the Hull Building Trades Federation formed by these labour unions. The injunction restrained the officials in question from picketing the Hull railway station, employers' works, and residences of the employed, for the usual strike purposes.

These cases differ from the Taff Vale case only in the one particular —that the name of the labour union concerned was omitted from the action, some of the officials only being entered as defendants. There were, however, at least two precedents for the inclusion of the union by name. In 1892 Mr. Justice Kekewich granted an injunction and gave costs against a body known as the Federation of Trades and Labour Unions connected with shipping, carrying, and other industries, and also against its secretary. Again, in 1895 the same judge granted an injunction against the London Building Trades Federation at the instance of Messrs. Trollope and Sons, as well as against certain individual members of that body.

It must be borne in mind that the Taff Vale judgment has decided nothing as to the merits of the particular case in question. It has merely decided that a labour union in its own name can be made a party to a legal action. The case itself will now go for trial, and every question involved, except the right to sue, will be open. There are to be settled at least two questions of vital interest. The first is that raised in Lyons *v.* Wilkins, and there decided against the labour unions—viz., whether it is or is not illegal to watch and beset premises where men are, or to or from which they are proceeding, for the purpose of persuading them not to work or to cease working for a particular employer. The second point is whether the officials proceeded against had the authority of the union for what they did. Although indisputably they had authority to organise the strike, the rules of the union provide that strikes are to be carried on by lawful means, and the defence will doubtless cite the judgment of Mr. Justice Stirling in Walters *v.* Green, which lays down that, labour unions being legal bodies, *prima facie* their officers could not be presumed to have authority to do or sanction anything other than what labour unions might lawfully do. The fact, however, is that the conducting of strikes is one of the primary purposes (and a perfectly lawful purpose) of the union, and it may justly be argued that, when the union instructed its officials to carry out this lawful purpose, it took the risk of any unlawful acts which might be committed in aid of the strike.

There are other subsidiary questions which must arise; among them the question of how the union funds are to be attached, and whether the trustees of the union must also be named in the action. There is also the question what funds can be attached, and whether alleged provident and benefit funds can be involved.

SOME POINTS FOR EMPLOYERS.

Reference has been made to the cases of Charnock *v.* Court and Walters *v.* Green to show the clumsiness of the method of obtaining justice by proceeding against a multitude of officials of labour unions, and entering all the members of an association as parties to the action. By the Taff Vale decision procedure is much simplified. It is now said that the funds even of an unregistered labour union could be attached by means of what is called "a representative action"—that is to say, by suing the executive of the union as representing the members. Apparently also a registered labour union might be proceeded against by the same means, although this is not likely to be done in view of the much simpler method of suing the union in its registered name.

In this connection the case of Bailey *v.* Pye may be referred to. It will be remembered that the plaintiffs, a firm of glass merchants, obtained judgment in 1897 for £1,218 damages (including costs) by the acts of the defendants, officials and members of the National Plate Glass Bevellers' Trade Union, as well as a perpetual injunction. The total amount Messrs. Bailey recovered by executions levied against the principal defendants was £5. This case is one of the strongest conceivable from the point of view of injustice done without reparation, for, although the case for the union was defended out of the funds of the labour union at fault and of ninety-nine other labour unions giving financial support, no recovery of the damages awarded was possible.

An important point on which there is at present no legal decision is whether labour unions can be made liable for wrongful acts done by one of their officials, not merely without express authority, but contrary to the instructions of the executive.

Another point which has been raised in some quarters is whether the Taff Vale judgment may not facilitate the practice of collective bargaining. A large number of agreements between associations of masters and workmen already exist, but it has always been supposed that these are binding morally only, and are not enforceable at law. The question arises whether labour unions can make legally-enforceable contracts in reference to the terms of employment of their members. It is suggested that they cannot, because the judgment in this case is in tort and not in contract. This, however, is hardly to the point. The judgments are all based on the ground that there is an implied power of suing and being sued, and this, it would appear, is as applicable to contract as to tort. The further question arises whether the Trade Union Acts contain any express limitation on this implied power. As is well known, the fourth section of the Trade Union Act of 1871 prohibits legal proceedings for directly enforcing certain contracts, and it is safe to surmise that the object of the framers was to prevent the enforcement of any contract relating to labour to which a union was a party. It may be questioned, however, whether this intention has been actually carried into effect, as the only relevant words—viz., those of the fourth sub-section of the fourth section—are: "Any agreement made between one trade union and another." The effect of these words would clearly be to deprive of any legal validity an agreement, say, between the Engineering Employers' Federation and the Amalgamated Society of Engineers; but on the plain meaning of the words they certainly would not invalidate an agreement between the Amalgamated Society of Engineers and one of the engineering firms, or between the Amalgamated Society of Railway Servants and a railway company.

Finally, it must be remembered that employers' associations are in constitution and in the eyes of the law on the same footing as labour unions, and therefore subject to the same liabilities while enjoying the same privileges. There are, however, three important points of difference. Employers' associations are (1) usually in their origin combinations for defence against aggression, (2) mostly unregistered, (3) generally not owners of large accumulated funds. It is, therefore, hardly to be expected that their newly-discovered importance as a legal entity will alter in any material way their usual characteristics or ordinary methods of procedure. It is reported that, in the opinion on the Taff Vale judgment given to the Parliamentary Committee of the Trades Union Congress by Counsel, "a great advantage has been obtained under the judgment in giving power to labour unions to sue a vindictive employer who might try to break up or otherwise injure a labour union." But it is very unlikely that occasions of this nature will arise at all frequently. Scores of cases against labour union officials can be recalled, but it is difficult to find any serious case brought by labour unionists against employers or officials of their associations. At the same time, it would be well for employers and their associations to remember that there exists in the Linaker libel case (in which the Amalgamated Society of Railway Servants was held liable in damages for a libel published in a newspaper belonging to the Society) a precedent which could be used against associations owning official organs.

THE RESULTS IN BRIEF.

COERCION AND INTIMIDATION.

Allen *v.* Flood and Quinn *v.* Leathem, taken together, decide that with unlawful and malicious intent (*a*) to bring about a strike or lock-out, or (*b*) to induce customers to discontinue dealing with a tradesman, or (*c*) to threaten to do so, is illegal; and that those injured by such proceedings can recover damages against the persons responsible, and equally so whether there is a conspiracy or not. It is also illegal to circulate "black lists" of employers not to be worked for or dealt with, or of workmen not to be employed.

PICKETING.

Such watching or besetting as constitutes what is known as "peaceful picketing" is decided by Lyons *v.* Wilkins to be unlawful, unless it is done (in the words of the Act) "in order merely to obtain or communicate information."

LABOUR UNION LIABILITY.

Taff Vale Railway Company *v.* Amalgamated Society of Railway Servants decides that a labour union (although it is not a corporation) can sue and be sued in respect of wrongs committed by or against it.

It is to be noted that all the cases referred to (except Lyons *v.* Wilkins) are decisions of the House of Lords, and are therefore final and binding throughout the United Kingdom. The point raised in Lyons *v.* Wilkins will probably come before the House of Lords in the probable further proceedings to be taken by the Taff Vale Railway Company for the recovery of damages from the labour union against which the injunction has been obtained, and we shall then possess a body of decisions on labour law of the highest possible authority. And these decisions safeguard the interests of employers in almost every vital particular.

APPENDIX.

For the information of employers of labour it may be convenient to cite the following Sections of law, Imperial and local, dealing with picketing :—

THE CONSPIRACY AND PROTECTION OF PROPERTY ACT, 1875.

Under this Act, as tested by the above cases, picketing has been declared illegal. The Section under which such action usually falls is as follows :—

> "*Section 7.* Every person who, with a view to compel any other person to abstain from doing or to do any act which such other person has a legal right to do or abstain from doing, wrongfully and without legal authority,—
>
> 1. Uses violence to or intimidates such other person, or his wife and children, or injures his property ; or,
> 2. Persistently follows such other person about from place to place ; or,
> 3. Hides any tools, clothes, or any other property owned or used by such other person, or deprives him of, or hinders him in, the use thereof ; or,
> 4. Watches or besets the house or other place where such other person resides, or works, or carries on business, or happens to be, or the approach to such house or place ; or,
> 5. Follows such other person with two or more persons in a disorderly manner in or through any street or road,
>
> shall, on conviction thereof by a court of summary jurisdiction, or on indictment, as hereinafter mentioned, be liable either to pay a penalty not exceeding twenty pounds, or to be imprisoned for a term not exceeding three months, with or without hard labour.
>
> Attending at or near the house or place where a person resides, or works, or carries on business, or happens to be, or the approach to such house or place, in order merely to obtain or communicate information, shall not be deemed a watching or besetting within the meaning of this section."

LOCAL BYE-LAWS.

As an instance of the efficiency of local provisions in some districts, the following bye-law of the Stafford County Council may be cited. A clause such as this can certainly be utilised to suppress abuses of picketing :—

> "No person shall, alone or together with any other person or persons, after being requested by any person annoyed by his conduct, or by any constable instructed by such person, to move away, so act in any street or public place as wilfully to obstruct, insult, or annoy any foot-passenger."

BURGH POLICE (SCOTLAND) ACT, 1892.

As another example of legislation under which action can be taken we may quote the Scotch Police Act, which applies to all burghs in Scotland. The following clauses seem to cover any offences which are not sufficiently dealt with under clause 7 of the Conspiracy Act above referred to :—

> "*Section 381.* Every person who in any street (and for the purposes of this section 'street' shall include any harbour, railway station, canal, depôt, wharf, towing-path, public park, links, common, or open area or space, the strand and sea beach down to low-water mark, and all public places within the burgh) commits any of the following offences shall be liable to a penalty not exceeding forty shillings for each offence, viz. :—
>
> *Subsection (33).* Wilfully jostles or annoys any person.
>
> *Subsection (53).* Stands or loiters on the footway, or sits or lies to the obstruction or annoyance of the residents or passengers on the footway or street."

"Wilson showed to the [Trades Union] Congress and advised every delegate to read and mark a little book entitled 'The Case Against Picketing.'"—*Star.*

Fourth and Enlarged Edition. Price 1s. 6d., by post 1s. 9d.

THE CASE AGAINST PICKETING.

BY

W. J. SHAXBY.

Contents:—

"The manual will be of great service in informing employers of labour and non-unionists how far the law, as it stands, affords them protection."—*Yorkshire Post.*

"The book should be read alike by employer and employed; in fact, it should have a place in the library of all connected with the industrial work of the country."—*Glasgow Evening Times.*

"The pamphlet is admittedly written in defence of the Individualist as opposed to the Socialistic point of view, but it is written with every consideration for the 'rights of Labour.'"—*North British Advertiser.*

"Perhaps, however, the case could not have been stated more concisely or more clearly; and, while we differ from the author's conclusions, we commend his work to those who desire to see the strongest arguments that can be used on the other side."—*Reynolds' Newspaper.*

"It should be consulted by every person who has, or is likely to have, difficulties with his workpeople."—*Textile Mercury.*

"A careful digest of the law on the subject of picketing, and also a summary of all the conclusions which have been arrived at concerning it. The question is really in a nutshell."—*Colliery Guardian.*

"The book is one that should have a wide circulation."—*Engineering.*

Copies of above can be obtained from "The Liberty Review" Publishing Co., Limited, 17, Johnson's Court, Fleet Street, London, E.C., or from 7, Victoria Street, Westminster, S.W.

Form

LIBERTY & PROPERTY DEFENCE LEAGUE.

(To uphold the principle of Liberty, and guard the rights of Labour and Property of all kinds against undue interference by the State; and to encourage Self-help versus State-help.)

ANNUAL REPORT, 1894-95.

(THIRTEENTH FINANCIAL YEAR.)

PUBLISHED BY THE
LIBERTY AND PROPERTY DEFENCE LEAGUE,
7, VICTORIA STREET, LONDON, S.W.

Liberty and Property Defence League.

(To uphold the principle of Liberty, and guard the rights of Labour and Property of all kinds against undue interference by the State; and to encourage Self-help *versus* State-help.)

COUNCIL—1895-96.

THE RIGHT HON. THE EARL OF WEMYSS, *Chairman.*

Sir FREDERICK BRAMWELL, Bart., F.R.S.

Sir W. J. R. COTTON.

The Hon. BARON DIMSDALE.

Alderman Sir JOSEPH DIMSDALE.

The Right Hon. Sir MOUNTSTUART E. GRANT DUFF, G.C.S.I.

The Right Hon. EARL FORTESCUE.

ALFRED HEWLETT, Esq.

Sir WILLIAM LEWIS.

The Right Hon. LORD PENZANCE.

H. C. STEPHENS, Esq., M.P.

Sir EDWARD W. WATKIN, Bart.

And Representatives of the Chief Defence Societies of the various industries and interests federated with the League.

Hon. Treasurer: WALTER FARQUHAR, Esq.

Acting Secretary and Parliamentary Agent: FREDERICK MILLAR.

Liberty and Property Defence League.

ANNUAL REPORT, 1894–5.

COUNCIL:—The Right Hon. the Earl of Wemyss, *Chairman;* Sir Frederick Bramwell, Bart., F.R.S.; Sir W. J. R. Cotton; The Hon. Baron Dimsdale; Alderman Sir Joseph Dimsdale; The Right Hon. Sir Mountstuart E. Grant Duff, G.C.S.I.; The Right Hon. Earl Fortescue; A. Hewlett, Esq.; Sir William Lewis; The Right Hon. Lord Penzance; Henry C. Stephens, Esq., M.P.; Sir Ed. W. Watkin, Bart.; *Hon. Treasurer:* Walter Farquhar, Esq.; *Honorary Secretaries of the League; The Chairmen (or their Nominees) of the 187 Defence Societies, Companies, and Corporate Bodies in Federation with the League.*

Acting Secretary and Parliamentary Agent: FREDERICK MILLAR.

GENERAL PROGRESS.

THE twelfth Annual Meeting was held at the Westminster Palace Hotel on the 13th of December, 1894, when the Right Hon. Sir Mountstuart E. Grant Duff, G.C.S.I., late Governor of Madras, presided, and delivered an address. At the conclusion of the address the Earl of Wemyss, as Chairman of the Council, presented to the meeting the Report of the Council (including the Reports of the Parliamentary and Finance Committees) for the past year. The usual resolutions adopting the Report and proposing a vote of thanks to the Chairman were variously moved and seconded by Sir Roper Lethbridge, Mr. Geoffrey Drage, Mr. Martin Wood, Mr. George Livesey, Lieut.-General Traill Burroughs, Earl Fortescue, and Mr. C. Z. Burrows.

The past year has been the most eventful in the history of the League.

A few days prior to the last Annual Meeting, Mr. W. C. Crofts, Secretary of the League from its foundation in 1882, died suddenly at his residence at Portsea Place. In the autumn of 1873 Mr. Crofts and a few others, who saw most clearly the growing tendency towards Socialism, and who keenly dreaded its further development, formed themselves into a Society for the purpose of drawing public attention to the dangerous principle underlying measures of a repressive or paternal character, and to the necessity for common action against the common enemy that threatened the very existence of personal freedom and private property. Nine years later Mr. Crofts, accompanied by Mr. Donisthorpe, called on Lord Elcho, now Lord Wemyss, who had at that time written a letter to the *Pall Mall Gazette* urging the necessity of forming an Association for the maintenance of individual freedom, and for the security of property, and to resist State Socialism. The result of this meeting was a resolve to establish such an Association or League, and on July 5th, 1882, a large and influentially-attended meeting of members of both Houses of Parliament, representatives of professional, mercantile, industrial, and other bodies who had signified their concurrence with the objects of the movement, was held at the Westminster Palace Hotel, under the Presidency of Lord Elcho, M.P. (now the Earl of Wemyss). At this meeting it was resolved that the name of the Association should be "The Liberty and Property Defence League," and Mr. Crofts was appointed Secretary.

As the Chairman of the League stated in his speech at the last Annual Meeting: "No office was ever in a better administrative state than was the office of this League under Mr. Crofts. My ideal of an office," continued his lordship, "is one where the chairman has nothing to do. In such an office everything is in perfect working order, and absolute confidence is reposed in the discretion, judgment, and ability of those employed, such questions only being reserved for the consideration of the Chairman as require his special notice, and as they deem it necessary to bring before him. Thus has the work of the office of this League been well and satisfactorily done during the past twelve years. I venture to say that no greater blow could have happened to this Society than that which we all lament in the death of our friend, Mr. Crofts. In him we lose as a League a most excellent Secretary, and I, speaking personally, lose a most valuable and trusted friend. His loss is, indeed, irreparable." At a meeting of the Council held on December 12th, 1894, the following resolution relating to the death of Mr. Crofts was, on the motion of the Chairman, adopted: "That the Council record on their minutes their deep sense of the irreparable loss they, the League, and the cause they endeavour to uphold, have sustained through the death of Mr. William Carr Crofts; that they mourn in him a secretary who zealously gave to the service of the League his remarkable ability, energy, and industry, and who, in the discharge of his duties, ever showed the most reliable discretion and the soundest judgment; and they further mourn in him the loss of a personal and much trusted friend."

THE LATE MR. W. C. CROFTS.

In December, 1894, Mr. Geoffrey Drage (late Secretary of the Labour Commission, and now M.P. for Derby) applied for and received the appointment of Secretary, in succession to Mr. Crofts; but after a few months he resigned the Secretaryship. Since that time Mr. Frederick Millar, who was Mr. Croft's assistant, has, as Acting Secretary, most zealously, ably, and efficiently carried on the Secretarial and Parliamentary work of the League. Death has also robbed the League of two of its most distinguished and valued members, the Earl of Pembroke and Mr. H. D. Pochin, both of whom had been connected with the Council, and the Executive and Parliamentary Committee, of the League since its foundation. Several noteworthy additions have been made to the Council by the election of the Right Hon. Sir Mountstuart Grant Duff, G.C.S.I., Sir William Lewis, A. Hewlett, Esq., and Alderman Sir Joseph Dimsdale. The latter gentleman and Mr. W. J. Carruthers Wain (President of the Tramways Institute) have been elected members of the Parliamentary and Executive Committee.

As was anticipated in the last Annual Report, the relegation of the Irish question to the middle distance of the political field has resulted in an enormous increase in the work of the League, both in amount and importance, beyond that of any previous years. So-called social reformers of all sorts have at last succeeded in getting into the foreground for the exhibition and furtherance of their various schemes of philanthropy and regeneration by Act of Parliament. While one of the two great political parties is, from its composition and connections, more ready than the other to fall back upon State action as the best means for furthering the progress of society and for remedying social evils, the other has, to a certain extent during recent years, been pursuing a policy of bidding against the pseudo-Liberals by promises of State-help in the supposed interests of the people. The spirit of emulation thus engendered results in the hands of successive Governments being forced by the Opposition to introduce measures into Parliament of a more or less Socialistic and objectionable character; and, under the euphemism of "social reform," both political parties have more or less committed themselves to a legislative policy, the aim of which is to make political capital out of the credulity of the working classes. It cannot be denied that under the present extended suffrage the temptation to take advantage of popular ignorance is one to which the statesman and the politician is very prone to yield, and there are few men in political life whose self-control is strong enough to save them from taking the State Socialistic short cut to supposed popularity and power.

The disinterested work of the League in exposing the mischievous and dishonest character of these vote-catching proclivities of political parties has naturally made the League the object of much abuse and misrepresentation. By the Radical-Socialists, the "Progressists," and the "New Unionist" Labour party, the League has from the first been singled out as their natural enemy, and during the past year the testimony of the Radical-Socialist press to the good work of the League in opposing objectionable legislation has been somewhat voluminous. One noteworthy example of such testimony is that of the *North British Daily Mail*, which, on February 25th, 1895, published a leading article under the heading, "How Good Bills are Blocked." After referring to the weekly list of Bills opposed by the League and its federated Societies, and to the printed instructions given by the League for securing opposition to those Bills, this Radical-Socialist organ exclaimed: "This is how the wheels of the blocking machinery are set in motion. The obstruction of desirable legislation is made a matter of deliberate and elaborate organisation......Every measure in the League's list is a measure of social reform, and every one of them is to be blocked in the first place, and then opposed and voted against when a debate or division on the second reading can no longer be prevented."

It may here be noted that in the Radical-Socialist press the League is invariably referred to as a Tory organisation, while, as a matter of fact, the League is in no way a political organisation in the party sense of the word, and its work in opposing Socialistic legislation has all along been conducted irrespective of party politics. The principles which the League was established to maintain are the principles of true Liberalism—the principles of the Liberal party before 1870; the objects of the League being "To uphold the principle of Liberty, and guard the rights of Labour and Property of all kinds against undue interference by the State, and to encourage Self-help *versus* State-help." These are objects with which every true Liberal must be in hearty accord. It is because the whole of one party and a section of the other pretend that the Liberal principles of freedom of contract and self-help must be laid by, while a good innings is given to State aid and the expediency of the hour, that the action of the League in resisting legislation opposed to true Liberalism is characterised by the Radical-Socialists and Tory Democrats as reactionary and deserving of public condemnation.

The result of the General Election which took place in July was a distinct triumph of League principles over the doctrines of State Socialism and public plunder. The verdict of the country against State Socialism and predatory and restrictive legislation was decisive. This, indeed, is admitted by the Radical-Socialist press. Commenting on the result of the election, the *Daily Chronicle*, the leading organ in the Metropolis of the Radical-Socialist and "Progressive" parties, said: "What the electorate desire is pure negation, mere preservation of the *status quo*, absolute unqualified Conservatism. They take no more account, they have no more belief in, the social policy of Mr. Chamberlain than they are grateful for the Factory Act of Mr. Asquith, or the Budget of Sir William Harcourt."

Immediately after the election another London Radical and "Progressive" paper, the *Star*, opened its columns to correspondence on the question, "Why We Lost." In this correspondence no attempt was made to disguise the fact that the rout of the pseudo-Liberals was due to the late Government having saddled itself with every fad in the kingdom, and with "pandering to the hopes of every little Bethel." Strong language regarding the Local Veto Bill was generally indulged in; defeated candidates and indignant voters alike declared that to the measure which would "rob the poor man of his beer" the loss of seats everywhere was due. Against the Labour policy of the pseudo-Liberals several correspondents strongly protested. "Each of us workers," said one of them, "wants to do his own work in his own way, in as many or as few hours per day as he pleases, for as much or as little as he can get." That is, the working classes want freedom to labour—no interference with their natural right to work up to their full capacity. It was because the Liberal party—the true Liberal party—stood up for freedom of labour that the working classes hitherto largely supported Liberal candidates at the poll; but the party which has usurped the name of Liberal has for years past been playing into the hands of the "New Unionism," and working men who value their liberty refuse to countenance the so-called Liberal programme, and now use their political power to make that programme impossible of realisation. Another correspondent wrote: "Those large principles of freedom from which the Liberal party takes its name are still believed in by the mass of the people, and it is because of the falling away, for years past, from these principles in matters which intimately concern the life of all classes that the party has been weakening, and has at length utterly collapsed." There is no mistaking such utterances as these, and they deserve to be well considered by both political parties.

Immediately after the dissolution, the Parliamentary and Executive Committee of the League held a special meeting for the purpose of considering what steps should be taken to bring the views of the League and its federated Societies before the electors. A draft of a Manifesto to the Electors (of which the following is a copy) was submitted to the Committee, and adopted. Copies of this Manifesto were, by special arrangements with bill-posting firms, posted on the hoardings in the principal constituencies in the United Kingdom; and, in the form of a handbill, the Manifesto was distributed at the meetings of both Unionist and Radical candidates:—

GENERAL ELECTION.—1895.

TO THE ELECTORS.

DO NOT VOTE for a Candidate who would pauperise the whole nation by a system of Old Age Pensions condemned by, and fatal to, existing Friendly Societies.

> Insist on Candidates explaining the difference, as regards being pauperised, between a man of sixty-five getting half-a-crown out of the Imperial Exchequer, under the proposed Old Age Pension scheme, and a man of sixty-four receiving, under the existing Poor Law, half-a-crown in out-door relief from the rates.

DO NOT VOTE for a Candidate who would forcibly limit a full-grown man's natural right to work up to his full strength for the good of himself and his family, alike below and above ground.

DO NOT VOTE for a Candidate who dares to tell the working classes that wages can be regulated and apportioned by Parliament. Can Parliament regulate the ebb and flow of the tide, in nature or in trade? A so-called "living wage" to some often means "no wage" to others.

DO NOT VOTE for a Candidate who would not give the fullest protection to non-Unionists, who, for the sake of their families, are willing to work for wages below the so-called Trade Union rate. Free Labour, remember, as compared to Trade-Union Labour, is as 9 to 1.

Do Not Vote for a Candidate who would prevent laundry and other women from working, as at present, for their own and their families' support, possibly for that of a sick or disabled husband.

Do Not Vote for a Candidate who would allow the rich man to drink his fill at a club, but would "rob a poor man of his beer."

Do Not Vote for a Candidate who, by encouraging General State and Municipal trading, would stop individual enterprise, invention, and national progress, waste national income, raise rates, and promote jobbery and corruption.

Do Not Vote for a Candidate who would take property of any kind from individuals or corporate bodies without full compensation, or confiscate the property of the few wherewith to buy the votes of the many.

Do Not Vote for a Candidate who would break or forbid Contracts. Free Contract is the soul of Commerce and the life of Labour.

SHORT ELECTORAL CATECHISM.

If the Candidate is a *so-called* Liberal, ask him if the term "Liberal" is derived from "Liberty."

If he answers Yes, ask him where "Liberty" is to be found in *so-called* Liberalism, except in the liberty it takes with property, contracts, and individual freedom, putting free-born Englishmen and women in State or Municipal swaddling-clothes, "*shadowed*" by male or female inspectors.

Ask him if the *so-called* Liberalism now is not the reverse of the Old Liberalism, which freed men from State restrictions, and left the individual free to work out his destiny as seemed to him best.

Ask him if the *so-called* "Progress" of the New Liberalism is not really the progress of the crab—Backward ! !

If a Liberal Unionist, ask him in what *his* Liberalism differs from the foregoing New Liberalism.

Ask both *so-called* "Liberals" and "Liberal Unionists" to explain the difference between the "New Liberalism" and Socialism ; also between Socialism and "New Unionism."

Ask them, further, if they intend to support or truckle to "New Unionism," which would seize all private property (without paying for it), allow no private trading, and get all the "instruments of production" into the hands of a labour-governed State, which is to be sole manufacturer, trader, and employer.

If a Conservative, ask the Candidate if he intends to *flirt* with Socialism—as unfortunately many of his party do—or fight it to the death, and stand by the Liberty our fathers won for us.

Vote only for those Candidates who are in favour of Free Labour, Free Contract, Liberty, Justice, and the Rights of Property of all kinds, including Men and Women's Property in their own Industry.

Printed for and Published by the Parliamentary Committee of the Liberty and Property Defence League, representing 184 Defence Societies and corporate bodies connected with the chief industries and interests in the Kingdom. Central Offices: 7, Victoria Street, Westminster.

July, 1895.

The League lecturers and agents were actively engaged during the election addressing meetings in opposition to the Radical-Socialist and New Unionist candidates. By these means, and by the efforts put forth by the Societies federated with the League, everything possible was done to bring home to the minds of the electors the gravity of the political situation.

The first session of the new Parliament opened on August 12th, 1895. On September 4th the Chairman of the League, at the request of the Parliamentary and Executive Committee, representing the various industries and interests of the United Kingdom, called attention in the House of Lords to the political situation, and to the late General Election, in so far as they bore upon Socialistic legislation. After referring to the Socialistic character of the now falsely so-called Liberalism, the Chairman passed on to the Conservatives and Liberal Unionists, and pointed out that the Socialist spectre dwelt also in their tents, and that they too had been taking sweet counsel with it. This serious aspect of the political situation was illustrated by quotations from the election addresses of several Conservative and Liberal Unionist candidates, and he declared that, if once the State embarked on legislation of the character advocated by these politicians, it would be impossible to prevent the nation being carried irresistibly down the Socialistic slide into the all-absorbing abyss of Socialism. Lord Wemyss concluded his speech in the following words: "So far as I have been able to ascertain, the real cause of the defeat of the late Government was the revolt of a free people against State and municipal interference with their individual freedom, property, and rights; for none are more opposed to such interference than the traders and the best and most intelligent of the so-called working classes of the United Kingdom. Such, as regards the recent election, are the views of those competent to form a sound judgment on such matters; and I know that Lord Salisbury has received similar information from the Conservative election agency. What, then, my lords, is the moral to be drawn from all this? What should be the course taken by my noble friend at the head of the Government, backed as he is by so large a majority? Why, to put his foot down, and forbid all immoral flirtation with Socialism by his party; to take his stand on individual liberty, free contract, and the freedom alike of labour and capital, knowing how history has shown that in freedom our national prosperity was born, reared, and flourished; that in freedom and abstinence from State and municipal interference it can alone continue to flourish and progress; that freedom of labour is the poor man's birthright and property; and, finally, that, if falsely so-called Liberals have cast the old flag of Liberty into the gutter of party politics, it will not only be the true policy, but the social duty, of the

Conservative and Liberal Unionist Government to take and raise it aloft, in the full faith that in so doing they will draw to themselves the support of a race on every page of whose history true, genuine, innate love of liberty is written—liberty that gives the real charm to life—liberty without which life itself would not be worth the living."

Since the speech referred to was delivered signs have not been wanting that the Government have taken to heart the true lesson of the election; and there is good reason to believe that under the new administration the country will enjoy an immunity from the schemes of State Socialism, the promises of which figured so prominently in the addresses and speeches of one or two leading members of the Unionist party during the election. The mischievous character of those schemes was fully demonstrated by the Chairman in his speech, copies of which may be had at the offices of the League.

Not the least satisfactory feature of the late election was the crushing defeat sustained by the representatives of the "New Unionist" and "Independent Labour" Parties. With the exception of Mr. John Burns, whose majority at Battersea was reduced from 1,559 to 253, and Mr. J. H. Wilson at Middlesborough, the candidature of none of the aggressive "New Labour" men was successful. The total poll of the thirty-three representatives of the Socialist Labour Party amounted to 48,371, or on average per constituency of 1,476. This is less than 1 per cent. of the entire electorate. The mischief-making and strike-promoting tactics which these self-styled labour leaders have pursued for several years past have at last been properly appreciated by the more thoughtful section of the working classes. Realising the senselessness and wickedness of the policy of stirring up strife between employers and employed, the working classes have withdrawn their support from the men who have been misleading them all along, and at the present moment the profession of "labour leader" in this country is not in a flourishing condition.

From the details of the work of the Parliamentary Committee of the League, which are given in the Parliamentary Report (see pp. 22–37), it will be seen that in the last session of the last Parliament the number of measures against personal liberty, freedom of contract, and proprietary rights was exceptionally large. The steps taken by the Parliamentary Committee to oppose these measures were very successful, and the thanks of the League are due to those members of Parliament who, throughout the session, co-operated with the Parliamentary Committee in preventing these measures becoming law. On February 15th, 1895, the Chairman of the League Parliamentary Committee presented to the House of Lords the Licensing Act Amendment Bill, drafted by the late Lord Bramwell, to secure uniformity in the granting by way of renewal or transfer of licences for the sale of intoxicating liquors. The Bill was read a first time. On May 11th, 1895, a petition in favour of this Bill, signed by the chairmen and secretaries of all the associations connected with the Liquor industry in the United Kingdom, was presented to the House of Lords by the Chairman of the Parliamentary Committee, and ordered by the House to be printed. As there appeared to be no possibility of the Bill getting through its various stages in the late Parliament, it was not proceeded with.

The net result of the changes which have been made in the Office staff have been chiefly to impart new life into all the League's undertakings. No new departures in policy have been made; and while the work, both general and Parliamentary, is still conducted on the principles laid down at the inaugural meeting on July 5th, 1882, it is increasing year by year in amount and importance. At a meeting of the Parliamentary and Executive Committee, held on August 14th, 1895, a proposal was adopted to establish a Press Correspondence Department at the offices of the League for the purpose of sending to the press original letters on subjects of interest to the League and its Federated Societies, and replies to all letters, etc., advocating Socialism or in support of principles contravening the objects of the League. This new department has up to the present worked very satisfactorily, and nearly 300 letters signed by an official of the League have appeared in the London and provincial press during the few months the department has been in existence. The original letters dealt with such topics as "The Benefits of Competition," "The Source of Wealth," "Municipal Ownership: Its Fallacy," "Local Indebtedness," "Old Age Pensions," "Socialism and Morality," "A French View of Collectivism," "The Liquor War in New York," "The Voluntary Schools Question," "The Growth of Officialism," "How Industry is Fettered," "Unearned Increment," "The Land Tax," and "The Land Nationalisation Fallacy." It is indubitable that work of this character, supplemented as it is by the work of the Lecture Department of the League, is productive of good results in opening the eyes of the public to the dangers of Socialism, and to the evils of undue State interference with the rights of freedom and property.

FINANCE.

Finance Committee:—Walter Farquhar, Esq., Chairman; the Earl of Wemyss; Sir Myles Fenton; Henry C. Stephens, Esq., M.P.; George Palmer, Esq.

The audited Balance Sheet for the year ended 31st October last, submitted by the Finance Committee, gives so far a very gratifying result, the total of the subscriptions and donations received during this thirteenth financial year being considerably more than half as much again as the amount for the preceding year, and by several hundreds of pounds the largest yet subscribed in any year to the League's funds.

Such an increase in receipts has in itself naturally brought about a corresponding increase in the League's work. The work has further been greatly increased this year by the unprecedentedly heavy Parliamentary Session, involving very considerable expense on the part of the League in printing and postage, by the General Election, and by the introduction of Lord Wemyss' Licensing Act Amendment Bill into the House of Lords. All this has caused the League during the past year to "live" fully up to its income; and although every possible economy has been practised, the actual expenditure has exceeded the total receipts by nearly £300.

Speaking generally, the increase in income shows the growing appreciation of the League's efforts and the real need for an extension of its work. It is to be hoped that the rate of increase of this past year will be maintained; and that the League may continue to grow in strength and usefulness. All members who have given such generous financial support during the past are earnestly invited to continue their assistance by renewing their contributions during the coming year, and by inducing many others to become members; and, above all, by themselves becoming regular annual subscribers.

Arrangements for the coming work of the League, more especially in Parliament, are greatly facilitated by knowing beforehand, approximately, the amount of income available for the current year. Nothing contributes more to this end than the system adopted by some of the individual members of the League of giving the League an order on their respective bankers for a subscription payable until further notice on the 1st of January of each successive year. Twelve per cent. of the League's subscriptions are received in this way; but it is felt that, if members realised to a greater degree the convenience to themselves of this plan, and the extent to which the League's work is facilitated thereby, the percentage of subscriptions thus paid would be very much larger. Standing Bankers' Orders for such payments, with instructions as to the mode of using them, can be had at the League offices.

The Balance Sheet, audited by the League auditors, and the subscription book, are open to the inspection of members at all times at the offices at Westminster.

INDIVIDUAL MEMBERS.

The number of individual members continues to increase. Of the total number of individual contributors to the League funds in 1894 nearly one-third are members who have joined during the last year.

Seven separate summaries of the League's Parliamentary work, from its inception up to this year, have been printed and extensively circulated. A new prospectus containing lists of the Council, Branches, Honorary Secretaries' statement of the League's objects, a summary of the advantages of membership and of federation with the League, and a classified list of the publications and literature on sale, has also been very widely distributed. Applications have been made to all contributors in arrear; and appeals have been addressed to those classes of the community that derive the greatest benefit from the League's work, such as bankers, shipping merchants, proprietors of iron works and coal mines, estate agents, brewers, etc. The response to these appeals has been most inadequate. The increase in the number of contributors to the League's funds has mainly been achieved by personal influence after repeated application.

Among those who have joined and contributed to the funds of the League during the past year are :—Miss Corbett, Mr. Daniel Crawford, Mr. Maurice Deacon, Mr. J. H. Dewar, Right Hon. Sir Mountstuart E. Grant Duff, Mr. Melville Fraser, Mr. H. Carr Gibbs, Mr. Henry C. Godwin, Mr. William Hall, Mr. Alfred Hewlett, Mr. Allan J. Hook, Mr. W. J. Leishman, Mr. George Livesey, Mr. P. MacSorley, His Highness the Maharaja Bahadur of Hutwa, Mr. John McNee, Mr. Robert McKinlay, Mr. Alderman J. Dundas Pillans, Mr. Robert Robin, Mr. J. H. Roger, Mr. W. T. Rothwell, J.P., Mr. C. F. Ryder, Mr. Charles Ryder, Mr. John Scouler, Mr. Prideaux Selby, Mr F. E. Shaw-Rooney, Mr. George Sherriff, Mr. James G. Speed, Mr. W. B. Thomson, Mr. D. Wans, Mr. Robert Younger, and the following firms :—Messrs. Anderson & Shaw, Ballinghall & Son, Bennett & Co., Bertram & Co., Thomas Breeds & Co., Brickwood & Co., Alex. Bryce & Co., Buchanan, Scott, & Co., Bullock, Lade, & Co., Carlisle Old Brewery Co., Ltd., Donald & Fisher, Andrew Foulds & Co., William Foulds & Co., John Fuller & Co., W. & A. Gilbey, Golder & Hunter, Robert Graham & Sons, James Gray, Sons, & Co., William Greaves & Co., Harding & Parrington, James Harvey & Co., J. Jeffrey & Co., W. P. Lowrie & Co., John Lowson & Son, G. & J. MacLachlan, William McEwen & Co., Marshall McEwan & Co., Muir & Martin, James Murray & Co, Murdoch & Co., Richmond Cavendish Co., Robertson & Baxter, D. & J. Robertson, Sacell Brewery Co., H. & G. Simonds, Smith & Ritchie, James Stewart & Co., Ltd., Steel, Coulson, & Co., Taylor & Ferguson, Ltd., Teacher & Son, J. & R. Tennent, Andrew Usher & Co., John Walker & Sons, Wigham Richardson & Co., Wilsons & Glenny, William Whitelaw & Son, George Younger & Son.

From this list it will be seen that a great number of firms have recently joined the League; this forms the special feature of the year's additional membership.

During the same period the League has had to record, with regret, the loss by death of the Hon. C. W. Fitzwilliam, Mr. J. Dunn, Mr. C. Barnett, Mr. W. H. Hardy, and, as already noted, the Earl of Pembroke and Mr. H. D. Pochin.

Both the Earl of Pembroke and Mr. Pochin had not only been most generous supporters of the League from the very first, but they had also taken an extremely active part in the League's work by joining the League Council and the Parliamentary Committee. It will be remembered that on June 24th, 1885, Lord Pembroke delivered the League's Presidential Address on "Self-Help and State-Help" at the Third Annual Meeting, and about the same time contributed to the League's published literature a valuable essay on "Liberty and Socialism," which had appeared in the *National Review*.

CORPORATE MEMBERS.

The number of Societies federated with the League is now 188, an increase of 28 new corporate members since October 31st, 1894. The 188 Associations, Societies, and corporate bodies now federated with the League represent every important interest and industry in the United Kingdom.

Throughout the year the League is in constant communication with these bodies, and during the Session of Parliament the League's work almost entirely consists in arranging, in conjunction with their committees and officials, opposition to the yearly increasing number of Bills brought before Parliament threatening their interests and the common rights of liberty and property. The federation of Societies and Companies for this purpose was the central idea in the constitution of the League; and particulars of the League's work in this connection are given in the appended Report of the Parliamentary Committee.

BRANCHES AND CORRESPONDENTS.

Since the last Report was issued, new Branches have been established in North-West London; in Bradford, Jarrow-upon-Tyne, Liverpool, and Nottingham; in Switzerland, and in New Zealand (Auckland). The appointments of Hon. Secretaries for the first time in new Branches are pending in several other places.

The Secretary of the League is in constant communication with the Corresponding Secretaries in various parts of the world, and much valuable information concerning the "Labour" and Socialist movements in foreign countries and the Colonies is by this means secured to the League for the use of members and lecturers.

Hon. Secretaries are provided with printed instructions indicating the methods to be employed for the development of their Branches and the extension of the League's influence in their districts. All the Branches are provided with a constant supply of pamphlets and leaflets for distribution in their districts, describing the principles and work of the League, and the advantages of federation and membership with it. Opportunity is taken by the League members and officials during the progress of Parliamentary, Municipal, or School Board elections in any constituency to publish letters in the local papers, explaining the principles of the League, and urging the voters to use them as guides in deciding upon the questions submitted to them.

PUBLIC MEETINGS AND LECTURES.

During the early part of the year it was decided that Mr. Geoffrey Drage should, on behalf of the League, deliver lectures in various parts of the country in opposition to Socialism. In January, February, and March, 1895, lectures were delivered at Alfreton, Bishop Auckland, Cambridge, Cardiff, Campden, Colchester, Crewe, Dewsbury, Halifax, Huddersfield, Hull, Ipswich, Leeds, Newcastle, Newport, Northampton, Norwich, Ossett, Pontypridd, Sunderland, and Yeadon.

The ordinary work in connection with the League Lecture Department has been carried on uninterruptedly throughout the year, and League lecturers have delivered addresses, undertaken debates, and given lectures at Battersea Town Hall, Battersea Park, Brixton and Kentish Town (Milton Hall) Branches of the Social Democratic Federation, Brondesbury Hall, Economic Club, Hammersmith Bridge, Hyde Park, Leyton Constitutional Club, Progressive Club (Isle of Dogs), Reformers' Club (Kennington), Regent's Park, St. Pancras Reform Club, Walworth, and other lecture centres. A portable platform for the League speakers is now in use during the summer months at open-air meetings in the London parks on Sundays and other days. Among the subjects discussed by the League representatives at these meetings were: "Land Nationalisation," "Fallacies of Socialism," "Is Socialism a Dream?" "Local Veto Bill," "Is Socialism Possible?" "Is the Present Commercial System Conducive to the Welfare of the Community?" "A Defence of the Competitive System," "Socialism and Poverty," "Socialism Opposed to Progress." At many of these meetings, both under cover and in the open air, leaflets and publications embodying the views of the League on current political topics were distributed, and resolutions in support of the League's principles were carried, in some cases by large majorities. The League has also been represented at meetings of Property Owners' Associations, at the Conferences on Women's Labour, at the Newcastle National Free

Labour Congress, and at meetings held by the Federated Societies in London and the provinces.

ANNUAL DINNER.

The Sixth Annual—or, as it should now be termed, Biennial—Dinner of the League was fixed to take place on July 17th, 1895, in the Great Hall of the Freemasons' Tavern. The dissolution of Parliament, followed by the General Election, rendered a postponement absolutely necessary. It is proposed to hold the Dinner as early as possible during the next session of Parliament, when it is hoped that very many members and supporters of the League in both Houses of Parliament will be present.

PUBLICATIONS.

During the past year the work connected with the Publishing Department has been much heavier than hitherto. The total receipts for publications sold are just double those of last year. The total number of publications printed and issued under the superintendence of this Department was about 240,000. Additions are continually being made to the stock of League publications, and revised lists of these are printed from time to time, and sent to members. These lists are also widely circulated for the purpose of drawing public attention to the valuable store of anti-Socialist writings produced or collected by the League, and to be procured by application to the Publishing Department. A list of the more recent Publications is given in the advertisements at the end of this Report.

"Liberty Leaves," written by members of the League, on the following subjects, are published by the League, and many thousands of them have been supplied during the year in various quarters in London and the country for public meetings and electioneering purposes: "Security of Existing Contracts"; "Are Trade Unions a Help or a Hindrance? An Address to the Workers of England"; "Self-Help *versus* State-Help: an Address to Working Men"; "Market Bargaining *versus* Trades Unionism"; "Compulsory Allotments"; "State Lessons in Coercion"; "State Education"; "Technical Education"; "Intermediate Education"; "Elementary Education"; "School Board Education"; "Employers' Liability"; "Taxation of Ground Rents"; "Land and Capital"; "Private Work and Public Waste"; "Anti-Theft: a Plea for the Security and Freedom of Contract"; "The Sweating System"; "Local Option"; "Liquor Traffic (Local Control) Bill"; "The Evils of Strikes"; "Free Libraries" (new edition); "Free Association"; Lord Halsbury on "Security of Contract, Freedom of Labour, and the Right of Private Judgment," etc., etc.

A specimen of these leaflets is sent to anyone gratis, on application; and quantities are supplied, where ordered, at a low rate.

The *Liberty Review*, a weekly journal of politics, economics, sociology, and Individualism, edited by the Acting Secretary of the League, and published at 17, Johnson's Court, Fleet Street, London, E.C., continues to widely increase its circulation, and is now becoming recognised as the only organ devoting its columns exclusively to an exposure of Socialist fallacies. The paper has no connection with the League, financially or editorially; but several members of the League, in addition to its editor, are on the staff of writers; and the political principles of the paper, advocated by forcible and able writers, are in accord with those held by the League. In its columns all legislative proposals affecting commercial and industrial welfare are subjected to exhaustive examination; and every attempt to harass or to confiscate the property of any body of traders, or of any corporate Association, is steadfastly resisted. The evil effects of past undue State interference with the conduct and management of railways, mines, the shipping trade, the liquor trade, and other national industries, and with the ownership and disposition of landed and other property, are exposed, with a view to demonstrating the pernicious character of the legislation which certain factions and parties are organised to promote. The various large interests of London and the country, federated through their representative organisations with the League, would do well to make it the medium of expressing to a more extended audience their views upon political questions particularly affecting themselves, now too often confined to their respective trade journals. A limited liability company was formed in December for the purpose of developing and further increasing the circulation of the *Liberty Review*. On and after February 1st, 1896, the paper will be published at one penny, and several new and attractive features will be added to its pages. Applications for shares in the *Liberty Review* Publishing Company should be addressed to the Secretary of the Company, 7, Victoria Street, S.W.

The following is a list of the more important publications issued by the League during the year:—

1. In connection with the general work of the League (113,000).

Leaflets (93,000).
- "Facts for the Socialists."
- A Liberal M.P. on "Socialism"—"Liberty Leaf," No. 46.
- "Trade and Socialism"—"Liberty Leaf," No. 47.
- "Radical Testimony to the League's Good Work in Opposing Objectionable Legislation"—"Liberty Leaf," No. 48.

"Municipal Spoliation, or the Ratepayer Doubly Robbed."

General Election Manifesto.

Pamphlets (20,000). "Old-Age Pensions." By Geoffrey Drage.

Address by Sir Mountstuart E. Grant Duff at Twelfth Annual Meeting, 1894.

"Pretensions of Socialism." By Yves Guyot.

"The Control of Labour." By Yves Guyot.

"Nationalisation of Land." By Lord Bramwell. Seventh edition.

"The Socialist Spectre." Speech by the Earl of Wemyss and March in the House of Lords, September, 1895.

All of the above pamphlets are sold at the nominal price of one penny each. The Leaflets, Annual Reports, and Parliamentary Papers are distributed gratuitously.

2. In connection with the Parliamentary Department (43,000).

Summaries of Parliamentary Work.

Alcohol.

Trades and Manufactures.

Land, Houses, and Agriculture.

Shopkeepers and Warehousemen.

Shipping.

Coal and Iron.

Railways.

Lord Wemyss' Licensing Bill Amendment.

Weekly Tables of Bills (Nos. 1–17).

3. In connection with Office Work (64,000).

Of these papers it would be wearisome to give details. It is sufficient to say that they consisted of credit notes, rules, advantages of membership and of federation circulars, whips, posters, election and annual dinner circulars, programmes of proposed work, a revised prospectus, list of publications, etc.

Other pamphlets or literature accepted or purchased for sale and distribution during the year number about 20,000. The following is a list of some of them :—

"Trades Unionism." By James Birks.

"Local Migration of Crofters." By George Malcolm.

"Liberty Review Yearly, 1895."

"Modern Labour." By J. Stafford Ransome.
"Socialism and Marriage."
"Labour and the Popular Welfare." By W. H. Mallock.
"Labour as an Agent in the Production and Distribution of Wealth." By W. H. Mallock.
"Memorandum on the Administration of the Poor Law." By the Earl of Wemyss.
"Insoluble Problems." By E. Stanley Robertson.
"A Few Facts about Mutual Insurance Societies."
"A Plea for Liberty." Edited by Thomas Mackay.
"God's England or the Devil's." By Rev. G. Brooks.
"The Tied House Question."
"Lord Wemyss' Licensing Bill: A Rejoinder to the U.K.A."
Liberty Review. (Weekly issues.)

The publications of the League are sold by booksellers in London, Manchester, Nottingham, Edinburgh, Dublin, Glasgow, Leeds, Birmingham, Liverpool, Sheffield, Leicester, Oxford, Cambridge, Doncaster, Derby, etc., and in nearly all the great provincial centres. All the hon. secretaries are supplied with parcels for gratuitous distribution in their districts in connection with the work and development of their respective branches; and this free distribution is extended to local parliaments, debating societies, working men's clubs, mechanics' institutes, etc., etc.

In addition to the publications printed by the League, a supply on sale or return is kept at the Central Offices of publications written by members and supporters of the League, but not printed by it, dealing with political, economic, and social questions in accordance with the principles of the League.

REFERENCE DEPARTMENT.

Extracts from the press continue to be regularly made in the offices of the League of facts showing the evil effects of past State interference, and the indications of fresh measures of the same character, which are classified and indexed in separate volumes under the following heads:—(i.) ships; (ii.) railways, canals, and vehicles; (iii.) mines; (iv.) manufactures and trades (including companies, etc.); (v.) land and houses; (vi.) labour, including Trade Unionism, Socialism, pauperism, co-operation, eight hours day, arbitration, employers' liability, alien immigration, unemployed, wages, etc.; (vii.) liquor; (viii.) amusements; (ix.) education; (x.) professions; (xi.) local government; (xii.) State failures. Under each head are also arranged the Acts of Parliament, blue books, and noteworthy pamphlets connected with the respective subjects. The attention of members of the League is especially directed to this department, to which a large mass of material has been added during the past year. The collection and classification of these press cuttings and other materials having been regularly maintained from the foundation of the League thirteen years ago, the League is now in possession of information on all heads of over-legislation, and especially as to the growth of Socialism in England and abroad; information such as, there is no doubt, could not be had elsewhere, similarly arranged for constant reference and use. All these materials are open to members of the League at the Central Offices every day between 10 a.m. and 5 p.m. Briefs of required information from any of these sources are drawn up and supplied to any member of the League on application. An alphabetical catalogue of books in the League's library has been drawn up, and is kept up to date. The Library consists of standard works on political, economic, and social subjects, together with a considerable number of Blue Books, Acts of Parliament, and pamphlets. The latter have been arranged and catalogued under such heads as the following: Economic Theory, Education, Individualism, Labour, Land and Property, Socialism, Temperance and the Drink Question, Trade Unionism, State Interference, etc.

Recently there have been collected and bound for the Library complete sets of all the League's publications from its commencement in 1882. The sets comprise the following volumes:—League Pamphlets (in five volumes); Liberty Leaves, Annual Reports, Parliamentary Reports, Reports of Annual Meetings, Tables of Bills opposed, supported, or promoted by the League and its federated Societies, Summaries of Parliamentary work, etc. The Library also contains bound and indexed volumes of the *Liberty Review*.

The Council confidently submit this Report to the favourable consideration of the members of the League.

December 31st, 1895.

PARLIAMENTARY REPORT, SESSION 1894–5.

Parliamentary Committee :—The Earl of Wemyss ; The Hon. Baron Dimsdale ; Alderman Sir Joseph Dimsdale ; The Earl Fortescue ; Sir Edward W. Watkin, Bart. ; Henry C. Stephens, Esq., M.P. ; George Palmer, Esq. ; W. J. Carruthers Wain, Esq. ; and Representatives of the chief Defence Societies of the various industries and interests federated with the League.

Parliamentary Agent :—Mr. Frederick Millar.

Shortly after the beginning of the session the Parliamentary Committee resumed the issue of their Table of Public and Private Bills before Parliament, in fulfilment of the plan approved at the Conference of March 9th, 1892, and commenced in the session of that year. The Table was printed and circulated each week, Bills requiring the opposition of the League and its federated Societies being added to the list on each occasion, as the attention of the Committee was successively called to them by the various Societies. The Table, which gives the stage of each Bill, is drawn up primarily for the use of the Defence Societies, instructions being included as to the manner of conducting the opposition, and the heads being given of the grounds whereon the opposition should be based in each case. Copies were also sent each week to all members and supporters of the League in both Houses of Parliament. In all, since February, 1895, seventeen editions, numbering 21,000 copies, have been issued.

This action of the Committee was further supplemented by the circulation among Members of Parliament, the Press, and the public of printed memoranda, whips, notices, etc.; by the publication and distribution of pamphlets and leaflets relating to over-legislation in general, or to special instances of it ; by letters written from the Central Offices to the London and Provincial Press ; by personally procuring the assistance of members and supporters of the League in Parliament in opposing Bills objected to, in whole or in part, by Societies federated with the League ; by addresses, speeches, and resolutions at public meetings through the agency of the League Lecture Department; by consultations and arrangements for concerted action with the Societies federated with the League, and with the leading representatives of the industries attacked; and by arranging for the drafting and presentation to Parliament of petitions against any of the Bills on the weekly Table, wherever desirable, on behalf of any of the Societies federated with the League.

The following is a list of some of the more important Bill thus opposed by the Committee and the federated Societies:—

LAND AND HOUSES.

CORPORATE ASSOCIATIONS (PROPERTY): Property belonging to any non-trading Corporate Association to be deemed to be held on trust; and the members for the time being shall not terminate the existence or divide the property thereof without leave of one of the Superior Courts. *Objection:* It is contrary to public interest to treat non-trading bodies formed by private association as if the property acquired by them were not their own, but held on public trust; and it is also an arbitrary interference with existing legal rights. Resolved by the League Committee that the Bill be opposed as in former years, and that resolution be communicated to City Livery Companies federated with the League. At the instance of the Committee, four notices of motion for rejection of Bill on second reading placed and maintained on the House of Commons papers throughout the session, and formal objection made to the Bill on each occasion it was down for second reading. 21,000 printed summaries and objections sent to federated Societies, Members of Parliament, Press, and elsewhere. Dropped before second reading.

LIVERY COMPANIES (CITY OF LONDON): On February 26th Mr. J. W. Benn gave notice that on Tuesday, March 26th, he would "call attention to the administration of the funds of the City Livery Companies of London, and move a resolution." The representatives of the City Companies on the Parliamentary Committee of the League were communicated with, and the Parliamentary Agent of the League had arranged to have the motion opposed, and to send a whip to League members and supporters in the House of Commons requesting them to vote against the motion. The motion, however, was eventually dropped.

CROFTERS' HOLDINGS (SCOTLAND) ACT (1886) AMENDMENT: To be extended to yearly tenants who were excluded under that Act. *Objection:* Interferes with freedom of contract and violates written contracts already existing. Opposed at instance of Highland Property Association and Orkney Landowners' Association. 18,500 printed summaries and objections sent to federated Societies, Members of Parliament, Press, and elsewhere. Dropped before second reading.

CROFTERS' HOLDINGS (SCOTLAND) ACT (1866) AMENDMENT (No. 2): In place of Sub-Section 1, Section 34, Crofters' Holdings (Scotland) Act, 1886. "Crofter" to mean any tenant residing on a holding not exceeding £30 annual rental in a crofting parish. *Objections:* Would break existing contracts, leaseholders being now included for the first time. It is held to be unreasonable to choose this time for legislating further in this direction, seeing that the Government had made the whole question the subject of a Royal Commission. Opposed at instance of Highland Property Association and Orkney Landowners' Association. Promises personally obtained from several members in Commons that they would object to and oppose Bill. 21,000 printed summaries and objections sent to federated Societies, Members of Parliament, Press, and elsewhere. Dropped before second reading.

FARM SERVANTS (SCOTLAND): To compel owners of farms in Scotland to provide every building used as a dwelling or sleeping place for farm servants with a regulation accommodation in the way of cubic contents, fire-places, etc. *Objection:* Would break existing contracts. There is no need for such legislation, and, if passed, it would cause great inconvenience and expense to all parties concerned. Opposed at instance of Highland Property Association and Orkney Landowners' Association. 18,500 printed summaries and objections sent to federated Societies, Members of Parliament, Press, and elsewhere. Lapsed owing to prorogation intervening.

HYPOTHEC (SCOTLAND): To abolish the right of Hypothec. *Objections:* There is no public desire for alteration of, and it is inexpedient to make any change in, the present law. In the event of the right of Hypothec being abolished, landlords would have to insist upon rents being paid in advance, or tenants finding security for same. Would check investment in building, and cause an increase of rent—all to the tenant's detriment. Opposed at instance of Glasgow Landlords' Association and Partick Landlords and House Factors' Association. 16,650 printed summaries and objections sent to federated Societies, Members of Parliament, Press, and elsewhere. With the assistance of two Members of Parliament an objection was made to the Bill on each occasion, and it was down for second reading. Lapsed owing to prorogation intervening.

INDUSTRIAL AND PROVIDENT SOCIETIES (PURCHASE OF FEE SIMPLE): To empower any Industrial or Provident Society to force the lessor to sell to it the freehold of its lease at a price to be fixed by the

County Court. *Objection:* Would break existing contracts and enforce a redistribution of proprietary rights between individuals, unattended by any benefit to the public. Opposed in conjunction with the Property Protection Society. 20,250 printed summaries and objections sent to federated Societies, Members of Parliament, and elsewhere. Dropped before second reading.

LAND TENURE: To apply many of the objectionable principles of Irish land legislation to this country. Opposed at the instance of the Manchester, Salford, and District Property Owners' Association, and in conjunction with the Property Protection Society. 7,700 printed summaries and objections sent to federated Societies, Members of Parliament, Press, and elsewhere. A motion for the second reading of the Bill was made on May 15th, and carried by 218 against 189—majority 29. On the previous day a special whip and statement of objections to the Bill were sent by the League to League members and supporters in the House of Commons. The Bill made no further progress, and lapsed owing to prorogation intervening.

LAND VALUES (TAXATION BY LOCAL AUTHORITIES): Vacant land (in addition to houses) in London and other towns (except market gardens) to pay a rate on a sixty years' building ground-rent, such ground-rent being not less than four per cent. on the capital value. Rate on empty houses to be levied from owners. Such rate to be a charge upon the freehold, any existing contract made before the passing of the Act to the contrary notwithstanding. Scotland and Ireland exempted. *Objection:* Would put an unfair burden on those so unlucky as to own houses and building land for which there is no demand; and would break existing contracts. Opposed in conjunction with the Property Protection Society. 19,500 printed summaries and objections sent to federated Societies, Members of Parliament, Press, and elsewhere. Dropped before second reading.

LEASEHOLDERS (PURCHASE OF FEE SIMPLE): To empower lessee of any lease (not being a yearly lease at the open market rent), or of any life lease of buildings and land not more than three acres in extent, to compel lessor to sell to him the freehold reversion at price or perpetual rent charge fixed by County Court. Covenants and agreements binding purchasing lessee not to demise or sell, nor to make structural alterations, etc., etc., without consent of lessor, to be void. *Objection*: Would break existing contracts. Opposed at instance of Glasgow Landlords' Association, and in conjunction with the Property Protection Society. 21,000 printed summaries and objections sent to federated Societies, Members of Parliament, the Press, and elsewhere. Dropped before second reading.

Leaseholds: To enable lessee of property to violate existing contracts, and to set off the value of any improvements made to premises for his own convenience against claim for dilapidations. To empower a judge of the High Court to authorise any alteration in premises lessee is desirous of making, but which lessor refuses to sanction. Opposed in conjunction with the Property Protection Society. 18,500 printed summaries and objections sent to federated Societies, Members of Parliament, the Press, and elsewhere. Lapsed owing to prorogation intervening.

London County Council (Tower Bridge Southern Approach), Section 36 [Private]: Lands not to be taken by the Council for the improvement to have an improvement charge placed on them in consideration of any enhanced value which, in the opinion of the Council, they would receive from the improvement. Council within seven years to assess the charge such lands were to pay, which was to be equal to 3 per cent. per annum upon half of their enhanced value. Notice of the assessment to be served on the owners, lessees, and occupiers. Objections made by them to be decided by an arbitrator appointed by the Local Government Board, whose award to be final. Council to collect the charge so assessed or awarded from the occupier, who might deduct such amount from the rent payable by him. Owner, lessee, or occupier might compound for the annual charge at 33 years' purchase. *Objection:* Created new and arbitrarily defined areas of taxation; and imposed a charge *in presenti* for conjectural benefits *in futuro.* Thus properties would be permanently depreciated in capital value by being made subject for ever to a "betterment" charge which no increase of rental value afterwards justified, and even where the improvement resulted in "worsement." Made an exception of town landlords in order to deprive them of a portion of the additional value ("unearned increment") accruing to their property, in the same way as it accrues to every other kind of property wherever the price of a commodity has been raised through any expenditure thereon of the ratepayers' money by the Municipality. Opposed in conjunction with the Property Protection Society, and a special whip sent to League member and supporters in the House of Commons against amendments moved on behalf of the London County Council. 20,250 printed summaries and objections sent to federated Societies, Members of Parliament, the Press, and elsewhere. Lapsed owing to prorogation intervening.

Occupying Tenants' Enfranchisement: Every occupying tenant with lease of 20 unexpired years, except person residing in premises belonging to his employer, or in flat or divided holding, or occupying it as a pensioner, "or from philanthropic considerations," empowered to buy by compulsion the freehold reversion, at price fixed by County Court, or at a regulation rent charge. Covenants and agreements binding purchasing lessee not to make structural alterations, etc., etc., without consent of lessor, to be void. *Objection:* Would break existing contracts. Opposed at instance of Highland Property Association, Glasgow Landlords' Association, and in conjunction with the Property Protection Society. 21,000 printed summaries and objections sent to federated Societies, Members of Parliament, and elsewhere. Dropped before second reading.

SMALLER DWELLINGS (SCOTLAND): No dwelling-house under £15 rent within a burgh to be let for longer than one month (the period to expire at 12 noon on the 28th of a month) unless with a garden attached, any agreement to the contrary notwithstanding. Rates to be paid by landlord. *Objection:* It was intended by this Bill to augment artificially the supply of small dwelling houses let on leases shorter than one year. In Glasgow more than one-third of such houses are let on monthly leases; a proof that the supply is ready to adjust itself by the natural process to any increased demand for shorter leases. The Bill would infringe the rights of private contract without any public benefit, and inflict great hardship on many yearly tenants of houses without gardens under £15 rental, who wish for the continuance of leases by the year in their own cases. Opposed at instance of Glasgow Landlords' Association, Edinburgh and Leith House Factors' Association, Dundee Landlords and House Factors' Association, Association of House Factors in Glasgow, Partick Landlords and House Factors' Association. The Bill was "blocked" each time it was down for second reading. 17,500 printed summaries and objections sent to federated Societies, Members of Parliament, the Press, and elsewhere. Dropped before second reading.

PUBLIC HEALTH ACTS AMENDMENT: To enable Local Authority to subject owners of property to the expense of cleansing, maintaining, repairing, or replacing drains used in common by several owners, and which, by recent decisions, have been held to be sewers, and, therefore, vested in the Local Authority. The Bill was an attempt by Local Authorities to relieve themselves of expenses which they ought properly to incur. They are under no grievance, as the existing law is quite sufficient in fairness for all practical purposes. Opposed at instance of Manchester, Salford, and District Property Owners' Association, Liverpool Land and House Owners' Association, Building Societies' Association, in conjunction with the Property Protection Society. 12,500 printed summaries and objections sent to Members of Parliament, the Press, and elsewhere. Lapsed owing to prorogation intervening.

Mines (Eight Hours): No person to work more than eight hours in the twenty-four underground in any mine; the eight hours to be reckoned from bank to bank. *Objection:* Interfered with the freedom of adult males in the disposal of their own labour. 21,000 printed summaries and objections sent to federated Societies, Members of Parliament, Press, and elsewhere. Dropped before second reading.

RAILWAYS.

Return Tickets: Passenger return tickets issued by Railway or Steamboat Companies to be available at any time from date of issue. *Objection:* Seeing that Railway Companies are directly interested in creating facilities for their passengers within the limits of sound economy, the interference of Parliament with such matters is likely to do more harm than good. 20,250 printed summaries and objections sent to federated Societies, Members of Parliament, the Press, and elsewhere. Lapsed owing to prorogation intervening.

SHIPS.

Merchant Shipping Act Amendment (No. 2): To apply Section 7 of the Railway and Canal Traffic Act, 1854, "to all contracts made for the carrying of animals by sea." This section provides that a Railway Company shall be liable for loss from injury to any animals or goods in the receiving, forwarding, or delivering occasioned by the negligence or default of such Company or its servants, notwithstanding any notice, condition, or declaration to the contrary; subject to a proviso that no greater damages shall be recoverable for the loss or injury to an animal beyond the sum of £50 for a horse and £15 for each head of cattle, unless the person sending the animals declares a higher value and pays a reasonable percentage thereon to the Company in respect of the Company's extra risk. *Objections:* The effect of the Bill would be to prohibit shipowners from inserting in contracts for the carriage of animals by the sea the "negligence clause" that is invariably inserted in such contracts. The effect of this clause is to provide that, if the shipowner has taken all possible care to send his vessel to sea in a seaworthy condition, he shall not be responsible for loss resulting from the perils of the sea, even although such loss may, in some degree, be attributable to the negligence of the crew. The Bill would give an undue advantage to foreign over British vessels. Opposed at instance of the Chamber of Shipping of the United Kingdom. The necessary steps were taken to have the Bill objected to on each occasion it was put down for second reading. 19,500 printed summaries and objections sent to federated Societies, Members of Parliament, the Press, and elsewhere. Lapsed owing to prorogation intervening.

RETURN TICKETS : Passenger return tickets issued by Steamboat or Railway Companies to be available at any time from date of issue. *Objection :* Seeing that Steamboat or Railway Companies are directly interested in creating facilities for their passengers within the limits of sound economy, the interference of Parliament with such matters likely to do more harm than good. 20,250 printed summaries and objections sent to federated Societies, Members of Parliament, the Press, and elsewhere. Lapsed owing to prorogation intervening.

STEAM ENGINES (PERSONS IN CHARGE) : Empowers the Board of Trade to prevent anyone having the charge of a steam boiler of more than five-horse power (except in private houses, or vessels on the high seas under the Merchant Shipping Act), unless such person has obtained a certificate from the Board of Trade by examination ; or application with proof of practical experience. Certificates by examination are to be ranked as first-class ; certificates on application, with proof of practical experience, are to be ranked as second-class. *Objection :* This Bill, introduced by the "labour leaders," will give the highest ranks of labour a monopoly of the market ; and in case of shipping in dock will prevent the less skilled labourers from taking temporary charge of donkey pumps, steam winches, etc. ; a duty for which they are sufficiently qualified by experience, without having to incur the cost of a certificate. Opposed at instance of Chamber of Shipping of the United Kingdom. Steps were taken to have the Bill blocked, and 21,000 printed summaries and objections sent to federated Societies, Members of Parliament, the Press, and elsewhere. The Bill was ultimately referred to the Select Committee of the House of Commons, who decided to drop it.

TRADES AND MANUFACTURES.

FACTORY AND WORKSHOPS : *Clause 5* placed on the employer the onus of seeing that the conditions of any place in which work sent out from his factory was carried on are in a healthy state. *Clause 13* still further limited the time during which adult women may work overtime. *Clause 14* prevented women from taking work home with them from the factory in which they had been working during the day. *Clause 19* provided for the inclusion of laundries under the Act. *Clause 26* gave power to the Home Secretary to forbid any person working in a dangerous trade. *Objections :* These clauses were drafted with the intention of protecting the labour of adult women. But the protection they would give was of a nature calculated to defeat its object, as, instead of protecting women in the performance of their work, it would prevent them from obtaining work to perform. The proposal to include all hand laundries would bring many hardships to bear on a line of work which is the chief opening of poor women suddenly cast on their own resources. Moreover, the laundry trade is one least capable of rigid hours ; and limitation in this respect will ruin thousands of small industries. Opposed at instance of the Women's Employment Defence Committee, Croydon Laundry Women's Union. 18,500 printed summaries and objections sent to federated Societies, Members of Parliament, the Press, and elsewhere. The Chairman and the Parliamentary Agent of the League Committee attended meetings organised in opposition to the clauses of this Bill, and were constantly in communication with the officials of Societies, and with individual firms interested in opposing the Bill. Steps were taken to give effect to the League's opposition at opportune stages in the progress of the Bill, and after amendment the Bill received Royal Assent.

SHOPS (EARLY CLOSING): Shop to mean a barber's shop, and any building, booth, or stall where goods are sold by retail. On application in writing from not less than two-thirds of shopkeepers to be affected, local authority might make an order closing all or any class of shops in the district (except public-houses with on-licenses, refreshment houses, tobacconists, and newsagents' shops), on any specified day in the week, at or after 1 p.m., and on all or any other days at or after 6 p.m. A shop wherein trades of two or more classes are carried on to be so closed for all such trades at the hour whereat the order directs closure for any one of such trades. Offences to be prosecuted under the Factory and Workshop Act, 1878. *Objection:* The natural regulators of closing are the buyers, as is shown by the variations in the hour in the quarters of London and large provincial towns inhabited by different classes. This Bill placed the regulation in the hands of the sellers, who would thus create an artificial position prolific in difficulties and disturbances for everybody, and in loss for themselves. Opposed at instance of National Federation of Off-License Holders' Associations. 21,000 printed summaries and objections sent to federated Societies, Members of Parliament, the Press, and elsewhere. Lapsed owing to prorogation interven ng.

BOROUGH FUNDS ACT (1872) AMENDMENT: To enable Municipalities, in contravention of the Borough Funds Act, 1872, to use the moneys of ratepayers, without their consent, for promoting or opposing Bills in Parliament. *Objection:* Would remove a useful check upon the extravagance of municipal Socialism, and upon the growth of municipal monopolies, at the expense of private enterprise. Opposed at instance of Provincial Water Companies' Association, and Liverpool Land and House Owners' Association. 16,650 printed summaries and objections sent to federated Societies, Members of Parliament, the Press, and elsewhere. Dropped before second reading.

Architects' Registration: A "General Council of Architectural Education and Registration of the United Kingdom," to be established with branches for England, Scotland, and Ireland. Members of General and Branch Council to have their fees and travelling expenses. Registration fees shall, after paying expenses of registration, be applied to support of museums, libraries, lectureships, etc.; or to building offices, examination halls, etc. An applicant for admission, after passing of Act, must be twenty-one years old, and have served not less than three years with a registered practitioner, and have passed a regulation examination. An apprenticeship entered on after passing of Act must be under indenture to a registered practitioner, to be recorded on registration list by payment of £2 fee. After 1st January, 1892, no one to use name of architect unless he is registered, on pain of a fine of £20, and £50 for repetition of offence. Inspectors shall attend examinations to report upon the efficiency of such examinations. Boards of examiners and inspectors to receive remuneration. No unregistered person to be able to recover professional charges in court of law. No municipalities or local bodies are to appoint architects acting under them, unless registered after a special examination. No architects' certificates are to be valid unless the architect signing is registered. Opposed at instance of Royal Institute of British Architects. 16,650 printed summaries and objections sent to federated Societies, Members of Parliament, the Press, and elsewhere. By the assistance of Members of Parliament, four permanent notices to move the rejection of the Bill were placed on the paper of the House of Commons. Second reading dropped.

TRADE IN ALCOHOL.

Grocers' Certificates (Scotland) (Abolition): To abolish licenses granted under the Forbes Mackenzie Act, 1853, to grocers and provision merchants for sale of excisable liquors for consumption off the premises. No person holding certificate for sale of such liquors to carry on business of grocer or provision merchant, or any such business, although conducted on different premises. *Objection:* It is through the retail grocer that the middle and working classes obtain their supplies of alcoholic drink for consumption at home; and the suppression of this trade would cause great hardship and inconvenience to the families of those classes, especially in the more rural and thinly peopled parts of Scotland. Opposed at instance of Scottish Licensed Trade Defence Association, National Federation of Off-License Holders' Associations. 21,000 printed summaries and objections sent to federated Societies, Members of both Houses of Parliament, the Press, and elsewhere. Dropped before second reading.

GROCERS' LICENSES ABOLITION: To abolish licenses now in force for the retail sale of spirits, wine, and beer by persons who keep shops for the sale of goods and commodities other than foreign wine. *Objection:* These licenses have been of great benefit and convenience to the middle and working classes, and no trustworthy evidence has ever been given that they are productive of the evils alleged against them by the promoters of this Bill. Opposed at instance of National Federation of Off-License Holders' Associations, Licensed Victuallers' Defence League of England and Wales, Federated Brewers' Association, London Off-Licenses Association. 11,600 printed summaries and objections sent to federated Societies, Members of Parliament, the Press, and elsewhere. Dropped before second reading.

INTOXICATING LIQUORS (LICENSES): Between passing of Act and 1899, Licensing Justices not to grant licenses to premises not licensed at passing of Act, if number of licenses exceeds regulation proportion to population. In 1899, and every subsequent year, Justices only to grant licenses not exceeding the following proportions: In Urban district, one license to under 1,000 population; two to over 1,000 and under 2,000; three to over 2,000 and under 3,000; one additional to every additional 1,000 or fraction. In Rural district, one license to under 600 population; two to over 600 and under 1,200; three to over 1,200 and under 1,800; additional license to additional 600 or fraction. At same time Justices to offer such licenses for five years for public competition, highest tender not necessarily accepted. During first ten years monies so received to be paid to "Licenses Liquidation Fund"; such monies to be distributed to license-holders during three years preceding 1889; balance to be paid to Chancellor of Exchequer. On requisition of one-tenth of ratepayers, by a majority of municipal or county voters, at poll by ballot, premises may be closed from 10 p.m. to 8 a.m., and altogether on Sundays and Parliamentary election days. After 1898, by a majority of three-fourths, prohibition may be enforced. Such resolutions may be rescinded after five years. Justices may grant special licenses to railway refreshment rooms, hotels, etc.; otherwise Act not to apply to theatres, passenger boats, canteens, medicated and methylated spirits, and liquor sold by wholesale. Act not to apply to Scotland or Ireland. Opposed at instance of National Federation of Off-License Holders' Associations, Manchester Brewers' Central Association, London Licensed Victuallers' Central Protection Society, London Off-Licenses Association, Licensed Victuallers' Defence League of England and Wales, Northern District League of Beer and Wine Trade Associations.

20,250 printed summaries and objections sent to federated Societies, Members of Parliament, the Press, and elsewhere. Dropped before second reading.

INTOXICATING LIQUORS LOCAL VETO (IRELAND): The Mayor or sheriff in the urban or rural districts of Ireland, in any year, from not less than one-tenth of the voters, is empowered to take a poll as to the adoption, by a majority of two-thirds in Ireland, of one of three resolutions—viz.: (i.) spirits, wine, beer, porter, ale, cider, perry, and sweets, to be prohibited; (ii.) number of licenses to be curtailed; (iii.) new licenses not to be granted. On adoption of first resolution, sale of alcoholic drinks will be punished, on conviction, by penalties or imprisonment. Opposed at instance of Belfast and Ulster Vintners' Association, Dublin Licensed Grocers' and Vintners' Association, National Federation of Off-License Holders' Associations, Federated Brewers' Association, London Off-Licenses Association, Licensed Victuallers' Defence League of England and Wales. By assistance of Member in Commons, notice of motion for rejection of Bill on second reading was placed on paper. 21,000 printed summaries and objections sent to federated Societies, Members of both Houses, and elsewhere. Withdrawn before second reading.

INTOXICATING LIQUOR TRAFFIC (LOCAL CONTROL): At a poll taken by ballot, on requisition of one-tenth of local government electors of area, a majority of two-thirds of persons voting might enforce total prohibition of sale of alcoholic liquors in area. Poll also to be taken on a resolution to limit the number of licenses in any area. While a prohibitory resolution is in force, no ordinary license to be granted in respect of any premises in area. While a limiting resolution is in force licenses not to be granted in the area to a number in excess of three-fourths of the number existing at the date of the poll, without prejudice to the discretion of the Licensing Justices to grant a less number of licenses than the said three-fourths. A subsequent poll on question of prohibition not to be taken for three years. During term of prohibition, at poll taken by ballot on requisition of one-tenth of electors, two-thirds of persons voting might pass resolution for abolishing total prohibition after three years from commencement of Act; after that time resolution not to come into force within one year from passing. By similar processes, excepting that the majority is to be a bare majority instead of two-thirds, total Sunday closing to be enforced; and subsequently abolished. The areas to be boroughs (where undivided), wards, parishes (in country); and in London—sanitary districts, wards, or parishes. Act not to apply to railway refreshment rooms, hotels for travellers and lodgers, eating-houses for meals, nor to Ireland. No compensation.

Objections: A change in the law of the land, like the one proposed here, affecting so profoundly the mode of life of all in the area, should not be made unless by the recorded votes of at least a majority of all in the area entitled to vote, and unless adequate compensation is given to traders whose business is injured or destroyed as a result of the enforcement of an adopted resolution. The loss to the excise revenue caused by the adoption of prohibition in any area would have to be made up by additional direct taxation levied from abstainers and non-abstainers alike in such area and over the whole country. Opposed at instance of National Federation of Off-License Holders' Associations, Scottish Licensed Trade Defence Association, Federated Brewers' Associations, London Licensed Victuallers' Central Protection Society, London Off-Licenses Association, Licensed Victuallers' Defence League of England and Wales. Steps were taken to give effect to the League's opposition if occasion arose, and 12,500 printed summaries and objections sent to federated Societies, Members of both Houses of Parliament, the Press, and elsewhere. Dropped before second reading.

LIQUOR TRAFFIC LOCAL VETO (ENGLAND): On the demand of one-tenth of the voters in any district a poll of the voters to be taken by which a majority of the voters polling could prohibit the granting or renewal of licenses for the sale of alcoholic drinks for five years, at the end of which time another poll might be taken. But if the prohibitionists lost the poll, they could demand another poll in two years. *An objection:* A change in the law of the land, like the one proposed here and in other cases, affecting so profoundly the mode of life of all in the district, should not be made unless by the recorded votes of at least a majority of all the voters in the district. Opposed at instance of National Federation of Off-License Holders' Associations, Beer and Wine Trade National Defence League, Federated Brewers' Associations, London Licensed Victuallers' Central Protection Society, London Off-Licenses Association, Licensed Victuallers' Defence League of England and Wales, Country Brewers' Society. By the assistance of a Member in the Commons, notice of motion for rejection of Bill on second reading placed on the paper. 21,000 printed summaries and objections sent to federated Societies, Members of Parliament, Press, and elsewhere. Dropped before second reading.

LIQUOR TRAFFIC LOCAL VETO (SCOTLAND): On the requisition of not less than one-tenth of the householders, one of three resolutions may be adopted by a majority, viz.:—(i.) that the sale of alcoholic drinks be prohibited; (ii.) that the number of licenses be reduced; (iii.) that no more licenses be granted. Opposed at instance of Scottish Licensed Trade Defence Association, London Off-Licenses Association,

National Federation of Off-License Holders' Association, Country Brewers' Society, Licensed Victuallers' Defence League of England and Wales, Federated Brewers' Association. 21,000 printed summaries and objections sent to federated Societies, Members of Parliament, and elsewhere. Dropped before second reading.

Public-houses, Hours of Closing (Scotland): Extends the restrictions of the Licensed Premises (Earlier Closing) (Scotland) Act for closing hotels and public-houses at 10 p.m. to towns of over 50,000 inhabitants, which were exempted by Parliament in 1887. Opposed at instance of the Scottish Licensed Trade Defence Association. 21,000 printed summaries and objections sent to federated Societies, Members of Parliament, the Press, and elsewhere, and the Bill blocked on each occasion it was put down for second reading. Second reading dropped.

Sale of Intoxicating Liquors on Sunday: To compel the closing of all hotels and public-houses throughout England during the whole of Sunday. *Objection:* Experience of such legislation in the case of Wales and Scotland shows that it tends to force drinking facilities into working-men's clubs and private gatherings, with demoralising results. Opposed at instance of Federated Brewers' Associations, Licensed Victuallers' Defence League of England and Wales, Beer and Wine Trade National Defence League, Northern Districts Beer and Wine Trade Defence League, National Federation of Off-License Holders' Associations, London Licensed Victuallers' Central Protection Society, London Off-Licenses Association. 21,000 printed summaries and objections sent to federated Societies, Members of Parliament, the Press, and elsewhere. Dropped before second reading.

Sale of Intoxicating Liquors: Licensing Board to be established for every district consisting of between seven and twelve members elected by district, and half that number appointed by Licensing Justices, to hold office for three years. All licensing powers to be transferred to Board from Licensing Justices. Licences to be for consumption on or off the premises, with powers of renewal and transfer at discretion. After five years, poll to be taken for prohibiting on and off licenses in district by majority of two-thirds of voters polling. Number of new licenses to be limited to one license per 1,000 inhabitants in towns, and one per 500 in country; and old licenses to be reduced to that proportion. Compensation for extinguished licenses to be given at first licensing after commencement of Act only. Board to compel closing at 10 p.m. on week days and during the whole of Sundays. Opposed at instance of National Federation of Off-License Holders' Associations, London Licensed Victuallers' Central Protection Society, London Off-Licenses Association, Licensed Victuallers' Defence

League of England and Wales, Federated Brewers' Association, Beer and Wine Trade National Defence League. 17,500 printed summaries and objections sent to federated Societies, Members of Parliament, and elsewhere. Dropped before second reading.

SALE OF INTOXICATING LIQUORS (IRELAND): Brought in by Ulster Unionist Members. To compel the closing during the whole of Sunday of all places for the sale of alcoholic drinks in Dublin, Belfast, and the other towns exempted by Parliament in 1878 from the operations of the Irish Sunday Closing Act. Opposed at instance of Dublin Licensed Grocers' and Vintners' Association, National Federation of Off-License Holders' Associations, Licensed Victuallers' Defence League of England and Wales, Belfast and Ulster Vintners' Association, Country Brewers' Society, London Off-Licenses Association, Federated Brewers' Association. 21,000 printed summaries and objections sent to Members of Parliament, federated Societies, and elsewhere. Read a second time, and referred to Standing Committee on Trade; but the stage of consideration was not reached before the dissolution.

SALE OF INTOXICATING LIQUORS TO CHILDREN: To make a penal offence to sell or deliver alcoholic liquors to persons under sixteen. *Objection:* This would inflict a vexatious hardship on the working classes by depriving them of the services of their children as messengers, and re-open the question as settled by Parliament in the Intoxicating Liquors (Sale to Children) Act, 1886. Opposed at instance of National Federation of Off-License Holders' Associations. By assistance of Members in Commons, arrangements made for permanently "objecting" to the Bill. 11,600 printed summaries and objections sent to Members of Parliament, the Press, and elsewhere. Dropped before second reading.

WINE AND BEERHOUSE ACT AMENDMENT: To repeal section 19, Wine and Beerhouse Act, 1869 (which precludes justices from refusing to renew on-licenses, except for bad character of applicant, previous forfeiture for misconduct, or disorderly character of house), and section 7, Wine and Beerhouse Act Amendment Act, 1870 (which extends application of section 19 of Act of 1869 to transferred licenses); and to empower justices to refuse renewal of retail on-licenses on any grounds appearing to them sufficient. Opposed at instance of Country Brewers' Society, Federated Brewers' Associations, Beer and Wine Trade National Defence League, Northern Districts Beer and Wine Trade Defence League, National Federation of Off-Licensed Holders' Association. By assistance of Members of the House of Commons, a standing block was placed on the Bill. 1,350 printed summaries and objections sent to Members of Parliament, federated Societies, Press, and elsewhere. Dropped before second reading.

BILL PROMOTED BY THE LEAGUE.

Licensing Act Amendment (House of Lords): The object of this Bill is to secure uniformity in the granting by way of renewal or transfer of licenses for the sale of intoxicating liquor. By section 19 of the Wine and Beerhouse Act, 1869, it is enacted that it shall not be lawful for Justices to refuse certain licenses except upon one or more of the grounds stated in section 8 of the said Act. And whereas, in consequence of the provisions of the Beer Dealers' Retail License Act, 1880, and an Act of 1882 to amend the same, doubts have arisen as to the discretionary power of Licensing Justices and a diversity of practice prevails, and license holders have been subjected to uncertainty and expense, the Bill proposes that Licensing Justices shall not be at liberty in the case of premises licensed at the time of the passing of this Act to refuse the renewal or transfer of a license for the sale of any intoxicating liquors in any such premises except upon one or more of the grounds specified in section 8 of the Wine and Beerhouse Act, 1869; but nothing herein contained shall limit or extend their discretion in the grant or refusal of applications for a new license. When an application for a renewal or transfer of a license is refused, the Justices shall specify in writing to the applicant the ground of their decision. This Bill, which was drafted by the late Lord Bramwell, one of the judges in the celebrated case, Sharpe *v.* Wakefield, was brought in the House of Lords by the Chairman of the League Parliamentary Committee and read a first time. During the session several conferences took place between the Chairman, the Parliamentary Agent of the League, and representatives of the Brewers, Licensed Victuallers, Wine and Spirit Merchants, Beer Retailers, and Off-License Holders' Associations in Great Britain, with regard to the progress of the Bill. Petitions from nearly 200 Associations representing every branch of the Liquor industry in the United Kingdom were presented to the House of Lords by the Chairman of the League Committee. On May 28th the Parliamentary Agent of the League accompanied representatives of Associations federated with the League in a deputation to the Prime Minister on the subject of the Bill. 19,500 printed summaries of the Bill were sent to Members of Parliament, federated Societies, the Press, and elsewhere. Subsequently it was determined that, in view of the pending dissolution of Parliament, no further steps should be taken to press the Bill forward, but that it should be re-introduced early in 1896, and a vigorous effect made to get it placed upon the Statute-book. On the motion of the Chairman of the League Committee, the petitions presented to the House of Lords in favour of the Bill were ordered to be printed as a Return and laid on the Table of the House.

December 31st, 1895.

You will help the work by tearing this off and enclosing with amount to **LLOYDS BANK**, Limited, **HERRIES, FARQUHAR BRANCH;** or to the Secretary, Liberty and Property Defence League, 7, Victoria Street, London, S.W.

LIBERTY AND PROPERTY DEFENCE LEAGUE.

To the Manager, LLOYDS BANK, Limited, HERRIES, FARQUHAR, Branch,
16, St. James's Street, London, S.W.

Please place the accompanying Sum of ....
to the Credit of the League in my name.

Name ....

Donation ... ... £ : :

Address ....

Annual Subscription ... £ : :

Total ... ... £ : :

....

Date ....

A Donation or Subscription of not less than 5s. entitles Contributor to League Membership and all publications for one year from date thereof.

LIBERTY & PROPERTY DEFENCE LEAGUE.

(To uphold the principle of Liberty, and guard the Rights of Labour and Property of all kinds against undue interference by the State; and to encourage Self-help versus State-help.)

ANNUAL REPORT, 1897.

(FIFTEENTH FINANCIAL YEAR.)

PUBLISHED BY THE
LIBERTY AND PROPERTY DEFENCE LEAGUE,
7, VICTORIA STREET, LONDON, S.W.

1898.

Liberty and Property Defence League.

(To uphold the principle of Liberty, and guard the Rights of Labour and Property of all kinds against undue interference by the State; and to encourage Self-help *versus* State-help.)

COUNCIL—1897-98.

Liberty and Property Defence League.

FIFTEENTH ANNUAL REPORT, 1896-7.

THE Council submit the following Report of the League's progress and proceedings during the past year to the consideration of the members of the League:—

MEMBERSHIP.

The number of **Individual Members** continues to increase. The number of **Societies Federated** with the League is now 207, being an increase of 7 since December 31st, 1896. The 207 Associations, Societies, and corporate bodies now federated with the League represent every important interest and industry in the United Kingdom.

Throughout the year the League is in constant communication with these bodies, and during the Session of Parliament the League's work almost entirely consists in arranging, in conjunction with their committees and officials, opposition to the yearly increasing number of Bills brought before Parliament threatening their interests and the common rights of liberty and property. The federation of Societies and Companies for this purpose was the central idea in the constitution of the League; and particulars of the League's work in this connection are given in the appended Report of the Parliamentary Committee.

BRANCH EXTENSION.

Early in 1897 several meetings of influential employers were held in **Nottingham** for the purpose of forming a strong local branch of the League. A Provisional Committee has been formed, and a statement of objects adopted. Full particulars can be obtained from the secretary, 7, Victoria Street; or from Mr. Amos Waters (Midland agent of the League), 205, Pym Street, Nottingham.

FINANCE.

The audited **Balance-sheet** for the year ended October 31st last, submitted by the Finance Committee, shows that the total of the subscriptions and donations received during this fifteenth financial year fell below the average of the previous years. Several reasons help to account for this. First and foremost it is a result of the "Jubilee year," with its many claims on public generosity. In this respect the League has not been the only sufferer. Secondly, the League has to combat the prevailing impression that with a Conservative Government in power things will "go easy" for a few years. But the socialist measures introduced and carried during the Session of 1897 ought to convince the property-owning classes that in respect to legislation of this character one political party is little, if any, better than the other. To check aggression individual effort is necessary, and concentration of effort is necessary. "It is energy that achieves, and it is energy alone that defends." The coming Parliamentary Session gives promise of a fruitful crop of "Labour" Bills, which, in their ultimate effect, should they become law, must touch every employer, workman, producer, consumer, and ratepayer. If the good work of the League, in opposing all legislation subversive of sound principles and socialistic in tendency, is to be maintained, generous financial support must be forthcoming.

The balance-sheet, audited by the League auditors, and the subscription book, are open to the inspection of members at all times at the offices at Westminster.

THE ANNUAL MEETING.

The **Fourteenth Annual Meeting** was held at the Westminster Palace Hotel on March 2nd, 1897, when Mons. Paul Leroy Beaulieu presided and delivered an address. At the conclusion of the address, in the absence (through illness) of the Earl of Wemyss, chairman of the Council, Sir Frederick Bramwell presented to the meeting the Report of the Council (including the Reports of the Parliamentary and Finance Committees) for the past year. The usual resolutions adopting the Report and proposing a vote of thanks to the chairman were vigorously moved and seconded by Mr. T. Dundas Pillans, Colonel Montague Clementi, Mr. L. Cranmer-Byng (chairman of the Individualist Club), Mr. John Hunt (president of the Licensed Victuallers' National Defence League), the Earl Fortescue, and Mr. G. A. Laws (general manager of the Shipping Federation).

PRESS AND PLATFORM WORK.

The ordinary work in connection with the League **Lecture Department** has been carried on uninterruptedly throughout the year, and League lecturers have delivered addresses, undertaken debates, and given lectures at a great number of public meetings held in the halls and parks of London and suburbs, and at working men s political and social clubs in the provinces. The League has also been represented at several congresses and meetings of property-owners' associations, and of the Federated Societies in London and the provinces.

The **Press Correspondence Department**, established for the purpose of addressing to the press original letters on subjects of interest to the League and its Federated Societies, and replies to letters and articles advocating socialism, or in some way contravening the principles and objects of the League, has continued its successful work in opening the eyes of the public to the dangers of Socialism, and to the evils of undue State interference with the rights of freedom and property.

PUBLICATIONS.

During the past year the issue and sale of **Publications** has been well maintained. Among other publications issued, "Property in Land: A Defence of Individual Ownership," by J. C. Spence (price 1d.), has been reprinted. New publications are :—"Liberty and Property: The Two Main Factors of Human Progress," by Paul Leroy Beaulieu (price 1d.), and "Trade Unionism in Relation to Wages," by James Birks (price 6d.). In connection with the Parliamentary Department twenty issues of Tables of Parliamentary Bills under consideration were widely distributed.

A list of the publications on sale at the League offices is given in the advertisements at the end of this Report. Special reference must be made to an excellent and most readable booklet (price 1s.), entitled "Conservatives or Socialists?" by J. Buckingham Pope, which is the most forcible protest against the Workmen's Compensation for Accidents Bill (of 1897) yet produced in book form; and also to a concise statement of the law as regards picketing and its abuses, published as "The Case against Picketing" (price 1s. 6d.), by W. J. Shaxby, a member of the League staff.

Mention should be made of the *Liberty Review*, a monthly journal of politics, economics, and sociology, edited by the Secretary of the League, and published at 17, Johnson's Court, Fleet Street, London, E.C. The *Liberty Review* is now recognised as the only organ devoting its columns exclusively to an exposure of socialist fallacies. The paper has no connection with the League, financially or editorially; but several members of the League, in addition to its editor, are on the staff of writers; and the political principles of the paper are generally in accord with those held by the League. In its columns all legislative proposals affecting commercial industrial warfare are subjected to exhaustive examination; and every attempt to harass or to confiscate the property of any body of traders, or of any corporate association, is steadfastly resisted. The evil effects of past undue State interference with the conduct and management of railways, mines, the shipping trade, the liquor trade, and other national industries, and with the ownership and disposition of landed and other property, are exposed, with a view to demonstrating the pernicious character of the legislation which certain factions and parties are organized to promote. The various large interests of London and the country, federated through their representative organizations with the League, would do well to make the *Liberty Review* the medium of expressing to a more extended audience their views upon political questions particularly affecting themselves, now too often confined to their respective trade journals.

THE INDIVIDUALIST CLUB.

Although the League is in no way connected with the **Individualist Club,** founded at the end of 1896, the staff and many members of the League have personally rendered every assistance in their power towards its successful start and growth. The Club, as a propagandist body, has widely circulated several printed statements, among them being a valuable memorandum upon the socialist tendency of modern legislation, and a strong protest against the Workmen (Compensation for Accidents) Bill. At its weekly social gatherings (now held in the Chapter Room at Anderton's Hotel) the debates—reported from time to time in the press—have done good work. They have dealt with many current topics, such as "Socialism" (opened by Mr. Bernard Shaw), Education (opened by Sir Richard Temple; and again by Mr. G. Brown), Free Trade (opened by Sir Henry Howorth, supported by Colonel Sir Howard Vincent), Woman Suffrage (opened by Miss Helen Blackburn), the Factory Acts (opened by Miss Ada Heather-Bigg), the Dock Companies' Superannuation Scheme (opened by the Hon. Sidney Holland), and the Irish Land Bills (opened by Mr. S. Murray Hussey).

A VERY IMPORTANT SERVICE; A NATIONAL FEDERATION OF EMPLOYERS.

The most important work of the League during the past year has, without doubt, been the part it has taken in the formation of the **Free Labour Protection Association.** The necessity for a national confederation of employers having for its primary object the repression of the tyranny of trade unions had, during the last few years, become so urgent that no sooner was the idea mooted than it met with the unanimous approval of the heads of the various industries who were consulted on the subject. A private meeting of influential employers and representatives of Employers' Associations in the United Kingdom was held at the League offices, 7, Victoria Street, Westminster, on July 16th, 1897, to discuss a proposal to form such a confederation. The chair was taken by the Right Hon. the EARL OF WEMYSS. On the motion of Colonel H. C. DYER (President, Employers' Federation of Engineering Associations), seconded by Mr. G. A. LAWS (General Manager, The Shipping Federation, Limited), the following resolution was unanimously adopted :—

> "That, in the opinion of this representative meeting of employers, it is desirable to form a Free Labour Protection Association, having for its objects—
>
> "I. To test systematically the efficiency, or otherwise, of the existing laws for the protection of Non-Unionists, and, if necessary, to obtain an amendment of such laws.
>
> "II. To watch all strikes, and ensure the observance of the law in all disputes between employer and employed.
>
> "III. To oppose all legislation injuriously affecting the trades and industries of the United Kingdom.
>
> "IV. To seek the attainment of these objects through the corporate action of the Association ; by the federation of *(a)* employers, whether individuals, firms, or corporate bodies ; *(b)* existing or future Employers' Associations for the protection of separate interests ; and in such ways as shall at any time appear necessary or desirable."

A Committee, consisting of the following gentlemen, with power to add to their number, was appointed to give effect to the foregoing resolution, and to draft the constitution and rules of the Association :—

The Right Hon. the EARL OF WEMYSS.
Sir WILLIAM T. LEWIS, Bart.
Mr. H. D. GREENE, Q.C., M.P.
Colonel H. C. DYER (President, Employers' Federation of Engineering Associations).
The Hon. W. W. VIVIAN (Dinorwic Quarries).
Mr. ALEXANDER SIEMENS (President, London Association of Engineering Employers).
Mr. GEORGE LIVESEY (Chairman, South Metropolitan Gas Company).
Mr. T. F. RIDER (President, National Association of Master Builders).
Mr. G. A. LAWS (General Manager, The Shipping Federation).
Mr. W. SHEPHERD (President, London Central Association of Master Builders).

Of this Committee several members, it will be noticed, have for many years past served on the League Council ; and Lord Wemyss, chairman of the League Council, has consented to act as chairman of the Executive Committee of the Free Labour Protection Association, and

Mr. Frederick Millar, the secretary of the League, to act as secretary to the Association. A movement of this important and far-reaching character, at a time when the world of trade and commerce is seriously struggling to free itself from the hampering and harassing conditions which the socialist trade union leaders have for some time past been endeavouring to force upon it, is the most valuable development outside Parliament that the League's influence could possibly have secured. And this help, rendered to employers and employed in their fight with trade union socialism, is of itself sufficient justification for the League's existence during the last fifteen years.

PARLIAMENTARY REPORT, SESSION 1897.

Parliamentary Committee:—The Earl of Wemyss, Baron Dimsdale, Alderman Sir Joseph Dimsdale, the Earl Fortescue, Sir Edward W. Watkin, Bart., Henry C. Stephens, Esq., M.P., George Palmer, Esq., Lord Rookwood, W. J. Carruthers Wain, Esq., and Representatives of the chief Defence Societies of the various industries and interests federated with the League.

Parliamentary Agent:—Frederick Millar.

Shortly after the beginning of the Session the Parliamentary Committee resumed the issue of their Table of Public and Private Bills before Parliament, in fulfilment of the plan approved at the Conference of March 9th, 1892, and commenced in the session of that year. The Table was printed and circulated each week, Bills requiring the opposition of the League and its Federated Societies being added to the list on each occasion, as the attention of the Committee was successively called to them by the various Societies. The table, which gives the stage of each Bill, is drawn up primarily for the use of the Defence Societies, instructions being included as to the manner of conducting the opposition, and the heads being given of the grounds whereon the opposition should be based in each case. Copies are also sent each week to all members and supporters of the League in both Houses of Parliament. In all, since February 1897, twenty editions, numbering over 20,000 copies, were issued.

This action of the Committee was further supplemented by circulation among Members of Parliament, the Press, and the public of several thousands of printed whips, notices, and memoranda; by publication and distribution of pamphlets and leaflets relating to over-legislation in general, or to special instances of it; by letters written from the Central Offices to the London and Provincial press; by the personal procuring of the assistance of members and supporters of the League in Parliament in opposing Bills objected to, in whole or in part, by Societies federated with the League; by addresses, speeches, and resolutions at public meetings through the agency of the League Lecture Department; by consultations and arrangements for concerted action with the Societies federated with the League, and with the leading representatives of the industries attacked; and by arranging for the drafting and presentation to Parliament of petitions against any of the Bills on the weekly Table, wherever desirable, on behalf of any of the Societies federated with the League.

The following is a list of some of the more important Bills thus opposed by the Committee and the federated Societies:—

LAND AND HOUSES.

The **Borough Funds; Places of Worship (Leasehold Enfranchisement); Smaller Dwellings (Scotland); Crofters' Holdings (Scotland) Act (1886) Amendment; Land Values (Towns Assessment); Leaseholders (Purchase of Fee Simple) (No. 2); Leaseholders (Purchase of Fee Simple); Occupying Tenants' Enfranchisement (Purchase of Fee Simple); Industrial and Provident and Incorporated Building Societies (Purchase of Fee Simple);** and **Local Government Act (1888) Amendment** Bills were reintroduced and put down for second reading; but, being persistently objected to and "blocked," they were either "dropped" before second reading, or lapsed owing to prorogation intervening. These Bills, all of which proposed to break existing contracts, were opposed by the League at the instance of such bodies as the Highland Property Association, the Orkney Landowners' Association, the Glasgow Landlords' Association, the United Property Owners' and Ratepayers' Association of Great Britain, and in conjunction with the Property Protection Society. Over 20,000 printed summaries and objections respecting these Bills were sent to the press, Federated Societies, Members of Parliament, and elsewhere.

The **London County Buildings** Bill: The object of this Bill was to enable the London County Council to provide new offices for its staff, and to acquire the whole of the south side of Trafalgar Square, from Drummond's Bank to Cockspur Street, and the hinterland back to the new Admiralty buildings on the east side and the park on the south-west, taking in the site of the present County Council Offices, and wiping out the thoroughfare on which they stand. *Objections:* (1) That the proposed site is altogether out of proportion to the requirements of the London County Council. (2) That, in view of the extreme probability of the Council's authority and powers being delegated to district councils and local municipal bodies, in response to the growing demand of London parishes for charters of incorporation, the proposed accommodation will not be needed. (3) That the injury done to the businesses now being carried on in Trafalgar Square will be irreparable, and the compensation likely to be awarded would not recompense the evicted. (4) That to involve the ratepayers of London in wasteful and wanton expenditure, amounting to nearly a million and a half, would be wholly unpardonable.

At the request of the property-owners and shopkeepers in the affected area, the Parliamentary Committee took steps to oppose the Bill. A pamphlet dealing exhaustively with the subject was published by the League, and a copy was sent to every member of the House of Commons, with the result that a strong feeling of opposition to the measure was aroused. The Bill was put down for second reading on February 18th. On the previous day a special "whip" was sent to members of the House of Commons, asking them to support the motion for the rejection of the Bill. The second reading was rejected by 227 votes to 146; majority, 81.

The **Working Men's Dwellings [H.L.]** Bill: Empowered the local authority to borrow from the Public Works Loans Commissioners, and to make advances of not more than £150 to any one workman for the acquisition of the dwelling-house in which he resides. *Objections:* This Bill, and the two similar Working Men's Dwellings Bills introduced into the House of Commons—one of which was withdrawn, and the other down for second reading when the prorogation took place—were wholly unnecessary. The working-class demands for the purchase of dwellings are adequately supplied by private enterprise. The Bill passed through Committee, was read a third time in the House of Lords, and sent to the Commons, in which House it did not reach the second reading stage. In the meantime, the Chairman of the League Parliamentary Committee "capped" this socialistic absurdity by introducing a Bill "To provide facilities for the acquisition, by *occupiers and* *occupying ratepayers*, of their dwellings." The introduction of this "logical" Bill undoubtedly had something to do with the fate of Lord Londonderry's measure, of which, it is to be hoped, nothing further will now be heard.

The **Land Tenure (Wales and Monmouthshire)** Bill: Proposes to establish a Land Court in Wales and Monmouthshire for the purpose of settling the rents of agricultural holdings; provides for reference to an agricultural judge selected by the Board of Agriculture from a list drawn up by the County Councils. Proposes that a tenancy shall not be determined at the wish of the landlord unless the ground is required for certain specified purposes, and that, when a landowner resumes occupation for any other purpose than "the benefit of labourers in respect of cottages, gardens, or allotments," the tenant shall be entitled to compensation for disturbance. *Objections:* The principle, that the question of rent as between landlord and tenant may be settled compulsorily by an authority external to the contract of tenancy, has failed in Ireland. It is undesirable that the law regulating the relations of landlord and tenant, at present identical in England and Wales, should for the future be entirely distinct in the two parts of the country. Compensation for disturbance is, in England, a new and objectionable doctrine. These and other objections were embodied in a "Statement," and sent by the Parliamentary Committee of the League to members of the House of Commons; and on the day preceding the motion for the second reading of the Bill a telegraphic whip was sent to League members and supporters in the House of Commons, urging them to speak and vote against the measure. On May 19th the second reading was rejected by 278 to 154; majority, 124.

RAILWAYS.

The **Coroners' Inquests (Railway Fatalities)** and **Railway Return Tickets** Bills were again put down for second reading; but, being persistently blocked, the former was dropped, and the latter lapsed owing to prorogation.

MINES.

The **Mines Eight Hours** Bill again proposed to interfere with the freedom of adult males in the disposal of their own labour, by prohibiting any person from working more than eight hours in the twenty-four underground in any mine. The Parliamentary Committee of the League took active steps to have the Bill opposed. The second reading was rejected by 227 votes to 186, Wednesday, May 5th, 1897.

TRADES AND MANUFACTURES.

The **Shops Early Closing**, the **Shop Assistants (Half-Holiday)**, and the **Shops** Bills all aimed at interfering with the natural regulation of closing shops, and attempted to enforce a rigid observation as to closing, which would cause much disorganization in established trade arrangements, and would tend to stop the general movement in the direction of early closing being effected voluntarily. Each Bill was opposed by the Parliamentary Committee on behalf of the Voluntary Early Closing Association, and of various associations of shopkeepers. Each Bill was dropped before second reading.

The **Gold and Silver Plate Licences** Bill proposed to abolish the license at present necessary for any trader who sells articles composed wholly or in part of silver or gold. It was opposed at the request of the National Retail Jewellers' Association and the National Association of Pawnbrokers of Great Britain, with such success that it was speedily withdrawn.

SHIPS.

The **Merchant Shipping Act Amendment** Bill was introduced as usual.

The **Merchant Shipping (Certificated Officers)** Bill allowed no British ship to proceed to sea from any port without certificated officers. British vessels of over 500 tons to carry master and two mates, and of over 1,000 tons to carry master and three mates. British subjects only may hold certificates.

The **Steam Engines and Boilers (Persons in Charge)** Bill empowered the Secretary of State to prevent anyone having the charge of a steam engine or boiler of more than 5-horse power (except when used exclusively for domestic, agricultural, or farming purposes, or on H.M.S., railways, steamships, and roads), unless such person had obtained from him a certificate by examination; or on application with proof of practical experience. Certificates by examination were to be ranked as first-class; certificates on application, with proof of practical experience, were to be ranked as second-class. This Bill, introduced by the "labour leaders," would give the highest ranks of labour a monopoly of the market, which, in the interests of wage-earners generally, is not desirable. The Bill was wholly unnecessary and uncalled for; there is not, and never has been, any genuine demand for it among working men; it is unsupported by facts or statistics; it may work enormous injury and injustice to every employer in the United Kingdom using steam power.

All three Bills were opposed at the instance of the Chamber of Shipping of the United Kingdom and the Shipowners' Parliamentary

Committee. Over 24,000 printed Summaries and Objections were sent to Federated Societies, Members of Parliament, and elsewhere. The Bills were persistently "blocked" at the request of the League, and were eventually dropped.

The Steam Engines and Boilers (Persons in Charge) Bill affords good illustrations of the blind manner in which the House of Commons frequently passes legislation which happens to be initiated and supported by the so-called "Labour" members. That the second reading of a measure of this kind should have been carried by 203 votes to 137 surprised a good many people when the true character of the Bill was made known to them by the League in a Memorandum which was issued on the subject and distributed among members of Parliament, the press, and the general public. Seeing that the House refused to proceed any further with the Bill, it may indeed be questioned whether any but a small proportion of the majority who voted for the second reading really knew what it was they were voting for. The following is an extract from the Memorandum issued by the League :—

> The Bill, if it became law, could not prevent explosions, accidents, or loss of life. Occasional causes of such calamities are carelessness, drunkenness, malice, etc., on the part of men in charge of boilers and engines. During the last twenty years no accident attributable to ignorance or incompetence on the part of "persons in charge" has occurred in the United Kingdom, *except in trades exempted from this Bill.* Why its promoters are willing to exempt those trades is explained further on. The Bill does not provide any test for ascertaining whether a person offering to take charge of engines and boilers is careless, a drunkard, malicious, etc., while an ample and unerring test in respect to experience, capability, etc., of such persons already exists, no other being required. Owners of expensive boilers and engines never have given, and never will give, charge of their property to a mechanic without first inquiring into the mechanic's fitness for his work. No owner of machinery can possibly want to have an explosion or accident on his premises, which might wreck his machinery, stop his business, and involve him in heavy damages.
>
> There is no demand among trade unionists, engineers, or working men for this Bill. Its very existence and its purport are unknown to 999 out of every 1,000 working men in the United Kingdom to-day. Resolutions in favour of this Bill have regularly appeared on the Agenda Paper at Trade Union Congresses for many years past, and have been "run through," without discussion, at the bidding of the well-known group of agitators who manipulate those Congresses—like resolutions in favour of land nationalization, or

other schemes in which trade unionists take no interest, which they have never instructed their supposed representatives at these Congresses to deal with at all.

The Bill was drafted and devised many years ago by a small group of so-called "Labour" leaders—actually socialist agitators—who live and thrive on strikes and social discord, when not drawing salaries from Radical party funds, on the off-chance that Parliament might let it slip through some day. The object—the sole object—of the Bill is perfectly plain and manifest. Since there is no active agitation at present among agricultural labourers, the so-called "Labour" leaders are willing to exempt agricultural machinery—actually the most liable to get into incompetent hands.

If the Bill became law, it would be used by socialist agitators in the following very practical way:—No engine could be started in the majority of factories, or in any steam-power-using enterprize in the United Kingdom, unless an officially "certificated person in charge" handled the throttle valve. Knowing what power this enactment would give them, the "Labour" leaders would, by their usual agencies—threats, coercion, and terrorism—insist on every qualified man in the kingdom joining a "Certificated Engineers' Trade Union." The Union once thoroughly organized, a small group of irresponsible socialist agitators in London, calling themselves "Labour" leaders, would find themselves possessed of statutory power to *stop every factory or enterprise depending on steam power in the kingdom in one day*. That socialist "Labour" leaders are perfectly prepared, and anxious, to abuse power in a similar way was proved recently, on a smaller scale, during the abortive cab strike. Efforts were then made to stop, or control, the issue of drivers' licenses by the authorities, on the sham plea that the public were not "safe" in the hands of newly-licensed men; really in order that the agitators interested might be able to prohibit cab and omnibus traffic in the Metropolis until their demands were conceded. This Bill gives to the same group of agitators who figured in the cab strike a like weapon to that which they attempted to obtain from the police authorities.

If the Bill became law, thousands of employers, especially mine-owners, would be absolutely at the mercy of a "Certificated Engineers' Trade Union," and of the agitators controlling it. Were the often-threatened "general strike" to be attempted by the Socialist Labour party, there might be plenty of perfectly competent and trustworthy men without "certificates" willing to take temporary charge of pumping, ventilating, etc., engines; this Bill would prohibit any of them going to work until examined and certified by the class of persons who now-a-days figure as Home Office inspectors. It might be objected that certificates could be easily and quickly obtained by competent men in emergencies. But employers would do well to bear in mind that, as shown during the recent debate on the Bethesda quarry dispute, the agents or "Labour" officials under the Board of Trade are mostly socialist agitators on half pay; while, under a so-called Conservative Government, the Department itself has been used to further socialist attacks on "capitalism." Employers and steam users ought, therefore, to consider seriously what their position is likely to be should the tremendous weapon provided by this Bill fall into the hands of some future Socialist-Radical Government, with a "Labour" Home Secretary and a host of pensioned socialist agitators acting as examiners under this Bill, and able to grant, delay, or withhold engineers' "certificates" to suit the purposes of a Strike Committee.

The **Trawlers Licensing** Bill proposed that no fishing-boat, being a trawler of twenty-five tons and upwards, shall put to sea from any port in the United Kingdom unless licensed by the Board of Trade. License to be suspended on conviction of offence of illegal trawling, the owner or master fined a sum not exceeding the estimated market value of any boat used during suspension of license. *Objections:* The Bill was a harsh and unnecessary restraint of trade, and shifted the responsibility of an illegal action from the shoulders of the master of the vessel on to the unoffending smackowner, who has no opportunity to control his property when once it leaves the harbour. It was opposed by the League at the instance of the Great Grimsby Smackowners Association, Limited, and the Lowestoft Trawling Smack Protection Society, Limited, and, being persistently blocked, lapsed owing to prorogation.

TRADE IN ALCOHOL.

As in the previous Sessions, the **Grocers' Certificates' Scotland (Abolition); Liquor Traffic Local Veto; Liquor Traffic Local Veto (Scotland); Sunday Closing (Wales) Act, 1881, Amendment; Sale of Intoxicating Liquors to Children**; and **Wine and Beerhouse Acts Amendment** Bills were introduced into the House of Commons, and put down for second reading. Each Bill was systematically "blocked," and was either dropped before second reading or finally lapsed owing to prorogation intervening.

Details of these Bills have already been given in previous Parliamentary Reports. They were opposed this session at the instance of the Dublin Licensed Grocers' and Vintners' Association,

Belfast and Ulster Vintners' Association, Federated Brewers' Association, Licensed Victuallers' Defence League of England and Wales, the Beer and Wine Trade National Defence League. National Federation of Off-License Holders' Association, Scottish Licensed Trade Defence Association, Northern Districts Beer and Wine Trade Defence League, and other bodies ; and over 20,000 printed summaries and objections respecting each Bill were sent to the press, Federated Societies, Members of Parliament, and elsewhere.

Sale of Intoxicating Liquors (Ireland): To compel the closing during the whole of Sunday of all places for the sale of alcoholic drinks in Dublin, Belfast, and the other towns exempted by Parliament in 1878 from the operations of the Irish Sunday Closing Act. This Bill was opposed by the League at the instance of the Dublin Licensed Grocers' and Vintners' Association, and the Belfast and Ulster Vintners' Association. In co-operation with the various liquor Trade Associations in England, the Parliamentary Committee of the League took steps to have the Bill opposed on the motion for second reading; and, in addition to statements of objections to the Bill, special telegraphic whips were sent to members of the House of Commons, urging them to oppose the second reading. In previous sessions the second reading of this Bill was carried by large majorities. Owing, however, to the action of the League and its federated Societies, the majority in favour of the second reading in the present instance was reduced to twenty-nine—201 members voting for, and 172 against, the second reading. The continued opposition of the League and its federated Societies resulted in the withdrawal of the Bill.

Sale of Intoxicating Liquors on Sundays: To compel the closing of all hotels and public-houses throughout England during the whole of Sunday. Experience of such legislation in the case of Wales and Scotland shows that it tends to force drinking facilities into working-men's clubs and private gatherings, with demoralizing results. The Bill was opposed by the League, and statements of objections to its provisions were circulated among members of Parliament and elsewhere. On February 10th a telegraphic whip was sent to League members and supporters in the House of Commons, and the motion for second reading was defeated by 206 to 149; majority against, 57.

Injuries to Workmen (Employers' Liability): This Bill provided that where a workman was injured in pursuit of his employment, whether by the negligence of his master or of his fellow-servants, or as the result of a pure accident, compensation should be paid by his employer. At the request of the Liverpool Shipowners' Association, the Parliamentary Committee of the League opposed this Bill on the ground that, if passed, the measure would be one of far-reaching application, and would bear very heavily upon shipowners, mine-owners, and, indeed, all classes of employers. It was estimated that the cost of compensation to shipowners alone would not be less than £500,000, and the promoter of the Bill admitted that the cost to each sailing ship would be £48 per annum. The Bill was full of traps, penalties, novel risks, and hindrances, which would press hardly upon struggling employers of labour and manufacturers, and the only people likely to benefit from such a measure would be the foreign manufacturers, who are not handicapped by similar legislation. Copies of a statement of objections to the Bill were circulated among members of Parliament, and, at the instance of the League, the Bill was persistently blocked during the time it appeared among the Orders of the Day. The Bill was ultimately dropped.

Workmen (Compensation for Accidents): This Bill, which was introduced by the Government, proposed to make an employer liable to pay compensation for injury to a workman, even though that injury was directly due to the fault or disobedience of the workman. Provided for settlement of disputes on the subject by reference to arbitration. The Bill applied only to employment on, in, or about a railway, factory, mine, quarry, or engineering work; it allowed contracting out only on certification by the Registrar of Friendly Societies that such scheme is not less favourable to the workmen than this Act. In conjunction with its federated Societies, the League opposed the Bill, on the grounds that it would inevitably reduce wages, since the foreign consumer will not pay an enhanced price for coal and such other of his imports as could be produced in his own country or obtained elsewhere more cheaply; it would foment strikes, promote accidents, and encourage carelessness, malingering, and idleness; and that it would lead to the extinction of voluntary accident funds. It was held that upon small capitalists the effect would be most disastrous, if not ruinous, and that it would dispose employers to seek relief from their individual responsibility by insuring heavily against risk, and rejecting, at the instance of the insurance companies, the old, infirm, and incapable workmen now retained from kindly motives. As contracting out was only permitted by license, the Bill distinctly interfered with freedom of contract. The League opposed the Bill at various stages in the House of Commons, through which House it passed with amendments. In the House of Lords the Chairman of the League Parliamentary Committee gave notice that he would move the rejection of the second reading of the Bill; but, in deference to the wishes of Lord Londonderry and the coal-owners, the motion for the rejection of the Bill was withdrawn. It was thought that, by persisting in the motion, the efforts of those who were seeking to amend the Bill might be frustrated. At the third reading stage the Chairman of the League Parliamentary Committee moved the rejection of the Bill, in order that a protest on behalf of the League and its federated Societies might be made against legislation of this character.

CONCLUDING REMARKS.

This resume of the year's work shows that the League has not been idle, and that, by the concerted efforts of its members and Federated Societies, a great mass of mischievous and predatory legislation has been successfully opposed. By securing the co-operation of all persons individually opposed to the principle of State Socialism in all or any one of its instances, and by concentrating into a system of mutual defence the forces of the Defence Associations of the various industries in the country, and of independent Companies and Corporate Bodies, the League seeks to resist all attempts on the part of the State or the Municipalities to restrict freedom of contract and freedom of labour, to harass private enterprise, or to unduly interfere with the rights of property. In carrying on this good and necessary work the Council invite the support of all persons who sympathize with the sound political and economic principles the League exists to maintain. This work, entailing as it does a heavy expenditure, cannot be continued with any degree of success unless those in whose behalf it is undertaken subscribe liberally towards the League funds. Persons and Corporate Bodies wishing to join the League are requested to send their subscriptions, with address, to Lloyds Bank, Limited (Herries, Farquhar, Branch), 16, St. James's Street, London, S.W.; or to the Secretary, Liberty and Property Defence League, 7, Victoria Street, London, S.W.

December 31st, 1897.

PUBLICATIONS SUPPLIED BY THE

Liberty and Property Defence League.

OFFICES :—7, VICTORIA STREET, LONDON, S.W.

Nationalization of Land. By LORD BRAMWELL. Seventh Edition. 1d.
Drink. By the same Author. 107th thousand. 1d.
Economics *versus* **Socialism.** By the same Author. 1d.
Labour Capitalization. By WORDSWORTH DONISTHORPE. 6d.
Municipal Socialism. By W. C. CROFTS. 1d.
Duties of the State. By the HON. DAVID DUDLEY FIELD. 1d.
The Man *versus* **the State.** By HERBERT SPENCER. 1s.
Land Nationalization. A Correspondence Discussion. 1d.
For Freedom. Three Lectures on the Fallacies of State Socialism. By J. McGAVIN SLOAN. 6d.
Prohibition in Canada and the United States. By Professor GOLDWIN SMITH. 6d.
Socialism in England. By the EARL OF WEMYSS. 1d.
Modern Municipalism. By the same Author. 1d.
The Socialist Spectre. By the same Author. 1d.
Trade Unionism and Free Labour. Speeches by LORDS WEMYSS, BRAMWELL, and FORTESCUE. 1d.
Is Socialism Desirable? Debate between Miss ENID STACY, B.A., and Rev. A. SETON, M.A. 2d.
A Plea for Liberty: An Argument against Socialism and Socialistic Legislation. 2s.
Capital, Labour, and Taxation. By C. McKAY SMITH. 2d.
A Criticism of the Theory of Trade Unions. By T. S. CREE. Third Edition. 2d.
Trade Unionism: A Criticism and a Warning. By JAMES BIRKS.
Trade Unionism in Relation to Wages. By the same Author. 6d.
Old Age Pensions. By GEOFFREY DRAGE, M.P. 1d.
The Pretensions of Socialism. By M. YVES GUYOT. 1d.
The State Control of Labour. By the same Author. 1d.
Socialism and Social Discord. By W. H. MALLOCK. 1d.
Land Nationalization. By the Hon. L. F. HEYDON. 1d.
A Shorter Catechism of the Land Question. By JOHN D. SPENCE. 1d.
On Liberty and Property. By the Right Hon. SIR MOUNTSTUART E. GRANT DUFF, G.C.S.I. (late Governor of Madras). 1d.
Conservatives or Socialists? By J. BUCKINGHAM POPE. 1s.
Property in Land: A Justification of Individual Ownership. By J. C. SPENCE. Second Edition. 1d.
Liberty and Property: The Two Main Factors of Human Progress. By PAUL LEROY BEAULIEU. 1d.
The Case Against Picketing. By W. J. SHAXBY. Third Edition. 1s. 6d.
Socialism in France. By J. T. FINDLAY. 6d.
An Eight Hours' Day: The Case against Legislative and Trade Union Interference. By W. J. SHAXBY. *(In the Press.)*

Complete List of Publications, Particulars as to Membership, Copies of the Annual and Parliamentary Reports, and set of "Liberty Leaves," Free on Application.

No. 7. 50,000. SENT FREE

THE FARMERS WANT TO KNOW.

Challenge of the State Grange of Pennsylvania to the Home Market Club of Boston, and Its Reply.

Counterstatement Proving the Enormous Cost of the Protective System, and Which Falls as an Unjust Burden Upon Agriculture—Why a Tariff on Imports Cannot Protect the Staples of Agriculture, and Why an Export Bounty Can.

In the minutes of the last meeting of the State Grange of Pennsylvania, held at Williamsport, Pa., December 10, 1895, appears the following resolution or

CHALLENGE.

WHEREAS, Report 1999, House of Representatives, Fifty-third Congress, Third Session, page 13, contains the following:

First, the American Protective Tariff League requested Brother David Lubin of Sacramento, Cal., to contribute to the funds of said League.

Second, a contribution of $1,000 was accordingly handed to the President of the Bank of D. O. Mills & Co., with instructions to pay same to said League, provided that a committee of five named, or to be impartially selected, would decide (a) that the present system of protection by a tariff on imports is just and equitable to the producers of agricultural staples as long as there is a surplus of these staples to export, (b) or that a bounty on exports of agricultural staples would be unjust or inequitable as long as there is a protective tariff on imports; and,

WHEREAS, The said League, in reply to the offer, stated that it would be submitted to its Executive Committee, but, so far as known, took no further action in the matter; and,

WHEREAS, on September 4th of this year, seven thousand farmers gathered at the Interstate Harvest Home meeting at Maryville, Missouri, did submit the above questions to the said Tariff League; and,

WHEREAS, The State Granges of California and Missouri, at their last annual meetings this year, also submitted the above questions to the organization named, to all of which no reply was made; and,

WHEREAS, Deeming correct answers to the above questions not alone of vital importance to the producers of agricultural staples, but to the American people; and,

WHEREAS, The American Protective Tariff League and the Home Market Club are assumed to be well versed in the operation of protection by a tariff on imports and are assumed to be representative exponents of protection; therefore, be it

Resolved By this State Grange of Pennsylvania, at its regular annual meeting held at Williamsport, Pa., that we respectfully, earnestly and urgently request said Tariff League and the Home Market Club to forward to the Secretary of this State Grange for general publication, replies to the following questions:

First, can a tariff on imports directly or indirectly protect the home market prices of agricultural staples as long as the surplus is sold for export, and the export and home price for these are the same?

Second, if it cannot, must not this unprotected industry pay for the cost of protection of the protected industries?

Third, is not such a system of protection injuriously unjust and inequitable to the producers of agricultural staples?

Fourth, will not a bounty on the export of agricultural staples for the protection of their prices in the home market be just and equitable so long as protection by a tariff on imports is in operation?

Resolved, That a copy of this preamble and resolutions be at once mailed to the

President and Secretary of the American Protective Tariff League, No. 125 West Twenty-third street, New York City, and to the President and Secretary of the Home Market Club, No. 56 Bedford street, Boston, Mass.

Passed by the State Grange of Pennsylvania at Williamsport, December 10, 1895.

[The American Protective Tariff League made no reply to the above challenge.]

On February 1st, 1896, the undersigned received a communication from Worthy Master, Leonard Rhone, of the State Grange of Pennsylvania, drawing attention to an enclosure, which was a reply to the above challenge by the Home Market Club of Boston, as follows:

THE HOME MARKET CLUB.

EXECUTIVE COMMITTEE.

CHARLES A. SCOTT, President.
ALBERT CLARKE, Secretary.
BEVELEY K. MOORE, Treasurer.
JOHN SHAW, Quincy.
JOHN HOPEWELL, JR., Boston.
O. H. SAMPSON, Boston.
FREDERICK E. CLARKE, Lawrence.
GEORGE L. HOOPER, Lowell,

56 Bedford and 53 Avon streets.

BOSTON, Mass., January 14, 1896.

MR. J. T. AILMAN, SECRETARY OF PENNSYLVANIA STATE GRANGE PATRONS OF HUSBANDRY, Thompsontown, Pa.

DEAR SIR: Your favor of December 30th, enclosing a copy of some resolutions adopted by the Pennsylvania State Grange, December 10, 1895, propounding certain questions to the Home Market Club, was duly received and the same has been candidly considered. It gives me pleasure to reply to the questions, in the order propounded, as follows:

1. Yes, we think that a tariff on imports of agricultural staples, of which our country has a surplus for export, can and does protect the home market price of such staples, to some extent, because seaboard markets and those along the Canadian border would often be supplied by foreign products instead of our own, if there were no duty. Two factors would cause this: (1), proximity and the small cost of transportation, and (2), the convenience and economy to vessels of having return cargoes. It is not claimed that the extent of protection by duties is so great as it would be if we had no surplus for export, but it is considerable.

2. This question is partly answered above, by the showing that it is based in part upon a wrong premise. But a further answer is this: There are no unprotected industries. Protection of the home market is or should be applied to every industry that is subject to foreign competition. The cost and also the benefit of it then diffuse themselves upon all classes according to the extent of their consumption. The great development of our country and the constant reduction in the prices of manufactures prove that the benefit is much greater than the cost. The fact that farmers can buy all kinds of goods which are now made in this country on a commercial scale at prices relatively lower than the prices of farm products, when compared with prices for both which prevailed before protection had developed home competition, shows that the agricultural class fully shares the benefit. If any other class gets a greater benefit it is the operative class, which, as statistics in Massachusetts show, derives a little more from manufactures than capital receives. But this has so greatly increased the purchasing power of this class that the home market for all the products of our farms has been developed even more than agriculture. Under any economic condition it is impossible that all classes and individuals should fare exactly alike, but protection by duties, when impartially applied, insures to all an equal opportunity throughout our national domain. All the rest must depend upon themselves.

3. Such a system is not unjust to the producers of agricultural staples, (1), because it does not tax them any more than it taxes all other consumers; (2), because it does not force them to produce a surplus for export, as greater purchases of foreign manufactures tend to do, and (3), because it continually increases the home market so that consumption is rapidly overtaking production, thus bringing the time nearer when duties on wheat will be as protective as duties on barley, fruits or vegetables.

4. A bounty on exported farm products would not, in our opinion, permanently help the prices of such products in the home market. It would not be paid directly to the farmer. Its first effect would be to enable the exporting merchant to cut prices abroad just enough to sell his stock. This, of course, would depress the foreign price, so that the farmer would get little or none of the bounty and

would be taxed his share to pay it. In this connection it should be observed that only a small number of our farmers raise anything for export. The greater number—three-fourths of the whole at least - would therefore be taxed to help the others and receive no benefit; on the contrary, if the bounty raised the price of wheat, the millions of farmers who buy flour would have to pay the advance. A second effect of the bounty would be to enable foreign manufacturers to reduce the wages of labor, on account of their cheaper loaf, and thus they could the more easily overcome our duties and crush some of the industries in this country. This would hurt the farmer's home market far more than the bounty would help it. A third effect of the bounty would be to invite similar legislation by other countries with which we compete, or to lead them to place higher duties on all imports from this country so long as we pay export bounties. We have set the example for such legislation ourselves. So, by one or both means the hoped-for benefit from the bounty would be completely neutralized,

Thus we have endeavored to answer each of your questions, fairly and as fully as seems necessary to acquaint you with our views. Much more, of course, can be said on every aspect of the case, and under another cover I send a pamphlet which contains a discussion of it by Mr. Lubin and Mr. Alexander R. Smith on the one hand and by the writer on the other; also, a copy of the January number of the *Home Market Bulletin* containing the conclusions of economists who recently heard the matter at Washington.

In behalf of the Home Market Club, I have the honor to be, very respectfully yours, ALBERT CLARKE, Secretary.

REPLY BY DAVID LUBIN,

OF SACRAMENTO, CALIFORNIA.

It shall be my endeavor to reply to the above as clearly and briefly as possible.

The Home Market Club says that it has "candidly considered" the above challenge. Very good. Let us now see if its answers are equally candid. It starts out by saying: "That a tariff on imports of agricultural staples, of which our country has a surplus for export, can and does protect the home market price of such staples." This assertion is plain and clear-cut, but, unfortunately, not true; besides, it lacks candor. The Secretary of the Home Market Club made a similar statement at the conference held in Washington, D. C., on December 20th and 21st, 1895, on this Proposition, and called upon Professor Gunton, teacher of economics in New York, to sustain him. The professor (though reluctantly) admitted that agricultural staples producing a surplus were sold in the United States at the world's international free trade prices, not alone for the surplus exported, but for the greater quantity sold for home use as well, and whether sold to free-trade buyers for export or whether sold to those who were protected and protectionists for home use. However, the Home Market Club, in its reply, modifies its statement somewhat by using the words "to some extent." Let us ask to what extent? The "United States Statistics, Treasury Department, imported merchandise entered for consumption, 1890-1893," on page 25, fourth item, shows that the United States only collected $1,973 37 duty on wheat. What kind of wheat? Can the Home Market Club tell? Is it not the kind principally from Manitoba, which, as a rule, is used for special purposes, such as in the manufacture of macaroni, etc.? This same item in the statistics shows that the duty is 20 per cent. Can a Canadian afford to sell us ordinary marketable wheat at 20 per cent. less than the world's price—when he can obtain the world's price in Canada, and also from buyers for export to England, the very same price that we receive in the United States? What idiotic policy would have a Canadian sell us his wheat 20 per cent. less than he can get for it?

It may be true that in a few instances the Canadian may be so geographically situated, for instance, some range of mountains or other obstruction before him may serve as a barrier in disposing of his crop to the English or home buyer; that because of this barrier he may still find it to his advantage to cross the boundary line to our side and pay the 20 per cent. duty, and have that much deducted from the world's price. Apart from these two reasons given, there are none other why

Canadian, Argentine or Russian wheat should come into our ports, even though there were no duty, for if we sell our surplus at all it must be sold in direct competition with the world's surplus. This is now well known to the Secretary of the Home Market Club, for the able authority which he brought to the Washington Conference amplified and thoroughly explained this fact, that our agricultural staples producing a surplus were sold in the home market (the entire product, mind) at the world's international free trade prices. The conclusion, therefore, is clear that a tariff on imports cannot protect the staples of agriculture so long as we have a surplus for export. So much for this point.

In the second paragraph the Home Market Club says: "There are no unprotected industries." This is not true, for corn, cornmeal, cotton, tobacco, wheat, flour, hops and other agricultural staples of which we export a surplus, as has been shown above, are unprotected.

In the same paragraph the Home Market Club says: "Protection of the home market is or should be applied to every industry that is subject to foreign competition." Very good. This certainly is candid. But the Home Market Club forgot to tell us how the prices of agricultural staples in this country could be protected against the direct competition in the home market of the prices of similar products of Argentine, India, Russia and Egypt!

In the same paragraph the Home Market Club also says that "the benefits of it (protection) then diffuse themselves upon all classes." The Home Market Club has forgotton to tell us how any benefit of protection reaches the producers of agricultural staples. It has also forgotten to tell us in what position it places the producers of these staples if they are unprotected!

Promising in the beginning of its letter to be candid, the Home Market Club should have told us that the unprotected must pay for the protection of the protected industries. However, there is no accounting for taste or style. Some advocates start out by saying that they will be candid, that is, truthful, and are really so. Others start out with the same assertion, but very shortly after forget all about it.

Let the members of the subordinate Granges of Pennsylvania carefully read this document and decide which side is really candid; which side truthful.

ON WHOM DOES THE BURDEN OF PROTECTION FALL?

The Home-Market Club in the beginning of its third clause claims that protection, limited to a tariff on imports "is not unjust to the producers of agricultural staples, because it does not tax them any more than it taxes all others concerned." This is manifestly untrue. It not alone taxes them more, but places the entire tax indirectly resulting from the protective system on their shoulders. The protected make a profit by it much greater than the cost to them for higher prices. This is the reason why the protected are so anxious to vote for protection. But when it comes to the unprotected producers of agricultural staples, they pay for protection and sell at free trade prices. The difference, caused by this, is the actual cost of the protective system, which the producers of agricultural staples pay, and which fact no capable and honest political economist can deny or refute.

In this same paragraph the Home Market Club says that the protective tariff "does not force them (the producers of agricultural staples) to produce a surplus for export." This is quite ingenious, but let us ask the Home Market Club, what Protectionists would do if there were no surplus of agricultural staples to send abroad at free-trade prices? With what would we pay for our imports, for our coffee, teas, spices, drugs, raw materials and other things that we must have? Would it be with protected knives at $8 a dozen, which are worth in England $3 30 a dozen? Let the Home Market Club please answer! Does it not also know, that while manufacturers have it in their power to make goods in advance, send out drummers on the road and just make enough to sell at a profit, that agricultural producers can do no such thing? What sections of the country then shall cease producing the staples to get them below the export line? Shall it be Virginia with her tobacco,

Georgia with her cotton, California with her wheat, or Washington with her hops? Shall these States become uninhabited again? What kind of logic, what kind of reason, what kind of sincerity have we in this statement of the Home Market Club? It refuses to have protection and enhancement of the home price for agricultural staples by an Export Bounty, and in the only way by which protection can be had for this great industry, but hints that it would not object to this enhancement by a tariff on imports if there were no surplus! All this time it must know that this surplus is first of all absolutely necessary, and secondly that our economic and geographical conditions do not permit the doing away with the surplus. For the same reason, we may frankly question its sincerity when it says that the time is coming when consumption must rapidly overcome production. This might happen under free trade, provided free trade can furnish sufficient manufactures for export at free trade prices to pay for our imports.

WOULD AN EXPORT BOUNTY PROTECT THE FARMER?

In section four, the Home Market Club says: "A bounty on exported farm products would not, in our opinion, permanently help the prices of such products in the home market. It would not be paid directly to the farmer." The opposers of this proposition seem to have kaleidoscopic skill in dodging. At the Washington Conference they opposed the Export Bounty on the ground that it would raise the home price to the poor man, the consumer, and in this instance it is opposed on the ground that it would not raise the price in the home market at all. Now which is it?

That the Export Bounty would not be paid directly to the farmer if he did not export, is true. But this does not prove that the farmer would not receive in the home market, as he does now, the world's price with the addition of the Export Bounty.

OPINION OF THE SECRETARY OF THE CHICAGO BOARD OF TRADE.

An Export Bounty on the staples of agriculture would give the producer, as at present, the world's price with the addition of the Export Bounty, the same as the millers in France receive every penny of the Export Bounty on their flour at the present time. That this is true, is amply corroborated by the statement of Mr. George F. Stone, given in his official capacity as Secretary of the Board of Trade of the City of Chicago, as may be seen from Report No. 1999, House of Representatives, Fifty-third Congress, Third Session, page 39, a portion of which is here reproduced:

Q.—Mr. Stone, it is desired to ask you a few questions in your official capacity as Secretary of the Board of Trade of the City of Chicago.

What effect would a Government Bounty on the exports of wheat have with regard to the general price of wheat throughout the United States?

A.—It would, in my opinion, increase the price per bushel.

Q.—It is said that the speculators would get the 5 cents or 10 cents export bounty, or at least the greater part of it?

A.—If a bounty of 5 cents or 10 cents a bushel should be given by the Government on all wheat exported from this country, in my opinion, the farmer or producer, would receive the full benefit of that bounty and not the speculator or exporter. It would simply enable the buyer to pay that much more than he otherwise could pay or would be justified in paying. Competition would force him to pay all he could to the farmer to obtain his wheat. The fierceness and intensity and volume of competition, by the very force of circumstances, by the very necessities of the case, would drive the 5 cents or 10 cents bounty proposed by the Government into the pockets of the farmer, or producer. There it would land and from there it could never be wrested by speculators or by anybody else.

Q.—It is also said that the ship-owners would get this 5 cents or 10 cents, or the greater part of it?

A.—I believe the answer to that is fully embraced in the reply which I have hereinbefore given.

Q.—It is also claimed by some that the 5 cents or 10 cents would come in some way to the producer for the quantity which would be exported, but that there would be no advance on the greater quantity remaining for home use?

A.—It is a mistake, in my opinion, to say that the 5 cents or 10 cents per bushel bounty, which it is proposed to give, would be confined in its beneficial result to the quantity or volume of grain exported. It would affect the price of the entire crop, for the reason that grain is a surplus crop in this country, and consequently the price per bushel of this grain is fixed and controlled by the export price of this grain, and this export price, of course, I will here say, parenthically, is made in competition with all the other surplus wheat-producing countries in the world. No domestic buyer will pay one single fraction of a cent more for a single bushel of wheat than the buyer for export will pay. The latter makes the price for the entire crop. If no more were raised than was required for home consumption the price would depend upon the domestic demand; but the export demand, inasmuch as the demand for food can never be interrupted for any length of time, and this continuous demand for wheat, so far as a surplus wheat producing country is concerned, fixes the price of the entire crop of this cereal of this country. No class of domestic buyers, of course, can be made to pay any more than the price offered by the export demand, the domestic and the export demand being ever present in the market.

GEORGE F. STONE,
Secretary of the Board of Trade of the City of Chicago.

December 20, 1894.

Further on, in the same paragraph, the Home Market Club states that the Export Bounty "would depress the foreign price." Well, supposing for the sake of argument it would? What then? It would then become an engine to curtail foreign production and at the same time protect the home producer of agricultural staples by giving him that much higher price above the lowered world's price, and would, by this means, just reverse the destructive method now in operation. Some protectionists claim that while the producers of agricultural staples cannot be directly protected by a protective tariff on imports, they are thereby indirectly protected, because it enables the payment of a higher wage rate, greater consumption and consequent increase of the home price of these products. But whose price? What price?—The world's international price, of course! Therefore, if there is any foundation for the claim of indirect protection, where does it lead to? To this: that the Argentine, Indian, Russian and Egyptian producers have their prices raised artificially by our present protective system. Does it benefit our producers? Not at all, for the little advance in the world's price as the indirect result of protection by a tariff on imports costs them many more times that probable advance. It is clear profit, however, to the foreign producers in every country of the world, but not to ours. This, once for all, sweeps away every vestige of support from any claim, not alone of direct protection by a tariff on imports, but of indirect protection also.

There is not an honest, capable economist in the United States, England, France. Germany, anywhere, who can refute this; and it cannot be refuted, because it is true. If it is true it should be known to every producer of agricultural staples in the United States, and—as you all know—it is being made known quite thoroughly.

The Home Market Club does, not, however, seem to be quite so sure that the Export Bounty would not raise the home price of agricultural staples, for it warns the farmers who buy flour that they would have to pay the advance. Well, these farmers would surely find it no hardship to pay the advance. Is it not a greater hardship, a greater injustice to compel the unprotected farmer at the present time to pay for the protection of the protected?

A WORD WITH FARMERS WHO PRODUCE FRUITS, DAIRY PRODUCTS, GARDEN TRUCK, POULTRY, ETC.

There is another view of this question which requires the earnest attention of farmers who produce products which are not exported, and it is this: Unless the staples of agriculture are as profitable as other farm products, what will be the result? Would it not be general diversification? Would not vast bodies of land in the West and South be put into the production of hay, potatoes, poultry, livestock, vegetables, fruits, dairy products and such other things now produced in those sections adjacent to large cities? What would happen in that event? Would that not lower the price of those products below the profit point also? Would it not besides lower the price of lands and improvements? Most assuredly. Has not this kind of competition already been felt in the East? Let the producers of dairy products in Herkimer County, New York, the potato growers in Accomac County, Virginia, answer! The fruit-growers of California, Delaware and Michigan will soon learn to their sorrow what "diversification" means when the fruits grown in the now unprofitable cotton fields in the South come into Eastern markets! And what Eastern farmer can say that it has not already lowered the prices of his product, his land and his improvements? Even this is but a small sample of what will follow, unless the production of agricultural staples be made more profitable than at present. It can be made more profitable by one of two methods. One is by absolute unrestricted free trade, and the other is protection by an Export Bounty.

Further on in the same paragraph the Home Market Club makes a statement that "the effect of the bounty would enable foreign manufacturers to reduce the wages of labor on account of their cheaper loaf." Is not our tariff of over 40 per cent., (which almost doubles by profits of the middlemen added to it,) high enough to keep out foreign competition? If not, it only manifests the deplorable injustice of the present protective system, and its enormous cost to the producers of agricultural staples.

The Home Market Club is not candid enough to admit, however, that should England obtain a cheaper loaf by an Export Bounty, this bounty would at the same time tend to crush out foreign competition in the production of agricultural staples, but by reason of the Export Bounty, our own producers of these staples would be protected in the home market.

A REASON THAT IS NOT VALID.

In paragraph 4 the Home Market Club gives a strange reason why the producers of agricultural staples should not be protected by an Export Bounty, saying "that only a small number of our farmers raise anything for export." Do not a small number of manufacturers produce suspenders, or knives, or pins? Yet every producer of agricultural staples must pay protection prices for suspenders, knives or pins, and many thousand other things which are protected.

But the Home Market Club is mistaken in its estimate. That there are many farmers who produce staples for export can be ascertained by the United States statistics, which shows that out of $800,000,000 exports annually, over $600,000,000 are in staples of agriculture, and $200,000,000 in mining, fish, manufactures, forest and miscellaneous.

The Home Market Club further on warns farmers who do not produce the staples by saying that they would be "taxed to help others (the producers of agricultural staples), and receive no benefit." In this the Home Market Club is mistaken. Apart from the question of equity, there is a very good reason why the producers of agricultural staples should be protected.

To leave them unprotected, and at the mercy of a declining world's price, is to drive them in large numbers into the production of the non-staple products, which must speedily result not alone in driving the non-staples of agriculture below the profit point, but also to greatly shrink the value of the land and improvements besides.

This is actually taking place now. Thousands of acres formerly profitably employed in raising cotton, corn, wheat, tobacco and hops, are now being put to use in root crops, hay, berries, fruits, dairy products and live stock.

This crowding into these branches of agriculture has already caused a serious shrinkage, but not near as much as it is likely to do as time rolls on.

The shrinkage is a much greater loss by far to the producers of non-staples of agriculture than any cost for protection by an Export Bounty.

Intelligent Eastern agriculturists are beginning to understand this.

Protectionists, like the Home Market Club, ought to realize that conditions have changed; that something must give; that the time has come when we must admit the producers of agricultural staples into the sacred precincts of real protection, or we must promptly abolish the whole of this system. Not alone does justice demand it, but the necessity of the times demands it.

WE ARE CONFRONTED BY NEW CONDITIONS.

The Home Market Club intimates that the Export Bounty on the part of our Government would cause retaliation on the part of foreign Governments. This objection has little, if any economic value. If foreign Governments are to retaliate, it is not at any internal arrangement, which would not interfere with foreign trade or foreign nations, which is simply intended to raise the home price in our own country. They have much more reason to retaliate on protective duties, which partially or entirely prohibit the sale of their goods in our own country. Take it in the case of England for instance: She admits our goods freely without hindrance, without toll, without duty, but, as will be shown, a dozen knives worth $3 30 in England is made to cost $8 a dozen in the the hands of the importer in this country.

In concluding this reply to the Home Market Club, an endeavor will be made to sustain question "two" of the "Challenge," which is as follows: "If a tariff on imports cannot protect the staples of agriculture must not this unprotected industry pay for the protection of the protected industries?"

To this the Home market Club replies first by saying, "There are no unprotected industries." This, in spite of the fact that its own chosen authority at the Washington Conference actually proved that agricultural staples were sold in the home market at international prices. But let that pass. Further on in the same paragraph it says: "The fact that farmers can buy all kinds of goods which are now made in this country on a commercial scale at prices relatively lower than the prices of farm products, when compared with prices for both which prevailed before protection had developed home competition, shows that the agricultural class fully shares the benefit."

Before the Home Market Club can hope to sustain its assertion, it will be obliged to refute the following facts and figures given in the article below. There are many importers, manufacturers, jobbers and retailers within a radius of several blocks of the office of the Home Market Club. If the Club can refute this, they will require very much less of the "campaign fund" than otherwise.

The language and terms used in the article are so clear and simple as to require no special study to understand them.

Let the Home Market Club's reply be equally clear and simple.

DOES PROTECTION ENHANCE PRICES OF IMPORTS AND OF DOMESTIC MANUFACTURES IN THE HOME MARKET? IF IT DOES, IS NOT THIS ENHANCEMENT PRIMARILY AT THE EXPENSE OF THE STAPLES OF AGRICULTURE, AND INDIRECTLY AT THE EXPENSE OF ALL OTHER AGRICULTURAL INTERESTS?

The Sacramento *Bee* in its issue of Thursday, February 13th, contains an important editorial headed "Japanese Competition," and quotes from a report that $50,000 wages in cotton manufactures in this country is equaled by $17,500 in Japan. The *Bee* shows that, unless Japanese manufactures are excluded by tariffs, the free entrance of Japanese goods would tend to lower our wage rate to the Japan level, and says "no decent American citizen wants that to be done. Similar opinions were recently expressed by a meeting of business men in San Francisco.

This is but an echoing of the more pronounced Eastern demand for higher protective duties. It would seem from all this, that it is in our power to overcome the destructive tendency of foreign competition by raising the tariff. A simple device surely, and one seemingly patriotic. Were it really effective in overcoming the destructive tendency of foreign competition, then, indeed, would statesmanship have a light task.

Unfortunately, however, there is another side to the story. Protection, as a means of maintaining a maximum rate of wages, is only effective when the purchasing power is sufficiently abundant to maintain a steady demand for labor. And the purchasing power, whence is it derived? In free trade England, from the profitable sale of her manufactures in foreign countries. In the United States, the primary purchasing power comes from agriculture—chiefly from the staples of agriculture.

That the purchasing power is diminished by our present system of protection there can be no question, for protection, limited to a tariff on imports, while it protects by enhancement everything protected, can neither protect directly nor indirectly the staples of agriculture, as is well known. Being unprotected, and paying for protection diminishes the power to buy, therefore reduces the purchasing power.

Any diminution of the purchasing power, must, however, counteract the benefits of protection, so far as the wage rate is concerned, and give us instead, low wages on the one hand, and abnormally high prices on the other. If this is true, then protection under our present system becomes an oppressive engine of extortion, enriching the few and impoverishing the millions. That this is really true, can be made manifest to everyone as indisputable evidences are at hand to prove it. At this time space will only permit me to give a single example, which can be multiplied by thousands.

The *Bee* quotes from a report showing that $50,000 wages in cotton manufactures in this country could be equaled in Japan for $17,500. This information is interesting, but not nearly as important to the State and to the Nation as are the questions and answers which follow:

AN ACCURATE ILLUSTRATION OF THE OPERATION OF THE PRESENT PROTECTION SYSTEM, SHOWING HOW IT UNJUSTLY AND OPPRESSIVELY BURDENS THE FARMER.

Q.—What would a California farmer receive for his wheat or hops if the quantity he had on hand was quoted in Liverpool as being worth $13,751 10?

A.—He would receive in Sacramento or in San Joaquin Counties about $10,500 for it,

Q.—If farmers in the West bought pocket knives at retail, costing in Liverpool at wholesale, $13,751 10, how much would they have to pay for them?

A.—Fifty thousand dollars.

Q.—Is there not some serious mistake here?

A.—No.

Q.—Why would wheat and hops bring so much less here than in Liverpool?

A.—Because there is deducted the cost of commission, interest, insurance and transportation on the wheat and hops from the place of production to Liverpool.

Q.—Supposing they are not exported, but sold to the Buffalo Brewery, Smith's or the Phœnix Mills here, or the Sperry Mills in Stockton, how much would these products bring?

A.—Not a penny more, for these products are sold at the world's free trade international prices.

Q.—Have we not a protective tariff?

A.—Yes.

Q.—Does it not protect?

A.—Yes, everything but agricultural staples. These a tariff on imports cannot protect directly nor indirectly.

Q.—Do not politicians and others say that it can?

A.—Yes; but some do not know, and others trample on the truth?

Q.—Is that example which you gave of the knives true?

A.—Yes, absolutely true, pocket knives costing $13,751 10 at wholesale in England retail for $50,000 in the United States.

Q.—What causes this enormous increase?

A.—The protective tariff, as may be seen from the following: 4,167 dozen pocket knives at $3 30 per dozen makes $13,751 10, to which add duty 50 per cent. and $2 per dozen, then add 15 per cent. profit on the total for the importer, 20 per cent. for the jobber's profit and 25 per cent. retailer's profit, and the total will be $50,000. If this is too much trouble, you can figure up one dozen, as follows: Cost in England, $3 30 duty, 50 per cent. and $2; 50 per cent. is $1 65, and the $2 is $3 65, and $3 30, makes a total cost to importer $6 95, on which add importer's profit 15 per cent. ($1 05), making cost price to jobber $8. Now, add

20 per cent. profit for jobber ($1 60), jobber's selling price to retailer is then $9 60, to which add 25 per cent. retailer's profit ($2 40), makes the dozen knives $12 or $1 each. As knives imported and of domestic manufacture of the same quality are sold at retail on a par value, it follows that the domestic price is artificially enhanced to the price of the foreign knife, with duties and compounded profits on duties by middlemen added thereto.

ACTUAL COST OF PROTECTION.

The following figures will give a correct idea of the cost of the protective tariff. These figures do not represent a single item of actual cost of material, labor or transportation. They are simply the cost of the protective tariff and compound profits on top of the tariff, which the unprotected farmers must pay whether they actually buy them, or whether some other persons buy them, so long as agricultural staples are unprotected.

Four thousand one hundred and sixty-seven dozen knives at $3.30 a dozen, duty $2 a dozen and 50 per cent.

Fifty per cent. on 4,167 dozen knives makes $6,875 55, to which add additional duty of $2 a dozen, or $8,334.

These added together make—	$6,875 55
	8,334 00
Total cost of duty at Custom House	$15,209 55
Profit on duty by importer, 15 per cent	2,281 43
	$17,490 98
Profit on duty by jobber, 20 per cent	3,498 20
	$20,989 18
Profit on duty by retailer, 25 per cent	5,247 29
Grand total of duty and compound profits on duty	$26,236 47

All of which is artificial enhancement by the protective tariff.

Q.—Where is the basis for these figures?

A.—The United States statistics, the George Wostenholm (I. X. L.), Sheffield, England, catalogue, and the usual profits of the middlemen. In summing up, I wish to say that protection by a tariff on imports swells the price of the English knife from 27½ cents to $1—52½ cents of which composes the cost of duty with compound profits on the duty. But, 27½ cents of agricultural staples may be had by the protected manufacturer for about 22 cents or less.

Q.—Are you sure that there is no mistake here?

A.—Quite sure.

What benefit does the producer of agricultural staples receive from this one-sided system? Absolutely none; on the contrary, his substance is devoured by it to enrich ambitious manufacturing corporations. Nor does the mischief of this one-sided and unjust system end here; it is but the beginning.

The shrinkage in the primary purchasing power takes the life out of all farming values, diminishes the demand for labor, and cuts the rates of wages right and left.

Shall we, then, have free trade? No; for that would be like "jumping from the frying-pan into the fire." We should have protection, but it should be a just and equitable protection. If imported and home manufactures are enhanced in price by a protective tariff, then we should have a system which shall also protect by enhancement in the home market the staples of agriculture. A tariff on imports cannot do this, it can be done by a bounty on the exports.

Protection by a bounty on exports is not new or untried. It is in operation in Germany, France, Russia and Austria. It is just as effective a mode of protection for agricultural staples as a tariff on imports is for the protection of manufactures. Eastern economists freely admit this. What they object to is the fact that it will enhance the home market prices of agricultural staples, and yet they ask farmers to vote for protection.

A CHALLENGE TO THE DEFENDERS OF THE PRESENT PROTECTIVE SYSTEM.

The American Protective Tariff League asked the writer of this to contribute liberally to its protection fund. One thousand dollars was accordingly deposited in the Bank of D. O. Mills & Co., with stipulation that it could have it on condition that the League could prove the present protective system just, or if it could prove protection to agricultural staples by an Export Bounty unjust. This offer was not taken up. Not because the League did not want the money, but because it knew that it could not sustain its unjust, one-sided system.

If there be any competent economist in this city, in this county, in this State, in this Nation, who can prove the present protection system just, or protection by an Export Bounty unjust or impracticable, then such a person is at liberty to take up this challenge, to be decided by the public at a meeting for that purpose.

If what has been set forth is true, then in that event it behooves all patriotic American citizens, especially those engaged in agriculture, to demand justice and equity in protection, and demand it in no uncertain terms.

How strange it is that the Western man living in a section, the primary industry of which is the production of agricultural staples, should feel so keenly the threatened competition of manufactures from Japan, and yet have so little to say in regard to the destructive competition which has already struck the producers of agricultural staples. Surely, there is either a lack of understanding of this condition, or a lack of patriotism. Which is it? Are the manufactures made of such sacred stuff that the mere threatening of foreign competition will shake up Boards of Trade and Chambers of Commerce in an endeavor to jump up the tariff on manufactures, and have so little to say on that industry—agriculture—which gives value to labor; which determines the price of city and country real estate, of securities; which determines the prosperity, the progress and the very life of the Nation? What does this mean? There is but one explanation.

Manufacturers are organized and have champions and leaders, all of which gives them the legislation which they demand. Shall we, then, vote to advance the prices of things which the Western and Southern States must buy, when we know that the West and South are at the mercy of the declining world's prices? Do we not see that this same cause, which animates the fears of protectionists, the competition of cheap labor in Japan, has already struck the Western and Southern producer by the unequal competition, from the direct international prices of Argentine, India, Russia and Egypt in the home market?

They tell us that machinery is now being employed for manufacturing purposes in Japan.

Why do not these Chambers of Commerce and Boards of Trade tell us that agricultural machinery is being sold to the cheap land and labor countries at the rate of five million dollars a year by the United States, and that many more millions are sold yearly by Germany, France, England and Austria to those countries?

Let up hope that the time will soon be here when agricultural leaders will arise who will have courage enough to advocate agricultural interests with the same spirit and vehemence which is now employed by protection manufacturers and their political servants. DAVID LUBIN.

Sacramento, February 19, 1896.

The Home Market Club, and the American Protective Tariff League are respectfully requested to refute the above!

CONCLUSION.

In conclusion, it is desired that every intelligent member of the Order of Patrons of Husbandry in Pennsylvania and in the United States ponder well over this matter. Let no one be biased or governed by preconceived notions. Let all consider well the arguments which have been used against it, and those in favor of it. It is a weighty matter for the farmers of the United States. More than that; it is a matter of the deepest importance, not alone to the farmers, but to all the people—to this Republic. Above all, to the farmers who produce the non-staples of agriculture. These very farmers should heed this Proposition with as much attention and earnestness as those who produce the staples. It is absolutely impossible for them to make a profit so long as the great mass of land in the United States is cultivated below the profit point in production of staples.

Should the farmers of the Nation conclude that this Proposition is just, equitable and expedient they must do more than simply assent to it.

The writer of this article asks for no reward of office, or money for this work. He believes it to be right, and, above all, the means whereby this Republic may be perpetuated. It is this belief which has induced him to devote his time, means and whatever energy he may possess in this cause. But in order that any practical results may follow it is absolutely necessary that the farmers of the Nation co-operate with him, and that promptly.

At this time the Hon. Grove L. Johnson, who introduced the Export Bounty Bill in Congress, earnestly and urgently requests that petitions favoring this Proposition be sent on to Congress by the thousands. In order that these should be productive of good they should contain the seal of the Grange or Alliance and be sent on without any loss of time whatever. The sooner the better. These petitions should not alone be signed by farmers, but by merchants, bankers, workingmen, professional men and by women.

Following is a Copy of Petition to be sent on to Congress

They should be copied as a heading on a suitable sheet of paper, and one each sent to the Senator, the other to the Representative of the District.

If to a Representative, address like this: (inserting name of your own Representative) Hon. Grove L. Johnson, House of Representatives, Washington, D. C.

If to a Senator, address like this: (inserting name of your own Senator) Senator George C. Perkins, United States Senate, Washington, D. C.

PETITION

"We respectfully petition the Congress of the United States to pass H. R. Bill No. 2626, for the protection of Agricultural Staples by an Export Bounty, in order to equalize the benefits and burdens of the protective system."

Women have the same right to petition as men.

Granges and Alliances can send in petitions as organizations, with the seal of the Grange or Alliance on the petition.

Sign, Circulate and Forward on the Petitions to Congress.

☞ **Extra Copies and other printed matter on this proposition mailed free. Address**

D. LUBIN, Sacramento, California

From Johns Hopkins Univ.
Oct. 1, 1896

Von Thünen's Theory of Natural Wages

BY

H. L. MOORE

JOHNS HOPKINS UNIVERSITY, BALTIMORE, MD.

Reprinted from the (Harvard) "Quarterly Journal of Economics,"
Vol. IX., Nos. 3 and 4, April and July, 1895

VON THÜNEN'S THEORY OF NATURAL WAGES

BY

H. L. MOORE

Johns Hopkins University, Baltimore, Md.

Reprinted from the (Harvard) "Quarterly Journal of Economics,"
Vol. IX., Nos. 3 *and* 4, *April and July*, 1895

BOSTON
GEO. H. ELLIS, 141 FRANKLIN STREET
1895

VON THÜNEN'S THEORY OF NATURAL WAGES.

I.

THE CLASSICAL THEORY AND VON THÜNEN'S FORMULA.

No scientific work could be more beneficent than that which would solve the problem of natural or just wages. The clashing interests of the capitalist and laborer in the division of the product of industry result in conflicting claims in the distribution of that product, and the lack of a scientific solution of the problem renders it possible that each may claim a moral basis for his actions.

Several vigorous attempts have been made to throw light on this question; and among those who have made important contributions to the subject, Thünen holds a conspicuous place. His theory contains much that is interesting and valuable; and the object of this paper is (1) to give this theory a critical consideration, and (2) to show his contribution to the theory of natural wages.* In order, however, that we may be placed in a position to form a correct estimate of Thünen's work, a brief review will be given of the theory of natural wages held by his English contemporaries.

The characteristic features of the classical theory of natural wages are exemplified in the opening paragraph of Ricardo's chapter on wages. The first sentence of that paragraph shows the manner in which the classical economists reasoned upon the subject. "Labor," says Ricardo, "like all other things which are purchased and sold, and which may be increased or diminished in quantity, has its natural and its market price." Here we find it im-

* For the bibliography of Von Thünen's Theory, see last page.

plied that labor is a commodity; and it is stated that labor, like every other commodity, has its natural and its market price. The classical economists taught that the natural price of a commodity is its cost of production: hence they inferred that the natural price of labor is its cost of production. But, when they came to define the cost of production of labor, they met with difficulty, and, as Marx * has shown, substituted for the cost of production of labor the cost of production of the laborer.

The second sentence of Ricardo's paragraph presents two more features of the classical theory. "The natural price of labor," Ricardo states, "is that price which is necessary to enable the laborers, one with another, to subsist and to perpetuate their race, without either increase or diminution." Here we find, in the first place, that Ricardo made no attempt to consider the equity in the case. Although he admitted that the price of labor "varies at different times in the same country, and very materially differs in different countries," yet he made no attempt to discover the reasonable or just wages. He was concerned only with facts and with the operation of natural law. In the second place, we observe that he defined natural wages without reference to the product of the laborer. Natural wages, according to his definition, depend upon the requirements of the laborer. These, however, vary at different times and in different places with "the habits and customs of the people."

In summarizing, the following may be named as characteristic features of the classical theory of natural wages:

1. Labor was treated throughout as a mere commodity.

2. Natural wages were defined without reference to equity, the operation of natural law being the main fact considered.

3. Natural wages were defined without reference to the product of labor. The requirements of the laborer

* **Marx**, *Das Kapital*, Band I., 2 Auflage, pp. 599. *Cf.* Schmidt, *Der natürliche Arbeitslohn*, p. 13.

as limited by his surroundings were regarded as determining his natural earnings.

While these doctrines were being taught by the classical school, Thünen was working upon a theory that was in many respects new. He claimed that the teachings of economists concerning wages were based upon the existing system of distribution. But, because under the existing system the laborer might be had for the bare means of subsistence, he could see no reason on that account for calling the bare means of subsistence natural wages. He was profoundly convinced of the evils resulting to the laboring class in consequence of the prevailing theory; * and this fact was one of the chief reasons leading him to undertake to discover the just or equitable wages, the wages agreeable to the nature (*naturgemäss*) and to the destiny of man. †

To simplify his investigations, or, rather, to make his investigations possible, he makes use of the isolated state. This state, isolated from the rest of the world by means of a wilderness, is in a plain of uniform fertility. Its only city, in which are concentrated all of its non-agricultural industries, is located at its centre. It has neither railroads nor navigable waters, and perfect competition pervades the entire state. The study is based upon the supposition that the isolated state is in a static condition.

Before entering upon Thünen's mathematical work, we must get well in mind the meaning of the terms he uses.

1. He takes rye as his measure of value, and selects a Berlin *Scheffel* of that grain as his unit. 2. He considers all laborers of the same class equal in strength, skill, intel-

* The light in which he viewed the classical theory may be seen from one of his letters of 1830 in Schumacher's *J. H. v. Thünen: Ein Forscherleben*, p. 117.

† *Der isolirte Staat*, II. 1, p. 193: "Ja, ich habe gefunden das tiefere Eindringen in die Frage, Welches ist der naturgemässe Arbeitslohn? in den letzten Studien unmittelbar zu der Frage über die Bestimmung des Menschen führt."

ligence, etc. 3. In wages proper — *i.e.*, in the reward for labor itself (*für die Arbeit an sich*), and not including interest upon any capital that the laborer may possess in the way of household effects — he distinguishes two parts. One part is that required for the means of subsistence of the laborer and his family. This part is designated by the symbol a. The other part, designated by the symbol y, is the surplus that the laborer earns above his means of subsistence. The symbol $a + y$ is used to express the wages for one year's labor of a laboring family. 4. By "product of labor" he means that part of the gross product which is shared by the laborers and capitalists alone, that part of the gross product remaining after deduction of profits, costs of management, insurance, etc. This product, divided by the number of laborers employed, gives the "product of labor" of one man. He designates the "product of labor" of one man by the symbol p. 5. By capital he means a product of human labor, employed in production.

We are now ready to follow him in his work. He approaches the problem by asking whether higher wages can exist at the margin of cultivation in the isolated state than exist in real life. He supposes, for the sake of argument, that the wages of the laborers on the marginal farms are raised, and then tries to discover the result of the change.

The income from the marginal farms before wages were raised just covered wages and interest upon invested capital. No ground rent was paid. If now wages are raised, ground rent will become a negative quantity, and the cultivation of marginal lands can be continued only at a loss. Perfect competition, however, pervades the isolated state; and no producer will continue to cultivate marginal lands at a loss. Consequently, producers will no longer invest capital in making improvements; and, as soon as buildings and other improvements have become dilapidated, they will abandon the marginal farms. The laborers from the marginal lands will then crowd into employments nearer the city. Competition sets in between the new laborers and the old; that is, between the laborers from the marginal farms and the laborers already employed nearer the city. But the old laborers already existed in such numbers that the product of the last laborer just covered the wages that he received. If the new laborers are to find employment, wages must be reduced below their former level. The attempt, therefore, to raise wages has worked to the laborer's detriment.

One might suppose, from this argument, that the laborer of the isolated state fares no better than the laborer of the modern state. But Thünen causes the reader to observe that he has reached the above conclusion only by supposing the rate of interest unalterable. If the rate of interest can be lowered, wages may be raised, and cultivation still continued upon marginal lands. The wages of the laborer in the isolated state are dependent upon causes determining the rate of interest. The knowledge, therefore, of the natural wages depends upon the knowledge of the law determining the connection between wages and interest.

I shall give here a brief outline of Thünen's course in the subsequent part of his work. His prime object is to get a mathematical expression for natural wages and for natural interest. To do this, he attempts first to get an algebraic equation expressing the interdependence of wages and interest. Having obtained this equation, he can proceed in any one of three ways to determine the unknown quantities; *i.e.*, the quantities representing wages and interest. He can find a second equation containing the unknown quantities, and then combine the two; or he can find an independent expression for interest, and then by substituting in the equation obtain wages; or else he can find an independent expression for wages, and then by making the substitution in the equation obtain interest. We shall see that, having found the equation, he selects the last method just described to obtain the value of the two quantities.

But first the equation expressing the relation between wages and interest must be found. Thünen approaches this problem in § 13, a section that has been grossly misunderstood and misinterpreted. This section has a meaning only when considered in connection with the main object of Thünen's work. The problem that he has before him is to discover the natural wages of the *ordinary* laborer, a laborer without a store of capital to invest, having only his labor with which to secure his maintenance. In order to find the equitable or just wages of such a laborer, he places him under conditions where the rate of wages is dependent upon the laborer's own course of action. As, however, the laborer has no store of capital, the conditions under which he can secure natural wages must be conditions where, without a store of capital, he can determine the rate of wages. Now the purpose of § 13 is indicated in the heading of that section,—"The Reduction of the Efficiency of Capital to Terms of Labor" (*Reduktion der Wirksamkeit des Kapitals auf Arbeit*). Thünen tries to show how the co-operation of capital in the production of a commodity may be reduced to terms of labor, and in doing this he lays the groundwork for the development of the formula expressing the interdependence between wages and interest.

He proceeds as follows: If an amount of capital Q, expressed in terms of rye, dollars, or any other measure, is divided by the year's wages of a laborer $(a + y)$, the wages being expressed in the same terms as the capital, then we shall find "how large the capital is, expressed in years' labor * of a laboring family, or how many years' labor of

* There is an inaccuracy here that has confused Thünen's critics. By dividing capital by wages, we do not find the value of the capital expressed in terms of years' labor, but in terms of wages.

a laboring family a capitalist with Q capital can control." * An amount of capital equal in value to the year's wages of a laborer he considers a unit of capital: hence, if $\frac{Q}{a+y}=nq$, Q will represent nq units of capital. He supposes that the capitalist lends Q to an undertaker, who invests it in some industry. If he employs n laborers, each laborer will use $\frac{nq}{n}=q$ units of capital.

Now, Thünen says, if from the gross returns of the industry "all expenses of the undertaker are deducted with the single exception of wages and interest, and if from the remainder business profit is subtracted, there is left the part of the product which we have called product of labor." † The "product of labor" of a man using q units of capital he designates by the symbol p. The question is, In what proportion will the capitalist and the laborer divide the "product of labor" between them? This question Thünen attempts to answer as follows: —

The n laborers employed in the industry bring forth a product np. Of this product the n laborers receive as wages $n\ (a+y)$. After the deduction of wages the capitalist receives as rent ‡ $n\ [p-(a+y)]$. The rent, divided by the capital employed, gives the rate of interest, which we shall designate by z.

$$\text{Then, } z=\frac{n\,[p-(a+y)]}{nq\,(a+y)}=\frac{p-(a+y)}{q\,(a+y)}.\text{§}$$

Thünen changes the form of this equation somewhat, in order to show the proportion in which the capitalist and the laborer share in the product p. From the equation $z=\frac{p-(a+y)}{q\,(a+y)}$ the following may be obtained: $qz\ (a+y)=p-(a+y)$; $(a+y)\ (1+qz)=p$; or,

$$1.\ a+y=\frac{p}{1+qz}=\text{share of laborer.}$$

* p. 124.

† *Ibid.*

‡ Thünen speaks of the earnings of capital as *Rente*, and the earnings of land as *Landrente*. These two terms I shall translate throughout this paper as rent and land rent, respectively.

§ p. 125.

To obtain the share of the capitalist, we must subtract from the product p the share of the laborer. Hence,

2. $p - \frac{p}{1+qz} = \frac{p+pqz-p}{1+qz} = \frac{pqz}{1+qz} =$ share of capitalist.

From equations 1 and 2, we can find the proportion in which the shares stand to each other: $\frac{p}{1+qz} : \frac{pqz}{1+qz} :: 1 : qz$. This result may be thus expressed: The earnings of one year's labor are to the earnings of q units of capital as 1 is to qz. Therefore, the earnings of one year's labor are to the earnings of one unit of capital as 1 is to z.

We shall have to follow Thünen but a little further to find how he applies the result which he has just obtained. He is going to make use of the law of substitution * as applied to labor and capital.

"In the production of one and the same product p, a part of the capital may be replaced by an increased amount of labor; and, *vice versa*, a part of the labor may be replaced by an increased amount of capital. Capital appears as a coworker, and enters into competition with the laborer. But it is in the power of the undertaker who employs n laborers with the capital Q, to give to the relative capital q, which one man uses, any desirable value † by increasing or diminishing n. The undertaker, knowing and following his interests, will increase the value of q just so much, until the costs of the work done by capital and the work done by men stand in direct proportion to their respective efficiency in production." ‡

Thünen therefore concludes that the respective efficiency of labor and capital is the measure of their earnings.

* Professor Marshall states that Thünen was the first to make use of this law in this connection. Cf. *Principles of Economics*, second edition, p. 556. Dr. Stuart Wood has recently applied this same law in the same relation with excellent effect. Cf. *Publications of American Economic Association*, vol. iv., No. 1.

† $\frac{Q}{a+y} = nq$; the number of units of capital used by one laborer is $\frac{nq}{n}$; therefore, by increasing or diminishing n, q may be made to have any desirable value.

‡ p. 126.

But, as we have just seen, he has proved that the earnings of a unit of labor are to the earnings of a unit of capital as $1:z$. The important inference that he draws from these facts is thus stated: "The rate of interest z is the factor by means of which the relation of the efficiency of capital to that of human labor is expressed";* *i.e.*, the rate of interest z is the factor expressing the relative efficiency of capital and labor. Now observe his final conclusion: "We are herewith placed in a position to reduce to terms of labor the co-operation of capital in the production of a commodity." † In these words he states, as plainly as could be stated, the chief results of his investigations in § 13; and, although he claims that his advantage over Ricardo consists in his ability to reduce the co-operation of capital to terms of labor, the validity of that claim has not been tested.

A little reflection will show the fallacy that he has committed. His conclusion does not follow from his premises. In his premises he states: (1) that, "in the production of one and the same product p, a part of the capital may be replaced by an increased amount of labor," and "a part of the labor may be replaced by an increased amount of capital," and that "the undertaker, knowing and following his interests, will increase the value of q just so much, until the costs of the work done by capital and of the work done by men stand in direct proportion to their respective efficiency in production"; (2) that the earnings of a unit of labor are to the earnings of a unit of capital as $1:z$. He infers from these premises that the rate of interest z is the factor expressing the relative efficiency of capital and labor. But here he draws a general conclusion from particular premises. It

*p. 127.

† *Ibid.* Notice also this sentence, p. 127: "Durch diese Reduktion ist es dann möglich, die Produktionskosten eines Erzeugnisses, insofern keine Landrente darin enthalten ist, ganz in Arbeit auszudrücken, und die Arbeit wird dadurch wahrhaft zum Werthmesser für die Tauschgüter."

will be admitted that in the production of a given product *a part* of the capital may be replaced by labor, and *a part* of the labor replaced by capital. It will also be admitted that, in the *margin of indifference*, the wise undertaker will employ capital and labor in such proportions that their costs will be in proportion to their respective efficiency in production. But it cannot be admitted that, because in the *margin of indifference* the efficiency of capital may be reduced to terms of labor, therefore the entire efficiency of capital can be reduced to terms of labor, or that the efficiency of capital in the production of any commodity can be reduced to terms of labor, or that z expresses the relative efficiency of capital and labor. It expresses the relative efficiency only at the *margin of indifference*, the margin where capital and labor may be indifferently substituted for each other. If, then, z does not express the relative efficiency of capital and labor, Thünen cannot infer that, by means of z, the co-operation of capital in production can be reduced to terms of labor.

We shall see later what use Thünen makes of this supposed law, but now we shall return to the main problem under discussion. In the section that we have just considered he obtains the equation $a + y = \frac{p}{1+qz}$. Although the quantities y and z occur in this equation, the expression in its present form is of no use; for the value of $(a + y)$ is dependent upon the value of z. Besides, p is not a constant quantity, but varies as q increases or diminishes; and the values of y and z depend upon the value of p. p, y, and z are therefore functions of q. The problem, then, is to find the values of p, y, and z for a given value of q.

In order to solve this problem, Thünen refers us to the isolated state. In the isolated state the laborers have it in their power either to work for undertakers or to lay out farms for themselves on the margin of cultivation. If the laborers are to be deterred from laying out new farms, and persuaded to continue in the service of their employers, their wages plus the interest on the capital needed to lay out a farm must be equal to what the "product of labor" of the farm would be after its completion. These conditions may be expressed mathematically. If wages $= a + y$, the rate of interest $= z$, "product of labor" of one man $= p$, the number of units of capital used by one man cultivating the new farm $= q$, whose value is $q\,(a + y)$, since each unit of capital has the value of one year's wages, then, in order for the laborer to be deterred from laying out the farm, this equation must exist: $(a + y) + q\,(a + y)\,z = p$;* or $(a + y) = \frac{p}{1 + qz}$; or $z = \frac{p - (a + y)}{q\,(a + y)}$. Here a, p, and q are known quantities, and y and z are unknown.

We have now obtained an equation expressing the interdependence of wages and interest. The next problem is to find an independent expression for wages. To enable him to find this expression, Thünen supposes that a number of laborers combine to lay out a farm on the margin of cultivation of the isolated state. This new farm is to be of the same character as those already existing in the state. The combination of laborers divide themselves into two groups, which we shall call group A and group B. The laborers in group A remain in the service of undertakers, and by means of the surpluses of their wages furnish the means of subsistence to the laborers of group B, who lay out the farm. In order to avoid confusion, we shall call the laborers in groups A and B capital-producers.†

In the course of a year the farm is completed, and la-

*It must be remembered that Thünen considers the isolated state under static conditions, for otherwise equilibrium would not be maintained even if the relation existed expressed by the equation $(a + y) + q\,(a + y)\,z = p$. In a progressive state the laborers would secure a large advantage in laying out marginal farms, owing to the growth in value of those farms, due to general progress. *Cf.* Professor J. B. Clark, "De l'Influence de la Terre sur le Taux des Salaires," p. 256 of *Revue d'Économie Politique*, 1890.

† Thünen calls the laborers in groups A and B *kapitalerzeugende Arbeiter* (p. 151).

borers are employed to cultivate it. The wages of each of these laborers must be so great that the income which each of them receives from his surplus when that surplus is placed at interest — *i.e.*, yz — will be equal to the sum received by each of the capital-producers as his share of the rent* of the farm; for, if this were not the case, the laborers would lay out farms for themselves.

These facts Thünen expresses in mathematical language, and is thereby enabled to obtain the formula: Natural wages $= \sqrt{ap}$. He uses the following symbols: —

Let $a + y =$ the year's wages of a laboring family, a and y retaining the same meanings that they have had throughout this paper.

$nq =$ the number of capital-producers in group B; that is, the number of men needed to lay out the farm. Thünen admits that, to lay out the farm, is needed not only labor, but also capital; but he summarily dismisses this difficulty by saying, "According to § 13, we can reduce the co-operation of capital to terms of labor" (p. 152). Later on I shall show that in the ascertainment of the quantity nq lies the error which vitiates the formula $\sqrt{ap}$.

As the farm is completed in one year, its value is equal to nq units of capital.

$anq =$ the amount consumed by the nq men in group B.

$\frac{anq}{y} =$ the number of capital-producers in group A, since the capital-producers in group A support those in group B by means of their surpluses.

Then $nq + \frac{anq}{y} = \frac{nq(a+y)}{y} =$ total number of capital-producers in groups A and B.

$n =$ number of men employed to cultivate the farm after its completion.

$n(a+y) =$ total wages paid n men.

$p =$ "product of labor" of one man, working with q units of capital.

$np =$ total "product of labor."

$np - n\ (a+y) = n\ [p - (a+y)] =$ total income from the farm for one year, or, as Thünen calls it, the rent of the farm. This rent is the property of $\frac{nq(a+y)}{y}$ men.

* Rent is used here in the sense noted above, and means earnings of capital, not land rent.

Therefore $\frac{\frac{n[p-(a+y)]}{nq(a+y)}}{y} = \frac{[p-(a+y)]\,y}{q(a+y)}$ = share of each of the capital-producers, or his portion of the rent of the farm. In this last expression all the quantities are known excepting y.

Now, it has already been observed that, for the laborers to be induced to work on the new farm, the income which each receives from his surplus when that surplus is placed at interest must be equal to the rent received by each capital-producer: hence yz must be equal to $\frac{[p-(a+y)]\,y}{q(a+y)}$. Capital-producers and laborers, therefore, have a common interest in making the above function as large as possible; and, when the function has reached its maximum value, the interests of capital-producers and laborers will be satisfied. The question is, then, For what value of y will $\frac{[p-(a+y)]\,y}{q(a+y)}$ have a maximum value?

Differential calculus enables Thünen to answer this question. He solves the problem by differentiating the function with respect to y, and then placing the differential equal to zero. He finds that the function will have a maximum value when $(a+y) = \sqrt{ap}$.

Having obtained the formula for natural wages,* he is able to find the expression for the natural rate of interest by substituting $\sqrt{ap}$ for $(a+y)$ in the equation $z = \frac{p-(a+y)}{q(a+y)}$.

*Thünen placed such great value upon the formula $\sqrt{ap}$ that he requested it should adorn his tombstone. According to Schumacher (*J. H. v. Thünen: Ein Forscherleben*, p. 322) his wish was respected: "Die Krone seiner Gesetze, das Resultat mühseliger Untersuchungen über das Verhältniss des Arbeitslohns zum Zinsfuss und zur Landrente, wie solches aus seinem Arsenale mathematischer Formeln siegreich hervorging:

Der naturgemässe Arbeitslohn = $\sqrt{ap}$

schmückt als Denkspruch seinen einfachen Grabstein im Hügellande von Mecklenburg, wie er in schöner Stunde selber gewünscht."

II.

CRITICISMS OF THE FORMULA: NATURAL WAGES = $\sqrt{AP}$.

THÜNEN'S theory of wages holds a peculiar place in German Economics. Important as the theory is, it is unmentioned in the majority of German works,—a fact which Falck and Komorzynski attribute to the abstruse mathematical character of his method. But even among the few critics that Thünen has had there is a lack of harmony concerning the correctness of his work: some accept his mathematical results in their entirety; others accept a part and refuse the rest; while still others reject his results *in toto*.

In the following pages my purpose is to endeavor to show that those critics who have offered the strongest objections to the correctness of Thünen's results have either overlooked the limited premises from which he started, or forgotten the hypothetical nature of his conclusions. At the end I shall try to expose the error which, so far as Thünen's own work is concerned, vitiates the correctness of his formula.

1. Let us examine first the position of Falck, who was one of the last to devote a monograph to Thünen's work. The main object of Falck's dissertation is to prove the mathematical inaccuracy in the formula for natural wages. He claims that the formula $\sqrt{ap}$ "is the keystone of Thünen's whole system"; and, if you reject it, his "system loses all practical importance." *

* Falck, *Die Thünen'sche Lehre vom Bildungsgesetz des Zinsfusses und vom naturgemässen Arbeitslohn*, p. 32.

He proceeds in his argument as follows: Thünen obtained the formula $\sqrt{ap}$ from the expression $\frac{[p-(a+y)]\,y}{q\,(a+y)}$. If we represent this expression by R, then

$$R = \frac{[p-(a+y)]\,y}{q\,(a+y)} = \frac{py}{q\,(a+y)} - \frac{y}{q} = \left[\frac{p}{a+y} - 1\right]\frac{y}{q}.$$

From the last expression we find, when $y = o$, the value of R becomes o. In other words, when wages are reduced to the bare means of subsistence, the rent of the capital-producer vanishes. This fact seems to startle Falck; and, forgetting that Thünen's work has nothing to do with actual conditions, but is based upon purely hypothetical conditions, he claims that the phenomenon indicated by the expression can have no economic cause, "since we can daily convince ourselves that, as a matter of fact, in many places wages are reduced not only to the bare means of subsistence, but even below that amount, while the income of the capitalist not only does not vanish, but may increase." * He infers, therefore, that there is a mathematical error in the expression; and he claims to prove the error by the following argument:—

"The formula $\frac{[p-(a+y)]\,y}{q\,(a+y)}$ was obtained from the formula $\frac{n\,[p-(a+y)]}{\frac{nq\,(a+y)}{y}}$. The numerator denotes the rent from the farm, the denominator the number of those among whom the rent is divided. But is the y of the denominator really equivalent to the y of the numerator?" He denies that the y's are equivalent, asserting that the "y of the numerator denotes the surplus that is paid to the laborer at this particular time; but the y of the denominator denotes the surplus of wages that existed before the laying out of the farm." "Only by placing these two y's equal to each other," he claims, "has it been possible for the rent to obtain a maximum value at a definite rate of wages." †

Falck is under the impression that the rate of wages which exists before the laying out of the farm is different

* Falck, p. 34. † *Ibid.*, p. 35.

from the rate that exists after the farm is completed. As this is an error into which several critics have fallen, it will be well to show that, in supposing a number of laborers to combine in laying out a marginal farm, Thünen proceeds on the assumption that natural wages exist in the isolated state before the farm is begun, and that the supposition is introduced merely as a means of ascertaining the mathematical expression for the prevailing rate of wages. Thünen attempts to place such conditions upon the isolated state, that natural wages not only can be realized, but are realized; and his main problem is to find the mathematical expression for such wages.

Let us briefly review the chief limitations that he places upon the isolated state. He assumes that the isolated state is in a static condition; that the laborers are equal in intelligence, skill, etc.; and that perfect competition pervades the entire state. He assumes that beyond the margin of cultivation there is a limitless territory whose fertility is equal to that of lands already under cultivation, and he maintains that the rate of wages and the rate of interest existing at the margin of cultivation determine the rate of wages and rate of interest throughout the entire state. With these conditions placed upon the isolated state, Thünen claims that the mere possibility * of laborers laying out farms for themselves will compel the undertakers to pay laborers wages that will be equal to what the latter could earn by laying out farms and cultivating them on their own responsibility.

He argues (pp. 146, 147), if the undertakers should attempt to lower wages, laborers would emigrate to the margin, and begin cultivation on their own responsibility. Since, however, the number of laborers is constant, this act on their part would cause scarcity of labor in the interior of the state, which would result in a loss to the

* "Die blosse Möglichkeit für die Arbeiter, sich in der Wildniss anzusiedeln ohne dass dies That wird," etc. *Der isolirte Staat*, Part II., p. 147.

undertakers. If, therefore, the undertakers desire to keep their laborers, they must pay them such wages as would make emigration to the margin of the state unprofitable.

Falck might claim that Thünen's supposition of a party of laborers combining to lay out a farm is an illustration of the manner in which the laborers would proceed to enforce higher wages when undertakers had reduced them below the natural limit. But this claim could not be sustained; for Thünen distinctly tells us that his investigations rest upon the supposition that the isolated state is in a static condition (*im beharrenden Zustand*, p. 146). By static condition he does not mean that the laborers are at war with their employers, trying to obtain natural wages. He means that they already receive natural wages. This follows from what he himself says concerning the static condition: "Im isolirten Staat haben wir . . . stets den endlichen Erfolg, also das erreichte Ziel, vor Augen gehabt. Mit dem erreichten Ziel tritt Ruhe und damit der beharrende Zustand ein; und hier erblicken wir Gesetzmässigkeit, während in der Uebergangsperiode Manches uns als ein unentwirrbares Chaos erscheint" (p. 35). He believes that natural wages already exist in the isolated state; and, as a means of discovering the mathematical expression for such wages, he supposes that a number of laborers, to whom it is a matter of indifference whether they labor for wages or cultivate a marginal farm on their own account, combine to lay out a farm.

We can now easily see the fallacy in Falck's objection. Falck rests his whole proof of the inaccuracy of Thünen's formula on his claim that the y of the denominator of the expression $\frac{n[p-(a+y)]}{\frac{nq(a+y)}{y}}$ has a different value from the y of the numerator. The sole reason that he offers to substantiate his claim is that the y of the denominator represents the surplus that the laborer receives before the farm is begun, and the y of the numerator represents the surplus that he receives after the farm is completed. This is no reason whatever why the y's are not equal. Because y represents two quantities, it by no means follows that those quantities are unequal. If the analysis that I have given of Thünen's method of procedure is correct, natural wages are assumed to exist in the isolated state both before and after the completion of the marginal farm; and consequently the y's in the above expression are equal.

2. Roscher * claims that even in the isolated state Thünen's formula $\sqrt{ap}$ does not represent natural wages; for, he says, if labor and capital are combined in different proportions in different industries, the laborers will not be justly rewarded if all receive wages $= \sqrt{ap}$. For example, if an artist, using cheap fuel, makes valuable vases out of cheap clay, it is not just or natural that he should receive wages equal to or less than the wages of an ordinary laborer. But Professor Roscher claims that the formula $\sqrt{ap}$ would bring about this relation, because a has the same value for the artist and the laborer, and p varies with the amount of capital used. Hence, when the laborer is employed in an industry where much capital is used, "product of labor," p, will be very great; and, if his wages $= \sqrt{ap}$, he may receive more than the artist who uses only a small amount of capital.

Komorzynski † holds that Roscher is right in saying that $\sqrt{ap}$ does not represent natural wages, where labor and capital combine in different proportions in production; but he shows that Roscher's illustration is defective, since he compares laborers of different classes, an artist and an ordinary laborer, whereas Thünen's investigations are concerned only with the ordinary laborer.

* Roscher, *Geschichte der Nationalökonomik in Deutschland*, p. 896.

† Komorzynski, "Thünen's naturgemässer Arbeitslohn," *Zeitschrift für Volkswirthschaft, Socialpolitik, und Verwaltung*, Dritter Band, 1 Heft, p. 53.

Now let us examine the argument offered by Roscher and approved by Komorzynski, that, where capital and labor combine in different proportions in production, $\sqrt{ap}$ does not represent natural wages even in the isolated state. In order to present the matter clearly, I shall use an illustration found in Thünen's own work,* where capital and labor combine in different proportions in production. In § 13 he announces the law that the price of commodities tends to conform to their cost of production, and attempts to illustrate the law by a comparison of the prices of mining and agricultural products. In the early part of his work he assumed that the mines of the isolated state lay in the neighborhood of the city; but, in order that he may illustrate his law by a comparison of the prices of silver and grain, he supposes, for the time being, that the silver mines are scattered about the state, that the last mine which is worked lies at the margin of the state, and that, further in the wilderness, mines of equal fertility to the marginal mine are found, but that they are not worked, because the product would not pay for the cost of production. This follows from the fact that the product of the marginal mine just covers the cost of production.

Now, it has already been observed that the product of the marginal farm just covers the cost of production. Then, since perfect competition pervades the isolated state, and laborers may work either at farming or mining, it follows that the wages of the farm laborer and the wages of the miner must have equal values. Hence, if we can find the wages of the former in terms of grain and the wages of the latter in terms of silver, we shall be able to find the exchange values of grain and silver at the margin of the isolated state.

Thünen's formula for wages is $a + y = \frac{p}{1 + qz}$. He supposes that the rate of interest — which, of course, is the same for owners of mines and owners of farms — is five

* Part II., pp. 131, 132.

per cent. In the above formula, and, indeed, everywhere else in Thünen's work, p represents "product of labor" *in kind*. When the laborers are employed in silver mining, p represents a certain amount of silver. When they are employed in agriculture, it represents a certain amount of grain. Thünen supposes that in the case of the marginal silver mine p equals $7\frac{1}{2}$ pounds of silver, and in the case of the marginal farm p equals 240 scheffels of rye. He then says, "Since different industries require different amounts of capital, q will represent different quantities."* He supposes that in mining $q = 20$, and in agriculture $q = 12$. By making these substitutions in the formula, we find that the wages of the miner $(a + y) = \frac{7\frac{1}{2}}{1 + 20 \times \frac{1}{20}} = 3\frac{3}{4}$ pounds of silver; and the wages, of the farm laborer $(a + y) = \frac{240}{1 + 12 \times \frac{1}{20}} = 150$ scheffels of rye. $3\frac{3}{4}$ pounds of silver, therefore, has the same value as 150 scheffels of rye; and $7\frac{1}{2}$ pounds of silver, the "product of labor," p, in silver mining, has the same value as 300 scheffels of rye.

Now, Roscher and Komorzynski would say $\sqrt{ap}$ does not represent natural or just wages, because the miner would receive as wages $\sqrt{ap} = \sqrt{a \times 300}$; while the farm laborer would receive $\sqrt{ap} = \sqrt{a \times 240}$. Whatever the value of a may be, it is the same for both; and consequently the miner would receive more than the farm laborer. Upon the face of it, this argument looks sound; but yet we should scarcely expect Thünen to make this blunder after telling us that throughout the isolated state all laborers receive the same wages, and that in different industries the quantity q, the amount of capital used, is different. As a matter of fact, I think it may be proved that the error lies with Roscher and Komorzynski. They attach

***Part II., p. 131. Falck attempts to defend Thünen against the criticism of Roscher, and says: "Der Herr Verfasser [Roscher] scheint hier vergessen zu haben, dass die Arbeiter des isolirten Staats Alle mit dem gleichen Capital ausgerüstet sind und dass daher ein verschiedenes Quotverhältniss geradezu undenkbar ist" (p. 55). The quotation above from Thünen, together with his illustration of different amounts of capital used in silver mining and in agriculture, show the absurd position that Falck has taken.**

an entirely wrong meaning to p when p occurs in the formula $\sqrt{ap}$. In the formula $\sqrt{ap}$, p means "product of labor" in agriculture at the margin of the isolated state, and in the formula $\sqrt{ap}$ it never means anything else.

In the beginning of his work Thünen gives a general definition of p as the "product of labor" of one man; that is, the product to be shared between the laborer and the owner of the capital which he uses. He proceeds with his work, and bases his investigations at times upon actual conditions, and at times upon the assumed conditions of the isolated state. In his investigations based upon actual conditions he develops the formula $z = \frac{p-(a+y)}{q(a+y)}$; but, as his object is to find the expression for the natural wages of the isolated state, he tells us that in its present form the expression $z = \frac{p-(a+y)}{q(a+y)}$ is of no use to him. But why? Because p does not represent a constant quantity, "but rises and falls with q. y and z, in turn, depend upon p. Hence p, y, and z are functions of q." * He then definitely and distinctly states the problem before him. "The problem is then," he says, "to find the value of p, y, and z for a given value of q." †

After announcing his problem, he immediately leaves his investigations based upon actual conditions, and goes to the isolated state. He then shows that, if the laborers are to be deterred from laying out marginal farms, this equation must exist $(a+y) + q(a+y)z = p$, where p equals the "product of labor" in agriculture on the marginal lands. "Here," he says, "a, p, and q are determinate, y and z indeterminate" (p. 141). With these quantities assumed as known, he proceeds with his investigations, and ends by declaring that natural wages $= \sqrt{ap}$. But what does p mean here? Evidently, it has but one meaning, the "product of labor" in agriculture at the margin of the isolated state.‡

* Part II., p. 139. † *Ibid.*

‡ Misconception with regard to the meaning of p as that quantity occurs in the formula $\sqrt{ap}$ has been a source of numerous errors, and it is important that

3. Komorzynski takes a peculiar position in his criticism of Thünen. Thünen tells us he considers his isolating method the most valuable part of his work;* but Komorzynski insists that the isolated state, with all its appurtenances, is an unnecessary part of Thünen's work, and serves merely to obscure his investigations and confuse his critics. Thünen believes that the formula for natural wages can be found only in one way; namely, by means of the conditions placed upon the isolated state.† But Komorzynski claims that Thünen unwittingly develops the formula in two ways: that the second method of obtaining the formula has nothing to do with the isolated state, but is based upon actual conditions; and, when the two methods are divested of all unnecessary suppositions, the

the point made above should be understood. Thünen's purpose is merely to investigate, under the favorable conditions of the isolated state, the influence of free land upon wages. His position is that, at the margin of cultivation in the isolated state, the determination of the rate of wages and the rate of interest will be in accord with the best interests of the laborer, and that the rate of wages and the rate of interest at the margin determine the rates throughout the state. If Thünen attempted to show anything, it was that wages at the margin equal $\sqrt{ap}$, where p equals "product of labor" in agriculture; and his claim is that the same wages will exist throughout the isolated state. "Wir behaupten, dass der an der Grenze des isolirten Staats sich bildende Arbeitslohn und Zinsfuss normirend für den ganzen Staat ist" (p. 142).

Thünen's assumption that the mines of the isolated state are situated near the city (Part I., p. 1) confirms the idea that it was his purpose to investigate under favorable conditions the influence of free land upon wages; for, if the mines had been so placed that the one whose product just covered its cost of production was situated at the margin of the state, and that a number of equally fertile mines were left untouched in the wilderness, then, instead of the laborers combining to lay out a farm on the margin, they would unite to work a mine. We might then make suppositions concerning the latter combination similar to those that Thünen made concerning the former combination; and, if we should use capital letters where Thünen used small ones, we should find, by following Thünen's method, that the wages of each miner would be $\sqrt{AP}$. But $A = a$, and P is greater in value than p, because more capital is used in the production of P than is used in the production of p. Hence $\sqrt{AP}$ is greater than $\sqrt{ap}$; and, consequently, it would be more profitable for the laborers to engage in mining than in agriculture. Thünen saw what the difficulty would be if he supposed the mines to be placed in this way; and for this reason he was careful, in making the illustration I have given in the text, to state that his supposition concerning the position of the mines was only temporary.

* Part I., p. xix. † Part II., p. 26.

ascertainment of the formula is found to rest upon two conditions which are common to the two methods.

The second method of obtaining the formula $\sqrt{ap}$ is, according to Komorzynski, as follows: In the part of his work based upon actual conditions Thünen develops the formula $z = \frac{p-(a+y)}{q(a+y)}$, and states that it expresses the rate of interest. In another part of his work he states that it is to the advantage of the laborer to have wages and interest bear such relation to each other that the laborer will receive the maximum income from his surplus when that surplus is placed at interest. Now, Komorzynski argues, since the surplus is y, and the rate of interest $z = \frac{p-(a+y)}{q(a+y)}$, the interests of the laborer will be subserved when yz, which is equal to $\frac{y\,[p-(a+y)]}{q(a+y)}$, obtains a maximum value. This takes place when $(a+y) = \sqrt{ap}$. He therefore concludes that Thünen's suppositions concerning the isolated state are all unnecessary, and all that is needed to prove that $\sqrt{ap}$ represents the best rate of wages for the laborer is to prove: —

A. That $z = \frac{p-(a+y)}{q(a+y)}$ expresses a general formula for interest.

B. That it is to the advantage of the laborer to have wages and interest bear such relation to each other that the laborer will receive a maximum income from his surplus when that surplus is placed at interest.

Why Thünen did not proceed in the manner indicated I shall consider later on. At present we shall consider Komorzynski's attempt to prove an error in the development of the formula $\sqrt{ap}$ on the ground that the conditions A and B are unsustainable.

A. He claims that the subtle error which vitiates the formula for natural wages is that $z = \frac{p-(a+y)}{q(a+y)}$ is not a general formula for the rate of interest. To fulfil the conditions of a general formula for the rate of interest, it must express the same rate of interest for all industries.

But Komorzynski says the above formula is not capable of doing this; for "wages $(a+y)$ and interest z are by means of Thünen's formula $z=\frac{p-(a+y)}{q(a+y)}$ brought into a relation which, in turn, varies with the changing quantities p and q. The quantity p, the surplus value of the product over the value of the capital consumed in production, and likewise the quantity q, . . . are different in different forms of production. From this it follows that the relation which, according to the formula, exists between the rate of interest z and the rate of wages $(a+y)$, will be different in different forms of production." * In other words, since the quantities p and q are different in different forms of production, he infers that the relation of $(a+y)$ and z expressed by $z=\frac{p-(a+y)}{q(a+y)}$ will be different in different forms of production; and therefore, since the formula does not express the same rate of interest for all industries, it is not a general formula for the rate of interest.

The error in the argument can best be exposed by means of the example that Komorzynski gives to illustrate his argument. The illustration is intended to show why the formula does not represent the general rate of interest. He says: "If the rate of interest is 5 per cent. and the rate of wages 400 florins, then, in three different forms of production, these equations may exist:—

$$\text{I. } \frac{5}{100}=\frac{2{,}500-400}{105\times 400}, \text{ where } p=2{,}500 \text{ and } q=105;$$
$$\text{II. } \frac{5}{100}=\frac{1{,}200-400}{40\times 400}, \text{ where } p=1{,}200 \text{ and } q=40;$$
$$\text{III. } \frac{5}{100}=\frac{460-400}{3\times 400}, \text{ where } p=460 \text{ and } q=3.$$

But, if $(a+y)$ should rise from 400 to 450, then the following unequal rates of interest would result:—

$$\text{I. } \frac{4.33}{100}=\frac{2{,}500-450}{105\times 450}; \text{ II. } \frac{4.16}{100}=\frac{1{,}200-450}{40\times 450}; \text{ III. } \frac{.741}{100}=\frac{460-450}{3\times 450}.\text{"} \dagger$$

* Komorzynski, p. 58.

† *Ibid.*, p. 59, note. There is a slight error in the original which I have corrected in the quotation given above. Where $\frac{.741}{100}$ occurs above, $\frac{7.41}{100}$ is found in the original.

This example, he claims, illustrates that the formula is not a general formula for the rate of interest, or, better, a formula for the general rate of interest, but that it represents the relation between wages and interest in specific industries.

The fallacy in the argument may be readily shown. Komorzynski has overlooked Thünen's definition of p. In his illustration Komorzynski makes p represent, in each of the three cases, a definite number of florins. This is evident from the fact that in each case he subtracts wages, expressed in terms or florins, from p. Furthermore, when he supposes wages to rise from 400 to 450 florins, he assumes that in each of the three cases p retains its value in terms of florins. In his illustration and throughout his whole article* he assumes that p represents a definite *value*. But Thünen distinctly defines p as "product of labor"; that is, "product of labor" in kind (pp. 80, 167). When laborers are employed in silver mining, p is expressed in terms of silver (p. 131); and, when they are employed in agriculture, p is expressed in terms of grain (p. 131). If, then, p means "product of labor" in kind, Komorzynski cannot assume that the value of p, or the price of p, expressed in florins, remains constant when the rate of wages changes. This error renders his objections useless; for if, after the rise of wages, the demands of the community require the continuance of production in groups I., II., III., the formula $z = \frac{p-(a+y)}{q(a+y)}$ (provided there is no other objection to the formula than that which Komorzynski offers) may still represent equal rates of interest for the three groups if p, remaining constant in quantity as "product of labor" in kind, may change its value or change its price in terms of florins.

B. Komorzynski also attempts to prove defective Thünen's supposition that it is to the advantage of the laborer

* For example, p. 58, "Die Grösse p, der Wertüberschuss des Productes," etc.; p. 55, "Hier bedeutet p den Tauschwert (erlangbaren Verkaufspreis) des Productes," etc.

to have wages and interest bear such a relation to each other that the laborer will receive a maximum income from his surplus when that surplus is placed at interest.* In brief, he claims that it is not to the interest of the laborer that yz should attain a maximum value.

His objection may be thus stated: The interests of laborers as to the relation of wages and interest vary according as they have saved during many or during few years. If they have saved during many years, they desire to have wages low and interest high. If, on the other hand, they are just beginning to save, they desire a higher rate of wages and a lower rate of interest. Hence there is no definite relation of wages and interest that, under all circumstances, is the best relation for the laborers. Concerning Thünen's supposition that it is to the advantage of the laborer to have yz attain a maximum value, Komorzynski says that it is based on the arbitrary assumption that the laborers save only during one year, and that all laborers have only an amount of capital equal to y.

This objection has much in its favor; but, before considering it, we must put Thünen in the right light. In introducing Komorzynski's criticism, it was stated that his position is peculiar, since he holds that, while Thünen believed he could obtain his formula for natural wages only in one way,— by means of the conditions of the isolated state,— he unwittingly develops it in two ways; that, when the two methods are disembarrassed of all superfluous suppositions, the ascertainment of the formula is found to rest upon two conditions, which are common to the two methods; and that the ascertainment of the formula by the second method is based, not upon the hypothetical conditions of the isolated state, but upon actual conditions. By the logic of his position, therefore,

* This question is also discussed by Knapp, G. F., *Zur Prüfung der Untersuchungen Thünen's über Lohn und Zinsfuss im isolirten Staate*, pp. 18–26; Roscher, *Geschichte*, etc., p. 896; Schmidt, C., *Der natürliche Arbeitslohn*, pp. 34–37.

he is forced to charge Thünen with holding that it is to the advantage of the laborer, under actual conditions, to have wages and interest bear such relation to each other that he will receive the maximum income from his surplus when that surplus is placed at interest. This charge cannot be proved. Thünen's hypothesis that there is a definite relation of wages and interest which is most desirable for the laborer is based upon the supposition that there is a direct interdependence between wages and interest. But he cannot be charged with claiming a direct interdependence between wages and interest under actual conditions,* for nowhere in his investigations based upon actual conditions does he make such a supposition. So far, however, as concerns the isolated state,— a state in a static condition, with constant capital, with constant population having constant wants and constant methods of production,— his claim of an interdependence of wages and interest cannot be denied.

Now, when the above objection is considered as directed towards Thünen's method of developing the formula on the basis of the isolated state, it has the merit, not of proving his investigations false, but of showing them to be painfully contracted and incomplete. In a state where there is a direct interdependence of wages and interest, it is true that, when laborers possess different amounts of capital, those who possess much will desire a different relation of wages and interest from those who possess little. It is also true that, when laborers have saved during many years, they desire a different relation of wages and interest from what they desired when they were just beginning to save. But, after we have admitted

* Komorzynski's error grows out of his misunderstanding of the formula $z = \frac{p-(a+y)}{q(a+y)}$, as that formula occurs in § 13. *If* Thünen claimed that the formula represents a general formula for interest under actual circumstances, and *if* he intended p to represent a constant price, as Komorzynski understands it, then we might charge him with holding that there is a direct interdependence of wages and interest under actual circumstances.

all this, we cannot deny that the laborers who are just beginning to save will be interested in having the relation of wages and interest such that they will obtain a maximum income from their surplus when that surplus is placed at interest. If, then, y equals the surplus, and z the rate of interest, we cannot deny that, when laborers begin to save, it will be to their advantage to have yz obtain a maximum value. Komorzynski's argument does not prove an error in Thünen's work: it merely shows its incompleteness.

4. I shall now attempt to point out a fallacy in Thünen's reasoning that vitiates his formula; and, in order to expose this fallacy, I must briefly review the chief points in § 13, that repeatedly misinterpreted section of Thünen's work. As I have shown in the early part of this article, Thünen's prime object in § 13 is to find means by which he can reduce to terms of labor the co-operation of capital in production. He proceeds to do this by saying, if an amount of capital Q is divided by the year's wages of a laborer $(a+y)$, we shall find "how large the capital is expressed in years' labor of a laboring family" ("Wie gross das Kapital in Jahresarbeiten einer Arbeiterfamilie ausgedrückt ist," p. 124). Although we see what Thünen means to say, yet his words do not express his meaning. By dividing capital by wages, he does not obtain an expression for capital in terms of years' labor of a laboring family, but in terms of wages. Further on in the same section (p. 128) he repeats the same idea by saying, in effect, that capital may be reduced to terms of labor by dividing the amount of capital by wages. This inaccuracy in the use of words continues throughout the chapter.

In continuing his work, he supposes that $\frac{Q}{a+y}=nq$, or $Q=nq\,(a+y)$. If the capital $nq\,(a+y)$ is used in a productive process where n laborers are employed, then, assuming that the "product of labor" of each man equals p, and the wages of each equal $(a+y)$, Thünen holds that the rate of interest is expressed by the formula $z = \frac{n[p-(a+y)]}{nq(a+y)} = \frac{p-(a+y)}{q(a+y)}$. By a manipulation of this formula he claims to prove that "z is the factor by means of which the relation of the efficiency of capital to that of human labor is expressed"; and hence he concludes, "We are herewith placed into position to reduce to terms of labor the co-operation of capital in the production of a commodity." Here he sums up in two sentences the result of his investigations in § 13. Notice, however, that above he spoke of reducing *capital* to terms of labor, while here he speaks of reducing the *co-operation of capital* to terms of labor,—two entirely different things, which we must keep distinctly separated. In a moment we shall find how Falck has fallen into error by confusing these two processes.

Now let us see what use Thünen makes of these results. To find the expression for natural wages, he resorts to the case of a number of laborers combining to lay out a marginal farm. One of the quantities that he uses to obtain his formula is nq, and the manner in which he obtains that quantity he states in these words: Suppose "the laying out of the farm required the year's labor of nq men. . . . Unquestionably, in order to provide a new farm, is needed not only labor, but also the use of capital; (but) according to § 13, we can reduce the co-operation of capital to terms of labor, and thus express the costs of laying out the farm entirely in terms of labor." *

What does Thünen mean by saying, according to § 13, the co-operation of capital may be reduced to terms of labor? Knapp understands him to signify that the co-operation of capital can be reduced to terms of labor by means of the rate of interest, and he states that such a reduction is impossible. This interpretation of Thünen's meaning I should urge as correct, and should base the claim (1) upon the general meaning of § 13, which is

* Part II., p. 152.

expressed in these sentences: *z* is the factor by means of which the relation of the efficiency of capital to that of human labor is expressed," and "We are herewith placed into position to reduce to terms of labor the co-operation of capital in the production of a commodity"; (2) upon Thünen's use of words. In the paragraph under discussion he says, "According to § 13, we can reduce the co-operation of capital [*die Mitwirkung des Kapitals*] to terms of labor"; and in the latter of the two sentences just quoted he uses the identical expression, the co-operation of capital (*die Mirtwirkung des Kapitals*).

Falck, however, takes exception to Knapp's interpretation, and states his objection by saying that in the first place, by dividing the value of capital by the value of a year's wages, the reduction of which Thünen speaks is possible; and in the second place, according to Thünen, the reduction is not effected by means of the rate of interest. Curiously enough, he informs the reader that, by referring to § 13 of Thünen's work, he may convince himself of the validity of his objection to Knapp's criticism. The truth of the matter is that Falck not only misinterprets both Thünen and Knapp, but he also misquotes Knapp. That he misinterprets those authors is evident from the fact that they speak of reducing the co-operation of capital to terms of labor, and Falck speaks of reducing capital to terms of labor. That he misquotes Knapp can be readily seen by comparing page 16 of Knapp with page 23 of Falck.*

If the interpretation that I have given of § 13 is correct,

* Knapp, p. 16: "Thünen bemerkt . . . das ein Grenzgut nicht nur durch Verwendung von Löhnen hergestellt werden kann; er glaubt aber . . . man brauche bloss 'die Mitwirkung des Capitals auf Arbeit zu reduciren,' so erreiche man das Gewünschte; diese Reduction, selbst wenn sie möglich wäre, geschieht nach Thünen nur durch den Zinsfuss, und da der noch zu finden ist, so bleibt also die Schwierigkeit ungelöst."

Falck, p. 23: "Schliesslich sagt Knapp, . . . 'Diese Reduktion (des Capitals auf Arbeit), selbst wenn sie möglich wäre,'" etc.

Knapp is speaking of the reduction of the co-operation of capital, and Falck quotes him as speaking of the reduction of capital.

it is easy to expose a fallacy in Thünen's reasoning that vitiates the formula $\sqrt{ap}$. Thünen's purpose in his whole work is to find mathematical expressions for the natural rate of interest and the natural rate of wages. The method by which he does this is first to find a formula expressing the interdependence of wages and interest in the isolated state. This formula $z = \frac{p-(a+y)}{q(a+y)}$ we shall call formula A. In this formula all the quantities are known except y and z. In order to find the values of y and z, he next attempts to find an independent expression for y, or what is the same thing, since a is known, an independent expression for $(a+y)$; and by substituting for $(a+y)$ in formula A obtain the value of z. The formula that enables him to find the independent expression for $(a+y)$ is $\frac{n[p-(a+y)]}{\frac{nq(a+y)}{y}}$. In this formula, which we shall call formula B, all the quantities are assumed as known excepting y. But how did Thünen obtain the quantity nq? He says: Suppose "the laying out of the farm required the year's labor of nq men. . . . Unquestionably, in order to provide a new farm, is needed not only labor, but also the use of capital; (but) according to § 13, we can reduce the co-operation of capital to terms of labor, and thus express the costs of laying out the farm entirely in terms of labor." When we refer to § 13 to see how the reduction is to be performed, we find that it is done by means of the rate of interest. The fallacy in the argument is evident. Thünen's whole procedure is a mere begging of the question. His problem is to find the values of y and z in formula A; and, to solve the problem, he undertakes to find an independent expression for $(a+y)$ by means of formula B, and by substituting for $(a+y)$ in formula A obtain the value of z. But, in order to get the quantity nq in formula B, he assumes that z is known. If, however, z is known, then, according to formula A, y is known. Thünen undertakes to find the value of the unknown quantities y and z; and, in attempting to solve the problem, he uses the very quantities that he wants to find as known quantities.

While this error renders useless the formula $\sqrt{ap}$, yet it enables us to see why Thünen did not proceed to obtain the formula in the manner indicated by Komorzynski, and shows us the continuity in his work. In the part of his work based upon actual conditions (§ 13) he obtains the formula $z = \frac{n[p-(a+y)]}{nq(a+y)} = \frac{p-(a+y)}{q(a+y)}$; and in another part he states that it is to the advantage of the laborer to have the relation of wages and interest such that he can obtain the maximum income from his surplus when that surplus is placed at interest,—that is to say, it is to the advantage of the laborer to have yz obtain a maximum value. Now, Komorzynski holds that in these few facts we have the data with which to obtain the formula for natural wages, and that Thünen need not have carried his work farther; for, he says, if it is to the advantage of the laborer to have yz obtain a maximum value, then, since $z = \frac{p-(a+y)}{q(a+y)}$, his interests will be subserved when $\frac{y[p-(a+y)]}{q(a+y)}$ obtains a maximum value, which is the case when $(a+y) = \sqrt{ap}$. But Komorzynski assumes that the value of q in the above expression is known; and, in making this assumption, he has fallen into error. In § 13 the denominator of the expression for interest is obtained by dividing a definite amount of capital, Q, by the rate of wages. $\frac{Q}{a+y} = nq$ or $Q = nq(a+y)$. Hence nq is unknown as long as $(a+y)$ is unknown; and, when nq is known, $(a+y)$ is known, because their product is the definite quantity Q. Since, then, the value of q depends upon the value of $(a+y)$, it is an error to attempt to find the value of the unknown quantity $(a+y)$ in the above expression by assuming that q is known.

Thünen's method of obtaining the formula leads us to believe that he foresaw this difficulty. His sole object in trying to reduce the co-operation of capital in production to terms of labor was to enable him to proceed with his work by considering nq a known quantity. When he attempted to find the expression for natural wages by assuming that a number of laborers combined to lay out a marginal farm, he did not begin by assuming that the value of the farm equalled Q, and by dividing that quantity by the rate of wages obtain nq; but he began by supposing that nq equalled the number of men required to lay out the farm. Knapp and Komorzynski * notice that he changed his method of obtaining nq, and, without seeing his purpose, charge him with inconsistency. By following his work, however, we find that he had a definite purpose in view; for, assuming that nq is known, he obtained an expression that is identical in form with the above expression from which Komorzynski obtains the formula $\sqrt{ap}$, but differs from it, in that nq, according to Thünen, is a known quantity.

Thünen's theory is valuable,† because it marks a decided reaction against the teachings of the classical economists, and yet at the same time avoids the extravagant doctrines of the socialists. His specific contribution to the theory of natural wages does not consist in his mathematical formulas, nor, indeed, in any positive conclusions that he obtains, but rather in his designation of the factors that must be considered in any scientific theory of natural or just wages. What these factors are can best be seen by contrasting Thünen's theory with that of the classical economists.

1. While the classical economists treated labor throughout as a mere commodity, Thünen regards the laborer as a *man*, and considers his wages as the means of satisfying

* Knapp, pp. 15, 25. Komorzynski, pp. 55, 56.

† It must be remembered that the first edition of *Der naturgemässe Arbeitslohn* appeared in 1850. For valuable suggestions concerning Thünen's contribution to Natural Wages, compare Schumacher's *Ueber J. H. v. Thünen's Gesetz vom naturgemässen Arbeitslohn*, pp. 18, 19; Mithoff (in Schönberg, *Handbuch*, Band 1), p. 640; Schmidt, pp. 2, 16.

his wants. The work that he undertakes is to find the wages that are agreeable to the nature (*naturgemäss*) and to the destiny of man.

2. While the classical economists regarded solely the operation of natural law, Thünen considers the equity in the case. He believes that natural wages exist in the isolated state when these two conditions are realized, (*a*) when the laborer receives the same income from his surplus when that surplus is placed at interest as the capital-producer receives from his surplus when that surplus is embodied in a marginal farm; (*b*) when the laborer receives the maximum income from his surplus.* Here Thünen makes a crude attempt to find an equitable basis for the division of the product of labor between the laborers and the owners of capital invested in concrete forms.

3. While the classical economists considered only the requirements of the laborer as limited by his surroundings, and disregarded the product of labor, Thünen holds that there can be no scientific theory of wages that does not make wages depend upon product. The fundamental idea in the formula $\sqrt{ap}$ is that wages must vary with the product.

A scientific theory of natural wages must regard the laborer as a man, consider the rights of the laborer and of the capitalist, and make the wages of the laborer depend upon his product.

* These two characteristics of natural wages are definitely stated, p. 204.

BIBLIOGRAPHY.

Johann Heinrich v. Thünen: *Der naturgemässe Arbeitslohn und dessen Verhältniss zum Zinsfuss und zur Landrente.* Part II. 1 of Thünen's *Der isolirte Staat in Beziehung auf Landwirthschaft und Nationalökonomie.* Dritte Auflage. Berlin. 1875.

J. A. R. v. Helferich: *J. H. v. Thünen und sein Gesetz über die Theilung des Produkts unter die Arbeiter und Kapitalisten.* Tübinger Zeitschrift für die gesammte Staatswissenschaft. 1852. pp. 393–433.

A. Leymarie: *Le Salaire Naturel et son Rapport au Taux de l'Intérêt, par M. Jean Henri de Thünen.* Journal des Économistes. 1857. t. 15, pp. 250–264.

Mathieu Wolkoff: *Nouvelles Observations au Sujet de l'Ouvrage de M. de Thünen sur le Salaire Naturel.* Journal des Économistes. 1857. t. 16, pp. 239–255.

Étienne Laspeyres: *Wechselbeziehungen zwischen Volksvermehrung und Höhe des Arbeitslohns.* Heidelberg. 1860.

Georg Friedrich Knapp: *Zur Prüfung der Untersuchungen Thünen's über Lohn und Zinsfuss im isolirten Staate.* Braunschweig. 1865.

L. J. Brentano:* *Ueber J. H. v. Thünen's naturgemässen Lohn- und Zinsfuss im isolirten Staate.* Göttingen. 1867.

H. Schumacher: *Ueber J. H. v. Thünen's Gesetz vom naturgemässen Arbeitslohne und die Bedeutung dieses Gesetzes für die Wirklichkeit.* Rostock, 1869.

W. Roscher: *Geschichte der Nationalökonomik in Deutschland.* pp. 879–902.

Georg v. Falck: *Die Thünen'sche Lehre vom Bildungsgesetz des Zinsfusses und vom naturgemässen Arbeitslohn.* Leipzig.

Carl Knies: *Der Credit.* pp. 125–131.

Th. Mithoff: *Der naturgemässe Arbeitslohn.* In Schönberg's Handbuch der politischen Oekonomie. Band I., pp. 636–640. Dritte Auflage.

H. Schumacher: *J. H. v. Thünen: Ein Forscherleben.* Zweite Auflage. Rostock u. Ludwigslust. 1883.

W. Launhardt: *Mathematische Begründung der Volkswirthschaftslehre.* Leipzig. 1885. pp. 138–140.

C. Schmidt: *Der natürliche Arbeitslohn.* Jena. 1887. pp. 16–40.

Maurice Block: *Les Progrès de la Science Économique.* Vol. II. 1890. p. 259 *et seq.*

J. Lehr: *Grundbegriffe und Grundlagen der Volkswirthschaft.* pp. 325–328.

Joh. v. Komorzynski: *Thünen's naturgemässer Arbeitslohn.* Zeitschrift für Volkswirthschaft, Socialpolitik, und Verwaltung. Dritter Band, 1 Heft, pp. 27–62.

*I have been unable to secure a copy of Brentano's dissertation. It is out of print.

THE

RELATIONS BETWEEN

CAPITAL AND LABOR

IN THE

UNITED STATES.

BY

JOSEPH NASH.

THE FIRST-PRIZE ESSAY AWARDED BY THE BOSTON YOUNG MEN'S CHRISTIAN UNION, 1878.

BOSTON:
LEE AND SHEPARD, PUBLISHERS,
1878.

Press of Rockwell & Churchill, 39 Arch St.

THE RELATIONS BETWEEN CAPITAL AND LABOR IN THE UNITED STATES.

BY

JOSEPH NASH.

THE FIRST-PRIZE ESSAY AWARDED BY THE BOSTON YOUNG MEN'S CHRISTIAN UNION, 1878.

BOSTON:
LEE AND SHEPARD, PUBLISHERS,
1878.

CAPITAL AND LABOR.

PRIZE ESSAYS ON THE RELATIONS BETWEEN THEM OFFERED BY THE CHRISTIAN UNION.

It was publicly proposed, a few months since, to offer to members of the Young Men's Christian Union, not more than thirty-five years of age, prizes of fifty and twenty-five dollars, to be paid out of a special fund contributed for the purpose, for the two best essays on "The Relations between Capital and Labor in the United States." The announcement stated that "essays are to be signed with fictitious names, and accompanied by a sealed envelope containing the real and the fictitious names of the writer. Eminent men will be selected as judges. It is expected that the successful essays will be made public in the Union building, or in some other manner. It is hoped that this will be the means of interesting many young men in, and inducing them to give serious thoughts to, this most important social question."

Much interest was manifested in the above proposition, many young men responding by preparing essays. General F. A. Osborn, Professor William P. Atkinson, and Samuel Wells, Esq. kindly consented to act as judges, and have devoted much time to the careful examination of the essays. From the judges the following decision has been received: —

BOSTON, February 7, 1878.

WILLIAM H. BALDWIN, Esq., *President of the Young Men's Christian Union:* —

DEAR SIR, — The committee to whom was referred the examination of the essays written by members of the Union on the subject of "The Relations between Capital and Labor in the United States," beg leave to report that they have carefully read the essays, which numbered seventeen in all, and are much gratified in finding that they exhibit evidence of considerable study and investigation, and also show that the ideas of the writers are generally sound and correct.

They unanimously recommend that the first prize be awarded to the writer of the essay marked "Themis;" the second to the writer of that marked "Junius, 1728;" and are pleased to be able to name for honorable mention the three essays respectively marked "Alleyn E.," "A Job Printer," and "Junius."

FRANCIS A. OSBORN,
W. P. ATKINSON,
SAMUEL WELLS,

The sealed envelopes, containing the real names of the writers, were opened Monday evening, February 11. "Themis" (first prize) was found to be by Joseph Nash, Boston; "Junius, 1728" (second prize), was by John A. Bennett. Names for "honorable mention": "Alleyn E.," F. A. Varney; "A Job Printer," Henry A. Kidder; "Junius," Henry J. Bowen.

Detached parts of this essay were read at the Union Hall, Boylston street, on February 18, 1878, which the Boston press characterized as "strong, suggestive, and original in style."

TO

The Boston Young Men's Christian Union

THIS ESSAY IS RESPECTFULLY DEDICATED, AS A SLIGHT TOKEN OF RECOGNITION OF THE PRACTICAL CHRISTIAN WORK IT IS DOING FOR THE YOUNG MEN IN THE CITY OF BOSTON, AND AT WHOSE INSTANCE IT WAS WRITTEN.

THE RELATIONS BETWEEN CAPITAL AND LABOR IN THE UNITED STATES.

We cannot regard but with solicitude, if not with alarm, the recent, violent and riotous events in the history and progress of labor in the United States. It is a new phase in our social order, that has for us, our country, and its institutions, a more than ordinary significance. Our civilization, in its political form, has been built of forces that are peculiar to itself. They give it certain elements of strength and weakness not to be found in the modern civilizations of continental Europe, which possess, in other respects, like characteristics; being developed and unfolded by the same expanding powers of religious rule, scientific discovery, intellectual growth, and economic prosperity.

Our government is made up of the people, by the people, and for the people. Whatever irritates and distracts any considerable number of its citizens comes close and quick in its sensitive pulsation to the heart and strength of our national life. With us government and people are synonymous terms. Like the brain and the body, they are bound together by innumerable and delicate nerves. Does the one suffer, then the pain is speedily communicated to every part of the body politic. We have no strong, conservative and centralized force that stands apart by itself, governed by a special sovereignty, and controlled by a limited authority, in the maintenance of public peace and order. Do the people strike at the government and the civil rule, then they fall.

We have no soldiers enlisted in their defence but them; no coercive power for municipal order and national unity but what they voluntarily contribute. Do the people make the assault upon our institutions, then Cæsar has fallen by the hand of his bosom-friend Brutus.

It would seem, then, that under such circumstances we must make some satisfactory solution of this difficult problem of capital and labor; that we must find some remedy for the disease, discover some palliative to sooth and allay its inflammation; for, should it continue to increase in its maddened intensity and purpose, who will set the bounds to what it may destroy, who limit the extent of the upheaval and change it may produce, in the present social order and political system of the government of the United States?

For labor to raise its rebellious hand in this country and under this government, formed in its deepest interests, and fashioned to its special needs, seems to us like the hand of an evil son raised to strike down the venerated father whose first care and thought were his welfare, success, and happiness. Well may we ask the question, if capital and labor cannot be united and harmonious under institutions and laws like ours, in a country so advantageous to their growth and increase as this, where is the land, or what the political system, under which this desirable result can be attained?

But, regret this recent trouble between capital and labor as we may, it has its lessons. The learning of them will form a kind of crisis in our national thought. Among other things, the struggle teaches us that the economic laws make no distinctions in nations or governments, in their rule and application. America has freedom and equality. She has millions of acres of rich and fertile soil yet uncultivated, exhaustless treasures of material prosperity yet untouched.

But labor riots here as well as in the most autocratic and imperial governments of Europe, where every acre of land is occupied, and every natural force pressed into the service for the accumulation of wealth, to minister to man's wants, necessities, and comforts. The economic laws are universal in their rule and sovereignty. They are confined to no nation or country in their jurisdiction. Disregard them in republic or monarchy, and the penalty is sure to follow.

As a people we are energetic and active. We hurry along, with a feverish intensity, in the pursuit of wealth and pleasure. We are not given to the study of causes. We are interested only in effects and events. We catch at the nearest way. We leap into the swiftest current, never thinking that in the fact of its swiftness lies the probability of a Niagara, near at hand, over which we may be hurled. We never anticipate or think of peril. The vessel sails under full canvas till she runs ashore; then we look about us for the why and the wherefore.

While we are not insensible to danger or misfortune, yet we require a strong electrical shock, such as this one of capital and labor has been, to set our reflective faculties in motion. If we heed the warning, it may serve a good and noble purpose in pointing out the way we may escape more fatal errors in the future.

The relations between capital and labor in the United States may have some few special and exclusive conditions that are only to be found in this country. They may consist in its climate, form of government, legislative policy, geographical position, or in some particular or material advantage which nature has bestowed upon the United States to the exclusion of all other countries. Each and all of these are important subjects of inquiry that bear more or less directly upon this controversy. But the greater importance of this question rests here, as elsewhere, in the analysis and consideration of the laws and forces that are universal in their application to the production of the capital and the remuneration of labor. All civilized communities have here a common cause, a common difficulty to encounter, a common obstacle to overcome.

The great capitals of nations and the markets of the world have been brought close to each other by the means of the telegraph. So rapid, facilitated, and frequent has become the communication, by the railway and the steamship, of the most distant parts of the world with each other, that all nations seem bound and linked together in a common brotherhood and purpose. No nation can long enjoy profit and advantages in which others do not soon participate. No country can suffer in the decline of its production and trade, or adopt artificial obstructions to exchange and intercourse, that will not be quickly felt by all with which it trades. The blow acts and reacts. It either intentionally or ignorantly hits the mark before it, but it often rebounds and comes back with a double force to strike the hand that sent it. This economic interest seems to be one of the silent and almost inscrutable ways of Divine Providence to raise all the nations of the world to a common level, in which they shall share their mutual benefits and privileges, whether they would or no.

Not only every country, but every age and cycle of time have characteristics of thought, manner, and work that distinguish them from all others. There are local influences, such as belong to the community, government, or nation, that we can comprehend, grasp, and measure, with some degree of certainty and truth. But there are also world influences, that, like huge levers, lift all the civilized races as a unit, and fashion all they touch to one universal mould. The force and direction of these influences we cannot always understand and predict. We cannot sufficiently separate ourselves from the all-pervading interests and prejudices that surround us to dispassionately consider and analyze them. What is the blessing of one age we denounce as the curse of the next. We run with no sight of the goal. We fall over a precipice, or land in a garden of roses.

This wide-extending influence we hold to be especially true of labor in the present century. Within the last fifty years there have been great changes and rapid strides in the social and material world. There have been great discoveries and marvellous inventions, that have almost annihilated space and time. But probably in no single phase has the change been greater than in the condition and circumstances of labor. This change in labor, in a large measure, has grown out of this new order. This new and increased application of the latent forces of nature to these powerful and wondrous constructions of mechanisms have made for it in the United States, as elsewhere, a new era and a new existence.

In this change man has been largely separated from the soil. Everything like dependent servitude has been zealously fought and largely overcome. Man's life, it is true, has become more independent, but often more responsible and precarious, in proportion as it has attained this end. The gaining of liberty often means the loss of bread. He has been drawn from agriculture to manufactures and commerce. At the beginning of the present century seven-eighths of the population of the United States was rural and engaged in farming. The last census showed that the balance is now as greatly against agricultural labor, as it was seventy or eighty years ago in its favor. Now, not more than one in seven of the people is so employed. In England the change has been still greater. Only three millions of her entire population gain their living by cultivating the soil, while she must annually import cereals to feed ten millions of her population. She expends yearly more than a hundred and fifty millions of pounds sterling for this purpose. About fifty per cent. of the population of France is still attached to the soil. England, it is true, under the present system of the division of her landed estates, cannot become an extensive agricultural country.

Under this new régime new trades and employments have sprung up, requiring special and skilful training, which when once acquired are seldom abandoned. There have been multiplied divisions of labor, having a special type and character. Each attracts unto itself its several artisans, who have attained a proficiency and celerity in its performance that they have in no other. The general character of labor, such as our forefathers possessed in settling the New World, has become special. Doubtless, in the new quality of labor, irrespective of machinery, the facility and capacity of production have been greatly increased. A few men now can do the work of a hundred of a century ago. The loom and the spindle have built up large towns and cities that but for their invention would never have existed. Machinery and commerce have brought within the attainment of the lower orders of society articles of consumption, comfort, and adornment, that two centuries ago a queen or a duchess could not have commanded. Queen Elizabeth dined on roast beef and beer; potatoes at the table of King James I. were a luxury; and the humblest citizen can now read by a light that royal eyes could not then enjoy.

It is out of this new order of the classifications and associations of labor, this ease and quickness of communication, that the trade-unions have had their origin, and derived their coöperation and unity. This vivid and strong contrast in the conditions of capital and labor, the employer and the employé, has been greatly intensified. Each has been amassed in greater quantities, and they have been brought in direct contact, where they were formerly more widely diffused. These new conditions have given a renewed impulse to the intensity of this modern antagonism between capital and labor. In this highly attained rapidity and cheapness of production, by these trained bands and classes of workmen, nations are rivalling each other in the race for wealth. It is out of this great economic saving of labor that the present order of civilization, in no small measure, owes its prosperity, power, and glory; its boasted superiority over those that have preceded it.

Whence arises this industrial conflict between capital and labor? Volumes have been written, commissions appointed, associations formed, courts organized, to answer this question; yet strikes continue, trade-unions multiply and increase, and labor grows more discontented, factious, and rebellious. It is not the few thinkers and writers who will settle this controversy, while the laboring classes are left in neglect and ignorance. It is not a burden that the few can sustain; but one where each member of society must press forward to bear an intelligent, human, and Christian part, or it falls to the ground.

A Christian humanity, an intelligent understanding of the primary laws of the science of political economy, or the science of the accumulation of wealth, we believe to be both involved in the relations between capital and labor in the United States. Whatever tends to the production of capital, the decrease in the supply and competition of labor, or to the contentment of labor in its present status, are lines of investigation that go directly to the deepest interests of this important controversy. Labor is entirely ignorant of the economic laws that govern and control the conditions by which it is remunerated. Capital is often hard, exclusive, and unsympathetic. The crystallization of society in its social form is, perhaps, one of the inevitable tendencies of time and human nature. Government sometimes assists, but cannot always resist, this influence. Often, like the atmosphere we breathe, we are unconscious of its existence. Societies, that have passed through many ages of opulence and wealth, naturally tend to autocratic assumptions of superiority and class distinctions. These often make labor feel that somehow it is disgraced and humiliated, with a curse upon its brow that it has done nothing to incur.

We cannot deny it, regret it as we may, that money in the United States is becoming the general basis of our social orders. It has here a boundless power and significance, that is, perhaps, to be found in no other order of civilization of modern times. Railway and other corporations can buy everything with their check-books, even, it would seem, almost the government itself. Large accumulations of wealth, that, under the direction of enterprise, integrity, and humanity, are the greatest blessings to the community and the State, are frequently becoming, by a sad perversion of the best objects and purposes of money, to be a great curse and misfortune. Unfortunately, by many it seems only the means to gratify a tinsel vanity and a hollow ambition. We can close our eyes to this fact and tendency, but they nevertheless exist. We can close our eyes to the sun, but that does not make the sun the less.

Labor does not, however, demand of capital an equality in a social sense. This is not the grievance of labor against capital. It is a humane interest and kindness that it seeks in its struggle, irrespective of the wages, be they high or low, by which it is remunerated. Labor wishes to be treated like flesh and blood, and not like a machine, to which political economy limits and prescribes it. And here we think it is that a solution of this problem, wholly by the science of political economy, will still leave much that is irritating and unsatisfactory. Human nature, in its essential characteristics and repeated phenomena, we believe to be no less a science than political economy. Whoever attempts to solve any problem directly connected with its passional life, that does not make it the form, if not the basis, of what would be demonstrated, is reckoning without his host. Political economy can do much, but it cannot do all, to bring capital and labor to a just, thorough, and intelligent understanding of each other.

The fate of the laboring man in regard to the amount of wages he shall receive hangs suspended between two causes, — that which produces capital, and that which reduces the competition of labor. Wages is but a relative term to the cost of living. Money wages may be high, yet of no advantage to the laborer. The proportionate expense of what he consumes may be so great that at the end of the week he has nothing to save out of his earnings. The cheapness of an article of necessity or luxury depends upon the number engaged in its production, the facility by which it can be produced at the least possible application of labor, and the demand for its consumption.

The ancient Greek laborer received nineteen cents per day. Yet, when a day's labor could buy a sheep, and six days' labor an ox, he was receiving comparatively high wages, to the laborer who gets two dollars per day, and a sheep costs him four dollars, and an ox twenty dollars. When sheep can be purchased at so small a sum there must be many engaged in their production, when compared to the demand for their consumption. At this price of meat the laborer could have his table bountifully supplied while earning the miserable daily stipend of nineteen cents. We know that there are many laborers of the present day, in continental Europe, who can earn three or four times this amount, yet rarely see meat upon their table. And we have no doubt that meat presses hard upon the wages of many a day-laborer in America. We fear that it will press harder in the future than it has in the past.

In the consideration of the wages that labor gets there are always two things to be considered: what it positively receives, and what it costs it to live. The economic sword is never sharpened only on one side. It always has two edges. While we follow the course and direction of one of those edges, we may be entirely ignorant of the execution and havoc that the unseen edge may be doing. As Bastiat, the French political economist, has said, "There is always the seen and the unseen." The seen is the number of dollars that labor is paid; the unseen is the purchasing power of those dollars, in the markets, of necessities and comforts. Both of these must always be contrasted and subtracted, one from the other, before we can have a just and accurate remainder to inform us of the true status of labor, to note its advancement or decline.

When we read that wages are any stated sum, in any particular age or country, our lesson is but half learned. We must next know how much meat or bread that sum will buy, to ascertain if labor is well or ill paid. An historian may quote the prices of labor, in different ages and countries, to show how much better off it must be in one age and country than in others. But this is a very false standard. One set of figures in the seen may prove a statement that would be an absolute lie in the unseen. We are often reminded of this when the different advocates of opposing industrial policies make exhibits of figures to maintain their different positions. These often may be but half the truth, and that the smallest half. It is the telling of a lie by omissions and silence. Is England losing in any industrial interest, look and see if she is not gaining double the amount in some other. Are the United States increasing in the business and manufactures of any protected article, be sure that some other interest, by its loss, decline, or contribution, is not more than paying for this increase.

Writers on political economy are not entirely unanimous on the wage-fund theory. Yet it seems to us that they substantially arrive at the same end, only differing in the ways they come to it. It is evident that capital must have its interest, or it will not be invested. The employer or the manager must have his wages or profits, or he will not work. If labor gets what remains, we cannot possibly see how it can obtain any more. The conflict is, perhaps, more directly between labor and profits as represented in the employer. For labor to deny capital its interest would be destroying the means and subsistence by which it exists.

The wage-fund principle of political economy teaches us that the amount of wages that labor will receive, at any given time, or place, or in any trade or occupation, is simply one of division; that capital is the dividend, the number of laborers the divisor, and what remains after the process of division is the quotient. There are only two ways to make this quotient larger. Increase the dividend, the divisor remaining the same, and the quotient will be larger. Lessen the divisor, the dividend remaining the same, and a like result will be obtained.

If there is a wage-fund of five hundred dollars, and there are one hundred laborers competing for its distribution, the result will be that each laborer will receive five dollars. But if there are five hundred laborers to be paid out of it then each one can only receive a dollar. It is self-evident that labor cannot get more than there is. All additions to capital, all investments of profits, in an extended and enlarged business, mean an increased demand for labor, or a higher rate of wages to those engaged. If there are two employers and only one laborer then wages will go up.

But if there are two laborers seeking work of one employer then wages will go down.

In the economic world much which seems to be lost is only transferred; what one has apparently lost, another has gained. An investment may be unprofitable, but the money that has established it, or has been seemingly sunk and lost, has gone to new hands. The railway may return no profits, but the wealth that has been expended in its construction has begun new enterprises or enlarged those already in existence, in the production of wealth and employment of labor. The railway failure we see; but we do not always see and follow the new distribution of wealth it has occasioned, and the silent forces it may have set in motion in the industrial world. The spirit of competition, and the ceaseless, voracious passion of selfishness, which the workman generally regards as his most bitter foe and relentless destroyer, are really his truest friends and most steadfast protectors. They are the heart of the great business world, the centre around which it revolves. They dispense light and warmth to the farthest parts of the world. Were it not for competition then capital would oppress and grind labor to the barest verge of subsistence, as the meanness or avarice of the employer might dictate. There would be no power to relieve it from its miserable and unfortunate condition. Were it not for selfishness, acting true to its grasping and covetous nature, then profits would cease to go to capital, enterprise would be abandoned, and business of all kinds would fall into decline and ruin. The laborer, finding nothing he could do for his support, would either have to starve or return to a state of semi-barbarism.

Labor is interested in the high rates of profits as much if not more than capital itself. These profits will again return to capital to increase the wage-fund to make higher wages, or to give employment to those pressing forward to enter the industrial pursuits. Here, if the laborer would cast his bread upon the waters, in the form of low wages, to increase profits, he will receive it back again in an enlarged capital. But it is also equally true that capital is interested in high wages, for through an increased consumption they will as inevitably find their way back to enlarge business and increase profits.

It is difficult for labor to understand and accept this law of supply and demand, this process of division, in determining the amount of wages it shall receive. It ascribes wages to the generosity or avarice of the employer. The laborer works hard and long, in the most disagreeable and life-destroying occupations, only to earn a scanty and beggarly subsistence. He sees his employer and the capitalist living in ease and luxury, engaging only in such tasks as taste or fancy may dictate. His judgment moves slow and reluctantly to a conclusion his feelings and his passions are so strong against, with apparently much reason on his side. He has no faith in the economic theory. The science of political economy to him is but a concerted conspiracy, continued from age to age in the interest of capital, to defraud labor of its just reward and honest remuneration.

But history shows us that wherever labor has been scarce then wages have always been high. In the reign of King Edward the Third the whole of England was afflicted with a plague of uncommon severity, and the people died in large numbers. Immediately after this event wages began to rise, and it was found necessary for legislation to interfere to regulate the price of labor. When the Puritans and the early settlers began to cultivate the New World, wages were high, and it was almost impossible to obtain workmen at any price. Governor Winthrop says in his journal that a laboring man could earn as much in three days as would keep him the seven. The merchants of the colony of Massachusetts Bay said they could better afford to pay the English manufacturers two hundred per cent. profit than to manufacture for themselves, so high was the price of labor. Here again the legislative authority of the colony interceded and fixed the sum that labor should receive, attaching a penalty to both the employer and employé who broke it. But if it is right, just, and wise, for parliaments and legislatures to fix the price of labor when it is scarce, then there are certainly the same reasons why labor should have the benefit of legislation when labor is plenty and wages low. But, doubtless, the best policy for governments to pursue is not to prescribe any industrial laws between capital and labor.

It has been truly said that they who would find truth must dig deep. The stones lie upon the surface, but the precious ore is deep down in nature's storehouses. There is much in the science of political economy that is in direct contradiction to what general opinion, popular belief, and superficial observation have formed of it. To throw aside these errors requires patience and diligence. This true and not this false instruction must be brought home to the door and threshold of labor.

Let us pause a moment to see how this law of supply and demand operates. Suppose there is a community of five thousand individuals, — three thousand are rich and two thousand are poor. The three thousand who are rich have meat; the two thousand who are poor cannot obtain it. The supply of meat is limited to three thousand pounds. The rich, being moved by humanity, gives each of the poorer members of the community enough to pay for a pound of meat, at its standard price, when only the three thousand are purchasers. What is the inevitable result? Why, the moment that the additional two thousand enter the market to purchase meat up goes the price, and they are just as far from their supply of meat as before, and would be until their purchasing power equalled that of the rich, or the supply of meat was increased.

This illustration, the principles of which are taking place every day in the economic world, not only shows us the law of supply and demand, but also shows us what is the true wealth of a country. Labor has generally a very erroneous and perverted idea of wealth. It calls it gold, silver, and greenbacks. But this is not so. They at best are only a symbol of wealth, an evidence of so much labor performed. If there are a thousand bushels of corn in a community or a country, all the gold and silver in the world would not make that thousand bushels of corn any more. If there are a thousand bushels of wheat in one balance, in proportion as you put in the purchasing power of greenbacks, or paper money in the other, up goes the price of wheat, and tons of paper money would not add a single grain to the quantity of wheat.

Paper money is comparatively worthless in the cheapness of its production. Gold and silver would be worthless, if they could be obtained on the same conditions. In our last war we saw how the increase of paper money made an increase of prices without a corresponding addition to value.

Professor Cairns, an English economist, has prepared a table in one of his works, by which he shows that since the discovery of gold in California and Australia, and its great increase in the monetary system of the world, there has been a proportionate rise in the prices of all articles of consumption. Should new mines be discovered, and gold more easily obtained than at present, then this rise in prices would still more rapidly increase.

This economic balance is a most delicate one, and will weigh to the hundredth part of a grain. In Australia a certain kind of boxwood is used, that is brought all the way from South America. This same wood grows in abundance in the immediate neighborhood, and costs nothing, only, to fell it. In the early history of the colony of Virginia that State attempted to exclude tobacco in its productions, and to encourage manufactures. But tobacco, in spite of all the legislation against it, was the master; and at the beginning of the Revolutionary War that colony exported annually a million of pounds sterling of this article, that largely maintained the balance of colonial trade. In our own time, wheat is shipped three thousand miles to Europe, while it may be sadly wanted in New York or Boston.

In the great commercial operations and industrial enterprises of the present age we cannot always see the delicacy and test the accuracy of this economic science, for want of figures and data, but which we believe always exists. It is of this force, that will draw a pin around the world, if it is for its interest to do so, and will not move a bushel of diamonds a sixteenth part of an inch, unless in obedience to some of the laws of its intricate structure, that labor should have some knowledge and insight, if we ever expect labor to understand its true position and interests in relation to capital. And this we think applies with almost equal force in the United States as in any other nation. It is true we have much teaching in this country, but comparatively little real deep and practical instruction. We seem content, in an astonishing degree, to glide upon the surface.

How to increase capital, the dividend of wages, is the objective point of all modern civilizations and nations. Capital is the all-pervading atmosphere that surrounds the economic life. It limits what can live and what must die. Does labor or population press hard upon capital, then there is suffering, misery, and death. Capital is the parent of industry, and assists in a new distribution of wealth. It gives work to the poor, employment to the idle, and makes an increase of population desirable and profitable. When capital and labor are mutual in their wants and needs then peace, plenty, and happiness abound, so far as the economic harmony can produce them. But have they grown out of proportion to each other, especially if labor is the larger of the two, then there is faction, strife, hunger, and crime. The prosperity and advancement of the present social and national systems seem closely linked with this increase of capital. And especially we of the United States, who claim that our civilization is in advance of every other, cannot give this part of the subject too much attention. When idleness and misfortune are the result of indolence, or a false pride and vanity, we certainly can have no sympathy, and can find no remedy for such an affliction. But when honest manly and womanly labor is forced to idleness because it has outgrown capital, and placed itself beyond succor, from this source, then we have arrived at a sad condition of economic development.

Capital is realized either from increase or economy, from the positive addition of something to the wealth of the community, or a saving in its annual expenditure. Increase your means, restrain and reduce your wants, and the result in both cases is the same. Although a contraction in the economic world may have the effect to do much injury to certain industries, yet it is much better that this gradual decline should come, than a general failure by the individuals of a community living beyond their means, or indulging in expenses that must end in ruin.

The people of that nation or country are no doubt the most prosperous who are the greatest consumers, and at the same time save and amass the greatest amount of capital. Such a condition as this in every community must be the standard of its national progress and superiority. Tables well supplied, houses healthy, agreeable, and pleasant, homes with an air of ease, plenty, and comfort,— these bespeak a season and a land where sunshine, warmth, and beauty have largely entered into the lives of the inhabitants. It is not how the few rich of every nation live, but what are the surroundings and comforts of the laboring classes, that are the highest tests of its true prosperity. Expenditure and economy are contradictory terms, and, if we can practise only one, it is far preferable to be economical.

That nation is most rapidly gaining wealth, in comparison and competition with the increase of the wealth of other nations, that is applying the economic forces to the industrial pursuits that are of the greatest advantage to her in the markets of the world. And here we know there has arisen a wide, earnest, and deep conflict of opinion and theory in regard to agriculture, manufactures, commerce, protection, and free trade. These various industries and national policies are advanced and maintained with much zeal and confidence by their respective partisans that they are the true ones; that in the adoption or rejection of some one of these theories lies the prosperity or ruin of the United States. One party asserts that the greatest and most rapid accumulation of wealth is in manufactures; another in agriculture; a third in commerce; a fourth believes in protection; and a fifth sees nothing but failure and ruin outside of free trade. But, as a nation cannot adopt and pursue all of these policies, it is evident that by many it can be fated only to general bankruptcy.

This industrial and national economic conflict has not confined itself to the United States alone, but has been agitated, discussed, and has divided since the days of the ancient republics. Under all kinds of governments and in all climates these policies have been advocated; one of them at one time successful, and at another defeated. A dogmatic assertion of the claims and advantages of either of these systems will probably never bring the converts of each to think more of their opponents or their systems. For the want of an all-comprehensive and accurate data, both in the seen and the unseen of the economic world, a result will not, probably, be soon reached that will admit of no dispute or contradiction in these controversies. In them, however, so far as they may aid or retard the accumulation of capital, may lie an important factor in the solution of the problem of "the relation of capital and labor in the United States."

We believe, in this matter, that the economic forces are stronger, and that the economic laws are wiser, than any that man can produce. Some writers maintain that in manufactures is the quickest and surest way to wealth. But this can be so only in a relative degree. The industrial balance is continually changing. How impossible the practice that all nations shall encourage and engage in manufactures. Let this be the custom, and it would soon be profitable to cultivate the barren soils of Greenland, and every small patch of ground would become a mine of wealth. It is in the harmony of the three great divisions of industrial labor that peace, plenty, and prosperity can only be maintained. This division cannot now be limited to a single nation, but must be enjoyed by all. You can pay no regard to this if you wish, but we think there is a greater power than man's puerile weakness that is directing the great engineery of life. In nothing is this power more signal than in the industrial world. In production and in the division and distribution of labor it is man's great mission to find out what nature demands of him. In proportion as he works in harmony with her, he prospers and lives; as he works against her, does he suffer and die.

The production of manufactures in the United States in 1790 has been estimated at twenty millions of dollars. The population then was about three millions. The value of the productions of manufactures in this country in 1870, making an allowance of thirty per cent. for an inflated currency, was three and a half billions of dollars, and the population was forty millions. In 1790 the value of the production of manufactures, per capita, in the United States was six and two-thirds dollars; in 1870 it was eighty-seven and a half dollars. The policy of the United States between these periods has been largely a protective one. Here certainly has been comparatively a large and rapid increase in the value of manufactures. But, in so far as this industry has been increased by protection, we believe that the agricultural interests and wealth have had to pay for it, to the utmost farthing. Agriculture has lost, manufactures have gained, by protection. The sum that by the policy of protection agriculture has paid for manufactures is the difference in the price it has had to pay for American manufactured goods, and what the same goods could be bought at in home markets from foreign manufacturers. Paul has been paid, but Peter has been robbed. There certainly has been a seen gain in the value of manufactures; but has there not also, at the same time, been an unseen loss in agriculture?

The national policy of England, in regard to protection and free trade, has been a somewhat changeable one. In 1650, when her great rivals, the Dutch merchantmen, were becoming the common carriers of the merchandise of the world, England passed a series of laws known as the Navigation Acts. These acts were the most rigid and severe in the interests of the protective policy. That nation wished to exclude her Holland competitors from trading in her colonial dependencies of America. These acts were warmly praised by commercial and political writers of the time. They were termed the *magna charta maritima*. But since then the free-trade policy has been adopted by that nation. By some it is claimed that the protective policy has been the palladium of her commercial prosperity; while others have been as strong in their assertions and testimony that the protective laws brought her to the verge of ruin; and the same regime, continued a few more years, would have plunged her into a bloody revolution, civil anarchy, and decay.

The protective policy, it is claimed by its advocates, keeps up the price of wages in the United States. Wages certainly have been higher in the United States than in England; but this we do not believe is wholly due to the legislation of protection. One of the reasons why wages have been higher in this country than in England is in the increased demand for labor. But let the national policy remain what it now is, for fifty years, we think that wages would fall by the inevitable law of supply and demand. It is impossible to prevent this result by an artificial barrier or protection. It is beyond the power of man to resist or control it. But where protection keeps up the price of other commodities, as well as that of labor, the latter loses nothing by its removal. Wages come down; but in the same ratio the cost of living is lessened. That which reduces the cost of what labor uses and consumes, in proportion as it reduces its remuneration, is of no disadvantage to labor.

The national policy may do much to accelerate or retard the accumulation of wealth. Whatever does this lies very close to this relation between capital and labor. The things that legislation can do to aid in the increase of capital are very few; but the things it may do to prevent it are very many.

If one country can manufacture cheaper and better articles than another, or all others, then that country ought to do it, not only for itself, but all the world. If one country can grow wheat cheaper than all others, then it should be the world's storehouse for this article, until some other country can excel it. But, even with free trade, England has not banished her pauperism and poor-rates. When one in ten of her population is a pauper, and, in hard times, one in six has to be assisted, then it would seem that this panacea, after a thirty years' trial, will leave much to carry on the conflict of capital and labor.

There is much in this struggle and competition of nations to do everything for themselves and neighbors, that resembles the selfishness of an avaricious man. He desires to grasp everything himself. It pains him to see friend or foe pursuing any successful industry or business. He has all he can do himself; but his greed outruns his judgment. It beclouds all his faculties. This might do if man was to live like Robinson Crusoe, independent of his fellow-men. But God and nature have decreed a different way. They have ordered that there shall be mutual help, assistance, and a mutual interchange of benefits and services. No nation, at the present day, can cut itself off from the rest of the world. Isolation is not independence. It is narrow, selfish, and small, — dwarfing the man or the nation that practises it. If we sell to England, France, or Russia, then there is nothing more inevitable than that we must buy of them, or give them what we produce. In interchange there is profit. When the profit ceases then the interchange will stop. In proportion as other nations are dependent upon us, just in such a proportion must we be dependent upon them; the service cannot long be on one side.

While we believe in protection and prohibition, to limit false and extravagant wants, and to correct the perversion of capital, yet we do not see why one nation should not partake of the special benefits that nature has made for all mankind. While we can understand that the infant cannot contend with the giant, we have yet to be convinced that it is cheaper for one nation to produce or manufacture for itself what it can buy at a much less cost from others. By the protective system the industrial occupations of a nation are no doubt multiplied and increased; but they are weakened just in proportion as they are not extended and broadened by some other force and interest than a merely artificial one. It may do very well to start a man in business who has the elements of success; but to keep one in business, who has not the experience, industry, and capacity to sustain himself, is an unprofitable and losing investment. So we think it is with protecting an industry by national legislation. We believe just in proportion as a nation is producing or manufacturing for itself what it can purchase in another market at a cheaper rate, just in such a proportion is it pursuing a policy of impoverishment and ruin.

A great deal has been said in our history about the American system. By this, as we understand it, America is to produce and consume herself. She is to cut all the economic cords by which she is bound to the trade and interests of foreign nations. Her wants and needs, and the means to satisfy them, are wholly to be found and brought forth from her own resources and industry. She desires neither to buy nor to sell to neighboring nations. She is young, vigorous, and prosperous, and does not wish to unite her youthful energies to the age and decrepitude of continental countries. But America in time must grow old, in the economic sense. She cannot resist age any more than can the individual. Her rich and virgin soil will not always yield productive crops at so little expense as at present. It will soon become worn out in the service, and will not give unto man, only what he has first given unto it, to renew and strengthen its wasted life. America, with her manifold interests, does not show that she is advancing towards that happy state of seclusion. With more than five hundred millions of her bonds, and other securities and stocks in the hands of foreign capitalists, an annual importer to the amount of more than a half billion of dollars, her economic life seems, as yet, closely connected with that of foreign nations. If to live by yourself, and upon yourself, means strength and prosperity, then the protective system is the true one.

We do not think, however, it is for a nation to decide by any course of arbitrary legislation upon what it has prejudged its interests. It is not for the legislative authority at Washington, London, or Paris to announce whether these several nations shall be agricultural, commercial, or manufacturing. There is a more wise and comprehensive wisdom than man's directing and controlling in this industrial selection. It is the economic power that never waits on legislatures for its instructions or orders. It is, no doubt, a poor trade to export wheat in exchange for French feathers and India shawls. But if the wives and daughters of the workingmen of the United States must have extravagant dress and useless gewgaws, it is best that they should have them as cheap as possible, or there should be a prohibitive tariff upon them so high that it would place them above their reach. We are not ruined by what we can't afford, but by what we think we can. This perversion of wealth is of vital importance in the relations of capital and labor in all countries; but it applies with double force in the United States, where the natural tendencies to extravagance receive a strong impulse in the freedom of the political form. But, fortunately, however strong the dose of poison by legislation that man may give to the economic life, it in a measure carries its own antidote with it. However deep the cut, the economic physician is at hand, with soothing medicines, bandages, and ligaments, to heal the wound as far as possible.

Political economists separate production into two divisions

or kinds, in its application and use; the production that is immediately absorbed and wasted, and that which turns into renewed capital, and becomes the source of other wealth. The greater part of the production of a country is annually consumed. Much of man's toil necessarily is being destroyed and wasted while he is engaged in the work of production. The fires of the body must be kept constantly supplied with fuel, or they go out. Healthy and wholesome food means a more efficient force, that has a greater capacity and endurance for labor. Yet out of the wreck of this annual havoc and destruction man could keep himself in as good a condition to perform his labor, indulge in all the comforts he now enjoys, and still make larger additions to capital, by saving, than are now often realized.

The amount that a people annually consume, in proportion to what they save in the form of capital or wealth, is very great. England, during more than eight hundred years of labor, has only accumulated about thirty billions of dollars. Each year she produces more than a third of this amount, so that, were it possible for the people to live without consuming, in less than ten years the entire wealth of England could be saved. The wealth of the United States in 1860 was estimated at about fourteen billions of dollars, and the annual production set down at something more than two billions, so that once in seven years the entire wealth of the country is produced. In 1870 the value of production was estimated at seven billions of dollars, and the wealth of the nation set down at twenty-five billions. This was a currency valuation, on which some allowance should be made. It is by reason of this great annual consumption that nations so rapidly recuperate their prosperity after a prolonged and destructive war. That which has been destroyed by the enemy would soon have been consumed by the inhabitants, had no war existed;—an observation in the economic conditions first made by John Stuart Mill.

Economy and saving in the production of capital belong to no class or order of the community. Interest or profit, as Mr. Senior has justly said, "is the wages of abstinence." But who economizes to meet this end? Who plans or directs their life with a view to the general good as well as their own comforts and pleasures? Perhaps seldom the rich and not always the poor. Here we think that the two extreme ends of society are sadly at fault.

From not fully comprehending and applying the laws of political economy to the practical affairs of life, there has grown up a false opinion as to what society can do to assist in the advancement and well-being of labor. It has become a kind of a settled conviction, in the order of public opinion, that the wretchedness, misery, and poverty of the lower and working classes is a predestined curse, which we cannot escape nor relieve; that the lowest forms of labor and want must often, if not always, go hand in hand; that industry must sometimes starve and die for the need of capital to set it in motion.

The reason is evident. There is much in the present order of civilization, in the United States as well as in other countries, that is a contradiction and a paradox. There is a Utopian spirit abroad that intensely desires to see labor benefited, and the lower strata of society raised above what it has hitherto attained. But if the majority in power and wealth have really any strong faith or abiding hope in this new condition, they must do something to develop it, besides to talk and write about it. They must bring work and sacrifice to the movement, for it will require of each all that can be summoned. There is no homely phrase truer in the science of political economy than that, "You cannot have your cake and eat it."

We do not deny that there is not much in the relation of capital and labor, that is not deep down, and high above our heads, in the depth and heighth of the economic forces, which we cannot readily understand. But there is also much in it that lies at our feet, shrouded in no intricacy, if we will stoop down and pick it up. To do this, we must at least bend our backs and stoop.

Pampered self-indulgence is a marked characteristic of the age. There seems a total inability to engage in any work that does not end in self-enjoyment, vanity, and show. We want the prize. We think how noble and beautiful it would be to win it in the cause of labor and humanity; yet we are not willing to make any effort in its attainment. Self is the most worshipped hero of the age. Self, no doubt, is the friend to labor in the motives to the accumulation of capital, but, pushed to its utmost limit, it can only exist on a vast strata of poverty, misery, and crime. Ancient civilizations prove this, as do many of those of Continental Europe. When the plough marked the limits of the eternal city there was no proud and haughty patrician, no oppressed and degraded plebeian. Poor-laws in England were comparatively unknown till the reign of Queen Elizabeth. Governor Winthrop reprimanded Deputy Governor Dudley for building an expensive house at Newton, lest the example should encourage others of the colony to do the same thing who could not so well afford it. Will the social and industrial system of the United States pass through the same phases that now characterize some of the European systems? To the observant there must be seen an all-prevailing element that is waxing stronger, and spreading its wings broader, that bears directly on this relation of capital and labor in the use of capital and application of wealth, which we believe God, in his own way and time, will correct, reform, and redress.

In regard to the use of profit, Mr. Perry, the American

economist, says: "Whoever transforms his property into capital establishes thereby a permanent fund whence he may draw an income and laborer's support in perpetuity; because the capital, though constantly disappearing in production, as constantly reappears in products with profits added,— a fact which shows the folly of the popular opinion; which regards more favorably the man who spends his money freely and unproductively than the man who, turning his money into capital, building a mill, or making some other permanent investment, creates by that means a fund in the community out of which permanent wages and permanent profits can be paid. The strength of the motives to abstinence in any country will depend largely upon the character of the government and the organization of society there."

These motives, Mr. Perry thinks, are strongest in the United States. But the recent response by the French peasant citizens and capitalists, upon the call of France, for a government loan amounting nearly to half of the debt of the United States, showed that economy and abstinence had been practised by that people to no small degree. French bonds did not have to seek a foreign market at a depreciated value of sixty per cent., as did many of the bonds of the United States during the late rebellion. There are, doubtless, many motives to save in the United States, that do not exist under other forms of government; but the motives to save seem also to promote extravagant expenditure in this country.

In the use and application of profits to productive and non-productive investment lies a great force in the industrial world that can revolutionize the present distribution of wealth, and remove much that is irritating and antagonistic between the different orders of society. It is impossible for any one to limit how wealth shall be spent by its possessor; but it is in what we term "the abuse of capital," that labor has not a groundless cause of complaint against capital. It is not within the economic province to consider this view of our question, in the relations between capital and labor; but it nevertheless is a vital one. While the non-productive use of wealth employs and pays labor, yet it dies with itself. There are two forces at work in benefiting labor in capital going to productive employments; the one economic and the other moral.

In the investment of capital to productive industry is a way to assist and advance the interests of labor. Does any member of society desire to benefit the workingman, let him, instead of buying a house that costs a hundred thousand dollars, take one that costs fifty thousand, and apply the other fifty thousand to the employment of producing and independent labor. If any rich and humane woman of society is grieved at the poverty and distress of the working-classes, let her deny herself the purchasing of diamonds costing thirty thousand dollars, which to true taste can never add to her beauty, and certainly not to her worth, and apply it to some productive industry, to increase the demand and remuneration of labor. What is the result of this application of wealth at the end of the year? Why, that the fifty thousand and the thirty thousand dollars have each gained unto themselves an additional sum, in the form of interest and profits, and honest labor has been employed and paid in the only way that wealth or capital should ever be applied to its maintenance; in a productive, independent, and honorable industry. More wealth must go to productive industry. This is what modern communism demands in an economic way in the distribution of property. More from self, show, and ostentatious luxury, to the general good and prosperity of the community. In this wealth loses not itself but gains in a legitimate accumulation.

But what does the laborer do in this matter of economy to produce capital? Is he entirely without blame? Certainly not. He is often a spendthrift and a prodigal, wasting his substance in alehouses, beer-shops, and rum-cellars, consuming it in bad habits that not only make him a physical but a moral wreck. In this consideration of our subject, we think not only in humanity, but in justice, some apology should be made for the laborer. When his day's work is done, he is at a loss, often, how and where he shall spend his evening. As has been said, "Amusement is a Christian duty." The workingman has no resources nor means to obtain the higher and more beneficial kind of amusement. He is unconsciously drawn into the lower, more ruinous and destructive. The laboring man does not seek the ale-house and the gin-shop from choice, to spend what may remain, or the whole of the wages of the day. He is forced there, from the dearth of a better companionship and a more ennobling influence, to hold him up to the instincts and impulses of his better nature. Then, again, the laborer has not the inducements to save and economize that other classes have. He says unto himself, "Why, my miserable, solitary pittance put by will never amount to anything. Let me drink and be merry, for to-morrow I die."

Both in this country and in England the sum annually spent by the laboring classes for alcoholic spirits, tobacco, and other articles, that it would be much better for them to throw into the fire, is as great as it is sad. In England the average tax of the laboring man is twenty-one shillings. Of this eleven shillings and four pence are paid for alcoholic spirits and tobacco, and only nine shillings and eight pence for all other expenditures. According to the authority of Mr. Levi, while the laboring men of England receive less than one-third of the total income of that country, yet they consume two-thirds of the total amount of wines, spirits, and tobacco. In 1860 the laborers of England spent upwards of seventy millions of pounds, almost a half of their entire earnings, in these capital and life destroying habits.

The amount expended for these products in England at the present day we have seen stated at one hundred and twenty-five millions of pounds, or between six and seven hundred millions of dollars. In this country the amount spent annually at the national drinking-cup has been stated as being more than six hundred millions of dollars, as in England, about half of the total wages, or income of labor. The cost of food in the United States is but a little in excess of what it costs to drink alcoholic spirits. This is a sad waste of capital by those who need it most, and are importuning wealth to supply it.

It is said there are points at which all sciences touch each other. But this science of political economy has strong, far-reaching, and magnetic forces. Its arms are long. They can almost clasp the universe. They stretch out so as to embrace much of the interest, welfare, and happiness of the human race. Its presence may not always be seen; but, concealed from common observation, it is sending its life-blood through the fibres, tendrils, and branches of the social, industrial, and even the religious and economic world, with a power and uniformity, but little realized, and not always felt or understood.

By its widespread circulation the emotional man is bound to the industrial man. Political economy regards man, we may say wholly, as a force in the material world, like the stroke of an engine, or the turn of a windlass. There are, however, humane relations of capital and labor, of which we have spoken, where this machinery connection and adjustment does not exist; where the humanity power is greater than the economic power.

Of this humanity relation between capital and labor we are indebted to Mr. Brasse for the following signal illustration: At the French exhibition, at Paris, in the summer of 1867, premiums were offered for examples of the most marked success that could be found of the harmony of capital and labor, employer and employé. Among many others, there was a striking illustration, showing that the labor of man is not always obtained and held on the same conditions as the turn of a shaft and the stroke of a hammer; that the humanity of capital is something in the problem, or, at least, can be made so. The most signal instance of this harmony, there brought to light, was that of Mr. Quitolf, a manufacturer of Portland cement at Stettin. When the war broke out in Austria his business became seriously embarrassed, and he was on the verge of ruin. On learning of his unfortunate situation his workmen united to a man in the labor of helping him out of his difficulties. To avert his impending bankruptcy they not only readily submitted to a reduction of thirty-three per cent. in their wages, but they cast all their hard-earned savings into the hazard to save their employer, making themselves the bridge on which he safely passed to more prosperous times. We shall not have to look far for the reasons of this action on the part of labor. It had been treated, not as a machine, but as flesh and blood. Mr. Quitolf had won for himself the grateful devotion of his workmen by the paternal interest he had always shown them. They had lived together in peace and union. Every Sunday, in the summer, Mr. Quitolf had been in the habit of going with his workmen, five hundred in number, to an island at the mouth of the Oder, where they were accustomed to spend the afternoon in singing choral music.

What would have been the solution of such a state of facts by political economy? At the first reduction of a half of one per cent. the workmen would have deserted their employer and gone over to his rival. And as to the investment of capital in such a venture, it could only have been obtained on a good and ample security, and that the rate of interest would have been in proportion to the insecurity of the loan. In nine cases out of ten, or perhaps in nine hundred and ninety-nine out of a thousand, the solution by political economy would be the right one.

We have no sovereigns in our political order. But there are sovereigns and master powers to which this man is never false nor turns traitor, be he workman, laborer, or the lowest and humblest of God's creatures. It is the sovereign of a noble and Christian humanity, as here displayed. If the humanity of the nineteenth century is what it professes to be, it should more often be seen acting as mediator between capital and labor. There are social and intellectual barriers in life, which it is impossible, and it is perhaps not desirable, should be thrown down. If, however, the social order becomes autocratic and controls the political order in the republic, then its rigidness and severity are often more strongly enforced than in an empire or a monarchy.

Messrs. Briggs, coöperative colliers in England, are doing a most successful work in the coöperation of capital and labor, making the stockholders in their business their workmen. Where formerly there were the breaking of machinery, strikes, riots, drunkenness, and often bloodshed, there are now peace, order, and prosperity, mutual esteem, respect, and confidence.

Other corporations and employers, in different parts of the world, have been equally successful in the harmonious and intelligent understanding that exists between capital and labor. At Halifax, Paris, in Germany, and among the slate interests of Wales, the coöperation of capital and labor has been successfully demonstrated.

We know of no such coöperation, on a large scale, that exists in the United States. There was some years ago such a coöperative system at Troy; but this we understand has since been abandoned. One reason for the absence of this coöperation between capital and labor in this country rests in the favorable circumstances that labor has hitherto experienced here; many laborers soon becoming small capitalists, and in their turn the employers of labor. But as population increases, and presses upon the industrial forces for employment, the condition of labor in the United States, in the future, will tend more towards a European development.

We do not say that there are not many valid reasons why this coöperation between capital and labor can never become a universal system in the relations of these two important interests. But some of the arguments brought against it should have no place in the discussion of this controversy. Many object to it on account of the trouble and annoyance it would give to the employer to permit the workmen to look over the books, and explain to them the true conditions and interests of business, in which labor has a share. This is just what labor should understand, and one of the great reasons why strikes, riots, and lock-outs occur is because they don't understand it. Such an argument as this can only be advanced in the general spirit of the selfish indifference and exclusiveness of the age.

When and where was any great movement accomplished but by trouble, patient submission, and heroic sacrifice? This problem may be as great as any age or time has been called upon to adjust. We must take care of this question, or it will take care of us. Is it unreasonable that this suspicious, child labor, suspicious because it is ignorant, should not wish to understand that it is getting its due? Once assure it that you are treating it fairly and honorably, and it will trust you, though you slay it. In Messrs. Briggs' establishment this confidence between capital and labor has been secured.

Political economy, in its highest development, means

freedom, liberty, and equality. It is always working in the interest and realization of these principles. The harmony of this science will sometime be more thoroughly comprehended and understood by nations and statesmen than at present. The freedom of labor can never be perfect. In the mobility of capital and labor, capital has the advantage of labor. Labor has heart, ties of blood, kindred, country, and locality, that trouble not capital. Capital can go from one investment to another, from one part of the world to another, comparatively without trouble or difficulty, in the great work and interest of equalization. But labor moves with more pain and slowness. This is fully shown in the excellent work by Mr. Brasse on work and wages.

Generally, we are averse to governmental or municipal regulations in the interests of the economic forces. But we think, in aid of the mobility of labor, much good might be accomplished in the establishment of industrial schools and colonization societies in every large city, not only of the United States, but of the world. They would greatly aid in taking labor from where it is not wanted, and sending it where there is a demand for it.

The industrial pursuits can and will regulate themselves. But in the United States, where the political form is so free, ambition is in danger of being overstimulated. There is a strong governmental tendency for labor to enter the higher grades of employment and professional life, where there is no demand for it. There is the need, but not the power. Ninety per cent. of the criminals are men who have been brought up to no trade. Industrial schools would often open the door to an honest education in labor, that would be a boon to a life that often finds itself wrecked in the course of its own choosing. It is driven to despair from what is false and unfortunate, rather than from what is evil or vicious.

This harmony in the industrial occupations must and should be maintained, to avoid the cry of hunger, the moan of misery, and the remorse of wrong-doing. While agriculture cannot extend itself more readily than manufactures without capital, yet agricultural occupations can be successfully increased, while those of manufactures and commerce have reached their utmost limit not only of capital but of population, and both wait for an increase of agricultural products before they can move. Workingmen and others are drawn into large cities from a wrong impression of their advantages and benefits. Once in them, they have no means to get out, especially if they have families. Often by this forced detention and poverty, crime is committed, with equal violence to the unfortunate victim as to the peace and interests of the Commonwealth. Jails are now as often the asylums of misfortune, the refuge of poverty, as the stone walls and iron bars to punish what is criminal in man. They should be considered as hospitals of economic and mental disease. Crime as often needs the physician as the prosecutor. Popular opinion is sadly at fault about this mobility of labor. It is not limited by green pastures and fertile fields, but by capital. You might as well say to labor, Go to the moon and cultivate there, as to say to it, Go West, or Go South. Even the early settlers of the New World had some capital to begin its cultivation. If wheat is burned for fuel in the West, and families are starving in New York or Boston, either there has been a wrong distribution of labor, or the highways of the country have been blocked by dishonesty, ignorance, and corruption.

The territory of the United States may be capable of supporting a population of three hundred millions, and yet not be more densely populated than continental Europe. But forty millions may press more heavily upon its capital for subsistence than would the three hundred millions, when the population of the nation shall have reached that limit.

We believe that such a movement, in the interests of the mobility of labor, has been inaugurated in the city of Boston. We think that such an organization in every large city would do more to settle the question, "How shall the country regain its prosperity?" than many more elaborate papers that might be written upon it and plans suggested.

The railways of a country have an important part to perform in the work of distribution. The highest intelligence and honesty should be exercised in their management. The highways of a nation are its veins of circulation. Are they obstructed, then every industry is paralyzed, and ruin begins. They should not be controlled by ignorant combinations and irresponsible monopolies. Both capital and labor demand of them that integrity that belongs to the government itself. In 1830 the number of miles of railway operated in the United States was thirty. In 1870 there were over seventy thousand miles, whose gross earnings amounted to $526,419,935. According to Mr. Poor, the railways of England pay five per cent. on the capital invested, while those of the United States pay more than ten per cent. If there is any industry that should be operated on a minimum of profit, it is that of intercommunication of one part of the country with another. If railways can be managed better by government than by private corporations, then the government should manage them.

Both capital and labor, however, have erroneous opinions and judgments as to the functions of governments in the conflict of the industrial forces. Governments, no farther than they assist in carrying out the purposes and designs of freedom, facility, and harmony in the economic forces, are powerless as an infant. All the governments in the world cannot, of themselves, raise a spear of grass or produce an ear of corn. All the exchequers, treasuries, printing presses in Christendom cannot create a dollar's worth of value. It can use capital in production or distribution only as private individuals may use it. It can subsidize steamship and railway lines. But unless there is a prescribed demand, or these steamships can carry merchandise as cheap as those of England, France, or Holland, then the steamships will soon lie idle in the docks, and be dismantled at the wharves. The government increases the rate of tax to make up what it has lost in the investment. Governments never pay back what they receive from the people. They spend it, and call for more. When there is no cash or assets, it gives notes on printed paper, rather than go into bankruptcy. The people of the United States, in national and municipal taxation, are taking the lead of nations in this respect. But a government can assist labor by keeping its plighted faith; having a sound and stable currency and monetary system; being scrupulously honest and thoroughly intelligent.

We fully appreciate the advantages and benefits of education in the efficiency and skill of labor. To this fact, no doubt, the labor of the United States owes much of its improved condition over that of continental Europe. But, then, there is a danger of pushing this matter of education too far beyond the arc of the economic circle. There is a limit where education will not improve labor in the attainment of an honest living. The first object of labor is to earn an honest and independent support. After this, you can point as high on the register of civilization as you wish. There may be a demand for manual labor, but none for intellectual labor. But the intellect, when once cultivated and refined, does not take up the tasks of hard toil as willingly as when brought up only to such an occupation. The statistics at Washington exhibit that labor is improved twenty-five per cent. by education. When, however, educated labor is in excess, the economic index will not fail to show it. But the great trouble is, that communities and nations go on suffering certain economic disorders, when they do not understand what afflicts them. Statesmen, philanthropists, and politicians apply the wrong remedies, that increase, rather than diminish, the disorder.

Labor is grieved at the injustice and wrong with which it feels that capital oppresses it. To defend itself, trade-unions have been organized on a large scale in England and this country. Fifty years ago in England not a thousand laborers belonged to them. At the present day a million are pledged in their support and purposes. International societies exist in every nation. Some of these societies have large sums invested in carrying out their designs. Some writers claim that these unions have raised the price of wages five per cent. within the last decade. Admitting this, the strikes, lock-outs, and forced idleness, they have occasioned must have more than offset this advantage, a single strike often costing labor alone hundreds of thousands of dollars. As organizations of mutual help and assistance they serve a good and noble purpose, and have sometimes prevented strikes rather than multiplied them. Under intelligent management and leadership they would be of great efficiency to the well-being of labor. But as a means to raise the price of wages, and put more into the laborer's pocket than they take out, we think they are helpless and pernicious. We do not say, that could labor press capital on all sides at the same time, but what capital might be forced to yield some of its rate of profits that it now exacts. This pressure must be universal, and extend to every part of the industrial world. If capital is bearded in one trade or locality, then there must be no refuge to which it can flee to obtain what it claims for itself. Like everything else, when there is no longer a demand for capital at a certain rate of interest, then it must take a lower rate.

Napoleon said "that the bank of France was established to loan money at four per cent." There are, however, limits to which the utmost concessions must be confined. There are minimum rates of interest and profit, below which, capital would not seek investment to compensate itself, and the responsibilities, toils, and cares of business. But should labor ever succeed in driving capital to such a condition, where it will not seek investment, then it will simply have been its own hangman and destroyer.

Labor has frequently manifested in the United States, and in Europe, an antagonism and hatred of machinery. We would ask it, why it is that the population of England within the last three-quarters of a century has been far greater than it had previously been since the Norman conquest, and the increase of wealth still more rapid? Why is it that the commerce and trade within the last forty years of three of the leading nations of the world, including the United States, has arisen from five billions of dollars to forty billions? Why is it that the lowest orders of society can now indulge in luxuries, comforts, and conveniences, that a king, a hundred years ago, could not bring to his palace? Why do towns and cities rise as by the wave of a magic wand? The relation of machinery to population, labor, and capital is an important inquiry that we can here only suggest. Destroy machinery, and labor would suffer as much as any other class of society. Machinery benefits labor in two ways: first, by accumulating capital for its subsistence; next, by diminishing the cost of articles consumed. As the economist Bastiat says, "Manual labor is lessened in one direction, only to be employed in another." The amount saved to the buyers by a cheapened production enables them to procure other comforts, and thus make a larger and increased demand. The standard of labor is not lowered, though that of the general well-being of society is raised. The labor performed by machinery and steam has been estimated as high as eight hundred millions of laborers. M. Chevalier, of France, calculates that the steam-engines of England alone do the work of forty millions of workmen. Take machinery out of the world, population would decrease, the cost of what we eat and wear would advance, and civilization would take a backward course.

In the decrease of the supply and competition of labor, there can be no conflict of opinion as to its effect on the price of wages. In this view of the question, public opinion and religious sentiment are as yet strongly opposed. It is considered as false and groundless; that God can, and will, take care of his own. We do not think that it is a very pleasant and satisfactory view to take; but that population in many communities presses heavily upon capital and the means of subsistence cannot be denied. From two to three millions of paupers in England, apparently, can have no part in the industrial system in that country. It is estimated that there are three or four millions of forced idle in the United States at the present time. This, as Carlyle says, "is one of the dismal sciences."

The world is doing but half its duty when it gives a man a loaf of bread. What it should do is to assist him to earn his own bread. Public or private charity, except to the sick, the lame, the blind, and the helpless, should be abolished, and banished out of this and every other country. It injures and demoralizes both parties, the giver and the receiver. We are not doing our highest duty to carry others' burdens, but to help them to carry their own. On this subject of over-population, we shall quote John Stuart Mill. He says:

"Unhappily, sentimentality, instead of common-sense, is the genius that usually presides over the discussions of these subjects. While there is a growing sensitiveness to the hardships of the poor, and a ready disposition to admit claims upon the good offices of other people, there is an all-but-universal unwillingness to face the real difficulty of their position, or advert at all to the conditions which nature has made indispensable to their physical lot. Discussions on the conditions of laborers, lamentations over its wretchedness, denunciations of all who are supposed to be indifferent to it, projects of one kind and another to improve it, were in no country, and in no time of the world, so rife as at present. But there is a tacit agreement to ignore totally the law of wages, or dismiss it with an exclamation of 'hard-hearted,' 'Malthusian;' as if it were not a hundred times more hard-hearted to tell human beings that they may, than that they may not, call into existence swarms of creatures who are sure to be miserable, and most likely to be depraved." It is not generally wealth that draws the largest number about the fireside, but it is poverty, living on the barest means of subsistence, that has the greatest number of mouths to share nothing but its hunger and squalor. Capital, however, knows no parentage. The world's children, whether rich or poor, are all alike to it. Some writers say that there can be no such thing as over-population; that population, whatever the rule of its increase, cannot possibly outrun the means of subsistence. In one sense this is true; no more can exist than can find bread. But if there is a perfect balance in the great industrial pursuits; if there is a free mobility of labor; if the various trades, occupations, and professions are evenly distributed in their employing capacity; if nothing obstructs, alarms, or intimidates capital, we would ask philanthropists and statesmen how, when, or where could they extend the employing resources, to set to work what should remain idle in such a condition of economic and industrial development? We recognize that such a state is not probable, and scarcely possible. As a last resort, there can be no doubt but what the problem will yield to the solution of a decrease of population in raising the price of wages.

But there should be no real antagonism between capital and labor. Capital is only produced by labor. If there was no labor, then there could be no capital. One is helpless without the other. Capital, when once accumulated, is the employment and support of labor. Does capital suffer, then labor is not prosperous. Is capital drawing no interest, then labor is earning no wages. Is capital lying idle in vaults, then labor is out at the elbow, and looks anxiously around for what it can get for dinner. If there is a conflict between capital and labor, then it is because labor does not understand its true interests and relations with capital. The eyelash does not fall more quickly over the pupil, nor the arm go more instinctively to the head at the approach of danger, than does capital seek shelter and contract itself when there is the least movement to injure its security, or threaten its protection. At violence it becomes paralyzed, and the more labor pursues it with the sword, the swifter it will flee from it. Does capital wish to get the best and most effective force out of labor in the creation of profits and wealth, it must be treated as something more than a machine.

Opulence and wealth are prone to forget what they owe to labor. Let labor cease for twenty-four hours and truly would riches take wings. Want would soon be in the best-stored larder. In a week your fine marble buildings and luxurious homes would be but charnel-houses. Wealth, rather than shunning labor when it meets it, should take off its hat to it and thank it for what it enjoys. Labor is the foundation, capital the edifice. Samson labor may pull down the pillars and supports of the social structure, and bring ruin to both, but undermost lies labor.

It may be thought by many that the freedom and equality of the political form in the United States will eventually become a saving power to labor in the triumph of a workingman's party; but we do not think that such will soon be the case. Labor, as yet, has not shown the intelligent choice of leadership that would save it, or work out its higher redemption and deliverance. This is often shown in the character and principles of the candidates it puts upon its tickets, and its communistic enunciations. If the laboring men had the national policy under their control, they would probably adopt such a course as would hasten it to ruin, and operate the most severely against their interests and prosperity. It is an intelligent power we need to preserve and save us; not ignorant power, however honest and manly. With the last two qualities left out, we have enough of the latter kind of power already.

Many centuries ago, in the history of the Roman commonwealth, a large number of the Roman citizens withdrew themselves to the Aventine hill in open mutiny to the civil order, with swords in their hands, mainly upon the issue of capital and labor. Valerius, who was one of the delegates sent to them by the Roman Senate to conciliate and address them said, "It's the shield you need, and not the sword." This is the spirit of the mottoes that labor should put upon its banners, rather than those we often see displayed there. It is the guidance of honest and intelligent protection that labor needs, rather than the leadership of demagogues, which is the surest and most certain way to anarchy and destruction.

A republican form of government is quick in its passions, and ambitious of crystallizations, in certain policies that are often hard and unjust. It, more than any other form of government, must keep itself fresh, healthy, and vigilant to its highest life. What is every one's business and interest is under the direction of none. There is no tyranny like the tyranny of a majority. In the Roman world, labor under Augustus was more prosperous and contented than in the last days of the republic. This has been experienced in other nations than Rome. This is the abuse rather than the best use of representative government, which, with certain restrictions and limitations, we believe will be the government of the future. A workingman, in writing of the late strikes and conditions of labor, in what he claims of the ballot that should protect it, says, "We are sick of this game; we are soul-weary of looking around for sympathy or a spirit of justice, and finding none."

Self-protection, you say, is the first law of nature. True; but do not be too short-sighted as to the means to secure that best and most durable protection. Every man is interested in the success of every other man. Every community should be interested in the prosperity of every other community. Somewhere the most opposite parts of society meet in the economic balance. The barber and the prince, the street-vender and the capitalist, come together here, if nowhere else. The most distant nations touch each other in their commercial exchanges.

The economic world moves in a circle. There are no squares, angles, or points, at which it reaches its end, and flies off into space. If any part of the circle is broken, or its life becomes stagnant, then the disease of hard times begins and continues, until industrial circulation has again been sent through every part of the economic body. Is business dull at London and there is a shrinkage of values, then its effect extends to New York, San Francisco, Boston, Paris, Berlin, Moscow, and Pekin. It is the seen over-production, the unseen idleness; no employment, no wages, decreased consumption, no demand. The harmony between the great industries has been destroyed. There is no demand for labor in manufactures and commerce; there is capital lying idle for investment, and honest hands waiting for something to do. These two must combine in agricultural production, to quicken and set in motion the other two great industries. Agriculture was before manufacture and commerce in the order of the industries. It is the fountain-head from which the other two gain their vigor and magnitude. The current of the channel is low, stagnant, and torpid. You must put more water into the source to give it a new impetus and force. The machinery has become too cumbrous and expanded for the motive-power that moves it.

Our late war may, in part, have been the cause of much of our present business depression. The government was a large employer of labor and consumer of production. When it ended, large numbers of men were thrown suddenly upon capital for employment that it had adjusted itself to do without. This surplus must be absorbed into new enterprises of agricultural investments.

But an inflated currency has done more than any other one thing to debase, debauch, and demoralize everything. When an increase of currency or the circulating medium is attended with a sudden rise in prices, it is an infallible test that it does no good to the industry of the country. An unlimited paper currency means bankruptcy. It costs little or nothing to produce it; its value depends upon legislative enactments. The purchasing power of money depends upon its quantity. If it consists of a comparatively worthless substance, then the supply must be limited. If coinage is unlimited, then its value will depend upon the cost of production of the material in which the monetary article consists. Labor should understand that its greatest and most vital interests depend upon permanence, stability, and confidence, as much as upon justice. These will carry even the most vicious system and heaviest burden with apparent ease; while the best monetary policies and measures that are continually dangling between defeat and success, caught by the gills in uncertain life, mean certain death. We say this not only of the monetary system, but of the political system, in the interests and welfare of labor. To change parties or administrations is of no benefit to labor only as the change will assist in a higher economic prosperity. Confidence is the life of capital. Constant agitations and fermentations frighten and alarm it. As Lord Mansfield said of the law, "It is not more to have it just than to have it certain."

Inflation is a great wrong; it is an economic crime to labor. It is a revolution in prices, and of itself, in the measure of money values. The greater the quantity of a debased currency, the more widespread the ruin. Contraction, it is true, is also often hard and unjust in the new adjustment. When a bankrupt nation enjoys five years of apparent prosperity, it is evident that a state of intensified bankruptcy must occur. There is no benefit in increase of prices with no corresponding addition to values.

Mr. Wells has written thoughtful papers on how the nation shall regain its prosperity; but we hope it will never return to prosperity based on the conditions it has experienced since 1861. We think in the relations of money to prosperity, values, labor, and population, there is yet much to be adjusted, in detail if not in principle. If the monetary system be national or international, then the financial condition of a country will depend upon its industrial laws and commercial exchanges. You are not prosperous because you have gold. You have gold because you are prosperous. Since the discovery of gold in 1848 trade has risen in a proportion of one to eight.

In no nation, in the ten years from 1861 to 1871, was there

ever so great a change in the manner of doing business as in the United States. How to make a fortune without labor or creating any real value, either in production or distribution, seems to be the great problem of the scheming business world. Speculative and worthless corporations are in every town and city. More than half the amount of the national debt has been sunk in worthless investments within the last few years. Knavery and idiocy seem to have largely entered into the commercial and financial world. We mortgage the future, spend the money in extravagance, and when the pay-day comes we are sorely troubled and perplexed. We are suffering from a disregard of the economic laws, an honest industry, and an honorable integrity. The pay-day comes, but our coffers are empty.

The conditions of capital and labor are governed by the same economic laws in this country as everywhere else. The superior advantages and prosperity of labor here we believe to be largely due to the great natural advantages of the material wealth we possess over other nations. Our liberal and advanced system of education has greatly aided in the worth and value of our labor. But unless the higher grades of employment are willing to return to the lower grades, it is only a question of time when it will tend in the wrong direction. Agriculture has done much for the prosperity of this country, and it yet has the power to do much more for it, if the people will not lose sight of this great source of wealth. In the Roman State, aside from the civil life of the forum, there were but two honorable employments: those of the farm and the camp. The comparatively high price of wages in the United States has come from causes that cannot always exist. The freshness, vitality, and vigor of the morning must give way to the heat of the noon-day, the twilight, and shadows of the evening. We must live on the interest and not the capital of our national, material wealth, if we would not have it vanish. The nation enters upon the second century of its existence, but with as much need of all that is heroic, humane, intelligent, and conciliatory, as it did upon its first. It is often more difficult to retain than to win. It seems to us that the recent strikes have proved that the political form of this country will not bear the pressure of some of the European orders. Perhaps it is well that it should not.

The immediate cause of the open conflict between capital and labor, so far as it applies to labor, comes from the ignorance of labor. There is a misunderstanding between these two interests; capital will not always understand labor, and labor cannot understand capital. Labor sins more through ignorance than intention; therefore a court having the confidence of capital and labor, rightly and intelligently administered, would be an efficient means, often, to adjust amicably the disputes and grievances of both. A court of this kind has been long established in France. Lord Brougham stated in Parliament, in 1859, that of twenty-eight thousand cases submitted to the Conseils des Prudhommes, twenty-six thousand eight hundred of them were settled without appeal. The science of political economy should become a popular branch of education in our schools. All classes of society should take more interest in it. It will help them to understand the wants, needs, and hardships of each other. It will bring them nearer together in thought, if not in personal relation. We do not live here as though we thought the class distinction was to disappear in the hereafter. Only by production or spoliation can property be obtained. Certainly, labor is not going to choose spoliation. Should it madly do so, then chaos has come again. The ballot-box will be thrown aside for the bayonet. The sword will be both our destroyer and our master.

It is hardly necessary to remind the labor of the United

States how much better it is paid and fares here, than in most other nations. In England the average wages of labor is not more than fifty cents per day. Nineteen pounds sterling is the average yearly income of the workingman to support himself and a family of five. In France, Switzerland, Germany, and Austria it is not much better. Woman in the industrial conditions of these countries occupies a different place than she does in the United States. In France out of 19,585,115 agricultural laborers, 9,860,820 are females. Labor must be more content to dress and care for itself according to its circumstances. It should not try to pattern the ways and expenditures of those who are wealthy. It should cut the acquaintance of fashion, which, at best, is but the rule of the "cap and the bells."

Our subject leads in every direction. We can but partially and disconnectedly follow it in some, and must pass over in silence many others. Nothing original can be said on this subject. At best we can but make new combinations of old material; set in motion what should know no rest; bring into the light what should never sink into the shade. To think that we could write a paper that would adjust all the difficult complications between capital and labor in the United States, would be only to prove how little we comprehended the greatness of our task. We can only suggest the ways by which we think some of its grating and irritation may be lessened. Wealth is especially the motive-power of the civilizations of the nineteenth century. Capital has outgrown its economic weight and province. It now reaches circles from which it hitherto has been excluded. To be rich, now, means to be the possessor of much more than money. Trade is no longer a reproach to social position or caste.

We have spoken of the economic and humane relations of these two great interests of capital and labor. In the economic, it is a strife of capital and labor; here we think that labor is greatly in error. In the humane or social consideration it is one order of society arrayed against the other for mastery. Here we think that capital must bear much blame. The church, that should do away with the class-line of rich and poor, often only seems to bring it out in stronger contrast, by placing itself beyond the reach of the poor. Labor knows where it is wanted. As was once remarked by a foreign envoy: "Where do your poor, the laboring men, go to church in the United States; or have you none?"

Distribution seems a more difficult question than production. An increased motive-power in the work of production can easily be supplied; but to find new markets in different parts of the world, new demands for what we produce, seems more complicated and difficult. These can only be made by industry, enterprise, cheapness in production, without lowering the standard quality. Trade must be made successful in honorable competition; whatever obstructs legitimate and healthy life in the economic forces and interests should be studiously avoided.

We sadly need in the United States more conscientious, independent, and intelligent labor. There is a dearth of this in our political and national councils. We are the most independent and dependent of nations. We look rather to our neighbors for approval than to our conscience. Never did imposture seem more frequent than at the present time, never were palaver and falsity so frequently to be found in high places. Tricksters and mountebanks seem to be at a premium. How to catch a vote is the purpose for which we trim our political sails to take every breeze from whatever quarter it may come. The dollar purifies all means by which it is obtained, however vile or base. We make drunk that we may destroy. We are dying of fawning flunkeyism and the flattery of the parasite. The man who is not true to himself will not be true to any party or interest long. The people of the republic, like the king of the monarchy, are not always right, and can do wrong. If they err not in the heart, they may in head and passion. Labor must be able to separate the false from the true, the dross from the gold. When its hero comes, it must know and honor him. In thought, it wants not the kid-glove dalliance of an artificial manhood or womanhood. It needs the warm, true, and flesh-like grasp of a Ruskin or a Carlyle; that while it holds it as a unit in the social, law-abiding order, yet fully appreciates its misfortunes and hardships, and lies close to its restless longings and anxious strivings. Our best life is not dead, but sleeping.

But with both capital and labor a gracious Providence metes out and awards its blessings with a more even hand than is generally supposed. In honorable and independent labor is man's brightest happiness; capital treads upon thorns that labor knows not of. Social forms of caste, based upon indolent wealth, is false in every particular. It carries its own curse with it. Manly labor is a sweet sauce, that can never come to pampered appetites of indolence and luxury. To work for something besides self is man's noblest mission. We are restless and discontented for what when gained brings us no peace or happiness. Our burdens are heavy, only because we have never borne the weight of others.

Our sympathies are with labor. As Mr. Harrison justly says, "They know by hourly experience, they only know, what social suffering exists. By suffering, their social sympathies are stimulated; by necessity, their practical instincts are developed. They are free from the restless egoism which is the misfortune of all who accumulate wealth; from the self-indulgent indecision which is the curse of all who live in idleness. Theirs is the highest form of sympathy, theirs the readiest powers of action."

For Mr. Harrison's word "all" we would substitute the word "many;" for certainly capital and wealth are often to be found with a Christian, tender humanity for misfortune, sorrow, and hardship. Poverty suddenly grown rich generally makes the severest taskmaster to labor. Labor should grant to capital what it claims for itself. The wealthy man draws a large income in interest from capital. This he has earned, or it has come to him by gift or inheritance. Does not labor as well as capital defend its own if there is any attempt to take from it by force what it has justly earned? We think it would. In fact, labor goes to unwarrantable lengths in destroying work that has not come within the rules of its trade-unions.

Work! work honestly and faithfully! Work at what you can, if not at what you would. Take the way nearest your feet, though hard and stony. After a season of worthy toil you may climb glorious heights, such as your most sanguine ambition never hoped to see or realize. Look up. As Emerson says, "Harness your wagon to a star." Lift yourself above your daily drudgery when it is over. There is nothing to prevent the laboring man from being a prince in thought and feeling, though a prince in station may be a brute. Seek the approval of a clear, manly and womanly conscience, rather than what is often the fickle praise and uncertain censure of public opinion. Do right. Let the world pass on the other side if it will.

At best, there are many undeserved misfortunes, calling for the strength and support of all that is humane; difficult problems, that stare at us with the Sphinx's impenetrability, when approached, even, by the combined action of all that is high and thoughtful. Labor must not lay to capital the fate that Providence has decreed it in the world. That social or religious order that shall absorb labor, the lower and middling classes, into itself, we think is assured the triumph of the future. The triumph will be deserved. It will be the success of the broadest humanity, and the highest element of a true Christianity, whatever be its covenant or creed. In the inequality of fortune, this all-pervading and Christian sentiment, if such can be attained, seems the only means of uniting all classes and conditions in a bond of peace, union, and harmony.

Let us not forget, that in whatever capacity we are called upon to act, either as capitalist or laborer, rich or poor, there seems but one universal allotment in which we all have our share, — sorrow, disappointment, and sacrifice; trusting in that sphere beyond the sight of mortal vision to right what here has been wrong, to redress what has been grievous, to reward us for the undeserved burdens we have here patiently borne.

Report of Commissioners

of the

State Bureaus of Labor Statistics

on the

Industrial, Social and Economic Conditions

of

PULLMAN, ILLINOIS.

SEPTEMBER, 1884.

REPORT OF COMMISSIONERS

OF THE

STATE BUREAUS OF LABOR STATISTICS

ON THE

INDUSTRIAL, SOCIAL AND ECONOMIC CONDITIONS OF PULLMAN, ILLINOIS.

At the annual convention of the chiefs and commissioners of the various bureaus of statistics of labor in the United States, held at St. Louis in June, 1884, it was determined to make a full and exhaustive investigation of the economic experiment conducted by Pullman's Palace Car Company on the plan projected by Mr. George M. Pullman, the president.

In carrying out this determination the convention met at Pullman, Illinois, in September following, and for three days studied all the economic, sanitary, industrial, moral and social conditions of the city.

Every facility was afforded for the closest scrutiny of every feature and phase of any and all the affairs the members of the convention saw fit to examine. The results of their investigations are embodied in this report, which is presented as a joint report through the various annual reports of the bureaus represented.

We have availed ourselves of material furnished the press by Duane Doty, Esq., a gentleman connected with the educational work of Pullman, and by other writers, but chiefly our report is the result of our own observations of things and conditions as we found them.

Our object in making the investigation was to give to the manufacturers and capitalists of our respective States official information relative to one of the most attractive experiments of the age seeking to harmonize the interests of labor and capital. It is no part of our duty to eulogize individuals; we have endeavored to learn results.

The enterprise of Herr Krupp at Essen; the philanthropy of M. Godin in the establishment of the Familistère at Guise, France; the humanity of Sir Titus Salt, that brought into existence the industrial town of Saltaire, in Yorkshire, England; and the broad Christian inspiration which resulted in the founding of Pullman have given the world, in the four greatest manufacturing countries, four magnificent schemes for the uplifting of a large portion of the people seeking a living through wages.

In all the countries named there have been many other experiments worth a careful study of all interested in social advancement. This is thoroughly true of our own country, and we might call attention with justice to the success at Peace Dale, R. I., at St. Johnsbury, Vt., at Willimantic, and Manchester, Conn., and at other points. But, for comprehensive plan, for careful recognition of all the strong points, and the fullest anticipation of all weak features, for the beauty of the executed plan, for the financial and social success thereof, Pullman city as the outgrowth of the newest of the great manufacturing nations stands at the head.

History.

The commissioners had no opportunity to consult Mr. Pullman personally, he being away at the time of our investigation, and we have, therefore, taken such statements of fact, as appear in our report, from documents already before the public.

Pullman's Palace Car Company was founded in 1867 with a capital of $1,000,000; its extended operations have been conducted on the strictest business principles, and have, from time to time, necessitated increases in its capital stock, until now its capital represents nearly $16,000,000, and $2,000,000 in debenture bonds; its palace cars are operated on upwards of 70,000 miles of railway in America and Europe. Its capital stock has been paid in dollar for dollar, and no watering processes have ever entered into the financial operations of the company. Its dividends have been regular and ample, and its affairs conducted on the same scientific basis that has characterized the construction of the works.

Four or five years ago Mr. Pullman determined to bring the greater portion of the works of the Company into one locality. To accomplish this he must leave the great cities for many reasons, and yet it was essential that a site should be selected where communication could be had with the whole country, and near some metropolitan place like Chicago. He wished above all things to remove his workmen from the close quarters of a great city, and give them the healthful benefits of good air, good drainage, and good water, and where they would be free, so far as it would lie in the power of management to keep them free, from the many seductive influences of a great town.

He was fortunate in securing about 4,000 acres of land on the Illinois Central Road, a dozen miles to the south of Chicago. This land was located in the town of Hyde Park, and here he built his city.

The Site.

The city is situated upon the west shore of Lake Calumet, which is a shallow body of water three and a half miles long by a mile and a half in width. This lake drains into Lake Michigan through the Calumet river, Lake Michigan being not more than three miles distant. The site of that portion of the city now fully covered with buildings is from eight to fourteen feet above the level of Lake Calumet. The soil is a drift deposit of tough blue clay ninety feet in depth, resting upon lime rock. The land gradually rises to the north and west to an elevation of twenty-five feet above Lake Calumet, this lake being usually from three to five inches higher than Lake Michigan. There is no land of a marshy character in this neighborhood. The bottom of Lake Calumet is of hard blue clay, from which the best cream-colored brick are made. It was deemed unwise to permit any sewage to flow into Lake Calumet, so the system of drainage adopted is what is known as the *separate* one.

On the 25th day of May, 1880, ground was first broken for the building of the Palace Car Works, and the city of Pullman. The land was an open and not over-promising prairie.

The first efforts were directed towards the scientific drainage of the future town. In old cities drainage follows construction, for the average village or city is but the haphazard conglomeration of odds and ends in the way of buildings, whose inartistic forms, defective construction, and inconvenient arrangements are supplemented by such drainage and sewerage systems as can be utilized. It is rare of course in the nature of things that drainage is thought of at the outset. It comes after a lapse of time when the soil has become charged with the accumulated filth of years, and all attempts at sewerage are more or less unsatisfactory.

The city of Pullman, on the other hand, has been built scientifically in every part, and is exceptional in respect to drainage and sewerage if in no other regard. For here the drainage preceded the population, and the soil is now as free from organic contamination as when it formed a portion of the open prairie. Every house has been constructed from approved plans, and under the supervision of competent builders and engineers.

The perfection of the site selected was accomplished through surface drainage, and the construction of deep sewers.

These should be described as a matter of logical order before anything is said of the buildings of the town.

Surface Drainage.

The atmospheric water goes from roofs and streets through one system of pipes and sewers directly into Lake Calumet. Brick mains from three to six feet in diameter are built in alternate streets running east and west, the intermediate streets being summits from which the surface water flows into the main sewers. The fall is sufficient to secure good cellars for all the dwellings in the city, the drain pipes leading from cellars being at least eighteen inches below the cellar bottoms. A two-foot cobble-stone gutter borders either side of every street, leading at short intervals of 150 feet into catch-basins, these basins, connecting either with the lateral or the main sewers. This system of surface drainage is calculated to carry easily an amount of water that would cover to the depth of one and one-half inches the entire area drained. For the drainage from lots six inch pipe is used, while for block drainage and for laterals pipe varying from nine to eighteen inches in diameter is used. The parks and play grounds are all thoroughly drained. The amount of vitrified pipe already laid in the town is as follows:—

Of 18 inch pipe, ...	4,500 feet.
Of 15 inch pipe, ...	6,500 feet.
Of 12 inch pipe, ...	6,600 feet.
Of 9 inch pipe, ...	16,000 feet.

There are also several miles of six inch pipe. In addition to the piping of diameters from six to eighteen inches, the necessary quantity of four inch tile has been used to carry water from cellars and down-spouts to the laterals from brick houses for 1,476 families. The lands surrounding the town are well drained by ditches.

Deep Sewers.

In every other street running east and west, and lying between the streets having brick mains for surface drainage, there are sewers made with vitrified pipe which lead to a large reservoir under the water tower, entering it at sixteen feet below the surface of the ground. These glazed pipe sewers are from six to eighteen inches in diameter and constitute another and separate system of drains which carries the sewage proper, by gravity, from houses to the reservoir. This reservoir has a capacity of 300,000 gallons, and the sewage is pumped from it as fast as received and before sufficient time elapses for fermentation to take place. The ventilation of this reservoir is perfect. Flues run from it to the top of the tower above it, and a flue leads from it to the large chimney which takes off the smoke from the fires under the boilers of the Corliss engine. The sewage is sent to the model farm through a twenty inch iron main, and, at the farm end of this pipe, it goes into a receiving tank, which contains a screen placed in a vertical position through which substances that are more than half an inch in diameter cannot pass. The pressure of the sewage upon the tile piping in the farm seldom, if ever, exceeds ten pounds to the square inch, provision being made at the pumping station and at the farm to relieve the pipes from greater pressure. About 100 gallons of sewage are now pumped daily for each person of the population. This seems a large amount, but when it is remembered that every tenement is provided with the best of closets and sinks, and that the water taps are all inside the houses, it will be seen that a large amount of sewage per capita is unavoidable.

The Model Farm.

About 140 acres of land have been thoroughly under-drained and piped for the reception of sewage with which these acres are irrigated by means of hose. Hydrants are placed at proper intervals so that the distribution can be easily effected. There is nothing offensive about this work, nor can one detect noxious odors at the pumping station or at the farm. All organic matter in the sewage is at once taken up by the soil and the growing vegetation, and the water, making from 100 to 500 parts of the sewage, runs off through the under-drains to ditches, which carry the filtered waters into Lake Calumet. Where the sewage water leaves the drains it is as clear and sparkling as spring water, and laborers often drink it. One acre of land will take care of the sewage made by 100 persons. The population is now only 8,500, but there is land enough already prepared to receive the sewage made by a population of 15,000. The pumps now at the pumping station can handle 5,000,000 gallons a day if necessary, and the main to the farm could carry the sewage for a population of 50,000. These pumps are now required to handle about a million gallons a day, coming from shops, homes, and public buildings. All waste products at Pullman are carefully utilized, being transformed by vital chemistry into luxuriant vegetable forms.

This farm is now a source of profit, and its products are sold in the markets of the country from Boston to New Orleans.

The Buildings.

With the scientific drainage and sewage system, in the construction of which nearly one million dollars ($1,000,000) were expended underneath the ground before anything appeared on its surface, came the erection of the works and the dwellings of the town. It is sufficient to say that the same care exercised in guarding the future health of the place has been bestowed in the erection of works and dwellings.

In the centre stands the water tower which takes a supply of water from Lake Michigan and distributes it through the town. Underneath this immense tower is the reservoir into which flows the sub-sewage of the place as described. Around the tower are located the principal works; to the south and north of the works, chiefly to the south, are the dwellings.

The appearance from the railroad as one approaches from Chicago is effective. The neat station; the water tower and the works in front; the park and artificial lakes intervening; to the right a picturesque hotel backed by pretty dwellings; the arcade, containing stores, library, theatre, offices, etc.; still further to the right, and beyond, a church which fits into the landscape with artistic effect.

The laying out of the whole town has been under the guidance of skilled architects aided by civil engineers and landscape gardeners.

The dwellings present a great variety of architecture, yet give harmonious effects. They are not built like the tenement houses of ordinary manufacturing towns where sameness kills beauty and makes the surroundings tame, but a successful effort has been made to give diversity to architectural design.

The streets are wide, well built, and wherever possible parked. The lawns are kept in order by the company; the shade trees are cared for, and all the police work is done under competent supervision.

Every care has been taken to secure convenience inside as well as outside the dwellings. The cheapest tenement is supplied with gas and water and garbage outlets. The housekeeper throws the garbage into a specified receptacle and has no more care of it.

The testimony of every woman we met was that housekeeping was rendered far more easy in Pullman than in any other place. In fact the women were in love with the place; its purity of air, cleanliness of houses and streets, and lessened household burdens, are advantages over their former residences which brought out the heartiest expressions of approval. The women of the comparatively poor bear most of the drudgery of life, enjoy the least of pleasures, and are most narrowly circumscribed, with little change in cares, scenes, or social surroundings. Pullman has really wrought a greater change for the women than for any other class of its dwellers.

All the works and shops are kept in the neatest possible order. The planing rooms are as free from dust as the street, blowers and exhaust fans taking away all shavings, dust, and debris, as fast as it accumulates. One notices everywhere the endeavor to save time and space in the construction of goods. As an illustration of the science which enters into manufacture we need only cite the shops where freight cars are built. All the timber is taken in in lengths at one end and is never turned around until it finds its proper place in a completed freight car, being carried constantly from one process to another in a direct line from its reception at one end to its utilization at the other.

There are 1,520 brick tenements in houses and flats. The frontage of all the buildings extends along five miles of solid paved streets, and there are fourteen miles of railroad track laid for the use of those in the shops and the town. The buildings are of brick or stone.

Industries.

The industries carried on and for which the city was built comprise the manufacture of Pullman Palace cars, and all classes of passenger and freight cars.

The Pullman car-wheel works, the Chicago Drop Forge Company's works, the Spanish-American curled hair factory, the Pullman Iron and Steel Company for the manufacture of iron and steel and of railroad spikes, and other works which are collateral to the principal business of the place, are located here.

The Allen paper car-wheel works, and the Union Foundry for making car wheels, car castings and architectural and general castings, have been conveniently located at Pullman.

Among the manufactures of the place should be mentioned that of brick. The Pullman company's yards turned out the past year about twenty millions of brick. The ice industry is also growing in importance. There is also an extensive Carpenter's shop, by means of which the erection of dwellings, public buildings, etc., here and in other places may contribute to the industries of Pullman.

Gradually the manufacture of all the parts necessary to the construction of cars in every condition is being added to the enterprise of the town. A laundry is being established for cleansing the vast quantities of linen used in the palace car service which will give employment to women ; it is the policy of the company to encourage the employment of women and young persons.

Population.

The rapid growth of Pullman is exhibited in the following tabular statement of the several enumerations of the population that have been made :—

Table of Nine Enumerations.

Dates of Taking the Census.	Families and Households.	Number of Men.	Number of Women.	Number of Children.	Total Population.
Jan. 1, 1881, .	1 family, .	1	2	1	4
March 1, 1881, .	8 families, .	31	14	12	57
June 1, 1881, .	102 " .	357	119	178	654
Feb. 1, 1882, .	321 households,	1,168	445	471	2,084
March 8, 1883, .	705 "	1,956	984	1,572	4,512
Aug. 15, 1883, .	910 "	2,878	1,039	1,906	5,823
Nov. 20, 1883, .	1,048 "	3,128	1,388	2,169	6,685
Sept. 4, 1884, .	1,295 "	3,817	1,773	2,613	8,203
Sept. 30, 1884, .	1,361 "	3,945	1,845	2,723	8,513

Of the population on September 30, 1884, 4,205 were born in the United States, 527 in the Canadas, 425 in England, 596 in Ireland, 170 in Scotland, 85 in France, 953 in Germany, 297 in Norway, 851 in Sweden, 212 in Denmark, 55 in Italy, 137 in other countries, such as Holland, Greece, and in Asia and Africa.

Omitting fractions, the religious preferences of the population may be expressed as follows :—

Presbyterian, ...	8 per cent.
Congregational, ...	2 "
Baptist, ...	4 "
Methodist, ...	8 "
Lutheran, ...	24 "
Episcopalian, ...	11 "
Catholic, ...	27 "
Dutch Reformed, ...	2 "
Universalist, ...	1 "
Swedenborgian, ...	1 "

The remaining 12 per cent. of the population includes those of other beliefs, but who expressed no religious preferences.

There are 75 pianos in the city, and the private libraries contain 30,000 volumes, while newspapers and magazines are freely taken in Pullman.

Of the 3,945 men here only about 900 are registered as voters (Oct. 29, 1884), and this is probably three-fourths of the voters residing in this city.

Nearly all the men accounted for on the population statistics are employed in the works of the company. Of course there are a few tradesmen and others. The total number employed in the works is about 4,000, but this includes some who live in surrounding villages, or who come down from Chicago.

Wages, Rents, and Living Expenses.

The wages paid in the works at Pullman are somewhat higher than those paid for like work in other places. They have been adjusted on the hour basis, and from such basis piece wages have been arranged. The attempt to justly equalize and adjust wages has sometimes caused complaint amongst the workmen, and in one instance a strike of small moment. The strike took place among the freight car builders who formerly received $18 for the construction of a car. Through a readjustment of the forces necessary to the preparation of the material of which the car was built, the price per car was reduced to $12, four men being able to build a car in 8 hours, the result being the wage of $3 per man for 8 hours work. Under this arrangement there was no cessation, no breaks in time ; in the old arrangement, when $18 per car was paid, the men made long waits for material, and did not earn any more, and often not as much, as at the present price per car, and with steady employment. But the first effect of the rearrangement of forces and consequent readjustment of prices was a strike of short duration. With this exception no strikes have occurred at Pullman city, and so far as we could learn there was no complaint regarding wages paid.

In the early days of the city, more men naturally were borne on the rolls than were actually necessary. In bringing the force employed to an economic basis, under which one man should be paid for one man's work, and only one man employed where only one was necessary, discharges or transfers took place, and this caused some complaint, but as the motto of Pullman is, "work for all, and all to work," that sentiment soon found lodgment and complaint ceased.

It costs quite as much to live in Pullman as in any other locality with which it can be reasonably compared. A two room tenement in a second story flat, but having all the conveniences of water and gas, and for sewage and garbage, rents for $4 per month, and a three room tenement, similarly situated, for $4.50 per month. Two room flats in small houses, large enough to accommodate five families, rent all the way from $5 to $8.50 per month, while two, three and four room tenements in large blocks rent from $6.50 to $10 per month. Four room tenements on the first, second, and third floors of three story flats, rent for from $11 to $13.50 per month, while four and five room tenements in two story flats may be had for $14 and $15 per month. Single five room cottages rent for from $16 to $19 per month, while single houses of from 6 to 9 rooms vary from $22 to $100 per month.

The average monthly rental per room in the whole city of 1,520 houses, having 6,485 rooms, is $3.30. In the manufacturing towns of Massachusetts, the average rental per room is $2.86 per month.

The rentals at Pullman are a little higher for the same number of rooms than in Chicago, but in Chicago the tenement would be in a narrow street or alley, while in Pullman it is on a broad avenue where no garbage is allowed to collect, where all houses have a back street entrance, where the sewage arrives at a farm in three hours' time from its being deposited, and where beauty, order, and cleanliness prevail, and fresh air abounds.

There are no taxes to be paid other than personal, and, when all the advantages which a tenant has at Pullman are taken into consideration as compared with his disadvantages in other places, the rent rates are in reality much lower.

The tenant is under no restrictions beyond those ordinarily contained in a lease, except that he must leave his tenement at ten days' notice, or he can give the same notice and quit. This short limitation has been established in order that no liquor saloons, objectionable houses, or anything likely to disturb the *morale* of the place, can become fastened on the community.

All the houses in Pullman city are owned by the company. This policy has been considered the best in the early years of the city in order that a foundation may be securely laid for a community of good habits and good order.

The men are employed without restriction. There are no conditions laid upon their freedom ; they are paid fortnightly, and they expend their wages when and where they see fit, their rent being charged against their wages. This, at first, caused some complaint, but the system is now generally liked, for when wages are paid there is no bother about rent bills, and the wife and the children know that the home is secure. Repairs, if due to the carelessness or negligence of the tenant, are made by the company at the lowest possible expense, and charged against the tenant. Of course, the company, like all landlords, expects to keep the houses in tenantable condition.

There has been some friction in this matter, but as the policy of the company becomes more generally and better understood, the complaint ceases.

Schools, Churches, Amusements, etc.

The company has erected a very fine school building having fourteen commodious rooms, which now contain about 900 pupils. The schools are under the charge of the school authorities of Hyde Park. They are in a prosperous condition and well accommodate the school population.

There are two or three religious societies, and the beautiful church which has been built by the company, while occupied by any sect or by any body that wishes to hold meetings there, is awaiting the occupancy of some society that chooses to lease it at a fair rental.

In the arcade is to be found a library handsomely fitted and well stocked with books.

The company have also provided a gymnasium, an amphitheatre for games, base ball grounds, and in the arcade is one of the most æsthetic theatres in the country.

All these influences are gradually elevating the society of Pullman city, and their influence is largely felt.

There is but little crime or drunkenness in Pullman, and one policeman, an officer appointed by the authorities of Hyde Park, constitutes the police force for 8,500 people. In two years but 15 arrests have been made; there is no general beer drinking, for there are no liquor saloons in the town. The hotel provides its guests with liquors, but under orderly restrictions.

There is no pauperism; two or three families, where the head had been taken away, or where some accident or misfortune had rendered it necessary, have been aided; but pauperism, as such, does not exist at Pullman.

HEALTH, ACCIDENTS, ETC.

In a Paper entitled "Pullman From a State Medicine Point of View," by Oscar C. De Wolf, M. D., commissioner of health, Chicago, read before the American Public Health Association at Detroit, at the session of November, 1883, we find the following significant statements:

"The town has now 7,500 inhabitants, and its average annual population has been 5,000. During the two years of its existence 69 persons died, its death-rate being therefore 6.9 per 1,000. The death-rate of the rest of Hyde Park (a village of which Pullman is legally a part, and which includes much rural territory) is 15 per 1,000. The causes of death were,—

Zymotic diseases,	23
Constitutional diseases,	3
Local diseases,	22
Developmental diseases,	3
Violence,	17
Unknown,	1
	69

"The large percentage of deaths by violence is due to the fact that Pullman is the centre of numerous railroads, and to the casualties attendant on its manufactures. The deaths under five years of age were thirty. Of these there died from zymotic diseases twelve, of which there died from—

Cholera infantum,	6
Diphtheria,	3
Scarlatina,	2
(Toy pistol) Septicæmia,	1
	12

"This favorable showing speaks for itself."

Dr. De Wolf's statement had reference to the two earlier years of the existence of Pullman. The last year presents as good a record.

From November 1st, 1883, to November 1st, 1884, there were 53 deaths in Pullman. Hence there was an average of 7.599 deaths per year for every 1,000 of population. For three years Pullman has had this low death-rate. The average for American cities is over three times this number and the average annual death-rate of the world is 32 out of every 1,000 of population. The average death-rate in the city of Mexico is 56 per 1,000 or eight times the rate in Pullman. Of these 53 deaths, 2 were of persons over 50 years of age, 2 of persons between 40 and 50, 2 of persons between 30 and 40, 4 of persons between 20 and 30, 4 of persons between 10 and 20, none of persons between 5 and 10. Eleven were of children over 1 and under 5, while 28, or more than one-half the deaths, were of children under one year of age. The healthful conditions here are unequalled by those in any city of the world. The lowness of the death-rate is remarkable. With one quarter of the physicians that ordinarily administer to a population of this size, Pullman has only a little more than one-quarter of the deaths usual in the same number of people.

The company has adopted a very broad and liberal policy relative to compensation for accidents received during or by means of work in the shops. At present it is contemplated to secure the insurance of all the employés of the company against accidents by the men taking out policies in worthy companies, from which insurance, in case of disability, they would receive $1 per day, Pullman's Palace Car Company guaranteeing to pay an additional $1 per day. This arrangement is perfectly just and must result in putting the men on the best possible basis as regards compensation for accidents. It is generous on the part of the company employing them because it is not by law liable for damages in case of accident.

Moral Influence.

Dr. De Wolf in the report already cited, in speaking of the influence of Pullman city on its inhabitants, says:

"The change in population from emigration amounts to one per cent. *per annum*. These emigrants go forth educated in a way that entitles them to be called sanitary missionaries. There are no special requirements to induce change in the habits of people taking up residence in Pullman, but it is a matter of common observation that insanitary habits—such as making yard cesspools, etc.—soon vanish under the silent but powerful influence of public opinion as shown in the habits of neighbors. Families with dirty, broken furniture soon find it convenient to obtain furniture more in accord with their surroundings. Men who are accustomed to lounge on their front stoops, smoking pipes, and in dirty shirt-sleeves, soon dress and act more in accordance with the requirements of society. All this is accomplished by the silent educational influence of their surroundings. There are no saloons in the town, and one great element of debasement is thus avoided."

Dr. De Wolf has spoken the truth, and another year's experience at Pullman has intensified the force of all he has said.

When Pullman city was first founded, many families came there who had been in the habit of living in a filthy, shiftless way. They came from tenements that were not neat, and that had no pleasant surroundings. Their presence in the new city was like a rubbish heap in a garden,— out of place, and unseemly. One may contemplate the feelings of Mr. Pullman on witnessing these evidences of unappreciation of all the beauty he brought into existence, and it would have been natural for him and for his coadjutors to have indulged in some fault-finding.

On the other hand, the untidy families were left to themselves. As they walked about the streets of Pullman city, and witnessed everywhere orderly ways, well kept lawns, tidy dwellings, clean workshops, and could turn nowhere without meeting order, they naturally began to make comparisons, and such comparisons have resulted in setting their own houses to rights. This is the influence of order and cleanliness everywhere. So the moral influence of Pullman city is an ever present lesson to every family that takes up its abode there. This perfect order and the cleanliness which comes of it is often felt as a restraint upon those who have been brought up under disorder and in uncleanliness, and sometimes causes a sigh for the looser ways and the consequent looser morals of other communities. Such people do not find the air of Pullman city congenial, and no obstacle is thrown in their way should they desire to leave.

These considerations make it easy to see how the company secures the best mechanics.

General Considerations.

We have given the history and the facts relating to Pullman city. There is a deeper side which requires a closer study.

The principle on which Pullman city is founded, and on which its success largely depends, is that in all industrial enterprises business should be so conducted and arranged as to be profitable to each of the great forces, labor and capital.

Mr. Pullman does not believe that a great manufacturing concern can meet with the highest economic and moral success where the profit is unduly large to capital, with no corresponding benefit to labor. The mutual benefit which comes from well adjusted forces is to his mind what brings the best success.

On the other hand, he has made no claim to being a philanthropist; the sentiment prevails in his city that true philanthropy is based on business principles and should net a fair return for efforts made.

Promiscuous charity has no place in the establishment of Pullman. Personally, the president of the company makes the favorable conditions, and, having made them, he then concerns himself chiefly in supplying his people with steady employment. The art interests, the moral interests, the social and the human interests, with favorable conditions supplied, take most excellent care of themselves. Incidentally his competent staff have an eye to all interests.

Mr. Pullman is no dreamer; he has studied the plans of socialists and reformers and the schemes of philosophers for the benefit of humanity.

Beginning at the bottom rung of the ladder and therefore familiar with the wants and aspirations of the workers of society, he has risen by the force of his own character and genius to his present position; he does not care to leave the world and look back upon his action and see that he has only offered a glass of water to the sufferer by the wayside, but he wishes to feel that he has furnished a desert with wells of living water that all may come and drink through all time. So he commenced with the foundation idea of furnishing his workmen with model homes, and supplying them with abundant work with good wages, feeling that simply better conditions would make better men and his city become a permanent benefaction.

He saw great amounts of money being used in speculative schemes, in stock operations, and in all the questionable ways which men take to increase their capital. He saw the energy, the enthusiasm, and the ability which entered into such operations. He could see no reason why all these elements could not be diverted into channels whereby the public should be the gainer and not the loser by great money operations. If capital could be invested in great industrial schemes like Pullman instead of in stock operations, but in such a way as to net a handsome profit to capital and thereby attract it, then not only would capital be safely, securely, and profitably invested, but it would bring even returns without the feverishness of the other method, and the great benefits which would come to the workingman, and thus directly to society itself, would be a positive and absolute gain.

Mr. Pullman's plans did not stop with the founding of an industrial city, but they contemplated establishing alongside great mechanical works where all the science of mechanics is practically applied in every day labor, technical schools where the young might learn the theory and see the application of great mechanical powers. There could not be a better location in the whole country for the highest development of mechanical skill. With technical schools successfully established, Mr. Pullman saw far enough in the future to contemplate a great university.

The great advantages of the geographical location of Pullman city warranted his vast plan; being the centre of the United States commercially, and not far from the centre geographically, he saw no reason why, with scientific works established and with well equipped technical schools, Pullman city should not only teach the nation the way to build up a magnificent class of workmen living under happy and moral conditions, but furnish the country with the most skilful foremen and leading mechanics. To accomplish successfully what Mr. Pullman has undertaken is to carry the world, so far as such men can reach it, to a higher level in civilization.

To do this it was necessary for him to open new avenues for the investment of capital, investments, which as we have said, not only return ample interest in the form of money dividends, but make a grander return in the form of happy homes, and happy hearts. Men must grapple with such enterprises in the belief that the life of the laborer should be something more than a weary round of hard toil, and in the belief that in aiding him to help himself and become a better man, a better brother, a better father, and a better citizen, they are rendering him the best possible service, and in the belief that individual charity, that is merely giving a man something, often does more harm than good.

The general management at Pullman of course partakes of the sentiment of its founder, a broad, comprehensive humanitarian. As we have said, without restrictions upon labor, but so far as we could see, always with justice; for instance, discharges are made with a view to being just; if one of two men must be discharged, other things being equal, the single man must leave and allow the married man to remain; or, if one of two men must be discharged, and each has a family, and one resides away from Pullman, and the other at Pullman, the resident is to be preferred.

All such matters give rise to complaints through superficial consideration, but the even handed justice which prevails is shown by an examination of all sides of the question.

After very careful investigation and the study of Pullman city from the standpoint of the manager, and that of the laborer, the mechanic, the physician, the priest, and from all points of view that we could muster, the question naturally arose, as it might arise in all men's minds who examine such institutions, what are the weak points in the plan? Superficially, we could see at once that the workman had no status as an owner of his home, but we could see that in the early years of Pullman city, if he had such a status it might be the means of his ruin financially. The company owns everything, manages everything; the employés are tenants of the company. This feature will be for some time longer the chief strength of the place, but in this strength lies its weakness. This feature is its strength so long as the industries of Pullman city belong to one great branch, the manufacture of one thing, or the things auxiliary to that manufacture. Now, should the industry of car building collapse or stagnate to any degree, the tenant employé is at liberty to remove at once; he has to give but ten days' notice to vacate his tenancy. He is free to take up his abode where he chooses, without the fear or the fact of any real property going down on his hands. But Mr. Pullman and his company have contemplated this very state of affairs, and are doing all in their power to bring in a diversity of manufactures so that if one kind of goods are not produced another will be. The industrial operations of the place, through Mr. Pullman's exertions, are being extended to the erection of houses, public works, and public buildings. The manufacture of brick, the capacity of all the works to turn out finish, and all the wood materials of buildings, and the other features mentioned under "Industries," have given the place a diversity of employment and of industry, which is leading it into strong and permanent industrial conditions. The result of these conditions, should the railroads of the country operate their own palace cars, will preserve the industral integrity of Pullman city. With these advantages, or, when these advantages come, the tenant employé at Pullman may become the owner of his home. For this purpose a large tract of land has been set aside, and when the time comes will be sold in small lots to the workman, his house built at cost, and he allowed to pay for it on easy terms; then, what would now be a weakness at Pullman will become its strength, and the plan of the city which has been projected on the basis of a population of 100,000 will meet its great success, and these two weak points, the lack of diversified industry and the lack of home ownership, will no longer exist.

To enable this feature of the purchase of homes to be carried out, a savings bank has been established having now deposits to the amount of about $100,000. This money is held subject to immediate call whenever the plans are perfected for the purchase of homes, and will be used in loans to the workingman. It is invested on call so as to be perfectly available whenever wanted. These deposits are entirely the savings of the workingmen of Pullman, and made during the period in which the bank has existed.

The Pullman establishment must, we think, impress the most casual observer as rare enough to be remarkable, and good enough to be commendable. Even superficially it presents a novelty and attractiveness which in themselves command approbation, but the closer scrutiny which we were permitted to give it developed the fact that its excellence was by no means superficial, that it is not only as good as it looks, but better, and that every promise has been made more than good.

Physically, it is better for the reason that its underground system is as complete and costly as the improvements upon the surface, so that there is not only a justification for the fair exterior, but a guarantee of its permanence, and of the welfare of the workers and dwellers in the town.

We found the *morale* of the place even better than we expected. Merely external appearances may not clearly indicate social conditions nor the motives and the policy of the management in such an establishment, yet, if the commissioners did not find that the whole plan was conceived and executed in a spirit of broad and unostentatious philanthropy, our observations and conclusions were at fault throughout. We must regard our investigation as having generously confirmed the good impressions of all those who are predisposed in favor of the Pullman enterprise, and it must disarm those who may have felt some degree of prejudice against it.

In order to arrive at any just estimate of the credit due the projectors of the industrial community under investigation, we were in duty bound to recognize the fact that the company merely proposed to manufacture railway cars for profit; no obligation rested upon them to enter upon any scheme of general beneficence or to jeopardize their financial interests by a costly experiment in the interest of their employés. For the initial disposition in this latter direction, however, they and all men like them deserve praise and encouragement. Having determined that such an experiment might justify itself in a commercial sense as well as on humanitarian grounds, it was still in their option to provide merely comfortable tenements for their men, plain structures for shops and ordinary facilities for cleanliness and sanitation, and for these even they would have deserved well, and yet they go much broader and deeper, and decide upon the most perfect methods of drainage for which their site afforded no facilities, and for a system of gas and water distribution to every house and apartment. They construct permanent streets, and an elaborate system of drainage. Not content with plain buildings, they exhaust the architect's skill in designing the greatest variety of forms for dwellings suited in size and appurtenance to all grades of employés; they erect costly and beautiful buildings for public uses, the church, library, and market house, public halls, theatre, savings bank, and stores; they furnish a park for field sports, amphitheatre for games, and every facility for recreation, physical and mental; and the place is neatly and attractively ornamented with lawns, shade trees, artificial lakes, fountains and flowers. In brief, they stop at nothing short of a model establishment constructed upon plans which are the result of the widest experience, and the best observation for which modern life affords opportunities.

While all this is done at a considerable outlay of money, which, to the ordinary manufacturer, might seem reckless, and commercially at least unjustifiable, the conviction grew upon us, as the details of this magnificent work became understood, that although no such motive has ever been proclaimed, there was really a noble and broad inspiration in the original conception of the undertaking beyond that of merely making the greatest possible amount of money, beyond that of mere personal glorification; an inspiration looking to an actual elevation of the standard of life among the working people who might be fortunate enough to be identified with it. Nothing could be more laudable from our point of view than this, and the Pullman company deserve well of their employés and of all men, not only for what they have accomplished for themselves and their own, but for the conspicuous example they have given the world of the nobler uses of great wealth. It is our view of the case moreover that even if they had attempted and accomplished much less, or even had made great mistakes, they would still deserve commendation for their manifest disposition to recognize the welfare of their employés as of the first concern to themselves. To the growth of such a sentiment among employers, and the practice of it in whatever degree circumstances may permit in smaller establishments, must we look for the real alleviation of the burdens which labor imposes upon those who live by it.

As to the question of earnings in the various grades of employment, and the cost of living within as compared with that outside the community, we are not, as we have already indicated, disposed to insist that the one be greater, and the other less, than elsewhere in order to demonstrate the advantages of the place. We should rather say that were there to be an actual money balance, or not, at the end of the year in favor of the average workman at Pullman, there must be a balance in his favor in all those things which go to make up comfortable and healthful living, in opportunities for the education of children, and their protection from dangerous influences; in the incentives to self-respect and self-culture, and in all the social, moral and sanitary influences which surround the life of every one at Pullman.

If the workman at Pullman lives in a "gilded cage," we must congratulate him on its being so handsomely gilded; the average workman does not have his cage gilded. That there is any cage or imprisonment about it is not true, save in the sense that all men are circumscribed by the conditions with which they surround themselves, and imprisoned by the daily duties of life.

It is quite possible that the Pullman community has been organized and developed thus far on a plan as comprehensive as commercial prudence permits, but when the experiment as now outlined shall have become an established success, it would be gratifying to see certain additional features considered, and if feasible introduced for practical test.

To make Pullman the ideal establishment of the theorists, in addition to the option of purchasing homes and the strength which must come from diversified industry, one would naturally expect that when this enterprise shall have survived adversity as well as prosperity, and the wise and beneficent policy now being tested shall have borne its fruit in a permanent community of intelligent and prosperous workingmen, it may then be found possible to advance them to a share of the profits of the business itself. However this may be, we think we are justified in the belief that, as long as the present management or the spirit of the present management exists, the beneficent features of this most progressive industrial establishment will be extended as rapidly as circumstances may ripen for them.

Let the model manufactory and the industrial community of Pullman city be commended as they deserve for whatever they are or what they promise to be. Let them be held up to the manufacturers, and employers of men, throughout the country as worthy of their emulation. Let Mr. Pullman and his coadjutors be assured of the good wishes of all those who seek the advancement of their kind.

CARROLL D. WRIGHT,
Chief, Massachusetts Bureau of Statistics of Labor.

JOEL B. McCAMANT,
Chief, Pennsylvania Bureau of Industrial Statistics.

HENRY LUSKEY,
Commissioner, Ohio Bureau of Labor Statistics.

JAMES BISHOP,
Chief, New Jersey Bureau of Statistics of Labor and Industries.

H. A. NEWMAN,
Commissioner, Missouri Bureau of Labor Statistics and Inspection.

JOHN S. LORD,
Secretary, Illinois Bureau of Labor Statistics.

WM. A. PEELLE, JR.,
Chief, Indiana Bureau of Statistics and Geology.

CHAS. F. PECK,
Commissioner, New York Bureau of Labor Statistics.

JOHN S. ENOS,
Commissioner, California Bureau of Labor Statistics.

JOHN DEVLIN,
Deputy Commissioner, Michigan Bureau of Labor and Industrial Statistics.

FRANK A. FLOWER,
Commissioner, Wisconsin Bureau of Labor Statistics.

E. R. HUTCHINS,
Commissioner, Iowa Bureau of Labor Statistics.

THOS. C. WEEKS,
Chief, Maryland Bureau of Statistics of Labor.

H. A. NEWMAN,
President of Convention.

HENRY LUSKEY,
Secretary.

THE RIGHTS AND DANGERS OF PROPERTY.

A

SERMON

DELIVERED BEFORE THE

Executive and Legislative Departments

OF THE

GOVERNMENT OF MASSACHUSETTS,

AT THE

ANNUAL ELECTION,

Wednesday, January 3, 1872.

BY ANDREW P. PEABODY.

BOSTON:
WRIGHT & POTTER, STATE PRINTERS, 79 MILK STREET,
(CORNER OF FEDERAL STREET).
1872.

THE RIGHTS AND DANGERS OF PROPERTY.

A

SERMON

DELIVERED BEFORE THE

Executive and Legislative Departments

OF THE

GOVERNMENT OF MASSACHUSETTS,

AT THE

ANNUAL ELECTION,

Wednesday, January 3, 1872.

By Andrew P. Peabody.

BOSTON:
WRIGHT & POTTER, STATE PRINTERS, 79 MILK STREET
(Corner of Federal Street).
1872.

Commonwealth of Massachusetts.

House of Representatives, Boston, January 10, 1872.

Rev. A. P. Peabody, D. D.

Dear Sir:—The undersigned have the honor to transmit to you the following vote, which was unanimously passed by the House to-day:—

"*Ordered*, That a Committee of three be appointed by the Chair to present the thanks of the House to Rev. A. P. Peabody, D. D., for his able and eloquent discourse before the executive and legislative branches of the government on the 3d inst., and to request a copy of the same for the press."

It will give us pleasure to report to the House that you have furnished a copy of the Sermon before named for publication,

While we remain, very respectfully yours,

HENRY S. WASHBURN,
W. F. ARNOLD,
J. D. HALL,
Committee.

Cambridge, January 12, 1872.

Gentlemen:—In reply to your favor of the 10th inst., permit me to acknowledge the courtesy and kindness of your communication, to express my thanks for the honor done me in the vote transmitted through you, and to signify my readiness to comply immediately with the request contained in it.

I am, gentlemen, very truly yours,

A. P. PEABODY.

Messrs. Henry S. Washburn, W. F. Arnold, J. D. Hall,
Committee of the House of Representatives of Massachusetts.

Commonwealth of Massachusetts.

HOUSE OF REPRESENTATIVES. January 15, 1872.

Ordered, That four thousand copies of the Sermon preached by Rev. Dr. Peabody be printed, under the direction of the Committee on Printing, for the use of the executive and legislative branches of the government.

W. S. ROBINSON, *Clerk*.

SERMON.

THOU SHALT NOT STEAL.—Exodus xx. 15.

We have reason for gratitude that our translation of the Bible was made while the Anglo-Saxon elements of our language were still in the ascendant; for their power of moral demonstration, rebuke and invective, immeasurably transcends that of the terms of Norman derivation. They come down upon the ear and the conscience with a sharp, incisive stroke, which can never ring from the more euphonious words gleaned from the classic tongues. Reserve these, if you will, as fit frames for the loveliness of virtue and the beauty of holiness; but let them not lend their always graceful drapery to relieve the hideous features of wrong and evil. Had stealing in all its forms and degrees never borne any milder name, there would have been much less of it to mourn and to brand.

But what has this to do with the occasion which has called us together, and with the august body which I have the honor to address? I answer, Much, every way. Your most important function as legislators is the protection of the rights of property. In our advanced civilization, life and personal liberty are guarded by the common sense of the community, and there is no danger of their being betrayed or ignored by any legislative body which shall owe its existence to popular election. We cannot conceive of a condition of things within the pale of Anglo-Saxondom, in which there should not be laws, honestly designed and reasonably well adapted for the prevention, detection and punishment of crimes of violence. At least, there is in no legislature a counteracting influence,—a disposition to frame laws for facilitating the commission of such crimes or the escape of the criminals. But the legislation which is the subject of earnest controversy, keen antagonism, close division and intrusive outside influence, relates for the most part, directly or indirectly, to property, private or corporate, or involves pecuniary rights, claims or interests. There is, moreover, in a large portion of the community, a strong tendency to the invasion of the rights of property,—a tendency which lies at the foundation of various *quasi* political parties or factions, and which has in numerous instances shaped the action of our national and State legislatures.

In this direction our general government has yielded to the very same demands that were restlessly urged by the agitators, revolutionists and incendiaries in the Roman republic. One of these was for agrarian laws, for the alienation and division of the public domain. Our agrarian laws have ceded the public lands with the most wasteful prodigality, sometimes indeed for the general good, but oftener in such ways as to feed the cupidity of individual speculators, or to enrich corporations that would else have found no lack of private capital. Another demand, constantly renewed with clamor by the indebted classes in Rome, was for the legal reduction or cancelling of all debts. This demand was satisfied on an enormous scale by the legal-tender act—unconstitutional, as still believe—passed during the late war, which was undoubtedly a bid for the votes of the masses in some future contingency; for, while incompetency is too often a passport to high official station, it can hardly be that the framers of this measure were weak enough to deem it wise, or even safe, in a financial point of view. Its aim, in all probability, as its immediate effect, was to authorize the liquidation of all existing debts in a currency of fluctuating and rapidly depreciating value. The issuing of a national paper currency was, no doubt, a necessity of that fearful crisis. But had the metallic standard of value been legally retained, the currency would have been kept much nearer its nominal value; its rapid and violent fluctuation would have been superseded; the imminent peril of national bankruptcy — our chief danger — would have been averted; and our public debt would have fallen short by at least one-third of its actual amount; while we should have been spared on the floor of Congress the disgraceful and infamous agitation of schemes for liquidating, in depreciated paper, obligations contracted in good faith — though at a ruinous sacrifice — for payment in coin or its equivalent. Worse than all this has been the debauching of the general conscience by the example of so gigantic a public wrong, the spirit of gambling that has been cherished in mercantile and pecuniary transactions, the extravagance which has grown from the inflation of nominal values, the power which has often been in the hands of a few unprincipled men to control and derange the financial relations of our whole monetary world.

But our present concern is with our own Commonwealth, and with the future rather than the past. I would first speak of the service which accumulated private property renders to the State, and then of the various forms of warfare against it.

There is a growing jealousy of large estates, and an increasing desire to invade them, and to approach a more equal distribution of wealth. There is good reason for this feeling where the right of primogeniture keeps landed property undivided, and where custom influences testators to make a similar disposition of personal estate. But where law and imperative custom redistribute large properties on the death of their owners, it is impossible that there should be excessive and harmful accumulation by individuals. With us, wealth is not inactive; even large private domains are kept for the most part under cultivation; and money is almost never suffered to lie idle. Is the rich man, as he ought to be, the willing steward for the benefit of his brethren? If so, his wealth is none the less useful, because he has charge of its expenditure; but in his hands it subserves numerous valuable purposes, which would be frustrated were it divided among many owners. This city and our whole State are full of the evidences of the generous use of riches acquired and held for no other end than benevolence. Our institutions of religion and of learning, our great public charities, embracing every form of human need and misery, and unostentatious, but munificent private charities, whose source often is first known when death arrests its flow, bear witness to the philanthropy which is the predominant characteristic of our rich men; and many of them are there, for whose wealth daily thanksgiving goes up to God from those who without its subsidies would be helpless and hopeless. There are hundreds of large estates whose loss or dilapidation would be felt as a wide-spread public calamity.

There are, however, some men whose generosity is in inverse proportion to their wealth, and whose only aim is accumulation. But what of them? They are their own enemies in denying themselves the sweetest, richest revenue they could have, and the treasure they might lay up in heaven. But they too are public benefactors, little as they mean to be so. They do not hoard their money,—if they did, it would not grow. They manage their property for the general good, and at the lowest possible cost of management. Every dollar of their capital is invested in industrial operations. Every dollar of their dividends is ploughed for, and dug for, and hammered for. They enrich themselves by feeding channels of supply for unnumbered mechanics, sailors, operatives of every sort. The very impulse that speeds them on their selfish ends enhances the demand for labor, and in the same proportion increases the wages and augments the comfort of the laborer. And when they die, their property oftener than otherwise falls into liberal hands that pay in full into the treasuries of public and private charity the overdue arrears.

Large properties are imperatively needed as safety-funds and movement-funds for the whole community. The ever-varying relations of demand and supply depend on so many, and often so latent, subtile and remote conditions, that no skill or care can foresee them or provide for them. Not from human fault or folly, but from the necessity of the case, there must be alternations of glut and scarcity as to every commodity that enters into commerce,—intervals when the business of late profitably pursued must be suspended, or continued at a loss. Accumulated capital alone can meet these crises, or furnish the means of meeting them, and they sometimes are so stringent as to put even the largest fortunes in jeopardy. In their less severe forms they occur much oftener than they are noted by the public. Industrial operations are continued and the operatives kept in employment through many seasons of excessive supply or slackened demand, solely because there are these reservoirs of wealth, which may be drawn upon at need, and will be replenished with an altered condition of the market. But without these, in the Utopia sometimes dreamed of in which there shall be no large capitals, strikes among employers would take place ten times as often as now among the employed; and the depressions below the desired level by failure, enforced idleness and starvation would make a much more diversified, though less picturesque social landscape than is now presented by the modest, in our country seldom over-lofty elevations, whence issue the streams that keep the valleys green. It might seem convenient and desirable to cut channels, by which the ever-flowing river should be divided into numberless rivulets that should twine through every village and by every farm-house between two mountain chains; but the first summer solstice would lay bare the bed of each one of the rivulets, would rob the clouds of their wonted supplies, and turn the whole region into an arid waste. In like manner, were large properties distributed, the wealth thus diffused would be rapidly dissipated, enterprise would die out, industry would languish, and the coveted universal competence would be merged in universal poverty, listlessness and misery.

Let us now examine some of the modes in which the war against capital is waged. Foremost among these is the reckless creation of public debts. The amount of national, State and city debt at this moment resting upon the city of Boston, is no less than one hundred and thirty-two dollars for every man, woman and child. The proportion of the national and the State debt due from Boston, in addition to the city debt, is about one-sixth of the entire valuation,—which means that the man who supposes himself possessed of a property of sixty thousand dollars in currency — in actual value some ten or twelve per cent. less — has really but fifty thousand, is by direct and indirect taxation annually paying interest on the remaining ten thousand, at a somewhat higher rate than he could himself borrow it for on good security; and, moreover, is paying a great part of that interest to foreign capitalists, from whom there comes back no return of benefit in any form to himself or to the country. The figures do not differ substantially for any of the towns and cities in the Commonwealth. A very large proportion of this debt is, indeed, the purchase-money of our ransomed Union, of freedom to the slave, and of a place among the nations no longer to be dishonored by a public wrong, sin and crime, which made liberty a baseless pretence, and republican forms a cloak for the vilest despotism. This burden, though much greater than it ought to have been, the patriotic citizen will bear cheerfully; and Heaven avert the day when the repudiation of any portion or description of our debt shall not be regarded with abhorrence!

Yet added liabilities should not be lightly incurred, as they are incurred, in not a few of our municipalities, for mere ostentation, for plans of so-called public improvement which have private ends in view, or for the imagined needs of a remote posterity, even in places where there are no elements of rapid growth, and as to matters in which posterity will doubtless be able to provide more judiciously for its own interests. It has escaped the foresight of some of our municipal functionaries that an abnormally heavy town or city debt may dwarf growth, discourage and repel an else incoming population, and thus make void the very purpose for which it is ostensibly contracted. It is, indeed, reasonable that a large necessary expense of one year should be distributed among several years; but it is unreasonable and in every aspect dishonest, most atrociously so in our smaller communities, that needless enterprises should transmit a funded and increasing debt to generations which will have outgrown the very improvements purchased by it, and will have pressing needs of their own that will be fully level with their tax-paying capacity. This is at least no way to merit the gratitude of posterity. Many of these modes of indebtedness are, I know, outside of the accustomed range of State legislation. Yet might there not be established by legal authority a proportion to the valuation of property, beyond which no debt hereafter contracted should be lawful?

There is, moreover, one form of indebtedness over which the legislature has control; namely, loans or grants by cities and towns to corporations. For an enterprise that gives certain or probable promise of speedy and lucrative returns, there is no lack of capital, and no desire or even willingness to invite the coöperation of municipalities. It is only in doubtful cases that such aid is solicited, and it is often asked where the immediate effect of the enterprise in hand will be the depletion of the town thus taxed, the drawing of its business to larger centres, and the enhancement of the cost of living by the attraction of domestic produce to larger markets. In such cases it is always easy to secure for the loan a majority or a two-thirds vote, even though the measure be opposed by all the large tax-payers. Is this right? Should not the owners of property have some voice in the mortgaging of their property? Should it be left to those who bear no appreciable part in the public burdens to increase those burdens at their will, or rather at the dictation or under the pay of interested parties? Universal suffrage inevitably places property to a very great extent under the control of those who have nothing to lose. Should not the legislature take heed how they enlarge this power?

Closely connected with our public debts, and growing in great part out of them, yet transcending by far the needs which they create, is the burden laid upon property by excessive taxation. We are probably the most heavily taxed people upon the face of the earth. Were we a stationary people, the weight would be more than we could carry. We barely carry it, it is doubtful whether we are thriving under it, now; but with a population rapidly increasing, and with new resources always in the process of development, we can remain elastic under a pressure else insupportable.

In our national government we have been cursed by a system organized in some departments and maintained in all, with prime regard to the extension of executive patronage. This may be seen conspicuously in our present system of internal revenue, in which the obvious aim is, not to adjust the modes of assessment and collection to the convenience of the tax-payers, but to provide for the largest possible number of officials and at the most liberal rate of compensation. There are other departments in which, with half the number of functionaries of tested capacity and approved integrity, the work could be better done; and there are numerous instances in which what are deemed the legitimate spoils of office — to say nothing of illicit peculations — far exceed the nominal and fully remunerating stipend.

In our own State the case is otherwise. Our highest functionaries, especially our judges, are inadequately compensated; and there are few, if any, instances in which public service is overpaid. At the same time, our annual and occasional grants for the promotion of liberal culture, and for the interests of humanity, when most munificent, are most to be commended. But there have been subsidies to bankrupt corporations, which do little credit to the wisdom of former legislatures, even if they leave their integrity unimpeached; and it is to be earnestly hoped that in this regard the past will furnish warnings, not examples.

In our towns and cities there is intense need of reform. Red tape is costing our citizens an enormous sum, and yielding to their officials an inordinate revenue. An item of paltry service will often cost a city from twice to ten times what it would cost any one of its inhabitants. There are in almost every city council and board of selectmen persons who are there simply for the opportunities thus afforded of making a better living than they could otherwise earn. If there be a mechanic not industrious, or skilful, or honest enough to find constant employment, he contrives, as a party fugleman, to be placed on some municipal board, in which he may exercise his talents lucratively on the public property, often to the delay and detriment of the public service. While within the memory of some who hear me civic charges were forced upon men who did not want them, and who bore them only at a personal sacrifice, now, that a man needs an office is often urged as a reason for giving it to him; and one is frequently supported at the town or city hall, simply because he is too genteel a mendicant to be sent to the almshouse. Nor are we in our own Commonwealth without instances of the pillaging of municipal treasuries by their legal guardians, for sumptuous and not always sober festivities, for utterly needless journeys and pleasure excursions, nay, for the very clothes that they wear at a public reception, and for costly photographs of the faces which they ought to be ashamed to show. In this entire department of fraud New York has indeed earned preëminent distinction, such enormous thefts being possible only in a vast metropolis; but toward this type of fame many of our smaller communities are evidently aspiring and tending, and remain in the rear for lack of opportunity, not of will. Perchance there is still in the hill-country, surrounded, but as yet unpierced by rail and telegraph, some little town, where Astræa is making her last sojourn, where in the old style a modest budget is warily canvassed and intelligently voted, and the *select*-men, the choice men, the real aristocracy of sense and character, exercise for their little public the same wise economy which they are constrained to practise in their own affairs, carefully audit all the bills they sanction, and account for every dollar to their constituents. If there yet be such a place, leave it, I beseech you, in its own charmed circle. Crush without mercy every project for replacing the old post-road that leads to it by quicker means of transit. Warn off from it the State geologist, lest he discover, in ore, limestone or emery, some lure for outside speculators. It may be that a pillaged State and a nation fallen among thieves will one day resort for lessons of political wisdom and honesty to this sole survivor among the town-governments, which were the procreant cradle of our republic.

The whole system of municipal knavery results from the fact—in itself alarming and threatening—that the property of every community is at the disposal of a majority, which hardly feels the burden, though it may hope in various ways to profit by the disbursement, of the annual taxes. It is perfectly well known that in some cases the promise of gainful employment on contemplated streets or buildings, in some, threats of discharge from factories, in some, direct and unconcealed pecuniary bribes, have alone secured the votes requisite for the choice of men or the passing of measures, in opposition not only to the property, but to the intelligence, sound judgment and moral sense of an entire community. Nay, it is a notorious fact that measures of the gravest import have sometimes been thus carried by a majority composed chiefly of imported and manufactured citizens, some of them not yet able to understand an English sentence, hardly any of them capable of comprehending the meaning of the vote they cast.

Now there is a limit, which overpassed, taxation begins to trench upon reserved capital, in keeping which intact and growing the public has even a more vital interest than individual tax-payers. This limit has been in some of our municipalities closely approached, if not exceeded. To exceed it is inevitable etiolation, decline and ruin.

These concerns may at first sight seem beyond the scope of legislation. But are they? The towns of New England were in earlier times pre-eminently capable of self-government; but if they have for any reason ceased to be so, may not their excesses be restrained, without doing violence to their just and safe liberties? Cannot their indiscretion be averted, while their reasonable discretion remains unimpaired? It is within the power of the legislature to set limits to the rate of taxation; to define the kinds of expenses which a city or town may or may not incur; to establish boards or modes of appeal with reference to extraordinary expenditures of doubtful utility; to lodge in some county or State authority a veto upon the street-making power, exercised, as it often is, wantonly, corruptly and injuriously; and to enact penalties at once severe and ignominious for fraud or complicity with fraud in municipal office, and for the use of threats, promises or bribes to influence voters.

I must pass to yet another form of the warfare upon property, namely, combinations and concerted aggressive movements of labor against capital, of the employed against employers. Here the agitation proceeds in part from ignorance, in part from wilful misrepresentation. There is not a vestige of the wrong and oppression complained of. Manual and mechanical labor is not only better paid here than anywhere else in the world, but its compensation exceeds that of mercantile and professional services. In these last, to be sure, there are a few great prizes, but not one to a hundred competitors. Take from the average income of a professional man a sum equal to the life-annuity that might have been purchased by the money expended in his education, and for his support during the unproductive years which would have been productive had he been a laborer,—subtract still further his strictly professional expenses, and those which are required by his position, but yield no benefit or comfort to him or his family,—you have reduced his earnings to a pittance which the man who shovels your coal would scorn to work for. Similar calculations as to persons employed in commercial operations would give a like result. When I say that labor is well paid, there is indeed one grievous exception, that is, the labor of women; but for this exception men are in no degree accountable. The sole reason why women are underpaid is that women who do not need employment are mean enough to underbid those who do need it; and the lowest price at which labor, as well as any other commodity is offered, must rule the market. But, with this exception, in the joint earnings of labor and capital, labor is now getting the lion's share, and is still clamoring and grasping for more. The revenue of machinery and labor-saving processes inures, immediately on the extinction of patent-rights, to the sole benefit of the laborer, and he has a just title to it either in money or money's worth or in time; but he now claims it in both. Persons of moderate income are already seriously embarrassed and straitened by the cost of necessary labor, and the screws of the inflexible and growing demand are turned by those who learned in trans-Atlantic homes to inflict, by being trained to endure extortion. How well they have learned the lesson is attested by the magnificent cathedrals and churches they are building, by their deposits in our savings-banks, by the rapid increase of their visible property, and by the disappearance of large amounts in remittances to their native country.

The demand of which I speak, if passively yielded to, will grow of its own necessity to a point at which a ruinous collapse is inevitable. As labor enters into the price of every commodity, the laboring man is increasing the cost of his own subsistence by the increase of his own wages, and every successful exaction is therefore a logical reason for increased exaction. Yet, on the other hand, with prices exorbitantly enhanced, general consumption must diminish, the scope for remunerative labor must be narrowed, and idleness, privation and suffering on an extended scale must be the consequence. It is toward this result that tend all exclusive and arbitrary trade-unions, strikes of operatives, and factious measures for obtaining control of the labor-market, which can be fair only when left free; for the actual worth of labor, as of flour or sugar, is determined by the ratio of the supply to the demand.

To keep the labor-market free requires in our time wise and wary vigilance on the part of our legislative bodies. Not only have they the often difficult task of so framing preventive laws that they cannot be evaded; but they are annually called upon to violate freedom and right, by sanctioning associations of laborers whose government is a truculent and cruel despotism, and by imposing arbitrary restrictions on the contract between the employer and the employed.

I have thus indicated some of the ways in which property is liable to depredation in our own time and country; and all the more liable because we have current among us certain traditional and imported maxims—belonging not improperly to other times and lands—which identify property with pride, rapacity, oppression, and, in general, with the attributes of birds of prey. In the American republic of the nineteenth century, if the old division of society into the preying and the preyed upon is not wholly obliterated, it is to the latter class, not to the former, that the rich belong.

I have chosen property and its dangers as my subject for this occasion, because there is no other subject that so intimately concerns the legislative body which commences its session to-day. The postponed business and the petitions on file relate almost wholly to pecuniary interests, and in many instances involve delicate and important questions of right between the public, existing or projected corporations, and individual citizens. In all such cases you will, I think, find your work greatly facilitated, if you will put the question of right before that of expediency, instead of attempting to grope the way to the right through the expedient. The single eye, says the Divine Teacher, is full of light; while, according to Him, double vision is no better than blindness. The single eye, seeking the right, can hardly fail to discern it. The cases of doubt and perplexity are generally those in which the endeavor is to find some creditable way of bending the obviously right in the direction of what is falsely imagined to be expedient.

'You will pardon me if I remind you that in our time there are many indirect methods of warping the honest opinion and sound judgment of a legislator, without his own consciousness. The man who takes an overt bribe must despise himself more heartily than he is despised by others. But there are insidious social influences—attentions, courtesies, flatteries—to which even the most upright purpose may yield unawares. Then, too, there is often an over-strong temptation to him who is earnestly pursuing some honest end to barter his vote and influence for a measure or enterprise which he does not wholly approve, in return for votes and influence in behalf of the measure or enterprise which he has most at heart. There is, also, to our poor human nature a profound significance in the Divine precept, "Thou shalt take no gift; for the gift blindeth the wise, and perverteth the words of the righteous." This is true, not only of the secret *douceur*, which no honest man will touch, but equally of gifts offered in open day, and to the entire body of which the donor—individual or corporate—may demand privileges or favors. The excursion planned for a retiring legislature, and so planned as to include not only its members, but their wives and children, and the strangers within their gates, and outside of them too, is not without a view to the votes of the reëlected members, and may bias the judgment of men who are incapable of conscious wrong. Claim, if you deem it your due, free transit for yourselves on the routes which you must traverse in the public service; but accept no gratuities from corporations that may be your suitors.

I have not forgotten that I was invited to address you as a minister of religion; and though I have not filled my discourse with sacred words, I have given utterance only to such views as bear in my own thought, and I am sure ought to bear in your minds, the sanction of religious obligation. The Divine law, as uttered in the thunders of Sinai, as reënacted by our Saviour, attaches inviolable sacredness to those rights of property which lie at the basis of social order, civilization and progress. This law I have, to the best of my ability, endeavored to interpret, in its application to the great questions and issues which may demand your serious consideration as the chosen trustees and guardians of right, justice and equity. Heaven grant that you acquit yourselves as "able men, such as fear God, men of truth, hating covetousness." May the record of your service be such as you can fully justify to your own hearts, and to God who "is greater than your hearts, and knoweth all things." The place on which you enter has been nobly filled from the earliest days of our provincial history. May the mantle of the fathers rest upon the children, and may the God of the fathers breathe into the children His own spirit of counsel and wisdom.

I rejoice to believe that nowhere upon earth is there higher honor paid than in our own State to political integrity and faithfulness. Last summer, as I frequently passed to and from my country lodgings, the railway train stopped at a little station in Maine, hard by a small, black, one-story cottage, where John Albion Andrew was born. All eyes were uniformly turned to that house in profound reverence, as they might have been to some sacred shrine, or some place of holy pilgrimage. Indeed, what shrine can be more sacred, what spot more holy, than that which formed and nurtured the budding virtues of him, who, with guileless simplicity, and with a single-hearted purity, in which even malice and rancor could find no ground for reproach, in the life and death struggle of our republic, consecrated his noble mind, his great heart, his unresting toil to the service of his God in the service of his country?

Long may it be ere like memories shall be recalled in sadness of our now retiring chief magistrate; but, whether in private life or in yet other high places of public charge and office, he will bear with him the gratitude and love by which man anticipates the Divine verdict on uprightness and fidelity in trusts of large and high responsibleness, held as in commission from God, and discharged "as ever in the great Taskmaster's eye." We are thankful that, in the chair of state which he vacates, the succession of personal and civic virtue and of Christian piety and philanthropy is not suspended; and so long as it shall be thus filled, there will be faith and hope in our traditional prayer, "God save the Commonwealth of Massachusetts."

NONPARTISAN INDUSTRIAL COMMISSION.

SPEECH

OF

HON. T. W. PHILLIPS,

OF PENNSYLVANIA,

IN THE

HOUSE OF REPRESENTATIVES,

THURSDAY, MAY 21, 1896.

WASHINGTON.

1896.

SPEECH

OF

HON. T. W. PHILLIPS.

The House being in Committee of the Whole on the state of the Union, and having under consideration the bill (H. R. 6119) authorizing the appointment of a nonpartisan commission to collate information and to consider and recommend legislation to meet the problems presented by labor, agriculture, and capital—

Mr. PHILLIPS said:

Mr. CHAIRMAN: The bill (H. R. 6119) now before the House is designed to better our industrial system. No demand of the people in any age has met with such general response as the demand for a better industrial and social organization of society.

No sentiment has attracted such widespread attention or has had such rapid growth. Our Government is republican; and to be effectual and durable it must have proper regard for all departments of human activity. Legislation must have just respect for the wage earner and for the wage payer, for the producer and consumer. This Government can not endure if more than one-half of its people are discontented, distressed, and suffering, for it is a Government of all and by all.

Mr. Chairman, this bill calls attention to the fundamental principle of our Government—the equality of man—and seeks a more equitable distribution of the burdens and benefits of our free Government. While it is not the function of the State to guarantee individual happiness, it is its function to guarantee each individual the right to pursue happiness, and so enact laws that one class may not be compelled of necessity to work solely for another class, regardless of their personal comfort and improvement. Rights do not belong to one class and duties to another. Physical, intellectual, and moral ability can not be made equal, but each capacity may be met; each cup, be it large or small, may be filled. Circumstances can not be made equal, but law can be adapted to circumstances.

Mr. Chairman, the danger to this Government is not external, but internal. In the progress of human society the battles of the world are shifting from conflict with nations to a conflict within nations for better government and more equitable laws. We must recognize the fact that more are now peacefully organized and enlisted in the cause of industrial equity than in all the armies of the world. The people of civilized nations will not always continue to fight for national honor and supremacy while their individual rights are not protected within the nation. National glory must henceforth be based more and more upon the prosperity and happiness of the individual citizen. After more than six thousand years of experience the people are beginning to learn that government belongs to them; that they are not owned by the government, but that they own the government, and that it must respect their rights by meeting their just demands.

If laws are derived from the governed, they should meet the just demands of all the governed. This nation took the most advanced stand in civilization, and is the best prepared to meet the industrial issues of to-day by building on the foundation it laid more than one hundred years ago by conforming law to its declared principles of right, freedom, and equality, and thus organize our social and industrial system upon a more just and equitable basis than has yet obtained in the world.

Mr. Chairman, in entering upon the discussion of the subject-matter of this bill I wish to make three observations in regard to man, which are stated in the first chapters of Genesis.

First, the unity of the race and equality of man was shown in creation; God created man and gave him dominion as man. He was to "subdue the earth," and "have dominion over the fish of the sea, over the fowls of the air, and over every living thing that moveth upon the earth." But he was not given dominion over his fellow-man.

Second, before God created man it was said: "And there was not a man to till the ground."

In the third place, man was told by the Creator: "In the sweat of thy face shalt thou eat bread till thou return unto the ground." To all, therefore, who believe in the Bible account of creation, which I believe is also in strict accord with science, fact, and history, these three things are indisputable:

First. That when God created man, he gave him dominion as man, not over his fellow-man, but over beast and bird and fish; over all animate nature below him.

Second. That he was to till the soil as his chief occupation.

Third. That his life was to be sustained by labor.

All this agrees with reason; shows equality in creation; that sustenance comes from the ground; that labor is the normal condition of man; and it is a fact that no man enters into rest unless it is upon his own labor or the labor of others. The government, therefore, that does not strive to meet these three great cardinal principles of reason and revelation in the highest possible degree will perish from the earth.

Mr. Chairman, this bill provides for the appointment of a non-partisan commission, to be composed of five members representatives of labor, five representatives of agriculture, five of manufacturing, and five of business. The importance of labor to our being and well-being can not be overstated. Labor is one of the foundation principles upon which organized society rests. All kinds of labor is necessary, from digging in the ditch to measuring space and counting the stars, yet the lower forms of labor are more intimately connected with our existence and needs. The most despised is often the most useful. The man who digs the foundation is more important to the structure than he who frescoes its walls. Without the grading of the roadbed there would be no stockholders, no locomotive, or railroad president. If all manual labor were to stop, if all wage earners were to cease work, there would be no value in property and a large part of the race would perish.

That our relations are most intimately bound up with the wage earner is shown by the many strikes and lockouts in recent years which have entailed great suffering and loss of property, as well as the sacrifice of life.

I submit a summary from Hon. Carroll D. Wright, Commissioner of Labor, on the subject of strikes and lockouts from January 1, 1881, to June 30, 1894, being a period of thirteen and a half years. For this period it will be seen that there were 14,390 strikes; that there were 69,167 establishments involved; that there were 3,794,406 employees thrown out of employment.

It will be also seen that the loss to strikers was	$163,807,866
For the same period in lockouts the loss to employees was	26,685,516
Assistance to strikers by labor organizations	10,914,406
Assistance in lockouts	2,524,298
Total loss to employees	203,932,076
Loss to employers for the same period by reason of strikes	82,590,386
Loss to employers for the same period by reason of lockouts	12,235,451
Total loss to employers	94,825,837
Total loss to both employees and employers	298,757,913

These figures represent the actual loss to the parties engaged, and do not represent the enormous loss which incidentally came to the community by reason of such disturbances; but the injury to society, the demoralization, suffering, and death, can not be estimated. All admit that something must be done, and a commission composed of those directly interested in this great labor problem, in my judgment, is the proper means through which to seek the cause of this violent disturbance and propose a remedy, as our legislative bodies are not meeting the issue. Again, Mr. Chairman, the agricultural industry is the most important of all industries. All civilized life depends upon the products of the soil. All food and clothing come from the soil; yet this most important industry is greatly depressed. The constant settling in the value of farm products and farm lands in recent years in a large portion of the United States has made great discontent and unrest among farmers. Many of them can not hope to have their children succeed them in husbandry, and they are exhausting their limited means to fit them for pursuits in the crowded town or city.

In 1870 the value of farm lands in the United States was	$9,262,803,861
In the same year the total value of all property in the United States was	30,068,000,000

The value of farm lands was, therefore, about 33 per cent of the value of all property.

In 1880 the value of farm lands in the United States was	$10,197,096,776
In the same year the total value of all property in the United States was	43,600,000,000

The value of farm lands was, therefore, only about 24 per cent of the value of property in 1880.

In 1890 the value of farm lands in the United States was	$13,279,252,649
In the same year the total value of all property in the United States was	65,000,000,000

The value of farm lands was, therefore, only about 19 per cent of the value of property in this later period. Thus in twenty years the farm lands settled from 33 to 19 per cent as compared with the total value of all property, and this notwithstanding the opening up of millions of acres rich in soil.

These are startling figures when we consider that the value of farm lands is not increasing in due proportion to all other property; that agriculture is the foundation of all other industries, and that 40 per cent of the toiling people are engaged in tilling the soil.

No country can prosper when the agricultural interest is suffering. This commission is needed by the farmers not only because of these facts, but on account of their growing discontent as shown by their various organizations and protests against unequal burdens and discriminating laws. Even if the agriculturists had nothing of which to complain or to adjust, they are needed in such a conference as this to aid in seeking a way out of the manifold labor troubles which so vitally affect their interests as well as those of the whole population.

In regard to the importance of the manufacturing industry, I will state that in 1890 the number of persons 10 years of age and upward engaged in all occupations was	22,735,661
Of this number there were engaged in manufacturing	4,712,622
Of this number there were engaged in agriculture	8,303,000
The total wage receivers of all classes were	14,920,525
The number of manufacturing establishments in 1890 was	355,415
Capital employed was	$6,139,397,785
Total number of employees was	4,476,884
Total wages paid was	$2,283,516,529
Cost of materials used was	$5,162,044,076
Total value of manufactured products was	$9,372,437,283

It will be seen from this statement that of the 22,735,661 of all occupations 4,712,622 were engaged in manufacturing and mechanical industries. More people are engaged in this industry than in any other, with the exception of farming. The greatest per cent of actual loss by reason of strikes and lockouts comes to those engaged in manufacturing and their employees. Great good should ultimate to those engaged in this industry by wise consideration of the violent disturbances which so vitally affect all concerned.

This commission is designed also to benefit all other business pursuits. The disturbed condition of affairs has entailed great loss upon the business community. The loss of $298,757,913, as shown in table quoted, in thirteen and one-half years to the laborers and the employers of labor is but a fractional part of the loss sustained by transporters, merchants, and others engaged in business pursuits. Business men have and will continue to suffer great depreciations in value and increasing losses unless a better adjustment is made. Business men need and business interests require a just and more satisfactory settlement of differences with those with whom they deal and upon whose labor and products successful business must depend. The better labor is protected in all its rights the greater will be the security for earnings. No intelligent business man can oppose any just and fair effort to harmonize conflicting interests in a legal and peaceable way, for all such must know and see from the history of the recent past that the great industrial problem may shortly be met by violence if not worked out in peace by law.

Mr. Chairman, this bill is designed to give an impartial hearing to those who complain of discriminating laws and unequal burdens. It is expected that it will be composed of the ablest and best of each class named. It will bring into conference representative men of labor, agriculture, manufacturing, and business, thus bringing together the aggrieved and those against whom the grievance is made, whose duty it will be to consider the disturbing causes and recommend laws looking toward a more just distribution of the burdens and benefits of our free Government. It is designed to be impartial, nonpartisan, seeking exact facts and conditions, and to conform legislation to the foundation principles of our Government—to place all men on an equal footing before the law.

I believe such a commission the most practical way to meet the issue. Our national and State legislative bodies are not so constituted as to give proper time to the consideration of the industrial questions presented in this bill. They have not met and are not meeting them, as discord, strikes, and violence are constantly increasing. These bodies are not made up equally of representative men, such as are proposed by this bill; they are besieged by men lobbying for special privileges, while none are lobbying for the good of all. If, therefore, such representative men as are proposed—men who suffer most from the great conflict of interest—can not agree in recommending more equitable laws looking to a peaceful solution of the question involved, it can not be solved by a free government in a peaceful way.

Mr. Chairman, I believe Congress is the proper body to authorize the appointment of such a commission, as it is composed of members coming from all parts of every State. However jealous we may be of the rights of the States, no one can object to such a commission making recommendations to Congress and furnishing information to the States which may be of the greatest value.

Again, the commission could utilize a large amount of statistical information gathered at great cost by various agricultural and labor organizations, and especially could use to great advantage the information collected by the various labor committees appointed in recent years, both State and national, in our own country, and by other nations most advanced in civilization. The facts so ably compiled by the Hon. Carroll D. Wright, Commissioner of Labor for the United States, would be of incalculable value. This, together with the findings of similar commissions appointed by 32 of our different States, could be utilized. It would also have the benefit of the completed work of the English royal commission of labor, and also the progressing work of the higher council of labor established in France, and the higher council of labor appointed in Belgium. Not only would it have the benefit of all such recently accumulated facts, but it would be in position to study the best laws of civilization and the best thoughts of the age, and thus be able to recommend more equitable laws than now exist, looking to the solution of the most vital and pressing political and economic questions of the age.

Labor statistical bureaus are of recent origin, and were first established in the United States—the first one in Massachusetts in 1869. They have since been established in 32 of our States. The first Commissioner of Labor, the Hon. Carroll D. Wright, was appointed under the General Government in 1885. The English royal labor commission was appointed by royal warrant dated April 2, 1891, and was composed of 27 members. The fifth and final report of this commission was made to both Houses of Parliament in June, 1894. The German commission of labor statistics was appointed in 1891, and it consists of 14 members, 168 civil servants, and 84 assistants. The higher council of labor was established in France in 1891. It consists of 50 members, chosen from among manufacturers, workingmen, and persons well informed upon economics and social questions. The Belgians' higher council of labor was appointed in 1892. It consists of 48 members, chosen in equal numbers from workingmen, employers, and specialists in economic science. Both these latter are authorized to examine into and recommend legislation. These foreign commissions are cited as precedents and to show that civilized nations are progressing along the line of our declared principles of equality which are recalled by this bill.

Mr. Chairman, after referring to these foreign commissions I wish to state that some of the most important results in our own history have been accomplished through the instrumentality of commissions, notably among which was the production of the Constitution of the United States. On the 28th day of March, 1785, the joint commissioners of the States of Virginia and Maryland met at Mount Vernon, under the auspices of Washington. These commissioners prepared the terms of a compact between the two States for the jurisdiction over the waters of Chesapeake Bay and the rivers that were common to both States, and, conforming to the wishes of Washington, they requested Pennsylvania to grant the free use of the branches of the Ohio River within its limits for establishing the connection between that river and the Potomac. The preliminary object of the commission being fulfilled, they took up matters of general policy and recommended to the two States uniform duties on imports, a uniformity of commercial regulations, and a uniformity of currency. George Mason was charged with a report of their doings to the legislature of his State—Virginia.

In pursuance with this, the legislature of Virginia invited all the States to appoint commissioners to meet at Annapolis on the first Monday in September, 1786. This convention became the ground of hope of the nation. No State north of New York was represented or south of Delaware, save Virginia. It was a meeting of central States, and it resulted in calling a convention of all the States to meet at Philadelphia on the second Monday of May, 1787. The result of this convention of commissioners was the forming of the Constitution of the United States which saved and perpetuated the Union.

There was great disturbance and distress then, and Congress and the States were powerless to meet the situation. It should not, therefore, be forgotten that it was a commission, an advisory body and not a legislative one, that wrought this great change and perpetuated this Government.

Now, under the Constitution, as then, under the Articles of Confederation, neither Congress nor the State governments are meeting the disturbed condition of our new industrial environments, and the only road open to us now, as then, is through a commission, an advisory body.

Mr. Chairman, the Committee on Labor did not consider the commission too large to represent a continent such as ours, with its vast and varied industries. The difference in climate, the difference between plain and mountain, the difference between North and South, East and West, give rise to great industries in one section that are not well understood in another; all of which should have representative men serve on the commission. Even the number provided for will not represent all, but it is believed that it will have reasonable knowledge of all the great pursuits of our country, and will be in full sympathy with all, so as to hear and recommend for the greatest good of the greatest number. [Applause.]

Again, the Committee on Labor do not think the appropriation required by this bill too large to secure and compensate such representative men as it requires. While the Government is appropriating millions of dollars for internal improvements, for material development, for defense on land and sea, it should not hesitate to grant such a comparatively small sum to investigate the industrial questions and recommend some remedial legislation for its industrial classes to prevent violent disturbances which cause so many million dollars of loss to the people.

Mr. Chairman, the question is one of equality. The equality of man was shown in creation, affirmed in redemption, and first declared as the foundation of human government in this new world one hundred and twenty years ago. This is the greatest political question of the nation and of the world. The barbarous ages are passed, feudalism is gone, serfdom has been destroyed, and slavery has perished from the earth, but the question of equality has come to the front, and is pressing for solution with irresistible power.

The history of the world teaches that God holds nations responsible to the standard they set up. Our standard was the highest erected since the dawn of time, yet it must now be apparent that this nation has been as false to its declared principle of equality as it was to its declared principle of freedom. [Applause.]

Mr. Chairman, when this nation was founded and equality declared there were only 3,000,000 of inhabitants who owned this continent, capable of sustaining in comfort one-half of the inhabitants of the civilized globe; yet in a hundred years we have exploited it and distributed its land and wealth most unequally. We have wantonly destroyed many of its forests, its animals, fish, and birds, instead of utilizing them for the benefit of man, and are now trying to replace them. We have unequally divided the public domain; have been prodigal of land, giving it by the millions of acres for development. This waste fitly ended in a great scramble for the last public lands in Oklahoma, where the strong bore down the weak and the man with the swiftest horse took possession not in right, justice, or mercy, but by physical force and endurance.

Mr. Chairman, with a continent vast in extent, incomparably rich in soil and mineral, teeming with vegetable and animal life; with its mechanically multiplied labor forces, capable of sustaining hundreds of millions of inhabitants; and yet with only 65,000,000 there have been and are yet large numbers out of work, seeking employment and finding none; many needy, hungry, and poor; all this with granaries and storehouses full of all the commodities of life; yet millions of laborers can not earn and have no money to buy. We have thus recently presented the anomalous condition that in the time of the greatest abundance we have had the greatest want. This can only be accounted for upon the ground of unequal opportunities, unequal privileges, and unequal distribution.

We have been as brave and patriotic as any people; we have fought three foreign wars and the greatest civil war in recorded time; we have been as generous to forgive as we were brave in battle; yet in business we have been prodigal of our inheritance and unjust in its distribution.

Mr. Chairman, the massing of capital and labor which has been caused by the discovery and use of steam and electric power and invention of modern machinery has brought us to face a new industrial problem of the greatest magnitude. History furnishes us with no precedent or example for its solution. This age is one of concentration, corporation, and centralization. It is an age of organization; and if organized capital deals with labor it must expect to deal with organized labor. Organization on the one hand implies organization on the other, so that there may be two equal parties to the agreement, otherwise the first party would dictate and the other submit. Ours is the contract system. While this is the best order of society that has yet obtained in the world yet men will not continue to contract as freemen while believing that they must submit as slaves.

There must be two parties to the contract.

Industrial corporations largely control the production and exchange of this continent. Massed capital and massed labor are largely controlling production, manufactures, and transportation, the very sources of supply and demand upon which all depend. These are now so frequently in conflict that all the relations of life are being disturbed. Society has rights which must be respected by both these contending forces, and its good order and peace demand a settlement which should be equitable, just, and durable. [Applause.]

Again, this centralization of capital and labor has produced a world-wide war of competition in which labor suffers, fortunes are wrecked, and homes are destroyed. Honorable competition is considered the life of trade, but the weapons which are more and more being used are cruel; they are reduction of wages and adulteration and counterfeiting. Low bids are made to secure large contracts, with no other hope to meet them than by the reduction in wages, and labor has lost in all these battles. Another weapon in this competitive battle is adulteration. This occurs in medicine, food, and raiment. There are adulterations and counterfeiting in all we eat, drink, and wear, thus endangering health, comfort, and life. While we have adequate laws to punish the counterfeiting of money, the more dangerous and damaging counterfeiting of the commodities of life goes unpunished. If passing pewter for silver or brass for gold is punished, the other should be more severely punished. The first means only loss in value, the latter means loss in value and endangers health and life. Dishonest men engaged in the war for gain grow rich in selling counterfeit commodities, while many honest competitors fail and their fortunes are wrecked.

Mr. Chairman, the war of competition, as now waged, instead of being the life of trade, too frequently means the death of one of the contending parties or a combination in which the people lose. Property won by fair competition or honest toil will be respected;

but won by special privileges, unjust competition, or fraud in adulteration can not be respected, and the time is fast approaching when such methods of acquisition will not be tolerated. The holder of such property can not atone in acts of charity, returning in part to the few that which he has wrongfully taken from the many. [Applause.] Philanthropy is one of the noblest traits of man; but it should be expended in teaching, in lifting up the race, in caring for the disabled, the suffering, and the helpless. All that others require is an equal chance in the race of life, with none to hinder and none to handicap. They require justice, not charity. [Applause.]

Mr. Chairman, it is most apparent that our laws have in no sense kept pace with the new discoveries, inventions, and developments of the age. The world has made more advancement in physical development and scientific discovery in the last one hundred years than it did in the preceding six thousand. While the founders of this Republic declared new principles, yet the laws they adopted were largely taken from a monarchy, and belonged to a darker age, when labor was oppressed, had no voice in the Government, and had not even the right of organization. We thus put our "new wine into old bottles," and they are bursting.

We say, "Government exists for the people," yet we adopted the laws of those who say that "the people exist for the government." New conditions confront us on every hand, in the concentration of capital and organized labor, in new improvements, in the instruments of husbandry, in the mode of manufacturing, transportation, travel, and communication. All these have been revolutionized within a generation. We have been offering premiums for inventions, discovery, and development, for labor-saving machines and devices of all kinds, until we have changed the whole order of industrial pursuits, of production and distribution. While we have had thousands inventing and discovering, we have offered no premiums for talent or energy; have had no men studying these new conditions and adjusting laws to our new environments; hence there is friction, discontent, and violence, destroying peace, property, and life.

Max Müller has stated that the word mankind is not found in human language before Christ. There was nothing in language to express the kinship of the race. It was Mede, Persian, Grecian, Roman, bond and free. But since the human race has learned its kinship and the word mankind has expressed this relation—this brotherhood—the laws of society must more and more recognize the obligations and rights growing out of this relation. Our Government is one government, our body politic being one body; when, therefore, any "one member suffers, all members suffer with it." When a number of the members of the human body suffer, and are not speedily healed, the body dies; so eventually will the body politic die if many members suffer. By not caring for others, we injure ourselves, as, for example, poverty and the want of sanitary conditions breed physical disease. This is true in a community, in a nation, and in the world. Even the world is bound together by ties of humanity which may not be disregarded without injury. Pestilence follows famine. This was recently demonstrated by the outbreak of cholera in Russia, which caused many deaths in other nations, and for a time affected the commerce of the world. If a small portion of the loss sustained by other nations had been spent in promptly relieving want, and caring for the afflicted in Russia, millions of money would have been saved, and the angel of death would not have spread its wings over the world. It must not be forgotten that in our body politic when one member suffers all the members suffer.

In the last analysis of human government it will be found that it must be based upon principles which meet the highest wants and guarantees the best good of all in view of our common origin, common interests, and common destiny. No self-government can exist without a community of interests. Equality can not be denied nor favors granted. Every man according to his ability must contribute part, otherwise he becomes a privileged person. No man can obtain true success who lives and acts solely for self. A purely selfish existence is worse than no existence. The highest happiness is to be and do for others, and no government of the people and for the people can fulfill its mission unless it has constantly in view the highest good of all. We in this self-government have plighted faith to each other. Every loyal citizen must be protected in all his rights, because he is a citizen and a part of this Government. No discrimination in favor of any individual, company, or class can be tolerated in such a Government, yet the cry of discrimination comes to us from every State and district over the whole continent, and it demands prompt consideration and just action. [Applause.]

Mr. Chairman, the Fifty-third Congress spent the larger part of two sessions discussing the silver question and the tariff issue, and a considerable portion of this session has been spent discussing the same subjects. These two questions, important as they are, constitute only a part of the great industrial issues; yet upon this fractional part Congress has consumed all this time, leaving the greater needs of the people unanswered. It will be found that when this labor question—the industrial issue—equality, which is the final problem of the world—is understood, that tariff and the coinage of silver are only a small part of it. In fact, we have been doing like the Pharisees of old, "Tithing mint, anise, and cummin," and have omitted the weightier matter of the law, "judgment, mercy, and faith." "These we ought to have done, and not left the others undone." As important as tithes, tariff, or silver may be, they are not all-important. The laborer and agriculturist are not organizing and protesting on account of the coinage of silver or the tariff issue, but on a question of right; and right, like truth, is eternal and will prevail. The levying of tariff will not settle it.

Protection against the product of the underpaid labor of Europe can never settle the question of equality and just distribution among our people. This has been demonstrated in both tariff and free-trade countries. In European countries, which are not disturbed by tariff agitation or the free coinage of silver, we find the industrial question to the front and threatening the very existence of nations. In all our discussions how often have we heard the rights of the laborer, the farmer, the manufacturer, and business man spoken of except in connection with tariff and free trade or the free coinage of silver? Yet their rights are superior to both, and the disturbed condition of the country can not be settled by the adjustment of these questions. I believe in protection, and have advocated it in this House upon both moral and economic grounds. I believe in bimetallism; in the widest possible use of silver with safety to our business interests, and that all dollars should be equal in value, but do not believe in either one or both of these measures as a cure for all the ills of society. I do not, therefore, believe in "cure-alls," but do believe in "all cures." [Applause.]

Again, too much of our law is made up of compromise measures. All compromise laws, from the Missouri Compromise to the present time, if not in all time and in all nations, have been disappointing if not disastrous. If there be any great compromise law in nature scientists have not yet discovered it. If there be any great compromise law in the Bible theologians have not yet expounded it. We can not compromise truth or principle, facts or figures. If there be no great compromise principle in nature, reason, mathematics, or revelation, compromises should not enter so largely into our law.

I believe that in the last analysis of this industrial problem, in view of our common origin, interests, and destiny, the golden rule will be its solution, and that a large per cent of existing laws will be stricken from the records by inserting, "All things whatsoever ye would that men should do to you, do ye even so to them." This is in strict accord with our declared principles of freedom and equality, and we must return and build again upon this everlasting foundation of justice, mercy, and right.

Mr. Chairman, the rights of woman must be more fully recognized in the future than they have been in the past. She is constantly entering new industrial fields and meeting their requirements with fidelity and ability. Her advancement in intellectual and moral pursuits is without a parallel in history. She is beginning to dominate along all the lines that lead to the betterment of the race. She has built and endowed more institutions of benevolence and charity for the relief of want and suffering in the past fifty years than were established by both sexes in all preceding time. Yet, notwithstanding all this, many of her sex still toil in sweat-shops, fighting an uneven battle for child and home with avarice and greed. This blot upon civilization must be removed, and woman's rights and influence be recognized in any future movement for the betterment of our industrial system. [Applause.]

The requirements of this enlightened age for a better industrial and social system must be met. Too many of the toiling millions are not properly housed, fed, clothed, and educated.

They must have homes, not hovels; must have proper food, clothing, education; must, in our unlimited fields of industry, have a chance to sow and reap and rest after toil; must share in the comforts of life, if they endure its burdens.

Mr. Chairman, it is painful to live in a land of such bounty and see so much suffering. It is distressing to feast while so many are hungry; to be clothed in comfort while many are clad in scanty garments or rags; to be sheltered in pleasant homes while so many live in hovels; to meet distress on every hand and be unable to relieve it. Individual effort can accomplish but little; only by united effort, upon principles of humanity and by doing unto others as we would have them do unto us, can our Government be established upon a foundation which no storm can move?

Mr. Chairman, all this can be done and more; not out of our

abundance, but out of our superabundance. This is sufficient to meet every physical want and relieve all distress that comes from man's inhumanity to man.

Mr. Chairman, while this bill seeks to meet the just demands of all classes, it must, however, be borne in mind that this is not a class government, not a government of laborers, farmers, manufacturers, transporters, or business men, but is a government of the people. No one class established this government in eight years of war; no one class saved it in four years of rebellion, and no one class can ever govern it unless it be by despotic rule.

Mr. Chairman, as this nation was the first on earth to declare the true principles of government, my greatest desire is that it shall be true to these principles and go on winning new fame and glory, through the ages, and that wherever its flag floats on sea or land it may be the symbol not only of freedom, but of equality. [Loud applause.]

I wish to call attention to the general desire of the people, especially of the labor and farm interest of our country, in favor of this measure, as shown by petitions, resolutions, and letters addressed to the Labor Committee of the last Congress, and also to the Labor Committee of this Congress, some of which I append:

NEW YORK, *January 7, 1895.*

MY DEAR SIR: It is with more than ordinary pleasure I note that House bill 7756 has been referred to the Committee on Labor, of which you are the honored chairman, and that the prospects are good for a favorable report from the committee to the House.

In my report as president of the American Federation of Labor, to the fourteenth annual convention, recently held at Denver, Colo., I took occasion to say the following in reference to the bill:

"A bill was introduced by the Hon. THOMAS W. PHILLIPS in the House for the purpose of creating a commission, to be appointed by the President, for the purpose of inquiring into the condition of industry, and to what extent the people have been deprived of the rights guaranteed by the Constitution of the United States and the Declaration of Independence. The bill prescribes that representatives from organized labor, business men, and farmers shall be appointed.

"The executive council indorsed the bill and organized labor generally approved it, forwarding resolutions to their respective Congressmen and Senators certifying to that effect. It is desirable that the bill before its final passage should receive the consideration of this convention to say whether any amendments may be required.

"Copies of the bill will be laid before the appropriate committee to which this subject may be referred."

The subject-matter was referred to the committee on president's report, which subsequently requested that a special committee be appointed for the purpose of expressing the sentiments of the convention thereon. The special committee reported in favor of the bill and recommended its indorsement by the convention. It also made the following recommendations:

"We would also recommend that, in case the said bill becomes a law, all matters indorsed by this body requiring Congressional action shall be submitted to the representatives of labor provided for in the bill, and that efforts be put forth by the executive council to secure the appointment of union men as such representatives.

"We would further recommend that all bodies affiliated with the American Federation of Labor petition their respective Senators and Representatives in Congress to vote for the passage of the above-named measure."

The report of the committee, I take pleasure in saying, was adopted by the convention by an overwhelming majority.

In all likelihood I may be in Washington during the coming week, and if I am I shall deem it both a pleasure as well as a duty to call upon you in connection with this bill and other measures in which the organized wage workers of our country are interested.

Truly, yours,

SAML. GOMPERS.

Hon. LAWRENCE E. MCGANN,
Chairman Committee on Labor,
House of Representatives, Washington, D. C.

PHILADELPHIA, PA., *December 14, 1894.*

SIR: Understanding that your committee have now under consideration H. R. 7756, introduced by Congressman PHILLIPS of Pennsylvania, being "A bill authorizing the appointment of a nonpartisan commission to collate information and to consider and recommend legislation to meet the problem presented by labor, agriculture, and capital," I beg leave to offer my personal and official indorsement of the propositions therein contained. It is not possible within the prescribed limits of a letter to give all my reasons therefor, but suffice to say for the present that it seems to me this would be a practicable way, not only of securing the best information as a basis for the making of laws conserving the interests of all classes, but would, to a considerable extent, do away with the necessity for various organizations of labor, capital, and agriculture sending committees to Washington to influence legislation and lobbying in the interest thereof. The prosperity of the urban working classes is so closely interwoven with that of the agriculturist and the manufacturer that I doubt very much if any of us know where the interests of each begin or end. Such a commssion as proposed by the bill would have the combined advantage of being representative of all classes, and securing information hardly accessible under other conditions.

The weight of recommendations from such a commission to the lawmaking power of States and nation would certainly be much greater than similar recommendations coming from any other source, inasmuch as it would be nonpartisan and representative of all classes.

Believing I voice the hearty concurrence of the large constituency I have the honor to be affiliated with and represent in the above indorsement, I am,

Very truly, yours,

JNO. W. HAYES,
General Secretary-Treasurer.

Hon. LAWRENCE MCGANN,
Chairman Committee on Labor, Washington, D. C.

HARRISBURG, PA., *December 22, 1894.*

DEAR SIR: My attention having been called to House bill No. 7756, Fifty-third Congress, second session, entitled "A bill authorizing the appointment of a nonpartisan commission to collate information and to consider and recommend legislation to meet the problems presented by labor, agriculture, and capital," and having examined the said bill with much care, I had it laid before the Farmers' Alliance council of this county, where it met, after discussion, with unanimous approval.

This week it was laid before the council of the Pennsylvania State Farmers' Alliance and Industrial Union, its provisions discussed, and the measure was practically unanimously approved.

The bill has been laid before a majority of the members of the executive committee of the National Farmers' Alliance and Industrial Union, and has their approval.

Personally, I hope it will become a law at a very early day, as the agricultural element of the United States, I am sure, will be greatly benefited by the labors of a commission appointed in the manner propcsed by the bill referred to.

Very respectfully,

H. C. DEMMING,
Secretary Executive Committee
National Farmers' Alliance and Industrial Union.

Hon. LAWRENCE E. MCGANN, M. C.,
Chairman of the Congressional Committee on Labor.

DES MOINES, IOWA, *December 18, 1894.*

DEAR SIR: H. R. 7756 having been called to my attention, I take great pleasure in informing you that it meets my most hearty approval.

It seems to me that the bill promises more for the harmony of conflicting interests at this time than any other measure now pending in Congress.

Thanking you for the introduction of so just and timely a measure, and trusting for its immediate passage, I am,

Respectfully, yours,

J. R. SOVEREIGN,
Grand Master Workman.

Hon. T. W. PHILLIPS, M. C.,
Washington, D. C.

INDORSEMENT OF THE NATIONAL FARMERS' ALLIANCE AND INDUSTRIAL UNION.

WASHINGTON, D. C., *February 7, 1896.*

A bill, known as the "industrial commission bill" (H. R. 21), has been introduced in the first session of the Fifty-fourth Congress. The position of the National Farmers' Alliance and Industrial Union on the proposition is as follows:

We favor the appointment of a nonpartisan commission to collate information and to consider and recommend legislation to meet the problems presented by labor, agriculture, and capital. Inasmuch as it is to be preliminary to proposed wholesome national legislation, and as the work of such a commission will gather many facts and figures into official form, all at the expense of the General Government, we indorse such legislative action.

In indorsing such a commission, however, we are firmly of the opinion that the appointment of the commission should be surrounded by such safeguards as to insure the appointment of members favorable to the industrial classes. The expenses of such a commission should be kept within the limits of strict economy.

J. W. BOWDEN, *Chairman.*
C. R. WHITE,
E. M. WARDALL,
Conference Committee N. F. A. and I. U.

Certified copy.

J. W. BOWDEN, *Chairman.*

OFFICE OF GENERAL ASSEMBLY, ORDER OF KNIGHTS OF LABOR,
Washington, D. C., January 20, 1896.

GENTLEMEN: We, the undersigned general officers of the Knights of Labor, acting on behalf of the entire organization, cordially commend to your favorable and prompt consideration the bill H. R. 21, introduced by Hon. T. W. PHILLIPS, of Pennsylvania, which is entirely acceptable to our members.

Most respectfully,

J. R. SOVEREIGN, G. M. W.,
M. J. BISHOP, G. W. F.,
JNO. W. HAYES, G. S. T.,
C. A. FRENCH,
T. B. McGUIRE,
J. M. KENNEY,
H. B. MARTIN,
Members of General Executive Board.

The COMMITTEE ON LABOR,
House of Representatives, Fifty-fourth Congress.

From the report of the committee on the president's report, made to the fifteenth annual convention of the American Federation of Labor, held at New York, N. Y., December 9 to 17, inclusive, 1895, the following extract is taken:

"Renewed efforts should be made to secure the passage of the Phillips bill, which was defeated at the last session of Congress, and a committee should be appointed by this convention to urge the passage of this bill."

WASHINGTON, D. C., *March 18, 1896.*

DEAR SIR: We have carefully considered the bill H. R. 21, commonly known as the bill creating a commission to inquire as to what legislation is necessary to the best interests of the people, and as it goes to the House from your committee we gladly lend it our indorsement.

It appears to us as a strictly nonpartisan and impartial measure, and we commend it because it singles out no class, creed, or party to conduct said investigation and proposes no legislation in favor of any class, creed, or party. Were it otherwise we would not feel that we could lend it our indorsement or approval.

Very truly, yours,

E. E. CLARK,
Order of Railway Conductors.
F. P. SARGENT,
Brotherhood of Locomotive Firemen.
P. H. MORRISSEY,
Brotherhood of Railroad Trainmen.
P. M. ARTHUR,
Brotherhood of Locomotive Engineers.
W. V. POWELL,
Order of Railroad Telegraphers.

Hon. THOMAS W. PHILLIPS,
Chairman Committee on Labor,
House of Representatives, Washington, D. C.

APPENDIX.

54TH CONGRESS, 1st Session. | HOUSE OF REPRESENTATIVES. | REPORT No. 1999.

LABOR, AGRICULTURE, AND CAPITAL.

MAY 26, 1896.—Committed to the Committee of the Whole House on the state of the Union and ordered to be printed.

Mr. PHILLIPS, from the Committee on Labor, submitted the following

REPORT:

[To accompany H. R. 9188.]

The Committee on Labor, to whom was referred House bill 9188, being the amended or substitute bill for House bill 6119, after having carefully considered the same, beg leave to report in favor of the passage of House bill 9188.

As this bill relates to the same subject-matter as House bill 6119, which was favorably reported to the House by the Committee on Labor at this session, attention is respectfully directed to the report (No. 387) accompanying the latter bill.

The bill as amended passed the House June 1, 1896, and is as follows:

54TH CONGRESS, 1ST SESSION.

H. R. 9188.

IN THE HOUSE OF REPRESENTATIVES.

MAY 23, 1896.

Mr. PHILLIPS introduced the following bill; which was referred to the Committee on Labor and ordered to be printed.

A BILL

Authorizing the appointment of a nonpartisan commission to collate information and to consider and recommend legislation to meet the problems presented by labor, agriculture, and capital.

Whereas many of those engaged in the various fields of labor and also many of those engaged in agricultural pursuits are organized and, together with those engaged in commerce, are presenting grievances to Congress and to the various State governments, seeking and demanding legislation in their behalf: Now, therefore, in order to give a hearing and to meet the requirements of this large number of citizens,

Be it enacted by the Senate and House of Representatives of the United States of America in Congress assembled, That the President of the United States is hereby authorized and directed to appoint a commission, to be called the "Industrial Commission," composed as follows: Three men representative of labor, three men representative of agriculture, three men representative of manufacturing, and three men representative of business. A majority of this commission shall not belong to any one of the political parties which took part in the last Presidential election. The President shall have the power to remove any member of said commission for inefficiency, neglect of duty, or malfeasance, or for any other reason duly set forth.

SEC. 2. That each division of three shall have the right to employ one legal adviser, whose compensation shall be the same as hereinafter provided for a member of the commission, and one secretary, at a salary of two hundred dollars per month; the commission shall convene in the city of Washington, District of Columbia, within sixty days after its appointment, and shall organize by the selection of one of its members as president, who shall designate from time to time one of the secretaries provided for in this section to act as secretary of the commission. The president and officers shall be chosen by a majority vote of the commission, and may be removed from office at any time by a vote of two-thirds of the commission; the president shall serve for such term as the commission may determine; a majority of the commission shall determine the composition of its standing committees and their duties, and shall appoint any subcommissions that may be required as provided for in section five, and committees and subcommissions shall report to the commission. The commission shall have power to make such rules as it may deem necessary for carrying out the purposes of this act.

SEC. 3. That it shall be the duty of this commission to investigate questions pertaining to immigration, to labor, to agriculture, to manufacturing, and to business, and to recommend to Congress such legislation as it may deem best upon these subjects.

SEC. 4. That it shall furnish such information and suggest such laws as may be made a basis for uniform legislation by the various States of the Union, in order to harmonize conflicting interests and to be equitable to the laborer, the employer, the producer, and the consumer.

SEC. 5. That the commission shall receive petitions and other papers on subjects pertaining to its duties and give reasonable time for hearings, if deemed necessary, and if necessary it may appoint a subcommission or commissions of its members to make investigation in any part of the United States, and it shall be allowed actual necessary expenses for the same. It shall have the authority to send for persons and papers and to administer oaths or affirmations. All necessary expenses, including reading clerk, shorthand reporters, messengers, rent for place of meeting, furniture and fixtures, and printing and stationery shall be allowed; however, not to exceed fifty thousand dollars per annum for expenditures under this section.

SEC. 6. That it may report from time to time to the President of the United States, and shall at the conclusion of its labors submit a final report.

SEC. 7. That the term of the commission shall be two years. The salary of each member of this commission shall be five thousand dollars per annum and actual traveling expenses from the home of each commissioner to Washington and return once each year.

SEC. 8. That any vacancies occurring in the commission by reason of death, disability, or from any other cause, shall be filled by appointment of the President of the United States.

SEC. 9. That a sum sufficient to carry out the provisions of this Act is hereby appropriated out of any moneys in the Treasury of the United States not otherwise appropriated.

2452

○

Respects of the Author.

From Miss Eliza Susan Quincy

MODERATE HOUSES FOR MODERATE MEANS.

AN

ARGUMENT

FOR

Cheap Trains as Essential to Independent Homes for the Working Classes;

AND AN

ADDRESS

BEFORE THE QUINCY HOMESTEAD ASSOCIATION:

TOGETHER WITH

THE ORGANIZATION OF THE QUINCY HOMESTEAD ASSOCIATION. AND THE REQUIREMENTS FOR ADMISSION.

BY JOSIAH QUINCY.

BOSTON:
WRIGHT & POTTER, PRINTERS, 79 MILK STREET,
(CORNER OF FEDERAL STREET).
1871.

MODERATE HOUSES FOR MODERATE MEANS.

AN

ARGUMENT

FOR

Cheap Trains as Essential to Independent Homes for the Working Classes;

AND AN

ADDRESS

BEFORE THE QUINCY HOMESTEAD ASSOCIATION:

TOGETHER WITH

THE ORGANIZATION OF THE QUINCY HOMESTEAD ASSOCIATION, AND THE REQUIREMENTS FOR ADMISSION.

By JOSIAH QUINCY.

BOSTON:
WRIGHT & POTTER, PRINTERS, 79 MILK STREET
(CORNER OF FEDERAL STREET).
1871.

THE QUINCY HOMESTEAD ASSOCIATION.

PREAMBLE AND RESOLUTIONS.

Whereas, The Hon. JOSIAH QUINCY has been and is making efforts to assist the working men, of moderate means, in obtaining homes outside the limits of the city of Boston; and

Whereas, There are certain measures before the State legislature, looking to the reduction of railroad fares for the benefit of the working classes; and

Whereas, The above-mentioned efforts, plans and measures seem feasible to us, and worthy of our attention, as being destined to meet with ultimate success; therefore

Resolved, That we unite together, under the name and style of "THE QUINCY HOMESTEAD ASSOCIATION," for the purpose of procuring homes for ourselves, on the plan proposed by Mr. Quincy, to wit: a small amount to be paid down, say at least two hundred dollars ($200), and the balance in monthly instalments, until, interest being computed, the whole amount shall have been paid, when a clear title to the property will be given.

Resolved, That all we do shall be on the coöperative plan, by which we are jointly responsible for the regular payment of monthly rent, paying like amounts down, like monthly instalments; houses to be after the same general plan and value, except that any individual member may add to the value of his or her house by paying actual cash for the said additional value.

Resolved, That all applications for membership shall be upon a prescribed printed form; that all applications may be received at a regular or special meeting of the Association; that all applications shall be referred to a regular or special committee of investigation, who shall report at next meeting, if possible, at which time each application shall be subject to a secret ballot, and one negative vote shall bar the applicant from admission.

Resolved, Any member absenting himself from three regular meetings, in succession, shall be considered as having withdrawn, unless he notifies the Secretary of his inability to attend.

Resolved, That the business affairs of the Association shall be kept strictly secret.

Resolved, That it shall require a two-thirds vote to alter, amend or add to these resolutions.

CHEAP TRAINS AND INDEPENDENT HOMES FOR THE WORKING PEOPLE.

ARGUMENT

BEFORE THE MASSACHUSETTS LEGISLATIVE COMMITTEE ON RAILWAYS, 1871.

MR. CHAIRMAN:—In the petition I have presented, and which you have done me the honor to print among the documents of the session, I pray the honorable bodies of which you are the organs to take into consideration "the justice, legality and expediency" of requiring the managers of the railways terminating in the city of Boston to carry mechanics, artisans and laborers, who have been driven, either directly or indirectly, from their homes, by the requirements of railroads, for a very reduced price. And first let me speak of the JUSTICE of the claim.

As I have stated in my petition, hundreds of families and thousands of individuals of the working classes, have been thus driven from their homes and forced to go into poorer, more expensive or more inconvenient lodgings. This is done by the grants made by your predecessors permitting these corporations to avail themselves of the power of the State in taking lands by eminent domain. This power is rarely, if ever, delegated, I will not say prostituted, in Europe, for the benefit of money-making corporations. Let me read you an extract from the London *Times* of the 24th of August, 1864: "From the city of London the working class are being fast driven away in the rage for railway enterprise and public improvement, no one knows where, but probably to crowd still more districts already densely populated. The value of ground in the city has increased to a fabulous extent; a building has been erected on land bought for the purpose, at the enormous rate of 1,800,000 pounds sterling (or over nine millions of dollars), the statute acre." Should a money-making corporation have asked Parliament, in such a case, to grant them the use of "eminent domain," their petition would have been treated with contempt. Let us look at the action of our own legislatures. I speak not of the power that has been used.

By Act of 1869, c. 291, the Boston and Lowell Railroad were authorized to take, and during the present summer will take, a block of land near their depot. There are two hundred houses, most of them occupied by several families, averaging at least ten tenants to a house. If, Mr. Chairman, the title of that bill had been "An Act entitled an Act to turn two thousand poor tenants, without compensation, into the street, for the benefit of the Boston and Lowell Railroad," it would not have passed without some such provision for their benefit as I now ask.

Again, by Act of the same year (1869, c. 461), the Boston and Albany Railroad are authorized, for depot and other purposes, "in any town or city, to purchase or take such lands and flats as and wherever they may deem expedient." Eminent domain is given without limit to an irresponsible corporation, with no provision for the rights of the tenants they have or may hereafter deprive of their homes.

Nor is this all. The last legislature appointed a joint commission, consisting of the Harbor and Railway Commissioners, to report a comprehensive plan for depots of the four railroads terminating on the northern side of the city. Several plans have been suggested, one of which at least will be laid before you at your present session. Every one of them contemplates taking houses that will turn hundreds of families out of their homes.

I do not mean to discuss the policy of the State in granting this power. But I maintain that justice demands at the hands of her representatives that, while they provide that the rich owners of the land shall be paid in full, they are bound to protect the interests of the poor tenants they turn into the street. Permit me to read an extract or two, as showing the difference between a monarchy and a republic in guardianship of this class:—

"In the House of Lords, on Friday, the 22d of April, 1864, the following sessional order was proposed by the Earl of Derby, and unanimously adopted, viz.: That it be an instruction to the committee, providing for any railway constructing in the metropolis, to require such railway company to run a cheap train morning and evening, the fare not to exceed one penny for the whole journey."

His Lordship also remarked that this rule applied already to the North London Railway, which may be seen on reference to their Act, 24 and 25 Victoria, c. 196, sect. 45. He further stated that the London, Chatham and Dover line voluntarily adopted the principle on his motion, by agreeing to run trains morning and evening, a distance of ten miles, for one shilling a week. In justice to the railway companies required to furnish this accommodation, it is provided that the number of workmen claiming this privilege shall not be less than one hundred.

Again, in the *Illustrated News* of Jan. 4, 1862, it is stated that on occasion of debate in the House of Lords on the 11th of March, 1861, Lord Ebury informed their Lordships that an arrangement had been made that day with three of the principal railway companies, by which they consented to convey not less than 1,000 passengers a day from any place within ten miles of London, and back, for twopence a day, thus offering a great inducement for the formation of suburban villages on a large scale.

It is remarkable, and not very creditable to our republican institutions, that the proudest peer in England, and her aristocracy by an unanimous vote, should thus care for the laboring classes, and that after an experience of more than thirty years, during which men of all parties have predominated, I should be the first to call the attention of the legislature to wrongs done to this most important class in the community, driven from their homes by legislative action.

As to the power of the legislature I have no doubt. The decision of the Supreme Court in the case of petitioners against the Eastern Railroad establishes, as I understand, their right, under the reserved right to alter, amend and repeal charters, the power to do whatever they may deem that the interests of the public require at the expense of the corporations. But I trust that no peremptory action will be necessary. From what I know of the managers and stockholders of the railroads I can have no doubt that they will be ready to do whatever they fairly can for the benefit of these classes, that does not establish a precedent or interference with their pecuniary interests. And there can be no doubt that if villages are hereby established on their lines, the friends and families of these tenants who will pay the regular fares will more than compensate for any additional expense, and that any abuses of their liberality can be prevented by their own or the action of the legislature.

My next request is that you consider the expediency of aiding the working classes to obtain homes in the country. Read the exhaustive report of the Bureau of the Statistics of Labor, and learn how thousands of the poorer classes dwell in this city. The greater part of their moral degradation arises from the utter impossibility of observing, in their miserable dwellings, the common decencies of life. Damp, dark, ill-ventilated houses are the prolific source of a large class of the diseases that enervate or destroy the health and strength of a class to whom these blessings are the conditions of their daily bread. If, Mr. Chairman, you wish, as I know you do, to see the laboring population healthy, sober, self-supporting, honest, chaste, religious, you must enable them to acquire homes, where health is not an exception, where decency is not an impossibility, where squalor and discomfort do not necessarily drive the husband and the father to the rum-shop.

I would that time permitted me to describe the exertions that have been made and the results that have been produced in other countries — at Mulhouse, at Penze, at Ackroydon, and elsewhere. I will quote but a single case: The Metropolitan Association for improving the dwellings of the industrial classes in London erected ninety cottages at Penze. A visitor says:—

"A more gratifying spectacle could hardly be offered to the friends of cottage improvement than this suburban village. An air of comfort and happiness pervades the whole group. The gardens that surround the dwellings are well planted, and the evident care bestowed upon their cultivation is a sure sign that the workmen themselves spend their evenings at home, instead of at the public-house. Besides these pleasant tokens of good, the visitor cannot help remarking the clean, healthy and happy appearance of the wives and children, so different from the squalid wretchedness which is inseparable from the dark alleys and fetid courts of a crowded town."

I cannot but hope, Mr. Chairman, that this petition may result in great benefits to the laboring classes. I have explained to several assemblies of working men a plan for enabling them, by depositing the difference between the high rents they now pay, and the interest on the value of their houses, in a savings bank, to procure a home at once, and in a few years to become its owner. I am happy to say that the plan has been deemed feasible, and met the approbation of the most intelligent among them, and associations are already formed into which the granting of this petition will breathe the breath of life. As a part of my argument I shall take the liberty of briefly stating the object and the mode of effecting it.

The success of the plan depends on two modes of action, which have long been acknowledged feasible, but which, as far as I am aware, have never been brought to bear on each other, or never been combined.

John Bright, Edward Ackroyd, Esq., in England, and Mr. Dollfus in France, undertook to solve the problem, "How a limited outlay of capital may materially assist in raising the general standard of workmen's houses, in any locality, to an extent far beyond the original capital employed." They procured land — obtained designs from an able architect — found parties willing to take the houses — formed a building association, and arranged with a savings bank, who agreed to advance three-fourths of the capital required, the principal to be repaid with annual interest in twelve yearly instalments. Where the purchaser was of good character but unable to advance the one-fourth of the purchase money, Mr. Ackroyd guaranteed the first three years' payments, after which his guarantee ceased, as the mortgage of the property was a sufficient security against loss.

All these men were manufacturers, and did what they did for the benefit of their operatives. We cannot expect a similar liberality from those who have not the same interests.

I hold in my hand a translation of the German law establishing the People's Banks, signed by the present Emperor of

Germany, and the greatest living statesman, Graf von Bismarck-Schonhausen. These People's or coöperative banks of Germany were established about twenty years ago, and there were in that country, in 1867, 2,600 of them, with 550,000 shareholders. Money and goods, in 1867, were entrusted to them on credit, amounting to 36,000,000 of dollars, and their business transactions amounted that year to 155,000,000. I have not time to explain to you fully the immense advantages that resulted from these associations, in enabling men, whose only basis of credit was their daily labor, to obtain small sums of money, either for trade or housekeeping, which they could not command at all, or only under hard conditions, from any other source. They enabled independent craftsmen to purchase at wholesale, for cost, the materials used in their manufacture; they enabled associated workmen to carry on manufacturing and agricultural pursuits on a large scale; to establish a common warehouse, in which each member is entitled and bound to expose, on his own account, the wares of his manufacture, and for procuring articles for family use and distributing them by means of coöperative stores or otherwise. All industrious persons who maintain themselves and their families are eligible as members of these associations. No one is allowed to hold more than two hundred dollars in stock. None are admitted but by vote. The basis of credit is a fund derived from monthly contributions, the amount of which is the measure of the sum for which the association can be indebted. It must always equal thirty per cent. of the association debt. But the great security arises from the personal liability of all members for debts due from the association. The law by which they are authorized consists of seventy sections, which guard the rights both of the public and the shareholders so effectually that there has never been a case of failure. The losses upon the millions used have only averaged one-fourteenth of one per cent., and the profits on the money deposited by the shareholders have averaged twelve per cent. per annum.

A German friend of mine, on returning to his native city of Cologne, was surprised to find the place in a great state of excitement. All the guilds of the several associations of working men were arranged under their several banners, in order to escort with due honor Mr. Schulze Delitzsch to his quarters. He naturally inquired who this Mr. Schulze Delitzsch was, whom the people thus delighted to honor, and what he had done to deserve it. He was not a soldier returning from successful war. He was not a millionaire who could bestow hundreds of thousands to give a small number of mechanics comfortable homes at a comparatively low price. He was a gentleman of moderate means. His whole merit was that by introducing these banks he had enabled the working classes to take care of themselves; and in doing that had opened the way to an independence which thus excited their gratitude.

I have now a petition before the Committee on Banks and Banking, which, if granted, will give to our working classes the great benefits that have been conferred by their law on the working men of Germany. Should it be reported, I am sure, Mr. Chairman, that you will give it your most careful consideration, and if approved, your most efficient support.

Now for the union and application of these principles. I go into a model tenement house, built by philanthropists who only desire to receive six per cent. on their investment, instead of twenty and thirty per cent. that are paid by the poor in other cases. The poorer class of the best condition are here provided with a small parlor, a kitchen, one chamber, and a recess, concealed by a curtain, for another bed. For this accommodation they pay three dollars and fifty cents a week, or one hundred and eighty-two dollars a year. I am satisfied, from replies I have received to an advertisement for suitable land, that, if this petition should be granted, they could obtain far better accommodations, with a few thousand feet of land for a garden, for one thousand dollars; the interest of which, seventy dollars, being deducted from the amount now paid, would leave over a hundred dollars to be applied annually to the payment of the principal.

But how shall this credit be obtained by the working classes who have no rich friends to help them and small reserves of their own? In Germany this question has been answered, as I have stated, by the coöperative banks, through which, by means of a system of mutual responsibility for loans, millions of dollars have been placed in the hands of working men, rendering them prosperous and independent, and developing the manly character that is now astonishing the world by its military results. Let us apply this principle to obtaining credit for the erection of houses. Take the first case to which I have alluded. If a man who is now paying three dollars and a half a week for his lodgings could obtain a house with equal or superior accommodations for $1,000, the interest on which, at 7 per cent. would be $70 dollars a year, and apply the difference between that and the rent he now pays, $112 a year, to a sinking fund, it is evident that within ten years he would have paid for and owned his house, his rent diminishing all the time.

A working man goes to a capitalist and makes the above statement, and adds, If I could obtain this money I should be able in a few months to procure a home, where the health of my children will be improved, where they will not be subjected to bad influences, and where I and my family will have an object for which to work and economize. The capitalist would reply, All that may be very true, but what security do you give me that you will take the house when it is built? I do not wish to invest my money in a small house, which I may have the trouble of leasing or be obliged to sell at a loss. You may reply, I have some money in the savings bank; if you will lend me the rest I will pay, say two hundred dollars towards the land and foundation of the house, and shall pay the rest in instalments as the work progresses. The capitalist may reply, So far your offer is satisfactory; but what security have I that you will continue to pay your rent? You are an honest, temperate man, a good mechanic, and perform your agreement if possible. But you may be sick; you may meet with an accident that will prevent your performing your contract. Is there no person who will be willing to guarantee the payment of your rent, at least until so much has been paid on the principal as to render a lien on the house sufficient security for the balance? You may reply, Yes. There are twenty—fifty—a hundred mechanics whose characters are as good, and whose individual responsibility is as great as my own, who for the sake of obtaining a house on these terms will be jointly and severally responsible that my rent, and the rent of all the other associates, shall be regularly paid and deposited every lunar month in a savings bank, from which deposit there shall be paid your interest semi-annually, and the balance carried annually to our credit; to remain, however, as security in the bank until all our contract with you is fulfilled, and the risk of thus guaranteeing the payment of rent would be small, after the first deposit, and diminishing by every payment that is made; and in case of default the association would have the right to take possession of the property and sell the subscriber's rights to some one who would undertake to fulfil his agreement.

What steps should be taken by persons who wish to avail themselves of such an association? If you are become liable for the payment of the rent of another, you of course desire to know the character and responsibility of your associate. Let a certain number of persons who work in the same shop or the same neighborhood form such an association, and admit any persons whom they are satisfied are honest, industrious and temperate, and who are earning enough to support their families, and pay regularly their present rent. I have spoken of a hundred associates, as a large number would be able to purchase the land and erect the buildings on far better terms than a smaller. But so large a number is not essential; ten or twenty responsible men could probably get the credit that is essential to carrying out the plan. There may be advantages in smaller numbers. If a village is to be established, it may be more agreeable that persons of the same occupation, nationality or faith should dwell together. Let there be several of these associations, to comprise persons who are naturally drawn towards one another, and let the rivalry be who shall show the neatest houses, the best organized society and best educated children. It is generally assumed that the members of such an association should be located on the same piece of land; but this is not essential. All that is necessary is that the house should be of sufficient value to render the payment of rent certain.

For many reasons it is desirable that those who thus associate should live together out of the city, obtaining a favorable location, and availing themselves of the advantages of buying and building by wholesale, and have an opportunity of organizing their society to their own satisfaction. From offers made to me in reply to an advertisement, I am satisfied that land can be procured within thirty minutes' ride by railroad on very favorable terms.

The association being formed and the refusal of the land obtained, the next and most important step is to raise the necessary funds. These may be obtained either of individuals or the savings banks. The latter hold about one hundred and twenty-three millions of dollars ($123,000,000), a very large proportion of which belongs to the working classes, and should, as far as is consistent with security, be used for their benefit. These institutions are authorized by law to lend money on mortgage of real estate, or on the note of an individual with two satisfactory sureties. The association would give both a mortgage on their property and their joint and several obligations to pay a sum agreed upon every month until the debt was cancelled. As His Excellency in his message states, great moneyed institutions object to lending small sums of money on account of the trouble in collecting the interest. This arrangement obviates the objection.

The great difficulty of forming such an association and carrying it out, results from want of confidence. Laboring men have earned their money hard and are unwilling to put it at risk. There is, however, one class of institutions that is entitled to and that has the confidence of the whole community—the savings banks. Should such an association be formed, I should hope not only to procure the money from them, but to constitute them, in a manner, the financial agents of the concern. I should propose that a committee of the association should be appointed to collect the rents, $3.50 a week, and deposit in a savings bank where interest is allowed. Supposing there are one hundred members; they have in a year together paid in $18,200; $5,600 will have paid the interest on the $80,000 borrowed, and $12,600, or $126 for each individual, paid on the principal of his debt, which is thus reduced from $800 to $674; this may be endorsed on his obligation, and at once reduce his rent $9.03, or may be left on interest in the savings bank until the whole debt is paid. Within three years one-half of the debt would be paid, and the property, without any other security, would be a guarantee for the payment of the rent.

Some will doubt whether the funds necessary for such a plan can be obtained. I am sanguine that they can. In the language of Burke, "There is nothing in the world really beneficial that does not lie within the reach of an informed understanding and a well-directed pursuit. There is nothing that God has judged good for us, that he has not given us the means to accomplish both in the natural and moral world. If we cry like children for the moon, like children we must cry on." Should such an association be formed, and a sufficient sum paid in to render the mortgage with the personal guarantee secure, philanthropists who cannot afford to dispense with the income of their property may confer a vast benefit on their fellow-men, without risk and without trouble. The weekly payments of the association into a savings bank will secure the interest and provide for the repayment of the capital. The painful necessity of collecting rents from the poor, which prevents capitalists from investing in this species of property, will be avoided, and the interest of the tenant in a house he owns will lead him to keep it in repair and provide for the taxes and insurance.

Mr. Chairman, I thank you and the other gentlemen of the committee for this opportunity of explaining my object in presenting this petition. You will be addressed by eloquent orators, paid to persuade you to make the rich richer. But I feel confident that as statesmen you will agree with me that the highest benefit you can confer on the republic is to elevate the character and condition of the working classes, by aiding them in obtaining INDEPENDENT HOMES.

HOMES FOR MEN OF MODERATE MEANS.

ADDRESS

BEFORE THE QUINCY HOMESTEAD ASSOCIATION, OCTOBER 4, 1871.

MY FRIENDS :—It gives me sincere pleasure to meet the families of your Association this evening. While we hold that the possession of a house is a condition almost indispensable to the highest usefulness and happiness of man, we must also acknowledge that the house can never be made a home without the coöperation of the woman who shares it. Here she finds the sweetest and fullest expression for her individuality; hence she exerts her widest influence. While we take a reasonable interest in the various schemes of coöperation put forward by zealous advocates to regenerate the world, let us never forget that the purest type of coöperation is found in the household. In these days, when competition is keen and demoralizing theories of life are publicly advocated, I think we can do our best work in upholding and strengthening the independent family as the only guarantee of a free state. If, then, this Association shall show that, by properly combining the savings of working men, comfortable homes are secured, it will be doing a work of great usefulness to the community in which we live.

At the commencement of this undertaking I told you that the first requisite of success was patience. And I have now to say that we have progressed as far and as fast as I anticipated. Your Association is composed of about fifty members, who have been admitted after a careful examination of their characters, wishes and prospects. I am told that there are several hundred more who are ready to join whenever you are ready to admit them. Many of the regular members have already deposited two hundred dollars each in the savings banks, and placed the books in my hands, to be used in payment for the land, whenever it is selected. Should the Association increase, as I am led to believe it will, to one hundred members, I shall have in my hands twenty thousand dollars in cash, which will give me great advantages in negotiating for land. It is not difficult to find a location in the country easily accessible by railroad to the city. In response to an advertisement, I had offers of more than fifty different pieces of land at various distances and at various prices. In some cases the owners of real estate have offered it without cost, looking for remuneration to the increased value of other lands by the location of a thriving village in their vicinity. The further we go from the city, the cheaper the land and the larger the lot for a garden obtained for the same money. Modern improvements have changed the relative position of places. A man who lives on a steam railroad, fifteen miles from the city, is, for all practical purposes of time and convenience, as near as one living three miles from his work, but who is obliged to depend on his own legs or a horse-car for his means of locomotion. From interviews I have had with the directors of several of the railroads, I feel confident that when we have decided on a location, they will either give a free ticket for several years to the head of each family, or run a cheap train, morning and evening, for the accommodation of the village.

I believe that the managers of our railroads are coming to realize the importance of building up villages by liberal reductions of fares. The enlightened policy of the Old Colony Railroad is even now creating one of the most beautiful and thriving settlements in the vicinity of Boston. The hills at present called Wollaston Heights, in the town of Quincy, which President John Adams used to say commanded finer views than any he had seen in Europe, are being covered with houses with a rapidity almost unprecedented. While a part of this success is doubtless owing to the able management of those controlling this settlement, and their guarantee that the community shall never know the nuisance of a grog-shop, a large portion must be attributed to the directors of the railroad, who promised, on an average, a free ticket for three years to each householder, provided fifty houses should be built. In three years the number of passengers between Wollaston Heights and Boston increased over four hundred per cent., and the income of the road from the families and friends of the householders over three hundred. The following are official returns :—

	Passengers.	Income.
For the year ending June 30, 1869, ...	3,376	$540 19
" " " 30, 1870, ...	8,617	1,160 70
" " " 30, 1871, ...	14,654	1,892 80
For three months ending August 31, 1871, . .	14,300	-

Thus in four years from the inauguration of this system, the paying passengers at that station will have increased from a little more than three thousand to fifty.

When the arrangements are made with the railroads, and the style and cost of the buildings decided, the financial question remains. That small houses in the country sell for much more than they cost is evident from the great numbers that are going up in every direction around the city. If I am rightly informed, houses that cost with the land from fifteen to eighteen hundred dollars, sell for from twenty-five hundred to three thousand dollars, and I have heard of cases where savings banks have loaned more than the whole cost of such buildings and considered the security ample. The managers of savings banks are trustees, and they would be false to their trusts if they loaned their money without adequate security. As far as it concerns us, their investments are limited by law to loans on real estate, and on the obligation of an individual, with two satisfactory guarantors. Most capitalists will lend two-thirds of the value of an estate on mortgage, if the signer of the note is considered responsible.

Now, what is the security your Association proposes? Let us take as an illustration the smallest house that would probably be constructed. The principle of course applies to houses of any cost.

In the model tenement houses apartments, consisting of a

parlor, a kitchen, a chamber and a recess for a bed, with certain privileges in the cellar, rents for three dollars and fifty cents a week, or one hundred and eighty-two dollars a year. A house with far greater accommodation can be built by an association for one thousand dollars, the interest on which, at eight per cent , is eighty dollars. A single house of this class would cost twelve hundred and fifty dollars, and would sell for more than its cost. If a single house can be built for $1,250, builders will contract to build fifty at a discount of from 20 to 25 per cent.

Fifty houses at $1,250 would be $62,500 ; at twenty per cent. discount they would be built for $50,000, or $1,000 apiece. The hundred dollars paid in would reduce the amount of the loan required to $900 on each house, or $45,000 in the aggregate, or about two-thirds of the value of the houses, supposing them to be worth only the $62,500 which would have been their cost if built singly. The subjoined calculation shows what would be the result if the loan were effected at 8 per cent., the interest and part of the principal being paid annually ; interest at 6 per cent. on deposits being credited, as this is allowed by several of the banks :—

Build fifty houses at $1,000 each, ...	$50,000 00
Pay $100 down on each house, ...	5,000 00
	$45,000 00

I pay 8 per cent. interest, or $3,600 a year:—

FIRST YEAR.

Rent of each house $3.50 a week, or $182 a year, say fifty houses, ...	$9,100 00	
Interest on deposits 6 per cent., average 3 per cent., ...	273 00	
Income, rents, etc., ...	$9,373 00	
Less 8 per cent. on $45,000, . . .	3,600 00	
		5,773 00
Carried forward, ...		$39,227 00

Brought forward, ...		$39,227 00
SECOND YEAR.		
Rents and income as above, . .	$9,373 00	
Less one year interest on balance of loan, say $39,227, at 8 per cent.,	3,138 00	
		6,235 00
		$32,992 00
THIRD YEAR.		
Rents and income as above, . .	$9,373 00	
Less one year interest on balance of loan, say 8 per cent., . . .	2,639 00	
		6,734 00
		$26,258 00
FOURTH YEAR.		
Rents and income as above, . .	$9,373 00	
Less one year interest on balance of loan, say 8 per cent., . . .	2,100 00	
		7,273 00
		$18,985 00
FIFTH YEAR.		
Rents and income as above, . .	$9,373 00	
Less one year interest on balance of loan, 8 per cent., ...	1,518 00	
		7,855 00
		$11,130 00
SIXTH YEAR.		
Rents and income as above, . .	$9,373 00	
Less one year interest on balance of loan, 8 per cent., ...	890 00	
		8,483 00
		$2,647 00
SEVENTH YEAR.		
Rents and income as above, . .	$9,373 00	
Less one year interest on balance of loan, 8 per cent., ...	211 00	
		$9,162 00
Less balance of loan, . . .		2,647 00
Surplus on hand, ...		$6,525 00
Debt extinguished.		

You perceive by these figures that in little more than six years the debt would be paid in full, and that at the expiration of two years there will have been paid interest and over $12,000 on the principal, and the debt reduced from $45,000 to $33,000, which is about one-half of the cost of the houses. Savings banks are authorized to lend on the note of an individual with two sureties. You propose to give a note, a mortgage, and fifty sureties; and those not men who to-day are supposed to be worth a million, but who, by a turn in the stock market, may to-morrow be bankrupts. The income of the men you propose is during their lives as certain as the continued necessities of mankind, and in case of death, the "Unity Mutual Life Insurance Company," of which most of you are members, will furnish the means for paying up his rent and securing the property to his family.

This Association propose to build fifty houses of a better class, which, if erected singly, would cost $2,000 each, or $100,000; assuming that there would be a discount of twenty-five per cent., as I am assured by builders would be the case, if contracted for together, the cost would be $75,000; of this each member pays down $200, or $10,000 in the aggregate, reducing the amount required on mortgages to $65,000, or about two-thirds of the value of the houses if erected singly; assuming that you obtain the money at seven per cent. and receive interest on your deposits as before. According to the following statement, the debt would be reduced in two years to one-half of the value of the houses, estimating them at the cost if erected singly, and the whole debt extinguished in a little more than six years:—

Build fifty houses at $1,500 each, ...	$75,000 00
Pay $200 down on each house, ...	10,000 00
	$65,000 00

Interest at seven per cent. is $4,550.

FIRST YEAR.

Rent of each house at $5 per week or $260 a year, is, ...	$13,000 00	
Carried forward, ...	$13,000 00	$65,000 00

Brought forward, ...	$13,000 00	$65,000 00
Interest on deposits, say 3 per cent., .	390 00	
Income, ...	$13,390 00	
Less interest on $65,000 at 7 per cent., .	4,550 00	
		8,840 00
		$56,160 00
SECOND YEAR.		
Rents and income as before, ...	$13,390 00	
Less interest on balance of loan at 7 per cent., ...	3,931 00	
		9,459 00
		$46,701 00
THIRD YEAR.		
Rents and income as above, ...	$13,390 00	
Less 7 per cent. interest on balance of loan,	3,269 00	
		10,121 00
		$36,580 00
FOURTH YEAR.		
Rents and income as above, ...	$13,390 00	
Less 7 per cent. interest on balance of loan,	2,560 00	
		10,830 00
		$25,750 00
FIFTH YEAR.		
Rents and income as above, ...	$13,390 00	
Less 7 per cent. interest on balance of loan,	1,802 00	
		11,588 00
		$14,162 00
SIXTH YEAR.		
Rents and income as above, ...	$13,390 00	
Less 7 per cent. interest on balance of loan,	991 00	
		12,399 00
		$1,763 00
SEVENTH YEAR.		
Rents and income as above, ...	$13,390 00	
Less 7 per cent. interest on balance of loan,	123 00	
Surplus, ...	$13,267 00	
And debt extinguished.		

When a location is selected and arrangements made with the railroads for free tickets or reduced fares, and not until then, the members will be called upon for an assessment to pay for their house-lots, which will not exceed the amounts proposed. Each member will receive a deed and give a bill of sale mortgage on his own house for the amount he requires — in one of the before-mentioned cases for nine and in the other for thirteen hundred dollars — the money to be received as the work progresses, so as to keep the lender always secured. In addition to the individual responsibility of the signer of the note, *the members of the Association agree to be jointly and severally responsible that the debt and interest, in the shape of a rent, shall be paid regularly on each and every note at the times and in the amounts agreed.* In case of neglect of an individual, the bank would, at the request of the Association, sell under the mortgage, the purchaser paying the surplus, if any, to the original owners. Such an arrangement would require the bank to keep but one account until the end of each year, when the interest would be deducted and his proportion of the surplus of the deposits indorsed on the note of each individual.

As by this plan no member parts with his money until he has a deed of his house-lot, and as the payments of rent are made directly to the lender, there would seem to be hardly a possibility of loss.

In the foregoing calculation I have made no addition for insurance, taxes and the railroad ticket for the owner of the house. My object is to render all that the tenants do as simple as possible, so that they may have no responsibility but that of paying their rent as it accrues. To provide for this I should propose that in addition to the payment of the interest there should be deducted from the amount paid in, a sum equal to the insurance and taxes, and after one-half of the value of the house is paid, a further sum sufficient to pay for the railroad ticket. This would postpone the ultimate payment for the house, but would simplify, in a great degree, the duty of the tenant.

A friend of mine, who has studied what is called the labor question with some attention, comes to the conclusion that one of the most practicable ways of protecting a man's rights as a laborer is to protect his rights as a capitalist. The working man who denies himself and lays by part of his wages should command the best business intelligence to secure him a productive investment. While walking through streets of magnificent stores and luxurious dwellings, we ask the question, Who furnishes the money for this lavish expenditure? A great part of it is supplied by the savings banks. And these banks represent the surplus not only of the mechanic and artisan, but also of the hod-carrier and the washerwoman. Now, it is recognized by all other banks that he who keeps a large deposit has a good claim to a discount. Should his bank refuse a capitalist such an accommodation he would at once transfer his account to another. The laboring classes in Massachusetts have on deposit over one hundred millions of dollars! There is a competition among savings banks to attract depositors. It should be determined among their patrons to withdraw their deposits from such banks as refuse to lend to persons of moderate means upon good security, and to place them in those that will offer the working man this important aid.

The savings banks at the West are managed by persons who deem it to be their duty to assist their depositors in obtaining independent homes. I have circulars issued by such institutions in Toledo and Chicago. These offer premiums for the best plans of houses adapted to persons of moderate means. They announce, in capital letters, "Money loaned to those who deposit with the institution and who wish to build houses." They publish plans, elevations, specifications, and "a bill of items furnished by a practical builder, showing the actual cost of a house." These houses can be erected there for from $375 to $1,500 apiece. A three hundred and seventy-five dollar house is not a palace, but it gives as much accommodation as is obtained in the city for three dollars and a half a week, and is so constructed that it can be made a part of a larger building whenever the tenant is able to construct one. I have had an offer to build a house with four rooms for $400, provided a large number were contracted for together. Now, on the plan adopted by your Association, the tenant would pay down $100 for a lot. This, if containing 2,500 feet, land at $400 an acre, would cost but about $25, leaving $75 for incidentals.

He borrows on mortgage, with the guarantee of his associates,			$400 00
He pays annually, by weekly instalments to the savings banks, $3.50 × 52,		$182 00	
Interest at 8 per cent. on $400,	$32 00		
Insurance and taxes,	20 00		
		52 00	
To be carried to the sinking fund annually,		$130 00	
In three years,		$390 00	
Add interest on deposits,		17 62	
			$407 62

At the end of three years he has paid for his house and can afford forever after to pay his fare on the railroad. The above is in the expectation of being able to obtain a free pass for the owner of the house for three years. My hope of so doing is based on the great benefit that would accrue to the public, and, as in case of the Old Colony, a prospect that it would greatly increase the income of the road. At the last session of the legislature I presented a bill, asking for working-men's trains, at rates similar to those granted in Great Britain. The counsel for the railroads did not deny the power of the legislature to grant the petition, but stated that the managers of the railroads would be very liberal to such associations if they were authorized by law to make such a discrimination between their passengers, and an Act was accordingly passed. In the interest of the railroads I advocate a free pass for the head of the house for three years, on certain specified trains, to associations that would put up fifty houses on the line of the road, as there would then be no necessity for making any alteration in regular fares. From letters I have received, and papers that have been sent me from St. Louis, Toledo, Pittsburg, Chicago and San Francisco, I have no doubt that similar associations to yours will be formed at many places in the West, and hundreds of houses be thus erected by the savings of working men in other parts of our common country.

The homestead of the laborer is the best form in which capital can be invested. It pays a large percentage, and is of the highest advantage to the State and the individual by elevating the family relation, upon which the prosperity of both must depend. I therefore maintain that the working man who lays by something every year should be able to buy *credit* with his savings. And I am confident that an association such as you have formed — a company of working men of good honorable character and responsible for each other — can offer the amplest security.

APPLICATION FOR MEMBERSHIP

TO

THE QUINCY HOMESTEAD ASSOCIATION.

---

1. What is your full name?
2. Residence.
3. Occupation.
4. Place of business.
5. Date and place of birth.
6. Are you married or single?
7. If married, how large a family have you?
8. Whom do you offer as references? (Name, .) (Address, .)
9. Do you understand Mr. Quincy's plan?
10. Are you prepared to pay $200 as the first instalment, when called for by Mr. Quincy?
11. Are you temperate in your habits?
12. Do you enter into this Association with a speculative view, or for the purpose of procuring a *home* for yourself and family?
13. What railroad do you prefer?

Signature of applicant.

Proposed by

The investigating committee report

ADDRESSES AT THE TENTH ANNUAL COMMENCEMENT
LELAND STANFORD JUNIOR UNIVERSITY
MAY 29, 1901

THE GOSPEL OF WORK

GEORGE MANN RICHARDSON
Professor of Organic Chemistry, Leland Stanford Junior University

---

LELAND STANFORD'S VIEWS ON HIGHER EDUCATION

DAVID STARR JORDAN
President, Leland Stanford Junior University

PUBLISHED BY THE UNIVERSITY
STANFORD UNIVERSITY, CALIFORNIA
UNIVERSITY PRESS
1901

THE GOSPEL OF WORK.

George Mann Richardson.

Horace Greeley is said once to have made the remark: "Of all horned cattle, the college graduate is the most to be feared."

There still lingers in some quarters a decided prejudice against the college graduate. You who are going out from us to-day as graduates will no doubt be made to feel this. It rests with you, in part, to determine whether the next class that goes from the University shall find this prejudice greater or less than you will find it. It is not very difficult for us to see some of the reasons for this lack of confidence. In the first place, I do not believe that it is in most cases a prejudice against a higher education or against educated persons, except as it is owing to a confusion of terms. It is common to assume that the college graduate is necessarily an educated man or woman, but this is a fundamental error. It has thus far been found impossible, even in our best and most thorough colleges and universities, to devise any system of exercises, requirements, or examinations which will make it perfectly certain that the holders of their diplomas shall be educated men and women.

An education is, in one respect, like a contagious disease —not every one who is exposed to it takes it. The diploma which you receive to-day is merely a certificate that you have been exposed to an education; whether you have taken it or not, your future life alone will determine. Undoubtedly a great part of the prejudice against the college graduate comes from direct contact with the uneducated college graduate, and in so far as this is the case, I believe

Horace Greeley was right,—such college graduates are, to say the least, to be viewed with suspicion.

The chances are that any young man who has spent four of the best years of his life in college and has neglected to make good use of his opportunities, will continue to follow the same course after he graduates; and such are not the kind of people for whom "the world stands aside to let pass."

The most important principle for our guidance in life is a thorough realization of the law that nothing that is worth having is to be had without work. When this law has been completely accepted and becomes part of our moral fibre, other things will be added unto us:—we have started on the right road.

Ignorance of this law or the effort to evade it is the cause of much disappointment, misery, and crime. There are no short-cuts to knowledge, to power, or to happiness. "Eminence in any great undertaking implies intense devotion thereto, implies patient, laborious exertion, either in the doing or the preparation for it. "He who fancies greatness an accident, a lucky hit, a stroke of good fortune, does sadly degrade the achievement contemplated and undervalues the unerring wisdom and inflexible justice with which the universe is ruled." Those who are continually seeking an unearned happiness are the people that the world can best spare.

An education which is itself acquired by hard work cannot be considered as a device for getting along in the world without work: it merely makes our work the more effective, it enables us to work at the long end of the lever,—but work we must. Genius is sometimes looked upon as a substitute for hard work, but this too is an error, as we shall quickly recognize when we read the biographies of a few men of acknowledged genius. In fact, most men of this class have exhibited an astonishing capacity for work. On the other hand, it is really surprising how closely the results of application and energy resemble the results of genius.

Any system of education which fails to develop in the individual a clear recognition of this great law of work must remain unsatisfactory. The individual who fails to recognize this law or who does not act according to it cannot be considered as educated.

The old system of education, in which the time was spent in studying Latin, Greek, and mathematics, was an excellent system for those to whom it appealed, as is proved by the grand characters that have been developed by it. It was, however, a very wasteful system, as many of the young men who went to college did not become interested in this particular kind of work. Some of this latter class, however, were nevertheless educated by the contact with earnest and educated men and by the countless other educational forces continually at work outside of the classroom at every college.

But too large a number of men succumbed to the habit, formed by four years' practice, of doing lifeless things in a listless way.

An abundance of leisure is a trial to which few men are equal; it is a trial that should not needlessly be thrust upon young people before habits of work have been established.

As the weakness of the old system came to be recognized, new subjects were added to the college curriculum to make it more generally attractive, or, as some would say, to make it "broader." There were added a little modern language study, a little history, a little political economy, a little science, and so on, until the older college course was so diluted that it offered very little training in serious scholarship, and the results very well illustrated the old adage, "He who embraces too much, holds but little."

While the old difficulty was far from being overcome by these changes, a new difficulty, a lack of thoroughness, was introduced. "A broad education,"—what crimes have been committed in that name!

The demand still frequently voiced for a fixed course of study which shall best fit the "average man" for the life of to-day is wholly irrational. It is not worth while to exchange the tyranny of the old fixed course of study for the tyranny of a new fixed course of study.

Owing to the endless variety of human characters and human tastes, and owing to the present extent of human knowledge and human activities, such a course of study is an absolute impossibility. Such a process for producing machine-made men would be prodigally extravagant of human material. In thus attempting to produce a uniform product, the very best part of the mental equipment of many men would be cut away or hindered in growth to make them fit into a system which at best is artificial. The best preparation for the life of to-day is to know well something worth knowing,—if possible, to know it better than any one else knows it. Such a knowledge is attained only when the work necessary to it strikes a responsive chord in the individual mind.

Our American universities are tending in the right direction, it seems to me, in offering the student a wide range of studies and then allowing him to select for himself those to which he will devote his attention. A university with unlimited means should extend knowledge and offer instruction in every worthy subject. A subject to be worthy must be, first, such that its serious study offers good mental training, and second, such that a knowledge of it tends toward human advancement. But the university with unlimited means is an ideal which has no realization.

It is the first duty of a university to do *well* that which it undertakes. There is no doubt but that much of the criticism which has been called forth by this introduction of "electives" into the university curriculum is more than justified by the consequent crippling, owing to inadequate means, of work previously undertaken, and to an equipment wholly inadequate to do justice to the new work. The expansion of the curriculum under such conditions is thoroughly dishonest, and the results are most deplorable. It is a vulgar form of self-advertisement to which no university should stoop. Desirable as it is to have a wide range of studies from which the student may select, expansion of the curriculum in any given institution is justifiable only when the work already undertaken is adequately done.

Since all universities are hampered from a lack of funds, it is eminently desirable that all universities should cooperate in this expansion of their curricula, and instead of following the old and narrow policy, dictated by petty jealousies, of establishing new departments because they have been established elsewhere, let each university look to develop where other universities have not developed, so that somewhere, here or there, the student will be able to find the thing he needs for his highest development.

With ample opportunities for studying worthy subjects the student should be able to find in the university that thing which will best enable him to find his sphere of greatest usefulness in the world, that thing which awakens his enthusiasm, — and it is not of great importance what the thing is; it is the *awakening* that is of supreme importance; *that* is the first great step towards a sound education.

One student will gain inspiration from the great epics of Homer, Dante, or Milton; another will be thrilled and incited to higher effort by reading the earth's history in the earth's crust; a third will have his soul stirred and be able to detect nature's immutable laws by the study of the venation in the wings of insects. Any work which is thus capable of inspiring men to new and nobler effort can ill be spared from our educational system.

James Russell Lowell is reported to have said that his admiration for Dante lured him into the little learning that he possessed; while the direction of Darwin's work was determined by his desire to know all about coral reefs. As often as not it is the teacher, and not the subject taught, that first arouses the interest of the student.

Thomas Jefferson said of one of his old teachers, that the presence of that man on the faculty of the College of William and Mary fixed the destinies of his life. The university that has a Mommsen, a Lowell, or an Agassiz in its faculty is in the possession of a power for good that is beyond estimation. How important it is that the student should be able to arrange his work so as to come into intimate contact with such men!

The fear is often expressed that with such possibilities of choice the student may not choose wisely, — that he will over-specialize, that he will be too narrow in his selection; and, strangely enough, this fear is most frequently expressed by those who look back to the older classical system as probably, after all, the golden age of education, and who look upon the new changes as an unwise catering to a popular demand. Will there ever again be such magnificent specialization as when the student pursued the study of Latin for three years in the preparatory school, for four years in the college, and as much longer as his schooling extended?

Indeed, it was, in my opinion, just this specialization that enabled the older system to produce such excellent results. The thorough and extended study of a subject produces the best kind of training.

"The only true enthusiasm lies in specialization, and the effort to compass the whole realm of knowledge ends in bewilderment and failure." The fear of narrowness that leads to a scattering, that kills enthusiasm and produces superficiality, is far more to be dreaded than narrowness.

It is serious study that broadens; not the study of any specific subject or of many subjects. Thorough knowledge of any kind begets respect for, and sympathy with, thorough knowledge of every kind. The mastery of one subject gives strength to master another.

So long as universities refuse to give place in their courses to the trivial, the superficial, and the sham, over-specialization is a danger that need have no terrors.

The student who enters the university and selects his studies with a view to their bearing upon his future calling is pursuing a thoroughly rational course. After spending four years in the serious study of things, even though they have a direct bearing upon his life-work, if the mind of the student is still narrow, then there is no implement in the educational workshop with which it can be broadened. It is well for us to remember in this connection that there are minds which no system of education yet devised seems to broaden, minds which never gain the power to look upon any subject except from the bread-and-butter point of view.

In an address, delivered not long since, Professor Charles Eliot Norton deplored the tendency of our times as exhibited in the decay of principle in our public men, and as an antidote to this he recommended a more universal and a more thorough study of English literature. Even among those who believe the evils pictured to be true, many would be inclined to smile at the remedy suggested.

Yet the remedy is a good one. Its value lies not in any specific quality of English literature as distinguished from other branches of knowledge, but rather in the inspiration, the uplift, and the appreciation of truth that comes from earnest and thorough study of any worthy subject.

The advocates of the older system of education are now for the most part ready to admit that recent changes are perhaps justifiable upon purely utilitarian grounds. Indeed, when we look about and note the wonderful material advancement made possible by a more general and a more exact knowledge of natural laws, it would be captious to deny this. But many of them still believe that, when it comes to the development of real culture, the new education can only helplessly appeal to the old.

In consequence, we hear much about so-called "culture studies" as distinguished from others, which, by implication at least, stand on a distinctly lower plane. In this connection allow me to quote from a recent editorial in the *Nation* called forth by certain changes in the entrance requirements of Columbia University intended to permit the substitution of an increased amount of mathematics for some of the Latin previously required.

" President Low's recommendation," says the writer in the *Nation*, "will certainly be cited and appealed to as a precedent by lesser colleges and universities; and in many a Western faculty Columbia and Cornell will be held up as bright examples of modern tendencies in the education in the East. . . . We have before us the problem of articulating the public school with the college. It is no easy task. Western universities (most of them are really colleges), growing up under local conditions and holding utilitarian or scientific ideals before them, have not been vexed by the problem, but our stronger Eastern universities and colleges have it still to work out.

"While these institutions have met the modern demand for scientific training, they have also sought to retain their ideals of culture, and most of them have succeeded in the effort. The modern public school, being nearer the popular heart, has sacrificed ideals of culture to those of science, so that, while the ordinary public schools can send up to the college or university students prepared to continue their education along scientific lines, most of them are unable to furnish the necessary propædeutic for culture. President Low's idea of a solution is simply and frankly to follow Western experience; to unify the two along the line of physical science and utilitarian aims — a line of least resistance — and let the culture go. . . . Thus, when we are forced to the conclusion that our classical machinery of elementary culture is inadequate to modern intellectual life and to our modern educational conditions, we think we must abandon culture, at least elementary culture, altogether, and devote the earlier years of training to a preparation for the pursuit of science. Small wonder if those of us who cannot ignore the value of culture are thus compelled to oppose the development of science as the only means of retaining what culture there is in our educational system."

According to this writer, it would appear that culture is something that cannot possibly be attained by the study of any science. Does culture, then, consist of a certain number of definite attainments, the possession of which means culture, and the lack of which excludes culture? Is it possible that a certain prescribed course of study produces in all minds the uniform results which we call culture, while in all other things we observe the most striking differences in the ways in which different minds react toward one and the same discipline?

Is not culture rather a combination of character and attainments? A true basis for culture in the individual is a sincere love of truth, and a firm belief that all truth is safe.

Emerson says of the possessor of culture: "He must have a catholicity, a power to see with a free and disengaged look every object." Culture is found among men of the most widely different training, and it is also frequently lacking in men whose training has been all that thought could suggest.

May we not therefore justly conclude that there are many roads leading to culture, and that, owing to the great diversity of minds and characters among men, when we limit the number of these roads we simply diminish the number of persons who attain culture? The evidence seems clear that there are many who attain culture by a study of the ancient languages and literatures who never would attain it by a study of the physical sciences; likewise there are many who reach culture through a study of the physical sciences who never would reach it by a study of the classics.

Why not leave both avenues of approach unobstructed?

The folly of keeping a Pasteur at writing Latin verses is quite equalled by the folly of keeping a Tennyson at peering through a microscope.

The notion is prevalent that such freedom of choice, which renders possible the easy following of one's own inclination, cannot possibly furnish the same discipline as may be had by the student's being forced to pursue some line of work that may perhaps be more or less distasteful. It is doubtless true that human beings, like other things in nature, tend to follow the line of least resistance. Yet it is by overcoming resistance that we gain strength. There is here a real danger to the student which can be avoided only by the constant vigilance of the university authorities.

Only worthy subjects adequately cared for should be found in the university curriculum.

As has been already stated, the most important thing to be acquired in a general education is the habit of work, and this is most easily and most surely acquired by doing work that is congenial. This habit once acquired, all work assumes a different aspect, and growth in all directions is henceforth possible. On the other hand, the attitude toward work and the habits acquired by enforced contact with uncongenial work are apt to dull enthusiasm, to stifle ambition, and future growth becomes much more problematical.

It is quite human for the man who has enjoyed the privileges of the older classical education and who has drawn therefrom inspiration, pleasure, and appreciation of the beautiful, to look upon the trend of modern education with misgivings and suspicion and to raise his voice in a cry of warning. It is perhaps equally human for the scientist who has likewise drawn from his work, and without the aid of the classical education, inspiration and pleasure and appreciation of the beautiful, to lose patience with the claims of superior excellence advanced for the classical training. Is it not time, however, for educators to borrow a page from one another's experience, and to recognize once for all that the desirable qualities that we class under the head of education and culture are not produced in different minds by identical processes? May we not welcome every new field of knowledge and recognize its power for training youth? May we not look upon it as some new tool in our workshop by means of which we may be able to reach some minds that it has been impossible to reach with the old implements?

This joining of hands upon the part of educators will require some exercise of culture, some "power to see with a free and disengaged look every object." We must make some effort in order to understand one another. We must remember that our estimate of the relative importance of things is largely a result of our point of view, and that the same things appear quite differently from different points of view.

Human knowledge has now vastly outgrown the grasp of any single mind ; ignorant in some departments of knowledge the most scholarly and the most industrious must remain, and that without shame. Let no one deceive himself with a superficial omniscience. The next best thing to knowing a thing well is to know that we do not know it.

Why should educators waste time and energy in trying to compare the values of different forms of knowledge, when their lack of omniscience renders them incapable of forming just judgments? Our own specialty is obviously to each of us the most important form of knowledge ; let us show this faith that we have in our specialty not by criticising or ridiculing other forms of knowledge which we are incapable of understanding, not by hindering and checking the growth of other things, but rather by advancing that specialty to our utmost by honest work and earnest endeavor.

Many of the faults ascribed to over-education and its unfitting of people for their true spheres in life can be directly traced to the undue importance which has in the past been attributed to particular forms of knowledge and activity and to a consequent implied degradation inflicted upon equally meritorious forms of knowledge and activity. Aristotle's dictum that "all manual work is degrading," that "all paid employments are vulgar," has cost the world dear by the long maintaining of false ideals.

Slowly, however, more just views are prevailing, and already the men who do the world's work are meeting with the esteem due them from all right-minded persons.

The student who is graduated from a university where he has had large freedom of choice in the selection of his studies has less excuse for remaining uneducated than one who has been forced through a prescribed curriculum, much of which may have possessed no interest for him. Upon you, therefore as graduates of Stanford, rests the increased responsibility of proving yourselves to be educated men and women. It may safely be assumed that a considerable majority of you have formed the habit of work, that you have accumulated a fund of useful information, and that in accumulating it you have learned how knowledge is obtained. You are then prepared to walk on your own feet and to think your own thoughts. But no one supposes that your education is ended. If that were the case this would have been called "Ending Day" instead of "Commencement Day."

In closing, I will, if I may, leave with you this short prescription for happiness: Choose your life-work with care, with deliberation, if need be; but when it is chosen, enter upon it with zeal. Let your attitude toward your work be such as was recently advised by President Hadley from this platform, "Not how much you can get out of it, but rather how much you can put into it." Be not overparticular about the importance of your first position — the important thing is not where you begin but where you end. At first the chief thing is to begin. Do not flatter yourself or discourage yourself by comparing your own progress with the progress of your neighbor or your friend, but rather live up to your own best all of the time, and that best will constantly grow better and your progress and ultimate success will take care of themselves. Fix your eyes upon the advantages that you have, rather than upon those that you have not.

Finally, "Look forward, not backward; look up, not down; and lend a hand."

51ST CONGRESS, } SENATE. { MIS. DOC.
1st Session. } { No. 212.

IN THE SENATE OF THE UNITED STATES.

AUGUST 14, 1890.—Presented by Mr. Carlisle and ordered to be printed.

LETTER OF THE COMMISSIONER OF LABOR TRANSMITTING A STATEMENT SHOWING THE DIRECT COST OF LABOR IN THE MANUFACTURE OF ONE TON OF STEEL RAILS IN THE UNITED STATES, GREAT BRITAIN, AND ON THE CONTINENT OF EUROPE.

DEPARTMENT OF LABOR,
Washington, D. C., August 13, 1890.

SIR: I have the honor to acknowledge the receipt of your letter of August 8, in which you ask for a statement showing the direct cost of labor in the manufacture of 1 ton of steel rails in Great Britain and on the Continent of Europe, such statement to be prepared in the same way as that sent to Senator Edmunds on the 6th instant, relating to the cost of steel rails in the northern district of the United States. In reply I send you herewith three statements:

First, an analysis of costs in 1 ton of standard steel rails made in the United States. This analysis is based mainly on establishment No. 1, reported on page 35, House Miscellaneous Document No. 222 of the present session, and is substantially a copy of the statement sent to Senator Edmunds on the 6th instant. I have repeated it here because it was hurriedly made for Senator Edmunds, and the proper credit for the value of scrap produced in the ingot and rail departments was not made. The cost given in the statement of the 6th instant related to total gross cost of 1 ton of 2240 pounds of steel rails in the northern district of the United States. This statement shows the total net cost of such a ton of steel rails. It varies but 11 cents from the total cost given as for establishment No. 1, page 35 of the document referred to.

As stated, this statement is based mainly on establishment No. 1. It is not wholly so, because of the impossibility of tracing from the schedules relating to establishment No. 1 the labor cost of all the materials entering into the manufacture of 1 ton of standard steel rails; so labor cost has been taken from several establishments making steel ingots. Using an average as derived from these several establishments makes a variation of but 11 cents in the result. This fact clearly establishes the soundness of the analysis of cost as based on establishment No. 1, and as reported on page 35 of the document referred to. The credit for the value of scrap produced raises the per cent. of cost of direct labor in the production of 1 ton of standard steel rails from 45 per cent., as stated in the letter from this Department of the 6th to Senator Edmunds, to 47 per cent., as shown in the last item in the statement herewith sent.

Second, a statement showing the analysis of costs in one ton of standard steel rails made in Great Britain. The calculation in this statement is based on establishment No. 11, page 35, House Miscellaneous Document, No. 222. In this case we started with the cost of steel rails as given in the establishment just referred to, and were able to trace the costs back through the preceding processes of making the blooms, ingots, pig-iron, coke, coal, and limestone, because all these elements were made under the direction of the same company that made the rails, and we had schedules covering all these costs. As to the iron ore, we did not have the exact mine from which it was taken, but we did have a representative mine in the same district from which it was taken, and we also had the cost for transportation given, so that the element of possible error in calculating costs is of necessity very slight.

As to "profit to producers," shown in the item relating to iron ore, a part of this is accounted for by the royalty or rent paid to the owners of the soil, which amounted to about 60 cents for the amount of ore shown in the statement. The remainder was made up by deducting the costs as calculated from the ore schedule from the cost delivered at the furnace, as charged in the pig-iron schedule. You will notice that the total net cost of 1 ton of steel rails, as stated in this analysis, is $18.614, while the cost, as shown in establishment No. 11, page 35 of the report referred to, is $18.588, or a difference of only 2.6 cents.

The labor at the establishment for which this analysis is made is paid less, I am informed, than at most other steel-rail establishments in Great Britain, but we were obliged to take this establishment, as it was the only one having a schedule for standard rails and for the previous processes, and furthermore, it is a representative establishment, whose production largely governs the price of standard steel rails. The other statement (No. 10) for Great Britain, on the same page, is for light rails, and the processes are not comparable fully with those for making standard rails.

Third, a statement of analysis of costs in 1 ton of standard steel rails made on the Continent of Europe, this statement being based mainly on establishment No. 3, page 35, House Mis. Doc. No. 222. The rails covered by this statement are standard steel rails, like those in the first and second statements just described. In making this analysis for the Continent of Europe we were enabled to follow the processes back, as in the case of the English establishment, until we came to the pig-iron, when, owing to the incompleteness of the pig-iron schedule for establishment No. 3, we found it necessary to use another schedule for the cost of converting materials into pig-iron.

For the costs of materials themselves, except limestone and iron ore, we had data from establishment No. 3, and we used the schedules of that establishment. For the limestone we had the cost as reported at the pig-iron furnace, but had no schedules for the Continent of Europe showing the amount of labor, etc., in 1 ton; so we used the cost as reported at the furnace, and subdivided that cost into its elements in the same ratio as that indicated in the limestone schedules for the northern district of the United States. The iron ore used was the same kind as that used in the English case just given; so we used the same schedule from which to ascertain the cost of it.

In other respects the same plan was pursued as in the English case, except that it was found that the cost of pig-iron, as charged in the ingot mill, amounted to $1.46 more than as figured from the materials; so we were obliged to charge that amount to the profits going to the pig-iron produced. The net cost of standard rails per ton, as given in the schedule for establishment No. 3, with which we started for this analysis, is $19.576, while as shown by this careful calculation it amounts to $19.635, an excess of 5.9 cents only by the use of other factors to supply those missing in the schedules of establishment No. 3.

I desire to say, in forwarding you these statements, that I have made hem up for three localities, instead of for two as requested, because of the resolution introduced yesterday by Senator Edmunds and now pending. Should that resolution be adopted I could not at present more fully answer it than I have done in this letter. The facts called for by you and by Senator Edmunds in the letters of the 6th and 8th insts., on account of the difficulties which I have intimated here, could not have been incorporated in the preliminary report, House Mis. Doc. No. 222. In the completed reports I am in hopes not only to give more elaborate analyses on the basis of these sent herewith, but for certain typical establishments, those that largely regulate prices, I anticipate being able to trace back through all the processes of manufacture the various labor elements entering into the production. The difficulty of doing this is at once discernible on a very casual examination of the facts.

You will pardon me if I call your attention to one analytical feature which should be observed in the use of the analyses herewith forwarded. Labor cost in one ton of steel rails—I mean after all the materials have been assembled in the steel-rail works and are ready to be subjected to the proper manipulations for the production of standard steel rails—should be less per ton relatively in this country than in Great Britain or on the continent, because American producers of standard steel rails dispense with at least one expensive process still adhered to by the foreign producer; and, furthermore, our materials, ore, etc., are purer than those used in most other places, so the quantity of ore, for instance, required for the production of a ton of standard steel rails is less in this country than in other places, and of course the labor required to produce one ton of steel rails is, so far as the purer materials are concerned, less here than abroad.

By reference to the statements herewith submitted it will be seen that in establishment No. 1, for the northern district of the United States, 4,137 pounds of iron ore were necessary for the production of one ton of standard rails, while in establishment No. 11, for Great Britain, 5,127 pounds, or nearly 1,000 pounds more, of iron ore were necessary for the production of one ton of the same kind of rails than in the United States, while on the continent of Europe, in establishment No. 11, 5,701 pounds, or nearly 1,600 pounds more of iron ore were necessary for the production of one ton of standard steel rails. Very many of those things which appear to be incredible when studying the total figures given disappear on a close examination of the analysis, and reasons for the figures can, as a rule, be found in the analysis if properly studied.

The establishments selected for the statements herewith forwarded are thoroughly representative, and are far more indicative of the true conditions surrounding the production of standard steel rails than any of the others given in the preliminary report referred to.

Of course, as remarked in a letter from this Department to Senator Edmunds, the cost of making rails, over and above what is in the previous statements denominated "direct labor cost," is largely resolvable into labor; that is, a very large percentage of the items above direct labor are labor in some form, but it is difficult to separate the elements, as in transportation, for instance.

Trusting that the statements herewith handed you fully answer your communication of the 8th,

I am, very respectfully,

CARROLL D. WRIGHT,
Commissioner.

Hon. J. G. CARLISLE,
United States Senate.

ANALYSIS OF COSTS IN ONE TON OF STEEL RAILS MADE IN THE UNITED STATES.

[Based mainly on Establishment No. 1, page 35, H. R. Mis. Doc. 222.]

Materials and successive stages of conversion.	Expenditures for direct labor.	Other expenditures.						Total.
		Officials and clerks.	Supplies and repairs.	Taxes.	Transportation to point where used.	Timber.	Difference between foregoing actual costs and costs as charged at the blast furnace—presumably profit to producers.	
For production of 4,137 pounds of iron ore	$2.142	$0.124	$0.807	$0.081	$4.893		$2.926	$10.973
For production of 1,497 pounds of limestone	.205	.018	.025	.001	.318		.036	.603
For production of 4,808 pounds of bituminous coal	1.973	.068	.149	.013		$0.042		2.245
For conversion of above coal into 3,532 pounds of coke	.598	.076	.072	.009	.738			1.493
For conversion of above ore, limestone, and coke, and 233 pounds of cinder, into 2,649 pounds of pig-iron	1.576	.134	.718	.054				2.482
For conversion of above pig-iron and 79 pounds of scrap and ferro-manganese into 2,488 pounds of steel ingots	1.689	.120	.503	.011				2.323
For fuel (1.11 tons bituminous coal) for conversion of above pig-iron, scrap, and ferro-manganese into 2,488 pounds of steel ingots	.912	.032	.069	.006		.019		1.038
For conversion of above steel ingots into 1 ton (2,240 pounds) of steel rails	1.540	(*a*)	1.000	.050				2.590
For fuel (1.17 tons bituminous coal) for conversion of above steel ingots into 1 ton (2,240 pounds) of steel rails	.962	.033	.073	.007		.020		1.095
Total cost of above processes	11.597	.605	3.416	.232	5.949	.081	2.962	24.842
For cost of 233 pounds of cinder entering into the pig-iron (this is for material and is additional to its conversion included in line 5, above)								.094
For cost of 79 pounds of scrap and ferro-manganese entering into the steel ingots (this is for material and is additional to its conversion included in line 6, above)								.937
Total gross cost of 1 ton (2,240 pounds) of steel rails								25.873
Deduct value of scrap produced in the ingot and rail departments								1.207
Total net cost of 1 ton (2,240 pounds) of steel rails								24.666

a Not reported.

STATEMENT SHOWING THE PROPORTION OF COST ATTRIBUTABLE TO DIRECT LABOR IN THE PRODUCTION OF ONE TON OF STEEL RAILS.

Item	Per cent.	Amount
Total cost of ore, limestone, and coke (coal included) for 2,649 pounds of pig-iron		$15.314
Cost of direct labor in production of ore, limestone, and coke (coal included) for 2,649 pounds of pig-iron		4.918
Per cent. of cost of direct labor in production of ore, limestone, and coke (coal included) for 2,649 pounds of pig-iron	32	
Total cost of converting the above materials, and 233 pounds of cinder, into 2,6 9 pounds of pig-iron		2.482
Cost of direct labor in converting the above materials, and 233 pounds of cinder, into 2,649 pounds of pig-iron		1.576
Per cent. of cost of direct labor in converting the above materials, and 233 pounds of cinder, into 2,649 pounds of pig-iron	63	
Total cost of converting the above pig-iron, and 79 pounds of scrap and ferro-manganese, into 2,488 pounds of steel ingots		3.361
Cost of direct labor in converting the above pig-iron, and 79 pounds of scrap and ferro-manganese, into 2,488 pounds of steel ingots		2.601
Per cent. of cost of direct labor in converting the above pig-iron, and 79 pounds of scrap and ferro-manganese, into 2,488 pounds of steel ingots	77	
Total cost of converting the above steel ingots into 1 ton (2,240 pounds) of steel rails		3.685
Cost of direct labor in converting the above steel ingots into 1 ton (2,240 pounds) of steel rails		2.502
Per cent. of cost of direct labor in converting the above steel ingots into 1 ton (2,240 pounds) of steel rails	68	
Total net cost of above ore, limestone, coke (coal included), cinder, scrap, and ferro-manganese, and of converting them into 1 ton (2,240 pounds) of steel rails		24.666
Cost of direct labor in the production of ore, limestone, and coke (coal included) and in converting them and the cinder, scrap, and ferro-manganese, into 1 ton (2,240 pounds) of steel rails		11.597
Per cent. of cost of direct labor in the production of ore, limestone, and coke (coal included) and in converting them and the cinder, scrap, and ferro-manganese into 1 ton (2,240 pounds) of steel rails	47	

ANALYSIS OF COSTS IN ONE TON OF STEEL RAILS MADE IN GREAT BRITAIN.

[Calculation based on establishment No. 11, page 35, Misc. Doc. H. R. 222.]

Materials and successive stages of conversion.	Expenditures for direct labor.	Other expenditures.						Total.
		Officials and clerks.	Supplies and repairs.	Taxes.	Transportation to point where used.	Timber.	Difference between foregoing actual costs, and costs as charged by establishment where used. Presumably profit to producers.	
For production of 5,127 pounds of iron ore	$0.860	$0.025	$0.185	$0.030	$4.166	....	$2.241	$7.507
For production of 941 pounds of limestone	.163	....	.016	....	.041	....	....	.220
For production of 4,778 pounds of bituminous coal	2.083	.110	.308	.062	....	0.334	....	2.897
For conversion of above coal into 3,532 pounds of coke	.440	.039	.298	....	....	....	....	.777
For conversion of above ore, limestone, and coke, and 341 pounds of scrap cinder, etc., into 2,912 pounds of pig-iron	.784	.019	.754	.016	....	....	....	1.573
For conversion of the above pig-iron, and 383 pounds of scrap and spiegeleisen, into 2,798 pounds of steel ingots	702	.060	.942	.007	....	....	....	1.711
For fuel (361 pounds of bituminous coal and 171 pounds of coke) for conversion of above pig-iron, scrap, and spiegeleisen into 2,798 pounds of steel ingots	.279	.015	.052	.008	....	.041	....	.395
For conversion of above steel ingots into 2,700 pounds of steel blooms	.492	.030	.419	.004	....	....	....	.945
For fuel (810 pounds of bituminous coal) for conversion of above steel ingots into 2,700 pounds of steel blooms	.353	.019	.052	.011	....	.057	....	.492
For conversion of above steel blooms into one ton (2,240 pounds) of steel rails	1.368	.025	.348	.003	....	....	....	1.744
For fuel (672 pounds of bituminous coal) for conversion of above steel blooms into one ton (2,240 pounds) of steel rails	.293	.015	.043	.009	....	.047	....	.407
Total cost of above processes	7.817	.357	3.417	.150	4.207	.479	2.241	18.668
For cost of 341 pounds of scrap, cinder, etc., entering into the pig-iron [this is for material and is additional to its conversion included in line 5 above]								.286
For cost of 383 pounds of scrap and spiegeleisen entering into the steel ingots [this is for material and is additional to its conversion included in line 6 above]								2.387
Total gross cost of 1 ton (2,240 pounds) of steel rails								21.341
Deduct value of scrap produced in the ingot, bloom, and rail departments								2.727
Total net cost of 1 ton (2,240 pounds) of steel rails								18.614

STATEMENT SHOWING THE PROPORTION OF COST ATTRIBUTABLE TO DIRECT LABOR IN THE PRODUCTION OF ONE TON OF STEEL RAILS.

Item	Per cent	Amount
Total cost of ore, limestone, and coke (coal included) for 2,912 pounds of pig-iron		$11.401
Cost of direct labor in production of ore, limestone, and coke (coal included) for 2,912 pounds of pig-iron		3.546
Per cent. of cost of direct labor in production of ore, limestone, and coke (coal included) for 2,912 pounds of pig-iron	31	
Total cost of converting the above materials and 341 pounds of cinder, scrap, etc., into 2,912 pounds of pig-iron		1.572
Cost of direct labor in converting the above materials and 341 pounds of cinder, scrap, etc., into 2,912 pounds of pig-iron		.784
Per cent. of cost of direct labor in converting the above materials and 341 pounds of cinder, scrap, etc., into 2,912 pounds of pig-iron	50	
Total cost of converting the above pig-iron and 383 pounds of scrap and spiegeleisen into 2,798 pounds of steel ingots		2.106
Cost of direct labor in converting the above pig-iron and 383 pounds of scrap and spiegeleisen into 2,798 pounds of steel ingots		.981
Per cent. of cost of direct labor in converting the above pig-iron and 383 pounds of scrap and spiegeleisen into 2,798 pounds of steel ingots	47	
Total cost of converting the above steel ingots into 2,700 pounds of steel blooms		1.437
Cost of direct labor in converting the above steel ingots into 2,700 pounds of steel blooms		.845
Per cent. of cost of direct labor in converting the above steel ingots into 2,700 pounds of steel blooms	59	
Total cost of converting the above steel blooms into one ton (2.240 pounds) of steel rails		2.151
Cost of direct labor in converting the above steel blooms into one ton (2,240 pounds) of steel rails		1.661
Per cent. of cost of direct labor in converting the above steel blooms into one ton (2,240 pounds) of steel rails	77	
Total net cost of the above ore, limestone, coke (coal included), cinder, scrap, and spiegeleisen, and of converting them into one ton (2,240 pounds) of steel rails		18.614
Cost of direct labor in the production of ore, limestone, and coke (coal included), and in converting them and the cinder, scrap, and spiegeleisen into 1 ton (2,240 pounds) of steel rails		7.817
Per cent. of cost of direct labor in the production of ore, limestone, and coke (coal included), and in converting them and the cinder, scrap, and spiegeleisen into 1 ton (2240 pounds) of steel rails	42	

ANALYSIS OF COSTS IN ONE TON OF STEEL RAILS MADE ON THE CONTINENT OF EUROPE.

[Based mainly on Establishment No. 3, page 35, Mis. Doc. H. R. 222.]

Materials and successive stages of conversion.	Expenditures for direct labor.	Other expenditures.						Total.
		Officials and clerks.	Supplies and repairs.	Taxes.	Transportation to point where used.	Timber.	Differences between foregoing actual costs and costs as charged by establishment where used—presumably profits to producers.	
For production of 5,701 pounds of iron ore	$0.957	$0.028	$0.206	$0.033	$3.744		$3.815	$8.783
For production of 1,582 pounds of limestone	.174	.016	.021	.001	.086			.298
For production of 4,927 pounds of bituminous coal	2.326	.175	.315	.042		$0.480		3.338
For conversion of above coal into 3,509 pounds of coke	.590	.051	.047	.024	.064			.776
For conversion of above ore, limestone, and coke into 3,061 pounds of pig-iron	1.246	.021	*a* .381	(*a*)			1.476	3.124
For conversion of above pig-iron into 2,612 pounds of steel ingots	.512	.110	.852	.012				1.486
For fuel (782 pounds of coke) for conversion of above pig-iron into 2,612 pounds of steel ingots	.649	.050	.081	.016		.107		.903
For conversion of above steel ingots into 2,580 pounds of steel blooms	.203	.049	.240	.049				.541
For fuel (217 pounds of coke) for conversion of above steel ingots into 2,580 pounds of steel blooms	.180	.014	.022	.005		.030		.251
For conversion of above steel blooms into one ton (2,240 pounds) of steel rails	1.043	(*b*)	*b* .448	.010				1.501
For fuel (474 pounds of bituminous coal) for conversion of above steel blooms into one ton (2,240 pounds) of steel rails	.224	.017	.030	.004		.046		.321
Total gross cost of one ton (2,240 pounds) of steel rails	8.104	.531	2.643	.196	3.894	.663	5.291	21.322
Deduct value of scrap produced in ingot, bloom, and rail departments								1.687
Total net cost of one ton (2,240 pounds) of steel rails								19.635

a Taxes are included in "Supplies and repairs" not separable.

b Salaries paid officials and clerks are included in "Supplies and repairs" not separable.

STATEMENT SHOWING THE PROPORTION OF COST ATTRIBUTABLE TO DIRECT LABOR IN THE PRODUCTION OF ONE TON OF STEEL RAILS.

	Per cent.	Amount
Total cost of ore, limestone, and coke (coal included) for 3,061 pounds of pig-iron		$13.195
Cost of direct labor in production of ore, limestone, and coke (coal included) for 3,061 pounds of pig-iron		4.047
Per cent. of cost of direct labor in production of ore, limestone, and coke (coal included) for 3,061 pounds of pig-iron	31	......
Total cost of converting the above materials into 3,061 pounds of pig-iron		3.124
Cost of direct labor in converting the above materials into 3,061 pounds of pig-iron		1.246
Per cent. of cost of direct labor in converting the above materials into 3,061 pounds of pig-iron	40	......
Total cost of converting the above pig-iron into 2,612 pounds of steel ingots		2.389
Cost of direct labor in converting the above pig-iron into 2,612 pounds of steel ingots		1.161
Per cent. of cost of direct labor in converting the above pig-iron into 2,612 pounds of steel ingots	49	......
Total cost of converting the above steel ingots into 2,580 pounds of steel blooms		.792
Cost of direct labor in converting the above steel ingots into 2,580 pounds of steel blooms		.383
Per cent. of cost of direct labor in converting the above steel ingots into 2,580 pounds of steel blooms	48	......
Total cost of converting the above steel blooms into one ton (2,240 pounds) of steel rails		1.822
Cost of direct labor in converting the above steel blooms into one ton (2,240 pounds) of steel rails		1.267
Per cent. of cost of direct labor in converting the above steel blooms into one ton (2,240 pounds) of steel rails	70	......
Total net cost of above ore, limestone, and coke (coal included) and of converting them into one ton (2,240 pounds) of steel rails		19.635
Cost of direct labor in the production of the above ore, limestone, and coke (coal included) and in converting them into one ton (2,240 pounds) of steel rails		8.104
Per cent. of cost of direct labor in the production of the above ore, limestone, and coke (coal included) and in converting them into one ton (2,240 pounds) of steel rails	41	......

O

THE ADVANTAGES

—OF—

EDUCATED LABOR

IN MISSOURI,

By S. WATERHOUSE.

A Lecture delivered at Washington University,
April 26th, 1872.

EDITION—10,000 COPIES.

ST. LOUIS:
E. F. Hobart & Co., Printers and Stationers, 615 Chestnut street.
1872.

THE ADVANTAGES

—OF—

EDUCATED LABOR

IN MISSOURI,

By S. WATERHOUSE.

A Lecture delivered at Washington University,
April 26th, 1872.

EDITION—10,000 COPIES.

ST. LOUIS:
E. F. Hobart & Co., Printers and Stationers, 615 Chestnut street,
1872.

PREFACE.

THE following lecture on "SKILLED LABOR" is published in compliance with the accompanying request of the St. Louis Board of Trade, the recollection of whose personal courtesies will be gratefully cherished by the author of these pages.

OFFICE ST. LOUIS BOARD OF TRADE, April 30th, 1872.

PROFESSOR S. WATERHOUSE, *Washington University:*

DEAR SIR: I enclose herewith the resolutions passed by this Board at its meeting on the 29th inst., and trust that you will accede to this request, and furnish for publication a copy of your very able and interesting address on "Skilled Labor."

I was individually deeply interested in the facts it contains, and believe much good will result from giving it a wide circulation at home and abroad.

With assurances of my very high personal regard and also that of the Board over which I have the honor to preside,

I am your friend and obedient servant,

B. R. BONNER, PRESIDENT.

At a meeting held April 29th, 1872, the following resolutions were unanimously adopted by the St. Louis Board of Trade:

Resolved, That we regard the recent Lecture of Professor Waterhouse on Skilled Labor of such public value as to merit our official sanction, believing that its impressive facts and convincing reasonings would, if widely circulated, exert an important influence upon the material interests of Missouri. Therefore

Resolved, That the President of the Board be instructed to wait upon Professor Waterhouse and solicit a copy of his address for publication.

THE ECONOMIC VALUE

OF

SKILLED LABOR IN MISSOURI.

Of the useful and æsthetic arts, some were discovered and others adopted by our city for the promotion of the public interests.——
Nor do I wish to speak upon subjects whose discussion will confer no practical benefit, but rather upon those topics whose treatment will tend to ameliorate the condition of mankind.

ISOCRATES.

While feeling a reverent admiration for the higher departments of abstract thought and æsthetic culture, I do not sympathize with the fashionable depreciation of utilitarian studies. In some minds the grandeur of a thought seems to be proportioned to its uselessness, but it may be doubted whether knowledge for its own sake is better than knowledge for the sake of mankind. The progress of civilization, in which industrial art has been so important a factor, attests the truth that a devotion to material interests is not necessarily sordid. It is upon the foundations of *practical* thought that education and religion have reared their finest structures. Even the halls of this University owe their existence to the commercial success which amassed the means of their erection—to the intelligent and appreciative liberality which devoted to the service of culture the wealth which business sagacity had accumulated.

The postulate of Archimedes is a universal need—to move the world there must be a material stand-point. The creative genius which devotes its energies to cheapening the necessaries of life is an efficient ally of moral progress. The successful conduct of any business demands and develops a special scholarship, which is not less valuable as a means of discipline, because it is so useful as a source of wealth. The business man may be narrow, but so may the scholar; and in either case, the narrowness results not so much from the necessities of the vocation, as from the character of the man. But to comprehend the broader relations of trade and manufactures requires a depth of insight, breadth of induction, mastery of facts, knowledge of political economy, mechanics and chemistry that will test the capacities of the best minds. The executive ability, soundness of judgment and knowledge of human nature which are essential to a symmetrical and useful development of faculties are evoked, not by processes of abstract thought, but by the experiences of business life. A recognition of the fact that some of the best trained minds in every community have been disciplined exclusively in the schools of active industry will not permit me to speak with disparagement of the professional scholarship which a devotion to business develops.

THE TRIUMPHS OF SCIENCE.

Applied science has transfigured the world. With Midas' touch it has created the wealth of nations and transmuted every object into gold. It has apprenticed the elements, invested the earth with a nervous system, endowed machinery with the attributes of intelligence, utilized the resources of nature, disciplined mental powers to greater efficiency, elevated and beautified human life. It has brought nations into nearer neighborhood, enlarged their exchanges and strengthened their friendship. It has relieved the severity of human toil, multiplied domestic comforts and increased the means of refined enjoyment. From the analysis of a planet to the observation of microscopic life, there is no department of physical research which it has not invaded. On every field of battle with ignorance it has won rich spoils of victory. It has fortified our faith with stronger proofs of a divine cause and broadened the borders of Christian civilization. Indeed, the spiritual efficacy of mechanical and chemical appliances has been one of the potent forces of modern reform.

It would be difficult to exaggerate the moral power of machinery in ameliorating the condition of mankind by the diffusion of knowledge and the promotion of culture. But it is the economical aspect of our subject which to-night solicits attention.

CAPITAL AND LABOR.

I shall be obliged to omit the discussion of the relations between capital and labor. Even a brief treatment of this topic would exceed the narrow bounds of a single lecture. This omission, however, occasions less regret from the fact that the relations between capital and labor are less susceptible of control by discussion than the immediately practical interests which to-night demand consideration.

RAW MATERIALS AND WAGES.

The enhanced values of manufactured products strikingly illustrate the wealth-creating energy of skilled labor. Ceramic art converts a few grains of comparatively worthless kaolin, quartz and feldspar into a Sevres vase costing $5,000. Metallurgical skill transmutes ten cents' worth of iron ore into $10,000 worth of steel springs. Textile craft increases a hundred fold the value of the materials which are fabricated into point lace, Cashmere shawls, Brussels carpets and Gobelin tapestries. Belgian lace-thread, even before it has received its highest value in the finished beauty of the gossamer tissue, is worth five hundred dollars a pound. From a window-pane to the field-glass of a telescope, from the toy wagon of a child to the mammoth engine of an ocean steamer, from a photograph to a Titian, there is not a production in the whole range of articles of use or virtu that does not show the influence of skilled labor in appreciating the value of raw materials.

The effect of dexterity upon wages is also equally conspicuous. The inexpert workman always receives the lowest remuneration. But as the hand gains a deftlier cunning, and the mind a clearer intelligence, so the rate of compensation advances. The ignorant laborer who can barely earn a living may acquire a scientific skill that will enable him not only to amass a fortune, but also to promote the material interests of the world.

THE FORTUNES OF INDIVIDUALS.

Nearly a century ago, there lived in an English hamlet a lad whose history fitly illustrates my argument. His father was a humble laborer. By unremitting toil, he was barely able to procure the means of subsistence for himself and family. In his ceaseless struggle with poverty, he was cheered by no hope of preferment, no leisure for healthful recreation, no opportunity for self-improvement. The son was early compelled to assist his father in procuring the means of livelihood. At the age of nine, he was earning two pence a day; at fourteen, he was tending the furnaces of a colliery engine; at eighteen, he did not know a letter of the alphabet; but before he was twenty, partly by unaided efforts and partly by instruction in night schools, he had mastered the elements of reading, writing and ciphering. From this time his progress was rapid. Quickened by the impulses of genius and guided by a natural aptitude for mechanics, he devoted himself assiduously to the study of civil engineering. As his scientific attainments qualified him for more important positions, he was promoted to higher trusts, till at length he became one of the foremost engineers of the age, the father of the railway system, and the builder of great public works. Wealth, fame and usefulness crowned his success. With a natural patent of nobility, far grander than the title of princes, he could well afford to reject the hónor of knighthood. Skilled labor had received its reward.

His son was reared under more favorable auspices. A scientific education, enriched by the experience of his father, was a rare discipline for the duties of professional life. The energies of his powerful mind, utilized by technical training, left their impress upon the fortunes of mankind, and constructed upon both continents works of public usefulness and enduring fame. These examples, so memorable in the history of civil engineering, are full of weighty suggestions. The father and son were gifted with an extraordinary similarity of natural endowments. The chief difference in their careers was due to the effect of scientific teaching. More than one-third of the father's life, with all its possibilities of usefulness, was squandered through want of education. For many years after he had reached manhood, and while he might, if he had been properly educated, have been building the great highways of commerce, he was toiling with slow and painful progress through the rudiments of mathematics. And during all these years the world was losing the service of his splendid abilities. His lack of early training was a life-long impediment. His progress was often obstructed by problems whose solution would have been facilitated by an acquaintance with the formulæ of science. In the first years of professional service, his mind was perplexed with practical difficulties which a knowledge of mechanical and physical laws would have enabled him easily to surmount. The scientific information, which cost the unaided engineer years of valuable time and dearly-bought experience, could have been acquired in a few months in a technological school.

But the son spent his earlier years in training his faculties for professional service, and, at an age when his father had scarcely mastered the alphabet, he was a learned engineer and the superintendent of important public works. His great powers were fully utilized for the benefit of mankind. None of his time and usefulness was lost through lack of early instruction.

It would be difficult to illustrate by more impressive examples the value of technical instruction.

But while a genius like that of the Stephensons is granted to few men, the principles of political economy which their lives inculcate measurably apply to the humblest departments of skilled labor. There is no pursuit so lowly that its follower may not increase the utility and value of his services by the acquisition of an intelligent dexterity.

THE WEALTH OF EUROPE.

Before discussing the application of skilled labor to the resources of Missouri, it will be well to investigate the polytechnic causes of foreign wealth. Differences in the various countries of Europe in wages, rates of interest and expense of living affect the cost of production, but they do not alone account for the relative superiority in manufactures. The nations which enjoy the most favorable industrial conditions are not always the foremost in manufacturing prosperity. The great secret of European success is skilled labor. It is this which develops national wealth and controls the tidal movements of commerce. Without it, no country can maintain an ascendancy in any department of manufactures. An active, vigilant, progressive competition would soon wrest the sceptre of industrial supremacy from the hand of an unskilful rival.

In Europe, skilled labor is fostered by the State. Hundreds of industrial and polytechnic schools have been liberally endowed and sustained by the government. The polytechnic buildings at Stuttgart and Munich cost 1,000,000 florins each, and the liberality of their endowment equals the splendor of their construction. Under the imperial government of France, an annuity of $200,000 was given to three technological schools, while a yearly grant of $400,000 was bestowed upon academies of higher art. Since 1852, the South Kensington Museum of Industrial Art has cost the British government $5,000,000, and the yearly appropriation for the encouragement of technical skill is $400,000. Emperors have deemed such institutions worthy of liberal patronage, and prime ministers have labored to ensure their success. The means of public-spirited citizens and the services of distinguished men of science have been devoted to their advancement. The result sanctions the wisdom of these efforts and expenditures, and attests the profitable economy of skilled labor.

The copious wealth which flows along the channels of successful manufactures springs from a polytechnic source. In Europe there is scarcely a fine or useful art that is not fostered by special schools of instruction. Technical academies promote the growth of every leading industry. There are "schools for instruction in the arts of designing, engraving, coloring, dyeing, silk and ribbon weaving, lace making; of the making of horological instruments of various kinds; stone-cutting and general carving; of manufacturing the most delicate patterns and elegant forms of glassware; of working the metals—both useful and precious—into nearly every variety of form, for the consumption of the most refined and cultivated nations—schools, likewise, of various grades for instruction in the principles and practice of the more complex and comprehensive arts of mining, engineering, agriculture, etc." These schools are taught by skillful professors, furnished with libraries of technical science and equipped according to their varying requirements, with laboratories, workshops, museums of models, and collections of materials in the crude state and in the various stages of manufacture. It may be stated, as an evidence of imperial liberality in providing facilities for artistic illustration, that the French government recently distributed to the schools of Paris 35,000 models of the finest workmanship and taste for the instruction of little children in the art of drawing and design. It is obviously impossible, within the limit of an hour's discussion, fully to describe the peculiarities of the several schools. The precision of detail must yield to the vagueness of generalization. In all of these institutions, learned professors elucidate the principles and applications of industrial science. Every step, in the best processes of converting raw materials into the finished product, is traced with minute care and philosophic exposition. The wastefulness of unskilful methods and the economy of scientific treatment are demonstrated. In the manufacture of fine silks and woolens, France stands pre-eminent. In lustre and brilliancy of impression, in exquisite taste, in beauty of design and harmony of colors, French fabrics rival the productions of the artist's pencil. This supremacy is not due to accident nor to the happy conceptions of untrained inventive skill. The consummate art which in these higher departments of industry controls the taste, fashion and trade of the civilized world, is the result of scientific study and discipline. Even the climatic and physical conditions under which the crude material is produced are carefully investigated, and every process of cleansing, bleaching, carding, spinning, weaving, dyeing and finishing is studied under the fullest illumination of modern science. Creative minds strive to devise better chemical methods, improved machinery, finer patterns and more elegant combinations. Elaborate expositions of the principles which control the harmonious blending of colors are illustrated by the finest products of textile art. Industrial æsthetics constitutes an important part of the course. The cultivation of taste begins in childhood. Little children are taught to observe every form of grace and symmetry, every beauty and variety of floral tint, every splendor of the sunset sky. The effect of this culture is discernible not only in the superior workmanship of the educated artisan, but also in the higher taste and general æsthetic refinement of the French people. But what are the commercial results of all this devotion to industrial science? France is to-day supreme in many of the higher branches of manufacture. The economical significance of this supremacy may be illustrated by a few statistics.

In 1863, the looms of Rheims produced $16,000,000 worth of woolen fabrics; 55,000 workmen were employed in this industry. In 1864, the value of the higher woolen manufactures of Roubaix was $40,000,000.

In 1863, France exported woolen goods of superior quality to the amount of $56,600,000. In 1866, the silk ribbons fabricated in the mills of Saint Etienne were worth $12,000,000. Out of a population of 90,000 people, 23,600 were engaged in this branch of manufacture.

In 1867, France sold $40,000,000 worth of silk goods to her British rival.

And in 1860, the exports of French silks amounted to $70,000,000, and the aggregate product was valued at $140,000,000.

Such are some of the practical results, representative of a wide range of manufactures, which are almost exclusively due to the influence of industrial schools. Wherever polytechnic instruction has been most general and thorough, there have sprung up those prosperous manufactories which have developed cities with an American rapidity of growth and raised impoverished populations to competence and the opportunities of education.

In 1830, Flanders employed more than 275,000 workmen in the manufacture of flax. But subsequently the mechanical improvements of other countries paralyzed this industry and involved a people, dependent upon it for their means of support, in suffering and ruin. In this extremity, the Belgian government resorted to the establishment of technical schools. The experiment was successful, and from that day the Belgian mills began to regain their former prosperity.

In 1851, the British government appointed commissioners to investigate the causes of decline in English manufactures. The report ascribed this decline to a conspicuous deficiency in technical instruction, and the government, seriously alarmed by the depression of manufacturing industry, loss of trade, and the conquests of foreign skill, at once instituted a general system of polytechnic instruction. The influence of this training soon manifested itself in the greater economy of manufacture, superior excellence of the product, and renewed vitality of trade. This example forcibly illustrates the importance of industrial schools. Cheap capital and fuel, together with educated skill, have made England the workshop of nations and given her almost a monopoly of all the lower grades of cotton and woolen goods. The value of this monopoly, which skilled labor will enable her to preserve, may be inferred from the following figures.

In 1867, England manufactured 380,000,000 pounds of wool, and the product, independent of worsted goods, was worth more than $100,000,000. In 1866, nearly 900,000,000 pounds of cotton were fabricated in English mills. The total value of the product was more than $500,000,000, of which $248,000,000 worth was exported. In 1870, British exports, almost exclusively manufactures, amounted to nearly $1,000,000,000.

It is not strange that the English government was alarmed by the jeopardy of such vast interests, and that it should strenuously cherish the technical art which was an effective means of their preservation.

DOMESTIC AGRICULTURE.

Skilled labor, which has been productive of such enormous amounts of foreign capital, is to-day the supreme material need of Missouri. The enrichment of its magic touch would be felt throughout the whole range of our industries, but nowhere would the economic worth of technical skill be more conspicuous than in the operations of agriculture. In this country there has been a strong prejudice against scientific husbandry, but this feeling cannot rest upon any tenable basis of fact or reason. The application of scientific truth to every other department of practical industry has proved of the highest economic value, That agriculture is no exception to the universality of this principle is shown by the surprising results which scientific farming has already achieved. Observe the progress in agricultural machinery. A few years ago, a friend of mine who was traveling in Greece saw some rustics vexing the earth with a knotted stick tied with ropes to the horns of oxen. The advance from this rude implement to the steam gang-plow of England is immense. The value of our improved reapers lies not only in the economy of human muscle and greater power of accomplishment, but also in that rapidity of operation which permits laborers to attend to other work till the full maturity of the cereal harvests, and then to garner them quickly with but slight exposure to damage by storm. The annual saving by this speedy rescue from the destructive force of the elements must amount to millions.

It is probable the world never before saw such perfect breeds of domestic animals as the scientific propagation of England has developed.

Skill in grafting, or in combination of varieties, has produced a marvellous improvement in the richness and delicacy of our apples, pears, peaches, grapes and strawberries. Through the beneficence of science, the modern laborer enjoys fruits of a more delicious and exquisite flavor than ever gratified the taste of an ancient epicure.

It is science that preserves the perishable fruitage of summer for the luxurious dessert of mid-winter, and concentrates meats and farina for Arctic voyage or sanitary use. It is science that, by the application of improved fertilizers, increases the bounty of our harvests, and restores the productive energy of exhausted soils. It is science that compels the sentinel lightnings to herald the approach of storms and to guard our property on land and sea against the elemental forces. Who then shall dare to say that science has been of no service to husbandry?

The European schools of agriculture are equipped with a liberality befitting their importance. The Russian school at Petrovskoi is sustained by an imperial annuity of $100,000. The Austrian farm at Krumau originally comprised 300,000 acres. All the schools devoted to agriculture are furnished with laboratories and workshops, improved implements and machinery, models and products; and the farms are supplied with the finest breeds of animals, the choicest varieties of cereals and vegetables, and the best selections of plants, vines and fruit trees. Some of these schools have factories for practical instruction in the manufacture of vinegar, starch, sugar, wine, etc. Thus, every branch of agriculture is enlightened by the tuition of science. The economic results of skillful tillage justify the expense of agricultural schools. It is hardly an extravagance of rhetoric to say that the chemical discoveries of Baron Liebig have increased the harvests of the civilized world.

I hope the time is not far distant when the European system will be extensively introduced into Missouri. Then its garners will overflow with the larger returns of intelligent cultivation, and its greater prosperity rest upon a scientific ground-work. Then the analysis of soil and vegetable, the special relations of climate to production, the conditions under which foreign plants and animals can be naturalized, and the applications of economic botany will be subjects of profitable investigation. Then the cultivation of fishes will be a lucrative employment. Then veterinary skill will measurably rescue our domestic animals from the ravages of epidemic disease, and entomological science, sensibly arresting the devastations of insects, will annually save a wealth of fruits and cereals that would be more than sufficient for the erection and endowment of an agricultural college. Then farming, raised to the dignity of a science, will furnish not only ampler means of material greatness, but also exhaustless resources of philosophic study and expanding thought.

COMMERCE.

Educated skill is the directive power of modern commerce. High mercantile success implies broad views and sagacious combinations. Only large, resourceful and well-informed minds can control the great interchanges of nations. The untrained merchant can seldom successfully compete with a well-disciplined rival. Commerce is no exception to the general truth that knowledge and skill are guarantees of victory. A wide range of professional learning lies open to the merchant. The mysteries of book-keeping; the principles of banking and insurance; local wants and products; the inter-relations of demand and supply; the causes of fluctuations in prices and rates of exchange; geography and channels of communication; processes of manufacture, adulterations, and the impositions of trade; common and international law; commercial history and political economy, challenge investigation and reward the intelligent student with broader visions of mercantile life and greater assurances of personal success.

The youthful merchants of Missouri should ever remember that the great prizes of commerce are always won by superior knowledge under the guidance of practical skill.

MANUFACTURES.

In treating the application of skilled labor to our manufactures, the multitude of topics that solicit consideration is simply bewildering; time permits but a hasty glance at subjects which only an elaborate discussion can render interesting.

The dexterity of English manufacturers enables them to purchase the cotton of India, pay the profits of production, incur the cost of manufacture, defray the expense of a double transportation, and yet under-sell the native products in a country where ten cents are liberal wages for a day's work. And American ingenuity has, in certain branches of manufacture, triumphed over the cheapness of British labor and capital, and profitably exported to England and the continent locomotives, sewing-machines, watches, and coarser cotton fabrics. It will, then, in this discussion, be assumed that skilled labor can achieve immediate success in many departments of productive industry, and an ultimate independence of European manufactories. Domestic skill will yet fabricate our wool, cotton, flax and silk into the myriad products for which we are now paying so costly a tribute to foreign looms.

In 1871, England bought of the United States more than $180,000,000 worth of cotton, and by the application of textile skill, realized a net profit larger than the original cost of the raw material. This single fact shows the possibilities of opulence which cotton mills in our own State would enjoy.

Iron of almost every useful variety is found in more than sixty counties in Missouri. According to the sober calculations of geology, this State contains 1,000,000,000 tons of iron ore, and 100,000,000,000 tons of coal. Yet the actual revenue which Missouri derives from this vast mineral wealth is far smaller than that of less favored regions. In 1871, this State produced about 85,000 tons of pig iron, worth something less than $4,000,000; in the same year England made from very inferior ores more than 6,000,000 tons of pig iron, worth in the *crude* state nearly $100,000,000. The annual productive value of the iron and coal mines of Pennsylvania is $120,000,000. Of the 2,000,000 tons of railway iron annually consumed in the United States, by far the larger portion is required for the roads of the Mississippi valley. While Missouri has such natural facilities for supplying this demand, most of these bars are imported, and the very rails that run to our mountains of iron were rolled in English mills. Capital and skilled labor will yet provide domestic supplies for every demand of hardware.

Possessing more than 15,000 square miles of coal, rich with inexhaustible stores of motive power, Missouri is yet largely dependent upon adjacent States for its supplies of fuel.

With galena enough in her mines to satisfy the wants of the whole Mississippi valley, our State imports lead from Europe and even from China.

Our abundant resources of copper, nickel, zinc, hydraulic cement, fire-clay and granite, are waiting for the hand of skilled labor to utilize them for the service of man. Vast quantities of cobalt, baryta, and ochres of every hue lie embedded in the soil of Missouri, ready for technical art to convert them into valuable paints. Our quarries are full of richly-veined and beautifully mottled marbles for the embellishment of our homes.

Kaolin, of superior purity for porcelain, and sand of the finest quality for glassware, exist in Missouri in exhaustless abundance. With these materials, skilled labor could create great and profitable industries. The example of Belgium, which twenty years ago produced 50,000,000 square feet of sheet glass per annum, Missouri would do well to imitate.

Iron pyrites, from which sulphuric acid is made, occurs in unlimited quantities in this State. This is a fact of great economic moment. No other chemical agent has such general use and value in the practical arts. The success of many of our most important industries depends upon a cheap abundance of this material. This acid is an essential element in bleaching, dyeing, calico printing, in the refinement of coal oils, and in the manufacture of super-phosphates, carbonate of soda, glass, soap, candles, etc. It is estimated that in Missouri alone the annual consumption of sulphuric acid amounts to 3,000,000 pounds. It is fortunate for our material interests that the State contains such exhaustless sources of this powerful industrial agent.

France is enriching itself by the annual production of 1,200.000.000 gallons of wine. Chemical analysis, meteorological observation, and practical experience show that we have a soil and climate admirably adapted to the culture of the grape. With 10,000,000 acres suited to the growth of the vine, the vintages of Missouri ought to equal in extent, quality and productiveness the best wines in Europe. But this great source of wealth can only be unsealed by the hand of skilled labor. The successful competion of some of our native brands in the wine markets of Europe reveals the brilliant possibilities of our grape culture.

Thus far only the utilization of our own resources has been discussed, but there is no reason for any such narrow limitation of our productive energies. The manufactories of England bring their crude material from every quarter of the globe.

I have long thought that St. Louis, with its comparative nearness, partial water transportation, and cheap coal, possessed unusual facilities for the reduction of the Rocky Mountain ores. Our northern rival has already established smelting works for this purpose. St. Louis has too long neglected a rare opportunity of establishing a great and lucrative industry. The mountains invite us to relieve their distended veins and infuse their golden currents into our own circulation. Only an unreasonable spirit of self-denial can induce us to decline so generous an invitation. The silver ores of Utah are carried to Pennsylvania, New Jersey, and even Wales for reduction. Two hundred and fifty car loads a month have been sent to Swansea, and recently one Welsh firm had at their works $600,000 worth of Utah ores. It is said that the ocean freight alone—$6.60 a ton in gold—is equal to the cost of refinement in this city. If our mountain ores can be profitably transported 4,000 miles for reduction, the financial success of smelting works at St. Louis cannot reasonably be doubted. Large quantities of these ores are now shipped to Wales by way of San Francisco and Cape Horn—a distance of not less than 15,000 miles. In 1870, the amount of ores exported from Utah and Colorado for foreign reduction, was more than 100,000 tons. This is an exhibition of energy which our citizens should emulate. Reductive works would also create kindred industries and our metropolis would become the great central manufactory of gold and silver ware. Artistic design and decorative skill are important elements in the value of such products.

CIVIL ENGINEERING.

Civil engineering is a branch of skilled labor too essential to be ignored in a formal discussion of the means of developing our resources. Its usefulness is conspicuous in the determination of legal bounds, in the sewerage which preserves the health of cities, in the drainage which reclaims malarious districts for fruitful tillage, in the water-works which supply towns with copious streams of healthful water, in the tunnels which undermine lakes and pierce mountains, in the bridges which span great rivers, in the canals which open new channels of communication between states and continents, in the railroads which facilitate domestic exchanges, in the steamships which bear the commerce of nations, in the machinery which impels the mightiest industries. But these works, without which our present civilization would be impossible, are the exclusive achievements of scientific skill. The civil engineer must be thoroughly conversant with mechanical drawing, the constructive principles of machinery, the tensile and compressive strength of materials, the dynamic effects of temperature and atmosphere, the static and hydraulic power of water—in fine, he must be familiar with mechanical forces, chemical properties, physical laws, mathematical science, and executive management, or he cannot command high success in his vocation. The calculations upon whose exact accuracy the erection of our great St. Louis bridge depends fill a large volume. But the skilled labor of the civil engineer is indispensable to a full development of the resources of Missouri. New avenues must be opened to our agricultural and mineral wealth. In many localities, our treasures of iron, lead and coal have but little present worth for want of means to transport them to market. The vast forests of excellent timber which cover the surface of southern Missouri are now comparatively valueless, in consequence of their inaccessibility. The skilful engineer, providing facilities of access and transfer, will be an important factor in our industrial development.

GEOLOGY, MINING, AND METALLURGY.

The millions which England and Germany have spent in the prosecution of geological surveys and the maintenance of schools of mining and metallurgy have proved an enriching expenditure. The technical science acquired in the schools and utilized in the surveys has developed a mineral wealth a thousand fold greater than the cost of instruction and exploration.

There are, in all the world, few richer fields for geological investigation than the mineral formations of Missouri; and in these fields only skilled laborers command employment. Economic geology will be one of the plastic forces of our greatness. The geologist will examine the water power of the state and guide the manufacturer to the best mill sites; analyze soils and reveal their adaptations; develop building materials, sands, clays, ochres, and cements; indicate the position and extent of mineral veins, ores and deposits; and, by his knowledge of formations, modes of occurrence, animal and vegetable fossils, save the inexperienced miner many useless and costly experiments. The geologist, verifying his scientific researches with the wonderful diamond drill, can point with unerring accuracy to the buried treasures of Missouri. Mining and metallurgy supplement the labors of geology. To construct tunnels, sink shafts, raise ore, expel gases, secure ventilation, remove water, manipulate compressed air and the new explosives, economize motive power and mechanical forces, analyze fuels and fluxes, construct furnaces, utilize waste gases, control the chemical operations of smelting and refining, forecast the cost of works, and understand the administration of mines, furnaces and workshops—these are duties whose economic discharge requires educated ability.

For the following examples of what skilled labor is capable of accomplishing in these departments of industry I am indebted to Prof. Potter. The ore in the district of Cleveland, England, has only 28 or 30 per cent. of iron. Our Missouri ores contain more than 50 per cent. of iron. Yet under the rigorous treatment of science, the Cleveland district produces from its inferior ore more and cheaper iron than any other region in the world. Where, less than a quarter of a century ago, there was not one house, there is now a population of 100,000 people, with an annual production of nearly 1,900,000 tons of pig iron.

The total value of the crude metals, coal and other minerals of Great Britain in 1870 was almost $240,000,000. Truly the results of skilled labor are not insignificant.

The lead ore of Freiburg, Saxony, is so extremely poor that in this country it would not, under existing conditions, pay the cost of reduction. But in 1867, an exhaustive scientific refinement extracted from 31,000 tons of ore 65,000 pounds of silver, 4,660 tons of lead, 1,200 tons of sulphur, 604 tons of zinc, 160 tons of arsenic, 70 tons of copper and 12 pounds of nickel and cobalt, with a total value of $1,393,885, and now a more skilful concentration in the treatment for other metals swells this aggregate by an annual addition of $30,000 of gold and bismuth, which even an analysis of the original ore failed to detect. Thus the economy of science compels an inferior ore, which here would simply be thrown away, to yield ten valuable and remunerative products.

Chemical superintendents are employed at most of the iron and steel works in Europe. Is it merely a coincidence that the greatest metallurgical and financial success is always found at those works which are under the constant supervision of professional chemists?

In foreign schools of mining and metallurgy, not only every

step from the opening of the mine to the completion of the metal product is elaborately taught, but the mind is trained to extreme vigilance of observation. Peculiar appearances of ore, novel behavior under treatment, the slag of the furnace, the dust of the refinery, and the gaseous condition of the surrounding air are carefully investigated for possible suggestions of more economical processes.

What wealth such skill, operating on the vast mineral resources of Missouri, would develop!

CHEMISTRY.

Chemistry, too, will be one of the great formative energies of our industrial prosperity. Many of the most brilliant and useful achievements in the domain of practical art have been wrought by economic chemistry.

This science sustains nearly the same relation to the industrial arts that air does to animal life. There is scarcely an article of use or beauty ever devised by the ingenuity of man that is not in some way indebted to economic chemistry. It is this science that provides comforts for the humble home and luxuries for the imperial palace; that reclaims waste lands and refines metals; that discovers remedies, disinfectants and anæsthetics; that derives from coal-tar the exquisite aniline hues, and forms the colors which embellish our fabrics and glow upon the canvas; that extracts the fragrance of a thousand flowers from the refuse of the stable, the flavor of pine-apple from putrid cheese, and the essence of pears and apples from fetid fusil oil; that forms artificial ice in tropic lands; that perfects the light which beacons mariners to safety; that works the infinitely varied miracles of telegraphy, photography and metallurgy; that moves mighty industries and cheapens the necessaries of human life. What chemistry has done to lessen the price of common articles a single example will illustrate. Formerly ultramarine was worth more than its weight in gold. But chemical skill has reduced the cost from $50 to 50 cents a pound. The annual value of the chemical products of France is $250,000,000. There is no more fruitful field of applied science than economic chemistry, and none which I would more earnestly urge the youth of Missouri to cultivate. But its vast harvests can be gathered by no unskilled hand. Only scientific culture can garner its golden fruitage.

ENTERPRISE AND INVENTION.

Thus even a general discussion of the applications of skilled labor to some of our leading interests forces the mind to a conviction of its transcendent value in every branch of industry. One of the grand advantages of polytechnic training is that the educated workman can avail himself of the best means of effecting his end. He wastes no capital in impracticable experiments and squanders no time in acquiring the costly lessons of untaught experience. No plans are disheartened or frustrated by ignorance of physical laws. But all the forces and economies of science are his business partners. Enterprize, too, is stimulated by a scientific knowledge of the means of accomplishment; and conceptions, which the unskilled mind might perceive but could not embody, are speedily realized through the agencies of science. But economy and productiveness are not the sole advantages of skilled labor. A technical education is a powerful incentive to invention and discovery. The significance of nature's hints is not always perceived by the unlearned mind, but the cultivated intellect trained to habits of scientific vigilance, is quick to take intimations. To the spirit of observation and inquiry which a professional culture develops the world owes many of its most wonderful achievements.

But few years ago, the polarization of light was regarded as a curious optical phenomenon utterly unrelated to human uses; but now, in all sugar refineries, the angle of rotation of a polarized ray is the unerring criterion of the requisite degree of refinement. The sensitiveness of certain chemical substances to the action of light was long a useless fact, but behold what a miracle skill has wrought!

Now photography not only fills the earth with art and beauty but also promotes science, depicting the magnified planet and animalcule with a delicate perfection that manual art can never equal. Its latest achievement is to form surfaces from which impressions can be *printed,* and the pictures, struck off just like steel plate engravings, retain the exquisite softness and fidelity of the photograph.

For centuries, a subtile and seemingly worthless force was allowed to squander its energies, but now, under the discipline of science, electricity guards our homes from burglary, protects human life in the regulation of railroad trains, moulds type, spreads golden beauty over the baser metals, secures the operations of agriculture, regulates the movements of fleets, and controls the commerce and politics of the world.

For years, the spectrum of flame was considered the valueless discovery of abstruse scholarship, but now spectral analysis is an important agent in one of our mightiest industries. In the manufacture of Bessemer steel, a powerful current of air is forced through the molten mass of iron, chiefly for the purpose of consuming the excess of carbon. A mistake of a few seconds in the length of the process would ruin the product. Only the most experienced and critical eye could determine, from an inspection of the flame, the exact moment of highest excellence. Such skill was rare and costly. But now the spectroscope affords a cheap and infallible means of telling when the work is done. While the carbon lines are visible in the spectrum of the flame, the operation is incomplete; but when these lines disappear, the process is finished, and the air-blast must be instantly arrested.

The spectroscope enables an ordinary workman to determine the precise moment when the requisite chemical change has been effected. Thus a curious physical discovery, apparently destitute of all practical value, has proved to be an efficient factor in a great industry. This novel use of the spectroscope is a beautiful illustration of the simplicity, certainty and economy of some of the processes of applied science.

To the infinitely varied applications of steam, whose motive breath vitalizes every industry, we now add some of the finest effects in the coloring of woolen fabrics, and even engraving, by means of the sand-blast.

These examples prove not only the practical usefulness of scientific truth, but also the expediency of cultivating the inventive faculty. A single discovery often enriches the world. A polytechnic education, stimulating the inquisitive and creative power of the human mind, tends to develop one of the most productive forces known to political economy. Scientific research may yet discover other agents as useful as hydrochloric acid in bleaching, mercury in the refinement of metals, or sulphuric acid throughout the range of industrial art. It may yet devise a cheap and effective means of eliminating sulphur from iron without coking the impure coal. It may yet utilize electric energy as a motive power. It may yet so improve machinery, simplify chemical processes, and reduce the cost of living as to secure for our State a golden pre-eminence in manufacturing industry.

ACTIVITY OF BUSINESS.

Now, most of our raw material is exported, and nearly all our domestic wants are supplied by importation. One of the beneficent results of the introduction of skilled labor would be a more general establishment of home manufactories. This would save the immense sums which we are now paying away for double freightage, reward the producer with the larger net gains of a domestic market, utilize our resources, retain within our own State the cost and profits of manufacture, and inspire every industry with prosperous life.

THE PRESENT DUTY OF MISSOURI.

Never in our history has there been a more propitious moment than the present for the introduction of skilled labor. In Europe, the increasing expense of living, and the greater difficulty and cost in obtaining ores and coal lessen the advantages of the foreign manufacturer, while the social, political and industrial condition of Europe favors emigration. Missouri should avail itself of the auspicious opportunity. The introduction of educated skill is worthy of legislative encouragement. Trustworthy expositions of our resources, issued under official sanctions which will command confidence should be disseminated in foreign lands.

DOMESTIC INSTITUTIONS.

But the acquisition of European dexterity ought not to be the limit of our endeavors. Polytechnic schools of our own should be equipped with every facility for the professional education of the youth of Missouri. George Stephenson once wished to emigrate to America, but was prevented by poverty. The accomplishment of his purpose might have changed the fortunes of the world. The financial value of such a man is beyond the calculations of political economy. But our polytechnic schools may develop Stephensons of our own.

PERSONAL CHARACTER.

If it be alleged that the tendencies of a technical education are sordid, the charge is refuted by the logic of experience Throughout Europe, it is found that industrial training not only surrounds the artisan with competence and physical comforts, but also begets in him a spirit of inquiry and greater general intelligence. It raises *all* its beneficiaries to higher planes, and some to lofty eminence. The mind which has gained an exact knowledge of any branch of practical science is stirred with a restless desire for a deeper insight into the laws and forces of physical nature; and the education that blesses the home with greater plenty and the means of mental culture also quickens the intellect with the spirit of scientific inquiry.

Before the establishment of technical schools, the industrial masses of Europe were generally poor and ignorant, and frequently profligate and lawless. Sunk often in sensual grossness, they were destitute of the virtues that ensure domestic happiness and the aspirations that guide to a higher life. But instruction, opening sources of purer enjoyment and disclosing possibilities of personal elevation, initiated a radical reform. It promoted civil order, public health, and private morality. Workmen who had been accustomed to squander their small wages in dissipation now spent their larger earnings upon the means of self-improvmeent; and strove to bestow upon their children the scientific culture whose practical value they had experienced in the advancement of their own fortunes. With a clearer perception of their industrial, civil, and moral obligations, they became more intelligent artisans, more orderly citizens, and more exemplary men—teaching by personal proof the grand fact that even an economic education promotes not only the material welfare of States, but also the higher interests of morality and civilization.

HIGHER CULTURE.

Wealth naturally precedes culture in the order of national development. It is idle to talk of the charms of literature to him whose utmost efforts can barely procure a living, or to speak of the beneficence of universities to communities which lack the riches to build and endow them. On every side great possibilities fail for the want of means to realize them. But the *wealth* derived from the practical arts should not be the ultimate object of human aspiration. Applied science is grandly useful in raising the masses to higher levels of happiness, and giving them the means and opportunities of intellectual cultivation. I have no fears that the wealth created by educated skill will be devoted to ignoble uses. History records no finer examples of intelligent munificence than those which embellish the annals of our own country. The consecration of private and public resources to beneficent charities, popular education and higher culture inspire an assured confidence that greater opulence would only be the means of a broader usefulness and a truer refinement. Then let the practical arts with utmost speed lay the material foundation of a higher civilization—a civilization that shall rise like the fair fabric of a Minervan temple, sacred at once to culture and adoration—a civilization whose spiritual wealth shall be far above all material riches, and whose refined art shall glorify the canvas with images of grace, chisel the marble into forms of celestial loveliness, and adorn the page with creations of poetic beauty.

From Dr. J. B. Angell

ARBITRATION

AND ITS

RELATION TO STRIKES.

BY

WILLIAM B. WEEDEN.

Arbitration and its Relation to Strikes.

AN ESSAY READ AT THE NATIONAL CONFERENCE OF UNITARIANS AT SARATOGA, SEPTEMBER, 1886.

BY

WILLIAM B. WEEDEN.

BOSTON:

PRESS OF GEO. H. ELLIS, 141 FRANKLIN STREET.

1887.

ARBITRATION AND ITS RELATION TO STRIKES.

BY WILLIAM B. WEEDEN.

A MAN of moderate but independent fortune, living in the suburb of a large village, awakes on a cold December morning, and finds the furnace fire out, the house chilled and cheerless in the gray dawn. He rings for a fire, but gets no answer. Then his wife sleepily tells him the condition of the family affairs. He had come home late at evening, and did not know of a certain unpleasantness occurring after supper. The mother with an infant had rebuked a nurse, whose duties conjoined those of a housemaid, for snapping the fingers of a sensitive, three-years-old girl, intrusted to her charge. The Most Worthy Nursing Mistress of the District Association of Nursery Maids had telephoned at once that nurses must have the right to snap children with the thumb and finger, or universal society would dissolve into its primitive elements of savagery. The mother — believing in the right of parents to discipline their own children, and not experienced enough to know that mistresses must obey their servants — discharged the rebellious maid. The cook was a fifth cousin of the nurse, and moreover, in the forenoon, had asked for more wages. It was not in human nature that she should remain silent in such a discussion, and she interfered loudly and effectively. She was an old hand,— of much influence in the higher circles of the order of cooks. While the mistress sobbed in the parlor, the telephone reported the discord of the family at head-quarters. The Most Ancient Master of Gastronomic Artists had signified that an economic deficiency in wages, combined with a wound in the sensibilities of a fifth cousin, involved grave questions, affecting the whole permanency of the relations of capital and labor; that, pending the question of wages, an apology must be rendered by the mistress, or not a chop could be broiled or a dish washed in that household. Hence, the deadlock in the affairs of that mistaken housekeeper,— the oppressor of her kind.

The wife and mother proceeds to build the kitchen fire, and attempt a breakfast. The father should have made the fire, and put the kettle on; but, unfortunately, having mail contracts, he must be at the railway station before breakfast, to superintend his own business. In the midst of the household reports, he runs to the stable for his horse and buggy, always ready at that hour. He finds the stable closed; and his excellent man, Patrick, lounging about, listless, yet respectful. In a shamefaced way, he said that he was sorry that he could not lift a finger for a gentleman who had always treated him well; but the interrupted privileges of the nursemaid, the outraged sensibilities of the thrifty cook, had convulsed the highest circles of the protective associations of the employed. The General Meddlesome Patriarch of the Amalgamated Order of Coachmen, Hostlers, Gardeners, Washerwomen, Cooks, Housemaids, Nurses, Butlers, and Scullions, had ordained that the whole domestic affair should be submitted to arbitration. Pending the decision, a general strike of the household was ordered. The Patriarch had considered, in council, a general strike of all the households in the village. But the telephone wires not working surely, on account of a storm, the more moderate thought it better to begin with the household in question. Only ten minutes remaining for the oppressor of his kind to get to his business, as he espies a man in the street, he offers him a half-dollar for instant help in harnessing the horse. The man answers reluctantly that, though he needs money to buy bread for his own family, the hostlers on either side of the street had warned him of a broken head, if he should interfere with the rights of labor in that stricken household.

Fables have illustrated truth since literature began. Though these incidents seem grotesque in the relation, they differ in no essential principle from daily occurrences in our industrial life, when it is disorganized by the irruption of strange and unnatural forces. These new powers, seizing the latest forms of organization,— created to construct,— turn them to the destruction of the organisms of industry. The sudden shock of a strike jars down the whole delicate fabric of industry, and deranges the social order on which that fabric rests. The mischief done,— the vital forces of production destroyed,— then a judicial procedure is proposed, and arbitration is summoned to award justice,— justice, where contracts are broken, property destroyed, personal rights and liberty overwhelmed by mob violence, either committed or apprehended and feared. There is not a tittle of exaggeration in the allegory. Industrial life is even more complex than domestic households. These fantastic situations, not present, but possible, only bring home to each individual man and woman the keen anguish which industrial leaders directly, the whole community indirectly, suffer from the arrogant action of hordes drilled to ape the ways of civilization, to use civilized forces to destroy the organisms civilization has built up.

The incidents of the fable are not chosen hap-hazard. The questions agitating society are not economic alone, or in the greatest part. Sentiment as well as self-interest impels men to attack the present social order. Wages are wanted, but more is wanted. A new deal is sought, not only in money and property, but in all the social advantages accumulated by experience and culture. The disturbances proceed not from the bitter cry of outcast society. It is well-paid labor which demands more and yet more, excluding and maltreating all orders of society not so well conditioned as itself. An enormous majority vote, using the secret methods of a despotism, is to crush the present order of society, and right the wrongs of labor.

For concrete information, let us review briefly the main facts of one strike as it occurred last spring. This deranged or suspended totally the industries of half a dozen great States,—the territory of an empire. The difficulty began in the discharge from the Texas Pacific Railway Company of a foreman in their shops at Marshall, named Hall. Captain Henry, of Cleveland, Ohio, was delegated by the United States Circuit Court to investigate the facts afterward. He stated that Hall was a "worthless workman by reason of his indifference to his duties, his attention being absorbed in studying the rules of the Knights of Labor, and devoting time to committee work for his order that should have been given to the railroad company." Captain Henry examined the company's books; and, under Hall's foremanship, the work in the shops "had cost the company fifty per cent. more than it did under his predecessor." The strike, first on the Texas Pacific, then on the Missouri Pacific, was ordered by Martin Irons. And who was he? Born in Scotland, a machinist by trade, a rover in fact, he had been a Knight of Labor about one year. After three months' service, he became Master of his Local Assembly. In a few weeks more, he was Chairman of the Executive Board of District Assembly No. 101. This made him virtual dictator of thirty Local Assemblies from Missouri into Texas, with about five thousand members, bound by oath to obey the orders of the Chairman. Irons made a written statement, to the Congressional Committee of investigation of this strike, of the reasons why he ordered it. He stated that delegates of the Knights of Labor were sitting at Marshall just before Hall was discharged. The discharge was regarded as a slight to the order, and Irons tried to get him reinstated. Passes for three to Dallas were given to Hall, where grievances and Hall's discharge were to be discussed. The board of Knights of Labor numbered five. Moreover, the passes were handed to Hall, and not to Irons. He regarded this act as another slight on the order, and declined to use the passes or to go to Dallas, telegraphing to that effect. He telegraphed again that, unless a reply came by two o'clock the next day, he should call out the men. He received no reply, and did call the men out. "Seeing it was useless to hope for an adjustment of grievances, he afterward called out the Missouri Pacific men." These are Irons's own statements, in substance. The Congressional Committee pressed him to know what the grievances of the men actually were, and what he had done for settlement of them before ordering the strikes. He reluctantly admitted that, in the only specific grievance ever submitted to Mr. Hoxie or his officers of the Missouri Pacific, he carried his point, and it was remedied. Now, we must understand that, in the vocabulary of the Knights of Labor, a "grievance" is a sentimental injury,—not only an injustice, but a wound. We must try to comprehend this Irons, an Oriental potentate,—in dirty shirt and brass jewelry, filthy, and reeking with tobacco,—and to appreciate his chivalric sensibilities as they were lacerated by slights to his order. Goethe thought highly of the manufacturers as "mediators" between the needs of labor and the hard instincts of capital. But this new order of elective kings displays the wrath of despots rather than the sympathy of intercessors or the equity of judges.

Despot is a hard name, but it may represent a very good thing. Despotism may mean good social order and the best adaptation of means to ends. What evidence is there that this new ruler would or could better the issues he raised, or that he even tried to comprehend them? In fact, 3,717 workers struck, assigning no definite reason, and forced out of employment 10,598 other workers on this railway system, who were contented with their lot. When Irons was questioned by the Congressional Committee of the number of strikers, he answered, "About five thousand." When asked how many more it affected, he said, "It is no concern of mine." Did he not know "that nine thousand men in the lumber business had to stop work on account of your strike"? "No: I don't concern myself with a census of the United States." Boycotts on the Texas Pacific and the Wabash systems were ordered, with as little consideration, according to his testimony,—"An injury to one in the order is an injury to all." "Missionaries" were sent out by the Executive Board to persuade men to strike. The results of the missions appear in the testimony of Joseph Cramer, who was ordered verbally, and afterward in writing, to report to the Master Workman at De Soto, Mo. The Master Workman ordered him to assist "to stop trains." He refused. "'Very well. You needn't do anything, but you can go and swell the crowd.' I replied, I didn't propose to violate any laws or make myself a criminal in any way. He told me I was a coward." This conversation was in the Knights of Labor hall. Cramer was afterwards expelled "for refusing to stop trains and damage the railroad property."

Every "missionary" has a gospel which impels him to his work. What is this new gospel? A witness before our committee read from shorthand notes a speech of Irons at a Knights of Labor meeting at East St. Louis. "Talk to the scabs. Go to their houses, and talk to their wives, and make them quit. Do everything you can to make them come out; and, if they won't, give them some pills, and —— them out. To hell with the Chinese! To hell with the scabs! We won in the Chinese fight, and we will win this."

It might be presumed from these utterances in a civilized country that a "scab" is a leper or unclean person, to be cast out from his kind. But he is simply a man holding his own opinion, and trying to exercise his right of judgment,—such a man as Philip and Alva, of Spain, roasted. Martin Irons is out of fashion just now; but turn to the testimony before our Committee of Litchman, First General Secretary of the whole order of Knights of Labor, who went to St. Louis as the authorized representative of Mr. Powderly. In defining a "scab," Litchman was asked, "Do you not acknowledge the right of any man to work and earn wages, and support his family?" *A.*—"When you put the question abstractly in that way, I must answer it, 'Yes.' But I do not acknowledge the right of any man, at the time a great conflict is raging between labor and capital, to step in between, and scab."

In this case, "stepping in" means the conduct of men like Cramer, regularly at work, trying to do their duty and obey law, and not men seeking a new job, as it sometimes means. The power is assumed and exercised by these labor associations of extending strikes and boycotts into the business of any and all innocent parties. This deserves especial consideration from all students of political philosophy, for it goes deep into the roots of social order. A dispute affecting labor in any way, once begun, no consideration of justice or mercy can restrain the will of the order. That works, *ex cathedra*, by direct inspiration, and can make no mistake. When the Missouri strike wavered, it was proposed to strike and boycott coal mines, to bring the railways to terms. Mr. Bailey, of General Executive Board Knights of Labor, was reported as saying they would repeat the programme until all coal mining was stopped in Illinois. "Will not that cause immense suffering among innocent people?" "Probably. So does war cause immense suffering among innocent people. If the coal company refuses to accede to our demand, it is they who are responsible for the consequences, not we."

It may be asserted that Irons is not a fair type of the controlling powers in this new *imperium in imperio;* that a new order of leaders is being developed, capable of leading laborers and capitalists—all society—into better and more prosperous paths. Men like Irons always take the initiative, when a crisis arrives. But consider Powderly, the master of them all. Is his course wiser, more consistent, and more masterly, though it may lack the tigerish ferocity of Irons? He palavers about his responsibility, greater than that of kings or presidents. What does he do? In the grasp of a strong intellect, like Gould's, he loses his initiative, and bends his policy to the stronger will. Then, beaten in tactics, he shrieks like a fish-wife. He shouts hard names, and appeals to the passions of unreason throughout the whole land. Is this the work of one greater than a statesman,—a democratic Bismarck? In spite of Powderly's orderly and amiable talk, in his heart he believes in the irresponsible force at his back. Irons testified, "Labor produces everything: capital produces nothing at all." Powderly's acts confirm the same dogma. In his talk about the militia, he did not reveal any capacity of seeing in the musket the right arm of the law. He saw a lot of individuals, each one a laborer, or who might be a laborer. Therefore, he would handle his musket as labor might direct, not as the law directs. Powderly has not the first conception of the organism of society, order, law, justice, or administration. Labor does not make a railroad, nor even a shovel. Labor does not create, it cannot create. Social order, civilization, law, accumulated capital, give his opportunity to the laborer. As a laborer, he has nothing but his hands.

No massing of forces, votes of majorities of Knights, or edicts of Lichmans and Powderlys, can reverse this eternal principle: Naked thou came into the world, naked thou shalt return. These prevalent notions that Labor is a sacred essence, and the laborer its high priest, superior to all law and all experience, are absurd. If not so tragical in their results, they would be ridiculous.

An observer from another planet would say, If your premises be sound, whence the conclusion? If this be the genesis of strikes, how comes it that strikes get headway, and inflict such injury? Here is the effect, present, effective. Where and whence is the cause? How can a highly civilized community give way to the passions of barbarism, and submit to barbaric havoc? We answer: The cause is not remote: it is nearer than most of us think, within reach of any average intelligence. The cause is in you, here, now,— latent, but potential.

Pure socialism has but few advocates. It has been well said that its apostles divide into two parties and pursue two ideals. The one is absolutist,— absorbing all the productive and directing forces of society, like banks, railroads, factories, and property, into the State, substituting "scientific stirpiculture" for the family. The other is democratic, tending to anarchism, making any individual will the sole authority, superseding all government, all combination for political or social ends,— a universal *laissez-faire*. Neither of these fancies, which dominate certain small fractions of people, possesses you. Nor do they possess the laborers and workingmen to any great extent. But they affect you in your daily walk and thought, as they affect the workman at his bench or in the halls of his order. A socialistic fervor is in the air. Each generation likes experiment, and the old proven ways are prosy and dull.

When the Texas and Missouri Pacific strike began, New York as well as other intelligent communities sympathized with the strikers. Men of business and the public generally said: Well, those fellows are not getting much. Jay Gould has a great deal. Let them get more. It is so easy to disgorge others' wealth. Such ample justice rules the average economic juror as he reads telegraphic reports of distant troubles, and calmly awards a dividend of others' goods.

But soft! The fungus became decay, rot and disease seized the body politic. Transportation throttled, eight hours demanded at the price of ruin, industry palsied, farmers ruined, with barns full of crops, builders halted, contracts stopped,— Heaven spare us! This is our property, our prosperity, our social order. We meant Jay Gould. Capital is so informed with order and prosperity, so linked in every chain that binds each part of the body politic into one whole, that even the hated capitalists became dear. In the twinkling of an eye, the trembling citizens, seeing the spectre of industrial anarchy hovering over their own firesides, turned, and thought the hard sense and worldly wisdom of Jay Gould was worth saving, however unlovely his whole character might be.

I alluded to the attempt of the Executive Board Knights of Labor to stop the mining of coal, and to compel the Missouri Pacific to terms. When the general eight-hour movement was projected, the labor managers intended, if necessary, to bring on a general cessation of industry, and thus to force a shortening of the hours of labor. Direct proof of this is unnecessary. Such was the dream of the International in Europe. It is the natural and inevitable evolution of the idea underlying the Knights of Labor movement. Such a body must drift toward such a crisis, to complete logically the purpose which starts to control all society according to the will of labor.

It was unfortunate that this purpose was not worked out and accomplished. The shock of the Chicago bombs and the deaths among the gallant police ended the concordant movement of socialism and labor agitation. This wholesale murder with foul weapons drew the line between violence abhorrent to all healthy public opinion and violence which might hope to divide an obtuse public and to array a party on the side of the labor agitators. But it would have made the solution of the American problem shorter and simpler, if a general suspension of transportation and industry had been precipitated. The Anglo-Saxons have learned how to deal with political problems tending toward revolution or anarchy. We should have then learned how to treat industrial anarchy, a much more terrible situation. If the strike had been consummated in the whole land east of the Mississippi, probably flour would have moulded in Minneapolis at the same moment that it was selling in New York at fifty dollars per barrel. There are five hundred thousand, possibly seven hundred thousand, Knights of Labor. There are some seventeen out of sixty millions who labor directly for their own support. It has been fairly estimated that, if the wildest theory of the most capable agitator could be realized, not over five to six millions could ever be massed into one organization, like the Knights of Labor. How long would the whole people have submitted to the rule of these five hundred thousand tyrants, as it rent their social system and brought actual famine into the land? The people, the whole people, would have made short work of the universal strikers.

Since the Chicago massacre, the Knights of Labor have shrieked loud, and spluttered that they did not believe in bombs or in anything else not nice. They have tried to avoid the odium of anarchy. It is true, as I have stated, that the Knights of Labor and hardly any workingman believe in socialism, pure and simple. Almost to a man, they believe in property, in the family, in some form of law and order which yet admits the disorder of their order. But the socialistic ideal affects their demands.

It is so commonly asserted that labor in itself and out of itself produces all the goods on which society rests that few consider how absurd and impossible the dogma is. Claimants should show at least one social system in which the laborer has produced the goods on which that system depended. In historic fact, how has labor been initiated, moved, or controlled? The savage directed his captive to labor; the barbarian directed his slave to labor; the fief-holder directed his vassal; the feudatory paid wage to his servant. As matters go to-day, who controls the workingman, laborer, trades-unionist? The employer? Not at all. Our admitted facts show that, though the employer may pay wages, just as a bank-teller pays a check, he has no control of the laborer beyond the certification of his wages in his contract. This is a disputed point in political economy. But I am considering the facts and the modern principles of action from the laborer's point of view and that of his especial advocates. In fact, the only absolute director and controller of the workingman to-day is the dollar. The mint-stamp of society, the direct force of money, is the only ruler recognized to-day by those holding the dogma that labor produces all things,— those purblind philosophers who cannot see that wealth is produced by all the powers of society, the mutual exercise of mutual desire, all together producing that living, constant demand for service, out of which labor, as labor, gets its opportunity and its reward. A short way to the dollar is the ultimate of the new doctrines and the new demands of labor.

The Knights of Labor, in convention at Cleveland, June 1, as reported, said, in a petition to Congress, "that, while human labor produces all wealth, those who have performed no honest labor have amassed the most of the wealth, and those who have performed the labor have least to enjoy; that we feel this state of things to be largely due to both vicious legislation and want of proper legislation by Congress. . . . In one part of the country, money is worth only two per cent. per annum; in another, twelve per cent.; in another, twenty per cent. . . . That you fix the measure of value by establishing a just, uniform, and invariable rate for money loaned." In the bill recommended to Congress with this petition was a provision "for the loaning of money by the government at three per cent. per annum."

This notion that a socialistic use of the powers of government, first in finance, and finally in all productive forces, will result in special benefit to labor, is one fallacy. Another is that the less there is produced, the more will be distributed; that less hours of work will afford more comforts and more culture (for a definite statement, see George Gunton in *Forum*, vol. i., p. 138). These two fallacies underlie the whole labor movement in our country.

I have outlined the motives and issues of strikes, and of the theories prompting the labor movement, not merely to arraign and condemn them. I would depict the actual forces working in the minds and passions of laborers on the one hand, and the attitude of the whole people, the tendency of public opinion, on the other, in order to explain the processes of arbitration, which is my main theme. Whatever our view of the present, we must take things as they are. Our present business is to search for any idea, any concept, which may promise to check the drift toward the chaos of strikes. Attempts to amend the situation proceed generally from theories, which class themselves in these three divisions: —

I. *Laissez-faire*, or unlimited competition; the individual right to let or hire, never interfered with, but always sustained, by legislation. To this, critics rejoin that legislation has already interfered largely with contract and with independent production; that the natural competition of each with each, of group with group, has been nullified by combinations of laborers on one side, and by closer and more thorough organizations of employers pending on the other; that peaceful industry is gone; that hostile camps have replaced the old quiet; that a new social order, though in transition, is nevertheless at work.

II. Co-operation and Profit-sharing. This method is expected by many theorists to absorb the better energies of capital, capitalizers, and laborers, to take away motives for conflict by a more harmonious joint action. Many instances of failure and a few notable successes can be shown here. Probably, most agree with Mr. Carnegie that, if successful, it would be remote; that now, under present conditions, there would be twenty failures to one success.

III. Arbitration and Conciliation. Those who have seen most of the actual conflicts of this generation, both here and in Europe, recommend arbitration, formally constituted and sanctioned by legislation, or by a public opinion more powerful than any law. It is practically established in the hosiery and manufactured iron trades in England. Indeed, both failures and successes can be cited in great numbers. But the advocates claim that, on the whole, the method gathers strength, and justifies itself.

At best, any change must be a choice of evils. If American industry had developed on its own lines, competition would have regulated the interplay of capital and labor. But alien elements have interfered. Together with the great benefits of immigration, we have received the defects and vices of a heterogeneous and undisciplined horde.

In this effervescence of social and industrial activity, arbitration fills the air. Every striker talks of it, after he has done all the mischief possible. Then he turns to this shibboleth, as if it were a panacea for all ills. The icy Mr. Gould appears to be as ready for this adjustment of difficulties as the most inflammatory agitator. What is it, what is in it, that it should possess the imagination of the time?

An arbiter is one who goes to see the matter in hand, hence an examiner or judge. Arbitrators are chosen by opposite parties in dispute to decide the difference. Two parties of arbitrators choose the final referee,—an umpire or odd-numbered arbitrator. Arbitrary and arbitrariness mean either capriciousness or despotism, will inspired by fancy or will absolute. Here the judicial essence is inverted, and becomes the desire of the disputant converted into irresistible force. Note the Knights of Labor development. A grievance exists. Call Knights of Labor to arbitrate it; the order is offended; a strike and stoppage of industry; destruction of property, violence, perhaps murder. If arbitration is to be the court of judicature of the coming generation, if the will of employer and the passions of employed are to be subjected to courts whose decrees shall be stronger than the common law, then society has something yet to learn. Order must be established before any court can sit, and established much more thoroughly, for a court of arbitration.

There have been efforts and tinkering by legislatures, but nothing like arbitration in its true sense, in this country. Conciliation in the form of arbitration has been effected in a few instances,—notably by Straiton and Storms, cigar manufacturers of New York, and by Mr. Washburne, among shoe manufacturers in Philadelphia. But a general submission of disputants to an even serene justice is far away from our present mood.

I assume that labor associations are permanent. That workingmen will cast themselves into one great Asiatic despotism, like the Knights of Labor,—this seems hardly conceivable. Or that they will federate in local and special assemblies, more like the English trades-unions. Either mode involves stronger and stronger combinations of employers for resistance. The strike is here, and well known. The lock-out has hardly begun, especially in our older communities. These combatants will be supported by you. Did labor *qua* labor create you? You hold the supplies, and finally recruit both Capital and Labor. Wisdom is shy and rare: we cannot expect much from her; but exhaustion and prostration may bring a desire for peace, and arbitration may accomplish itself. I think Mr. Weeks—the most experienced student of this subject—is correct, when he says the future arbitration must be voluntary, and not enforced by legislation. Legal or State arbitration has succeeded in France and Belgium. For that reason, it is not likely to succeed in a community differing so much as ours.

I have cast the thoughts suggested by this study into several propositions, as follows:—

I. Arbitration proper begins after all methods of conciliation, by conference or by negotiation of grievances, have been exhausted. Arbitration is a submission of the will of both parties to judges, disinterested and beyond the pale of dispute.

II. Arbitration implies an organized industrial system. The employers must be associated in fact or in sympathetic accord. The employed must be banded together, acting under trained leaders, trusted from long experience. The sanction would come from the deliberate action of these representative bodies, supported by the larger judgment of the whole people. Arbitration would be through a joint board, selected equally from disinterested representatives of employers and employed. The board would choose an umpire, and a decision of the majority must be binding on the disputants.

III. No strike, lock-out, or any suspension of work can be permitted while arbitration is pending.

IV. The right of employers to hire and discharge must be conceded.

V. No interference with employers or employed, by individual or joint action, by boycott, employers' black list, or violence of any kind, can be permitted by any of the parties to systematic arbitration.

VI. Voluntary agreement to submit to arbitration, backed by industrial sentiment and confirmed by public sentiment, will be a more effective sanction than any legislation.

It is easy to criticise these propositions, to show that they are impracticable under present conditions. It is as easy to prove that no progress is possible until workingmen and the general public shall be educated and disciplined enough to make some similar system effective. You may or may not like employers and capitalists, the present trustees of industry. You will not better them until you lift the whole constituency into a larger sense of law and order. No arbitration, no co-operation or profit-sharing, can be administered until labor agitators and workingmen are forced — yea, compelled — to see that they must respect the rights of others. Here is the key to the whole problem. The principle has been worked out politically. The State has enlarged its basis until it rests securely on the rights of all. It is for you and those like you to apply the principle to the industrial and social system which underlies the State. We washed our land in blood to right the slave. Have we not force enough, moral and physical, to protect the "scab" and "knobstick," with the victim of the boycott?

I do not argue with workingmen or labor agitators. They have their own modes of discussion. The matter is at the bar of public opinion. My question is with society as a whole. Preachers, publicists, politicians, and speculative thinkers have encouraged, by various means, the agitation in our country, until it has culminated in the organization known as the Knights of Labor. It is time that they show cause why. The consequence is on you, the issue is yours. You have to deal, not with a body of men and women in their capacity of citizens of the United States, but with a horde banded for one arbitrary purpose. This horde is not moved by the genius of a Timur or a Gengis. It is directed by the ferocity of an Irons, and animated by the feeble sentiment of a Powderly. Remand these disturbers of the public peace to the ranks of the people. Then arbitration and other forms of public order will be made easy, by the people and for the people.

REPORT

ON THE

Practical Operation of Arbitration and Conciliation

IN THE

SETTLEMENT OF DIFFERENCES BETWEEN EMPLOYERS AND EMPLOYEES IN ENGLAND.

BY JOS. D. WEEKS,

SPECIAL COMMISSIONER OF THE STATE OF PENNSYLVANIA,
ASSOCIATE EDITOR OF THE IRON AGE, ETC.

HARRISBURG:
LANE S. HART, PRINTER AND BINDER,
1879.

REPORT

ON THE

Practical Operation of Arbitration and Conciliation in the Settlement of Differences between Employers and Employees in England. By Jos. D. Weeks, Special Commissioner of the State of Pennsylvania, Associate Editor of the Iron Age, etc.

PITTSBURGH, *December 26, 1878.*

SIR: I have the honor to forward you the accompanying report of my investigations, the past summer, into the practical operations of arbitration in settling differences between employers and employed in England.

I found, at the beginning of my inquiries, that though there were at least three laws on the statute books of England on this subject, they were virtually dead letters, and, therefore, I directed my attention to the workings of the voluntary Boards of Arbitration and Conciliation, that exist in a number of the trades of that country, and have given, in this report, some account of their operations, with copies of the rules of the most important. These rules will be found in appendices to the report, together with the latest act of Parliament on the subject of arbitration.

The condition of the laboring class, and the strength and extent of the labor organizations, were subjects to which I was forced to devote considerable attention, in order to correctly understand and appreciate the workings of arbitration; but I have touched upon these subjects incidentally, and only so far as was necessary to an understanding of the difficulties to be overcome.

I have to make grateful acknowledgements of the uniform kindness with which I was met, and the readiness with which every facility was extended to me for acquiring information. I should make a special acknowledgement, however, to Mr. Rupert Kettle, judge of the county courts of Worcestershire; Mr. A. J. Mundella, M. P.; Mr. B. Samuelson, M. P.; Mr. Thomas Burt, M. P., representative of the colliers; Mr. Ed. Trow, secretary of the National Amalgamated Iron Workers Association; Mr. George Howell, formerly secretary of the parlimentary committee of the Trades Union Congress; Mr. George Broadhurst, present secretary of the same; Mr. Alsager Hay Hill, editor of the *Labour News*; Mr. W. H. S. Aubery, editor of *Capital and Labour*, and especially to Mr. Charles Wheeler, of Wolverhampton, who was most earnest in his aid and most helpful in forwarding my inquiries.

I would most respectfully suggest that this subject is worthy of a more extended investigation than I was enabled to give it in the time at my disposal, and I would recommend that some legislation be adopted to this end, and also that the inquiry be extended so as to include the workings of this principle in other European countries, as well as to the condition of labor.

Very respectfully,

JOS. D. WEEKS.

To His Excellency JOHN F. HARTRANFT, *Governor of Pennsylvania.*

SECTION I.

PRELIMINARY. CONSEILS DES PRUD' HOMMES.

ARBITRATION IN ENGLAND PRIOR TO 1860.

Industrial arbitration and concilation had their origin in France early in the present century. The system established was the outgrowth of the trade guilds which had existed in that country and regulated trade matters, in some cases from the Middle Ages. These were abolished during the last days of the monarchy of Louis XVI, a time when the constitution of industrial as well as political society was being overturned. After a few years of imperfect legislation, in 1806, at the request of the workingmen of Lyons and by command of the First Napoleon, courts of arbitration and conciliation were established by law. These, with some slight modication, have continued until the present under the title of "*Conseils des Prud' hommes.*" These councils are judicial tribunals, constituted under authority of the Minister of Commerce, through the Chambers of Commerce, which are established at important trade centers of that country. They are composed of an equal number of employer and workingmen members, each class electing its own representatives, with a president and vice president named by the Government. The authority of these councils extends to every conceivable question that can arise in the workshop, not only between the workman and his employer, but between the workman and his apprentice or his foreman. There is but one question they cannot settle—future rates of wages; but even this can be done by mutual agreement. Arbitration is compulsory upon the application of either, and the decisions of the court can be enforced the same as those of any other court of law.

The workings of these courts have been beneficial to French industry, especially in conciliation, by which more than ninety per cent. of all cases brought before the tribunals are settled. In 1847, the sixty-nine councils then in existence had before them nineteen thousand two hundred and seventy-one cases, of which seventeen thousand nine hundred and fifty-one were settled by conciliation in the private bureau, five hundred and nineteen more by open conciliation, and in only five hundred and twenty-nine cases was it necessary to have formal judgment. In 1850, of twenty-eight thousand cases, twenty-six thousand and eight hundred were settled by conciliation. There were, at the close of 1874, one hundred and twelve councils in France. This is a most satisfactory showing, but it falls far short of expressing the great benefit these councils have been to French industry, especially in removing causes of differences or in preventing them from growing into disputes. Their success is sufficient justification of the praise so lavishly bestowed upon them by M. Chevalier: "*Une des plus nobles créations dont notre siecle l'honore.*"

Tribunals similar to the *Conseils des Prud' hommes*, of France, are in existence in Belgium. Their success, however, has not been as marked as in France, owing in part, no doubt, to the fact that they have in some cases criminal jurisdiction.

In Great Britain, though a law somewhat similar in its character to that of France, and evidently framed from it, has been on the statute books since the fifth year of the reign of George IV, (1824,) so little use has been made of its provisions that its existence was practically forgotten. England did not possess the organizations necessary to its successful workings, and the compulsory features seem especially obnoxious to both employer and employed. As Mr. Rupert Kettle, to whom the cause of industrial arbitration owes such a heavy debt, says: "It is agreed that, according to the spirit of our laws and the freedom of our people, any procedure, to be popular, must be accepted voluntarily by both contending parties."* The history of arbitration and conciliation in Great Britain fully justifies this remark.

Previous to 1860, a year which marks an epoch in the history of industrial arbitration in England, it had frequently been applied to the settlement of industrial disputes. Legal sanctions, however, were never sought for the awards. They were loyally accepted without any constraint, except a man's sense of honor, and a certain *esprit du corps*, both among the employers and employed. These arbitrations were not only frequent, but in some trades were systematically used in every dispute which arose. The pottery trade furnishes a very good example of continuous and successful arbitration. In this industry, one of the most difficult in which to harmonize the conflicting views of capital and labor, by reason of the large number of trades into which labor is divided, and the peculiar customs that have come to be regarded as rights, in this trade there has not been a general strike since 1836, and the reason given is that disputes have been invariably settled by arbitration. The yearly "contracts for hiring," contained the following clause: "If any dispute arise between the parties as to the prices or wages to be paid, by virtue of such an agreement, the dispute shall be referred to an arbitration board of six persons, to consist of three manufacturers, chosen by the masters, and three working potters, elected by the workingmen." This clause does not provide for a board to settle future rates of wages, but both sides have formed what may be called the habit of arbitrating, and they have appealed to this principle in trouble. As a result, for over thirty years this clause has prevented strikes in this trade.

It is not necessary to extend this report by giving other examples, showing the history and success of arbitration, prior to 1860. It was often appealed to in many trades, though in none does it appear to have worked as well, or to have been tried so continuously, as in the pottery trade. There had, as the result of these trials, grown up, especially among the work people, a decided feeling in favor of industrial arbitration and a willingness to give it a trial, which, doubtless, rendered the attempts to establish it as a principle much surer of success.

SECTION II.

THE ESTABLISHMENT OF VOLUNTARY PERMANENT BOARDS OF ARBITRATION AND CONCILIATION IN ENGLAND.

DIFFERENCE BETWEEN ARBITRATION AND CONCILIATION.

As already stated, the year 1860, marked an epoch in the history of arbitration and conciliation in Great Britain, and gave it a new character, one more in accordance with the tone of modern thought and the changed relations of capital and labor. Late in that year, mainly through the efforts of Mr. A. J. Mundella, the first permanent or continuous board of arbitration and conciliation in England was established, in the hosiery and glove trade, at Nottingham. Mr. Henry Crompton in his admirable little work on "Industrial Conciliation," in speaking of the establishment

---

*Strikes and Arbitrations, page 26. London, 1866.

of this board says,* "Mr. Mundella must be regarded as the inventor of systematic industrial conciliation." In view of the fact stated in the previous section, that the large majority of cases brought before the *Conseils des Prud' hommes* were settled by conciliation in the private bureau, this claim can hardly be made for Mr. Mundella. The distinguishing feature of the board organized by his efforts, and at the same time the marked characteristic of arbitration since 1860, is that it is systematic conciliation or arbitration organized on a purely voluntary basis, without an appeal to legal processes, even to enforce its decisions. That is, its novelty is not that it is systematic—the French *Conseils* were that—but that it is both systematic and voluntary, and these the French prototype were not.

The voluntary feature of these boards is one to which I desire to call particular attention. Both Mr. Mundella and Mr. Kettle, to whom the cause of arbitration and conciliation in England owes much that it is, and who represent somewhat diverse views on the subject, agree that these boards should be voluntary, and not compulsory. Though there are acts of Parliament which provide compulsory legal powers, by which either side can compel the other to arbitrate on any dispute, these powers have never, in a single instance, so far as I could learn, been used; but the large number of differences that have been settled by arbitration in Great Britain in the last eighteen years, have all been voluntary in their submission, and in the enforcement of the award. Mr. Kettle would provide, that in certain cases, the awards should become part of the contract between the employer and the employed, to be enforced at law as any other contract; but as these contracts can be terminated by a short time notice, it does not take away from the voluntary nature of the arbitrations under what is known as the Wolverhampton system. How this voluntary feature has worked in practice, will be evident in the course of this report.

In discussing this subject, it is very important at the outset to distinguish between arbitration and conciliation. Though the former is a generic word, and the one more commonly used in referring to the system, there is an essential and important difference between arbitration and conciliation. Unless this is clearly impressed on the mind, and the scope and working of each clearly understood, it will be impossible to learn the secret of the success that has attended these boards, and the reason of their continued existence. Arbitration deals with the larger questions of trade, conciliation with the smaller. Arbitration with the whole trade, conciliation oftener with the individuals. Conciliation is not formal; it does not attempt to sit in judgment and decide in a given case what is right and what is wrong, but its efforts are, in a friendly spirit, to adjust differences by inducing the parties to agree themselves. It removes causes of dissentions and prevents differences from becoming disputes, by establishing a cordial feeling between those who may be parties to the same. Conciliation, in a word, may be defined as informal arbitration. Arbitration, on the other hand, is formal. It sits in judgment. It implies that matters in dispute by mutual consent or by previous contract have been submitted to arbiters, and an umpire, whose decision is final and binding on both parties. Mr. Crompton, in his work on "Industrial Conciliation," says* when contrasting arbitration and conciliation, "conciliation aims at something higher—at doing before the fact that which arbitration accomplishes after. It seeks to prevent and remove the causes of dispute before they arise, to adjust differences and claims before they become disputes. A board of conciliation deals with matters that could not be arbitrated upon, promoting

*Page 33. **Page 17.

the growth of beneficial customs, interfering in the smaller details of industrial life, modifying or removing some of the worst evils incidental to modern industry, such, for example, as the truck system, or the wrongs which workmen suffer at the hands of middle-men and overseers."

It is this preventive feature that gives conciliation a value beyond estimation. It is a most admirable and praiseworthy object to provide means for settling disputes when they have arisen. It is much more desirable to prevent them from arising, and the tendency of conciliation is to do this, by removing the old feelings of bitterness, by inspiring respect for each other and fostering, at the same time, a spirit of independence, and compelling a recognition of the dignity and worth of labor and the necessity and beneficence of capital.

And yet, after all that may be said in praise of conciliation, it is conceded, even by its warmest advocates, that back of all conciliation there must be arbitration. The time may come, and in the setttlement of certain questions, generally will come, when no friendly offices are sufficient to enable capital and labor to see alike. Self-interest renders it impossible for either to decide fairly, and something more than a master of ceremonies or a concilator is needed. There must be power to determine as well as hear. That is, arbitration must intervene, and its decisions accomplish what conciliation is powerless to bring about.

To show the workings of arbitration and conciliation, I have given in the following pages a detailed account of the organization and operation of several of the most prominent boards. The records are mainly those of arbitration, not of conciliation, as in war it is the battles that are recorded, not the skirmishes and movements for position.

SECTION III.

THE NOTTINGHAM SYSTEM OF ARBITRATION AND CONCILIATION.

The so-called Nottingham system of arbitration or conciliation owes its establishment to Mr. A. J. Mundella, at present one of the members for Sheffield of the House of Commons. Mr. Mundella has been most earnest and untiring in his efforts to make arbitration the prevailing and recognized method of settling all disputes that may arise between labor and capital, and it is not too much to say, that to his intelligent efforts much of the success that has attended conciliation is due.

The hosiery and glove trade, with which Mr. Mundella is connected, is one of the most localized in Great Britain, being carried on only in the immediate vicinity of Nottingham, in Nottinghamshire, Derbyshire, and Leicestershire. I need not point out that such a concentration of one class of skilled labor led to union, and a consequent power not always judiciously used. According to all accounts, the relations between employers and employed in these trades, prior to 1860, were as ugly as could well be imagined. From 1710 to 1820, there is a frightful list of murders, riots, arsons, and machine-breaking recorded, all arising out of industrial differences. An act was passed by Parliament, early in the century, punishing machine-breaking with death, and in 1816 six persons suffered this penalty. In the remaining forty years of the century and a half, from 1710, while the worst features of this industrial strife nearly or quite disappeared, the relations were in no wise improved, though the strife assumed a different form. Suspicion, distrust, hatred, were the sentiments cherished towards the manufacturers by the workmen; and arrogance, oppression, and an equally strong hatred were returned. War, or at least an illy-kept armistice, was the condition of the hostile camps. Strikes and lock-outs were constantly occurring, and no judicious, honest effort was made to end them. In 1860, there were three strikes in one of the three branches into which the hosiery trade is divided, one lasting eleven weeks. It was during this strike that the board of arbitration and conciliation was formed. Though the strike was confined to one branch, it was soon discovered that it was supported by the workingmen in the other branches, and, in what they considered self-defense, it was proposed by the manufacturers to lock out the entire body of workingmen in all branches. Some of the manufacturers, Mr. Mundella among them, shrank from the misery and suffering, and perphaps crime, that would be the result. "Some of us thought, says Mr. Mundella,* "that we might devise some better means of settling the thing. I had heard of the *Conseils des Prud' hommes* in France, and with one or two others I built up a scheme in my imagination of what I thought might be done to get a good understanding with our men, and regulate wages."

At a meeting of the manufacturers, a committee of three was appointed to invite the workmen to a conference, which they accepted. "We three," to quote Mr. Mundella again,* "met perhaps a dozen leaders of the trades union, and we consulted with these men, told them that the present plan was a bad one, that it seemed to us that they took every advantage of us when we had a demand, and we took every advantage of them when trade was bad, and it was a system mutually predatory. And there is no doubt that it was so; we pressed down the price as low as we could and they pressed up the price as high as they could. This often caused a strike in pressing it down and a strike in getting it up; and these strikes were most ruinous and injurious to all parties, because when we might have been supplying our customers, our machinery was idle, and we suggested whether we could not try some better scheme. Well, the men were very suspicious at first; indeed, it is impossible to describe to you how suspiciously we looked at each other. Some of the manufacturers also deprecated our proceedings, and said that we were degrading them, and humiliating them, and so on. However, we had some ideas of our own, and we went on with them; and we sketched out what we called a Board of Arbitration and Conciliation."

The result of this action was the formation of "The Board of Arbitration and Conciliation in the Glove and Hosiery Trade," the first permanent board established. The rules adopted were very simple,† and have worked so well in most particulars, that they have hardly been amended since the day they were made. The object of the board is declared to be to arbitrate on any question of wages that may be referred to it, and to endeavor, by conciliatory means, to put an end to any disputes that may arise. The board consists of twenty-two members, half operatives and half manufacturers, elected for one year, each class electing its own representatives. The delegates have full powers, and the decisions of the board are considered binding upon all. There is provision for a committee of inquiry to whom all differences must be referred before the board will act upon them. This committee has no power to make an award, acting only as conciliators. A month's notice is to be given to the secretaries, before any change

*Trades Union's Commission, 1867. Tenth report, p. 74.

†A copy of the rules will be found in appendix A.

in the rate of wages will be considered. Regular meetings are held quarterly. The chairman, in the original constitution of the board, had a vote, and a casting vote as well in case of a tie. This was one of the weak points in the organization, and, as the chairman was an employer, trouble resulted. Mr. Mundella, who was the first chairman of the board, speaking of this, says: "I have a casting vote, and twice that casting vote has got us into trouble. And for the last four years it has been resolved that we would not vote at all. Even when a working man was convinced, or a master convinced, he did not like acting against his own order, and in some instances we had secessions in consequence of that, so we said, 'Do not let us vote again, let us try if we can agree,' and we did agree."

In the Wolverhampton system this error was avoided. An independent umpire or referee was elected by the board, whose decision was final and binding in case of an equal vote by the board. The Nottingham board has also changed its rule, and the chairman no longer gives a casting vote, a referee appointed for the occasion being called in in case of a failure to agree. I cannot but regard the Wolverhampton system of a referee elected previous to a "dead lock," as much the better plan. This is the course adopted in the lace trade of Nottingham.

The proceedings under these rules are very simple. When any difference arises between employers and employed, the secretaries endeavor to arrange it. In the event of their failure, it is brought before the committee of inquiry, who try to settle it, and it being unable, it is then brought before the board. One of the invariable conditions of any arbitration is that work shall be continued pending the trial of the case. That is, that there shall be neither strike nor lock-out. The proceedings before the board are very informal. The members sit aronnd a table, workingmen and employers interspersed. The discussion is without ceremony and the differrence is settled by endeavoring to arrive at the best arrangement possible under the circumstances.

The most serious questions brought before this board are those of wages, which, considering the nature of the trade, are very difficult of adjustment. On this point and of the success that has attended its efforts to adjust wages, Mr. Mundella said in a speech at Bradford: "The articles manufactured in the hosiery trade are exceedingly numerous and varied in character. All work is paid for by the piece, at the rate of so much per dozen. From time immemorial these rates have been fixed by printed statements, and the battles formerly fought were as to whether masters or workmen should make these statements. Since the foundation of the board, all variations in prices, up or down, have been referred to it, and no statement is considered legitimate without the signatures of its members.

"It is very rarely that the price originally proposed by either masters or workmen is the price ultimately agreed to. Some alterations or concessions are generally made on both sides, and the price once fixed, is considered mutually binding. In times of depression, when foreign competition has interfered with any branch, a fair reduction has been generally submitted to, and in times of prosperity, when advances could fairly be given, they have been invariably conceded; but in order that the trade may not be taken by surprise, that manufacturers may finish their contracts in times of advance, and that no hasty decisions may be made against either party, we have a resolution on our minute-book, that a month's notice shall be given before any change of prices can be discussed. Owing to the variable character of the trade, small differences and disputes are constantly arising. Some extra work may be required in an article for which the workman may think a shilling would be proper compensation, while the manufacturer may think six pence is sufficient.

"If the workmen of any branch conceive that they have grievances to complain of, in addition to the ordinary representatives of that branch, a delegation may attend the board, and lay the case fully before them. The first business at our meetings is invariably to receive delegations. They retire after having made their statements, and the board proceeds to deliberate. We have never met without settling at least half a dozen questions, some important and some trivial, which, if allowed to remain open, would produce irritation."

The benefits this board have conferred on the hosiery and glove trades are incalcuable. A most friendly feeling has taken the place of hostility, and confidence and mutual respect exists, when formerly all was suspicion and hatred. This was not the result of a day nor was it accomplished without occasional lapses to the old state of things. The strifes of a century and a half are not so soon forgotten; but troubles in the board have been so infrequent and unimportant, that I am justified in saying that it is a complete success. Strikes and lockouts are unknown; contact has developed respect. The changed relations of employer and employed have been recognized, they have met about the same table as equals, and out of this has grown a condition of affairs that will make it impossible for the old conditions to return.

A large part of the credit of the success of this board, and of this change in the relations of the two classes, is due to the provision for regular meetings of the board. I do not hesitate to say that this is the most valuable feature of these boards. The great curse of industry, and the fruitful cause of difficulty, is a foolish obstinacy and a false pride. This arises in many cases from a want of knowledge and a lack of common courtesy in matters concerning both capital and labor, and in which both have an equal interest. This quarterly coming face to face, this meeting as equals—and, in all questions that can come before these boards, they are equals, and it is foolish to ignore this fact—and this discussing subjects of common interest as sensible men, seeking for the facts, and inclined to moderation and concession, if need be, have had a marvelous effect in removing this pride and obstinacy, and bringing about that respect and courtesy that must be at the basis of all friendly negotiations between capital and labor. These meetings have also given the men a knowledge of the conditions of trade and its necessities, which they could not get in any other way, and, from this knowledge, they have been led to moderation in demands or willingness to concede reductions that otherwise they would not have possessed. If the arbitration features were wholly removed from these boards, and they only retained this feature of quarterly meetings of recognized representatives of trades unions and of manufacturers' associations, their adoption, generally, in this country would be productive of incalculable benefit.

SECTION IV.

THE WOLVERHAMPTON SYSTEM OF ARBITRATION AND CONCILIATION.

Some three years after the establishment of the Nottingham board, a system of arbitration, differing from it in some essential particulars, was adopted in the building trades at Wolverhampton. This plan was worked out without any knowledge on the part of its chief promoter of what had been done at Nottingham. It avoided some of the errors of that plan; but at the same time it lacked some of its admirable features.

The building trades are peculiarly liable to industrial contests. These contests have been not only over wages, but over certain customs of the trade, which have been regarded as rights on the one side, and submitted to on the other from necessity. Building is so much a matter of contract, and the portion of time in a year in which it can be carried on so circumscribed from various causes, that strikes in its trades are very frequent. At Wolverhampton, prior to 1864, these strikes were of common occurrence, and seriously interfered with the business of the town. One in 1863, lasted seventeen weeks, and left a feeling of discontent that promised trouble at the opening of the building season in 1864. To avert this, the mayor called a public meeting of the trades to devise, if possible, some means of preventing the strike. A meeting was accordingly held, at which one branch of the building trade—the carpenters and joiners—appointed six delegates to confer with six delegates of the employers, and endeavor to arrange their differences, the latter appointing six delegates on their part. This was on the 14th of March, 1864. On the 21st of March, the twelve delegates met, and they then saw the propriety of choosing a chairman, who should have a casting vote, before they entered upon any other business. This was done by each party using a list of six names, and means were taken to determine by chance whether the "master's or the men's" list should have priority of consideration. As the first name upon both lists happened to be the same, a chairman was easily chosen. The chairman thus chosen was Mr. Rupert Kettle, judge of the Worcestershire county courts, a gentlemen most admirably fitted for the responsible position of arbitrator he has so often been called to fill; of clear insight, a judicial mind trained by his long experience on the bench, and a most happy faculty of graphic expression. His awards, to quote the language of Mr. Henry Crompton, were "remarkable for very vigorous analysis and skillful unraveling of complicated facts." For ten years Mr. Kettle devoted most of his time to arbitrating industrial disputes, until his judicial duties and private business compelled him reluctantly to decline longer to serve as arbitrator.

The scheme adopted by Mr. Kettle* was a simple but admirable application of the principles of common law. A code of rules is framed; these rules, signed by the arbitrators and umpire, are posted in all the workshops represented in the board, and a copy given each workman on his hiring, he being informed that it is the contract under which he is to work. If any question arises, it is referred to the board, or the conciliation committee under the amended rules, and it is by them decided. Any breach of the rules is a breach of contract, which can be punished the same as the breach of any other contract. It should be noted that this idea of a contract enters much more largely into the question of wages and the relations of employer and employed in England than with us.

These rules, as originally drawn, had no provision for conciliation. All disputes were to be referred to the full board, and the thirteen members brought together to settle the most trivial matters. This was soon found too troublesome, and the conciliation rule (rule No. 2) was adopted. Mr. Kettle says this has been "found in practice more useful than the arbitration rule."

There are two radical differences between this plan and the Nottingham system. The latter provides no method of enforcing the awards of the

*A copy of the rules will be found in Appendix B.

board, while under the Wolverhampton system, provision is made for their enforcement the same as any other contract. As to which system is the best is a question much discussed in England. It is evident that no board can force a manufacturer to run his mill at a loss, nor can he be accused of dishonesty or disloyalty if, when an award goes against him, he closes his mill or mine, if it can only be operated at a loss under the terms of the award. On the other hand, there can be no power to compel a workman to continue work unless he choose. So in these senses it is evident that no provision can be made for enforcing awards, and whether they shall be carried out must be a question left entirely to the will of the parties to the arbitration. Of course, when conciliation is used, there is no question; it must be in all respects voluntary.

There are circumstances, however, in which the awards can and should be enforced at law, and under a scheme that contemplates a code of working rules like those adopted at Wolverhampton, it is perfectly feasible to do so. These rules, and the penalties attached, do not contemplate that a workman may not be at liberty to terminate his contract with his employer, or *vice versa*. It will be seen that this can be done on very short notice; but while the relations of employer and employed continue, they are on certain terms, and when it is desired to end them, there is a business like way of doing it. That most outrageous custom of ceasing work in a pet, at a moment's notice, causing the loss at times of thousands of dollars' worth of half prepared material, as, for example, in the glass trade, when the pots are full of melted glass, cannot occur under these rules, or if it does, there is a remedy at law for breach of contract and damages for loss. Indeed, the business-like methods of some of these rules must commend them to the good common sense and judgment of business men. Mr. Kettle has done an immense service in insisting on the business character of these boards. As the system becomes more perfect, the aim will be to reach in a business-like way what is fair and just under the circumstances, and then to do it.

A second difference in the two systems, is the provision for the election of a permanent arbitrator or umpire. This is a feature which I regard as of the greatest value. Mr. Crompton in his work, though strongly favoring conciliation, confesses that "every board of conciliation must have an ultimate appeal of some kind."* Mr. Mundella found that his method of giving the chairman a casting vote caused trouble. The best plan seems to be the appointment of a standing umpire or referee. Whether he should attend the regular meetings of the board, is an open question. It seems that should he attend, much time and expense would be saved, and one of the objections to arbitration met.

Another of the rules embodied in this system is deserving of more than passing notice—it is the third. "Neither masters nor men shall interfere with any man on account of his being a society or a non-society man." The society men pledge themselves not to annoy, nor allow annoyance, to non-society men. The system of arbitration accepts the fact of combination among both employers and employed, and uses it as an agent to accomplish the ends it aims at—the establishment of peace and good will.

To show the practical workings of this board, it will be interesting to append Mr. Kettle's account of the first arbitration before it.

In November of the first year of its existence, a difference arose between one of the master builders and some of his carpenters as to the right con-

---

* Industrial Conciliation, page 24.

struction of one of the rules—that which provided for extra payment for working in winter months upon unprotected buildings.

Upon receiving a request in writing from each party to settle this difference under the rules, the umpire ascertained what day would be convenient to both sides, and then called a meeting of the delegates—who had, by the operation of the individual contracts of service, become in law the arbitrators in this dispute. He also, through the secretaries of the two societies, caused the master and the workmen between whom the dispute existed to attend the arbitration, treating them as the parties to an ordinary reference. At the time appointed, the arbitrators, the umpire, two men who represented the workmen, who were parties to the dispute, and the master from the works where the dispute had arisen, met. As the men were the complainants, they were asked (as plaintiffs) to state their case. The master answered, (as defendant,) giving his reading and view of the rule alleged to have been broken. The workmen's arbitrators were then asked—taking them in succession as they sat at the table—to express their opinions. The opinions of the master's arbitrators were then taken in the same way. It was a case of conflicting arguments upon construction. The umpire decided that the men had put the true construction upon the rule; and he offered to make an award which could be legally enforced; but the master said he would willingly abide by the result, and at once pay the men accordingly. In this the men, on behalf of themselves and their fellow-shopmates, cheerfully acquiesced, and so we are deprived of a precedent from this case of the procedure for enforcing such an award.

The Boards of Arbitration existing in England embody the best characteristics of both of these systems. While they differ in detail, their main features are the same. They are all voluntary. They are composed of an equal number of employers and employed, each class electing its own representatives. There is in all of the boards a provision for conciliation without convening the entire membership. Regular meetings of the board are provided for, whether there is any business to be transacted or not. And in some form or other there is a power to which either party can appeal without pride or shame, that has power to determine as well as to hear, and whose decisions are received without exultation or humiliation. That is an umpire. The practical workings of some of the boards will be given in succeeding chapters.

SECTION V.

ARBITRATION AND CONCILIATION IN THE MANUFACTURED IRON TRADE.

It is important to the purposes of this report to show the practical workings of arbitration and conciliation in some industries in which our State has a special interest. In two industries Pennsylvania stands preëminent among the States, viz: Those connected with the manufacture of iron and the mining of coal. It is also in these that labor troubles are most frequent, and the contests the most severe. If arbitration has been successful in averting or mitigating industrial strife in these trades in England, this fact should be a consideration of no small weight in favor of its trial here. In view of the circumstances, in none of the trades of England has arbitration and conciliation had a greater success than in these. This is especially true of the manufactural iron trades of England. The wages of all classes of labor in the English rolling-mills are settled, and have been for nearly ten years, by arbitration. An award has just been given in South Staffordshire, reducing the price of puddling, and other wages, and the North of England arbitration board has decided on a corresponding decline.

Some account of the establishment and practical workings of the Board of Arbitration and Conciliation in the North of England iron trade cannot fail to be interesting, as no severer test of the value of arbitration and conciliation can be found than in the circumstances accompanying its workings in this trade. This trade, including that of the Cleveland district, begun to assume importance as recently as in 1860. For ten years its growth was marvelous, and at the end of this time it rivaled many and surpassed most of the older centers of English iron manufacture. This wonderful growth, at a time when other districts were increasing, created a demand for labor that could not be met from the ranks of those already skilled in the various processes of iron manufacture, and workmen were drawn from all classes and grades of laborers. The result was a most heterogenenous collection of workmen. There were no ties of friendship or locality. There were none of those attachments that long companionship causes men to form among themselves and for their employers, and even for the very tools with which they work. "Earning higher wages than those to which they had been accustomed, unable to appreciate the difficulties incidental to a trade so liable as the iron trade to great and sudden vicissitudes."* The result of this state of affairs can be easily imagined. It was endless disputes; strikes were of frequent occurrence. In 1865–66, there was both a lock-out and a strike, the latter lasting four months, and in the end nothing was settled, except that capital could hold out longer than labor. "Between that time and the winter of 1868–69, repeated reductions in wages became necessary, and gave rise to feelings of resentment, which rendered it more than probable that any considerable increase in the demand for iron would be the signal for peremptory demands on the part of the workman."† Trade began to improve in 1869, and the demand came. To avert the trouble, arbitration was suggested, and on March 22, 1869, the board was formed, and has continued in successful operation until the present time, and, for these ten years, has settled the wages and other industrial questions in this trade.

‡ This board consists of two representatives from each works joining it, one chosen by the owners of each works joining the board, the other by the operatives. It chooses from among its members, a standing committee, to whom all differences are in the first instance referred, and whose recommendations in minor matters are generally accepted. This committee, however, has no power to make an award except by mutual agreement of the parties to the dispute. All questions not settled by it, are brought before the board as soon as possible. In cases of re-adjustment of wages over the whole district, on one occasion two arbitrators had been chosen, who intervened between the board and the independent umpire. The committee meets when there is any business. The board twice a year, or oftener if necessary. The expenses are paid equally by employers and employed. At the close of 1875, it represented thirty-five works, and thirteen thousand subscribed operatives. These works had nineteen hundred and thirteen puddling furnaces—more than all Pennsylvania, and half as many as the

* From a paper read by Mr. B. Samuelson, M. P., before the British Iron Trade Association, February 24, 1876, page 4.

† Mr. Samuelson's Paper, pp. 5–6.

‡ A copy of the rules will be found in Appendix C.

entire United States. During the year 1875, the standing committee investigated forty disputes. Since its organization there have been eight or nine arbitratons on the general questions of wages, and scores of references in regard to special adjustment of wages at particular works.

Since 1874 this board, and the adherence of the workmen to its decisions, have been put to a severe test, and to their credit, it should be said that, with a few unimportant local exceptions, they have been loyal to the rules of the board. It is a well known fact that strikes and lock-outs generally occur on a declining wages market, and the real test of the value of any method of settling wages is not on an advancing market, but a falling one. The first action of this board was, under the umpireship of Mr. Rupert Kettle, to decree an advance of 6*d.* From its formation in 1869 to 1874, wages were advanced from 8*s.* per ton, for puddling, to 13*s.* 3*d.* In 1874 the turn came; 9*d.* were first taken off. In the middle of the year 3*d.* added, and from that time there has been a constant decline in wages until now puddling is only 7*s.* per ton of twenty-four hundred pounds. That is wages have been reduced, under the action of this board, without any serious difficulty, forty-seven and a half per cent.

Does any one believe that this could have been peacefully accomplished without arbitration?

The success of arbitration in the South Staffordshire Iron Trade has not been as marked nor have its operations been as continuous as in the North of England. The Board was originally formed by the two iron associations in the district, representing employers and employed, viz: The South Staffordshire Ironmasters' Association and the local branch of the Iron Workers' Union. The Board represented only these Associations, no attempt being made to give a representation or to allow a vote in selecting representatives to those who were outsiders and non-unionists. This course—unlike that of the North of England, where the operative members are elected by the vote of all the employés of the works, unionists and non-unionists—was the cause of the failure of the first Board. "It was quite powerless to bind those men who were not in the Ironworkers' Union, even though the master himself was bound."

Out of this failure has grown an organization known as The South Staffordshire Iron Trade Conciliation Board, now some three years old. Profiting by the former experience, it has avoided some of the errors of the old Board, while retaining its valuable features. Its rules and constitution are not the same as in the North of England. The Board consists simply of twelve employers and twelve operatives, but every works joining the Board shall, if possible, have a representative of the employers and a representative of the operatives. The Board elects a president, not connected with the iron trade, whose duty it is to attend at meetings when questions are brought before the Board to be settled, but to take no part in the discussion, beyond asking explanations sufficient to guide his judgment.

Besides the president, there is a chairman and vice chairman, who are elected by the Board from themselves, but whose functions are not clearly defined by the rules. Instead of a committee of inquiry, the rules, which are not very precise, say, that "In case of any difference arising at any works, it is intended that it shall be settled by the works representatives, but in case of their failing, it is open to them to refer it to the chairman, vice chairman, and the two secretaries, who may call the Board together if they see fit."

The president of the Board is Mr. Joseph Chamberlain, M. P. for Birmingham, who has been quite successful as an arbitrator, and still retains the confidence of the operatives, though he has for several years been forced, by the state of the trade, to award reductions in wages. As the result of the discussion, at a meeting of the Board, held October 7, 1878, wages were reduced to the point mentioned above. At this meeting, Mr. Capper, one of the workingmen's representatives, stated that the reductions conceded since January, 1874, amounted to 52½ per cent. Mr. Chamberlain stated, however, that he had seen no reason to believe that any of his past decisions were wrong, or, in fact, that they were not such as were absolutely necessary, having regard to the state of trade. In the course of his remarks, he asked what was the intention and object of a Board of Arbitration? Surely it was to arrive at a fair decision, without the painful necessity of a strike. If this was so, he had to ask himself what would be the result of a strike, if there were no Board. Suppose, for a moment, there were no Board of Conciliation to settle the matter, and that the employers thought themselves entitled to ask for a reduction to 7*s.* of the puddlers' wages. Did anybody doubt, that grievous as such a reduction might be to the work people, they would, under the existing state of trade, be obliged, in the long run, to submit to it? He was there rather as a conciliator than as a judge, and the feeling he had, that if there were no board, the operatives at the present time must yield to the demands made by the employers did certainly weigh with him very much in considering the present application of the employers.

At a meeting of the Board, held since this report has been in press, the members on both sides expressed their continued confidence in the Board, and their implicit faith in Mr. Chamberlain.

As the two districts mentioned are among the largest and most important of the iron producing districts of Great Britain, I think I may confidently point to the success of arbitration in their iron mills, as giving strong grounds for predicting the success of arbitration in our iron works, were it tried. The fact that good feeling has been fostered, and severe reductions of wages accepted, without strikes, is abundant evidence of its value.

SECTION VI.

ARBITRATION AND CONCILIATION IN THE COAL TRADE.

The working of arbitration and conciliation in the coal trade is somewhat different from its history in the iron trade. The nature of the work in collieries does not admit of so many different trades as in iron working, and, as a result, there are fewer unions. They are larger, more united, and in a better position to enforce any demand they may make. Though this is true, and though, further, there is not, with possibly an exception, a permanent board in this trade, there are many cases, during the last few years especially, in which differences have been adjusted by temporary boards or an arbitrator. The awards have not always been loyally accepted. It is too much to expect that they would be. The fluctuations in this trade in the last five years have been both rapid and large, and the strain on any system that could be devised would have been too great not to have caused it to give way at times. Notwithstanding this, after a careful and thorough study of all the facts I do not hesitate to say, that arbitration and conciliation in the coal trade has been a success. The wonder is it has not failed oftener. There have been cases where both employers and employed have refused to submit their demands to arbitration, and there have been cases where the award, when made, has been rejected; but the exceptions are so few, that it can be fairly said that for some years, until very lately, arbitration has settled the wages question in the coal trade, and both sides have abided its results.

To illustrate its workings in detail in this trade I have selected the Northumberland, Durham, and South Wales districts.

In the Northumberland coal trade wages and other industrial disputes have been settled for some years by conference or conciliation between the mine owners and workmen, each side having its unions or associations. Since March, 1873, up to the close of 1877, a joint committee consisting of six employers and six workmen have settled all questions "of mere local importance affecting individual pits." This committee had no power to deal with the question of wages. When this was to be discussed a board was created for the occasion, consisting generally of two arbitrators for each side, presided over by an umpire. Mr. Rupert Kettle, who acted in this capacity at an arbitration in 1875, defined the constitution of the court very clearly. "We are one body of five, and if, by and by, it shall be found that you are two and two, and, therefore, cannot arrive at a conclusion, the decision will be with me; but until that time arrives you are the judges and I am only assisting you."

The last arbitration in this trade in Northumberland was in July, 1877, In May, of this year, the employers gave notice of a reduction and a withdrawal of the allowance of free house and free coal. The men refused to permit the reduction, and, also, an offer to arbitrate, and twelve thousand of the fourteen thousand miners in the district went out on a strike. So bitter were the men against arbitration that their trusted leaders who suggested it were hissed and hooted. After several weeks idleness they, however, agreed to arbitrate.

Two arbitrators were appointed on each side, with Mr. Farrer Herschell, M. P., as umpire. This arbitration was an important one, as introducing new considerations as reasons for reductions. The employers did not rely upon the claim that there had been such a reduction in the selling price of coal as to justify a reduction in wages, but claimed it on the ground that other districts had advantages over them in the greater number of hours worked per day, and days per week, which, added to a higher wage they were compelled to pay, placed them at a decided disadvantage in the market. The award was in favor of the men, but it recommended that the men in order to aid the pit owners to compete with other districts, should work six hours instead of five, at the face, twelve days per fortnight; to increase the out-put of large coal, and the throwing back of small coal. These recommendations practically discredited the umpires own decision, but they were faithfully adhered to by the employers, while the recommendations were carried out with little grace by the employés. A quarter of an hour was added to the working time, and the other recommendations were ignored.

This arbitration was a most important one in its results. On the 24th of November of the same year, notice of a reduction of twelve and a half per cent. was posted, and the miners, refusing to accept, went on strike on December 7. The employers refused to withdraw the notice, and also in view of the circumstances attending the last trial, refused to submit their case to arbitration. The men yielded so far as to agree to accept ten per cent., and arbitrate the remaining two and a half per cent., but this was refused, and, after eight weeks' strike, the men went to work at the full reduction. I have given this case in detail, as it is often referred to as showing the failure of arbitration. It certainly did not fail, for it was not tried, and no one who has had an opportunity to know the present feeling of the men, doubts that there is trouble ahead. The employers, maybe, have been justified in the course they took. As to its wisdom there is an opportunity for discussion.

In the Durham coal trade, a much larger one than the Northumbrian, arbitration is in full operation, though it has been subject to a most severe strain in the large reduction of wages that have been decreed. This district has been described as one in which "reason and calm discussion have preëminently taken the place of force." The miners in this region number some fifty thousand. Beginning with March, 1872, up to May, 1873, wages had been advanced fifty-eight and one half per cent. In May, 1873, the decline began, wages being reduced ten per cent. In October, 1874, Mr. Russell Gurney, Recorder of London, after a very exhaustive investigation, awarded a reduction of nine per cent. This was accepted, though not with very good grace. Mr. Kettle says he always expects a little sulking when the award is unpleasant. So great was the depression, that in February, 1875, only three months after the announcement of Mr. Gurney's award, another reduction was claimed, and five per cent. awarded. At the close of the same year, Mr. Hopewood, M. P., was appointed arbitrator, and awarded, in February, ten per cent. reduction. In May, 1876, a notice of a reduction of ten per cent. was given and arbitrated. In August, six per cent, and in February, 1877, ten per cent. more. In March, 1877, a sliding scale was adopted for two years. Under this it was provided that any differences that might arise were to be settled by reference. All these reductions have been accepted, not always pleasantly, but nevertheless accepted; and under the sliding scale the men are now working, referring questions as they arise to be settled by conciliation.

In South Wales, a strike occurred in 1875, lasting seventeen weeks, and involving one hundred and twenty thousand workmen, whose loss in wages was variously estimated at from £3,000,000 to £5,000,000. This was settled by conciliation. Immediately after this, as the result of an extended consultation, a sliding scale, based upon the selling price of coal, with a fixed minimum and maximum, was adopted; all other differences arising to be settled by arbitration. In 1876, several reductions resulted, which caused considerable dissatisfaction, and a vote of the members of the union was taken to get its views on continuing the scale, and abiding by its action. Eighteen thousand four hundred and seventy-five voted for it, and eight thousand nine hundred and thirty-four voted against it, though wages had been in some cases reduced thirty per cent. Late in 1877, the price of coal had fallen so low that the "Coal Masters' Association" asked the men to consent to lower the minimum of the scale five per cent., which they did, confirming their action in February, 1878, and again in June.

There have been other arbitrations than these in the coal trade all over Great Britain. In South Yorkshire and North Derbyshire, Mr. Mundella has arbitrated a number of disputes the present year. At Barnsly an eight months' strike was settled by Mr. Whitwell and Mr. Mundella. There have have been successful arbitrations in the coal trade at Ashton, Oldham, North Staffordshire, Cleveland, North of England, and Lancashire. In South Staffordshire, a sliding scale was adopted in 1874, but its working was not satisfactory, owing to the decline in coal being much greater than was expected. At Radstock there have been two awards, one by Mr. Kettle, and the other by Mr. Thomas Hughes, M. P. In North Wales there have been several arbitrations. In all these cases there has seemed to be an earnest desire on the part of the leaders of the unions to hold the men to the award, telling them that they were bound in honor, and threatening to withdraw from their positions if the men were false to their word. The Welsh colliers are rough, uneducated men, however, and have forgotten honor and interest, and rejected awards that have been made, and, at present, arbitration is not practiced in this district.

SECTION VII.

ARBITRATION IN OTHER INDUSTRIES.

I have spoken at length of the workings of arbitration in the coal and iron trades for the reason assigned—that they are the industries in which our State has so large an interest. It must not be inferred that it has been only in these that its success has been obtained and its adaptation for the purpose designed established. Of its workings in the hosiery trades of Nottingham and the building trades of Wolverhampton, I have also given an account in previous sections. Of its workings in other industries, I can give, for lack of space, only the most meager account, and that simply for the purpose of showing to what a diversity of cases arbitration is applicable. The lace trade of Nottingham has a board which was started very soon after Mr. Mundella's, in the hosiery trade. As the rules of this board are regarded by this gentleman as the model rules, they are given in full in the Appendix.* This board was a complete success for over fifteen years. Latterly there has been some dissatisfaction regarding awards, and a desire to repudiate them; but there has been no more difficulty than was to have been expected, or than there will continue to be, so long as human nature remains human. In the textile trades there have been but few attempts at systematic arbitration. The Macclesfield silk trade had a board suggested by the *Conseils des Prud' hommes*, as early as 1849. The failure of this board is to be attributed to the fact that, though organized to put an end to strikes and lockouts, it used them as a means to compel obedience to its awards. In other branches of these trades, notably the cotton trades of East Lancashire, a spasmodic kind of conciliation has been practiced in the past, but during the recent very disastrous lockout, though arbitration was proffered by the employés, it was refused by the manufacturers, on the ground that there was nothing to arbitrate, as unless they could get the reduction asked for they must cease work.

In the building trades, a number of boards have been established, and though it is in many respects a very complicated trade, their history has been such as to indicate their great usefulness in these trades.

Among other industries in which arbitration has been successfully tried, may be mentioned the potteries, iron and stone mining, iron tubing, quarrying, chemical, and boot and shoe. The best examples of the workings and success of boards, are, however, to be found in those industries treated of at length in preceding sections.

SECTION VIII.

THE ACCEPTANCE OF AWARDS BY THE PARTIES TO THE ARBITRATION.

A very important question to be answered in arriving at a true estimate of the value of arbitration and conciliation is, how have the awards of the boards been received? Have they been frankly accepted, and loyally obeyed, or have they been rejected, or if accepted, received sullenly, and

---

*See Appendix D.

obeyed grudgingly, and with a determination to renew the struggle in the near future.

So far as relates to conciliation, these questions are easily answered. From its very nature its awards or decisions can meet with but little opposition. When differences are settled, through the good offices of committees of inquiry, or the conciliation committees of these boards, it is without an award, and a decision is reached, because the parties themselves agree to such decision, and, of course, in such cases there is little or no opportunity for the rejection of the result. The same is true, though not so generally, where conciliation boards exist without a final appeal to an umpire or referee. In these cases the subject in controversy is settled by what the men call "a long jaw," and an agreement is reached by a compromise, or by coming to the best arrangement possible under the circumstances. This is a contest, to be sure, but it is of a far different character than a strike or lockout. It also offers an opportunity for rejecting a decision, and under the working of the Nottingham board, which is on this principle, there have been cases of such rejection. Mr. Mundella mentions one example of a small branch of the hosiery trade, employing some two hundred men, who made a demand, which the whole board deemed unreasonable, the representatives of this branch were outvoted, and, in a fit of ill humor, seceded from the board. They found themselves, however, isolated and deprived of all sympathy and support, both of their fellow-workmen and the public, and they soon expressed a desire to be restored to membership.

Where there has been formal arbitration and an award, especially in the coal and iron trades, I am constrained to confess that there are more cases of rejection or attempted rejection of awards than there should be. There should be no case of a refusal to accept an award made by a duly appointed umpire or a board. It is worse than useless to submit a case to arbitration, unless both parties agree to be bound by the result, and are prepared to act upon it in good faith. The parties to the arbitration are in honor bound to this course, however unsatisfactory the result may be, or however unwelcome the award.

It is unfortunate, also, that most of the repudiations of the awards have come from the workmen, and these have at times been coupled with most gratuitous insults to the gentlemen who have acted as arbitrators. A recent case of this kind is the action of the nut and bolt trades of Birmingham, in which Mr. Chamberlin acted as arbitrator. The award was not rejected, but Mr. Chamberlin was so grossly insulted, that he refused in an indignant letter to serve in a subsequent case in the same trade. Mr. Chamberlin said: "I have always been of the opinion that arbitration, as a means of settling such disputes, could only be successful where there existed on both sides a belief in the principle, and implicit confidence in the discretion, impartiality, and fairness of the arbitrator. In the present case, these conditions appear to be wanting, for you will recollect that when recently, at very considerable sacrifice of time and trouble, I settled a dispute which had arisen in your trade, my decision was made the subject of abusive complaint, and my honor was called in question, and improper motives were attributed to me."

Another example was the rejection of the award of Mr. Sergeant Wheeler, by the North Wales colliers, who stated in their resolutions that the reduction was "a gross imposition," and gave notice of an immediate demand for twenty per cent. advance. A three month's strike grew out of this.

In addition to these cases and others that might be given, there are some in which there have been cases of disloyalty to the Board at particular works. This has been true, even in the North of England. It is interesting, however, to find that the employers, in a recent document, submitting their case for a reduction of wages, most readily record their opinion that, with a few local exceptions, which do not affect the general principle, the operatives, as a body, have been loyal to the rules of the board, one of these rules being that, in the event of a dispute, the operative shall not abandon his work, but continue his employment pending its adjustment. And this is confirmed by Mr Kettle. He writes as follows: "Except in one or two instances of a few days' sulks at particular works, my award being against the workmen, I think all have been approved, and all, without exception, have been practically acted upon, and for six years the peace of the trade, generally, has not been interrupted."

It is also interesting to note that Mr. Chamberlain, at a recent meeting of the South Staffordshire Conciliation Board, stated, that during the three years that Board had been in existence, three successive reductions had been made in the wages of the operative, but in all these cases his award had been strictly observed, both by employers and employed.

The cases that have occurred when awards have been rejected have, without doubt, brought arbitration somewhat into disrepute. But there are some things forgotten by those who, for these few cases, condemn the principle. It should be remembered that the rejection of an award will be more widely known, and commented upon, than the acceptance of a score, and it must further be remembered that the test to which this principle has been subjected in the last five years, has been a most severe one. Wages in the coal and iron trades have reached, in some cases, a lower point than they have ever touched before. A reduction of ten per cent., or even five per cent., has come to mean want and misery, and human nature is often too strong for honor. The wonder is, that the awards have not been oftener rejected. Coming, as I did, from a district in which the iron workers are better paid than in any other district in the world; and seeing the self-restraint of the iron workers of England, in the face of constant reductions of wages, and the too evident fact that others were to come, I could but admire the honorable action of the men, and conceived the highest respect for the principle which enabled these great changes to be made without strikes and lock-outs.

SECTION IX.

ADVANTAGES OF ARBITRATION.

There are two or possibly three objects sought in the formation of boards of arbitration and conciliation. The first is to prevent differences between employed and employers from becoming disputes, and leading to strikes and lock-outs; and the second is to settle disputes that have unfortunately arisen, and to put an end to strikes and lock-outs, should they occur. The third object, which is possibly included under the first mentioned, is to promote mutual confidence and respect between these two classes. The only sufficient reason for the adoption of the principle is that it accomplishes these purposes.

Whether it has accomplished these objects in the trades in which it has been fairly tried in England, can be judged from the facts set forth in the preceding pages of this report. For myself, I do not hesitate to say that it is not only the best method yet devised, but the only rational one for adjusting the relative rights of employers and employed under the present constitution of industrial society. In making this statement, I do not forget the method by strikes and lock-outs, nor do I consider it. These methods are neither rational nor civilized. A victory or a defeat for either side, under the pressure of strikes or lock-outs, neither proves nor disproves the justice of a position assumed; but it is fair to infer that an award given by a board of arbitration, after due consideration, would be as near just and right as it is possible for human judgment to reach. It is to be observed, also, that a decision of a board should not be and in most cases is not regarded as a victory by one side, or a defeat by the other. There is no exultation over victory, no smart over defeat, nor a determination to wait for a convenient season and revenge. The burning questions that arise are settled in a friendly manner.

Another advantage of a permanent board of arbitration, with stated meetings, is that it furnishes an opportunity, seldom possessed without these, for the workmen to obtain a knowledge of the needs of trade and the demands of the future, both upon them and the manufacturers. Labor troubles are as often the result of a lack of information as to the true state of a trade as of any other one thing. It is true, that workmen may be told the facts rendering a reduction necessary, but they are not inclined to credit them, and believe that affairs are not as represented. In the working of the English boards, especially in fixing prices, notice is taken of the state of trade and competition with other countries and other districts, and the information thus gathered, not by the employer members, but by the board, is brought to bear in the settlement of wages. In his testimony before the trades unions' commission of Parliament, Mr. Mundella says: "We sent two of the workmen to France last year, and a third to Germany to see for themselves the prices paid there for that work. They came home and said, 'It will not do, we must be content as we are for the present,' and we produce on the table the articles made in France and Germany, and the men are convinced by their own senses of the justice of what we say and by their knowledge of the laws that govern trade, because this system has been a complete educational process for our men; they know as well as we do whether we can afford an advance or not; they know whether the demand is good or bad, and at what prices the article can be made in France or Germany, and they are accustomed to consider the effect of a fall or rise in cotton just as we do; and when they think that things are going well, they ask to share in the benefit, and when they think that things are going wrong, they are willing to take low rates."

Facts gathered in this way and supplemented by statements of those in whom the workmen have learned to have a degree of confidence, have a greater influence than unnumbered assertions of men who are brought together only to struggle for a victory.

This suggests another and a most important advantage of these boards. Accepting the fact that unions of workmen exist, and will doubtless continue to exist, it is only through boards of arbitration or conciliation of some kind that the trades unions and those of employers can meet except as antagonists. The manufacturer and his workman can never be brought face to face to discuss trade questions, except when their interests are hostile. With these boards there is a possibility of meeting as fellow members of the same trade whose interests are indissolubly joined.

Another and perhaps the most important advantage of these boards is the bringing of employer and employed together, and thereby increasing their respect and esteem for each other and the consequent growth of confidence. One of the greatest barriers to an understanding between capital and labor is a feeling on the part of workingmen that they are regarded as holding a servient position, and a feeling on the part of manufacturers that theirs is a dominant one. Out of these feelings, which are altogether too common, come a brood of evils that have cost our industries dear. Even when nothing is further from the mind than the thought of cherishing such sentiments as these, suspicion, ever quick to grasp an appearance for a reality, catches at some chance word, and all the horrors of a labor war are the result. Judge Kettle, in speaking of strikes from matters of sentiment, says:

"If in the common intercourse of life this is felt, how much more in the excitement of a trade dispute must men be sensitive to influences which clash with their just estimate of their own position; and still more keenly must they be felt, when those influences are directed to controvert the means taken to maintain what they believe to be their right."

For this want of confidence and suspicion, these permanent boards of arbitration furnish a remedy. Confidence is cherished. The intercourse of representative workmen with representative employers, as equals with equals, breaks down all class distinctions, removes suspicion, and makes the task of harmonizing differences a much simpler proceeding.

But the chief advantage of these boards is that they form an open market, where labor and capital can come together, and in a friendly spirit, fix what is "a fair price for a fair day's work" In these boards, the statements made by each side can be challenged, each others arguments answered, and estimates impeached. "I verily believe that, without limiting the influence of fair competition, boards of arbitration, properly worked, afford the best means of fixing the market price for a fair day's work. I believe, moreover, that their action has a tendency to secure the maximum prices which are consistent with steady employment, and that the presence of an umpire prevents the ruinous consequences to both parties which follow separation upon a disagreement."

SECTION X.

DIFFICULTIES OF ARBITRATION, AND OBJECTIONS TO THE SAME.

In the course of this report, I have incidentally referred to the difficulties that stand in the way of the successful workings of arbitration, and some of the objections to the same. It may not be amiss to group together some of these, and to consider others, selecting those that may be regarded as typical rather than taking up each objection in detail.

The chief obstacle encountered in the formation of boards of arbitration and conciliation, as well as in the earlier operations of the same, is suspicion and prejudice. These are the sources of some of the most bitter and ill-advised strikes and lock-outs that the history of industry has known, and it is this tendency to quarrel upon what Judge Kettle so aptly terms "matters of sentiment," that stands most in the way of arbitration. Happily, these feelings are passing away; a more intimate knowledge and a more generous estimate of the acts of each other are removing this suspicion and prejudice. Once boards are established, their very existence, as we have shown, tends to the removal of all sources of strife founded upon passion or ignorance.

Another difficulty that arises immediately upon the decision to form a board, is the selection of an umpire. Shall he be a permanent officer, or chosen to decide a particular case? Shall he be practically acquainted with the trade in which he is called to act, or is this not necessary, so that he have the other qualifications? These are questions that it seems almost impossible to answer from the results of experience. Judge Kettle, who has been a most successful umpire in some of the most important arbitrations in England, and especially in the coal and iron trades, has no practical knowledge of these trades. Mr. Thomas Hughes, M. P., (Tom Brown,) Mr. Herschell, M. P., Mr. Thomas Brassey, M. P., Mr. Russell Gurney, Mr. Henry Crompton, and others, are all gentlemen who are not practically connected with manufacturing or mining; but have been very successful as arbitrators. On the other hand, Mr. A. J. Mundella, M. P., Mr. Joseph Chamberlain, M. P., Mr. David Dale, and others, who have been just as successful umpires, are or have been very extensive manufacturers.

On the part of the workmen there have been very strong objections at times to what they term "a stranger referee;" but it will be found that the success of a referee will not depend upon his practical acquaintance with the trade, so much as it will upon the man himself. If he is at all fitted for his responsible position in other ways he can gain sufficient knowledge of the trade to enable him to give a just and intelligent decision. It seems, however, advisable that when it is possible, the referee should be an officer selected by the board, with a tenure of office the same as the board. It is not well to wait until the struggle begins, and each side, perhaps, is striving for victory and all they can get before the one who is to decide between them is named. It is best to select him when judgment and reason rule. In this country, I think little difficulty will be experienced in securing umpires. I think it possible to name men in our own State in whose fairness and judgment our iron and coal industries would be willing to confide.

When the practical operation of these boards are considered, a very serious difficulty is found in the absence of any recognized definite principle as a basis on which awards shall be made. For example: first and foremost among industrial questions, is that relative to the wages of labor. When this is before a board for decision, the question arises at once, what shall be the basis upon which the award shall be made? It is because of this very difficulty that arbitration boards exist. If there were such a basis definitely established, and universally acknowledged, the decision as to the wages at a given time would be a simple question of arithmetic or of bookkeeping. It is to endeavor to discover what is fair and right at a given time that these boards are organized. As a matter of information, it may be said that in the practical operation of the boards, while all the facts relative to prices, competition, demand and supply both of labor and products are considered, wages are generally based on the selling price of the articles produced. Mr. Kettle, in a noted arbitration in the coal trade, found a certain date at which the wages paid for work about the collieries were satisfactory to both sides. This became the ideal and served to fix, in a general way, a ratio of wages to prices that would be a satisfactory one to both parties. Due notice was taken of any changes that had occurred that should serve to increase or diminish this ratio, such as reduction in the hours of labor, increased expense from mine inspection laws, &c., and the arbitrator in his award endeavored to approximate this ratio as near as could be done without injustice or injury.

It has been objected to this course that it involves an exposure of secrets in connection with ones business, that a manufacturer should not be called upon to make. To arrive at the wages paid and prices received for any commodity at a given time, an inspection of books is necessary. This objection must arise from a misapprehension of what is really done. The books are not brought into the board, nor are the arbitrators as a body, nor any one of them permitted to inspect them. An accountant, sworn not to divulge the details, but only the results, and these only to the board, unless they direct differently, is elected. He ascertains not how much it has cost to produce an article, unless so agreed upon nor how much profit has been made, but what was the actual selling price of the commodity at the times desired. There can be no objection to this. No secrets are divulged, the accountant covering his work in such a way that it is impossible to trace a sale.

It is further argued as against arbitration that an umpire may make mistakes. They are human and consequently liable to err. What would be the result if they did? It would be a very careless or ignorant umpire, one who had no business to occupy the position, who would make a mistake of say two per cent. in his award. This would be if the award held for six months equal to about half a week's work—three days. Would not this loss be better than a strike or a lock-out for probably many times this? A more pertinent answer to this objection might be to ask the question, whether an arbitrator is any more liable to make a wrong decision than a strike or lock-out? That is, is cool deliberation more liable to err than passionate impulse?

There is another objection that I imagine will have more weight in England than in this country. It is that arbitration is an attempt to interfere with the operation of natural laws—by which term is meant the politico-economical theories of Adam Smith and his successors and followers. It is not germane to the purpose of this report to discuss the truth or falsity of these theories. It is enough for us to say that at present our knowledge as to industrial laws is extremely limited, and that the assumed facts upon which theories have been based, or from which these laws are deduced, have been questioned by some able political economists. However this may be, the law or theory is good only so long as the facts or phenomena remain the same. There is nothing eternal in an economic law, and, when the facts change, or are modified, then the law, which is only a statement of these facts and their relations, changes, or is modified. Would it be wise or truthful to say that the facts or phenomena of labor have not undergone a wonderful change in the past century? Have not elements been introduced that promise permanence, that have produced marked changes in the relation of labor to employment, and demand changes in the statements of these relations, or, in other words, of the laws? But no argument is necessary on this point. No one will deny that interference with these laws is possible. Demand or supply may be increased or diminished, and thus, by a deliberate interference, changes to our advantage or disadvantage made to occur.

Just here I suggest the vital question as to the advantage or disadvantage of arbitration is to be asked. We must acknowledge that just so long as labor maintains its present constitution, interference with these so-called laws will occur. Now, is it better to interfere with these laws by the peaceful and friendly methods of arbitration and conciliation or by the destructive and hostile ones of strikes and lock-outs?

SECTION XI.

THE RELATION OF TRADES' UNIONS TO ARBITRATION.

A most interesting and important study in connection with this subject is its relations to trade unions; that is, how do these societies regard arbitration and conciliation as a means for settling industrial questions? What part should they have in the formation of boards, the conduct of cases, and the enforcement of awards? Whatever may be one's views of trade unionism, it is a fact, and will doubtless continue to be one. It is more than probable that, not only in England, but in all countries, labor will tend more and more to combination, at least until there is some radical change in the relations of capital and labor, and the decisions, as to rates of wages and other economic questions, will be largely controlled by these combinations. I am aware that there are certain economic laws, the action of which no union can prevent however much it may hinder, and these laws will, in spite of unions, prevail; but even the outcome of many of these may be very much modified, and of others entirely moulded, by combinations. It is not germane to my purpose to enter into a discussion of how far unions can affect the rewards of labor. It is a fact that they do, and so great an authority as the Duke of Argyle, in his Reign of Law,* states that combinations of workingmen for the protection of their labor are recommended alike by reason and experience.

Such combinations cannot fairly be objected too. They are but unions of the workingmen's capital—labor, and it is a question if, after all that has been said about the evils of unionism, it is not better to have organized labor, which is always somewhat conservative, than disorganized labor which is radical, and which, when it unites, becomes a mob, with no past to conserve and no future for which to provide.

These unions have been a large factor in freeing labor in Europe from the industrial slavery of the feudal system, and in bringing about industrial independence under the restraint of an enlightened intelligence, and equitable customs and laws. Notwithstanding some of the black pages of the history of English unionism, it has been a benefit to English labor, and an important means of its advancement. It is destined largely to rule it and direct its future, and, in proportion as it surrenders its indefensible practices, will be its value.

It is these facts that make important the views of trades unions as to arbitration.

As to their views in general, it can be said that they have for years been its warmest advocates. The report of the trades union committee of the Social Science Association, made in 1860, is full of evidences of the truth of this statement. The two largest industrial interests in England to-day are the coal and iron. They have the largest and most ably managed of the unions of that country. In an interview which I had with Mr. Thomas Burt, once a miner, and now a member of Parliament, elected by the coal miners, he expressed his warm approval of the principle of arbitration.

Mr. Edward Trow, the successor of Mr. John Kane as secretary of the National Amalgamated Association of Iron Workers, writes me as follows: "With regard to my views on arbitration, I believe it is the only fair and honorable mode that can be adopted for settlement of questions between capital and labor; that where both parties meet with an earnest desire for a fair and honorable arrangement, and discuss the various questions in dis-

*The Reign of Law, by the Duke of Argyle, 16th edition. London, 1872. Page 373.

pute in a kind and conciliatory spirit, there is no fear of failure; but, on the contrary, the old feeling of mistrust and jealousy is banished, and confidence in each other is established.

"The fault in connection with arbitration is when workmen come to meetings, jealous and suspicious, believing that employers are their natural enemies, and employers, by not conversing with delegates in a free and friendly spirit, foster their suspicion, and only through this action is there any fear of failure. Arbitration in England is regarded with great favor by the workingmen, and only in a few solitary exceptions has it been refused, or its awards been rejected by workmen.

"If you wish arbitration to be successful, employers must meet delegates in a kind and conciliatory spirit, so as to gain the confidence of the workmen by proving that they only desire full and free discussion, and that no advantage will be taken of men for speaking their opinions. Let this be done, and arbitration will prove successful, and will be a blessing to employers and workmen."

The rules of this association which, at the time they were drawn up, numbered thirty-five thousand members, contains the following clause:

16. Arbitration to be offered in all disputes. That in the event of any misunderstanding or dispute arising with the members at any works and their employers, if connected with the North of England Board of Conciliation and arbitration, they shall, in the first instance, refer the particulars of their grievance to the general secretary, who shall investigate the claims of the applicants according to the spirit of the arbitration rules, and endeavor to settle the matters referred to him. In the event of the general secretary being unable to settle any question calculated to produce irritation betwixt employer and employed, he shall call upon the standing committee to hold a meeting at an early day for the due consideration and settlement of such matters in dispute; and, if necessary, the full board shall be summoned to settle the same.

If a dispute takes place at any works not connected with the Northern Board of Arbitration and Conciliation, the general secretary shall hold a meeting with the general council to consider and, if possible, to settle the same. If desirable, a deputation from the counsel shall visit the works, in accordance with the instruction given by the general council.

The Duty of Members to form Arbitration Boards.

17. Where works are not connected with the board, the members of this association shall use their influence with employers and others, to join the present board, and to form new boards to suit the local circumstances of such works and workmen. And in case any dispute should arise where a board of conciliation and arbitration has not been formed, the workmen, who are members of this association, shall, before any step be taken calculated to produce a loss of employment, first make an offer in writing to the employer or employers, to settle the question in dispute by an appeal to conciliation and arbitration. This is the organic law of one of the most influential of English trade organizations.

There is held yearly in England, a convention known as the Trades Union Congress, or, as it is familiarly called, the Labor Parliament. This is a very important body, composed of delegates from the various unions of Great Britain. At the ninth convention held in 1876, at which one hundred and thirteen societies, and five hundred and fifty-seven thousand four hundred and eighty-eight members were represented, the following resolution was carried:

"That this meeting, recognizing the benefits conferred on many of our great industries by the adoption of the principles of arbitration and conciliation, pledges itself to use every endeavor to extend the application of those principles to cases of dispute in which there may be a prospect of peaceful settlement by such means."

At the tenth session, held at Leicester, in 1877, at which one hundred and twelve societies and six hundred and ninety-one thousand and eighty-nine members were represented, the president elect, on taking his seat, said:

"The principle of appeal to facts and reasons instead of brute force is rational, and at once commends itself to the judgment of men. There is no wonder, therefore, that the principle of arbitration for settling disputes has grown very rapidly. In the hosiery trade in the midland counties, we were among the first who adopted it, and we do not regret having done so. The workmen sometimes have had adverse decisions; but on the whole it has worked better than the old mode. It is gratifying to find that the workmen generally are the first to adopt this intelligent and enlightened system. In some disputes which have arisen in the country, notably the West Lancashire strike, the employers refused to submit to arbitration, although the men suggested it on three occasions. My own experience as a member of one of these boards, has led me to this conclusion: If a board be properly constituted, and proper arrangements are made to give publicity to the facts of a case, the result generally will be a righteous award. I was glad to hear that the National Miner's Union have decided to offer arbitration in every dispute, and it forms a part of their rules It is a rational arrangement, and it would be a good thing if all would adopt it. I think, too, arbitration boards should be open to the press and the public. Workmen have nothing to fear from either the one or the other. We want right and justice to rule, and we are not afraid of publicity. When men and employers gather round a board to talk over differences and try to adjust them, they give evidence of their manhood. Beasts and reptiles fight and tear each other, and carry out the law of the strongest; but men reason and think, and by this means show their dignity, and arrive at much better conclusions and far less costly. Boards for settling disputes would not do away with unions, they would still be needed, and under increased necessity to enforce the decision of the board when given in favor of the workmen."

The constituency which these bodies represent is so large as to fully justify the statement that the trades unions of Great Britain are decidedly in favor of the principle of arbitration as a means of settling labor disputes.

In the practical workings of arbitration, trades unions have been found essential to its success. They have formed the center around which the entire body of labor, non-unionist as well as unionist, has gathered, and by which the workmen members of the boards have been elected. As the result of his long experience, Mr. Kettle says:

"I confess I see no organization but trades unions to fall back upon for the purpose of conducting the business of electing workmen delegates. It must be distinctly understood that I do not here intend that members of a trade society should elect the workmen's arbitrators. In all our staple trades there are unions, but the proportion of their members, to the total number of workmen, differs greatly in different trades. In all there are a greater number of what are called non-society men.

"All the workmen, whether unionists or not, should be represented at the arbitration board. I suggest that the trades' union organization is, at present, the most accessible means of carrying this out."

The organized union also gathers the facts upon which the arguments for the labor side are based, and it is in them that the moral power resides which has been found not only essential, but sufficient to the enforcing of the awards of the boards.

SECTION XII.

ARBITRATION AND THE STATE.

As has already been stated, arbitration and conciliation in their practical workings in England have been purely voluntary. Not only is this true of the submission of the dispute or difference, but of the acceptance and carrying out of the awards. The very nature of conciliation precludes the idea of legal sanctions for its awards, or a legal enforcement of the same. With arbitration it is different; its methods are nearer those of a court of law, and its decision somewhat of the nature of a verdict based on testimony, and it is possible to give them the force of judicial decisions, capable of enforcement, with penalties in case of evasion. Some of the warmest and most intelligent advocates of arbitration have insisted that arbitration should have this legal aspect, while others, equally friendly and intelligent, have argued that to take away its purely voluntary character would be to destroy its usefulness.

There are at present, in the statute books of Great Britain, three acts relating to arbitration. The first of these, passed in 1824, and generally referred to as 5 Geo. IV, cap. 96, and the others later, passed in 1867 and 1872,* known commonly, respectively, as Lord St. Leonard's and Mr. Mundella's.

The first of these acts is evidently based on the French law for the establishment of *Conseils des Prud'hommes*, and, like that, gives considerable powers of compulsory arbitration. There is no permanent board or council established, but a justice of the peace or a referee appointed by him acts as umpire or referee. The operation of the act is restricted to disputes in certain trades, and upon certain subjects; and, although it admits of very extensive application, yet the act has not been generally received with favor. It only provides for the settlement of existing and not future disputes, and contains a proviso that, "nothing in this act contained shall authorize any justice or justices, actting as hereafter mentioned, to establish a rate of wages, or price of labor or workmanship, at what the workman shall in future be paid, unless with the mutual consent of both masters and workmen." The time, also, within which complaint is to be made is, as to disputes about materials, within three weeks, and, as to complaints from any other cause, within three days.

As to the character of the awards, section thirteen of this act provides:

"As well in all such cases of dispute as aforesaid," (meaning those enumerated in the second section,) "as in all other cases, if the parties mutually agree that the matter in dispute shall be arbitrated and determined in a different mode to the one hereby prescribed," (that is by justices, referees, &c.,) "such agreement shall be valid, and the award and determination thereon final and conclusive between the parties, and the same proceedings of distress, sale, and imprisonment, as hereafter mentioned, shall be had towards enforcing such awards," (by application to any justice of the peace of the county, stewartry, riding, division, barony, city,

*The act of 1872 will be found in full in Appendix E.

town, burg, or place within which the parties shall reside,) "as are by this act prescribed for enforcing awards made under and by virtue of its provisions."

The proceedings to enforce awards are as follows: Section 47 enacts that, "If any party shall refuse or delay to fulfill an award under this act for the space of two days after the same shall have been reduced into writing, it shall be lawful for any such justice as aforesaid, on application of the party aggrieved, and he is hereby required by writing under his hand, according to the form (A) of the schedule hereunto annexed, or in some other form to the like effect, to cause the sum and sums of money directed to be paid by any such award to be levied by distress and sale of any goods and chattels of the person or persons liable to pay the same, together with all costs," &c. And in case there is no sufficient distress, "it shall be lawful for any justice, as aforesaid, and he is hereby required by warrant under his hand, according to the form (C) of the schedule hereunto annexed, or in some other form to the like effect, to commit the person or persons so liable as aforesaid to the common gaol or some house of correction within his or their jurisdiction, there to remain without bail for any time not exceeding three months."

Section twenty-five provides for committal to prison in the first instance, where the justices think the issuing of a distress warrant would "be attended with consequences ruinous or in an especial manner injurious to the defaulter and his family."

Section twenty-six provides for the release from prison upon paying by the person committed "to the governor or keeper of the prison the full amount of the sum awarded, with all reasonable expenses incurred through such refusal or delay."

Section twenty-eight says: "No appeal or *certiorari* shall lie against any proceedings under this act," and section twenty that "no proceedings under this act shall be invalid for want of form."

The fees to be taken under the act are very low—2*d.* for a summons, 4*d.* for an order, 6*d.* for a warrant, 4*d.* for service of summons or order, 1*s.* for execution and sale, 3*d.* per diem for custody of goods, &c.

The act of 1867, commonly called Lord St. Leonards' act, is entitled "An act to establish equitable councils of conciliation to adjust differences between masters and men." Quoting Mr. Kettle's analysis of this act: "It proposes that the councils should be formed under license of the Home Secretary, granted upon the petition of masters and men in any particular trade or place; such petition to be based upon the resolution of a public meeting called for that purpose. This is subject to certain restrictive conditions as to residence and other qualifications. The bill provides that the petitioners shall elect the first council, and that succeeding councils should be elected each by registered members of the trade—masters and men—who shall be licensed by the council and have resided six months in the town, &c.; and as to men, have worked seven years in the trade. The bill further provides for the appointment of a chairman, (who must be unconnected with the trade,) a clerk, and other officers. It also provides for registration, polling, the holding of meetings, the making of by-laws, and other matters necessary to carry on proceedings as a body corporate.

"The provision for determining disputes is section five, and is as follows: 'That a quorum of not less than three (one being a master, and another a workman, and the third the chairman) may constitute a council for the hearing and adjudication of cases of dispute, and may accordingly make their award; but a committee of council, to be denominated the committee of conciliation, shall be appointed by the council, consisting of one master and one workman, who shall sit at such times as shall be appointed, and be renewed from time to time as occasion shall require; and all cases or questions of dispute which shall be submitted to the council by both parties shall, in the first instance, be referred to the said committee of conciliation, who shall endeavor to reconcile the parties in difference. When such reconciliation shall not be effected, the matter in dispute shall be remitted to the council, to be disposed of as a contested matter in regular course.'"

By the fourth section power is to be given to these councils to hear and determine all questions of dispute and difference between masters and workmen, as set forth in the 5th George IV, cap. 96, which might be submitted to them by both parties; and, as to which, the council is to have all the authority granted to arbitrators and referees by the before-mentioned act. The council are to be further authorized to adjudicate upon and determine any other case of dispute or difference submitted to them by mutual consent; but with the same proviso as in the act of George IV. against fixing future prices. Such awards to be enforced according to the provisions of the last-mentioned act. This bill of Lord St. Leonards would also establish a committee of two for the purpose of conciliation, in addition to the council before mentioned. The power would not be operative until a dispute had commenced, and then the two conciliators, or the two trade members of the quorum, would be in the position of ordinary arbitrators, and the independent chairman in that of the umpire. The defect in the system of Lord St. Leonards is that it does not make it obligatory to settle future disputes by the means provided in his act. His lordship had, no doubt, some good reason for confining his system to the settlement of existing disputes; but it is remarkable that the general law as to the binding effect of agreements to submit future disputes to arbitration has been finally settled by a most able judgment of his given in the case of 'Dimsdale *vs.* Robertson' (2 Jones and Latouche, 58,) given when his lordship was Lord Chancellor of Ireland.

The last act, that of 1872, we have given in full in the Appendix. This act was the result, in some measure, of the sentiment in England in favor of Mr. Kettle's plan. It is to be regretted that it was not passed as drawn up by Mr. Kettle. This act gives all powers consistent with freedom of contract for the establishment of permanent boards of arbitration, with authority to fix future rates of wages, and power to enforce their awards by legal process.

Notwithstanding the existence of these laws, I was unable to learn of any recent cases of their use, if, indeed, they have ever been used. Moral coercion, in case of any attempt to repudiate the awards and what Mr. Kettle so happily terms, "that aggregate honor of individuals, which our French neighbors call '*esprit du corps*,'" have generally been sufficient to secure the enforcement of an award. The love of justice and fair play, which has led the parties to agree to submit their disputes to arbitrators, has also led them to act in good faith when the award has been made. Still it would not be without its effect if some simple inexpensive legal method were provided for enforcing such of the awards of arbitration as in their nature are capable of such enforcement. I am aware of the impossibility of enforcing an award that relates to a future rate of wages, the most prolific source of disputes. In the very nature of the award, when it includes working rules or rates of wages, these rules or the contracts for hiring must be subject, so far as the individual is concerned, to termination on short notice, and therefore the award in its action, must be bounded by this notice, but it seems just and right that until such notice has been given and the contract ended in accordance with its terms, it should be conformed to, or penalties provided for its non-observance.

There is another obstacle to legal arbitration. An employé cannot be compelled to work unless he choose, nor a manufacturer to run at a loss. The advocates of the Wolverhampton system do not claim nor propose that this shall be done, but they wish to provide that one party shall not, on a moment's notice, discharge the other, nor shall the latter cease work without a moment's warning. This does not in any degree detract from the voluntary nature of arbitration. It simply is carrying out the evident truth that whilst one remains a party to an agreement, he is bound to abide by the terms. If he does not like the terms, his remedy is to free himself in the proper way. Legal arbitration in the sense in which Mr. Kettle advocates it only proposes to secure by legal means the performance of honorable obligations.

SECTION XIII.

CONCLUSION.

In the forgoing pages I have endeavored to give in as brief a space as possible the history and practical workings of Industrial Arbitration and Conciliation. My inclination and the importance of the subject would have led me at times to much fuller details and a more complete discussion of the subject, had I not rigidly adhered to a determination to include this report within such limits as would secure a reasonable probability of its being read. With such limitations, it has been impossible to more than touch upon the history and accomplishments of arbitration and conciliation. In fact, a large part of its history, especially that which relates to the working of conciliation, by which ninety per cent. of the cases are settled, is of such a nature that its details cannot be given. It can only be known by its results, and these have been a better and more cordial feeling between employers and employed, and a mutual coöperation and trust that promises the most satisfactory and speedy solution of some of the most vital questions that vex industrial society.

I have not forgotten that the present constitution of industrial society is not for all time. There are great and vital changes that must take place. There are even at the present time important re-adjustments in progress in the relations of capital and labor. These must continue, and with these changes new modes and new expedients must be adopted.

While this is true, the practical question for us is, what, in the present condition of the relations of capital and labor, is best calculated to harmonize those relations, and give to each its just proportion of the results of their united energies?

I believe that the practice of arbitration and conciliation will tend to these ends. As a result of the fair and open discussions of the boards, knowledge will be acquired, the views of each modify those of the other, and out of it, and as a result of it, will come such relations between capital and labor as will effectually put an end to industrial conflict.

Of the great value of arbitration and conciliation as means of settling trades' disputes, there can be no question. That it is infinitely to be preferred to the barbarous method of strikes and lock-outs, is scarcely a subject of argument. In the terse language of Mr. George Howell, formerly secretary of the Trades' Union Congress, "the whole question lies in a nut shell. Is brute force better than reason? If it be, then a costermonger may be a greater personage than a philosopher, and Tom Sayers might have been considered superior to John Stuart Mill."

I do not claim for arbitration that it as a wonder worker. It is not perfect. It is used by men that are very human, and who, under the present condition of things, are extremely selfish. For these reasons it will fail to accomplish all that is expected. Though it may fail at times, when it is fairly and honestly tried it will in most cases succeed; and under its action, wherever established, an intelligent coöperation between employers and employed will be effected, and steady employment secured at those rates of wages which the industrial conditions of a competitive market enables capital to pay.

As before stated, differences between capital and labor must constantly arise. They are here now. It is for our workmen and manufacturers to say how these differences shall be settled, whether by reason or by brute force. Decide they must, and in some cases soon. The solicitude to discover some more rational way of settling these differences than by the barbarous methods of strikes and lock-outs is shared equally by workmen and employers, and probably most of all by the on-looking public. While this end may be the immediate object of the solicitude of these classes, underneath it lies an earnest desire to find a permanent, honorable, reasonable solution of this and other phases of that most important of all human problems, the labor question. We are greatly in the dark on this subject. I believe we are moving toward the light. Looking back a hundred years, we can see the gradual brightening of what was then the darkest of all social problems, and need have no fears of the result. It may be delayed; but reason will rule and determine the nature of the relations of capital and labor. There are certain facts that we may refuse to acknowledge, and, refusing to own, may go on in the old way; but the new way of reason and a respect for the rights of each other will win. I believe that arbitration and conciliation will aid in bringing about the recognition of these rights. It is not an end nor a solution of the problem. It is on the way to the end, and is much nearer it than a strike or a lock-out. It will be a day of the greatest promise when in our State we shall put aside our preconceived prejudices and the notions of the past, when we shall realize that something higher than brute force has come into the affairs of men to adjust and harmonize them, and when acting on this belief, we shall urge forward an industrial reorganization on the basis of reason and right. There can be no nobler or more sacred work for men to do.

APPENDIX A.

BOARD OF ARBITRATION AND CONCILIATION FOR THE HOSIERY AND GLOVE TRADE.

Rules.

1. That a board of trade be formed, to be styled the "Board of Arbitration and Conciliation for the Hosiery and Glove Branches."

2. That the object of the said board shall be to arbitrate on any questions relating to wages that may be referred to it from time to time by the employers or operatives, and by conciliatory means to interpose its influence to put an end to any disputes that may arise.

3. The board to consist of eleven manufacturers and eleven operatives. The operatives to be elected by a meeting of the respective branches. The manufacturers to be elected by a public meeting of their own body. The whole of the deputies to serve for one year, and to be eligible for reëlection. The new council to be elected in the month of January, in each year.

4. That each delegate attend the Board with full powers from his own branch, and that the decision of the Board shall be considered binding upon the branch he represents.

5. That a Committee of Inquiry, consisting of four members of the Board, shall inquire into any cases referred to it by the secretaries. Such committee to use its influence in the settlement of disputes. If unable amicably to adjust the business referred to it, it shall be remitted to the Board for settlement; but in no case shall the committee make any award. The committee to be appointed annually.

6. That the Board shall, at its annual meeting, elect a President, Vice President, and two Secretaries, who shall continue in office one year, and be eligible for reëlection.

7. That the Board shall meet for the transaction of business once a quarter, viz: the first Monday in January, April, July, and October; but on a requisition to the President, signed by three members of the Board, specifying the nature of the business to be transacted, he shall, within seven days, convene a meeting of its members. The circular calling such meeting, shall specify the nature of the business for consideration, provided that such business has first been submitted to the committee of inquiry, and left undecided by them.

8. That all complaints submitted to the Board for their investigation, be embodied in writing, stating, as clearly as possible, the nature of the grievance complained of; such statement to be sent at least one week prior to the Board meeting.

9. That prior to any advance or reduction in the rate of wages being considered by the Board, a month's notice shall be given in writing to the Secretary, that such change is desired.

10. That the President shall preside over the meetings of the Board, and in his absence, the Vice President. In the absence of both President and Vice President, a chairman shall be elected by a majority present. The chairman to have a vote, and, in case of members being equal, the chairman to have the casting vote.

11. That any expense incurred by this Board, be borne equally by the operatives and employers.

12. That no alteration or addition be made to these rules, except at a quarterly meeting, or a special meeting convened for the purpose. Notice of any proposed alteration shall be given in writing one month previous to such meetings.

APPENDIX B.

RULES OF THE WOLVERHAMPTON BUILDING TRADE.

Rules for Regulating the Carpenters' and Joiners' Branch.

We, the undersigned, (A. B.,) umpire; (C. D., E. F., and four others,) arbitrators, appointed by the master builders; (G. H., I. J., and four others,) arbitrators, appointed by the operative carpenters and joiners, having fully and fairly discussed certain alterations in the rules proposed on behalf of the masters and men respectively, of which due notice had been given, do hereby certify that we have, by unanimous resolution, agreed upon the following rules, to come into operation on the 1st day of May next:

Arbitration.

Rule 1. That if any trade dispute shall arise between master and workman, such dispute shall be settled by the award of (C. D., E. F., and four others,) on the part of the master builders, and (G. H., I. J., and four others,) on the part of the operative carpenters and joiners, who are hereby appointed trade arbitrators, or by a majority of them; or in case they or a majority of them cannot agree, then by the award of A. B., who is hereby appointed umpire; and that in case any or either of the masters' arbitrators shall happen to die, or cease to carry on business in the town of Wolverhampton, or be ill and unable to attend to the business of arbitration during the continuance of these rules, then the surviving or remaining masters' arbitrators shall appoint another or other master builder or builders then carrying on business in the town of Wolverhampton, in the place of him or them who shall so have died or ceased to carry on business, or become incapable of acting; and in case any or either of the workmen's arbitrators shall happen to die, or cease to work as a carpenter and joiner in the town of Wolverhampton, or become ill and incapable of attending to the business of arbitration during the continuance of these rules, then the surviving or remaining workmen's arbitrators shall appoint other or another carpenter and joiner, then working in the town of Wolverhampton, in the place of him or them who shall have died or ceased to work, or become incapable of acting. And in case either or any of the masters or men appointed arbitrators shall be a party or parties to the dispute to be decided, other arbitrators shall, for the purpose of that arbitration only, be appointed in manner hereinbefore provided for filling up vacancies. That upon any dispute arising, either the master or workman may forthwith give notice to the umpire of the same, who shall thereupon summon the arbitrators to meet at some convenient time and place within seven days, for the purpose of hearing and determining the said dispute. At the meeting so to be held both parties, and such others as the arbitrators or umpire may think necessary, shall be heard; and both parties shall produce before the arbitrators and umpire such documents in their possession relating to the dispute as they or either of them shall require. The award of the said arbitrators, or a majority of them, or in case they or a majority of them cannot agree, then the award of the umpire shall be binding and conclusive upon all parties to the dispute arbitrated. The award shall be made within three days after the sitting, or if more than one, after the last sitting of the arbitrators. The award shall not be void or voidable for want of form; and may be referred back for amendment in form to the arbitrators or umpire, as the case may be, by any judge or magistrate. No proceedings whatever at law or in equity shall be taken against either arbitrators or umpire, or any of them, for anything done under this rule.

And lastly, that the arbitrations hereinbefore provided are intended between masters and workmen to be, and for all intents and purposes shall be, taken and held to be under the provisions of section thirteen of the 5th of George IV, cap. 96.

Conciliation.

2. That in case any trade dispute or difference of a private nature shall arise between any individual master and any individual workman or work-

men, by which the general interests of the trade are not directly affected, then in such case, before proceeding to arbitration under the last rule, the master shall nominate one of the hereinbefore appointed masters' arbitrators, and the workman or workmen one of the hereinbefore appointed workmen's arbitrators, who shall as soon as conveniently may be meet together, and endeavor, if possible, to arrange such private dispute or difference without proceeding to a formal reference, and in case they cannot so arrange such difference to the mutual satisfaction of both contending parties, the matter in dispute shall be determined by arbitration under rule one, as though no such meeting for conciliation had been held.

Society and Non-society Men.

3. Neither masters nor men shall interfere with any man on account of his being a society or non-society man. The society men pledge themselves not to annoy nor allow annoyance to non-society men.

Masters' Conduct of Business.

4. Each master shall have power to conduct his own business in the matter of the employment of any man he thinks fit, on any work he considers him capable of doing; in taking apprentices; in using machinery and implements; and in all details of the management of his business, not infringing on the individual liberty of the workman. Provided that, on any job where a number of carpenters and joiners are employed, their instructions shall be given by the employer, or, in his absence, by the general manager, through the carpenter and joiner appointed to take the lead of the job.

Wages, Payment by the Hour.

5. All time shall be reckoned and paid for by the hour, at the following rates: The class of men who have hitherto been paid five pence three farthings per hour shall be paid sixpence per hour, and other classes of men in proportion; but men working only on unprotected buildings shall be paid one halfpenny per hour additional for six weeks before and six weeks after Christmas day. Provided that when a man employed on unprotected buildings has the option of making up his full time by working in the shop, he shall be paid at the ordinary rate only, it being the intention of both parties that men of the same class shall have the opportunity of earning the same wages in each week.

Time of Work.

6. The shops and works shall be open from six o'clock in the morning till half past five o'clock in the evening for the first five working days in the week; and from six o'clock in the morning till four in the afternoon on Saturday, allowing one and an half hour per day for meals; but from six weeks before till six weeks after Christmas day, workmen on unprotected buildings, who are not provided with work in the shop to fill up their full time, shall work from seven o'clock in the morning till five o'clock in the evening, on the first five working days of the week, and from seven o'clock in the morning till four o'clock in the afternoon on Saturday, with one hour per day allowed for meals. Provided that for men who wish to be paid at the office on Saturday, between one and two o'clock, under the next rule, the hour of ceasing to work on that day shall be one o'clock instead of four.

Reckoning and Payment.

7. Time and wages shall be reckoned up to Friday night in each week, and wages shall be paid at the pay office at the shop, on Saturday, between the hours of one and two, to all men who require a half holiday; the men requiring payment then to walk to the pay office in their own time. Other men will be paid either at the pay office, at the shop, or upon the job, at four o'clock, as heretofore.

Overtime.

8. All time made at the request of the master between eight o'clock in the evening and five o'clock in the morning, shall be paid for at the rate of ninepence per hour, and on Sunday shall be paid for at one shilling per hour.

Distant Work.

9. Walking time shall be paid as follows: that is to say, if the distance of the work or job be within two miles from the High Green, Wolverhampton, the men shall walk in their own time. If more than two miles from that place, then walking time shall be allowed at the rate of three miles per hour beyond the first mile and a half. The men to walk back in their own time, except on Saturdays, when the wages are not paid on the job or place of work. Lodgings to be paid for at all jobs beyond four miles distance, at the rate of two shillings per week. Railway fares shall be matters of special arrangement between master and man.

Notice.

10. One working day's notice shall be given before a man leaves an employer, or before a master discharges a man.

Rules, How Long in Force, and How and When to be Altered.

11. These rules shall come into operation on the 1st day of May next, and shall continue in force for one year. Should either party require an alteration in these rules at the end of the time specified, notice shall be given to the other party of such required alteration, in the month of January next. If no such notice shall be given, then these rules shall continue in force until the 1st of May in the next year, and so on from year to year, until either party shall give notice to the other in the month of January in any year, that an alteration in these rules will be required on the 1st day of May next following such notice.

Printing, Publishing, and Proving these Rules.

12. That these rules shall be printed and posted up in some conspicuous place in each of the master builders' workshops in Wolverhampton, and that a printed copy of these rules, issued by the umpire, shall be read as evidence of the contract and submission to arbitration, between any master builder carrying on business in the municipal borough of Wolverhampton, and any carpenter and joiner, in any proceedings to inforce any award made under these rules, unless a special contract in writing shall have been entered into between the parties.

Dated this 31st day of March, 1866.

[Signatures of Masters' Arbitrators.]
[Signatures of Men's Arbitrators.]
[Signature of Umpire.]

APPENDIX C.

BOARD OF ARBITRATION AND CONCILIATION FOR THE NORTH OF ENGLAND MANUFACTURED IRON TRADE.

Rules.

1. The title of the Board shall be "The Board of Arbitration and Conciliation for the Manufactured Iron Trade of the North of England."

2. The object of the said board shall be to arbitrate on wages, or any other matters affecting their respective interests, that may be referred to it from time to time by the employers or operatives, and, by conciliatory means, to interpose its influence to prevent disputes, and put an end to any that may arise.

3. The board shall consist of one employer and one operative representative from each works joining the board. Where two or more works belong to the same proprietors, each works may claim to be represented at the board.

4. The employers shall be entitled to send one duly accredited representative from each works to each meeting of the board.

5. The operatives of each works shall select a representative by ballot in the month of December in each year, the name of such representative and of the works he represents shall be given in to the secretaries on or before the 1st of January next ensuing.

6. The operative representatives so chosen shall continue in office for the calendar year immediately following their election, and shall be eligible for re-election.

7. If any operative representative die, or resign, or cease to be qualified by terminating his connection with the works he represents, a successor shall be chosen within one month, in the same manner as is provided in the case of annual elections.

8. Each representative shall be deemed fully authorized to act for the works which has elected him, and the decision of a majority of the board, or of its referee, shall be binding upon the employers and operatives of all works which have joined the board.

9. At the meeting of the board, to be held in January in each year, it shall elect a president and vice president, one from the employers and the other from the operatives, also a deputy president and a deputy vice president in like manner, and two secretaries, who shall continue in office till the corresponding meeting of the following year, but shall be eligible for re-election. The president and vice president shall be *ex-officio* members of all committees.

10. At the same meeting of the board a standing committee shall be appointed, as follows: The employers shall nominate ten of their number, (not more that five of whom shall be summoned to any meeting of the committee,) and the operatives five of their number; The president and vice president shall be also *ex officio* members of the committee.

11. All questions shall, in the first instance, be referred to the standing committee, who shall investigate and endeavor to settle the matter so referred to it, but shall have no power to make an award, unless by consent of the parties. In the event of the committee being unable to settle any question, it shall, as early as possible, be referred to the board.

12. The president shall preside over all meetings of the board, and in

his absence the vice president. In the absence of both president and vice president a chairman shall be elected by the meeting.

13. All votes shall be taken at the board by show of hands, unless any member calls for a ballot. The chairman and vice chairman shall not be entitled to vote, but the works for which the chairman and vice chairman respectively were elected shall be entitled to nominate another representative in each case. If at any meeting of the board the employer representative or the operative representative of any works be absent, the other representative of such works shall not, under the circumstances, be entitled to vote.

14. In case of an equality of votes at the board, it shall appoint an independent referee, whose decision shall be final and binding; but whenever such equality of votes arises on the choice of independent referee, the original question shall be referred to and finally decided by the award of three indifferent persons, or a majority of them, one of such persons to be named by each section of the board, and the third by the two persons so named by the board, within fourteen days of such meeting.

15. The board shall meet for the transaction of business twice a year, in January and July; but on a requisition to the president, signed by five members of the board, specifying the nature of the business to be transacted, and stating that it has been submitted to the standing committee, and left undecided by them, he shall, within fourteen days, convene a meeting of the board. The circular calling such meeting shall specify the nature of the business for consideration.

16. All questions requiring investigation shall be submitted to the standing committee or to the board, as the case may be, in writing, and shall be supplemented by such verbal evidence or explanation as they may think needful.

17. No subject shall be brought forward at any meeting of the standing committee or of the board, unless notice thereof be given to the secretaries seven clear days before the meeting at which it is to be introduced.

18. The standing committee shall meet for the transaction of business prior to the half-yearly meetings, and in addition as often as business requires. The place of meeting shall be arranged between the president and secretaries in default of any special direction.

19. Any expenses incurred by this board shall be borne equally by the employers and operatives, and it shall be the duty of the standing committee to establish the most convenient arrangements for collecting what may be needed to meet such expenses.

20. The sum of ten shillings for each member of the board or standing committee shall be allowed for each meeting of the board or standing committee, together with such percentage addition as is for the time being made by order of the board to the standard wages. This sum shall be divided equally between the employers and operatives, and shall be distributed by each side in proportion to the attendances of each member. In addition each member shall be allowed second-class railway fare each way, and when an operative member is engaged on the night shift following the day on which a meeting is held, he shall be allowed payment for a second shift.

21. If any works desires to join the board at any other time than is contemplated in rules four and five, such desire shall be notified to the secretaries, and by them to the standing committee, who shall thereupon admit such works to membership, on being satisfied that representatives have been chosen in the manner prescribed by the rules.

22. No alteration or addition shall be made to these rules, except at the

first meeting of the board to be held in January in each year, and unless notice in writing of the proposed alteration be given to the secretaries at least one calendar month before such meeting. The notice convening the annual meeting to state fully the nature of any alteration that may be proposed.

By-Laws.

RULE 5. In the month of November in each year, the secretaries shall issue a notice to each firm connected with the board requesting them to elect representatives in the month of December, and shall supply them with the requisite forms.

RULE 10. The committee shall have power to fill up all vacancies that may arise during the quarter.

RULE 11. An official form shall be supplied to each representative, on which complaints can be entered. Either secretary receiving a complaint shall be required to forward a copy of the same to the other secretary, and the complaint shall be considered as officially before the board from the date of such notice.

RULE 17. This rule to be interpreted to mean that no case in which the committee are called upon to deal finally with a complaint from any member of the board shall be taken up without seven days' notice has been received; but this not to apply to routine business, or to such preliminary investigation of complaints as may be necessary.

RULE 19. The sum of 3d. per head, per quarter, shall be deducted from the wages of each operative earning 2*s.* 6*d.* per day and upwards (in case he does not object in writing to such deduction) on the first pay in the months of January, April, July, and October. Each firm shall pay an amount corresponding to the total sum deducted from the workmen. The contributions shall be forwarded on official forms, to be supplied by the secretaries, to the bankers (the National Provincial Bank of England) within one week from the pay when the money is deducted from the operatives.

RULE 20. If any member be compelled in the service of the board to attend meetings on two or more days consecutively, the sum of 3*s.* 6*d.* each be allowed per night. This is not to apply to any members living in the place where the meeting is held. Members attending meetings on any day except Mondays or Saturdays, and being that week employed on the night turn, to be paid for two days for each sitting.

The board earnestly invites the attention of all who belong to it, either as subscribers or as members, to the following instructions:

If any subscriber of the board desires to have its assistance in redressing any grievance, he must explain the matter to the operative representative of the works at which he is employed.

The operative representative must question the complainant about the matter, and discourage complaints which do not appear to be well founded.

If there seems good ground for complaint, the complainant and the operative representative must take a suitable opportunity of laying the matter before the foreman or works' manager or head of the concern, (according to what may be the custom of the particular works.) An official form on which complaints may be stated can be obtained from the secretaries.

The complaint should be stated in a way that implies an expectation that it will be fairly and fully considered, and that what is right will be done.

In most cases this will lead to a settlement without the matter having to go further.

If, however, an agreement cannot be come to, a statement of the points in difference must be drawn out, signed by the employer and the operative representative, (and, if possible, by the employer also,) and forwarded to the secretaries of the board, with a request that the standing committee will consider the matter.

It will be the duty of the standing committee to meet for this purpose as soon after the expiration of seven days from receipt of the notice as can be arranged.

It is not, however, always possible to avoid some delay, and the complainant must not suppose that he will necessarily lose anything by having to wait, as any recommendation of the standing committee or any decision of the board may be made to date back to the time of the complaint being sent in.

Above all, the board would impress upon its subscribers that there must be no strike or suspension of work. The main object of the board is to prevent anything of this sort; and if any strike or suspension of work takes place, the board will refuse to inquire into the matter in dispute till work is resumed, and the facts of its having been interrupted will be taken in account on considering the question.

It is recommended that any changes in modes of working requiring alterations in the hours of labor, or a revision of the scale of payments, should be made matters of notice, and, as far as possible, of arrangement beforehand, so as to avoid needless subsequent disputes as to what ought to be paid.

APPENDIX D.

BOARD OF ARBITRATION AND CONCILIATION FOR THE LACE TRADE FOR 1876.

Rules, as adopted at the Meeting of Delegates, held at the Mechanics' Hall, September 17, 1874, and amended July 10, 1876.

1. That a board of trade be formed, to be styled the "Board of Arbitration and Conciliation for the Lace Trade."

2. That the object of the said board shall be to arbitrate on any questions that may be referred to it, from time to time, by the joint consent of employer and workman, and, by conciliatory means, to interpose its influence to put an end to any dispute that may arise.

3. This board to consist of twelve manufacturers and twelve operatives, five of each to form a quorum. The manufacturers to elect six levers, three curtain, and three plain net representatives, and the operatives six levers, three curtain, and three plain net representatives, each to be chosen by their respective associations. The whole of the delegates to serve for one year, and to be eligible for reëlection. The new council to be elected in the month of January in each year. That when a special question arises,

upon which the members of the board have not sufficient information, it shall be competent for either side to introduce, after seven days' notice to the secretaries, not more than two extra delegates, who shall give information and enter into discussion upon such question; but, in every case, only members of the board shall vote. The above alteration shall also apply to special meetings of each branch. No changes shall be made in the extra delegates whilst the question is under discussion.

4. The decision of the board shall be binding on the parties to any dispute submitted by them.

5. That a committee of inquiry of six members of the board, three employers and three workmen, engaged in that particular branch in which the dispute arises, shall inquire into any cases referred to it, such committee to use its influence in the settlement of disputes. If unable, amicably, to adjust the business referred to it, it shall be remitted to the whole of the members of that branch upon the board, and, should no agreement then be arrived at, the case shall be submitted to a full board, but in no case shall the committees make any award. The committees to be appointed annually at the first meeting of the board.

6. That the board shall, at its first meeting in each year, elect a president, vice president, treasurer, referee, and two secretaries, who shall continue in office for one year, and be eligible for reëlection.

7. That the board shall meet for the transaction of business once a quarter, viz: The second Monday in January, April, July, and October; but on a requisition to the president, signed by three members of the board, specifying the nature of the business to be transacted, he shall, within seven days, convene a meeting of its members. The circular calling such meeting shall specify the nature of the business for consideration, provided that such business has first been submitted to the committee of inquiry, and left undecided by them.

8. The parties to any dispute remitted to the board shall, if possible, agree to a joint written statement of their case, but if they cannot agree, a statement in writing from each party shall be made, and in either case forwarded to the secretaries within seven days of the board's meeting.

9. That the president shall preside over the meetings of the board, and in his absence the vice president. In the absence of both president and vice president, a chairman shall be elected by the majority present. The chairman to have but one vote, and in case of numbers being equal, appeal shall be made to the referee.

10. That the decision of the referee shall be final and immediately binding on both sides.

11. That when at any meeting of the board the number of employers and workmen is unequal, all shall have the right of fully entering into the discussion of any matters brought before them, but only an equal number of each shall vote. The withdrawal of the members of which ever body may be in excess to be by lot.

12. That any expenses incurred by this board be borne equally by the operatives and employers, and the accounts to be produced and passed at each quarterly meeting.

13. That no alteration or addition be made to these rules except at a quarterly meeting or a special meeting convened for the purpose. Any member of the board intending to propose an alteration or addition shall furnish the exact terms thereof, in writing, to the secretaries twenty-eight days before such meeting, and the secretaries shall give twenty-one days notice of the same to each member of the board.

APPENDIX E.

ARBITRATION ACT OF 1872.

Masters and Workmen (Arbitration) Act. (35 and 36 Vict., Chap. 46.)

An Act to make further provision for arbitration between masters and workmen. 6th August, 1872.

WHEREAS, By the Act of the fifth year of George the Fourth, chapter ninety-six, intituled "An Act to consolidate and amend the laws relative to the arbitration of disputes between masters and workmen," hereinafter referred to as the "principal Act," provision is made for the arbitration in a mode therein prescribed of certain disputes between masters and workmen;

And whereas, It is expedient to make further provisions for arbitration between masters and workmen;

Be it enacted by the Queen's most Excellent Majesty, by and with the advice and consent of the Lords Spiritual and Temporal, and Commons, in this present Parliament assembled, and by the authority of the same, as follows:

As to agreements under this act.

I. The following provisions shall have effect with reference to agreements under this Act.

(1.) An agreement under this act shall either designate some board, council, persons or person as arbitrators or arbitrator, or define the time and manner of appointment of arbitrators or an arbitrator; and shall designate by name, or by description of office or otherwise, some person to be, or some person or persons, (other than the arbitrators or arbitrator,) to appoint an umpire in case of disagreement between arbitrators.

(2.) A master and a workman shall become mutually bound by an agreement under this Act, (hereinafter referred to as "the agreement,") upon the master or his agent giving to the workman, and the workman accepting, a printed copy of the agreement: *Provided*, That a workman may, within forty-eight hours after the delivery to him of the agreement, give notice to the master or his agent that he will not be bound by the agreement, and thereupon the agreement shall be of no effect as between such workman and the master.

(3.) When a master and workman are bound by the agreement, they shall continue so bound during the continuance of any contract of employment and service which is in force between them at the time of making the agreement, or in contemplation of which the agreement is made, and thereafter so long as they mutually consent from time to time to continue to employ and serve without having rescinded the agreement. Moreover, the agreement may provide that any number of day's notice, not exceeding six, of an intention on the part of the master or workman to cease to employ or be employed shall be required, and in that case the parties to the agreement shall continue bound by it, respectively, until the expiration of the required number of days after such notice has been given by either of the parties.

(4.) The agreement may provide that the parties to it shall, during its continuance, be bound by any rules contained in the agreement, or to be made by the arbitrators, arbitrator, or umpire, as to the rates of wages to be paid, or the hour or quantities of work to be performed, or the conditions or regulations under which work is to be done, and may specify penalties to be enforced by the arbitrators, arbitrator, or umpire, for the breach of any such rule.

(5.) The agreement may also provide that in case any of the following matters arise they shall be determined by the arbitrators or arbitrator, viz:

a. Any such disagreement or dispute as is mentioned in the second section of the principal Act; or,

b. Any question, case, or matter to which the provisions of the master and servant Act, 1867, apply:

And thereupon, in case any such matter arises between the parties while they are bound by the agreement, the arbitrators, arbitrator, or umpire shall have jurisdiction for the hearing and determination thereof, and upon their or his hearing and determining the same no other proceeding shall be taken before any other court or person for the same matter, but if the disagreement or dispute is not so heard and determined within twenty-one days from the time when it arose, the jurisdiction of the arbitrators, arbitrator, or umpire shall cease, unless the parties have, since the arising of the disagreement or dispute, consented in writing that it shall be exclusively determined by the arbitrators, arbitrator, or umpire.

A disagreement or dispute shall be deemed to arise at the time of the act or omission to which it relates.

(6.) The arbitrators, arbitrator, or umpire may hear and determine any matter referred to them in such manner as they think fit, or as may be prescribed by the agreement.

(7.) The agreement, and also any rules made by the arbitrators, arbitrator or umpire in pursuance of its provisions, shall, in all proceedings, as well before them as in any court, be evidence of the terms of the contract of employment and service between the parties bound by the agreement.

(8.) The agreement shall be deemed to be an agreement within the meaning of the thirteenth section of the principal Act for all the purposes of that Act.

(9.) If the agreement provides for the production or examination of any books, documents, or accounts, subject or not to any conditions as to the mode of their production or examination, the arbitrators, arbitrator, or umpire, may require the production or examination (subject to any such conditions) of any such books, documents, or accounts in the possession or control of any person summoned as a witness, and who is bound by the agreement; and the provisions of the principal Act for compelling the attendance and submission of witnesses shall apply for enforcing such production or examination.

II. This act may be cited as "The Arbitration (Masters' and Work men) Act, 1872."

MEMORANDUM.

The Uses of the Act.

Briefly stated, the uses of the Act are three, viz:

1. To provide the most simple machinery for a binding submission to arbitration, and for the proceedings therein.

2. To extend facilities of arbitration to questions of wages, hours, and other conditions of labor, and also to all the numerous and important matters which may otherwise have to be determined by justices under the provisions of the "master and servants' act," 1867.

3. To provide for submission to arbitration of future disputes by anticipation, without waiting till the time when a dispute has actually arisen, and the parties are too much excited to agree upon arbitrators.

Mode of putting the Act in operation.

1. A form of agreement must be drawn up and printed either by the employer or by the workman. Such a form is appended, (No. I.) But this form is not obligatory, and it may be varied to any extent not inconsistent with the provisions of the Act.

2. When the form of agreement is settled and printed, it will become binding on an employer and a workman, reciprocally, upon the employer giving to the workman—and the workman accepting—a printed copy. But the workman has forty-eight hours to consider and satisfy himself of the effect of the agreement, and if within that time he gives a written or verbal notice to the employer or his agent, that he rejects it, he will not be bound by it. If, after accepting the copy, he does not give such notice, then both he and the employer will be bound by the agreement during the agreed term of employment, (whether that term be a day, or a week, or a year,) and no longer. The agreement, however, may itself provide that six days' notice shall be given of an intention to terminate the employment. And, in any case, upon an expiration of an agreement, it may be renewed in the same manner as before.

3. In case any dispute of a kind to which the agreement relates, arises between the parties bound by it during the continuance of the agreement, the dispute will be heard and determined; not by the parties, but by the arbitrators in the mode prescribed by the agreement; or, if no mode is so prescribed, then at their discretion. The attendance of witnesses, and the production of evidence may be enforced in the manner provided by the Arbitration Act of 1824, (5 Geo. IV, c. 96.)

4. The award of the arbitrators may be in the annexed form, (II.) And it may be enforced in the manner provided by the Arbitration Act, 1824, (5 Geo. IV, c. 96,) by distress, or imprisonment, and otherwise, or it may be enforced by plaint in the county court.

5. An analysis is appended of the clauses of the Arbitration Act, 1824, which will be applicable for the purposes of this Act

Forms of Agreement and Award.

I. FORM OF AGREEMENT.

The Arbitration (Masters' and Workmen) Act, 1872.—A B., (here insert name or usual description of the employer's firm and the name of the works;) and C. D., (here insert the name and occupation of the workman.)

1. The arbitrators shall be E. F. and G. H. (or an arbitrator shall, on or before the day of . . . , 18 . , be named in writing by H. I. on the part of the employer, or by J. K. on the part of the workman.)

2. The umpire, in case the arbitrators are equally divided, shall be L. M. (or shall be the person for the time being holding the office of . . . . . or shall be appointed by N. O.)

3. In case a person by whom anything is to be done under this agreement as an arbitrator or umpire, or as a person appointed to nominate any arbitrator or umpire, dies or declines to act, or becomes incapable of acting, or is interested as a party or otherwise in the matter referred to him, a person shall be appointed in writing by P. Q., or if P. Q. do not appoint within three days after request in writing from either party to the agreement, then by R. S. to act in the place of the person so dying, declining, or becoming incapable, or being interested.

4. Six days notice shall be required of an intention on the part either of the employer or of the workman to terminate the contract of employment and service in respect of which this agreement is made.

5. The parties to this agreement agree to the following rules, (or to such rules as may be made by the arbitrators on the following subjects,) viz:

(*a.*) As to the rate of wages, (here insert any such rule agreed on.)

(*b.*) As to the hours and quantity of work to be performed, (here insert any such rule agreed on.)

(*c.*) As to the conditions or regulations under which work is to be done, (here insert any such rule agreed on.) The penalties for the breach of the above rules shall be the following, (here insert the penalties.)

6. The following disputes arising between employer and workman during the continuance of this agreement, shall be determined by arbitration under this agreement, viz:

(*a*) Any such disagreement or dispute as is mentioned in the second section of the Arbitration Act, 1824, (5 Geo. IV, c. 96,) except (here insert a description of any such disagreements or disputes which it is intended to except.)

(*b.*) Any question, case, or matter to which the provisions of the Masters' and Servants' Act, 1867, apply, except, (here insert a description of any such question, case, or matter which it is intended to except.)

7. The arbitrators or umpire shall hear any matter referred to them in the following manner, viz: (Here insert any regulations by which it is desired to govern the proceedings of the arbitrators or umpire, *e. g.*, that they shall decide on written statements from each side, or that they shall hear oral evidence.)

8. The following books, documents, and accounts shall, on demand by the arbitrators or umpire, be produced, and submitted for examination, subject to the conditions hereafter mentioned, viz:

(*a.*) Books, documents, and accounts. (Here insert a description of them, or any such books, documents, and accounts as the arbitrator or umpire think fit to demand.)

(*b.*) Conditions. (Here insert any condition as to the mode of production or examination.)

II. FORM OF AWARD.

The Arbitration (Masters' and Workmen) Act, 1872.

Award.

We, A. B. and C. D., (name the arbitrators or umpire,) the arbitrators or umpire in the matter in dispute between, (here state the names of complainant and defendant,) do hereby adjudge and determine [1] that (here set forth the determination.)

(Signed) A. B.
C. D.

This . . day of . . . . , 18 . .

([1]. *Note e. g.*—That A. B. left his employment without due notice, and that A. B. shall pay to C. D. the sum of . . . . . . for his breach of contract; or that C. D. dismissed A. B. without due notice, and that C. D. shall pay to A. B. the sum of . . . . . . for his breach of contract)

Analysis of the Applicable Sections of the Arbitration Act, 1824, (5 Geo. IV, C. 96.)

§ 9. Attendance of witnesses by a justice of the peace by summons or commitment.

§ 23. Acknowledgment of fulfillment of award by the person in whose behalf it is made.
§ 24–30. Performance of award may be enforced by distress or imprisonment.
§ 31. Costs and expense to be settled by the arbitrators.
§ 32. Exemption from stamp duty.
§ 30–34. Protection of arbitrators, &c., from actions.

CONTENTS.

THE CLAIMS OF CAPITAL CONSIDERED.

By William Brown.

The conflict between labor and capital becomes more and more the struggle of the age. On both sides there are titanic powers engaged in what appears to be headlong and indiscriminating war. There may be now and again a lull in the contest—there may be some kind of truce proclaimed—some good sort of people may approach the combatants and induce them for a season to lay down their arms. But to the calm looker-on it is evident that all the fine talk about mutual forbearance, sympathy and good will, is only a makeshift; that each party returns to work with its passions but restrained for the moment or for the occasion; and with not only the expectation of a speedy renewal of the contest, but with a determination, when the time again comes round, to fight it out to the bitter end. Is it not one of the strange things in this strange world that industry should thus be constantly arrayed against its own productions—the wealth of the world in constant antagonism to the producers of that wealth? After all that has been lost and won, can it be said that either party is in a better position, or permanently secure from further strife?

Providence is constantly calling us, by the events transpiring around us, to consider our ways. The struggle between capital and labor, whatever be the issue, ought to direct the minds of thoughtful and reflecting men to a subject of unquestionably the first importance in relation to the general well-being of society. On the surface of this question, and amidst the contending factions there, we shall glean little or nothing. We must dig deep for the information requisite to enable us to form a correct judgment of the matters in dispute. I propose therefore in the present paper to make some examination into the claims advanced by capital, with the view of ascertaining if in any way or in any measure, industry, out of its resources, can yield to these claims; and will endeavor at the same time, to weave into my argument some essential principles in political economy, without a proper consideration of which, the great questions at issue will never be satisfactorily settled.

I need not trouble the reader with any long quotations from the economists in definition of the term "capital." It is sufficiently understood I daresay by the general reader. The following extracts from Mr. Mill's Principles of Political Economy will for the present suffice.

"It has been seen in the preceding chapters that besides the primary and universal requisites of production, labor and natural agents, there is another requisite without which no productive operations beyond the rude and scanty beginnings of primitive industry are possible: namely a stock, previously accumulated, of the products of former labor. This accumulated stock of the produce of labor is termed capital. The function of capital in production it is of the utmost importance thoroughly to understand, since a number of the erroneous notions with which our subject is infested originate in an imperfect and confused apprehension of this point.

"Capital, by persons wholly unused to reflect on the subject, is supposed to be synonymous with money. Money is no more synonymous with capital than it is with wealth. Money cannot, in itself, perform any part of the office of capital, since it can afford no assistance to production. To do this, it must be exchanged for other things, and anything which is susceptible of being exchanged for other things is capable of contributing to production in the same degree. What capital does for production, is to afford the shelter, protection, tools and materials which the work requires, and to feed and otherwise maintain the laborer during the process. These are the services which present labor requires from past, and from the produce of past labor. Whatever things are destined for this use—destined to supply productive labor with these various pre-requisites—are capital."

The above extract may be taken as representing the views generally held by economists on the subject of capital. The definitions may be considered as in some measure correct. They are not such as, in the use of exact language, I would employ. I think a better and more guarded definition can be given—better in so far as it would close every door against the entrance of those "erroneous notions with which our subject is infested," of which complaint is justly made by Mr. Mill. I have elsewhere had occasion to remark that political economy, more than any other science, has been worm-eaten with that incautious language which a modern writer has aptly declared to be "the dry rot of the world." Bearing upon, as it does in every direction, the most vital interests of humanity, this great science demands, and can be satisfied with nothing short of, perfect accuracy in thought and expression on the part of all its expounders.

I define capital simply as *the produce, the tools, and the appliances of labor*. As a question of property, capital is the produce of labor—as a question of productive agency, it is its tools and appliances. This definition embraces all that can be said and all that can be demanded. The capitalist himself may feel alarmed at so simple a definition, and may be inclined to regard it as one of those "hard sayings" with which restless people are continually troubling the world. But as the sweetest kernel may sometimes be found in the roughest shell, so the most precious truths have not seldom come to us enclosed in the hardest sayings.

Having made this statement, I think it is fair, before proceeding further, that I should set forth what I consider the weak points in Mr. Mill's definition above quoted, a definition more or less objectionable according to the interpretation which it may legitimately bear.

He states that money in itself cannot perform any part of the office of capital, since it can afford no assistance to production; that to do this, it must be exchanged for other things; and that anything which is susceptible of being exchanged for other things is capable of contributing to production in the same degree. If this language be not wholly ambiguous, it sets forth that money, when exchanged for other things, then and only then becomes an agent in production; and that anything susceptible of exchange is, from that very fact, exalted to the rank of a productive agent. Now, money, in a high degree, is susceptible of exchange, and must therefore be included in the latter statement. There are thousands of products on which you may cast your eye every day as you pass the shop windows, which could not by any stretch of fancy be considered as productive agents; and yet they are all susceptible of being exchanged, else they would not be exposed for sale. The usefulness of the tools to the workman does not consist in the fact that they may be sold for money, or exchanged for other things, but that they are properly fashioned and fitly made by industrious hands to aid these hands in continued production. I think it is quite evident that there has been a notion floating in our author's mind—some indefinable idea, something intangible which he calls capital, and which he proclaims as superior to and independent of money, tools, and materials. He does not tell us what it is. It may be a myth: and we fear that thousands of good people, who think they know all about the matter, are in the same position with regard to this myth It is not industry. It is no product of labor. It was never seen by mortal eyes, and yet men everywhere stand in awe of it. They would not dare to utter a word or pen a sentence to prejudice or discredit the existence of this ghostly shadow which flits around every mart, which casts its mysterious influence over every Exchange, and which, like others of its kind insensible to either lead or logic, fills us all with some indefinable sort of fear and robs us of our very manhood. That Mr. Mill had some such idea in his mind is evident from his own words. What capital does for production, he says, is to afford the shelter, protection, tools and materials, which the work requires, and to feed and otherwise maintain the laborers during the process. If words have any meaning, what does all this imply but that there is something which is called capital, something over and above industry, which furnishes shelter, houses, factories, etc; not the tools and materials themselves, or the industry which produces them, but something else which "affords" or furnishes the tool and materials; not the food and other means of maintenance for our bodily frames, but something outside of labor which feeds, clothes, and maintains these frames. Can it be money itself to which he has reference? I can hardly say. His language on that head is that money is not synonymous with capital. And yet, in other parts of his writings, he leaves one under the full conviction that he fell into the error of attributing to money the power of feeding, clothing, and maintaining industry.

Mr. Mill seems to have taken all the good things which industry can produce, and, placing them in the laboratory of his mind, or rather in the crucible of his imagination, immediately there is separated something without form and void; having neither body nor parts; acknowledging to neither length, breadth, nor height; giving not the slightest evidence that it has ever been touched by the hand of labor: and forthwith we are commanded to bow down and cry, This be thy God, O Industry! Is there a man, with a spark of intelligence, to obey such a summons?

It is no trifling or light matter which now engages our attention. The subject is of such momentous and far reaching importance, and leads us away down into the midst of a world of such misery, wretchedness, and unrequited toil, that we may well be excused if we bring before the reader another extract from Mr. Mill.

"Suppose, for instance, that the capitalist is a hardware manufacturer, and that his stock in trade, over and above his machinery, consists at present wholly in iron goods. Iron goods cannot feed laborers. Nevertheless, by a mere change of the destination of these iron goods, he can cause laborers to be fed. Suppose that with a portion of the proceeds he intended to maintain a pack of hounds, or an establishment of servants; and that he changes his intention, and employs it in his business, paying it in wages to additional work people These work people are enabled to buy and consume the food which would otherwise have been consumed by the hounds or by the servants; and thus without the employer's having seen or touched one particle of the food, his conduct has determined that so much more of the food existing in the country has been devoted to the use of productive laborers, and so much less consumed in a manner wholly unproductive."

Now, if this be not a deliberate shutting of one's eyes and running full tilt against the impregnable walls of political economy, I do not know what is. It is not simply a mistake, an error—it is a thorough subversion of the method and order of political economy; an attempt to blot out industry itself from its position as the great factor in the world's production. It is not by a change in the destination of iron goods, or of any other goods, that a capitalist can cause laborers to be fed. It is not by paying wages to work people that workers are enabled to buy and consume the food which would otherwise be consumed by hounds and servants. It is not the "conduct" of the capitalist which has determined that so much more of the existing food has been devoted to the use of productive industry. The truth is, the bits of money paid by the capitalist are powerless in the case. The power is wholly on the other side. The production is entirely with the laborers. They do not use the capitalist's money; neither do they eat the capitalist's food. It is their own money they spend—it is their own food they consume. If the capitalist places tools in their hands, he takes good care that the workmen pay for their use through either of the only two possible channels—reduction of wages, or enhanced price of the things made. Wages are always paid in money, and the workmen have given full value for that money. The capitalist hands over to them certain little coins upon which he bestows no toil from the moment they come into his possession till the moment they leave—the workingmen hand over to him the substantial evidence of a full week's personal toil and exhaustion. Whatever doubts may arise in the mind as to the earnings and toil of the capitalist, and as to the legitimacy of his great rewards, of one thing we may be certain—the men leave behind them, at the week's end, full and substantial value for the pittance they carry to their homes. At the same time I may be permitted to say that I am just as certain the noble mind of John Stuart Mill did not fully realise what was written when his pen traced the lines which I have transferred to these pages; and which, unhappily, are not by any means fitted to restore the beautiful temple of industry, so long laid in ruins.

All attempts thus to frame the system of political economy, or any of its great principles, on the life or death of a pack of hounds, or of a lot of domestic servants, or of a number of half-starved laborers, must, in the end, only expose our system, if not ourselves, to the ridicule of critical and intelligent men.

Industry is anterior to capital, and must, in the nature of things, be continually anterior to it, seeing that it is a principle (now happily being recognised more and more) that there is no value without labor. The savage who first fashioned a bow and arrow or hollowed out a canoe, illustrated the truth of this principle. It must ever be so. The fact that industry has gradually framed an immense quantity of tools and other good and serviceable material, will never subvert the natural order of things. Were the proposition or theorem of Mr. Mill true, that industry is limited by capital, then there never would have been any capital. To say that industry is limited by the very things it fashions is manifestly absurd. If any philosophic statement is really necessary on the subject, I would reverse the theorem of Mr. Mill and say that *capital is limited by industry*—that whatever is yielded or has been yielded by industry may be assumed as having had its limits clearly defined by industry itself. When a man is toiling up a mountain, and a friend in passing gives him a lift to its summit in his waggon, on condition, we will say, that he drives and guides the horse ; no one would allege that the journey had been limited, when it had been actually aided, by the horse and waggon. If to produce merchandise be the goal of life, as the top of the mountain was the goal of the journey, then capital, as I understand it, aids industry towards that goal. The power of physical endurance indeed presents a limit to industrial effort. Increasing age and feebleness will gradually impose a limit to effective force. Although it may be said, and said truly, that the fishes and wild animals and berries which sustain savage life are in a certain sense anterior to industry ; yet it is also true that, as an industrial question, the labor necessary to secure them is anterior to the produce—the labor is first exerted, then the results appear. Those who hold that industry is limited by capital do not mean to set forth the simple truism that every created thing necessarily has its limits. They mean to propound something very different from that—indeed, so far as labor is concerned, a most dangerous and destructive heresy. To say that industry is limited by capital, in the sense in which the economists use the phrase, is to say that the parent is the offspring of the child ; that capital is the master and man the slave ; that dead inert matter rules and reigns ; and that intelligent and strong-limbed men must implicitly obey. In short, it is to put the dead in the place of the living ; to take from industry its birthright, its blossom, and its crown.

Another of Mr. Mill's fundamental propositions regarding capital is, that it is the result of saving. This, he says, is the source, or relates to the source, from which it is derived. " We may say that all capital, and especially all addition to capital, are the result of saving." After what I have already stated, I think few, if any, of my readers will feel inclined to pin their faith to so foolish a proposition. But seeing that it has been elevated to the rank of an axiomatic truth in economic science, we do not wonder that this has further been set forth, with all due solemnity, — a sort of twin brother,—that, when industry *abstains* from using its productions, then it is on the high road to prosperity,—a statement diametrically opposed to truth. It seems to me very strange that Mr. Mill should apparently have been so anxious to divert the mind away from the only true source of production, *labor*. By what sort of arguments does Mr. Mill seek to establish his proposition ? By such as these : that, were all persons to spend all they produce, capital could not increase ; that farmers, even in the simplest states of society, must save a little for seed over and above their personal consumption ; that all that any one employs in carrying on labor other than his own must have been originally brought together by saving ; that, in a certain state of society, the increase of capital has usually been derived from privations which, though not generally called by that name, are essentially the same with savings; and so forth. Some of these are plain and simple truisms, and have little or no relation to economic science. Not one of them bears out the proposition that capital is produced or increased by saving. In fact, industry not only produces the capital, but cares for it afterwards, keeps it in repair, and thus "saves" it for use. Nobody will dispute the fact that, if a factory or piece of machinery is not burned up or otherwise destroyed, it will be found standing in its place ready for its work; in fact "saved;" just as nobody will dispute the fact that a horse is a horse and a cart is a cart, or that you cannot both eat and have your cake. Mr. Mill seems to think that all persons can spend all they produce, and that, in such a case, capital will not increase. *All* persons could not spend, in the sense in which Mr. Mill applies the term—that is that there should soon be nothing left for anybody—even in "personal indulgences" *all* they produce. The thing is impossible. But most producers part with all they produce in exchange for equivalents. It is incorrect to say that "all that any one employs in carrying on labor, other than his own, must have been originally brought together by saving." It was originally brought together by purchase or by labor. The man who has it, got it originally by exchanging for it his labor or the fruits of his labor, else he should not have it at all. Here is just an example of that "incautious language" which not only leads so many readers astray, but brings into reproach a science which presents before the enquiring mind a field of investigation not surpassed in interest by any department of thought.

Over against all these statements I place the simple economic truth which a child may understand—that industry is the "source" of capital, and capital the "result" of industry.

But Mr. Mill could not shut his eyes to the obvious fact that every thing produced by mortal hands gradually decays and disappears; that "dust to dust" is written over both man and his works. He therefore advances another theorem, that though capital is saved, it is nevertheless consumed. To save it for yourself you must, he says, have it consumed by some other person, not by yourself. Are we, then, to believe absolute impossibilities? If laid by for future use, he urges, it is not saved, it is then only hoarded. Why there should be any real distinction of this kind between the flour I sell to a laboring man to be immediately consumed by himself and family, and the flour I keep past me and consume in say three or six months hence, is a species of economic legerdemain I cannot comprehend. What is there involved that should cause the one transaction to be spoken of approvingly, the other in terms of reprobation? Mr. Mill makes a vast deal out of what he calls the unproductive consumption of the good things of this life, such as wines, equipages, and fine furniture. He speaks of them being "destroyed" by being consumed, so as to lead one to infer that they are as effectually put out of existence as if some stout fellows, club in hand, had smashed them to pieces, bottles, equipages, and all. The thing is too preposterous to bear investigation. Is one man to be reviled because he makes for himself a handsome turn-out—even though it be a four-in-hand, livery, cocked hats and all—and another to be praised because he is content with a creaking old cart? Is one man to be reproved because he grows a field of grapes, and turns out some puncheons of generous wine; the other to be praised because he aspires no higher than a draught of good cider, or mayhap is content with a glass of milk from his cow? Is one man to be railed at because he makes for himself by his labor, or purchases for himself by the produce of his labor, a set of nice, polished, and comfortable furniture; and another praised because he is content to lie on a rough plank? There is no "destruction" in either case. The very object for which all labor is undertaken, personal satisfaction, has been equally attained in each of the cases supposed. To say that it would be better to have the labor which is expended in the production of all these good things diverted into some other channel, such as the production of more tools for the workmen, or capital so called; or to say, as Mr. Mill says, that society collectively is poorer by the amount expended in these things, is to say what is manifestly untrue. It would be to sweep away much that makes life pleasant and enjoyable; much that tends to the advancement and refinement of society. Setting morals aside, and looking at it only from an economic point of view, I could not have a word to say against the man who spends ten thousand a year on hunters, hounds and racers, so long as he expends the produce of his own labor. An economist whose recent death we all mourn held that abstract political economy is susceptible of reduction to a single equation—in the same way as Lagrange reduced abstract mechanics—the fundamental idea of which is, that every person seeks to employ his productive powers in the way which will yield him most. Whilst questioning the propriety of attempting such a reduction of this noble science, we may yet accept of the statement so far as it goes, or so far as it is related to production. And so it stands out in bold antagonism to the proposition of Mr. Mill. The position held by the economists, that "had men always consumed their produce in the gratification of their immediate wants and desires, there would be no such thing as capital at all."* is so startling that one can scarcely believe it to have been advanced in sober earnest. There is not the least truth in it. It subverts the very order of nature. It puts aside, as of no moment, the very end and aim of all industrial effort. It is to gratify their wants ahd desires that men work and consume the produce of their work. Men do not eat up their ploughs and spades and harrows; they do not swallow their steam engines and their ships; but they clothe and feed themselves generally as well as they can, and they love to decorate their homes. The reverse of the statement of the economists is the truth. If men had *not* always consumed their produce in the gratification of their wants and desires, no such thing as capital would ever have existed; and they would all soon have descended to the position of miserable starvlings. It is the steady production of all that is good, and the no less steady consumption of these good things which go, if men would but live and let live, to clothe industry with its productive powers, and to yield it to those satisfactions after which it constantly strives.

How is it possible, as Mr. Mill alleges, to save your products for yourself by having them consumed by some other person? The products are gone when they are consumed. Those who have consumed them have purchased them. They have but put an equivalent in their place. The original producer or owner has got an equivalent for them, something else in exchange, that is all. Is it

* Ency. Brit. 8th Ed. Art. Pol conomy.

not a fact worthy of most attentive consideration, that the economists, in their desperate efforts to build up the present system, have been compelled to drag to ruins every vital principle in political economy, exchange among the rest?

Mr. Mill has a fourth fundamental proposition respecting capital, namely, that it supports and employs productive labor. This theorem must embrace money itself, for he speaks of capital "or other funds" devoted to the sustenance of labor. As I do not wish to weary the reader, and as what I have yet to say will bear upon the point, I feel as if the best answer I can give at the moment to this proposition is, that, in the sense in which it is advanced by Mr. Mill, it is not true.

Here I part company with Mr. Mill, for how can two walk together except they be agreed; and it is far from a pleasant task thus to have to criticise one whose writings have, in many respects, done so much for the science of political economy. And yet, notwithstanding all the influence of his great name, much of what he laid down as fundamental principle must eventually disappear in presence of calm and sober reflection. For it is quite plain to me that Mr. Mill, like many before him, and like some others since, frequently though unconsciously suffered the powers of his great mind to be overborne by the vulgar, arrogant, and commonplace maxims of the commercial world. He is not alone in having taken up ideas, those regarding capital, so called, which go far to vitiate much of what he and others have written on the subject. I have in the course of my reading become more and more impressed with the necessity of watching like jealous sentinels at the very portals of our science, for once an error creeps in there is no saying whither it may lead. Well would it have been for us, humanly speaking, had the "little ones" of the daughter of Babylon been taken in their infancy and dashed against the stones. A vulgar error in political economy, as in Scripture interpretation, only needs to be sent forth with the endorsation of a great name, and forthwith a crowd of lesser mortals join the cry, and centuries may pass away ere it is run to earth. What would my readers think of me were I to parade before them the naked savages of New Guinea as samples of civilization and christianity? Or were I to enter a lunatic asylum, and shutting my eyes and ears to the outer world, proceed to reason as if what I witnessed there were a fair representation of human life and society? Would that be anything more absurd than to accept of the ignorant, degraded, hand to mouth multitudes, struggling all day long for their daily bread, and retiring at night like the beasts of the field to their miserable lairs, as the true and legitimate fruits of the workings out of industrial and economic science? And yet it is reasoning from just such data that has led numerous economists to fall into such errors and absurdities as these: to exalt money at the expense of labor—to view it as practically a productive agent—to invent the myth of the wages fund—to claim separate and distinct rewards for the tools and appliances of labor—to set money, true money, aside—to give the name of money to bits of paper, and thus to make the very acknowledgment of debt to industry a means of payment, so called, of its just demand—to set forth that "credit," or the getting of the proceeds of labor into one's hands without payment, is actually a blessing to industry—to fall into the perilous sort of security which accepts of what we see around us as the natural and inevitable condition of things—to exercise, by sprinkling a few gold pieces around the base of the mighty mountain of paper, the heinous and constant deception of what is facetiously called "the specie basis" (that "cunningly devised fable" which has led such multitudes astray)—to perpetuate, under the pretence of paying by paper promises to pay, a universal suspension of payment, thus convicting us as a nation of being, like the Cretians of old, "always liars"—and to say and do many other things at which reason and morality alike revolt. In a word, the economists have labored hard and brought forth, not a mouse, but a monster.

I will now advance two distinct propositions or theorems on the subject of Capital, and then proceed to lay down a few principles in political economy, which, though they may be new to most if not all of my readers, in my judgment throw so clear a light over the whole field of Capital as, I trust, will induce those who love truth for truth's sake to follow up the very interesting subject for themselves.

1st. Capital, *as such*, cannot receive any reward from Industry.

2nd. Industry, *as a productive agent*, cannot afford any return to Capital.

Each of these theorems is the corollary of the other. If one is true, both are true. And if both are true, then it follows that there never was and never can be an equitable or other division of profits between labor and capital, between industry and the things which it produces. In that case, if capital be divorced from the producer, there cannot but be unceasing conflict between the two.

There is no such thing in nature, and therefore no such thing in political economy, as demand for labor. What is there to demand it? Is there anything outside of labor itself to demand it? Do men work for others or for themselves? Can money demand labor? Money is simply a product of industry, in general and gratuitous use by industry in the exchange of its products. It is produced by industry, is emphatically *for industry*, and surely must be owned by industry. It is designed for circulation throughout all the fields of labor, so that wherever a product of labor is found, there also will be found or ought to be found, another product of labor, money, with which to buy. In its universal and gratuitous use to industry, money may be said to be its very slave. It is where it should be when it is in the hand of industry; for the absolute title which labor gives to the products of its own toil can never be destroyed. Would there be any reason in calling such a thing as this, or calling buying with such a thing as this, a demand for industry? A series of buyings, on the part of the capitalist, from the raw material all through up to the finished product, is not production, for buying a thing or selling a thing is not producing it. It is simply an exchange of money for the products of labor, and the buyer, as such, is never the producer. You may please to call this continued series of purchases *investing*, but there is no production in it at all, not even to the extent of the most slender thread. Labor can only sell its products. *For* these there is a demand; and *of* these there is a supply. If you buy a human being from some one who claims to own him, and set him to work for you, you will have a slave in your possession. He never owns property, the produce of his toil. You simply keep him in life for the sake of what his labor will yield, by giving him a bare sustenance out of the things he produces; but it is impossible he can ever rise above the position of a slave. And yet, as you must well know, it is his labor which keeps you in life. If a system prevails by which the generality of men receive only days wages, and never *own* the things they produce, their position will practically be similar to that of the slave. They will get the bare necessaries of life, nothing more. A home, a dwelling, with all its pleasant surroundings, they will rarely if ever own. They will remain strangers to all elevating and refining influences. They will see all the good things they create—the good houses, the good clothing, the good food, the good equipages, the good furnishings of all kinds—continually passing away, as if by some inevitable law, out of the hands of the many into the hands of the few, out of the hands of the producers into those of the non-producers. The stately steamships which they build will rarely carry them across the ocean on a visit of pleasure, or of recreation for their wearied frames. *Is not this the very condition in which we now find the industrial world?*

It is impossible, under our present system, that it can be otherwise. It is a provision in economic science that the human race is to be greatly advanced in culture, condition, and refinement, by the universal exchange of the products of every land, and by the profits realized in such exchange. If the whole earth had been of the same temperature and yielded the same products, there would have been but little occasion for different nations to seek each other out in order to exchange their various commodities. The diversity of climate, surface, and natural products, sustains foreign trade, and vastly increases the intercourse between nations. Now, men exchange their products with each other in order that they may secure a profit by the exchange. If there were no profit, there would be no exchange. But what is this profit? Men like to make as much of it as they can, but how few of them ever consider what it really is. I think the best definition I can give of it is, that it is *labor saved*. It is not a definition cumbered with words, but it tells the whole story. To save labor, we must labor. Men exchange the products of their toil for other products of toil, because they see that they can save their labor by so doing—they find it cheaper to exchange than that they should themselves make the things they are in quest of. Thus we are compelled to throw our skill and energy into one channel, and in that particular channel or branch of industry we naturally become proficient. This definition, so simple, brings before us at a glance the prolific source of all those vast emoluments which are represented by the general term "income"; all of it the fruit of industry; all of it the wealth of labor. Of course the true profit in every case is secured when the two products are exchanged at their true value—that is, at the value of the actual labor embodied in each, reckoned in but never arbitrarily measured by that article of universal use and desire which is taken from the mine; and which, though it be called a *medium* of exchange, yet exchanges nothing but the labor value it contains. It is evident, also, that this profit or saving of labor is a most powerful and important factor, though silent and unseen, in the progress of our race, bestowing upon us vast resources beyond all computation. And thus also we see how it comes round that the products of industrial skill and effort flow into the very channel—that of exchange—through which these beneficent forces are brought into full and best play.

Now, so far as the products of manual or muscular labor are concerned, it is obvious that the profit should fall to the lot of those who have actually embodied their personal toil in the making or necessary handling of the commodity to be exchanged. Wherever needful actual labor is given, there profit should accrue.

Mr. Mill has, I think, entirely missed the point in his definition of profit. He is not alone, however, in this respect. He says, " the cause of profit is, that labor produces more than is required for its support." Now, this cannot be true, however well it fits in with the ideas of capital. Labor does not produce more than is required for its support. What object would it have in doing so? A shoemaker makes more shoes than he can himself wear out, but that fact is not the cause of his profit. He makes more shoes than he can consume, but he needs other things in exchange for the shoes. How could industry make profit out of useless surplus which would have to lie and rot? It is as striking as it is instructive to see with what regularity all the great staples of life are produced and consumed, consumption following as closely on the heels of production as night follows day. Even the luxuries of life are all called for and consumed, else they would not be produced. Has half famished industry, as we daily witness it around us, more than it needs for its support? Would it not be glad to have a great deal more of even the necessaries of life, let alone its comforts and luxuries? The truth is, my definition of profit is too simple for the economists. Simple and truthful though it be, it plays sad havoc with a multitude of fine but baseless economic theories.

If these principles be correct, it becomes a question of gravest importance how or to what extent the laboring population, our working hired millions, can possibly receive profit on their labor. They make nearly everything that is produced. All the labor value that these things contain flows from their hands. But do they ever *own* the things they make? or do they ever exchange them? The ownership falls immediately into the hands of parties who have not labored and produced, and by them they are exchanged. And if it be needful, as it seems to me beyond all doubt it is, that the laborer or producer should personally *own* the things he makes in order to secure the lawful profit by their exchange; and if, as is the fact, the workers never own, these things; then it follows that the millions of actual producers are inevitably shut out from all profit on their labor. This great source of elevation and progress is practically closed against them. The wealth, whatever it is, goes into another channel and falls into other hands. Industry *produces* it and *loses* it—capital claims it and gets it. Under such a system the doom of the working classes is effectually sealed. Though they produce the world's wealth, they have, in the way of reward, no part or lot in the matter. As a body it is impossible they can ever rise above that low plane of existence on which, from the cradle to the grave, they spend their unambitious, sad, and hopeless lives. Hence also we perceive how it is that all the vast resources, in the shape of machinery, now in the hands of industry, allied as these are with some of the most powerful forces of nature, have failed appreciably to affect for the better the condition of industry itself. Nations without values to exchange will either remain in an uncivilized state or become extinct. Industry, in the persons of its producers, never *owning* and exchanging the products of its toil, is reduced to the position of a beast of burden. Capital, the product of industry, and designed to be its best friend, thus becomes, in the hands of the non-producers, its most dreadful oppressor, never halting even for a moment in its insatiable demands, but ever crushing our poor humanity beneath that hopeless bondage out of which death is the only escape. This is industry in ruins; and industry in ruins is, without doubt, humanity itself hastening rapidly to destruction.

But it may be urged that if the laborer gets $5.50 a week, and it only costs him $5 to live, he has gained 50 cents on his labor for the week. This would not shew that he gained a profit out of the things made. It would only disclose the fact that he had been able, by extraordinary pinching, or denying himself some of the necessaries of life, to keep his expenditure within his income by 50 cents. Nothwithstanding all that may be urged as to the little savings of a few of the more skilled hands, it is a notorious fact that the great bulk of workers are constantly living on the edge of poverty, and that the slightest stagnation soon brings them to actual want.

Think, also, of the radical difference between selling the products of industry, and selling, as it is called, a day's or week's labor, or labor separate from its products. Do men, in each case, meet on equal terms? Far from it. In selling the products of industry men do indeed meet on equal terms. If the thing is not wanted at the moment, there is no pressing hurry. It can lie a while. Labor is fairly matched with labor, service with service, value with value. But in the other case men meet on unequal terms. On the one side is the gigantic power of capital, of accumulated wealth; the factories, the houses, the machinery, the tools, the means of transport, all in the hands of non-producers—on the other helpless industry, wearied and anxious, wasted, broken down, with suffering at the door: on one side all earth's goodly products to fall back upon, on the other famished children it may be crying for bread. There could not be a more unequal conflict. In the disposal of commodities there may be a law of demand and supply, where each party brings with him his own supply and his own demand, but here it would be a shameful perversion of language to speak of any natural law of supply and demand as existing at all. If commodities are not in demand, they will simply cease to be made. But if labor, in its present sad condition, ceases to be "employed," as it is termed, it will cease to live. The forces at work are different, as well as the objects on which these forces are expended. On the one hand products of industry matched against products of industry—on the other hand all the products of industry arrayed against industry itself in the persons of its producers; in other words, against human beings.

Here we are brought face to face with the great question of human labor considered in the abstract, or as apart from the proceeds of the toil of the active, intelligent and responsible being in whom it is lodged. Can it be sold as a commodity can be sold? Have we considered how closely man's moral and material interests are linked together? Is it consistent with his dignity, independence, rights, and progress, that he should sell his labor otherwise than through the *produce* of his toil—that the great bulk of the world's commodities should never be owned by the people who toil for them—that *the man* and the material produce of his hands should be brought to the same level? It is a question of profoundest interest. I have my own thoughts on the subject, but for the present I must leave the problem in the hands of the reader. We know, at all events, what a wise man said on the subject long ago,—" Also that every man should eat and drink, and enjoy the good of all his labor; it is the gift of God: there is nothing better than that a man should rejoice in his own works."

It will help us much in our investigations if we bear in mind that it is not the material of which products are made, but the labor embodied in the product, which is sold. This truth comes too seldom to the surface. We appropriate nature's gifts—we sell only men's labor. From the richest and rarest of her products (the diamond for example) down to the cheapest and commonest of them all, the same truth prevails: it is labor only which can be sold. I would invite the capitalist especially to take this great truth in hand, and see whither it will lead him, and what it will do with all that he so fondly calls his own.

It may be necessary to remind my mercantile readers that they also must submit to the inevitable laws regulating value and exchange. Political economy has no special rules for them. They can be paid on no other principle than that on which the laboring man is paid. If they think that the mere touch of their fingers, or the mere act of purchase, separates in some mysterious manner a large portion of the world's wealth for their pockets, they are deeply mistaken. They can claim for their labor; for all *they* have got to exchange; for all the value *they* add to commodities; and for no more. Can one expect to reap where he has not sown? The broker who spends a few hours of each day rushing up and down the street must account for his labor just the same as the farmer who follows his plough. The laws of value and of the exchange of values embrace each with the same firm grasp. Labor demands at the hands of every man a service of some sort; and it must be a true industrial service if it is to come within the circle of exchange. Trade is but buying and selling. Exchange is the appointed channel through which a profit comes to industry; and though it cannot come unless an exchange is made, yet it does not come simply because the exchange is made, but because an exchange is effected of things in which certain parties have embodied a determinate amount of labor value. If any one presumes to intercept a portion, whether great or small, of that profit flowing to the producer through this, nature's own channel, he must, it is very plain, be able, by a labor title and by no other, to establish his claim to the share he appropriates, otherwise he will wrong labor *by taking that which does not belong to him.* Commerce is not a vast grab-bag into which a man may thrust his hand at pleasure. Possession is not necessarily ownership. Broad lands do not become yours because some marauding baron of old looked over them from some distant height, and said to sundry of his followers: All this will I give you if you will fall down and worship me. Property got by fraud or violence must ever be a source of reproach and shame; property got by values incorporated with it by other hands can never be a cause for boasting; property accumulated as the result or equivalent of personal toil must ever be a source of honorable pride and satisfaction. The eye of truth itself can discover no flaw in the title conferred by an exchange of labor value for labor value; but it is a questionable sort of title which comes with property whose price has been greatly depressed by the urgent necessities of the man whose toil it represents. Are there many commercial transactions really able to pass through the ordeal of labor? Have we much property in possession able to stand the fiery trial, and to produce, on demand, labor's grand and unimpeachable title?

The next proposition which I have to make is one of great importance with reference to the question of capital. It bears directly upon it, and, so far as it goes, presents an insuperable obstacle to its claims. It is this—*that in every act of exchange the profit is on the side of the man with the labor, not on the side of the man with the money.* I have elsewhere laid this down as a principle in political economy, and given, with some fulness, the argument in support of it.* Money is an absolutely unproductive commodity. Labor is finished with it from the moment it leaves the mint. Its general service to the human family in helping barter or exchange, and in placing in the hands of industry at all times absolute security for its work or for its goods, no arithmetical terms can fully embrace. But in its special work in the act of exchange between man and man, it can bring back nothing to its holder except the labor value embodied in the coins. Though we are in the habit of calling it a *medium* of exchange, it exchanges nothing outside of itself. Of course, if it did not circulate, men would not desire it. But it does circulate, and it does own value; and these are the reasons why industry accounts itself safe in investing its labor in it for the time being. Labor itself will permit no questionings on the point; for it considers itself, and justly so, absolutely safe in such an investment. With gold and silver in hand it not only feels secure, but *is* secure, and in the midst of the wildest panic, is perfectly serene. Nothing can equal a labor title, and gold and silver have that title perfect. Labor knows it gave toil for its specie—it knows the specie is always in demand—and with that in its hand, it can laugh in the midst of the greatest commotion. But profit on the bit of money, there is none. That was all settled for when it passed from the mint or from the hand of the man who dug it from the mine. Profit can only accrue when labor is spent; never when money is spent. It may startle the reader to tell him so. It is true nevertheless. And it is well that it is so; for industrial prosperity for the world does not consist in the quantity of money in existence, nor in the accumulation of money in particular hands, but in the quantity of good things produced by labor, and distributed wherever other labor establishes its claim to a share. I need hardly pause to point out how or to what extent this important economic truth bears on the subject of capital and its claims. The reader may intuitively make the application. Fixed and circulating capital are the two divisions generally made of the subject by the economists. Money is consequently held by them to be capital, and entitled to rewards. But if the principle I have laid down be correct, it can receive no return from industry; and there is surely no other conceivable source from which it can be supplied. And then, let it be borne in mind, the laborers are always paid their wages in money, or in what pretends to be money. It needs no argument to shew that the worker gives toil, and that the man who gives a bit of money, gives an article on which he has bestowed no toil. If he claims a profit because he has given a bit of money in exchange for labor, as all capitalists do, he claims what labor can never give without most serious loss and suffering.

* New Catechism on Political Economy, p 36.

Money, instead of being a blessing to industry, will then be turned into an instrument of oppression. In exchanging a pair of boots for a pair of pants, the tailor and the shoemaker each receives his full labor back again, and a profit besides, because each has brought skilled and effective labor to bear on the things made, and labor is mutually saved by the exchange. The skill of the tailor is transferred to the shoemaker, and the skill of the shoemaker becomes the property of the tailor. But in exchanging the boots for a five-dollar piece, the owner of the money can claim no profit, because he bestows no labor, skilled or otherwise, on the piece. Where he has given no labor, it is certain he can claim nothing for labor saved. Hence money conveys a profit *to the producer* for the things he makes and exchanges, but can never impart profit to the person who simply pays it away. When that producer comes, in his turn, to part with the money, he parts with it without a profit.

It is plain, then, that if the capitalists, or anybody else, claim a profit on the mere exchange of money, of this so-called circulating capital, they claim what labor, at any rate, never can afford to give.

It may not be out of place to consider, in passing, what really constitutes the capital of the Bank of England. It is made up of three things: specie, paper, and credit. As related to industry, the first is real, the second valueless, the third a myth. It may have some other things in possession, such as bills discounted, or, in other words, vast claims against the commercial and manufacturing classes, and which the industrial classes are constantly in the act of paying out of their hard toil. But the three things mentioned are those by which it principally does its work. The specie has been all produced by the hand of toil. It has been got by much labor. It is the property of industry. It ought to be in the hand of industry, busy exchanging the products of industry. It could not be more out of its place than stowed away in a bank vault. The Bank of England never gave a bit of genuine labor for a single sovereign or bar within its vaults. I do not say that it has been gathered in there out of the hand of industry *for the known purpose* of destroying industry; but I say that the effect of its being so gathered is to destroy industry. The next thing is the bit of paper, nicely engraved, promising to pay industry its money on demand. As related to industry, that bit of paper must not only be valueless, but ruinous; for, so long as it floats, it suspends payment, draws vast returns out of labor, and thus uses the capital of labor to ruin labor. It is absolutely impossible that you can ever hand to me a bit of paper in exchange for my labor, without you making a gratitious use of my toil for the time being. It is generally held up as an honorable and creditable thing for the Bank of England to pay specie on demand. Why should it be so considered? The money does not belong to the bank—it belongs to industry. Trace it back to the man who produced it; or trace it down from that man till it was intercepted by a bit of paper. Is there anything creditable in the Bank paying back to the man of labor the gold which belongs to him, and which the other has originally got out of his hands in exchange for a bit of paper? Is this all that can be said in favor of specie payments, or of a return to specie payments—a question which is at this moment convulsing this western continent? Is it such work as this that we are satisfied to call creditable and honorable? Has industry any real interest in such a question? Not one whit. Paper men may worry themselves to death over the subject, but what interest has the great world of industry, the toiling millions, with the question of specie payments, *so called?* Will it be better paid by one sort of nicely engraved paper being substituted for some other sort? Will it be paid any better by a bit of paper called a promise to pay than by a bit of paper called a legal tender in payment? What difference will it make to toil? That is the question at issue. Then there is the thing called credit, a myth so far as industry is concerned in its production or handling, but, alas! not a myth so far as industry suffers by its exactions. It is a fine word, a most honorable word, a most plausible word. Did industry ever produce it, or handle it, or see it? Industry says: Your credit is said to be good, when you can get much, very much, of our money and goods into your possession without payment; and you make us constantly pay tribute for the exercise of your credit. Who is it, think you, that pays the vast sums on account of this credit? It is all paid by the men who toil, and by none else. The statesman thinks the strength of the British nation lies at the back of the Bank of England. I pity his delusion. Alas! the weakness of the British nation is *in* the Bank of England. The violated laws of political economy are the terrible things with which that nation has yet to deal.

The rudest implement ever fashioned by savage hands, to aid in moving the soil, was a step in the creation of capital. It relieved, so to say, from the necessity of scratching the ground with the fingers for the reception of the seed. It was a veritable production of capital, and in that respect not different from the construction of the most complicated and skilfully prepared piece of machinery. The savage into whose brain there first flashed the idea of making a hoe, and who first fashioned and employed such an implement, would at once be placed in a position superior to his fellows. Until similar hoes were made throughout the community, his rewards of toil would be in excess of those of his companions. To make him a live capitalist, it would only require some sort of paternal government (such as we are blessed with in these days) to take into its head that the best way to promote the general prosperity of its subjects is to create monopolies for particular branches of industry, to invent a patent law, and thus deny to all the other members of the tribe the privilege of making hoes. But the inventive faculties of industry, once aroused, can never sleep more; and so another step forward is taken. A spade, or something after the model of a spade, is fashioned; and this relieves from the necessity of scratching the soil with the hoe. A third step is taken; and some Tubal-Cain not only sends forth the plough, but instructs other artificers to do the same. According to the definition of the economists, these three well known and ancient implements of husbandry are entitled to be ranked among capital. Inde.d, when we consider how much the human race from the earliest ages has been indebted to the plough for its very sustenance, and how widely that instrument is distributed throughout every nation, may we not conclude that, as a labor-saving instrument, it takes precedence of all others ever made, or likely to be made, and stands in the front rank of capital.

There is thus not the slightest difficulty in comprehending how capital is created, and how it is at once the produce and the property of toil. It is simply an aid to industry, and so far must be considered as the tools and appliances with which further production is to be accomplished; and, in this respect, if we are very fastidious about the matter, as embracing also all that shelters, clothes, and feeds industry.

The important question now comes before us, In what manner and to what extent can capital itself receive rewards from industry?

The capitalist says that he is entitled to receive a return from industry for the employment or use of capital: I say that industry can never afford to give a return to capital.

The capitalist says that the employment of his capital in the hands of industry, and the reception of a distinct and separate reward for himself as the owner of that capital, is a blessing to industry: I say that the employment of capital by industry, in its own hands, and for its own behoof, is a blessing; but that the giving of a distinct and separate reward to capital is a curse instead of a blessing to industry, and can never generally be done without industry being brought, as a direct consequence, to utter degradation and slavery.

The capitalist says the profit can be divided between those who do the work and those who own the machinery: I say that profits can never be so divided without serious injury to industry.

The capitalist says the profits may be doubled by the employment of capital, so as to give one profit to the laborer and another to the capitalist: I say that it is impossible for labor ever to get a double profit out of the exchange of its products, and that every legitimate exchange transaction yields on each side only a single profit.

The capitalist says it is better for him to "give employment" to thousands of laborers than to let them starve: I say it is better to do so, much better; better that men should work and earn even wages than not to work and starve; but that this is no argument at all on behalf of the claims of capital, and does not throw the least ray of light into our subject.

These propositions, as I have put them, are distinct and antithetic. If one stands, the other falls: both cannot be true: either industry or the capitalist must be relegated beyond the sphere of political economy.

I think I need hardly say to the intelligent reader that the question is not, Ought I to give the use of my capital without fee or reward? or, Ought the working men to make use of my capital and give me no return? Happily, the economist is not called to adjudicate upon questions of that sort. What men may do or will do belongs to another department of thought. Our duty is to expound the principles of our science, and to show what industry can do and what it cannot do.

It seems necessary also, just at this point, to remind the reader that industry receives its rewards, or equivalents, from the produce to which it gives birth. Out of that source alone can it be paid. I suppose there can be no dispute with the capitalist on this point; for I will admit, as the capitalist will also admit, that if capital is entitled to a reward, it can be got out of no other source than the produce of industry. The more ample things made by the use of capital will bring in the more ample returns than if the tools in aid of labor had never been fabricated. Simple and self-evident though it be, it yet seems necessary to keep continually in mind that industry can only get its returns and its profits out of the things produced by human hands, by industry itself; a truth which the general use and circulation of money has no doubt helped largely to hide from view. For the use of money, whilst it practically simplifies every transaction of exchange, to the careless or superficial observer appears as if it reduced the science to only endless complications or a confusion of tongues which nobody can understand. Neither must we omit to estimate the powerful influence exercised over many minds by that intangible and incorporeal thing called credit; which, so long as it is only talked about outside of industry, is harmless enough; but which, the moment it issues in getting hold of the products of industry, such as money or anything else, without payment, and then adds to the price of everything consumed by the producer, is a most hurtful and destructive thing, mythical though it be. Credit, when it continually keeps possession, without payment, of the products of industry, is doing a mean thing: credit, when in addition it makes industry actually *pay for the use of its own products*, is doing both a mean and an unjust thing.

As is well known, it has been found somewhat difficult to give a proper definition of the science of political economy—to restrain it within proper bounds. Its infinite value to the human race seems to mock all our efforts to confine it within scientific swaddling bands. The true economist rejoices in its grand embrace, and will not trouble himself much about precise or positive lines of demarcation. But define it as we may, it deals with human beings as the producing agents to whose lot, and as a recompense for whose toil and energy, all returns must finally, nay directly, fall. It never can be claimed that a spade as a spade, a plough as a plough, a thrashing machine as a thrashing machine, or a marine engine as a marine engine, are entitled to profit or reward. The profit must ever accrue to the active and intelligent being who presides over all; of whose inventive genius and skilful labor these are the products; and without whose guiding hand and watchful presence and constant co-operation, all the tools and machinery in existence would be nothing but so much useless lumber. The capital itself can no more claim a reward than can those active forces of nature which the skill and ingenuity of man render obedient to his will. Capital has no more claim to take anything out of the hand of industry, than the sun has as a recompense for yielding its heat or the moon its light.

It will help to throw further light upon the subject if we also keep before us the interesting truth so clearly and logically set forth by Mr. Mill—that man's labor in its totality from first to last consists in nothing but moving things into position, or from place to place. Every turn of the spade, every stroke of the hammer or the brush, every movement of the plough, every twist of the thread, every sweep of the scythe, illustrates this simple truth. All that man can do is to bring matter into its right position—nature does the rest. He may *think* till he can think no more about his work; about making a spade, about hammering a plough, about constructing a bridge, about building a ship; his thinking must issue in a product before he can be paid in a product. From the lowest to the highest piece of mechanism, from the simplest up to the most complicated, the same truth prevails. There is no exemption in favor of capital, or of the use of capital. It is for this movement of the mortal frame, for the muscular force requisite—in other words, for the expenditure of toil, or for the sweat of the brow—that men are and ever must be paid. All physical toil requires some mental toil, some thought, more or less. If men are to be paid in a physical product, such as money, the visible product must be the offspring of physical toil, conceived in the mind, thought out there, and issuing through the hand. The thing produced, as we say, by the hand, is the fruit in every instance of the combined efforts of brain and muscle, and must be accepted as payment in full for all that goes before—for all that brain and hand have jointly contributed towards the product. There is a sweet and everlasting partnership between the hand and the brain of every human being; and the fruits of that partnership are the endless things useful and beautiful which confer joy and comfort, refinement and satisfaction, to society in general. The hand and the brain can no more be divorced than can the workman and his tools. I admit that industry may be so degraded in ignorance and so reduced by oppression, that brains may arrogate all the wealth, comfort and profit, leaving only bare life to industry. But this never can be done without the violation of natural laws and of natural rights, and the introduction into human society of a train of misery whose terrible issues can only be fully known to the divine mind.

But the capitalist may now urge, Does not the case of a skilful inventor who, by the use of some new machine, turns out products at a vastly increased rate, upset all your theories about men being paid for actual toil? At first blush it appears to do so, but it does not do so. If men were *not* paid according to the produce turned out, then they would not be paid for their *toil*. If one improves his knitting machine so that he turns out a hundred pairs of stockings in the same time as he used to turn out fifty, the price of stockings will tend to fall. Unless he were secured a monopoly of stocking making, he would not long retain any advantage over his fellows, for nothing can ever prevent human labor so distributing itself as to become generally equalized in its rewards. Unless men arbitrarily interfere with natural laws, no department of labor can long continue in the ascendant over other departments. Just as money, true money, has a tendency to distribute itself abroad wherever products of industry are offered for sale; so labor has a tendency to equalize itself throughout every department of toil. There is no measure of the value of labor but labor itself. Every product of toil must submit to be measured by all other products of toil. I do not set aside the efficacy of skill in all works of industry. The most skilful worker is the best worker, and will reap the best rewards. The "skill" of the mind will be shown through the skill and "cunning" of the hand. The expert workman who does his work as well as his fellow and in half the time, will get a better payment. Yet both are paid *for* their labor, *for* the amount of toil—that is, the one has a certain return, in visible products, for his toil; the other has a certain, and larger, return for his toil.

But is it money which *really* pays the great world of industry for all its toil? Without money we cannot, in the ordinary sense, be paid. The digging of money from the mine will pay its producers, or make them richer than if they had not done any work at all. And, after that, it will be the medium, but the medium only, through which profits are brought to every toiling hand. Its general distribution at this moment would give to each family but a trifling amount. So that it's not being paid in money which makes the world richer. One form of economic wealth is, as I conceive it, that there be such a conjunction of skill and toil in the same individual and throughout every branch of industry, that there shall yet issue, among other things, *a universal relaxation of labor*, and our race be saved from that severe and continued toil which leads only to debasement and ignorance. And here, in passing, I would throw out the thought that exchange, and what is secured to industry by the principle of exchange, seem to have been designed by our allwise Creator to restore to us the waste of the sweat of the brow—to return to the race, *in the form of profit*, far more than it can ever expend in the shape of personal toil I have been long impressed with the fact that all the laws of political economy have a merciful side. There is a deep and beneficent design in the interdependence of human labor, as well as in the interchange of blessing which all producers are unconsciously compelled to bestow upon one another in the act of production and exchange. I expect that the old truth is as fresh and vigorous as ever—that the way to fill our barns and burst out our presses, is for industry to consecrate its first fruits to the cause of suffering humanity in every land. I am quite convinced that thoughtful men will yet unfold the whole subject from points of view which will command our deepest interest and attention. The period is approaching when, to the pulpit especially, the industrial and economic ethics of the Bible must be for the time being of paramount importance.

The man who works is the true and only producer. All that *his* toil brings forth, aided or not aided by implements or tools, is *his* property, unless it can be established that there are other reasons outside of production itself, which confer a title to a share of the products of his toil for people who do *not* work. If the fact of the *ownership* of capital establishes a claim to a large share of the products of industry, we may be quite sure that as an economic truth it will fall in with every other economic truth.

On the one side we have the claims of the capitalist: 1st. That he should have a share of the products of industry, because he owns the capital or appliances; 2nd. That he should have a share because others use and employ what belongs to him. These two grounds, I think, fairly set forth and embrace his claims.

On the other side we have the claims of industry, antagonistic to those of capital as just set forth: 1st, That all the tools and appliances of industry are designed and have been constructed specially to aid the worker in his work; and 2nd, That he cannot give a share of the produce of his toil, such as capital claims, to those into whose hands his tools may have fallen; in other words, that he cannot give away what he produces with the aid of the tools, without being reduced to the position he would be in, were he still compelled to struggle for a living without tools at all, or with only those of the rudest description.

The laborer may urge, and surely with the utmost propriety, that it is unnatural to divorce him from his tools; to compel him to support himself and family by his personal toil; and out of the same toil, to have him give away all profits on his work to the very tools designed and constructed for the help of industry; for it is virtually doing this so far as he and his labor are concerned. May he not say, and say well, If the rate of profit you secure for the capital, the tools, and machinery of our work, is such as to cause it to double itself in ten or twelve years, ought I not to see my position as a producer advanced at a corresponding rate? Ought I not by this time to have good clothes, good food, a home of my own, and my family in comfort? Ought I not to be sharing, along with you, in all the precious things I produce? Ought I not to see my children, if not myself, rising in the social scale, and inheriting a share of all that is going? Ought I not to be now getting quit of my ignorance, my rags, and my wretchedness? Why should the ground which I till not yield to me her strength? Is the very curse of Cain upon me that I and my children after me should be as fugitives and vagabonds in the earth? Why should the little ones whom I love be taken from their childish play to be ruined in body and mind, and yoked to repulsive labor? How is it that the very order of nature should be reversed, and the idler be rich and ever accumulating more riches, and the toiler be poor and familiar for evermore with poverty? Why should all these vast industrial resources only issue in reducing me and my fellow laborers to mere days wages and mere days labor? What good do we get out of them if we never own any of the things we make? Is it not *our* labor which doubles *your* capital? How is it that we have lost the ownership of the very tools with which we work? How is it that the working millions, producing all that is handled in every market, should still remain poor, very poor, and the few fortunate ones, who neither toil nor spin, be rich, very rich?

These may be hard questions, and we may be troubled at their presence; but never were more legitimate or more pressing enquiries presented before the minds of thoughtful men. They must be answered sooner or later, and he is far from being a wise or a prudent man who shirks the investigation. And they will be answered when political economy, in the person of its expounders, ceases to play the courtier in presence of capital. God forbid that, with such a world of suffering at our doors, we should any longer barter the pure gold of this noble science for a lot of sounding brass.

But the truth lies at our hand. The working man is not able, by his own work, to produce for himself and also for the capitalist. It is beyond his capacity to do so. The very tools, in that case, instead of being an aid become an oppression to him. To be able, as some may say, by an ingenious turn of the wheel of fortune, to take all the appliances of labor, all the inventions of industry, out of its hands, and then put them back again with a demand that all the visible produce of labor shall go into the pockets of others than those who toil, is an utter subversion of what is just and right, a complete destruction of every principle in political economy. You may urge that possession is nine points in law, but I am bound to tell you, on the part of the working world, that this, accomplished, will ruin industry so thoroughly that there will not be much to choose between white slavery and black.

The increased production flowing from the employment of these aids to industry does not come to hand on the ground that the worker *owns* these resources or aids. The ownership is invested in the hand which has toiled and fashioned. It is simply the fruit of industry. Wherever the commodity goes, the ownership goes with it, so long as the labor title, or title of service can be produced. When that fails, ownership also fails. The occupancy is there because the ownership is there; and the ownership is there because the title which labor gives is a complete title. The ownership is one thing; the employment of all the implements and tools is another and quite different thing. The laborer who owns his tools has increased production, not because he owns, but because he works with them. It is certain, therefore, that there can be no increased production (but the reverse) when capital gets possession of the tools and hires men to work for day's wages. The increased produce appears, not because all these things are owned, but because men work with them. The ownership has therefore no relation to production, except, it may be, as a stimulant to those who own and work at the same time. Production is caused neither by the owner as such, nor by the ownership. Production flows forth, not because things are owned, not because things are hired, not because men are hired, but because men work. If, with the employment of certain agricultural implements, the farmer is able to support himself and family in decency and comfort, he can do no more if the ownership of his capital passes away into other hands. The yield will just be the same. Indeed, it will, if anything, be decreased; for the stimulus to toil will be lessened, and those hopes and inducements to labor which are inspired by a full return for one's work, and by the pride and happiness of owning property, will cease to operate. The farmer's returns, which formerly were sufficient to keep his family in comfort and independence, will now be so diminished by the returns demanded by capital, and by the manner of rating or estimating these returns in the form of a centage on the money value, that he and his family will be reduced to all but beggary. And all this because the capital, so called, which at one time aided him so well, now calls for and obtains by far the largest share in a definite amount of produce, not increased but rather diminished in volume and value by the change in the disposition of the capital. The plough which in the hands of its owner turns over its two acres a day, cannot turn over any more because it happens to fall into other hands. The bit of ground which, by means of labor spent on it, supports a man in comfort, cannot at the same time support an idler in wealth. What a terrible means of oppression does capital become when it is thus turned with grinding and destructive force upon the very hands which produce it; not only arresting all those powerful moral and social influences calculated to flow from healthy and well requited toil, but opening a wide door for the entrance of all that is vile and base and calculated to disorganise society. It will not do for you to urge, in justification of what we see around us, and as so many have urged before you, that if capitalists did not provide labor with tools, labor would perish. For I might ask you, How did capitalists come to get possession of all the tools and instruments of labor? Was it by cunning or wit? Labor, from the very beginning, has produced all the tools and machinery. Surely it could not be mere accident that has thrown everything one way. Some great principle must have been violated to bring before us so extraordinary and unnatural a spectacle as a complete divorce between labor and its tools. I might thus hedge you up from question to question, until you were at last driven to the wall; or obliged to acknowledge, what indeed is the truth, that industry has from the beginning lost its capital, and must continue to lose it, by the utter perversion of every principle in monetary science; by that cunning which, shrinking from hard toil, or any toil at all, has never ceased, since the world began, to play fast and loose with honest and unsuspecting industry.

Whatever stress you may lay upon the circumstance that you are the owner of the capital, the fact remains that it is the laborer's toil which brings in your returns. That cannot be disputed. It is out of his toil that you are paid. For if he did not work for you, then you would have to take the tools in hand and work for yourself. And if you did so, you would just have the produce of your labor as your reward. You would take the workingman's place, and you would get the workingman's reward. Political economy must ever regard the worker as the producer, to whom a reward single and indivisible must fall. It is to the worker, and to the worker alone, that the reward must ever come. It is therefore impossible that industry can ever pay you, or pay even itself, on the ground of ownership.

Again, I might ask, What about the decrease in production caused by the capitalist ceasing to work? I suppose he was formerly a producer. He could not be a capitalist (setting inheritance aside) unless he had been a producer, for surely he must have given value to the people in exchange for the people's capital. The strange thing in the whole affair is—what has become of all which is alleged to have been given in exchange for the capital? Can any one lay his hands upon it? Do you say the multitudes have consumed it in food? That cannot be; for what they have produced is worth far more than their food and clothing. The capitalists are all fed too, and well fed, but in addition they have managed to get hold of all the good things made by toiling hands; and furthermore, by means of paper, to carry a claim against industry, the principal of which is so vast that the present resources of labor could not liquidate it for a century to come. You say the capitalist looks after his property. But there is no production in that. Everybody is bound to look after his property, and everybody does look after it. Could you ask your neighbor to pay you for looking after your own property? Does production consist in buying the same goods, or the same stocks, ten or a dozen times in the course of a day? Are gambling and gambling debts production? How much production is there in Wall street or Lombard street? Is there any in speculation? These are the fields in which many a capitalist wastes his life. *But where is the production?*

When a full and fair profit is obtained by each of two workmen in the exchange of the product of his work, it is evident that there is not room for further, and perhaps larger profits, for every one of perhaps half a dozen people over the same products. The first and principal profit is secured by the producers. The labor of transporting to destination will legitimately be paid. But now is it possible that additional profits can be given to those who do nothing but speculate in the great staples of industry?

The writer of the article on Political Economy in the last edition of the Encyclopœdia Britannica asks, in the defence of capital, and with a triumphant air, "What could the most skilful agriculturist perform without his spade and his plough? a weaver without his loom? or a house-carpenter without his saw, his axe, and his planes?" There would be very little "performance" indeed. There might be enough to keep life in the body of the producer; there would certainly not be so much as a bite for the hungry capitalist. The one, at all events, would live because he still did some little work; the other would perish from the face of the earth. The one would, at the worst, have a hut and some skins to cover him; the other would go naked and without shelter. Capital, in putting such questions, pronounces its own condemnation.

But will Capital now permit Industry to ask a few questions? What would capitalists do if there were no workingmen to make the spade, plough, loom, axe and other tools? What would capitalists do if there were no persons willing to toil in the mine for gold, on the land for food, in the bowels of the earth for fuel, or in the forests for timber? What would capitalists do if they produced nothing to exchange for the gold, the food, or the fuel? What would capitalists do if industry refused to give away its tools and machinery, its clothing and food and furnishings, unless for an equivalent in labor value? In a word, what *could* capital do without industry?

I now ask every intelligent reader if he is not prepared, with myself, to repel with scorn the gratuitous assumptions of these writers, that something they call "Capital" found Industry a beggar, fed it, clothed it, and fostered it into life and vigour; when the truth is that Capital is indebted to Industry for its very existence.

From all that has been stated it is quite evident that modern workmen (and, alas! the children of modern workmen) are subjected to severe, constant, and depressing toil in order to provide the vast returns demanded by capital. Let us just glance at what capital takes, and what industry receives. I am willing to abide by the verdict of any unprejudiced on-looker. Are not the workingmen, as a body, just kept out of the breakers, nothing more? Do they get anything beyond a bare living, with a hard struggle at that? Are not suffering and poverty their inevitable lot? Contrast their position with that of the capitalist. Mark how the principle of accumulation, once begun, continues to swell the hoard. The veriest simpleton, one who knows as little of any department of industry as an unborn child, has only to invest in a successful banking institution, and he begins forthwith to draw out of industry. The anxiety of the workingman is to keep himself and family in life—the anxiety of the capitalist is to add to his abounding and increasing wealth. See how one man reaps as much as two or three hundred producers. One of these capitalists has just died in New York, leaving property worth one hundred millions of dollars. Where is the equivalent, the other one hundred millions of dollars *given* in exchange for the one hundred millions *taken?* Is it in the shape of rents of houses? Is it houses, then, which *pay* rent? Let me tell you, it is out of the toil of human beings that rents are taken, and that industry has nothing left to represent these one hundred millions it has given. It ought to have that amount somewhere in houses or other property; for if labor has given this vast sum (and of that there can be no doubt) to one man in New York, it ought to have a corresponding sum to represent it. Do you think it has gone to the laboring classes in food and clothing? It has gone no such road. Mr. Astor did not feed the workingmen of New York. These workingmen fed themselves by their own labor. But they have left in one man's hands as much as would feed the whole population of New York for two or three years. You see then how interesting the investigation really becomes when we begin to institute a search for the equivalents of capital. I am quite in earnest in my desire to have you investigate the question of rent as a return for capital. You will find that the dwellings, the very homes of the people, or what should be their homes, as well as their tools and machinery, are all passing into the hands of capitalists through the violation of the same laws. In this investigation one illustration is as good as a thousand. The same pernicious system which takes away a man's spade, can take away his plough, his horses, his stables and barns, and at last his house or home. And is not labor, to a very large extent, now really destitute of house and home? If my labor fails to provide for me a home I can call my own, then the labor of my life has proved a failure, and other people, by some means or other, but not by labor, have got the best produce of my life's toil.

I have studied these questions long enough to know that capital has acquired its vast accumulations mainly through the practical destruction, as an industrial instrument of exchange, of the money provided for industry and produced by industry. The economist has investigated to little purpose who has failed to perceive the almost unlimited power thrown by such means into the hands of a class. Capital (or some intangible thing called credit) has gathered up the true money out of the hand of industry (leaving a fiction in its place) and concentrated and employed it for its own ends largely in the fields of speculation and gambling; and through the enormous increase of mere buying and selling, repeating of transactions over the same goods, selling and buying millions worth of stocks in the course of a day, multiplying "paper" without end for discount, and concentrating all these enormous payments into a few so-called monied centres, has actually deceived people into the notion that nature has failed in providing a sufficient quantity of money for our wants. And there are not wanting those on this side the water, who, apparently in the extremity of their despair of ever understanding what all this confusion is about, do not hesitate to launch their anathemas against even the gold and silver. I do not say that it was through the destruction of its money labor first began to be oppressed; but this I say, that it is by such means the oppression has, in modern times, become concentrated, systemised, and vastly intensified. Any government which has thus practically destroyed the true money of its people, and cast the gold, or most of the gold, into the vortex of speculation and gambling, has entered on a path so full of perils that I tremble to think of the result. The road may be a long one to travel, but sooner or later the end must come. Every step in that road is strewn with the wrecks of industry; and these wrecks not only tell of the sufferings of the lowest ranks of society, but of the ruin of millions above them who began life with bright and joyous hopes. Now, it is deeply interesting to trace the manner in which capital exercises its cruel and unrelenting oppression on labor. It is said to double itself in a certain period, say in eight or ten years. A capitalist who invests his money in stocks or shares expects it to be doubled in about that time. There are certain bank stocks which, on the original shares, are doubled every five or six years. The language in which all this is set forth has become incorporated with the daily life of society. All these vast returns come out of labor. There is no other conceivable source from which they can be taken. Personal toil, aided by its own appliances, or what ought to be its own appliances, produces the whole. The products of industry, it is admitted, have been greatly increased by the employment of machinery. Industry is now able to accomplish a great deal more than it formerly did in the same space of time; but capital steps in and demands a full profit, a certain rate per cent., out of the entire value of all the tools, factories, houses, warehouses, implements, and machinery employed; and all this continued from year to year, so long as these various appliances exist. That is to say, labor builds a house rated at a thousand pounds; capital demands from labor, and gets for that house, during a course of years, fifty thousand or a hundred thousand pounds. Labor has put a value equivalent to a thousand pounds, and no more, into the building. Capital, under the name of rent, compels labor, some way or other, to pay a continuous tax so long as the house will shield from wind and rain, amounting, it may be with compound interest, to two or three hundred times the actual labor value embodied in it. Labor builds a warehouse or factory worth ten or twenty thousand pounds; under the demand which capital makes for its inevitable rate, labor continues to pay, whilst the building stands, an amount which may be counted by the million. And so with tools and every kind of machinery and appliance. *The things produced by labor thus become instruments of oppression to labor.* The working millions, instead of being benefited by capital, are thus reduced to such a struggle to obtain a living, that the painted and feathered savages who hunt over our western plains, in their wild exuberance and joy, have a happiness to which the wearied and anxious toilers are total strangers. And so, poor blind humanity, age after age, continually grinds in its prison-house. Now, if labor owned all its tools and appliances (as it certainly ought) what a different state of things we would witness. The working man would then begin to advance through the only legitimate way by which industry can ever advance—that is, he would, either by himself or in equitable co-operation with his fellows, own and sell the produce of his own toil, wrought out by his own hands, and with the aid of his own tools. He would own the house, and the thousand pounds worth of labor invested; and he and his children after him would not only sit rent-free for life, but every eight or ten years (if the estimated return of capital be taken as the true rate of increase) he would have resources at command equal to another dwelling worth a thousand pounds. The working men would, singly or in co-operation, own the warehouses, factories, and all the tools and machinery, and the constant strain which capital now lays upon them would be turned to their advantage. They would own all the goods they make, and would derive the profits on the sale of these goods. The purchasing power of industry would be increased a hundred-fold. The masses, under the rigor of the reign of this capital, are so poor that they may be said to have hardly any purchasing power at all. Their constant anxiety is to keep soul and body together. What can they do as patrons of luxuries or the fine arts, or even of the vast mass of things which go to make up the general comforts of life? But let them simply own their tools and machinery and factories—enjoy, without paying for the use of, that which is their own—and see the change which would take place. The gaunt poverty and the crime which are now the reproach of our modern civilization would disappear as if by magic. The mighty and wealthy world of industry would empty every market in a day. There would be a call for goods, and the best of goods, which would set every wheel in motion, and stimulate every mind into thought and activity. The wealthy would have about as many *visible* comforts and luxuries as ever; those now poor and degraded would be lifted to the same plane. All would work, and all would receive, under the increased stimulus of new and improved machinery, everything good to their heart's content. Machinery would be so perfected and arranged that repulsive work on any large scale, would hardly ever require to be performed by direct manual toil. The wide gulf which now separates us into different ranks and classes, our modern caste, would disappear. Education and all the refining arts of civilization would take hold of and leaven society. Think of the complete change in our literature, and of the demand for pure and stimulating works, with the great majority of men at once thinkers and readers. What a renovation there would be of the bookseller's shelves! Where could a market then be found for the disgusting products (literature we cannot call it) of diseased imagination? That which, in the hand of the capitalist, is now the most terrible instrument of oppression to our race, would confer upon industry resources of such incalculable and beneficent power, that nations might then be said to be born in a day. And, last and most blessed effect of all, the uncounted resources of industry, instead of being concentrated on self and accumulation, would overflow in unmeasured largess to every land.

The average centage which is demanded and obtained by capital appears to be the average division of not only all the profits of industry, but of all its products too, *after a provision is made to keep industry just in life.* If capital be some great and independent force acting in antagonism to industry; that is, if it be not industry itself, but something outside of industry, whose interest it is to take all it can possibly obtain from the producers, then we may be certain that it will get industry so thoroughly into its power, that anything which may be given to it beyond bare existence must be looked upon in the light only of a gratuity.

The great and substantial truth *that utilities cannot be sold*, here forces itself upon the attention, and we must follow it out in whatever direction it leads. It has been somewhat timidly approached by the later economists. But if it be a principle in political economy, we may be sure that it will never lead us astray. I have never seen any reason to doubt that close and critical examination will result in its being generally received as an accredited doctrine, and perhaps one of the most important in the whole range of the science. If utilities are all gratuitous, it follows that nothing but labor, as represented by its productions, or as embodied in its handiwork, can ever be sold; that payments withheld, or given in consecutive periods, can never increase or diminish the real value of a commodity; and that no article, from a needle to an anchor, from a palace to a cottage, can ever, *on any ground whatever*, receive, *permanently*, more from labor than the labor value embodied. If you will but reflect over the subject, you will come to perceive that to speak of the value of the use of a thing is really as absurd as to speak of the weighing of a sunbeam, or of measuring in money, a mother's love. Industry, as a productive agent, can never both produce the property and pay for the use of the property. If it is compelled to do so, then its tools or appliances are not aids to industry, but the reverse. The economist must use terms in accordance with the principles of the science; and when we speak of value it must ever refer to commercial or industrial value, or, what is perhaps a safer phrase, *value in exchange.* It is not utilities which are sold, but human labor. And around that human labor, as the grand centre and regulator of all, everything that is represented by that uncertain phrase "demand and supply" must continually revolve.* The consciousness which men in general entertain of the amount of toil they have embodied in what they have to sell, holds in its inexorable grasp all demand and all supply; so that men, as a rule, will neither give away their goods for less than an equivalent, nor continue to produce things for which there may be no demand, or to produce them in similar or greater quantities when there is a less demand. We do not reflect at all as we ought to do, that in every exchange, demand and supply co-exist in each of the parties to the exchange, so that four factors of equivalent power are ever at work regulating the movements of the whole machine. Demand, among civilized men, can never remain, as a rule, at the mercy of supply, nor supply at the mercy of demand. On some far away coast, an Indian may exchange an otter skin for a glittering bead, but it is not an exchange of value for value. Civilization in this instance, as in many others, has only over-reached ignorance and barbarism.

It appears from all the foregoing considerations, that a "wage-fund theory," for which a place in the realms of political economy has lately been so strenuously sought, has no tangible ground on which to rest, and no certain or reliable principles to present to the mind. The system of days wages, as we now know it throughout all the fields of industry, comes before the philosophic eye only as a ruin—it may be a vast and splendid one, but yet only a ruin.

There is but one refuge more into which capital endeavors to retreat. It lays claim to a return on the ground that profits may be divided between itself and industry, or on the ground that profits

---

* "Utility and value are mere accidents of a thing arising from the fact that somebody wants it...... Money must have utility as the basis of value." "Money and the Mechanism of Exchange" by Professor Jevons. The learned Author would have us believe that mere desire or clamor for money—the crying of the public baby—imparts to money the "accident" of value, and that utility, not labor, is the basis of value! Probably he has not given much consideration to labor as the source of all value. Apart from this and some similar errors, Mr. Jevons has produced an important treatise on monetary science. Nothing could be clearer or more to the point than his remarks on International Money, and to American statesmen especially what he has to say on "The future American Dollar" ought to prove of profound interest in the present agitated state of the public mind. He says: "The most easy and important step which can now be taken towards an international money, consists in the assimilation of the American dollar to the five-franc piece. There is little doubt that the adhesion of the American Government to the proposal of the Congress (Monetary) of 1863 would give the holding turn to the metric system of weights, measures and moneys. It is quite likely that it might render the dollar the future universal unit. The fact that the dollar is already the monetary unit of many parts of the world gives it long odds. In becoming assimilated to the French écu, American gold would be capable of circulation in Europe, or wherever the French napoleon has hitherto been accepted. It may seem unpatriotic in an Englishman to advocate a change which may lead to the defeat of the pound sterling, but I look upon any one scheme of unification as better than none. Whatever may be the ultimate results, I desire to see assimilation between the French and American systems

may be doubled. I do not think that capital could venture on more inhospitable ground than this. It seeks a sorry refuge. Political economy at once seizes the intruder and decapitates him at a stroke. The true remuneration of labor, as has been shewn, is not what is paid in wages, but is the amount of the things produced, the visible product of handiwork. The industry of the world can never be remunerated except through the total industrial products of the world. As the products collectively are the remuneration of all the toilers, so each particular product is the remuneration, either in itself or by an equivalent, of him who has produced it. In any other light than this, the phrase "the cost of labor" is a solecism. The entire mechanism of exchange consists simply in an exchange of services. These exchanges, from beginning to end, must proceed on the principle of equity. If there is a double profit for one of the parties, then there is no profit at all for the other party. If there is a double profit for the one half of the number of producers, then there is not a scrap left for the other half. Such a principle, it is evident, would at once strangle all exchange. And so of the claim on the ground of partition of the profit. Industry may, out of accumulated resources, give away what it pleases in charity, pleasure or amusement, or indeed for anything it may desire; but as a productive agent, held in check and regulated in its profits by a healthy and untrammelled competition, it can never afford to give away to capital half or any portion of its profits. The increment of profit has no natural tendency to resolve itself, as so many economists imagine, into certain parts or divisions, a portion for this, a

---

adopted as soon as possible. For reasons subsequently stated, I consider the dollar so good a unit that it would be mere national prejudice to oppose it, were there a fair chance of its general adoption. Even if it were not generally adopted, it would be a great step in advance if Great Britain, America, and France were to agree to coin gold money identical in weight and fineness, which might circulate indifferently as sovereigns, five-dollar pieces, and five-franc pieces." Professor Jevons adds that he considers the gold dollar and five-franc piece too small to be coined in gold, as they suffer too much by abrasion. It may interest the reader, and perhaps add some weight to the foregoing, if I here reproduce what I stated on this important subject some years since. "The decimal system of curreny, with which, happily, we in this Dominion are now so conversant, even though it be confessedly artificial, is yet one we would not like to see displaced. Some years since we went, all at once, and with extraordinary facility, from the old and cumbrous method of computation by pounds, shillings and pence, to the simple plan of dollars and cents; and thus a common system prevails over all North America. The example of the United States conferred upon us this great boon, and the advantage to both our international and domestic commerce has been very great. I conceive it would be a great advantage to the people of the United Kingdom if they should at some future day adopt the decimal currency, and prefer the dollar as the central unit, around which so large a portion of the commerce of the world has revolved. I think it would be well if all nations were to bring their coins into decimal relation, and to adopt the dollar as the monetary unit, with, to us, its familiar range of decimal multiples and subdivisions. But this is only *our* national idea; and the French people will cling to the familiar franc, and the English people to the no less familiar pound; and although the pound sterling of England, the five-dollar gold piece, or half-eagle of America, and the proposed twenty-five franc piece of France, approach each other in value, they are not the same thing precisely, and it is just the precise equivalent that is wanted in a system of international coinage."—INTERNATIONAL COINAGE AND THE STANDARDS OF VALUE.

second for that, and a third for something else. It can only faithfully evidence itself by the general advance and well-being of industry, or of those who work and produce—not by accumulations of money, but by all the visible comfortable surroundings of industry. Skill and energy are the two forces which we bring to bear in the act of production. One who works harder or more skilfully than another, will have more of the good things of this life, not because he has made a greater profit than the other, but because he has had more things to exchange. He will indeed have, in sum, a greater profit collectively than the lazy or indifferent worker, but he will have it because he has had more things to exchange with others more diligent or equally diligent with himself. 'Tis but poor profit that is made out of the lazy portion of the community. They will remain poor, not because they have small profits or half profits, but because they have few things to exchange. When each works well, all fare well. The principle of exchange has no premium for the ignorant or indifferent worker. The man who produces only one pair of shoes a day cannot expect to exchange them against the five pairs produced by some other in the same space of time. The value of our labor is seen in what we produce. The five pairs of shoes will not seek to exchange against the one pair, because value ever seeks for an equivalent. The five pairs will naturally seek to exchange with some other things produced by some one equally skilful and energetic. Here like clings to like. The owner of the one pair will get his profit according to the labor saved to him in the exchange; the owner of the five pairs will get his profit also according to the labor saved to him—a single and indivisible profit on each transaction. The true way to save our labor, and thus to earn profit, is to work skilfully and well. For labor to share its profits with a class who do not produce (for in these days there is a great deal of working, so called, the *business* of mere "busybodies," which is not production but its opposite) is just as unnatural as to attempt to double its profits. In either case the inevitable tendency would be to the destruction and ruin of industry. To say that industry, under the reign of capital, gets a share of profits, is to say what is not true. It does not get the smallest remnant of profit. All the profit is swept into the coffers of the capitalist, much of it to be reissued in further oppression of labor, an oppression which has its limit only in the capacity of industry to bear the strain. *

---

* I quote from the Report of Commissioners on Hours of Labor: Commonwealth of Massachusetts, 1866:

"The average wages of males throughout the United States in these descriptions of labor—manufacture of Cotton, Woollen, Clothing, Shoes, &c—in 1860, were, males, $316; females, $176 per annum."

"The wages in the cotton mills, of the six New England States, deduced by the method stated, from the census of 1860, give:—

Wages for males, per annum.......................... $285 75

Do Females do .... 158 75"

The average rate of wages over the whole of the United States is given at 91½ cents per day.

A letter to the Commissioners from one of the best paid journeymen mechanics, a first-class shipcarpenter, states that with his family of eight persons, he has been driven to "a system of economy which has left painful evidences of its severity," and has been compelled to remove his children from school to contribute towards the support of the family.

I suppose there is no one more competent, at least on this continent, to judge of the emoluments of workingmen than Mr. E. H. Rogers, who was

I have purposely avoided any lengthened reference, in the present paper, to what is generally understood by brain work or intellectual labor. I have hardly felt it necessary that it should engage our attention, as I think it does not materially affect the argument. It has come under our observation for a few moments only as related to the visible products of toil, or, in other words, as in a sort of "silent partnership" with the hand. This part of the subject is far from being devoid of interest, but requires more consideration than I can at present devote to it. The equivalents of manual labor are not difficult to distinguish. A gold dollar is the exact equivalent of another gold dollar, and a bushel of barley, as nearly as may be, of another bushel of barley. Most people, and even some economists, think that gold is dearer than silver, and diamonds, in their price, more precious than flour; and even some governments, professing to be very wise,have,on this and other grounds, demonetised their silver; but a day's labor of digging silver is just worth a day's labor of digging gold, and the labor of producing diamonds is just worth the labor of producing flour. The equations in each case are at our hand. But who is acute enough to discover the unit of value when we come to compare material products with immaterial? Is there any true *ratio* of exchange between things so different? If there be no ratio, can you arrive at an equation? What is the exact money value of a *thought?* Has it money value at all? Can you measure it in a quart or a peck? We pay *more* for a song from Jenny Lind than from some ordinary singer—more for a good than for an indifferent teacher; but where is the standard of value? *How much* is a song worth? In reading this article,you will pay for the paper on which it is printed, for the ink, for the type setting, for the press work, the folding, the stitching, or, in other words for the labor embodied in all these processes, but I am sure I could not tell you what, if any, is the mint value of any thought there may be in it, and as little can you. The thought may have commenced before some of my readers were born. I am conscious of no small amount of brain work, and yet the thought has no dimension, no weight, no parts at all. You cannot manipulate it, or place it in your scales, or adjust it by your most delicate balance. It may have a general relation to other thought, or special relation to thought on economic science, but what relatoin has it to a bit of money? Any value of this kind you place upon it must be merely an arbitrary value. The only manual labor I have had with it is in handling the pen, and that you know is not worth mentioning. You cannot pay me for what some may call my "time," for I have none of it to sell, and political economy cannot turn *time* into a commodity. The present work has been to me emphatically a labor of love, and I dont think that I could be repaid in anything but similar coin. Has nature made such a

---

one of the Commissioners on Hours of Labor, appointed by the State of Massachusetts. He says, in the above Report. "With constant thoughtfulness this income ($1.25 per day, Sundays included) necessitated an economy penurious in its character, often failing to meet the demands of health in clothing; and throwing the support of aged parents on more favored relations." "Wages," he adds, "as at present paid are not an equitable return for labor performed. It is universally understood that the laborer has only a living. The idea of what a living is, is comparatively elevated in this country; but figures show that the wages of labor do not reach on the whole that point."

dividing line between Intelligence and Work as that one party shall be able to say, We have all the intelligence and must get all the products of toil, except what is just able to keep you, Work, in life? Has she sacrificed Labor in her desire to endow Intelligence? Is the one to be gainful to the other, or does it exist only to oppress its partner in toil? What good things is it possible for cunning or shrewdness to leave, as exchange, in the hands of industry? It is among those everchanging values whose stability has been all but destroyed by the present mercantile system (undoubtedly a system of the most dangerous communism) that our modern man of business rears his fortune, and when he dies, the pulpit and press applaudingly clap their hands and hold him up, so far as his gains are concerned, as a bright model to the rising generation. But where is the production? What has industry reaped for all that it has given, or rather that has been taken away from it. What has he left behind? A lot of money in his will? or a vast deal of service in the hands of his toiling fellow men? Shall I use my "wit" in taking what does not belong to me? One man, we will say, is engaged within doors in some light pleasant fancy work; or he may be "a professional man" writing a few letters, or sweeping dollars by the hundred into his coffers by the mere stroke of his pen; and he looks down from his window on another toiling in a deep and filthy cavity in the street, clearing away some obstruction which threatens miasma and disease to a whole neighborhood. Who gets the best return? Which of the two *ought* to get the best return? I do not say they ought to change places. Each may be in his right place. All I ask is who should be best paid? The economists are careful to tell us that risk and disagreeableness are important elements in determining prices. Do they determine prices or values in this case, or in ten thousand like it around you every day? We know that it is hand-work which really does pay for all the brain-work which claims and receives payment. As we generally understand the term, payment, it could not otherwise be paid. But there should be an interchange, a true commerce, a just reciprocity, ought there not? None should be burdened. The brains should surely be coming over, by this time, to the side of the hand. If products pay *for* intelligence, then intelligence should be largely the property of toil. But is it so? If brain takes away the produce of hand surely hand should get the produce of brain. Industry by this time should be so well taught to do its work as never more to need a teacher. We are fond of talking of our mental labor, and of what we should get for that labor, but it is all simply *thought*. As regards visible products it is not worth a rap till you put out hand and let us see some fruit. I fully believe in brains taking industry by the hand; but, within the range of industrial application, I have as little faith in brains without industry as in industry without brains. Separate them and you destroy them. Can you tell me to what extent intelligence or intellect has itself suffered by being divorced from work? How has society fared? Perhaps we have a weakling, a silly nondescript, where we might have had Spartan brain and vigor. Is not the mutual helpfulness of the family circle to be carried out into the larger circle of general humanity? What if we have hitherto missed a great economic truth in the general constitution of society as a colony of workers? Is it the design of Providence that this great industrial hive is to be helpful to the weak, the needy, the less-favored, the far-off heathen of every land? Is this the grand design of industry, or of the exchange of the products of industry? If so, it will be fulfilled. What if it should be part of the order and method of the science itself, that intellect, in all that it is competent to accomplish separate from the toil of the hand, is to be the gratuitous servant of humanity? Would it in anywise lessen its true value or take from its dignity? If industry finds its satisfactions in material products, where should intellect find its satisfactions? Did you ever reflect that it is from the tillage of the field that the greatest amount of values is realized? Is the greatest amount of values returned there? You see, then, how many grave and grand questions there are yet to challenge our attention and investigation. Do you think you can settle them by shelving them? Are you vain enough to think that questions such as these will remain for ever buried in the dark? Let us be humble. We know nothing yet as we ought to know.

Before closing this paper, it is right to state that Mr. Mill seems to have assumed, throughout his writings, the existing relations between capital and industry as the natural foundation on which to rear his entire system of political economy. It is no doubt through this assumption that he has been led to lay down principles which, when really put to the test, are found to be very rickety indeed. It is this which vitiates page after page, and prevents his work being, in any great degree, a reliable guide towards a perfect understanding of the leading elements of political economy. As this science is fast becoming the most important of the day, I think it is of the highest consequence that students in our schools and colleges should be put upon their guard in reading Mr. Mill's "Principles," as a text book. And yet, notwithstanding all this, I hope, and doubt not, that Mr. Mill will long continue to be read. His laborious application; his simple, massive style; his clear logic; his extensive information; his evident sympathy with workingmen; the master thoughts on some important economic subjects which he has thrown out so far in advance of his day; and the mass of important instruction he has given to the world; must ever entitle him to the gratitude of mankind. And though it is inevitable that the fabric he raised with so much diligence will have to be taken down and rebuilt on a different model, much of the material which he so patiently gathered and so skilfully prepared, will ever continue as a monument to his name. As to living economists, I cannot express half what I feel in regard to the solemn responsibilities of the hour.

I confess that I am somewhat sorry for capital. It seems such a pity to destroy so pleasant a delusion. It has hitherto passed as a respectable sort of personage. His retainers have, during the last twenty or thirty years, given him some hard knocks. There can be no question as to which side has fared worst in the strife. Capital as well as industry has cudgels in his hand, and sometimes it is worse to be locked out than to be locked in. There has been plenty "striking" going, but there can be little doubt which of the two has got the most bruises. The sad thing is that amidst all the din the voice of reason cannot be heard. If capital has truth on its side it will remain—if it is built on error it will pass away. And I can say to both capital and industry that there are more thoughtful men than ye wot of pondering over these momentous questions. It is a hopeful sign of the times that there is everywhere abroad a spirit of free inquiry and scrutiny, a spirit which is growing from day to day. The capitalist who refuses investigation will only gather around him greater perils. For I suppose there is nobody so silly as not to perceive that there are perils. If the economists in their long and labored endeavors, and under the names of capital, credit, and so forth, have conjured up nothing but a spectre to crush the industry of the race, and to scare free inquiry, we have only to take the shadow in hand to know what it really is. These sort of things are only fearful in the dark—the light of day puts them all to flight. "He that doeth truth cometh to the light." Who can doubt of the ultimate triumph of every vital human interest over error and wrong?

It is neither my inclination nor my duty to enter upon a tirade against capital. Railing accusations are generally fruitless things, and can only react in injury to the cause which we advocate. We must remember that we are all the victims, more or less, of the system under which we have been trained. We cannot charge the capitalist with doing a wrong thing when he hires laboring men, and pays out wages. I do not feel called upon to say that the capitalist is doing a wicked thing when he invests his means in any of the recognized enterprizes of the day. He is perhaps, in the circumstances, doing the best thing possible. I am conscious of the same respect and kindly feeling towards capitalists as towards working men; and I am aware of the noble and spotless lives led by very many of them. But I think it is of the utmost consequence that both Capital and Industry know exactly where they stand, and what they have to stand upon. Let us have a calm and thorough investigation of the whole subject. The *interest* of money is not to be weighed for a moment against the interests of truth. We can do without the one—we can never do without the other. The views I have set forth in this paper are worthy of the most careful consideration; and I hope, moreover, they are able to stand examination. If these views be sound, there is one thing the capitalist can do—he may look with a more favorable and kindly eye on working men, as the real producers of his wealth, and may give to them a larger share than they now enjoy of the produce of their toil. I hardly know anything better which I could recommend capitalists to do. If Corporations had souls—which it is said they have not—I would be inclined to say to them also that there is nothing at any rate which would bring them in more true enjoyment. Blessed is the hand which relieves poverty, but more blessed still is the hand which lifts workingmen above poverty.

It may be said of humanity in general that men born into the world launch upon life under the necessity of earning their bread by the sweat of the brow. It is the inevitable condition of existence from which the race can never escape. It is the mark which this old world must carry to its grave. As all must live, so all must labor. Physically a man lives by bread alone. It is from his own labor, and not from that of his fellows, that he must provide for himself food, clothing and shelter. Labor gives the true title to all property, to everything framed by human hands. What comes to you by inheritance, still comes to you, or ought to come to you, with that labor title intact. All that is above and beyond, the higher and better things, are for the higher and better life. The soil of the hand, the sweat of the brow, the rude bargainings of commerce, cannot touch them,—they are removed by their very nature beyond the common-place circle of things merchantable and perishable. For it appears as if no really equitable adjustment could ever be made between the thoughts of the brain and the toil of the hand. It is, as I have already said, only when these thoughts of the brain find expression through the labor of the hand, that the products stand on a common platform where values can be rightly appraised. Where is the economist who would venture to *price*, in perishable gold, those high ministries which directly contribute to spiritual culture? Does it not seem that the higher and more powerful the ministry, the further it is removed, by that very circumstance, from the comparatively mean measure of earthly values? Therefore, although it is within reason that they who minister about holy things should live off the things of the temple, it is not the less true that carnal things reaped can never be the measure of spiritual things sown. For things spiritual can only be reckoned in terms spiritual. It was not the bit of money cast into the treasury which gave it the value: it was that which lay behind which made the very small gift a very large gift in the eye of Him who seeth not as man seeth. Why should the spirit of earthly ambition or gain annoy us with either its computations, its cavillings, or its lamentations, when we choose to break our alabaster box? And herein lies a truth for all workers, whether in the pulpit or the pew, who would forget self in their efforts after the good of their fellow creatures, and who desire to live superior to those low-born motives, which, it is to be feared, too often impel men of great talent and power to sell themselves to "the highest bidder." Let earnest and thoughtful men ever keep before them this high ideal, and they shall not fail to leave a lasting impression for good on their own and succeeding generations. The men who have laid the world under the greatest charges have themselves been "chargeable to no man." Christianity itself would have been strangled in its cradle by a modern endowment. It must ever be so. For there does seem, after all, to be a kingly sphere, into which things sordid may not enter—where the baubles of earth and the babblings of commerce are alike out of place—a quiet and humble sanctuary consecrated by the great travail of the mind, and where mightier bolts are being forged than have ever rung to the workman's hammer.

I confess that the condition of industry in this our boasted age of civilization lies like a heavy burden on my soul. I cannot shake it off. It haunts me night and day. I have no faith that the therapeutics of modern commerce will ever heal its wounds, or cause life and health to course through its veins. In patient study and painstaking investigation lies much of the renovating power. It may be that we will have to build the wall in troublous times. Surely industry expects of us that we expound the principles of political economy in such a way as to secure to it the fruits of its own toil. The science itself has been handed over to the dominion of mob law, and has become the sport of every scatterbrain who imagines that he has a call to pronounce, at first sight, upon the subject. In this western world we are at this moment flooded with a literature which gives but too certain and sickening evidence of the truth of what I have just stated. I need not waste words in urging upon the cultured men who read these pages the vast importance of the matters I have brought under review. I have but endeavored, according to my humble ability, to open a door here and there to the great temple of economic truth. How inviting is the field! And what a glorious exercise to both the intellect and the heart to grapple with such mighty problems! The claims of labor must call forth the warmest sympathies of every true-hearted man. Ought it not greatly to mitigate the rigor of the judgment we are accustomed to pass even upon the lowest and most abandoned classes of society, when we consider the character of the system of which they are to so large an extent the unhappy victims? Where is the man to refuse a sigh or a tear over melancholy and broken-hearted toil—over countless millions of our fellow creatures for ever divorced from all that makes life bright and joyous—over the majestic temple of industry in utter desolation and ruin? I am sure every humane reader must join me in the hope that the day may soon arrive when the science of political economy shall be rescued from its present chaos and disorder, and remodelled and established on such a basis that the sad inheritance of hopeless and unrequited toil which has been for so many generations transmitted from father to son, may be exchanged for those ample, equitable and sure rewards destined to make millions of hearts happy, and to throw the light of joy and gladness over every land and into every home.

Note.—All letters, newspapers, reviews, &c., intended for the Author, are requested to be addressed to the care of Mr. Lovell, as above. Friendly readers can render important assistance by contributions, however small, in aid of the printing and circulation of these tracts.

Left at Univ. Exhibit
Chicago, 1893

Origin and System

OF THE

Workingmen's Loan Association

Workingmen's Loan Association,

Office, No. 1 Beacon Street, Room 63,

BOSTON, MASS.

OFFICERS.

CHOSEN APRIL 20, 1893.

PRESIDENT.

ROBERT TREAT PAINE, ... 6 Joy Street

VICE-PRESIDENT.

FRANCIS B. SEARS, ... 53 State Street

TREASURER.

R. T. PAINE, 2d, ... 1 Beacon Street

CLERK.

ARTHUR LYMAN, ... 53 State Street

OTHER DIRECTORS.

EDMUND BILLINGS, ... 987 Washington Street
HENRY B. CABOT, ... Fiske Building
WILLIAM ENDICOTT, 3d, ... 113 Devonshire Street
CHARLES W. HUBBARD, ... 133 Essex Street
ARTHUR S. JOHNSON, ... 7 Commonwealth Avenue
JOSEPH LEE, ... 53 State Street
ARTHUR LYMAN, ... 53 State Street
HERBERT LYMAN, ... 95 Milk Street
JOHN F. MOORS, ... 111 Devonshire Street
ROBERT TREAT PAINE, Jr., ... 113 Devonshire Street
FRANCIS B. SEARS, ... 53 State Street
CHARLES L. YOUNG, ... National Union Bank
SAMUEL CARR, Jr., ... Ames Building
(Appointed by the Governor.)
CHARLES C. JACKSON, ... 24 Congress Street
(Appointed by the Mayor.)

WORKINGMEN'S LOAN ASSOCIATION.

The Workingmen's Loan Association received its charter from the Commonwealth of Massachusetts on March 8, 1888, and was organized April 19 of the same year.

In Boston, as in all large cities, there were numerous money-lenders lending at exorbitant rates of interest upon chattel mortgage of furniture and of other personal property. The rates of interest charged by them varied from three per cent. to ten per cent. per month.

Under such rates of interest the borrower could seldom pay up the principal of his loan, and year after year he would go on paying a heavy interest and never lessening his debt,— often, in the end, to have all he possessed taken from him when the lender demanded his principal. There was no company or person affording the opportunity of borrowing on such security at reasonable rates.

It was for the purpose of providing such an opportunity to people of moderate means to borrow upon easy terms that this company was formed.

It was designed that the company should transact a business, but a business conducted economically, at the very lowest rates that would yield a fair return to the capital invested in the enterprise.

The charge for interest was at the outset fixed at one per cent. per month; and this rate has been constantly adhered to in all loans that the company has made on chattel mortgage, upon which almost all of the loans of the company are secured. The system was adopted of requiring with each payment of interest the payment of an instalment of the principal equal to about five per cent. of the loan, thus encouraging the borrower to save and to pay off his loan.

Before the company was organized, Robert Treat Paine had caused to be conducted an experimental work, beginning on Aug. 1, 1887. At the time when the company was organized the loans outstanding made by him amounted to the sum of $10,778.89; and these loans were transferred by him to the company upon its beginning business, with a sufficient guaranty against loss.

The company began business with subscriptions to its capital promised to the amount of $66,600: this amount was raised later in the year to $78,200. The capital was called in gradually, and was loaned readily, borrowers eagerly seeking the advantages that were offered. The total number of loans gradually grew until in March, 1889, less than a year from when the company began business, the whole capital was loaned. The profits of the first year afforded the payment of a dividend of two per cent. and a small surplus. During the second year (1889–90) the capital stock was $78,500; and $25,000 was borrowed at a low rate of interest (4½ per cent.), and used in the business. Losses proved heavy during this year; but the profits were sufficient to pay four per cent. upon the stock.

The company had the same capital and used the same amount of borrowed money in the years 1890–91 and 1891–92, as in 1889–90. The results, however, were more successful; and six per cent. dividends were paid each year. In the year 1892–93 the company extended its business,—having in use at the end of the year $89,500 paid on account of capital stock and $28,000 borrowed money. During this year the office of the company was changed to a more central financial location. This change has brought to the company many more borrowers,—more than the present capital of the company can supply.

During this latter year a six per cent. dividend was paid to the stockholders, with a moderate surplus remaining. It should be noted that the company pays full taxes to the State upon its capital stock. The amount paid in taxes in 1892–93 was $1,051.27. The total number of borrowers on April 1, 1893, was fourteen hundred and ninety.

The results accomplished during these five years have been encouraging. Loans have been repaid very fast, averaging about one year and a half in duration. The company has made since its beginning $449,673.15 of loans; and of these $326,837.09 have been paid off. In 1892–93, $80,591.81 of loans were paid off, or about four-fifths of the total amount of the loans existing at the beginning of that year. Nothing could speak more strongly for the merits of the system than the speed with which borrowers have been able to pay off the principal of their debt. The charge for interest amounts to so little upon small loans as to be lightly felt, and a loan of the company seldom proves to be a heavy burden. Often illness or misfortune comes, when even an honest and industrious man cannot meet his payments. In such cases, wherever it is possible, the company relaxes its demands, and gives him time until his circumstances shall improve.

The relations of the company with its borrowers have generally been friendly. In most cases, the borrower's feeling is one of cordial appreciation of the efforts of the company to promote his welfare.

Methods of Doing Business.

The charge for interest is one per cent. per month. An additional charge is made on the making of each loan, sufficient to cover all money expended in investigation and recording the mortgage, and to give the company in ordinary cases $1.65 for the time spent in appraisal and drawing papers. Nearly all of the loans of the company are made on the chattel mortgage of furniture and household effects.

These mortgages, in pursuance of the law, are recorded in the city or town hall where the borrower resides, and also in the city or town hall of the place where he principally does business. A few loans were made by the company in the beginning of its existence on pledges of jewelry; but this practice has been discontinued. Loans are occasionally made on insurance policies having a cash surrender value, on second mortgages of real estate, indorsed notes, stock and other securities. On March 1, 1893, approximately one-thirteenth of the total value of the loans of the company outstanding had been made on such miscellaneous securities, and the remainder, or twelve-thirteenths, on the chattel mortgage of furniture.

Each applicant for a loan is questioned with great care. If the circumstances seem favorable for making the loan desired, he fills out a blank application, giving his residence, previous residence, business, good references, and other desirable information, and leaves a deposit of thirty-five cents.

An appraiser then goes to his abode, examines his security, and makes a schedule of the articles to be mortgaged, placing against each article the price that it would bring in an auction-room. A loan may be made to the amount of three-quarters of the total value so estimated; and this margin is, in almost all cases, required. The schedule, with the appraised values set upon each article by the appraiser, is entered by him on the back of the application, and filed in its proper place for future reference.

The borrower is required to show receipted bills for his furniture or to account satisfactorily for the absence of the same, in order to prove his ownership, and to show that, if bought on instalment, it is fully paid for.

The records are then examined to ascertain whether there is any existing mortgage on the property. In most cases, inquiry is made of the persons referred to or of other persons as to the character of the borrower.

If the investigation proves the loan to be a desirable one, the borrower signs a mortgage and note for the amount borrowed, and receives the money less the expenses charged.

Where the borrower is married, the signature of both husband and wife is required; and, generally, a general clause is inserted in the mortgage covering all furniture and household effects of every kind in his house.

Payments of the interest and instalments of the principal are made monthly, and receipts given for the same. In case of default for more than ten days, a notice is sent, with a charge of ten cents for the same, if it is the first notice. If the first notice proves futile, more imperative notices follow, for which a charge of twenty-five cents is made.

No investigation of the property mortgaged is made after the appraisal. The notices sent serve to inform the company of any change of abode of the borrower, as in that case they are returned to the company by the post-office; and, by the attention that the borrower pays to these notices, a very good estimate can be made of the danger of losing the loan, and the measures of the company shaped accordingly. In nearly all cases, the deterioration of the property is more than made good by the monthly payments of principal made on each loan, so that a constant inspection is found not to be necessary.

The borrower's name is entered on a card, with his address; and on the back of the card there are entered in pencil the amount of interest and the date when it is due. The amount and the name of the month are changed from month to month, the interest growing less as the principal is paid off. These cards are so arranged as to show exactly what borrowers are delinquent at any time. They serve, therefore, as a convenient reminder of what loans are in arrears; and the amounts and date upon the back of the cards show exactly what interest is due and at what time.

The risk of the company from the danger of loss by fire of the goods mortgaged is met by requiring an insurance in its favor in the case of the larger loans. In the case of loans under $100, a small yearly payment is made by the borrower instead of taking out an insurance policy. The receipts from this source are credited to a "Risk Fund." The company, however, has been careful not to assume the position of an insurer. The charge is fifty cents on loans under $50 and $1 on loans of from $50 to $100. Sometimes this system is extended to loans from $100 to $200.

Risks of the Business.

The company has charged off since its organization as bad debts $4,133.44, and has at present estimated bad debts amounting to $1,106.73, a total of $5,240.17.

The amount of losses that it has suffered shows the risks to which lenders on such security are subject.

Many of the losses have occurred in the case of loans on other security than furniture mortgage; and experience has proved that the safest way of conducting such a business is to confine loans almost entirely to chattel mortgage of furniture and household effects. It has been found that furniture can be sold at auction quickly and easily. It generally brings the prices at which it is appraised. It is estimated that only one-quarter of the purchase price of the furniture is loaned upon it by the company. The loan is thus so small in comparison with the value of the furniture to the borrower that there is a strong incentive to pay the loan.

Loans on horses, carriages, boats, pictures, merchandise, stocks in trade, druggists' stores, and machinery, have been made by the company, and have generally proved unfortunate.

Loans are seldom made on furniture in storage, as the storage charges are a constantly increasing lien on the furniture, if their payment is neglected by the borrower. Loans are avoided to people of constantly changing residence or disreputable character; and to certain of the foreign races, especially where their residence in the city has been of short duration. Constant care is needed to protect the company against lending on goods encumbered by lease or mortgage.

With all the care that can be exercised, losses will occur: certain bad borrowers disappear with their furniture: it is found too late that the security is encumbered: furniture is destroyed or worn out or sold. These losses are one of the necessary expenses of the business, and only great vigilance upon the part of the officers of the company can keep them down to a moderate sum.

Many inquiries have been made of this company by men in other places who have been interested in its work, and have desired to found similar institutions elsewhere. It is hoped that the success of this company in Boston, during the five years of its existence, may help to induce people in other cities to create similar companies to give working men and women facilities of borrowing money, at reasonable rates of interest, to meet their varying needs.

LOANS.

	No. loans made.	Amount loans made.	Amount loans repaid.	Amount loans at end of year.
1888-89	781	$99,398.38	$22,143.83	$77,254.55
1889-90	909	94,177 52	67,097.29	104,334.78
1890-91	875	81,043.15	80,944.24	103,375.84
1891-92	840	73,506.26	76,059.92	99,866.98
1892-93	1,092	101,547.84	80,591.81	119,709.06
Total	4,497	$449,673.15	$326,837.09	

RECEIPTS, DIVIDENDS, AND GENERAL EXPENSES

(NOT INCLUDING INTEREST PAID AND TAXES).

	General expenses.	Interest received.	Charges received.	Risk fund received.	Dividends paid.
1888-89	$2,484.62	$4,367.66	$337.58	$53.00	2%
1889-90	4,334.34	10,456.49	734.92	108.57	4%
1890-91	4,331.12	12,133.92	732.67	302.75	6%
1891-92	4,368.23	12,029.06	802.77	347.46	6%
1892-93	5,822.03	12,555.81	1,659.64	609.81	6%
Total	$21,340.34	$51,542.94	$4,267.58	$1,421.59	

TRIAL BALANCE, MARCH 31, 1893.

Dr.		*Cr.*		
Loans	$119,709.06	Capital stock		$78,500.00
Cash	1,602.63	Prepayments upon stock not issued		8,700.00
		Notes payable:		
		Hospital Life Insurance Co.	$25,000.00	
		Third National Bank	3,000.00	28,000.00
		Dividend No. 9		2,355.00
		Unclaimed balances		73.55
		Risk fund (against our loss by fire)		1,000.00
		Bad debts (estimated)		1,106.73
		Undivided profits from the year 1892-93		1,576.41
	$121,311.69			$121,311.69

INCOME ACCOUNT, 1892-93.

Payments.			Receipts.		
1893. Mar. 31.	General expenses	$5,822.03	Undivided profits,* March 31, 1892	$1,921.43	
	Interest paid Hospital Life Insurance Co. @ 4½%	1,125.00	Credited by vote of Directors to "Bad Debts (estimated)"	1,921.43	
	State tax	1,051.27	Interest received		$12,555.81
	Interest paid Third National Bank	52.33	Profit and loss, sundry profits		1,659.64
	Credited to "Bad Debts (estimated)" account	300.00	Risk fund received during the year	$609.81	
1892. Oct. 15.	Dividend of 3%	2,355.00	Add risk fund, March 31, 1892	811.78	
1893. Apr. 19.	Dividend of 3%	2,355.00	Total risk fund received	$1,421.59	
	Profit for year, credited to "Undivided Profits"	1,576.41	Credited to profit and loss	421.59	421.59
			Balance risk fund (against our loss by fire)	$1,000.00	
		$14,637.04			$14,637.04

*The amount to the credit of undivided profits on March 31, 1892, was reserved by vote of the Directors to meet probable losses on a schedule of the bad and doubtful loans then existing, as stated in the last report for the year 1891-92. This amount, therefore, of $1,921.43 has been credited to a new account, "Bad Debts (estimated)," and to this new account has been credited $300 from earnings of the current year to cover losses actual and probable (in addition to those in above schedule).

BY-LAWS.

ARTICLE I.

OFFICERS.

The officers of the Company shall be a President, a Vice-President, a Treasurer, a Clerk, and a Board of Directors, not exceeding sixteen in number, including the officers first mentioned, who shall be members thereof *ex officio*, and including one Director to be appointed by the Governor of the Commonwealth, and one Director to be appointed by the Mayor of the city of Boston, conformably to section four of the charter of this corporation. After the first election, all officers shall be chosen by ballot at the annual meeting of the Stockholders, and shall hold their offices until their successors shall have been qualified. Vacancies occurring during the year may be filled by the Directors.

ARTICLE II.

PRESIDENT.

The President, or in his absence the Vice-President, shall preside at all meetings of the Stockholders and of the Directors.

ARTICLE III.

TREASURER.

The Treasurer shall have charge of the funds of the Company; shall give bond in such sum as the Board of Directors may determine, with sureties for the faithful discharge of his duty; shall keep all its books except the records of meetings; and exhibit a statement of its affairs at the annual meeting of the Stockholders, and whenever required by the Directors.

All moneys belonging to the Company shall be deposited in its name in some bank in Boston approved by the Directors, and shall be drawn therefrom only by checks, signed by the Treasurer or such other person as the Directors may designate by vote, who shall pay no bills unless approved in writing in such manner as the Board of Directors may determine.

ARTICLE IV.

CLERK.

The Clerk shall notify all meetings of the Company and of the Directors, as hereinafter prescribed, shall keep a record of the proceedings of such meetings, shall keep a record of all leases and deeds, and shall present at the annual meeting a full report to the Stockholders of the doings of the preceding year.

ARTICLE V.

DIRECTORS.

The Directors shall have full power to manage and control the affairs of the Company, and may, by a vote of a majority of the whole Board, remove any officer. They shall hold meetings quarterly. They shall procure a suitable seal for the Company, to be kept by the Clerk.

ARTICLE VI.

MEETINGS.

The Company shall hold its annual meeting on the third Thursday in April, at such time and place as the Directors may appoint. The Clerk shall notify each Stockholder of the time and place of the annual or any special meeting that may be called, by advertising such time and place in some newspaper in Boston, at least four days before said meeting, and by such other notice, if any, as said Directors shall by vote from time to time, or any time, direct.

Five members present in person shall constitute a quorum, provided that not less than one-half the capital stock is represented ; but a majority of Stockholders present and voting may adjourn any meeting from time to time until the business shall have been finished. Absent members may vote by proxies in writing; and at all meetings each Stockholder shall be entitled to one vote for each share owned by him.

The meetings of the Directors shall be notified by delivering, at least twenty-four hours before the time fixed for the same, a written or a printed notice to each member of the Board, or by mailing the same to such address as shall in writing be designated to the Clerk by the individual member, provided, however, that a meeting of the Directors shall be held without previous notice after each annual meeting.

Five Directors present shall constitute a quorum. In case of the absence of the President and Vice-President at any meeting of the Stockholders or Directors, a President *pro tempore* shall be chosen.

Special meetings of Stockholders or Directors shall be called by the Clerk, on the written request of the President, ten Stockholders, or three Directors, respectively, or by a vote of the Board of Directors.

ARTICLE VII.

INDEBTEDNESS.

No officer, agent, or member of the Company shall incur any debt or make any contract in behalf of the Company, except by authority given by vote of the Directors, duly certified in writing by the Clerk.

ARTICLE VIII.

CERTIFICATES.

Certificates signed by the President, or in his absence by the Vice-President and Treasurer, shall be issued to each Stockholder on payment in full of all assessments on stock, in the following form : —

CERTIFICATE.

Workingmen's Loan Association.
of
is proprietor of shares
in the Workingmen's Loan Association, which shares are transferable by a conveyance in writing, recorded by the Treasurer of said Company.

President.
Treasurer.

[L.S.]
Boston 18

(and on the reverse) a blank form, by executing which the same may be transferred as follows, subject to the other provisions of these By-laws.

For value received, I hereby sell, assign, and transfer to
of shares in the
Workingmen's Loan Association.
Dated at Boston, this day of 18
Recorded in Book page with transfers of
Workingmen's Loan Association this day of
18

Treasurer.

ARTICLE X.

AMENDMENTS.

The By-laws may be amended by a vote of the Stockholders at any meeting thereof, provided that the proposed amendment shall have been inserted in the notice of such meeting.

ACT OF INCORPORATION.

In the Year One Thousand Eight Hundred and Eighty-eight.

CHAPTER 108.

AN ACT

To incorporate the Workingmen's Loan Association.

Be it enacted by the Senate and House of Representatives in General Court assembled, and by the authority of the same, as follows:—

SECTION 1. Robert Treat Paine, Charles W. Dexter, John S. Blatchford, Francis C. Foster, John D. W. French, I. Wells Clarke, George W. Pope, Charles H. Washburn, Robert Treat Paine, second, Thomas T. Stokes, and Henry R. Gardner, their associates and successors, are hereby made a corporation by the name of the Workingmen's Loan Association, to be located at Boston, for the purpose of loaning money upon pledge or mortgage of goods and chattels or of safe securities of every kind, or upon mortgage of real estate; and all the powers and privileges necessary for the execution of these purposes are granted, with all the powers and privileges, and subject to all the duties, restrictions, and liabilities set forth in chapter one hundred and five of the Public Statutes, and in all the general laws which now are or hereafter may be in force in relation to such corporations.

SECT. 2. The capital stock of said corporation shall be twenty-five thousand dollars, to be divided into shares of one hundred dollars each, and to be paid for at such times and in such manner as the board of directors shall decide: *provided*, that no business shall be transacted by said corporation until said amount of twenty-five thousand dollars is subscribed for and actually paid in; and no certificate of shares shall be issued until the par value of such shares shall have actually been paid in in cash. The said corporation may increase its capital stock, from time to time, until the same amounts to five hundred thousand dollars.

SECT. 3. Said corporation is hereby authorized to borrow money on its own notes not exceeding the amount of its capital paid in, and for periods not exceeding one year.

SECT. 4. The government of said corporation shall be in a board of directors, chosen as the by-laws may prescribe, conformably to law: *provided*, *however,* that one director shall be appointed by the governor of the Commonwealth, and one shall be appointed by the mayor of the city of Boston.

SECT. 5. All loans shall be for a time fixed and not more than one year; and the mortgagor or pledgor shall have a right to redeem his property mortgaged or pledged, at any time before it is sold, in pursuance of the contract between the parties, or before the right of redemption is foreclosed, on payment of the loan and rate of compensation to the time of the offer to redeem.

SECT. 6. The corporation shall give to each pledgor a card inscribed with the name of the corporation, the article or articles pledged, the name of the pledgor, the amount of the loan, the rate of compensation, the date when made, the date when payable, and the page of the book where recorded.

SECT. 7. The commissioners of savings-banks shall have access to the vaults, books, and papers of the company; and it shall be their duty to inspect, examine, and inquire into its affairs, and to take proceedings in regard to them in the same manner and to the same extent as if this corporation was a savings-bank, subject to all the general laws which are now or hereafter may be in force relating to such institutions in this regard. The returns required to be made to the commissioners of savings-banks shall be in the form of a trial balance of its books, and shall specify the different kinds of its liabilities and the different kinds of its assets, stating the amounts of each kind, in accordance with a blank form to be furnished by said commissioners; and these returns shall be published in a newspaper of the city of Boston, at the expense of said corporation, at such times and in such manner as may be directed by said commissioners, and in the annual report of said commissioners; *provided, however,* that said commissioners may cause any examination to be made by an expert under their direction, but at the expense of the corporation.

Approved March 8, 1888.

FORM OF MORTGAGE USED BY THE CORPORATION.

KNOW ALL MEN BY THESE PRESENTS,

THAT ....

of ....in the county of ....and Commonwealth

of Massachusetts, vendor, in consideration of ....

..................................Dollars paid by the WORKINGMEN'S LOAN ASSOCIATION, vendee, a corporation under the laws of said Commonwealth, the receipt whereof is hereby acknowledged, do hereby grant, sell, and deliver unto the

said vendee the following goods and chattels :...

And all beds, bedding, carpets, crockery, china, glass and silver ware, and every

article of household furniture now owned by..................., and situated in house

No.. and that may be owned and added

by ....to said goods and chattels during the continuance of this mortgage.

TO HAVE AND TO HOLD, all and singular, the said goods and chattels to the said vendee, and its successors and assigns, to their own use and behoof forever.

And..................hereby COVENANT with the vendee that..................the lawful owner of the said goods and chattels that they are free from all encumbrances,

....

and that....................will WARRANT AND DEFEND the same against the lawful

claims and demands of all persons..

PROVIDED, NEVERTHELESS, that if..................shall pay unto the vendee the sum of...Dollars, in one month from this date, with interest at one per cent. per month, as stated in a note of even date herewith, signed by................, and shall pay said sum with interest at said rate at any other time that it shall become due under the provisions of this mortgage, and until such payment shall keep the said goods and chattels insured against fire in a sum not less than the amount of this mortgage for the benefit of the vendee, in such form and in such insurance companies as it or they shall approve; and shall pay to the vendee any sums which it may pay for any such insurance; shall not waste or destroy the said goods and chattels, nor suffer them or any part thereof to be attached on mesne process; shall not, except with the consent in writing of the vendee, attempt to sell or to remove from aforesaid house the same or any part thereof, and shall not make any change of place of abode without giving previous notice in writing to the vendee, then this deed and said note shall be void.

But upon any default in the performance or observance of the foregoing condition the vendee may sell the said goods and chattels at public auction or private sale, first having given notice of the intention to sell by mailing such notice, postpaid, ten days, at least, before such sale, to the address given to the vendee, by the vendor , or................representatives, or publishing such notice once a week for three successive weeks in some newspaper published in said .... And out of the money arising from such sale the vendee shall be entitled to retain all sums then secured by this mortgage, whether then or thereafter payable, which it is agreed include all costs, expenses, and counsel fees incurred or sustained by it in relation to said note, or any extension of the same, or to the said property, or to discharge any claims or liens of third persons affecting the same, rendering the surplus, if any, to.. and holding vendor to pay any balance that may be due thereon.

And it is agreed that..................and..................heirs, executors, administrators, and assigns will keep the condition of this mortgage; that upon any breach of the condition, or upon any loss or destruction by fire or otherwise, of the above property, in whole or in part, the above note, with interest apportioned to the time thereof, shall become due and payable; that the property is conveyed under this mortgage under the above conditions and agreements further to secure the vendee for any other sums that are or may become due to it from......................., besides those above described; that the vendee or any person or persons in its behalf may purchase at any sale; that until default in the performance or observance of the condition of this deed,......................may retain possession of and use the mortgaged property, but after such default the vendee may take immediate possession of said property, and for that purpose may enter forcibly, if necessary, and without being guilty of any trespass or tort, or liable in any way therefor, upon any premises on which said property or any part thereof may be situated, and remove the same therefrom; or may as aforesaid at all reasonable times before or after such default enter any such premises for the purpose of inspecting the above mortgaged property; and the assigns of each party shall have all benefits and be subject to all burdens of such party under this mortgage.

IN WITNESS WHEREOF, the said vendor,..

hereunto set......................hand and seal this ....

day of....................in the year one thousand eight hundred and ninety-...............

Signed and sealed in presence of

.... }

.... } ....

.... } ....

....189 ....h ....m..........................

M. Received and entered in records of Mortgages of Personal Property in the clerk's office of the..of..

....

....

WORKINGMEN'S LOAN ASSOCIATION,

63 Albion Building, No. 1 Beacon Street,

BOSTON.

APPLICATION FOR LOAN.

Name in full.

Amount of Loan?

What Security?

Where is it situated?

Where is your present residence?

How long have you resided there?

Previous residence during the last five years?

What is your business?

Where?

Have you receipted bills for the property?

Does all the property belong to you?

Is there any encumbrance on it?

Name two references.

What amount of principal will you pay monthly?

Do you agree to pay interest promptly?

Is your property insured, and for how much?

Will pay .... yearly, in place of insuring, but such payment shall not make company an insurer in any event.

Signature, ...

Dated, ...189

The borrower must rely, for any extension of the time of his Loan, upon his own punctuality and good faith in dealing with the Association.

Deposit..

Examine..

Take ....*Horse-car to* ....*Street.*

From Mrs. Geo. S. Morris
June 1896

[From the Wisconsin Academy of Sciences, Arts, and Letters]

DISTRIBUTION OF PROFITS.

A NEW ARRANGEMENT OF THAT SUBJECT.

[BY PROF. A. O. WRIGHT.]

The following is offered as a new arrangement of the subject of distribution of profits, differing in some important particulars from the arrangement given in any work on political economy with which the writer is acquainted.

In civilized communities nearly all Production requires the union of capital and labor. The proceeds of production are then distributed in various ways between the capitalist and the laborer. In actual practice the capitalist and the laborer may or may not be the same person; but in theory we may separate the shares of capital and labor. There is still a third party concerned in production, the business manager, who stands between the capitalist and the laborer, and by his skill in superintendence increases the proceeds of the business, and thus makes himself a sharer in the proceeds.

The share which always belongs to the capitalist is called interest, when it is paid for the use of money, and rent when it is paid for the use of real estate. The rate of interest and the rate of rent vary according to fixed laws which I need not give here. The share which always belongs to labor is called wages (or in some cases salary). This also varies according to well-known laws. After deducting interest or rent, as the case may be, and wages, including the salary of the business manager, the net proceeds are the real profits of the business. In some cases instead of profits we should say losses, but this does not change the conditions of the problem. Whoever receives the profits should also bear the losses, and generally does. There are then two questions in regard to every kind of production: first, what are the profits (or losses); and second, who gets them. In solving these questions I make the following five cases, each of which presents a different phase of the question :

CASE I.

In this case, capitalist, business manager and laborer are combined in one person. Examples of this case are farmers who own land and furnish their own labor; mechanics who own their own shops and tools and do their own work; and merchants who own their own stores and stock in trade, and keep no clerks. This case is the simplest in practice and the most difficult in theory. As one person combines the functions of capitalist, business manager and laborer, there is no distribution of the proceeds. No one pays interest or wages to himself. The question, who gets the profits, is easily answered. But the question, what are the profits, is much harder to answer, and indeed the producers who come under this class rarely attempt to answer it. They confuse together interest, wages and profits in one lump sum, and often fail to separate their personal or family expenses from the expenses of the business, or to account for the proceeds of the business which they or their families consume.

To find the true profits of such a business, not only should all business expenses be deducted from the gross proceeds, but also interest on the capital invested and wages for the labor done. The farmer, mechanic or merchant, as the case may be, owes himself as a capitalist interest on the capital invested. He also owes himself as business manager and laborer, wages for labor performed. But all products of the business consumed in his family should be added to the gross proceeds of the business, and charged to family expense account.

In this case a real business loss is frequently concealed under the profits of capital and labor. The producer thinks he has made so much out of his business, when in fact the business has made nothing, and his receipts are really less than interest and wages should be. So also a real business profit is frequently concealed under extravagant personal or family expenses.

But it does not always follow that a farmer is losing money who does not clear the interest on his land and stock, and wages for his labor. He has the advantage, if he is free from debt, of receiving interest without the trouble and risk of lending money or renting a farm, and he has work all the year round. He can put in odd hours and days of labor for himself where he could not in working for some one else. The great advantage of small farms held in fee simple is that more work can be put on them than could be done by hired labor. This is an advantage both for the farmer and for the whole community, as the case of France since the revolution shows.

CASE II.

In this case capitalist and business manager are the same person, employing one or more laborers. This case differs from Case I only in the employment of laborers; and as a farmer's, mechanic's or merchant's business grows, it naturally runs into this case.

In this case there is no distribution between capitalist and business manager. The net profits of the business are found as in Case I, except that the labor is partly or wholly paid for, according as the proprietor himself works or not. This payment of labor thus makes wages visible as a business expense. But the proprietor's own labor, as manager or laborer or both, must be accounted for as in Case I.

The remuneration of the laborers hired is generally (a) wages. But it may be (b) a share in the gross proceeds or in the net profits, or (c) partly wages and partly a share in the proceeds or profits. As the gross proceeds are so much more easily estimated than the net profits it is found in practice usually better to give a share in the proceeds in those cases where the laborer receives a share of the results of the business. Thus on the cotton plantations in the south, since the war, the negro laborers are often given a share in the crop, a thing which they can easily understand and in which they cannot easily be cheated; whereas if they are to have a share in the net profits it would be easy to cook up the accounts so as to cheat them, and with the utmost honesty on the part of the planter it would be hard for him to make the negroes understand the accounts he kept. But the simplest and most obvious way is to pay the laborer wages, reserving to the proprietor interest on the capital invested, salary as business manager, wages as far as he performs labor, and the profits, if there are any. In many kinds of business it would be hard to introduce any system of sharing the profits with the laborer. Thus in a printing office, where the workmen are constantly wandering from one office to another, or on a farm where in harvest and threshing extra men must be hired, or in a store where the amount of sales and the net profits are both matters that often must be kept secret from the public and from rivals, — in all these cases it would be hard to introduce any system of giving the laborer a share either in the proceeds or in the profits of the business. But where such a system can be introduced it has obvious advantages over the system of wages. It produces a greater interest in the business on the part of the laborer and therefore more faithful work and greater care to prevent waste. It is the usual practice in the great mercantile houses to give the best clerks a partnership, that is, a share in the profits. The hope of this is a constant incentive to the younger clerks, and the offer of a partnership prevents the best clerks from carrying their customers to rival houses or setting up in business for themselves.

CASE III.

In this case the capitalist employs the business manager and the laborer, giving them (a) wages or salary, (b) a share in the profits or (c) a combination of the two. The capitalist takes interest, and the net profits (or losses) of the business. In this case the interest is concealed by the profits, but can be easily separated.

Thus if a capitalist builds a woolen mill, and employs a superintendent and several laborers, he usually pays a salary to the first and wages to the secoud. But he may give the business manager a share in the profits, thus virtually making him a partner. Or he may make him formally a business partner, reserving the title to the mill, and rent for it, to himself. Or he may give both the superintendent and the hands a share in the profits. The usual practice on a whaling ship is for the owner to receive one-half the oil and whalebone, and for the other half to be divided among the captain and crew, in so many "lays," or shares to each.

A variety of this case is where the capitalist is a corporation, as in the case of a railway company, an insurance company, a national bank, a city newspaper or a manufacturing company. In this case interest and profits combined appear as dividend. In a large corporation there are often several business managers, each with his department of the business. Very generally the managers are also stock-holders, and receive dividends in that capacity as well as salaries as managers.

The questions raised by the subject of stock companies and their dividends, are important questions in Distribution. But they call for a separate treatment, and are omitted in this paper.

Another variety of this case is when a number of persons are associated so carry on a co-operative store. Usually the capital of each partner is quite small; but for the purpose of carrying on the co-operative store they are capitalists, even if they earn their living as laborers. They simply club together their individual savings, so as to make a mercantile association, and then employ a manager and clerks, and sell to one another and to outsiders on such terms as they choose to offer. In England these co-operative stores have been quite successful.

CASE IV.

In this case the manager carries on the business, borrowing money or goods of the capitalist or renting land or buildings of him and employing laborers. In this case the distribution is, to the capitalist interest or rent, to the laborer wages, and to the manager salary for his services and the net profits (or losses.) It should be noted that the case is very rare where the business manager can borrow money, buy goods on credit or rent land without capital of his own as a basis of confidence. On that capital he should also have interest.

The best example of this case perhaps is the system of agriculture in England. There the capitalist is the landlord, who rents land for a term of years, generally now for twenty-one years, under definite conditions in regard to crops and improvements, and for a fixed rent in money. The business manager is the farmer, who receives salary for his services, interest on the capital he invests in the shape of stock, tools, improvements on the land

and advances made to the laborers before his crops are sold, and the profits (or losses) of the business. The laborers receive wages, often miserably inadequate.

A very common example of this case in this country is where a merchant as business manager invests a small capital and buys goods systematically on credit, renting a building and hiring clerks. In this instance the capitalists are the owner of the store who receives rent, and the wholesale dealers of whom goods are bought on credit, who receive interest directly, or indirectly in the enhanced price of the goods, and perhaps also the bank of which the merchant secures accommodation loans from time to time, paying a high rate of interest. The business manager is the merchant who receives interest on the capital he has invested, salary as business manager, wages as salesman, and the profits (or losses) of the business. The clerk or clerks receive wages. I need not say that the result of doing business in this way is in nine cases out of ten a net loss, which falls either upon the merchant or fully as often upon his foolish creditors, the wholesale dealers.

A variety of this case which almost deserves to be set off as a case by itself, is when the business manager gives the capitalist a share of the proceeds or of the net profits in lieu of interest or rent. The most familiar example of this is where a farm is rented on shares. This is the usual method in the United States of renting farms, when they are rented at all. It is also, under the name of Metayer rent, the usual method in France and Italy. In this method of carrying on business, the distribution to the laborer is wages; the distribution to the capitalist is rent in the form of a share of the crop, which on the average of years is more than a fair money rent. But this is usually more than offset by the tenant's neglect to keep up the land, as he holds only from year to year. And the distribution to the business manager who in this case is the tenant, is interest on the capital he has invested, if any, wages for his own labor and net profits (or losses) after paying any laborers he has hired and giving the landlord his share of the crop.

CASE V.

In this case an association of laborers borrow capital and employ a business manager who may or may not be one of their own number. This case is a favorite one with many persons in theory, but it has never thus far been found to work well in practice. To avoid misconception, it should be noted that corporative stores do not come under this case. The laborers who organize a corporative store, do not as a rule work in the store, and are therefore in regard to that business not laborers, but capitalists. They are really a stock company to carry on a mercantile business and therefore come under case III. as we have already seen.

But when journeymen shoemakers, for instance, form a co-operative association, they come under this case. As in all kinds of business, capital is needed to begin it and to carry it on. This capital may possibly be obtained in one of three ways: (a) By borrowing money of some capitalist, which could not be done ordinarily; or (b) by renting a shop and buying materials on credit, a hazardous undertaking both for the association and for the capitalist; or (c) by combining their separate earnings, which would be the usual method. In this case the association as a combination of capitalists employs its own members as business manager and laborers.

This case in the last form differs from case I only in being the case of a combination of individuals instead of a single individual, that combine in one the three functions of capitalist, business manager and laborer. But in this case, while there is no distribution between the association and outsiders, there is a question of distribution between the members of the association. Of the various methods which might be adopted, the following is the most in accordance with the principles of political economy. Let the members be credited with the capital advanced by each as so much stock in the association; let the members be paid for their services at the market rates, and if possible, by the piece and not by the day, and after paying these wages and other expenses, let the members divide the profits or losses on the basis of the capital advanced by each, like any stock company. All these five cases have their place in the transactions of business, and every form of productive industry must fall under some one of them. I summarize them in closing:

Case I. Where the same person is capitalist, business manager and laborer.

Case II. Where the capitalist and business manager are the same person, employing laborers.

Case III. Where the capitalist employs the business manager and laborers. All business corporations are a variety of this case.

Case IV. Where the manager carries on the business, borrowing or renting of the capitalist and employing laborers.

Case V. Where an association of laborers employ themselves and furnish their own capital.

www.ingramcontent.com/pod-product-compliance
Lightning Source LLC
LaVergne TN
LVHW021218110826
845150LV00002B/197

* 9 7 8 1 4 2 5 5 6 4 5 3 7 *